The Xanadu System

How to Get Paid $30,000 a Year to Travel*
*Without Selling Anything

by Craig Chilton

New Worldwide Edition
for 1995-97

1997 Upgrade

5th Edition
Printing 3-A -- May, 1997

IMPORTANT!!
Please Do This Right Away!

As the new owner of this book, it is important that you **REGISTER** your ownership. This will entitle you to receive many benefits for which you otherwise would not qualify. One example of this is that ownership of this Handbook is a prerequisite for enrollment in Driver Placement Network.

Your Registration Number is printed on the label below. Please note that the number is followed by a hyphen. *After* the hyphen, you should neatly PRINT the appropriate letter combination from this **list,** to show *how you obtained* the book:

- **CS** -- *Cash Paid* directly to the Author or Publisher (but not in a bookstore).
- **BK** -- Purchased at a *Bookstore, off the shelf.*
- **BO** -- *Ordered through a Bookstore,* and then purchased there.
- **AS** -- Purchased at an *Author's Signing session, at a bookstore.*
- **CC** -- *Credit Card* purchase, *by Phone.*
- **PB** -- Purchased *by Mail,* directly *from the Publisher, by check or money order.*
- **FC** -- Purchased *by Mail,* by dialing an *"800" number,* and **then** sending a *check or money order to a Fulfillment Center* (such as BookMasters, or a similar site).
- **CT** -- Purchased from another company's *catalog,* flyer, or ad.
- **GF** -- Received the book as a *Gift.*

970004674BM-__

IF you purchased the book at a *bookstore,* please tape the sales receipt *over* this message. Some bonus offers may require that documentation. (Then you only need to photocopy this page.)

Then -- *Please return your Registration Card.* If card is missing, you may register by calling us and providing your complete Registration Number: (319) 234-0676. (Ownership *IS* transferable at a later date, if you wish. To do this, you need only to notify us.)

© **Copyright 1995, 1997 by Craig Chilton** 5th Edition, Printing 3-A: May, 1997
ISBN 0-933638-09-4

All rights reserved. No part of this publication may be reproduced or utilized in any form or by any means, electronic or mechanical, including photocopying, recording, or by any information storage and retrieval system, without permission in writing from the author. Certain specific exceptions to this are explained within the book, and permission is granted for reproduction and/or distribution of the *applicable* material -- *strictly within the guidelines provided* in those locations.

Since 1989, the term "Road Rat," and its cartoon caricatures, having been used exclusively and continuously by that time by Craig Chilton and XANADU Enterprises for more than ten years (since 1979), are pending as registered trademarks of XANADU Enterprises, and cartoons may not be used in any manner or reproduced without the express permission of the author or publisher unless accompanied by the symbol, ™. The words may be used without permission, but each word must begin with a capital letter, and the phrase be accompanied by ™. Origin should be acknowledged in cases where such normally is deemed appropriate.

Published by:	Road Rat Cartoon Caricatures in This and Previous Editions by:	Cover Art for This Edition by:
XANADU Enterprises	Ronald Henley	Steve Hanson
P.O. Box 3147	506 Scott's Glenn	7623 Poplar Lane
Evansdale, Iowa 50707-0147	Springfield, Oregon 97477	Cedar Falls, Iowa 50613
Tel. (319) 234-0676	Tel. (541) 741-1272	Tel. (319) 277-3976

*In Loving Memory of Mom & Dad,
Whose Love and Patience Made It Possible for Me –
and Through This Handbook, for You,
and for Untold Thousands of Others –
to be Truly Enabled to Achieve the Great American Dream.*

TABLE OF CONTENTS

Dedication	iii
Table of Contents	v
About the Author	vii
EXTREMELY IMPORTANT!! **(Read This *FIRST!*)**	ix
Introduction	xi

PART I --- GETTING THE JOB ... 1

1. Availability of Work ... 1
   Table: "Comparison -- Trucking vs. RV Delivery" ... 9
2. General Requirements ... 17
3. Possible Impact by Swings of the Economy, and by War ... 24
4. "Home, Sweet Home..." ... 27
5. On the Road! ... 32

PART II --- PERFORMING THE JOB ... 38

1. Getting Started ... 38
2. Getting the Most from a Unit ... 43
3. The Care & Feeding of Breakdowns ... 45
4. "And the Northern Lights were a-Runnin' Wild..." ... 54
5. Delivering the Unit ... 62
6. Sex & the Single Road Rat... & How a *Couple* Can be Successful ... 65
7. The Good, the Bad, and the Rinky-Dink ... 72
8. Some *Really* Special Tips! ... 78
9. Rat to the Future! Computer Trip Planning ... 92
10. **$200 - $800 BONUS:** A Great Way to Start Seeing the *World!* ... 104

PART III --- GETTING HOME ... 109

1. *INTERLOCK:* The *Round* Trip for Pay! ... 111
2. *MAXIMIZATION:* For Those Who LOVE to *FLY!* ... 120
3. The "Class 'A' CDL Option" -- How to be a "Road Rat *Extraordinaire!*" ... 133
4. The "ECONOMY" Method... Lessons from "**The Ameripass Team!**" ... 135
5. Road Rat in *Training* -- The *Amtrak* Adventure! ... 145
6. Alternate Ways to Travel for Pay ... 152
7. Condensed Answers to Some of the Most-Asked Questions ... 156

APPENDIX #1: THE JOB MARKET ... 161

1. Understanding the Company Listings ... 161
2. Highway of Adventure... Linking *Alaska* to the *Lower 48!* ... 173
3. Manufacturer & Selected Dealer LISTINGS: ... 179
   - -- USA: Manufacturers & Selected Dealers ... 179
   - -- CANADA: Manufacturers & Selected Dealers ... 293
   - -- EUROPE: A Selection of Manufacturers ... 301
   - -- AUSTRALIA: Manufacturers, Selected Dealers, & Transporters ... 302
4. Transporter Companies of the USA and CANADA ... 311

APPENDIX #2: THE TECHNICAL STUFF ... 321

THE *LATEST* INFORMATION!! ... 337

ABOUT THE AUTHOR

Craig Chilton is a graduate of Central College, Pella, Iowa, and has pursued studies in Geography, Geology, and Anthropology at universities in Arizona, New York, New Jersey, North Dakota, and Mexico City.

He was awarded an NDEA Federal Grant for a special course in Urban Geography at Rutgers University, during which he conducted field studies in New York City.

He has completed all course requirements for two Masters Degrees at the University of Northern Iowa (Geography and Geology). While attending school there, he served a term as Executive Editor of the university newspaper, *The Northern Iowan*. In planning his master's thesis for geography, the author researched an extensive geo-sociological study that took him to universities in all of the 50 states. A book for general consumption is planned as a spin-off to the academic work.

The author has been travel-oriented throughout his lifetime; a fact readily apparent to readers of his more recent works, of which this Fifth Edition of this handbook is his fourteenth. In 1976, he explored the Alaska Pipeline during the latter stages of its construction, from Fairbanks to Prudhoe Bay. The result was his seventh book, *7 Days on the Kamikaze Trail*, which provided a unique behind-the-scenes look at life in that dynamic project.

While completing his graduate studies at the University of Northern Iowa, Craig simultaneously worked as a technical writer for the Research & Development Division of Chamberlain Manufacturing Corporation, in Waterloo. The six books written in that capacity were his earliest, providing him a firm foundation for a writing career. The First Edition of this book was his eighth published work, followed quickly by the ninth, which was a small *supplemental* guide for RV delivery persons. (It followed Energy Hoax II, in 1979, and was designed to help drivers to cope with the soaring gasoline and diesel fuel prices of that dismal era. Today, this industry has built-in safeguards that would prevent a recurrence of that from being a problem, in terms of pay scales.)

Before settling into a lifestyle based on writing and travel, Craig served honorably in the U.S. Air Force as a navigator and meteorologist. He then taught elementary school in Arizona and in Lancaster, California. Later he taught social studies and science at the middle school level in East Greenbush, New York. While doing his graduate work in Iowa, he was awarded an assistantship, the duties of which included instructing undergraduate and graduate students in computer applications and techniques within the field of geography.

Craig currently is finalizing the writing of his first novel, which he started in 1983. He hopes to present the most realistic fictional account of nuclear war yet written, and in the course of researching the Eastern Bloc component, has made nine trips since 1987 to the Soviet Union/Russia, Outer Mongolia, China, and to several nations, such as Kazakhstan, Azerbaijan, and Ukraine, that formerly were part of the USSR. Those travels included several fascinating rides across Asia on the Trans-Siberian Railroad. Keeping up with the phenomenal geopolitical changes since 1989 "has been daunting, yet ultimately challenging... this novel will be as up-to-date as tomorrow's headlines!"

EXTREMELY IMPORTANT !!

You MUST READ... AND FULLY UNDERSTAND... THE INFORMATION ON THESE PAGES, BEFORE GOING FARTHER.

Your SUCCESS IN USING THIS HANDBOOK DEPENDS ON THIS !!

If you love to travel, this job will seem much more like a perpetual vacation with pay to you, than it will seem like work. I know. I did this *full-time* for 10 years... and it never seemed like work.

However, you must understand that this is a very real JOB. You will be providing a valuable service to those for whom you drive, and you will be fairly compensated for doing this.

As employment, this job depends upon many factors common to seeking and performing other jobs. Please keep the following in mind as you proceed:

1. Even though you will not be performing sales work while doing this job, you will have to do the usual sales work of selling your potential employers with respect to your qualifications as a driver, and your enthusiasm for performing your work well. **It is vitally important that you approach potential employers with a positive, cheerful attitude.** No one wants to hire a negative person. This goes for making telephone contacts as well as when approaching them in person. *If you're having an off day, wait until later to make the approach.*

2. Appendix 1 of this book is a compilation of all the companies we've been able to research which are potential users of drivers, or which probably have drivers somewhere in the loop when it comes to getting vehicles from their site to their customers or dealers. **Their appearance in this book indicates only that they EXIST. Their presence in this manual should by NO MEANS be construed as evidence that they currently employ drivers, either as employees, independent contractors, or via the use of transporter companies.** Even if the data indicates that they DO have drivers or retain the services of one or more transporter companies, you must remember that this was data provided when we interviewed someone at that company by phone. This publication is not responsible for the accuracy of the data thus provided, and we have seen cases where data was furnished incompletely or erroneously. The XANADU Enterprises staff does the best job it can to ensure that the

facts it obtains are accurate, but such errors do sometimes slip through, and when dealing with so many thousands of companies, there is no way this can be prevented completely.

Next, please be aware that some of these companies may never have used drivers. We include such companies if it is evident that there is a reasonable chance that this situation could change. Over the years, we have observed that companies tend to experiment quite a bit. Many companies that have used their own drivers have switched later on to using a transporter company instead, for example. And vice-versa. We observed such a change a few years ago in the case of one of the largest and best-known manufacturers of RVs, Winnebago Industries. For many years, they had had their own corps of several hundred independent-contractor drivers, but in recent years, they have been availing themselves instead of the services of transporter companies, and today use no drivers of their own whatsoever.

So please **be very polite and friendly** when approaching the companies listed in the Appendix. If a company tells you they don't use drivers, *accept* that fact graciously, and immediately move on to another company. Always remember that a company's presence in these listings implies **ONLY** its existence. They owe you nothing.

Remember, too, that only perhaps 5% or less of those companies have ever even **seen** one of these Handbooks. Their complete experience with it in *most* cases is the telephone interview one of our staff members held with one of their own staffers, as well as whatever contact potential drivers have made with them while seeking employment. **Unless you happen to speak with the *same* person with whom the XANADU staff talked, it is most likely that the person to whom you speak will not even know about us.** So leave them with a good impression of your approach to them. Even if they aren't in need of a driver when you speak with them, the favorable impression you leave can be helpful to another driver applicant at a later date -- and may even help *you* at some future time to arrange an "Interlock" trip. (You'll learn the value of "Interlock" later in this Handbook.)

Finally, be SURE to read the pages in APPENDIX 1 which *precede* the company listings THOROUGHLY AND CAREFULLY before beginning to make your contacts. Approximately 98% of the questions people have had for us after obtaining this book would have been answered immediately if only they had read THOSE pages carefully!

One last word. We live in an age of skepticism, due to the scams and rip-offs that pervade our society... and our own Congress hasn't been setting very good examples for us in recent years, either. So many, upon hearing about this job, are skeptical from the start, figuring it's too good to be true.

Fortunately, that's very easy to remedy, because the proof surrounds us every day! We see *cars* on the back of trucks, but we *almost never* see an RV, an ambulance, a school bus, or even a limousine being transported in that fashion. Since we know these don't sprout like mushrooms in the lots of dealerships and driveways of customers, that means they have to be *driven* there by people like you and me! So make your job applications *confidently*. There are millions of those vehicles in existence -- and it takes a *big* workforce to deliver them. New jobs open in this field continually!

INTRODUCTION

𝔚elcome to XANADU!

When the original edition of this book came off the press in 1979, the hit movie of that name was still more than a year in the future. The fact that this work is subtitled, *The Xanadu System*, then, is reflective of Coleridge's original concept, when he created the word as the name for an exotic pleasure dome in his work, *The Kubla Khan*.

Over the ages, we have come to regard Xanadu as synonymous with the word, "utopia."

Now... if "utopia" deals with a perfect and flawless world of peace and ease, in which war, hunger, and poverty no longer exist, and wherein Murphy's Laws have all been repealed, then let us apply "Xanadu" to the effect that rapidly manifests itself after one decides to deliver recreational and specialized vehicles.

Owners of this Handbook who study it well have a BIG edge over the vast majority of Road Rats now in the field. Most people now doing this work who do *not* have this guidance work for very modest wages: typically between only $12,000 and $15,000/year for full-time workers. But single Road Rats who are *using this book* can easily earn between $30,000 and $52,000/year *without working any harder!* (*Couples* working full-time earn substantially more.) The difference is that the Handbook owners *already know* the secrets of success, so *don't have to learn them the hard way.* They learn in just *hours and days* what it takes others months and even *years* to discover. Also, this book will enable you to **avoid** the *extra lower-income-related problems* that are faced by those who start this job *without* it.

It is important for you to understand that the vast majority of the 100,000-plus drivers (counting all types of Road Rats) in this lifestyle who work in the USA and Canada are working at lower levels of income. This is because *at least 95% of those drivers (and probably more) have never heard of this book,* so have not yet learned the techniques they need to use to earn a *comfortable* living. This is one of the two primary factors that permits rapid turnover of these jobs, and therefore constantly provides openings for new drivers. An in-depth explanation of both factors is provided in Part I, Chapter 1, and I strongly encourage you to read *both* this set of introductory pages and that chapter very carefully before proceeding with the rest of the book. Having this knowledge of the basics as you continue will be helpful to you.

Consider this, now. *Most* who seek to pursue this lifestyle full-time, but have *no guidance* in the techniques that make it possible to earn a good living, will *drop out from sheer frustration in a short time* and seek some *other* line of work. By all rights, that should have been my own experience when I entered this lifestyle nearly two decades ago. But here's what made the difference...

My "Road Rat career" began as a summer job after my teaching year ended in early June, 1977. As luck would have it, my first position was with a transporter company rather than with a manufacturer. In those days, I didn't know the difference. It was nearly a year before I even *learned* that driving for a transporter company (which is essentially a broker -- a middleman operation) pays on average only *half* as well as does driving directly for a manufacturer or a dealer.

But I have no regrets, because if I *had* started working for good pay, I doubt that this book would have been written! Working solely for a transporter company forced me to live by my wits and search out the economic shortcuts. Within scant *hours* of being hired, during the very first run, I began keeping records of all that I was learning from my experiences.

By summer's end, still working for the transporter company at an earning rate of perhaps only $11,000/year, I was faced with either returning to schoolteaching, looking for a brand-new line of work, or continuing to plug along at RV delivery and see what developed. Returning to teaching was the logical choice, but I'd already done that for ten years at grade levels 6, 7, and 8, and that is an extremely stressful job with unrelenting pressure, hassles, and almost no free time. Although RV delivery still wasn't paying me worth a hoot, this newly-discovered lifestyle of unbridled freedom was a strong counterbalance to the economic pressure caused by the lower income. After three highly enjoyable and stress-free months of being able to set my own hours, explore the country at will on routes of my choosing, I was hooked. Money wasn't everything!

It should be mentioned, though, that one other factor influenced this decision: a strong sense of ***potential.*** Somehow, I was certain that vehicle delivery could pay substantially *better*... if I just kept improving my ways to go about doing it. Even by the end of those first three months, I'd begun developing some new techniques.

The first year was difficult, filled with experimentation, trial and error. By early 1978, discovery of the "Interlock" system was still in the future, and "Maximization" almost two years beyond that. Interlock isn't possible without a source of potential return trips. No handbook yet existed to *provide* such listings; it would be 1979 before I wrote the *first* (and still the only) complete handbook and guide to this lifestyle. By all rights, I should have given up in frustration before I ever made the key discoveries. (In fact, looking back on it all, that's probably why no one else had ever written a book about this before 1979. What was necessary was the *combination* of a person getting into this lifestyle who enjoys writing... *and* that same person having the willingness to work for peanuts for 18 months while learning the secrets of this lifestyle's success... just because he had a gut feeling that the potential for earnings was far greater, if only the proper ropes could be learned.)

To make a long story short, after a year and a half I had learned many of the principles necessary for earning a decent income, and my own earnings had by then reached $30,000/year. I gathered all of my notes from my experience, researched the 333 RV manufacturers that I was able to discover (without the aid of a computer, by the most rudimentary methods you can imagine), and published the first edition of this Handbook. And *that* moderate earnings figure from 18 years in the past is where the book got the title it still bears even today, five generations of Handbook later -- in this 1997 Version.

By 1980, I'd discovered Maximization, and by using it primarily, but in combination (to a lesser degree) with Interlock, my income escalated to $52,000/year and levelled off there for the next six years, while I continued to drive full-time. As I improved the Handbook and brought out its later editions, I retained the original title because anyone who follows the guidance in this book and drives full-time should be able to earn *at least* $30,000 a year. Most drivers who own and *use* this book can earn considerably *more*, and therefore are pleasantly surprised.

So **the purpose of this book is to provide you with a *gateway* to new opportunity and adventure,** whether you are 18 or 88... or any age in between... at a comfortable wage level. Remember, you have more control over the hours, days, weeks, and even months that you work than at least 99.9% of all other gainfully-employed people. Think about the *other* dreams you may have had for your life, and recognize the fact that a combination of substantial time off *and* a good income can enable you to *additionally* pursue those *other* avenues. For example, consider writing and photography. This lifestyle is *tailor-made* to help you pursue such other vocations! So if you use your newly-discovered freedom creatively, *you may well discover that you can use this as a gateway to doing just about anything in life that you've ever wanted to experience!*

And that's what *The Xanadu System* is all about... **Freedom!**

PART 1
GETTING THE JOB

1

Availability of Work

This is a complete Handbook and Guide for one of the most incredible jobs on earth. It is the type of position that most people dream about, but don't realize exists. (From here on, when reference is made to this book, it usually will be called, simply, "the Handbook.")

The position is almost unknown to those outside of the field. This is because practically no one ever gives conscious thought to the way recreational and specialized vehicles reach their respective dealerships and destinations.

Chances are you have never seen a motorized vehicle of a recreational or specialized nature being transported on a truck. That is because *they almost never are,* due to their size, height, or greater transportation costs. Almost invariably, they are *driven* from their thousands of points of manufacture, to their *tens* of thousands of dealerships and customers, throughout the USA and Canada. And in Australia and Europe, as well as many other parts of the world, this is done the same way.

People usually learn about this lifestyle in either of two ways:

A. Something causes them to *realize* that they haven't seen such vehicles being trucked. Perhaps they've heard the author of this book as a talk show guest or in a newscast feature. Or maybe they happened to notice that an RV, fire truck, or other type of vehicle on the highway had a license plate bearing the word, "transporter," "manufacturer," or "dealer." And *then* made the association.

B. By word of mouth. Until late 1986 this is how *nearly all* prospective drivers first heard of this lifestyle. From those who were already doing it. This *still* is the way that *most* discover it.

By early 1997, though, the author's frequent appearances on talk shows across North America (and Hawaii... and in 1993 over a radio station in Moscow, Russia), were becoming more of a factor because they were increasing people's awareness of the job's existence. Some concern has been expressed to him in this regard, often in the form of a question asked of him on the air. It goes something like this:

"Don't you think all this new public awareness will cause saturation of the job market, making it more difficult for a new driver to enter this field?"

The surprising answer is... "Probably not."

Many variables need to be considered here. As a prospective driver, you need to understand these factors, and what they mean to you, both now and in the future.

First off, no one knows *exactly* how many of these drivers are at work. Even the Bureau of the Census likely would be hard-pressed even to guess the number of them that reside in the USA -- simply because their data would mix them up very thoroughly with *truckers.* There's a world of *difference* between the lifestyles of *these* drivers and truckers, but it's highly doubtful the Census Bureau makes that distinction.

The best we can do is make a *very educated* estimate, based upon the number of manufacturers in existence, the number of transporter companies which serve many of them, the rate at which vehicles are produced, and the frequency with which one can spot them out on the highways and byways. (We're all over the place, out there, if you know how to look for us, and can recognize us when you see us -- usually through your observation of a special type of license plate, or the lack of one. Paper stickers are used instead by some states, usually in the front or back window.) Also, and most importantly, the researchers here at XANADU Enterprises are able to obtain further insight when they interview by phone the thousands of companies that are listed in Appendix 1 of this book. So our estimate becomes *quite* a well-documented one, and falls close to 100,000 Road Rats* that work, full-time & part-time, in the USA and Canada, *not* counting the "on-call" ones. In Australia, we estimate the number to be between 1,000 and 3,000, but for Europe we have insufficient data to make such an estimate.

As you will see in this book, some Road Rats work directly for manufacturers. Others for transporter companies. Some work for both, continually, since most such drivers are independent contractors -- and that usually makes them free agents. (In that case, it is up to the driver whether or not he works for more than one company. This is covered in depth in Part III, Chapter 1.) And... there are untold thousands of Road Rats who work directly for the *dealerships* that *receive* the vehicles from the manufacturers. Such deliveries are known throughout the industry as:

    CPUs -- Customer Pick-Ups, and
    DPUs -- Dealer Pick-Ups.

It is important for you to know both of those terms, but it can get confusing unless you realize just how *little* difference there is between them. Anyone who works for a *purchaser* of vehicles is therefore *working for the **customer** of the factory from which he obtains it*... and therefore is doing a CPU. And if the factory's customer just happens to be a *dealership* (e.g., limo dealer, or RV dealer), then he is doing a DPU. (In other words, a *DPU* is simply *a more specific type* of *CPU*. The customer (in this case, a dealer) *sends him to the plant*, where he picks up the unit and then *drives it back* to his employer.) If you work for a manufacturer or a final assembly site, you can expect some competition from drivers coming in from outside to do CPUs and/or DPUs. In some locations, CPU/DPU competition is nonexistent or minimal -- which is the ideal situation for the drivers who happen to work for the factories. Unfortunately, there are many companies where CPU/DPU competition for available runs is predominant, or absolutely *fierce!* However, in such locations, dispatchers compensate by simply maintaining a driver force of the size necessary to deliver the *anticipated* flow of *non*-CPU/DPU shipments. In previous editions of this Handbook, we've made notations of CPU/DPU competition for those factories where it was known to exist, in the company listings. That became redundant because it exists to *some* degree for *almost all* of them, so in *this* edition, we just make that blanket statement to cover *most* manufacturing sites. **You are STRONGLY URGED to read pages 161-170 (in Appendix 1) VERY CAREFULLY before attempting contacts with companies.** The information in those pages must be considered along *with* the facts presented in this chapter, for the best understanding of the way this industry functions, and of the role of this Handbook within it.

---

*   "Road Rat" is an **affectionate** term for the drivers who deliver brand-new RVs and specialized vehicles. They use it to distinguish themselves from truckers -- much as someone who lives in a desert community often calls himself a "desert rat." The term was coined in the *first* edition of this book, and over the ensuing 18 years it has come into common and universal use throughout this industry. (Remember the trademark, though. If you write or print it, please do so in accordance with the last paragraph on page ii.)

So -- back to that question of the number of Road Rats in existence. The estimates provided above apply only to Road Rats working directly for manufacturers, modifiers, final assembly sites, transporter companies, and dealers. They do *not* include the people who perform CPUs that do *not* work for *dealers*. Those CPU drivers normally are not people who seek to be Road Rats in the first place. And they actually do *not* fit that description, as you will learn on page 10. (For right now, just trust me on this: you do *not* want to be a CPU Road Rat *unless* you are doing *DPUs!*)

A full explanation of this is provided on page 11, but in case you already were wondering... YES, you generally can work for *almost* as much money as a DPU Road Rat as you can working for the companies that *produce* the vehicles. But the procedure for locating the companies and making application is quite different, and Interlock opportunities for DPU Road Rats are almost nonexistent.

IMPORTANT! -- **At this point, if you have not yet read the Introductory pages of this book (ix-xii), please do so *now*, BEFORE continuing. The information they contain is *VITALLY IMPORTANT* to you, if you wish to perform this job!**

Strange as it may seem, a great **advantage** to you in seeking work of this type is the fact that the level of pay received by *tens of thousands* of Road Rats is down in the root cellar somewhere! For *you,* the good news is that perhaps *more than half* of all full-time Road Rats earn less than $15,000 per year. Many of them earn as little as $10,000 or less.

Why is that *GOOD* news? After all, this book's title indicates you can earn at least $30,000 per year. But now I'm telling you that *the majority* of those who are employed in this lifestyle are at or below the *poverty* level? Why!?

First of all, over 95% of all Road Rats have never even *heard* of this book -- and this is the *only* complete Handbook for this type of work that has ever existed. Of course, just *having* a copy of it is no guarantee of success, either. You need to **use and understand it**. As it says in the Introduction, you *either* can employ the techniques described herein and realize earnings from $30,000 to $52,000 a year, or more, right from the start. *Or* -- you can get into this field *without* being armed with this information... and scratch your way up out of the poverty level after a year or more, from learning many of these techniques the hard way. Uninformed drivers might have to work for several years to learn most of them, and still would not likely learn them all. And even if they did, it would be difficult to set up return Interlock runs *without* having access to the listings in Appendix 1 of this Handbook!

So the good news for you, now that *you* have joined the ranks of that tiny minority of Road Rats who *are* well-informed, is that **most people who are faced with doing things the hard way, drop out and seek work that is more lucrative, or in which advancement seems likely to occur at a faster pace. That is a *major* reason for there being so much turnover within the driving corps of some manufacturers, but *especially* of the *transporter companies*.** There are other reasons, too.

The *second-most important reason* for rapid turnover within the Road Rat workforce is the fact that about 30% of all such drivers are age 65 and over when they start. Drivers in that age group do a very good job, so *that* is *not* a factor. But consider *this*. **When people enter *any* workforce at an age between 65 and 80, they *won't stay in it nearly as long* as they would if they had entered that workforce at, say, age 25 or even 50.** A 65-year-old Road Rat may perform the work for weeks, months, or even for a few years. What he almost surely *won't* do is retain that position in the workforce for 25 years or more. As soon as he drops out of the workforce due to advancing age, that provides a *new* job opening for someone else -- of *any* age -- seeking to take his place.

Do *YOU* know of *any* other workforce in the world in which roughly *one-third* of all the workers are over 65? *I* don't. **This is perhaps the most retiree-friendly industry on the planet,** with the possible exception of the workforce comprised of security guards!

So let's combine those two factors, and see how good your chances are of being hired as a Road Rat within a reasonable period of time:

1. The earnings of 80% or more of Road Rats are almost at the poverty level because *they have little or no **initial** guidance,* and therefore a high percentage drop out after a very short time to do something else, as a result of economic need or due to becoming discouraged.

2. 30% or so of all Road Rats are between age 65 and 80 when they enter the workforce, and therefore will work, on average, for a period ranging from a few months to only a few years.

That results in a TREMENDOUS turnover in the Road Rat workforce! If there are 100,000 part-time and full-time Road Rats working at the moment you read this sentence, figure that by a year later, probably less than 40,000 of those *same* people still will be doing it.

What this means is that by NEXT MONTH, about 5,000 **new** Road Rats will be working, having *replaced* the ones that dropped out during the previous 30 days. If *you* want to be hired in any given month, all you have to do is find just **one** of those positions!

Let's take this a step farther. The *average* person living within the populous regions of America is within a reasonable driving distance of perhaps 35 manufacturers and transporter companies that use drivers to deliver vehicles. (To keep this example simple, we *won't* consider the many *dealerships* in the same area that probably would be using DPU Road Rats.) Of the 4,000 companies in America and Canada that are listed in Appendix 1, about 3,700 are manufacturers and transporters.

This means that during any given month, around 50 new driving positions open up for prospective Road Rats within a reasonable driving distance of most Americans living in the Lower 48 states. You might think that some of those might not actually be re-filled due to the modern trend of companies "downsizing" (a hokey buzzword of the '90s that simply refers to companies that are getting chintzier!). But that's not true in this industry. If a given number of vehicles are being built and shipped, there's no way they can be delivered by *fewer* drivers. That makes the Road Rat lifestyle *immune* to that factor.

When the positions are filled, many will be taken by Road Rat applicants who had taken the initiative to request that they be placed on those companies' *waiting lists.*

TIP: Getting on waiting lists is a very important job-seeking strategy!

The other major group of drivers that are hired are those who just *happen to be making contact* with a company to inquire about an opening at a time when the dispatcher either knows he's about to have one, or else has just had a position open up.

TIP: Making *contact* with companies on a *regular* basis is equally important!

Later in this book, you'll find that many different factors govern the availability of work in the Road Rat workforce. As you learn more about those, you'll develop a keen awareness for why making *frequent contact* with companies for which you would especially *like* to work is a very good plan.

JOB SEARCH TIPS:

For *best results* in getting hired either quickly, or within two or three weeks,

1. Tell companies that you want to check back with them regularly, because you are very interested in working for them. Then follow through, and *do* so! At least once a week, and twice, if they don't mind your doing that.

2. Ask to be *wait-listed* for a job opening as one of their drivers. Then **check the status** of your position on the wait-list, **weekly**.

NOTE: **If a person is in reasonably-good health, has a valid license, a decent driving record, and enjoys driving -- there is NO NEED for him or her to be living on a restrictive "fixed income!"**

That point cannot be made strongly enough!

If you are retired, or soon will *be* retired, and a loved one or friend has given you this book as a gift, *you may just have been given a new lease on life!* Many Road Rats continue in this lifestyle until their late 70's. Some reach their 80's before heading for that rocking chair. The facts stated earlier about retirees in this workforce are absolutely true: you probably *won't* be an active Road Rat 25 years from now. But with the information and guidance you now hold in your hands, there's no reason you can't be doing this at least through most of your 70s, if you so desire, and your health permits.

The fact is, the rocking chair is literally a *deadly foe* if you have retired recently. The retiree who keeps active and enjoys a healthy zest for life has a **much** better shot at a long and happy life than does the person who becomes sedentary. If you're unsure of this, ask *any* doctor for confirmation!

Fortunately, most retirees know this.

Unfortunately, most retirees *also* find that their age seems to be a substantial barrier to employment. In fact, in most fields, they quite literally *have* become unemployable.

Most fields. But **not** *this* one!

REMEMBER: **There is NO upper age limit for Road Rats.**

And -- retirees are strongly *desired* as drivers by prospective employers! Safety is the greatest concern for those involved in the manufacture and shipment of new vehicles. Actuarial tables of insurance companies verify that people between 65 and 80 are in the age group comprising the *safest* drivers!

Most companies want drivers who are stable and mature. *Careful* and *safe* drivers. Retirees are a perfect choice in that respect. So they are *eminently* employable. Some companies make it policy to have *only* retirees in their driving corps. (Fortunately for those who are younger, though, *most* are quite willing to hire safe drivers from across the *entire* age spectrum, 18 and over.)

Let's suppose for a moment that **you** have reached age 65. (For many, that means mandatory retirement, while for most others, age 70 is the limit.) Perhaps throughout your lifetime, you've dreamed often of traveling, but haven't managed to do it due to insufficient income, or to the rat-race nature of a job having all-too-short vacations.

For *you,* the world of travel has simply been in your *future.*

You just didn't *realize* it until now!

As a retiree, you can travel to your heart's content... and get *paid* for it.

***No more* "fixed income" problems!**

Now you can get out to *explore* those national parks, or *visit* friends and relatives in distant places.

And you can *set your own schedule.* Drive full-time, part-time, occasionally, or even just take a *rare* trip, now and then. It's easy to negotiate such things with most employers!

Okay... back to an earlier question: How much can increased awareness of this Handbook, due to the author's appearance on radio and TV talk shows and newscasts, affect the availability of work? Can that cause a surplus of applicants capable of overwhelming the number of available Road Rat positions?

The answer is that such an occurrence is fairly rare, and when it does happen, the effect usually is localized within a relatively small region. And it *always* is temporary. This is why...

If 20,000 people hear a talk show in which this subject is discussed, some who are interested will purchase the book. More will fall victim to skepticism, figure that such a job is "too good to be true," and will **not** purchase the book. (Consider the fact that I've written *many* books, but the primary reason for my writing *this* one was to enable other people to enjoy the unique Road Rat lifestyle that I have loved so much since 1977. So as you can well imagine, it saddens me to know that over the years that this book has been out, many thousands of people who *could have* greatly improved their lives -- did not -- simply due to their own skepticism. Skepticism often protects us, but when it reaches the level of cynicism it often slams the door on rare and valuable opportunities!) As a result, out of 20,000 listeners, perhaps only 40 people actually *purchase* the Handbook. Those are the ones who were interested in the lifestyle, *and* who were not so skeptical as to pass up the chance to look into it.

Out of those 40 people, perhaps 20 will read the Handbook *thoroughly.* The rest will either give it a *quick* read, decide they can't really leave the rut they're already in, and shelve the book... or worse, they'll put it on a shelf *unread,* and then forget it. It's tragic, but even though literally tens of millions of people are unhappy or downright miserable in their present jobs and wish their situation could change -- they STAY in that rut, just for the security it affords them. What a shame when you consider that we get just one shot at life, and then so many choose to pass up chances to make it better!

So of the 20 who read the book thoroughly, perhaps 4 will decide to become Road Rats.

That's a total of four new Road Rats resulting from 40 Handbooks purchased, or *one in ten.*

You'll recall that my estimate for the total number of Road Rats *working at any given time* was around 100,000. (That figure does not include "on-call" Road Rats, or CPU drivers *not* working for *dealers.*)

Since early 1987, this book has been disseminated at the rate of roughly 500 per month. So of the 500 people *each month* who obtain it, perhaps only *50* decide to enter the Road Rat lifestyle.

And since around 5,000 new Road Rats get started every month (while an equal number drop out), but only 50 are *prepared* with this knowledge, beforehand, you can see that this Handbook normally causes *no* competition for available jobs. For every 100 new Road Rats being hired, only ONE will have the book. And as a result, most of the remaining 99 who have to learn the *hard* way... will give up before very long, and seek a different job. And *that* will *continue* the cycle of new opportunity for future drivers! (Now you can see why my estimate that 95% of Road Rats that are working at any given time, have never even *heard* of this Handbook, was actually a *conservative* one.)

As for the 19,960 people who heard the show, but *didn't* buy the book (in this example we just used) -- *not* counting the skeptics -- this lifestyle really *isn't* for everyone. Some folks don't enjoy driving that much. So it's true that because of the talk shows and newscasts, many more people *have* become *aware* that this lifestyle exists. But almost *none* of **them** will *ever* compete with you in the job market.

Now -- what if you are a *college student,* or a *teacher?* It's all good news! You are in *demand!*

Specialized vehicles and RVs are manufactured and delivered *all year-'round*... but the volume is *greater* during the *summer months*. This gap is largely filled by college students and teachers, who have their long vacations at that time, and come out of the woodwork to help out the regular driver workforce.

TIP: **Given the normal 3-month-long summer vacation, college students and teachers typically are able to earn from $8-12,000. That's a very nice supplement to a teaching salary, and frugal students often can earn their tuition and fees for the coming school year this way.**

Most college graduates who learn about this job wish they'd known about the opportunity while they still were in school. That includes *this* author!

It was particularly interesting to us when our research turned up a manufacturer in Canada who specified that they need more college students to apply for summer driving jobs with them! We were told that they're often unable to find a student to drive for them on short notice -- so they wanted us to be sure and provide that information as part of their listing in Appendix 1. (We did.)

Okay -- what about the job itself? If a Handbook *this large* is needed to provide the instruction, doesn't that mean that the job is quite complex, and hard to learn?

We hear that about once or twice a year from purchasers of the book, and we're convinced that they either didn't read *this chapter,* or else they expressed their concern to us *before* they bothered to read the *book!* So for the benefit of purchasers of THIS edition who may have that idea, I'm going to repeat the paragraph that deals with that -- but *this* time, I'm going to make sure it gets *everyone's* attention:

The methods described in this book are *not* complex. Once you start driving, you will find nearly all of them second-nature to you within two or three weeks. You will become a very skilled Road Rat in that period of time, to the point that most functions of your new job will have become automatic.

There. *That* oughta do it!

Much of what you'll see in these pages is common sense, but *without* this instruction, all too many people would find themselves asking the question, after about three years of driving, "Gee! That should have been obvious! Why didn't I think of that *sooner?!!*" Not all "common sense" is accompanied by conscious awareness of same, when a person needs to draw upon it.

So I'd rather state the seemingly-obvious a bit too often, and be sure that everyone receives *all* the information they need, and sees the *tie-ins* of it to the specific circumstances they're likely to encounter. The alternative is to be a bit more brief, but in the process perhaps leave out something that would *then* turn out to be, for *someone,* an important oversight. This book is, by the way, a **major revision,** as owners of previous editions have no doubt already noticed. Over **95% of the material in this book has been revised** or completely re-written since the previous edition, including the data in Appendix 1, which nearly all was current as of late November, 1994, when this edition was sent to the printer.) (And... in this 3rd Printing of that same edition, in **May, 1997,** we *updated* roughly 100 of its pages and 500 of its listings!)

Let's get back to your own situation, and see some more of what this job can mean for you.

As a skilled and successful driver, you quickly will gain job security. Keep doing your job right, and your future is assured. In the fresh air of the Great Outdoors, which is all yours, there is no "rat race" climb up the corporate ladder, and no competition for your job. Isn't *that* a refreshing change?!

You can sit back in a comfortable bucket seat, drive, and see all North America on a perpetual vacation-with-pay that's beyond most people's wildest dreams!

There is a surprising number of differences between trucking and RV delivery, as shown in the table on the next page. RV driving has almost all the advantages of trucking, and practically none of the disadvantages. It is both interesting and important to note that *most* of the advantages enjoyed by *RV* Road Rats *also* are applicable to the Road Rats who deliver *other* specialized vehicles.

An interesting aspect of becoming a Road Rat is the versatility you will gain. A few of the unique advantages are listed below. Compare them to the conditions encountered in most, more conventional, jobs -- even other jobs that involve travel.

1. Many companies will allow you to take vacations, or days off, at will, on fairly short notice. Sometimes on even a few *hours'* notice.

2. Most companies allow you complete freedom to choose *any reasonable route* to your assigned destinations. (The longer the distance involved, the more you can vary your route without adding extra miles to the trip.)

3. You normally will have a wide latitude of *choice* with respect to your *destinations,* from the trips available at any given time.

4. You set your own hours. No more of the dreaded tedium of "9-to-5" hours or other similar syndromes of the rat race. You drive when you feel like it, stop when you feel like it, and sleep when you feel like it. (Isn't that nice? **Road** Rats are *exempt* from the rat race!)

5. With a galaxy of 4,000 potential employers, the North American Road Rat can easily gain access to most of the continent, including all of its beaches, national parks, and other points of interest. (It takes many *years* to explore even the high points of all that. I know!) The same is true for Australians and Europeans in *their* respective continents.

COMPARISON:
Trucking vs. RV Delivery

TRUCKING	RV DELIVERY
Special Training or Apprenticeship is Required.	No Training Necessary.
Commercial Driver's License (CDL).	Ordinary Operator's or Chauffeur's License if Vehicle is Under 26,000 lbs.
Truckers Frequently are Under Time Pressure.	Normally Set Own Schedule, within Reason.
Experience Normally is Required.	No Experience Necessary.
Investment Frequently is Required.	No Investment Necessary.
Truckers Often Encounter Route Restrictions.	RV Drivers Normally can Travel wherever Cars Can be Driven.
Time is Lost at Warehouses while Cargo is Loaded & Unloaded.	No Down Time at Destinations; Check-in Normally Takes Only a Few Minutes.
Trucks Normally Haul Freight.	The RV Itself is the Payload.
Major Repairs Take Days or Weeks	Breakdowns Rare; Repair Normally is Rapid.
Repairs Generally Quite Costly.	All Repairs are Under Warranty.
Much Paperwork is Required.	Paperwork is Quite Minimal.
Many Drivers Must Seek Lodging.	Drivers Sleep Right in the Coach.
Insurance is a Burden to Owner-Operators.	Insurance Almost Always Company-Furnished.
Few Luxury Items Normally Included.	Many Amenities are Standard.
Cruise Control is Almost Unheard-of.	Cruise Control is Almost Universal.
Automatic Transmission is Rare.	Nearly All RVs are Automatic.
Older Models Give Rough, Bumpy Ride.	Ride is Always Smooth & Comfortable.
Most Trucks Harder to Maneuver than RVs.	RVs Often Handle Better than Cars.
Truck Payments are a Monthly Burden to Owner-Operators.	No Payments to Make, nor Job-Connected Financial Obligations.
Only the Most Luxurious Trucks Have Spacious Beds.	Class "A" and "C" RVs Have Comfortable Beds in which to Sleep.
Trucks Must Stop to Weigh at Most Open Weigh Stations.	Occasional Port-of-Entry Stops are Required in Some of the Western States.
Seeking New Loads at Destinations is a Source of Much Lost Time and Aggravation to Many Truckers.	Return or Continuing Runs Not Required, But if Desired, "Interlocks" Usually Can be Established before Arrival at Destination.

Selecting a Company

There are four general types of employers of drivers. These are:

- A. Manufacturers/Modifiers/Final Assemblers of RVs and other specialized vehicles
- B. Dealers of RVs and other specialized vehicles
- C. Vehicle Transporter Companies
- D. Renters/Users of certain specialized vehicles.

Significant differences exist between these which should be considered before you apply for employment. Before we get into this, let's *eliminate* Item D from consideration, after which we'll discuss the others in order.

Item D refers to companies that have one or more of a given type of specialty vehicle as an integral part of their operations. Here are six examples:

1. Hospitals that have ambulances
2. Bottling Companies that have beverage route trucks
3. Funeral Homes that have one or more hearses
4. Firehouses that have one or more fire trucks
5. Limo *Services* (not dealers) that have one or more limousines
6. School Districts having fleets of school busses

I could go on and on, but you get the picture. Now, if such a company decides that it could save money, or that it would be handier simply to send one of its regular employees to the factory to pick up a vehicle, then the person who makes the pickup is *not* a true Road Rat. He is, in fact, most likely making the only such trip he'll ever make, and being a Road Rat does not normally fit within the parameters of his job description. All Customer Pickups (CPUs) are done in this manner. *Unless* you work for a *dealer* (doing DPUs), you are never likely to be a Road Rat doing CPUs.

The best way to illustrate this would be for you to imagine yourself going to a funeral home and volunteering to become their Road Rat. If you do, you'd better have a regular day job besides, or else before long you'll become a very *hungry* Road Rat! Most funeral homes do not need to purchase new hearses once or twice a week on a regular basis. So much for Item D. Now let's examine A, B, and C, in that order.

A. FACTORY ROAD RATS

Item A includes all manufacturers, modifiers (including converters), and final assembly sites for RVs and other specialized vehicles. It is the point from which the finished vehicle is shipped to the customer, or to the dealer who ultimately will sell it to a consumer. When a Road Rat works for such a company, he normally does so as an independent contractor. That means that his taxes are not withheld, and he therefore pays estimated taxes quarterly, and then files the usual return on April 15 along with everyone else. The best way for him to accomplish this is by having a qualified tax person or CPA do it for him. I recommend a CPA because such people have that extra amount of expertise which can enable them to legitimately save you hundreds, and perhaps thousands of dollars. You pay more for their services, but the investment generally repays you immediately, several times over. Additionally, by being an independent contractor, you normally are not entitled to employee benefits, such as health care. That's the bad news. The good news is that this type of company generally pays the *highest* wage to Road Rats, so by working for them, you can afford to establish your *own* plan of benefits! About 90-95% of Road Rats who work for manufacturers are paid between 30 and 35 cents per mile, *take-home pay,* before taxes. That means that a Road Rat making a coast-to-coast trip across North America generally earns around $1,000 or more for his efforts. Not bad for a job that only takes three to seven days, depending upon how you pace yourself! The pay is this good because there are *no middlemen* involved in the process; the Road Rat works *directly for the manufacturer.*

B. DPU ROAD RATS

This Road Rat is the *nemesis* of factory Road Rats, but most of the latter are too gracious to show it. (They just grit their teeth a whole lot whenever one appears.) The DPU Road Rat is the one who is sent *to* the factory to *pick up* a unit, which he then *drives back* to the dealer. Factory Road Rats wish all of the DPU Road Rats (along with the folks doing other CPUs -- Item D) would simply go away for good, because every time one of them shows up at the factory, it *eliminates* a run that the factory Road Rats otherwise would have had available to them. Strangely enough, it doesn't work the other way around, because dealers who have Road Rats doing DPUs generally get *all* their units from the factories that way, so the DPU Road Rats usually don't have the disconcerting experience of seeing a competing factory Road Rat on *their* turf! Like the factory Road Rat, the DPU one also is usually an independent contractor. However, they frequently are members of the sales force at the dealership, and in that event, *may* be actual employees, doing double duty. Road Rats who apply to dealerships for work should therefore be prepared to hear either of two reasons for not being hired: (1) The dealership has all its units delivered by the *factory,* or (2) The dealership always sends its *sales personnel* to pick up the units. You won't be able to cope with reason #2 unless you're prepared to become a salesperson -- but there *is* a way to cope with reason #1. When you hear reason #1, you can sometimes *negotiate!*

Dealers generally pay their sales personnel an hourly or negotiated wage for making a DPU, but if one is purely a Road Rat, then he or she generally is paid by the mile, just like the factory Road Rats. The difference is, they frequently are paid somewhat *less* than the factory ones. Because that's why most dealers that employ DPU Road Rats usually have them in the first place! They want to obtain units from the factories at a lower cost than the factories otherwise would charge them for the shipping! If the shipping cost is lower for the dealer, then he can *sell* the unit at a lower price, and that gives him a competitive *edge* over the dealer down the street whose deliveries are all made by *factory* Road Rats!

And *that's* where you can negotiate. When you run across a dealer who has all of his units delivered by factory Road Rats, you can suggest the possibility of *saving him money* by letting *you* do it for *less*. If he's willing to listen, see if he'll make an appointment with you so that you can analyze together how much the factories are charging him for the shipments. Once that figure has been determined, all you have to do is come in with a lower bid that would cover the cost of your transportation to the factory, your road expenses (mainly the fuel) back, and leave you with a decent wage of say, somewhere between 25 and 30 cents per mile. If you're really lucky, you might find that his costs for having factory Road Rats deliver to him might have been high enough that you can come in with a lower offer and *still* make between 30 and 35 cents per mile! Before all is said and done, though, be sure that it's arranged so that the dealer's *insurance* will cover both *you and the unit you're driving* while you're en route. He already has insurance on his premises and employees, and arranging this only calls for his obtaining a simple extension of his policy that will cost him little or nothing extra in premiums. *Be SURE that this is in place before you work for him.* Road Rats generally can NOT afford to purchase their OWN special insurance for the purpose of delivering new vehicles. (Factory Road Rats are always covered by their companies, with only the rarest of possible exceptions.) Whoever you drive for, be sure to carry along *proof* of insurance. If the police stop you for any reason, they'll ask for it in many states... and you cannot enter and drive across *Kansas* in a specialty vehicle, and sometimes even an RV, without showing this at a port of entry!

TIP: **REMEMBER that the DPU method has one important advantage: One who does not live near RV manufacturers, and who wants to return frequently to his present home, can often get into this field by working for a dealership right in his home area!**

C. TRANSPORTER-COMPANY ROAD RATS

These Road Rats are generally the lowest-paid, and therefore tend to be the most transient in terms of their longevity in this lifestyle. The irony is that most transporter companies generally have friendly and helpful people as agents and driver dispatchers, but they're caught between the proverbial rock and a hard place. Here's how this works.

The transporter usually has one or more factories for which they've contracted to deliver vehicles. This is a nice deal for the factories, because it doesn't cost them any more to have a transporter do this for them than it costs them to have their *own* Road Rats. By having a transporter do it, their own lives become simpler. When a factory Road Rat has a problem on the road, such as a breakdown, then a factory dispatcher has to work out the details with the service manager on the other end, and decide whether or not (in the case of a major breakdown) to bring the Road Rat back, or to pay him per diem and put him up in a motel while the unit's being repaired. And should a Road Rat have an accident, then his factory has to deal directly with the insurance company. Therefore, a transporter company is a middleman in more ways than one... it acts as a *buffer* that stands between the drivers and the factory in cases of problems like these. If insurance claims are involved, then that's the transporter company's problem, and *their* insurance that's affected, and not that of the factory.

What puts the transporter company in a bind is the fact that if they set the price of their services to a factory at more than it would cost for a factory to use its own drivers, then the factory simply will turn them down in favor of doing just that. In trade for a bit more hassle, the factory then would save money. After all, both factories and transporters make a point of hiring Road Rats with decent driving records, so accidents are very rare. And since the vehicles are brand-new, major breakdowns don't occur very frequently either. Now, out of the money the factory pays to a transporter company, the company must make enough to pay the wages of its office personnel, all the overhead, the insurance premiums (which are high!)... and pay the drivers. That leaves you, the Road Rat, with only about half as much as you would make if you worked *directly* for the factory, but you can see the problem faced by the transporter companies: If they pay the drivers more, the factories will consider their services too expensive, and they go out of business. If they pay the drivers less, no one will *be* their Road Rat, and they *still* go out of business. Even if they set their standards lower so that lower-caliber Road Rat applicants are hired, then they have drivers who are more prone to being irresponsible, or unsafe -- and as a result, their already-exorbitant insurance premiums go up... and they can't afford it anymore... and they go out of business! As you can see, the transporter companies have to walk a very fine line.

The above paragraph was written so that *all* Road Rats can have some appreciation for the situation faced by transporter companies and the lower-paid Road Rats who work for them. Now consider *this*:

Some factories have their own drivers, and some factories use transporter companies instead. It's been that way for decades. And we don't know what the ratio is from one day to the next, because so many factories are *switching* from one method to the other. Our guess is that for the foreseeable future, there probably will be no drastic pendulum swing one way or the other. In Appendix 1, the factories and transporters are in *separate sections*, so that you can distinguish when making your applications.

TIP: Be SURE to read the introductory pages at the beginning of *Appendix 1*, before going on to examine the listings. And please don't just SKIM that material. Read *all* of it VERY CAREFULLY!

You may wonder why a driver would seek employment with a transporter company if he can only expect to clear around 16 to 18 cents per mile (and sometimes even less). In my own case, as you've probably already seen, a transporter was one of the only two companies about which I knew existed at the time, and that was the one that hired me. But frequently, it's simply a case of being hired more *easily* there than at a factory or a dealership. Delivering vehicles is what transporter companies *do*. It is their *primary* function, whereas the main task of a *factory* is to *build* the vehicles, and it's the *dealer's* job to *sell* them. So transporter companies are very driver-oriented in the first place. And in the second place, because they're forced to pay them less, the transporter is always having to replace drivers that can't afford to keep going, with new drivers. So it is usually easier to find job openings there, than at the higher-paying locations. For example, how many Road Rats who earn $52,000 a year working for a factory are going to feel inclined to quit? When I found myself in that position, I stayed on for seven years, and left only because the factory went out of business! When a Road Rat gets himself into a position that sweet, about the only thing that's going to dislodge him is age. Sooner or later, everyone reaches an age where he or she is too old to drive safely, and then it's time to consider the rocking chair. But as I told you earlier, the saving factor here for prospective drivers is the fact that 30% of all Road Rats *already* are age 65 and over... so the turnover, even at factories, is fairly brisk! And that 30% is across the board -- it applies *both* to factories and transporter companies. So Road Rats seeking work at *transporters* have *two* advantages in their favor... underpaid Road Rats who quit in despair, and retirees who are starting to get too old to drive. Father Time ultimately catches up with us all -- but with this Handbook in your possession, *income* doesn't have to be a problem, even if you go to work for a transporter company. There are two ways to win, economically, if you work as a transporter-company Road Rat:

(1) Use it as a stepping-stone to becoming a factory Road Rat. Once you're driving, carry this Handbook along, as you would a road atlas, and then stop in and apply in person at factories all over the country as you encounter them in your travels. This is how I got my first job as a factory Road Rat... although in my case, it immediately *conformed* to (2), below...

(2) Establish a regular Interlock situation, with your transporter company on one end, and the factory on the other, of a route you can drive frequently for both companies. If the factory has dealers or customers in the region where your transporter company's office is located, and your transporter ships frequently to the factory's region, then you can have it made. In my own case, establishing this relationship up and down the West Coast immediately boosted my earnings to $800/week -- over a year before I even *discovered* Maximization (which *subsequently* paid me *$1,000* a week).

TIP: Don't sell transporter companies short. They can be VERY helpful to you as either a starting or continuing Road Rat! And remember, if you go to work for one, be a QUALITY Road Rat! Serve your employer well, no matter what he pays you. This book will assist you in your advancement, if you study it well, and use it to your best advantage.

Availability of Runs

Normally, factories are not wildly enthusiastic about having their drivers working for *competitors* in the *same immediate vicinity*, when runs are not available. Nor, for that matter, are transporter companies. Both like to have drivers that they can count on when they're needed, and both feel a natural resentment when a worker suddenly begins assisting a *competitor* to be profitable when things are slow on their *own* end. (In the case of Interlock, of course, the companies involved are far enough apart that no competition pressures are felt. In the only case where I've found a dispatcher that prohibited his drivers from practicing Interlock when making return trips, the company has since gone out of business.)

As in so much of life, there are trade-offs involved when one chooses to work for a factory or dealer, *vis-a-vis* for a transporter company. On occasion, if a driver works directly for a factory, and that factory has no units to ship for a period of time, the driver could be left hung out to dry. (Factories call it "laid off" when the situation applies to *hourly employees.*) This is a difficult situation, and holds the potential of fiscal disaster for the driver, if it should persist. Likewise, something akin to an Energy Hoax or a nearby major bank failure can badly impact sales at an *RV dealership* -- and that would do a bad number on a DPU Road Rat!

No matter how highly a factory or a dealer may regard a driver, it is an economic fact of life that neither can pay him if he can't do any work. One could hardly expect that.

On the other hand, even though less-adequately paid, the transporter-company Road Rat has a greater degree of job security at a time when a factory or some dealerships may be having problems. The majority of transporter companies serve a *number* of factories. So if one of those factories has a slump, a company-wide vacation period, or a production problem, the transporter company usually receives enough units from the *other* factories to keep all its regular drivers busy. (And, during periodic times of *surplus,* most transporter companies can call upon a list of local residents who are willing to take runs on an occasional or part-time basis. These frequently are retired persons. Factories, and sometimes dealerships who do DPUs, also usually maintain a list of back-up or standby "on-call" drivers.)

Unions

As far as we know, there still are no unionized Road Rats of any kind, of the types of Road Rats we've discussed so far, nor have I yet ever met such a driver who has been approached by a union for that purpose, or who has shown the least interest in belonging to one. Most delivery drivers consider their working conditions excellent, and their pay reasonable for work done. I can't imagine how a transporter company could really survive unionization of its drivers, given the economic tightrope such a company already walks. So it's doubtful that an attempt to organize a union in that situation would benefit anyone. There is virtually no real discontent to my knowledge, based on 17 years of observation. Most Road Rats enjoy their work, and those who don't usually stop being Road Rats.

There *are* a few places that drastically underpay drivers, or undercut driver opportunity by offering unpaid runs to local folks, in return for the "adventure" of making the trip. Fortunately, they are few in number, have runs available quite infrequently, and therefore would be of no interest to anyone wanting to unionize. And it's more like the (*non*-DPU) CPU situation; the drivers involved aren't really Road Rats.

"Should I Become a Road Rat?"

Only *you* know the answer to that question... and it is an answer you might not fully decide upon until you have read all the material in this book, and weighed the trade-offs. However, there are some important points to ponder, besides those discussed in the Introduction, and elsewhere.

It's a sad commentary on our society, but evidently America still has a lot of growing up to do. According to U.S. Government report issued in the mid-1980's, at the rate women currently are approaching a status of receiving equal pay for equal work, they can expect to finally be treated fairly in the workplace by the year 2035. *Fortunately,* though, that far-flung date actually seems to have *arrived* long ago with respect to the delivery of vehicles. I have neither seen nor heard of an instance wherein a woman working as a Road Rat for any company has earned any less than her male counterparts, or has been treated any differently.

And if you're in the rat race, there's hardly a better way to get *out* of it! This stress-free, laid-back lifestyle can enable you to climb out of the rut you've been in, and look objectively at your life options. Few people aspire to be Road Rats for the *remainder* of their *lives,* as fabulous as the experience is, except, perhaps, in the case of many of the retirees. But you may wish to *combine* it, as I have, with *other* activities. I've always loved to write, even though the pay sometimes left much to be desired, and tended to come in a "feast-or-famine" manner. But while a full-time Road Rat, I was able to earn a regular wage from my driving and still have adequate blocks of time, as I chose to designate them, for my writing. And, over the years, I've gotten many of my *best* ideas for future writing projects while driving down the road. Whenever an idea strikes me in that circumstance, I've been known to just pull over and stop, so that I could put those thoughts on paper, or dictate them into a cassette recorder. Remember what I said about using the Road Rat lifestyle as a **gateway to expanded opportunities!**

It's great for professionals and executives, too! You already know how it can improve the lives of teachers, as it did with me. But for **bankers?!** You'll enjoy *that* story in Part III, Chapter 4!

* * * * *

ABOUT THE CARTOON ON THE NEXT PAGE --

Every edition of this Handbook has included this cartoon, which dates back to 1979, when Congress still included speed limits in its "federal blackmail" list. (The 10th Amendment of the U.S. Constitution prohibits the enactment of federal laws in areas not defined by the Constitution; the individual states have the *right* to legislate in those areas. In recent years, Congress has unethically circumvented that right by threatening the loss of federal highway funds to states who don't comply with their wishes. And remember, too, that the federal government is only acting as a *broker* for those states' people's *own* tax money!) By early 1996, Congress had finally restored free rein to the states for setting speed limits... and you've just gotta **LOVE** the way *Montana* handled the whole thing. During the blackmail years (1974-95), if you were stopped for daytime speeding there, they gave you a "Failure to Conserve Natural Resources" ticket that carried a $5.00 fine and had no impact on your driving record! People were framing them and hanging them on their walls as a proud badge of independence! (No, unfortunately, I never got one. But it wasn't for lack of trying!) Best of all, when the blackmail was lifted, Montana responded by *completely eliminating* its daytime speed limits! (I had fully expected Nevada to do that, too, but they only went to 75 mph instead.)

On the down side, even though Big Oil (so far) has not teamed up with the government again to pertpetrate any new energy hoaxes, it *is* charging about 20 cents per gallon more for gasoline in early 1997 (at around $1.25 - $1.35) than it did just six months earlier. Road maps (which used to be *free,* remember?) now cost $2.50 and more. New England is notorious for having a high percentage of gas stations that charge 50 cents for *air* for your tires (so shop around!)... and in Pawtucket, RI, a *"Sunoco"* station has the *gall* to charge *its own customers* **25 cents** to use the *rest rooms!* (Good grief!)

Part 1 --- Getting the Job

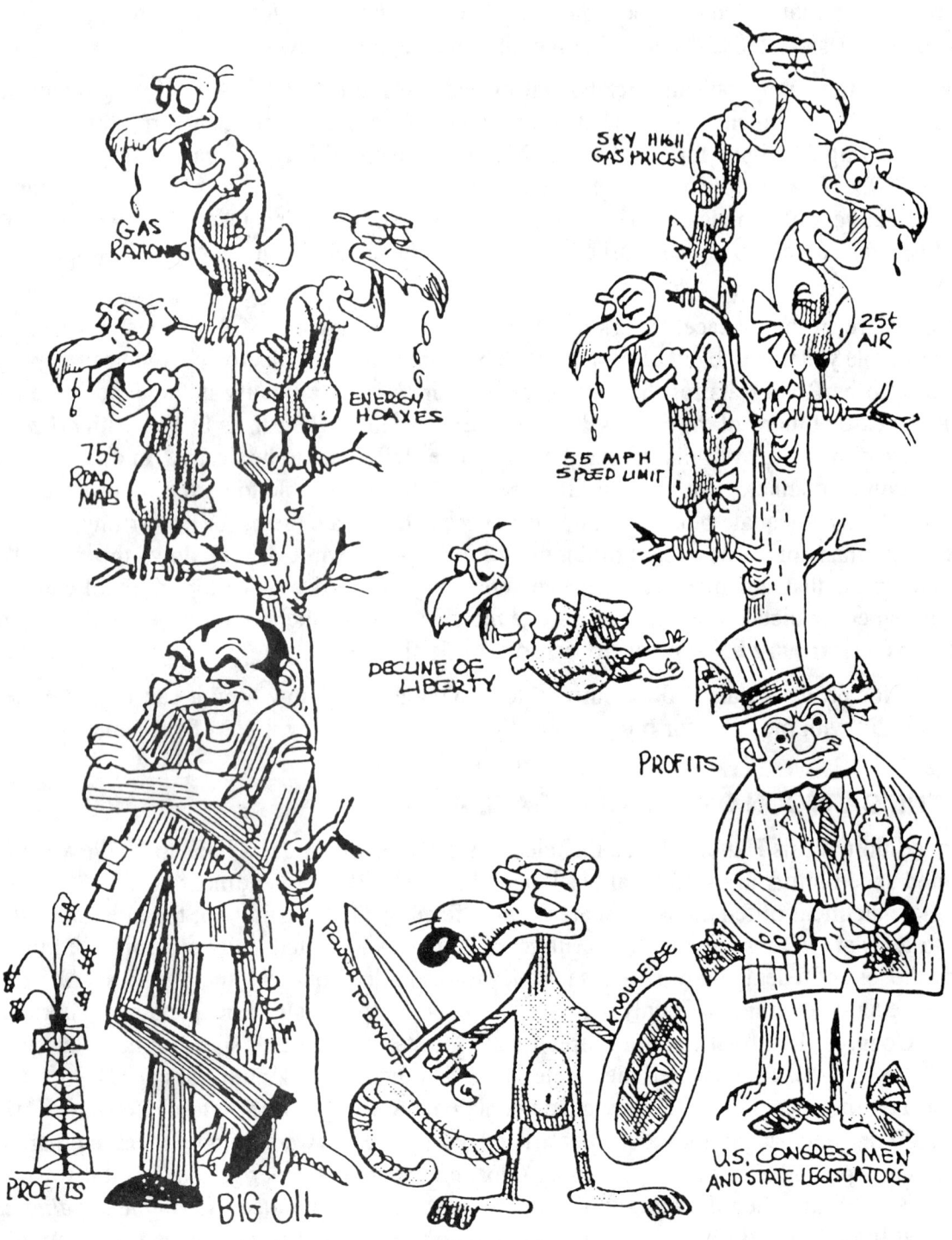

Road Rats don't appreciate price gouging!

2

General Requirements

The minimum requirements for becoming a Road Rat are surprisingly easy to meet. It is likely that perhaps as much as 90-95% of the population age 18 and over can qualify.

There are **practically no *educational* requirements.** In fact, I have even known some moderately successful people in this field who are functionally illiterate. On the other hand, I have known Road Rats who have Ph.D degrees. This is one of those rare jobs where people are almost never considered to be either underqualified or overqualified with regard to their educational backgrounds. There are certain criteria which must, of course be met -- but quantity and/or quality of one's education is not one of them.

***Sex discrimination* is all but non-existent.** Women make up 30% of the drivers in this workforce, and most companies having two or more drivers have drivers of both genders. The pay and working conditions almost always are equal for both.

There are only **five basic requirements** which you must meet in order to be hired:

1. *Minimum* Age: 18... *Maximum* Age: None! --

Some companies require a driver to be 21, and few still require one to be 25. In the latter case, this generally applies to those companies that require drivers to have the Commercial Driver's License, or due to insurance. Such companies are some of the transporter companies, and all companies which manufacture or modify vehicles weighing more than 26,000 pounds. For drivers who have a Class "A" CDL, there is new material in this edition of the Handbook that provides additional information about expanded opportunities. See Part III, Chapter 3. Because the majority of Road Rats are neither truckers, nor have trucker qualifications, however, the lower age limit of 18-21 usually applies at those companies where CDLs are not required of drivers. In the summertime, when production rates are higher, college students and teachers are in demand to supplement the regular, year-'round driver workforce. Most college students can qualify at companies that have the lower age limit at age 18.

There is *no* **maximum** age limit, which makes this an ideal field for people of retirement age who enjoy travelling! Nearly 1/3 of all Road Rats are over age 65! People in that age group generally fulfill companies' needs for having "on-call" drivers, who are called in periodically to work when the regular drivers all are on runs, and a driver is needed. But thousands of retirement-age drivers work full-time, as well!

2. A Degree of Maturity --

As in any situation involving responsibility for valuable property and the well-being of others, a normal amount of good judgment and common sense is expected of the employee. This is not necessarily a factor of chronological age. A mature and sensible college student having a good, safe driving record is welcomed as readily as is a retiree by a dispatcher. But "hot dogs" should wait until they "grow up" before seeking employment in this field!

3. A Valid Driver's License --

A valid operator's license from any U.S. state or Canadian province is a basic requirement. It can be from another nation if it is accompanied by an International Driver's License. Any class license is sufficient; this job does not require a driver to have a chauffer's license or CDL when driving vehicles *under* 26,000 lbs. is involved. However, an increasing number of companies are beginning to require the higher-grade driver's licenses in line with their own policies, or because some of the vehicles they ship exceed the 13-ton weight limit cut-off specified by the U.S. Department of Transportation (DOT). It should be noted that this Handbook deals primarily with legal requirements for driving in the USA. Weight limits and licensing requirements vary from country to country, but it is our understanding at the time of this edition's publication, in 1994, that ordinary driver's licenses still can be used as well in Canada for light-weight specialty vehicles and RVs.

4. A Relatively Good Driving Record --

Even a history of accidents or moving violations may not stand in your way with many employers, *if* it can be shown that your record *in recent years is good,* or if no serious accidents (in terms of injuries or major property damage) were charged to you recently. A general rule is that if one's record has been excellent for the last three or four years, even a DUI/OMVI/DWI (translation: drunk driving!) offense can be overlooked. Companies have two things to consider. They want safe drivers, and your demonstration of continued driving safety for three or four years can stand you in very good stead, even following a major infraction or a chargeable accident. You may have to seek work at more locations than average because of this, but it generally is possible for people in that situation to be hired. The other factor that companies consider in this regard is whether or not the driver can be hired under their insurance, without the driver's either (a) being rejected by the insurance company, or (b) causing an increase in the premiums that the company would have to pay for the insurance. In almost all cases, the company provides the insurance coverage for drivers, and the units they deliver, while en route. Surprisingly, though, just this year -- 1994 -- for the first time, we learned of a *possible,* but unconfirmed, exception to that, in Florida. We hope that this is not the beginning of a trend, because that could be very disruptive to Road Rats in the future! For now, though, it's a very isolated case, and we have been unable to verify it.

5. Reasonably Good Health --

Some companies require their drivers who travel interstate to have a DOT physical examination, and to carry the health card to this effect (furnished by the employer). The exam can be performed in minutes at nominal cost (generally less than that of a full physical exam), by any medical doctor. If no health certification is required of you, then you, yourself, should make the common-sense determination of whether or not you have a health problem. For example, sleep apnea would be very dangerous when performing this type of work. If you believe you would have no problem driving a minimum of eight hours out of 24, from a health standpoint, then this job should not be hazardous for you.

Getting hired can be an amazingly easy task. Frequently, simply walking into the prospective employer's office and stating your purpose is sufficient, and more than once I have been hired in less than two minutes this way. Even more surprising is the fact that many companies will hire you sight-unseen on the strength of a phone call... another experience that I have personally enjoyed.

On the flip side, it must be noted that some prospective drivers have made 50 or more contacts before getting that first run. Fortunately, that is the exception, rather than the rule, and most applicants get started after making an average of between 8 and 17 contacts with prospective employers. If you get hired on the first or second contact, consider yourself lucky. But if you happen to have the ill fortune to be on the *other* end of that spectrum, it is MOST IMPORTANT that you *DON'T GIVE UP!!*

TIP: **The go-getters who really *want* to become Road Rats almost always *succeed!***

During the course of the interview, it can be beneficial to let your prospective employer know that you have a copy of this Handbook, and that you will get extra guidance from it as you travel. Even if the dispatcher is not yet familiar with this book, he or she should be favorably impressed with the degree to which you take this opportunity seriously, and that you intend to pursue your work with enthusiasm and professionalism. If the dispatcher *is* familiar with the book, then he already will know that your use of it will make you a more efficient Road Rat, to the benefit of *both* yourself, and the company for which you will work.

A few other pointers:

1. Don't Take "No" for an Answer...

...if you really want to work for a specific company, AND if it appears that there is any chance at all that you can become a driver for them. If the company isn't hiring, but does use drivers, inquire again every two or three days, by phone, as long as they remain friendly to you. If there is more than one company in your area (or in the region in which you wish to work), make the rounds regularly. (Whether or not your first application is in person, follow-up calls by phone work very well.) Many of those who secured lucrative jobs on the Alaska Pipeline back in the '70s first lived in Fairbanks for up to five weeks, applying daily. Perseverance pays off.

TIP: **If you are granted an interview, return immediately afterward -- within minutes -- and leave a thank-you note that says: "Thank you for taking time to interview me. I'm looking forword to working for you." Give it to the secretary. And if you should be hired on the spot, the thank-you note then should read: "Thank you for hiring me. I appreciate it, and I'll do my best for you." These can ensure good rapport, right from the start, and it's a proven method in that regard!**

Let's examine two examples from my *own* experience. NOTE: *Don't* skip over this part. Each of these examples is valuable in its own right, and they are very different from one another. Keeping these in mind as you seek the work you want can be very helpful to you. So here goes! (I'll try my best not to bore you!) --

EXAMPLE A

"The West Coast Gambit"

In the spring of 1978, I had gained nearly a year of experience as a Road Rat. (This was without benefit of a Handbook, because this is still the only one, and I was still a year away from writing its *first* edition at that point. Most of the techniques contained even in that earliest edition hadn't been developed yet.) I was tiring of seeing only that part of America that is east of the Rockies. Except for an occasional run to Vancouver, BC, in Canada, most of my company's customers (which were RV dealerships) were east of the spectacular scenery of the West, and I was seeing primarily the Great Plains. Without burning my bridges behind me, I decided to see if I could drive for a *California*-based company for awhile.

So before departure, I secured a promise from my dispatcher (in Indiana) that I could *resume* working for him if things didn't pan out for me in the West. I was working for an agent of Auto Driveaway (a major transporter company), and my plan was to seek work with another agent of the *same* company, in San Bernardino. The odyssey began with a run to Golden, Colorado, in an RV. From there, I "chased the dog" (took *Greyhound*) to San Berdoo, using my *Ameripass*. I arrived early the next morning, and walked the five blocks to the office from the bus depot.

After presenting myself to the agent, Don Myers, and telling him of my experience in Indiana, I was in for a disappointment. Don told me that there were no runs available... and that the best he could offer me was $3.00 per hour if I wanted to join his other drivers that day, helping him ferry RVs to his lot from factories in the desert town of Hemet, 30 miles away.

"I'm already here, so why not?" I told him. About a half hour later, three other drivers and I hopped into his car to begin the long, hot, tedious chore. The sun soon was high in the desert sky, and the temperature topped a scorching 105 degrees. Over eight hours, we all schlepped a total of 16 coaches to Don's lot, which his regular drivers would proceed to deliver over the next few days to points all over the West.

I drew my $24 in pay from Don, thanked him, and picked up my suitcase from behind his desk, about to start my trek back to the bus depot. Then came the surprise.

"Before you go," Don said, "do you see that coach over there in the corner of the lot?" "Yes," I replied. "Well, how would you like to take that up to Tacoma, Washington for me, this evening?"

The whole day had been a TEST! Don had had that opening for a driver all along -- but he wanted to see if I'd be willing to do the tedious dirty work that sometimes goes along with being a Road Rat who works for a transporter company. When he saw that I did so willingly and cheerfully, even though there appeared to be NO chance that I'd be hired... he hired me. And it was a *very* important step up for me, as you'll learn when you read Part III, Chapter 1, on "Interlock!"

EXAMPLE B

"A Yankee in Rebel Country"

Well... I had to come up with *some* kind of enticing name for this, didn't I? And it *did* lead to this upstate New Yorker taking up residence in the former capital of the Confederacy for more than a decade... but we're getting ahead of our story!

Two of the worst periods of recent American history (except for wars) were the disruptive Energy Hoaxes that the U.S. Government successfully perpetrated upon the American people. The worst part of it was the fact that most were gullible enough to *fall* for it!! I *didn't*, by the way, and with Watergate in full swing, I was amazed that *most* people weren't taking such radical government claims with a *cubic acre* of salt by that time! I saw through the first one in 1973-74, right from the start, but mine was one of only two households, of which I had knowledge, that displayed *outdoor* Christmas lights in my city during that gloomy Christmas season. It was either peer pressure from believers, or else most of the people actually *were* being suckered by the Hoax! It seemed so *obvious,* and by *now* most people realize it. But amazingly, it happened *all over again* in 1979 -- and *again,* the people almost universally fell for it! Hopefully, the age of skepticism (or has that justifyably become *cynicism?)* in which we *now* live may have made us immune to *ever* being scammed *again* by yet a *third* Energy Hoax at some future date. (If we ever have another one, I urge you to please *remember* these words! It's just possible that sufficient *protest* might be capable of *neutralizing* it. Letters to newspaper editors for publication, and calls to hosts of talk radio stations can accomplish much!)

Energy Hoax II, in 1979, was *devastating* to the RV industry! And that was very bad news for *RV-*delivering Road Rats. Which I was, when the Hoax began. Suddenly, people all over the nation, once again actually *believing* the government (& Big Oil) lie that we had an energy shortage, started having concerns that gasoline *rationing* might be in the offing. And if gasoline were to be rationed, it would become tough for RV owners to roam around the land, because RVs have always (and especially back then) been notorious for getting lousy gas mileage. An issue of gasoline ration coupons could strand a family from Kankakee in Winnemucca! Knowing this, along with having been duped into thinking there was an actual "energy crisis," potential purchasers of new RVs suddenly began putting their plans to buy on hold. *En masse!* Within just a few months, many RV manufacturers were biting the dust forever, while innovative ones quickly switched to *new and diverse* product lines. A highly-astute company in Oregon kept afloat by temporarily changing over to the manufacture of quality *wood* stoves!

Road Rats find wood stoves rather tricky to drive, so I did what most of the "survivor" Road Rats did in '79. I sought a driving position with the manufacturer of a specialty vehicle that would be certain to be *unaffected* by EH II, no matter *how* far the government and Big Oil decided to carry their cruel and silly game.

Swan, Inc., a manufacturer of beverage route trucks that was located in Powhatan, Virginia (near Richmond) was paying its drivers 55 cents/mile, and the idea of working for them was highly-appealing to *this* particular Road Rat. Not only did they *pay* well, but beverage route trucks would stop selling only if Americans suddenly decided to give up drinking soda pop and beer! The place was Energy Hoax-*proof!* So I showed up in person to apply.

And was turned down.

"We have all the drivers that we need," the dispatcher told me, "but that could change in the future. It wouldn't hurt to check with us again from time to time."

For the next three months, I phoned that dispatcher twice a week. He was always friendly and encouraging, so I figured I had nothing to lose by being persistent. And sure enough, after *two* months, he voluntarily provided me with Swan's "800" number. That was a very good sign. (And I previously hadn't even been aware that they *had* such a number.)

At the end of the *third* month, they told me I could come in and share a run with a check driver, so they'd be sure I would be a safe driver in their types of vehicles. The vehicle was a heavy-duty pickup truck towing a long, 5th-wheel trailer having beverage bays on both sides. It was unique to the beverage industry. The check run went well, and I was immediately put to work. That was in late summer, 1979, and I worked for them right up until they went out of business in 1985. It was an excellent place to work, and when the company met its demise, it was due entirely to a case of management errors, and had nothing at all to do with Energy Hoax II, which by then had long since ended. During those six years, my average income was $52,000/year, before taxes, and the entire experience was most enjoyable.

The lesson to be learned from this experience is that if you, as a driver applicant, simply *persevere,* you not only can usually work in your region of choice, but sometimes even for your *company* of choice. It took me **three months** to accomplish that goal -- *but I never gave up!* And the result was six of the most fascinating and lucrative years of my life!

Oh, yeah. Almost forgot. The Capital of the Confederacy turned out to be a really nice place to live! Gets a tad warm and muggy in the summer, but you can beat that with air conditioning. The Science Museum in Richmond is great. And if you live in or near that city, you might want to check out the Museum of the Confederacy for me; I never did get around to seeing that, although I wanted to!

TIP: **If a desirable company gives you any encouragement at all,** *persist* **in the application process. As long as they remain friendly. For as long as it takes.**

* * *

Just one word of caution to close this segment. Use common sense in determining how frequently you persevere. If a company says, "We'd hire Adolph Hitler before we'd hire you," or, "We have no drivers, and we *never plan* to use drivers," then handle cases like these as follows: in the "Hitler" example, don't bother trying again with them. At least not for a year or two. (By then, maybe they'll have a new dispatcher.) In the second example, simply ask them *how* their units are moved if *they* have no drivers. If it's all done by CPU/DPU drivers, file that information away; you might be able to do an occasional return "Interlock" run for them. (See Part III, Chapter 1 for more information about that.) But if they tell you they use a transporter company, then ask them how you can get in touch with that transporter. Because if you're willing to work for a transporter, at least for awhile, then *they* might hire you, and you'd still be working out of your chosen *location*. In short, play it by ear. But if you're getting any encouragement at all from a dispatcher for whom you'd like to work, then by all means, do what it takes to start working there. Even if it takes weeks or months!

2. Don't be a Prima Donna...

If a manufacturer that pays 35 cents/mile has no openings, while a transporter company nearby that pays 18 cents/mile is willing to hire you, my advice is for you to sign on with the transporter company. Later, the factory may hire you on the basis of your experience, or, while working for the transporter, you may be able to set up an Interlock with another factory in a distant region. GET STARTED... and then improve your situation as time progresses. Your employers will admire your initiative.

TIP: **Do the *best* job that you can, for whomever you are working.**

Work as hard for 18 cents/mile as you would for 33 cents/mile. That should go without saying, but unfortunately, for many people in the America of the 1990s, the work ethic is not what it used to be. Any job worth doing is worth doing *right!* And you're going into this with your eyes open. Armed with this Handbook, you know *exactly* what to expect from the various types of employers! If you love to travel, being a Road Rat probably will seem to *you* like a vacation with pay -- but for those who *employ* you, you are *working*. (Furthermore, a good recommendation from a transporter company's dispatcher is every bit as valuable as one from a dispatcher who works for a factory, or from a dealer.)

3. Put Your Cards on the Table...

Tell your prospective employer right up front what you can do for him. Wherever vehicles are being moved, if the company is of any size at all, there almost always is room for most types of drivers... full-time, part-time, seasonal, weekend, those who'd like to take a run (or runs) during a vacation period, those who are on-call if needed... and even those who might choose to drive only once in the proverbial blue moon. It's important that your dispatcher understands *which* type of driver *you'd* like to be, so that he can schedule you accordingly. If he knows what you want to do, and can *count* on you to do it on the basis you specify, you have given him what he needs most: reliability.

For example, suppose that you'd like to drive full-time, but you know that your routine ideally would be to spend an extra two or three days at your destinations, between runs. Tell him this, and he likely will be able to accommodate you. Remember, you're being paid for the number of miles that you drive; you're not on the clock. This allows both drivers and dispatchers a lot of latitude, and this flexibility is the primary reason that Road Rats have more freedom than practically all the other working people on earth!

Finally, if you want to work during your vacation periods from another job, it is best to plan well ahead -- especially if you want to take your family on a trip to a specific destination, and *most* especially if you also wish to establish an Interlock trip for the return leg. In that event, you'll have two specific destinations to arrange... your vacation destination, and your return home again afterward. If you're doing the run by yourself, an Interlock return that gets you only to within several hundred miles of home is not a problem. But if your family is with you, getting *them* home those extra hundreds of miles can get expensive. For precise planning, allow yourself at least 4-6 weeks of lead time to set things up with companies on both ends.

3
Possible Impact by Swings of the Economy, and by War

As evidenced on page 21, energy hoaxes comprise one of two factors that can predictably and substantially impact this lifestyle. Economic upheavals comprise the other one.. Hopefully, the population learned a valuable lesson in gullibility from EH I in '73-74 and EH II in '79, but I'd hate to put money on it. You know the old saying that those who forget history are doomed to repeat it. And Americans seem to be better at forgetting such things than one could ever imagine! So if EH *III* ever comes down the pike and you're an RV-delivering Road Rat at the time, **run**, don't walk, to a factory that makes **non-recreational SPECIALTY vehicles!** You know how well that worked for me. I consider that to be is your **only** defense against an Energy Hoax if you're involved with RVs! EH II impacted the RV industry *severely* until nearly *5 years* after it started.

As strange as it seems, though, *economic* ups and downs (short, perhaps, of Great Depressions) have historically not had too adverse an effect on the RV industry. We've just emerged from a recession that affected much of the country, but except in the American Northeast (New England, New York, Pennsylvania, and New Jersey), it had little impact on the RV industry. It only affected *that* region because there were some major bank failures there, and *that* resulted in some of the RV dealerships going out of business. As for Great Depressions...? Well -- we've only had one in this century, during the decade of the 1930s, and that was before the RV industry existed. But my guess is that one of *those* would be catastrophic to this particular industry! The last such cataclysm ended long before I was born -- but anyone with a feel for history, regardless of their age, can appreciate the ghastly and momentous impact that *that* bleak decade had upon the entire human condition worldwide. If you don't know very much about it, I invite you to **read** *"The Grapes of Wrath,"* by John Steinbeck. The movie is a decent portrayal, but the **book** is *unforgettable!* So if the economic doomsayers are by any chance right, and the monetary balloon were to go up sometime during the next few years, all bets are off. Remember what I said in the last chapter: delivering *beverage route trucks* just *might* always be a good option, because soda pop and beer are one of the *last* things people would give up! But there's no way that the specialty vehicle manufacturers *alone* -- without the RV industry -- can employ 100,000 Road Rats, so act quickly if the time comes!

Before moving on from the economy to the effects of war, it can't hurt to speculate on the reason this industry seems to be impervious to recessions, almost to the point of being recession-proof. Our thinking is that it's one primary factor for RVs, and a different one for specialized vehicles. For RVs, it would seem likely that those who can afford to purchase brand-new ones probably are well-enough heeled to weather recessions, and maintain diversified investments. Therefore, the recessions have little or no impact on most people who are in a secure position financially -- so they buy their RVs as though the condition didn't prevail. As for *specialty* vehicles... these probably continue to sell well because they are vehicles that our society requires in order to continue functioning efficiently: school busses, utility trucks, straight trucks that haul cargo, hearses, etc. Only a major economic *upheaval* -- such as a depression -- would be likely to severely impact the *specialized*-vehicle industry.

Okay. Now let's take a look at war.

When I last wrote on this topic, it was to prepare a similar chapter for the 1991-92 edition of this Handbook (which unexpectedly lasted all the way into the middle of 1994 before this total revision was completed). That chapter was written on Feb. 27, 1991 -- the very day that Kuwait City was liberated by the Coalition forces of Desert Storm from Saddam Hussein. It was the last item prepared for that edition, and the book went to press immediately afterward. The chapter was included almost as an afterthought... in response to many inquiries from Road Rats and prospective Road Rats as to how we thought the war would affect their work. The analysis I wrote that day stood the test of time well, so I'll repeat it again now, *exactly* as it was first written six years ago. My reason for this is twofold. (1) Because it was written at the height of Desert Storm, the words are *reflective of how we perceive war when it is actually going on.* That's a difficult, if not impossible, mental state to achieve after a few years of peace. And (2) the analysis was *accurate,* so as the old saying goes, "If it ain't broke, don't fix it!" Some of this will be a bit redundant with some things stated earlier in this edition, but to keep the analysis intact, that's necessary. Here it is:

> On January 17, the New York Stock Exchange closed after the Dow Jones Average soared 114.6 points (the second-largest one-day gain ever during that first full day of the Persian Gulf War. Simultaneously, as everyone observed the thorough initial thrashing (or trashing, take your choice) of Saddam, oil prices dropped like a stone plunging from the World Trade Towers. (Down over $10/bbl. to July, 1990 levels -- the greatest one-day drop ever.) This was initial euphoria, of course, but America's optimism and high expectations of success were to be borne out over the weeks that followed to a degree above their highest expectations. Tonight, President Bush declared the war at an end. Across the nation, gasoline prices have fallen below $1.00/gal. for the first time since before Saddam's treacherous invasion on August 2nd of last year.
>
> What does all of this mean to the Road Rat?
>
> For openers, the government has demonstrated that America is no longer interested in becoming involved in morass-type no-win conflicts like Vietnam, and indeed, it appears that this quickly, the Persian Gulf War is history. With the tremendous resurgence of pride and patriotism that has swept the land over the last few months has come a new sense of optimism for the future. The stock market is generally a good indicator of that... and over the course of this short war, it went up almost 300 points.
>
> Fortunately for the RV industry, we did not see a repeat of the scenarios of two periods during the 1970s.
>
> We learned during the Energy Hoaxes of 1973-4 and 1979 that the RV industry can be severely impacted by oil crunches. Both times, it took years for recreational vehicle sales and production to return to previous levels. However, the hoaxes were characterized quite differently from the situation resulting from Iraq's invasion of Kuwait. This time, there was never even the slightest threat of gasoline rationing as before, nor did the notorious gas lines ever develop.
>
> Combine those favorable differences in the situation of 1990-91 with lessons we learned from the hoaxes, and the impact on the RV industry ranged from nonexistent at some companies and dealerships to only slight at others. Clearly, the events of the 70's taught us all that the world has plenty of oil and that shortages are either artificially-induced, short-term, or both. So this time, Americans simply didn't buy it. (Saddam's insane actions caused a legitimate problem, albeit clearly an over-rated one, but didn't disrupt world oil supplies significantly. In fact, as I write this, America has an oil glut!)
>
> This time, "Wolf!" was simply cried once too often, and we weren't about to fall for it. Fortunately for all concerned!

And as 1997 begins, thankfully, we *still* have no shortage of oil. That, despite the obvious fact that Big Oil is currently in one of it's phases of ripping us off from head to foot for it. In early summer, 1994, I paid $0.74^9 per gallon for regular unleaded at a Georgia gas station situated right at an interchange of I-75. But by August of that same year, prices around most of the country had reached their highest level in three years, at $1.20^9. Then, over the last couple of years, the price fluctuated within a few cents either way of $1.10^9 -- but it's 15-25 cents higher than that today. (I often wish that I could be a fly on the wall at some of Big Oil's highest-level board meetings, and then report to you what I learned *there!*)

It would not hurt to keep the word, "rationing," in mind. It is the perceived threat of *rationing* that scared off those who would have purchased new RVs between 1979 and 1983. The government had even printed up ration coupons by the millions and pictures of them had been run in newspapers and shown on TV. You see, folks who can afford higher gasoline prices aren't unduly worried when the *price* goes up. But *rationing* is another breed of cat entirely. If rationing ever comes along, the fuel-thirsty RVs will become driveway and yard ornaments for as long as that lasts. We probably will never see gasoline rationing, however, *unless* we first experience Energy Hoax III. So let's end this discussion on an upbeat note by reprinting the *predictions* that I made in **February, 1991,** which have been coming to pass:

> Today, America and Canada appear to be leaping vigorously out of the blue funk that pervaded the land last fall when recession was deepening and impending war haunted us with scary possibilities of chemical and biological warfare. Personally, I don't look for the recession to last much longer, and I believe we're already on our way out of it. Lower energy and fuel costs are putting more dollars into consumer pockets, and as buying increases, factories will produce more. Demand was low while consumers were cautious, so plants laid folks off and were selling their inventories. But the inventories weren't all that high to begin with, so stepping up production was only a matter of time. Spring is right around the corner, Americans are proud once again, energy prices are relatively low... and my bet is that for Road Rats (and 'most everyone else) the early '90s will turn out to be very good years!

So far, so good! *Now* let's include the *late* 1990s in that prediction!

*The most **successful** Road Rats are the ones who have -- and **USE** -- this Handbook!*

4

"Home Sweet Home..."

When it comes the length of time that one spends in this job, there are "short-term" Road Rats, and "long-term" Road Rats. Some take only one trip, as in the case of some CPU drivers, and vacationers, and others spend several days, weeks, months, or even years doing this. Depending upon whether or not you work for a company located close to your home, *and* the length of time you plan to spend pursuing this lifestyle, certain options regarding where you choose to hang your hat are better than others, and this chapter is designed to assist you in making those choices.

*The **short-term** Road Rat* is the person who gets into this for *a time-span that can range from **one day to 12 weeks**,* and sometimes longer. This includes the college students and teachers who choose to be Road Rats throughout their 3-month-long summer vacations. Normally, such drivers will not find it necessary to consider relocation, even if they happen to be working for a company on the other side of the continent. For up to three months, almost anyone can get by pretty well on the contents of two well-packed suitcases containing carefully-selected items. **Beyond three months,** you should consider yourself a ***long*-term** Road Rat, and *other* options may work *better* for you.

THE SHORT-TERM ROAD RAT

A. Home-Based

1. WEEKENDERS!

The nice thing about working for a company that's within easy driving distance of home is that you get home with frequency, which allows you to recycle clothing and other items within your luggage. Assuming you have a washer-dryer at home, this also frees you from interruptions in your routine to go to laundromats. So *what* constitutes "easy driving distance from home?" It depends on your own perception of distance. Most people probably would consider a drive of 25-30 miles to be no problem at all, but there are some who wouldn't even bat an eyelash at driving 150-200 miles routinely between their home and the origin point of their runs, as long as the runs were long enough to be worthwhile. For example, suppose that you work for a manufacturer that will always send you on runs that are at least 600 miles long. If your take-home pay is 35 cents/mile, a 600-mile-long run would pay you $210.00. Even if your own car were a gas hog that costs you $7.50 to drive 100 miles, you still could make the round-trip drive from home to a plant 200 miles away for $30.00, and your net profit from the run would be $180.00.

That might not sound particularly attractive, but consider *this* scenario for a moment: A person comes up to you one day and offers you a reliable *weekend* job, and he tells you the following...

"I'd like you to drive over to my factory after you get off work on Fridays from your regular job. It'll take you about four hours to get there, so you'll reach us at about 9 p.m. When you get there, the guard at the gate will let you park inside the compound, and then he'll give you a set of keys to a brand-new motorhome, and tell you where to deliver it. He'll also give you cash up front that'll pay for your gas, and for your return flight to my city.

"Your destination will always be between 600 and 750 miles from the plant," he continues. "Therefore, at an average driving speed of 50 mph, the trip will generally take you around 12-15 hours of actual driving time to accomplish. Suppose you decide to drive about three or four hours, and then sleep in the coach until morning. You then can drive the rest of the way on Saturday and return Saturday evening -- or you can deliver on Sunday, and fly back on Sunday afternoon. Then you simply give the paperwork, receipts, and remaining cash to the guard, hop in your car, and drive home. On Monday morning we'll mail your paycheck to you.

"You can do this on weekends of your choosing, and stay home on other weekends. Just let us know a day or two ahead of time, each week. That's all there is to it."

Would that be attractive to *you*? It would supplement the pay of your regular Monday-thru-Friday job by about $800/month, or by roughly $9,500.00/year, if you did it every weekend. And if you did it only *half* of the weekends of the year, you'd still add close to $5,000/year to your regular income!

Now consider *this*. The above example is an absolutely *worst*-case scenario! That's because *most* weekend Road Rats work for companies that are located within *an hour or less of driving time from their homes* -- which effectively makes their available weekend time for driving and sleeping about 6 to 8 hours longer than in the example above. Doing it *that* way is a piece of cake!! And literally *thousands* of Road Rats do it just that way.

2. SEASONAL

Even if you are a teacher or college student who devotes an entire summer to being a Road Rat, you can retain your home base while "living out of a suitcase." It's recommended that you pack enough clothes to sustain you for about two weeks between laundromat forays. One of the great things about being a Road Rat is the *informality* that goes with that territory. So bring *comfortable* clothes that fit the season. If it's summer, shorts and T-shirts are great, and it's easy to pack a good quantity of them into a suitcase. (One of the aspects of this that professionals and business people love is the opportunity to get out of those uncomfortable suits for a few days or weeks, and do a *job* that permits *casual* dress!)

One day back in 1988, I'd just finished doing a radio show in Kingston, New York -- which sits almost at the base of the Catskill Mountains -- and was about to leave the station when a man ran up to me, almost out of breath.

"I have a seasonal job in the Catskills," he told me, "that keeps me busy about eight months of the year. But the four months of winter every year gives me an uncomfortably-long dry spell with no income. When I heard your show, I jumped in my car and drove down here as fast as I could so that I could ask you if this job can be done in the wintertime!" (I didn't have the heart to tell him that he could have *phoned* in his question to me, live, while I was on the air!)

He was very happy to learn that **Road Rats are kept just as busy in the wintertime as during the rest of the year** -- and hopefully this was the complete solution to his problem.

It's true that production rates are higher for most of these vehicles during the summer, but the year-'round Road Rats never really notice that. They stay *steadily* busy all the time. But the influx of several thousand seasonal drivers in the form of college students and teachers almost perfectly *offsets* the higher rates of production during the summer -- and *that* keeps *everybody* comfortably busy!

3. OTHER PART-TIME

As a part-time Road Rat you can be just about as creative as you want to be. Just as long as you tell your dispatcher the basis on which you'd like to work, the dispatcher usually can accommodate you. (That, of course, assumes that the dispatcher can use part-timers -- and most of them can, to some extent.) Here are some ways that Road Rats work part-time, *besides* weekends and seasonally:

(1) **ON VACATION --**

Even if your vacation occurs just once a year, you can be a Road Rat during that time. You can even make it an annual event! It just takes a bit of advance planning, if you desire to go to one or more specific destinations. Remember that you should *allow a **minimum** of 4-6 weeks of lead time* so that you can arrange this with both companies.

Suppose that you live in Kansas City, have a two-week vacation, and would like to spend a week or so of that time in San Francisco. Furthermore, let's say that yours is a family of four. You know that the air fare would eat you alive, and renting an RV would probably cost you even more than that. What you really need is an RV that you can deliver to San Francisco, with the run starting on the day your vacation begins. And for the return, you need to set things up so you can leave San Francisco for your home area, three or four days before your vacation ends. That way, you'll have no transportation costs either way, you'll travel in the comfort of a brand-new recreational vehicle -- and best of all, you'll get PAID about $1,000 (and perhaps as much as $1,500) for your effort and your ingenuity! Your earnings could offset most of your hotel and meal expenses while visiting the "City by the Bay!" Instead of ending your vacation in credit card *hock* up to your eyeballs, as happens to most families, you actually can come out *ahead!*

By the way, if your vacation destination happens to be either in California or Florida, you'll be very happy with the rates if you desire to rent a car to give yourself more mobility while you're there. Weekly rates can be in the $65-80 range, with unlimited mileage. A couple of tips: Gravitate toward using companies like *Alamo, Dollar,* and *National,* and even *Rent-a-Wreck,* rather than the biggest ones because you'll often find better rates. And always tell them you want their *smallest, most economical* car. Most companies will try to rent you a larger one for a few dollars more. However, seasoned travellers have learned that frequently those small cars, limited in quantity in the fleets, will not actually be available, and you'll *end up* with the *larger* model at the *lowest* rate. And even if it doesn't work out that way, and you *do* get the small one, you can be comfortable enough in it for a few days, unless you have a large family. Another advantage to having a rental car: you get the mobility necessary to be able to stay in *economy* motels in the suburbs, rather than the pricey downtown hotels. That can save you between $50 and $100 a day, even when you add in the cost of renting the car!

EXAMPLE: In June, 1994, I attended a convention in Santa Monica, California for four days and nights. Although I had the opportunity to stay at the convention hotel for "only" $125.00/day, I rented a car instead for $22.00 a day -- and then drove each night into the San Fernando Valley and stayed in a clean, comfortable, economy motel for $25.00/night. My net savings was therefore about $75.00 a day, for **a total savings of $300.00!**

(2) **ON-CALL** --

This method is GREAT for *retirees,* and there are thousands who use it.

Most companies, from the smallest to the largest, have times when their driver or drivers ALL are out on the road, and they need to get a unit on its way before any of them are due back. If you have established yourself as an "on-call" driver, who can be called upon when that situation arises, this can nicely supplement your pension or social security. You may only get a run or two per year, or you may get a dozen or more. The only requirement is that you need to *be able to leave on short notice* -- sometimes within just an hour or two of being notified -- because that's what your being "on call" is all about, for your company. You don't always have to be *available*, though, because companies usually have more than one on-call driver. If you're tied up with something else and can't go, you simply tell your dispatcher, and then he'll try the next on-call driver on his list.

There are other very nice aspects to this. Unlike most driving positions, which require either that the position is open when the Road Rat applies, or that he or she must go on a wait list for a position, to be an on-call driver...

a. ...once you've qualified yourself as a good driver, over 18, with a mature and positive attitude, you generally can be placed *immediately* on the on-call driver list. (However, if they have other on-call drivers and they operate on a seniority system, runs may be rare until you've been on the list for awhile. It's not always that way, though. Many companies put their on-call drivers on a *rotating* list.)

b. ...you may find it pretty easy to be put on a list with a company that is quite close to where you live.

c. ...you may opt to apply for that position with *several* companies that are in your area. For regular Road Rats, that's inadvisable because two or more companies might want you to drive at the same time, and because companies in the same immediate area who make similar types of vehicles usually tend to regard each other as competitors. For the on-call driver, neither of those factors is likely to be a problem.

B. *Non*-Home-Based

Those who plan to work for several weeks or months in a location far from home will find it advantageous to rent a place to use as home base. Those who own or rent their homes can continue to live there, returning periodically to "re-group" (leave unnecessary items, replace clothing, etc.). However, it may be advisable to *consider renting a sleeping room within a private home* in the same community where your workplace is located. There are two advantages to this:

1. Many companies specify that they use only "local" drivers. Renting a sleeping room will meet that requirement. In fact, if you really want to work for a company that's far from where you live, and they tell you this, all you normally have to do to qualify is tell them that if they'll take you on, you'll immediately *relocate* to their community. The fact that you don't sell your house and *move* there lock, stock, and barrel is of no consequence. The main reason companies want drivers who are "local" is so they can get them on the road *on short notice.*

2. If you are going to be working with little prospect of getting home because your company seldom ships in that *direction,* this will provide you with inexpensive accommodations if you get back from a run and find you might have to wait a day or two, or until after a weekend before going out again. Motel expenses can add up quickly if you have to go *that* route as an alternative. But in most communities, there are private homes where you can rent a sleeping room by the week or month quite inexpensively. Sometimes for as little as *$25 per week,* for quite a beautiful room! Most *economy* motels charge that much or more for just *one night!* Also, this provides you with the advantage of keeping your clothes and most necessities in an orderly fashion, so that you can generally go on runs just carrying an overnight bag, and perhaps a sleeping bag.

THE LONG-TERM ROAD RAT

A. Home-Based

See the section on home-based **short**-term Road Rats. If you live in, and work out of, the same vicinity, it makes no difference *how* long you are a Road Rat.

B. *Non*-Home-Based

If you own your own house, and you've determined over a few months that you want to continue being a Road Rat for some years to come, then you may wish to consider several different possibilities. You can buy a house in your new community, move there, and sell the old one. Or you can rent a room, apartment, or house in your new community, move most or all of your belongings there, and rent out the house that you already own. Other possibilities may occur to you as well, and only you know what would be best for your own situation.

But -- suppose that you are only *renting* an apartment or a house in your original home town.

That simplifies things immensely!

In that event, you may wish simply to move everything to an apartment in your new location, and just let the old place go altogether. Or, you may wish to rent a smaller apartment, or a sleeping room in a private home, and then bring *just the most necessary of your belongings* to the new location. You can *store* the items you *don't* need from your old place, and this will allow you to keep moving costs and rent both to a minimum. Unless your storage space is large, the monthly fee for storing your major appliances and your larger items of furniture can be *more* than offset by a tremendous reduction in *moving* costs, and by being able to rent a much *smaller* place in your new location! This is also a nice option if you think that someday you'd like to *resume* living in your old home town. The *large* items will already *be* there, and therefore will only require a *local* move within the immediate area!

As far as getting your small, necessary items to your new location is concerned, you will likely find that a one-way trip with a rental trailer behind your car will accomplish this, thereby costing you perhaps only $100-300, depending on the size of the rental trailer, and the distance involved.

Remember, **as a Road Rat, you'll soon find that *distance* becomes meaningless to you. The entire continent will become your backyard!** Therefore, **you should *never* limit yourself geographically!** If it is *advantageous* to you to accept a job offer a long way from home, *go for it!* You can always work your way into a Road Rat position in a company in or near your old home town later, if you want. But you'll sometimes find that accepting a position in a far-off locale is a good way to get started *quickly!* And remember, when I first got started, it worked for me!

5
On the Road!

When a driver spends 90% or more of his time on the go, he needs to find quick and economical ways and places to eat and to meet personal needs, such as showers and laundry.

The least expensive way to eat is the same way you probably do when living at home: shopping at supermarkets. Careful shopping yields a wide variety of good and healthful food. (Be careful when shopping, not to buy any of that "healthy" food, by the way. Only *living* things can be health*y*, and I don't know about you, but I happen to draw the line at eating anything that's still breathing! On the other hand, foods claiming to be health*ful* can occasionally even be *good* for you. But more often, that's just hype, generated by con artists who probably take their lessons from those who perpetrate Energy Hoaxes. For example, take that cereal you'd need to eat 10 bowls of at one sitting to get your recommended vitamins and minerals for the day. Or would have to supplement with other foods. Wouldn't you just *love* to see the much-maligned "Shredded Wheat" or corn flakes makers team up with a *multi-vitamin* maker to tell us on TV that we can eat *their* product *one* bowl at a time *too,* to our heart's content and get the *same* nutrition that we would with the *hyped* product, simply by taking a *vitamin pill* with it?! Sorry -- I digress. You can tell I used to be a teacher! But then, Andy Rooney is so interesting, I thought I'd just have a little fun and imitate him a bit. I'd hate to see this book get boring!) Anyway, those health*ful* foods that can be eaten conveniently while on the road, and take up little luggage space, can include fruit drinks, many vegetables, luncheon meats, cheese, nuts, milk, soft drinks, etc., etc. The biggest limitation is food that needs to be heated or cooked. On the road, that can be inconvenient and/or impractical. *However...* if you keep the microwaves in motor homes *clean,* or use the ones at the mini-marts where you buy gas, even *those* foods can serve you well!

Here's how to do it without overloading your luggage.

Immediately before you leave, and after you have the vehicle you'll be delivering, buy a nice, *cheap* styrofoam ice chest. Most supermarkets sell the smaller ones for $1.50 or so, and if you'd rather go for a larger one, roughly $2.50 will usually do it. That's about the cost of a decent burger at a fast-food place these days. (Ah, for those days when burgers were universally just 15 cents!)

Then buy the groceries you want that should be chilled. If you don't already have them, you can also get foods that need no refrigeration, at this same time. Then get a bag of ice that'll fill the chest about halfway. You'll have to add ice about once every 24 hours while en route. (You are embarking on a perpetual vacation. Why not make a *picnic*, too?)

$$ TIP: Do you buy brand-name soda pop, like Coke or Pepsi? Carry along 4 of those 20-oz. bottles with the screw-on caps. Then buy a *2-liter* bottle of your favorite brand, chill it, and pour it into the smaller bottles. The soda then retains its carbonation, you can drink it at your leisure *and* while driving, and over time this'll SAVE you a FORTUNE!! That's the *least-expensive way* to buy brand-name pop! (Even if you never become a Road Rat, *this single tip* will save you MANY times the price of this book!) You can do *this* at home!!

It is a good idea to purchase two or three flexible plastic sandwich containers having tightly-fitting lids. With these, one can store everything needing refrigeration from salads to luncheon meat without danger of water seeping in from the melting ice. If you plan properly, you'll run out of the perishable foods at about the time you reach your destination. Then the only thing that'll have to go in your luggage for the return flight are the re-useable sandwich containers. Just before making delivery, toss the styrofoam ice chest into a dumpster; it's served its purpose. EXCEPTION: If you've arranged an Interlock return, the ice chest can survive and continue to serve you all the way home, and probably on your next outbound run. But the first time you'll need to take public transportation, you'll want to be rid of it. Retaining it simply isn't worth the hassle and extra bother on a plane, train, or bus.

Showers and laundry facilities can be found at nearly all of the large truckstops. The showers range in cost from free to $5.00 or so, in 1997. Soap and towels are provided, but *amazingly* few truckstops seem to have figured out that it would be nice to provide *washcloths,* too! It's one of those unfathomable mysteries for which no one seems to have the answer. Like why Elkhart and not Detroit became the RV-manufacturing capital of the world. Or how long the universe will survive. I don't know about you, but to me it just seems natural that if washcloths and towels go together with showers at home and in motels, they likewise should go together in truckstops! Maybe if we ask them about this often enough, they'll figure it out. As for laundry, their washers and dryers are often less expensive than those in laundromats. (Toss your clothes in and watch a favorite TV show in the trucker's lounge, or take a shower while you wait.)

By the way, if your concept of a shower at a modern truckstop is of the shower bays you experienced after gym in school, or in the service, you'll be pleasantly surprised. There's no comparison at all. (This might seem to be to be especially pleasing to the women, but believe me, men appreciate it just as much.) Typically, in such modern truckstops as "Union 76 Auto/TruckStops," and "Truckstops of America," you simply walk up to the fuel desk and give them the required towel deposit. In return, they'll give you a bath towel, bar of soap... *maybe* a washcloth (if you're lucky. You may want to bring your own) -- and a KEY! The key fits the lock of a personal bathroom that contains a shower, toilet, and lavatory. All the comforts of home, or a nice motel -- except, probably, for the missing washcloth. And it's all yours for as long as you need it. Upon returning the towel, they'll either refund all of your deposit or part of it, depending upon whether they charge a fee. Fueling truckers frequently can have this service at no charge, but the units Road Rats deliver generally haven't the capacity to meet the minimum fueling qualification. Besides, you usually won't want to buy *gasoline* at truckstop prices. You're generally much better off buying your gas at *cut-rate* gas stations, and simply *paying* the truckstop's shower fee. (Frequently, though, *diesel* fuel is as cheap *there* as it is at gas stations, so that's good to remember when you're delivering units that run on *diesel*. In that circumstance, be nice to the people at the fuel desk, and they may let you have a free shower in exchange for getting a fill-up, despite the smaller capacity tanks.)

Where are the modern truckstops? When on the interstates, you're never very far from one, and you'll soon compile a list of favorites. But for openers, you might want to stop at some major truckstop chains and obtain their FREE nationwide directories. They're usually available right at the fuel desk.

A good hot meal is welcome now and then, so enjoy yourself seeking out new worlds of cuisine while you travel. You'll probably come up with your own list of favorite eating places. My all-time favorite is the *King Fong Cafe*, a beautiful upstairs restaurant at 315 S. 16th Street, in downtown Omaha, Nebraska. I've often gone miles out my the way to eat there. The very BEST Chinese food I've ever had... and yes, I *have* eaten Chinese in San Francisco, L.A., and New York -- not to mention also Hong Kong and Beijing! I suggest the "Cantonese Shrimp Chow Mein," with *extra* black mushrooms. Out of this world! And you won't BELIEVE the huge portion you get, for well UNDER $10.00 (in 1996).   I'd tell you about some other favorite restaurants that come close, but I have to keep this book at a reasonable length. Anyway, if you like Chinese food, you're gonna just LOVE this tip I just gave you. You'll get hooked *instantly* on the *King Fong!*

Now for motels. If you work for a company far from home, and you haven't established a sleeping room base as yet, you may find yourself staying over from time to time in that community, between runs. Or, if you deliver a unit that's not comfortable for sleeping, such as a hearse or a school bus, then your company frequently will include a motel allowance in the expense money. (This is more likely in the case of manufacturers than with transporter companies.) Such an allowance is usually about what you'll need if you like clean, economy lodging such as the "Motel 6," or the "Econo-Travel" motel chains. If you wish, you can always upgrade for a few dollars more of your own money.

When delivering units in which sleeping would be uncomfortable, manufacturers frequently furnish a motel allowance as part of the expense money.

Now, this is kind of interesting. Over the years, there have been occasions when I've stayed in hotel rooms that rent for as much as $325.00 a night. Not that I ever *paid* that much, you understand. No one in his right mind would! When business folks stay in such digs for that price, you can bet that it's usually because their corporation is footing the bill. (So next time you pay top dollar for some name brand of widget, consider the fact that much of the money they extract from your wallet goes to pay for coddling executives and high-priced advertising campaigns. That's why *generic* products -- with only rare exceptions -- *are usually just as good, for a lower price.)* My experience with such hotels has been at special convention rates ($75-110 a night, usually) in cities where renting a car and using economy motels is impractical -- such as Chicago, New York City, and Washington, D.C. There's a good reason why I'm spending a perfectly good paragraph to tell you all this. Read and comprehend: The ritzy hotels and motels are only *marginally* better than ones costing only 1/10th as much, and frequently provide LESS service! The $325 hotel room in D.C. wasn't *nearly* as nice, as comfortable, as spacious, or as convenient in terms of available ice, newspapers, snack machines, etc. as the $28 room I often occupy at the "Knight's Inn" in New Cumberland, PA (on I-83, just south of Harrisburg). Would you believe that the $325 room contained a TV set with *basic* cable, *no* premium channels, and a selector box that would permit me to choose a movie that I could watch for an *additional $7.00?* You'd think that such a hotel would've left a complimentary copy of *The Washington Post* or something outside my door, too, wouldn't you? Guess what. Not even *that* simple amenity! And to add insult to injury, if I wanted to use the room phone for *local* calls, each call racked up another charge on my bill! For HALF the money they charged for that, I could go down to the lobby and use a PAY phone! (By the way, at *almost all* the economy motels, local calls are FREE. Almost all of the "Motel 6" chain now has FREE *"HBO"* -- and that "Knight's Inn" in New Cumberland has FREE *"Showtime."* These details could well have been written instead into the chapter called "The Good, the Bad, and the Rinky-Dink," (Part II, Chapter 7, in your future), because the things that "luxury" hotels and motels do to tourists and business travellers comprise the ULTIMATE in **rinky-dink!** But in that chapter, you'll find *other* valuable tips.

One more thing before leaving hotels and motels. If you're going to stay in them, pack at least one, and preferably two, HIGH-wattage light bulbs in your luggage! Most economy motels have this one shortcoming: they tend to provide bulbs that are so dim you feel like you're in a cave trying to read your book by the light of a distant campfire! I check this out as soon as I enter the room, and if they're chintzy with the bulbs (40 and 52 watts is typical), I replace one or two of them with 200-watt ones for the duration of my stay. *(Don't forget to switch them back when you leave!)* And do you remember that washcloth we talked about earlier? No problem at American *hotels and motels,* but be sure to pack one or two of them for *truckstops.* AND -- pack them when the time comes that you'd like to cash in some frequent flier points for a trip *overseas.* European hotels, for example, don't seem to have discovered yet that these have been invented. Picture this. You're staying in a tourist hotel in Moscow, such as the *Cosmos,* or the *Belgrad.* Or perhaps the priciest of all, the *Intourist,* which overlooks Red Square. Do you suppose ANY of those places provide washcloths? *Dishtowels,* yes. Washcloths, no. And I won't describe the toilet paper. You wouldn't believe me if I did. Russia's a fascinating land to visit, but if you go, bring along rolls of *that,* too! Be sure to install the toilet paper in the holder only at night, or while you're in the room, and then *switch it back* to the Russian toilet paper *before* leaving the room. *Hide* the American paper in your luggage. Otherwise, it disappears. I'm not sure Russia even *has* toilet paper the quality of ours (even though they have *ten times* the number of *trees!),* so the maids scarf it up the instant they see it, and simply replace it with more *Russian* T.P.

Did I just digress again? Nope. *This* time I stayed right on course. You see, a major part of the mission of this book is to give you a realistic feel for the *kinds of experiences* you'll have as a Road Rat. Most folks can't even DREAM of the kind of freedom a Road Rat knows! The only way I can impart this to you is to shock you a bit from time to time by relating experiences which have become *normal* to me, and which *will* become normal for *you*. Experiences that probably seem out of this world to you, as you consider entering this lifestyle for the first time. YES! You *can* visit Russia. YES! You *can* watch nomads on camels, and on horseback, riding across the Gobi Desert, from your train as you cross Outer Mongolia. YES! You *can* explore Europe by train for weeks at a time. YES! You *can* go to South America, or India, or Australia. *THAT'S* why this chapter is called, "On the Road!" Because it's not just the "road" as you are used to thinking of the word. It's the **Road,** with a capital **"R,"** that you'll experience as a Road Rat. And *Russia's* on the Road. *Europe's* on the Road. *Britain,* and *India,* and *Brazil* are on the Road. The whole **WORLD** is now on your Road, if you'll accept it! The frequent flier points will take you just about everywhere for free, and Road Rats collect an *abundance* of them!

I PRESENT YOU WITH THE PLANET. *That's* what you just spent less than $30 for. Your ticket to unimagined *ADVENTURE*.

Okay, one more thing before we end this chapter. Security on the road.

Do you remember hearing about that tourist in 1993 who was killed in a rest area in Florida? That was nearly 4 years ago as this is written, and I haven't heard of any more people being killed in rest areas, either in Florida or in any other state. So if I calculate correctly the number of people in America who travel on highways, and the number of trips that have been taken since that murder, I figure that the average person will be killed in that manner perhaps once every million *lifetimes*. Think about it. In their hunger to keep the news sensational enough for us to keep watching it, the media seem to be trying to scare us to death! When's the last time you witnessed a murder? Sure, they happen, but nothing in life is ABSOLUTELY certain. The fact is, that when we use just plain old common sense, we can go about our lives -- and our travels -- with little more risk to life and limb than our odds would be of being struck by lightning. When you park for the night as you're en route in an RV, lock the doors, park under the lights in a rest area, at a truckstop, or in some other decent locale, and get a good night's sleep. Simple as that. Remember what I said earlier about *hype?* Our society -- and especially television -- *thrives* on it. Use common sense, and don't worry. Be happy!

A normal precaution I take on the road, though, if I have any amount of cash with me, is to carry a dummy wallet containing no credit cards, a couple of bucks in cash, and without my driver's license. And I keep the *real* wallet with the cash, cards, and driver's license where no one is likely to find it, usually stashed within the RV or specialty vehicle. The dummy wallet also has a pointed reference to the ancestry of the potential thief, but that's where he wouldn't find it immediately. When he takes the time to *really* search the wallet later on, *that's* when you want him to experience such frustration. Not while he's still in your presence.

Hitch-hikers, of course, are a *no-no!* It was a lot of fun in the '50s and '60s, and when I was in high school and college, I explored America and even Mexico that way. But these days, that would be considered an unsafe pastime, and I'm not sure who would be more at risk -- the hitch-hiker or the ride-giver. But that's not all. Always remember that *your company's insurance won't cover you if you pick up a hitch-hiker* and then have a problem. So keep your job, and stay safe. Remember hitch-hiking's golden age with relish, but remember, too, that for the most part, that mode of getting around has gone the way of the 15-cent hamburger!

It really **IS** very safe out there on the road. And on the **Road!** You need only employ normal common sense and caution, just as you do on a daily basis in all other aspects of life. And **have a great time pursuing this Grand Adventure!**

PART II
PERFORMING THE JOB

1

Getting Started

Most companies make no provision for intensive orientation, student runs, or a period of apprenticeship. Drivers are hired on the basis of safety and maturity. The basic requirements of the job itself are quite simple, and your new employer generally (and correctly) assumes that you have sufficient intelligence and driving ability to perform adequately.

While most employers would like to see their drivers achieve economic stability and success, they simply do not have time to teach a ground school, and most know precious *few* of the techniques in this Handbook, so wouldn't be equipped to teach you in any case. They'll explain their basic policies, show you the check-out procedure for the vehicles, tell you how to handle the paperwork at the time of delivery, and then let you get started. That is sufficient to enable them to achieve *their* goal, and depending on the company for which you work, if that's *all* you do, you'll earn a wage that can range from marginal to pretty decent. However, **you can do much better!** It is up to *you* to get paid $30,000/year and *up,* as a Road Rat. Here's how:

This book is your "ground school." Your own initiative will enable you to achieve comfortable earnings, if you *study well* and then *use* its techniques.

Shortly after you are hired (probably immediately afterward), you will be assigned a coach or specialty vehicle to drive. About half of all Road Rats deliver recreational vehicles, and there are five basic types of those that are motorized, and two that are towed which are generally not trucked. Two other types of nonmotorized RVs, the pop-up camper trailer, and pickup-truck campers, are small enough that *they* usually *are* trucked, *except when delivered singly.* Because so many Road Rats are involved in RV delivery, a description of the first seven are provided here. Not described are the other (non-recreational) specialty vehicles. If you are to deliver RVs, you'll probably drive or tow one of the vehicles below. (The code number for each, as used in Appendix 1, is shown in parentheses.)

1. ***Bus Conversion (U)* --**

    Probably the most *luxurious* vehicle you'll ever encounter, these are constructed using the most professionally-made heavy-duty bus bodies (such as Prevost Car, and Motor Coach Industries) as the starting point. When completed, the vehicle is truly a home on wheels, with most of the amenities you can imagine, and maybe even a few you can't. They retail for around $400,000 and up. Because of their weight -- usually more than the DOT's cut-off weight of 26,000 lbs. (13 tons), it takes a special sort of Road Rat to deliver these. One needs to hold the CDL (Commercial Driver's License) and keep a log book. (But it's worth the extra effort!)

2. **Class "A" Motor Home (R1)** --

This is the most deluxe type of coach on the market, after the bus conversion. All of these share the general appearance of a solid, fairly rectangular, box-shaped unit, with no separate cab. (See the front cover of this book for an illustration.) Most of the Class "A"s currently built range from around 25-35 feet in length, and the recent models are easily distinguished from earlier models by their more rounded, streamlined design, particularly in front. This is the heaviest type of coach made (with the exception of the bus conversion), ranging up to about 9 tons in weight. CDL sometimes is a *company* requirement.

3. **Mini Motor Home (R2)** --

This somewhat lighter coach is built on RV truck chassis, generally of major American makes: Chevrolet, Dodge, Ford, and GM. Their trademark appearance is the separate cab compartment that has a bed or storage section constructed above it. (See the cartoon on page 143 for an example.) This type of coach has enjoyed tremendous popularity for about three decades.

4. **Micro-mini Motor Home (R3)** --

This is a miniature version of the mini, considerably smaller. Most are built on chassis of Japanese manufacture, such as Nissan or Toyota. In 1994, *none* were being built, but people in the know think that they'll soon be making a strong comeback.

5. **Van Conversion/Class "B" (R4/R4-B)** --

Hundreds of companies take basic van bodies and convert them into miniaturized motor homes. Some even build their own van bodies. There is a wide variety in floor plans. A van conversion is considered a class "B" RV if it is wired to enable regular house current hookups to be made and utilized at campgrounds or elsewhere. Outwardly, they appear the same.

6. **Fifth-Wheel Travel Trailers (R5)** --

These mount into a mini-fifth wheel assembly mounted in the bed of the towing vehicle. The Road Rat delivering these frequently has the option of driving a company-furnished tow vehicle, or one that he or she personally owns. Certain distinct advantages pertain to each method. See also page 118, regarding these, and the trailers in Item 7, below.

7. **Travel Trailers (hitch-mounted) (R6)** --

The same situation as with fifth-wheel travel trailers, above, except that these are towed by hitch mounting, and therefore generally are smaller.

Not too much structure and routine is necessary in the Road Rat business, which is one of the main advantages of the job. However, you will want to establish a pattern as early as possible of being able to find yourself *en route* somewhere on *Sundays,* except when you know in advance that you can deliver that day. Some dealers are closed on Sunday, and suddenly finding yourself with a full day of down time when you haven't planned for it can be very inconvenient. Remember, too, that your return plane ticket may incur a severe penalty if not used on the right date, or even be unchangeable!

It's not a bad idea to phone ahead and check with a dealer before getting on the road if it looks like your most comfortable arrival time will be on a Sunday. Dealerships are almost *always* open on *Saturdays,* however, so a likely arrival on that day of the week should be no problem. About the only time you have to watch out for a possible Saturday problem is when you're delivering a specialty vehicle to a customer. For example, you might find that you cannot deliver a school bus to a school district on that day.

Be sure you also know the hours and days when you can be dispatched by your company. Unless special arrangements for dispatching can be made ahead of time, you may find that you'll have to plan the scheduling of your return trips carefully so that you don't miss a run you could be making over a weekend, if desired.

In both California and Virginia, I had wonderful arrangements worked out that enabled me to be dispatched whenever I liked. One or both of these ideas may serve you well, also.

My dispatcher at Auto Driveaway in San Bernardino had Monday through Friday office hours, so he provided me with a key to the lot, and a prearranged drop spot where I could pick up the key to the next vehicle I would be assigned. All I had to do was call him during business hours, ahead of time, and give him my ETA. Then, even if I were to arrive at two o'clock in the morning on Memorial Day, I could still go directly to my coach, run through the checklist, put a copy of it for Don through the office door's mail slot, and leave.

At Swan, the plant was large enough to warrant a 24-hour security guard at the gate. If I came in when the facility was closed, he simply gave me the paperwork and keys per my pre-arrangement with the dispatcher, and I was on my way! (This was much like the scenario at the bottom of page 27.)

During those years while I worked full-time, 1977-1986, having this arrangement enabled me to earn thousands of dollars per year that I otherwise would have lost due to unnecessary down time.

Does that mean it was all work and no play for me during those years? No, for two reasons. First, because this job was always quite literally like a vacation to me. School teaching is very hard work, and prior to becoming a Road Rat, I'd gone through 10 years of that. My awareness of the extreme contrast between the two jobs was always strong. Secondly... I took days off whenever I felt like it. A few days in Seattle. A bus ride to the southern tip of the Baja California peninsula and back. It wasn't *all* driving, riding, and flying by any means. But most of that time, the days I took off were entirely ones of my *own* choosing. I was almost never forced into a down time situation by weekends or holidays. It was a wonderful feeling! I was living almost *completely* free of both the clock and the calendar! How many people do you know who can say that? Not even most truckers, because they must adhere to very tight schedules. But now that you know *how,* **you** can be as free as I was!

You need to find the routine that is best for you, however. That sort of freedom doesn't suit everyone. Some drivers work out of their home towns, and prefer to be *home* on weekends. And some drivers even like to take short runs of 100-400 miles and get home again the same evening! This is your choice, of course, but it is a pattern that probably would result in your earning significantly *less* than $30,000/year, even as a full-time driver. (Most drivers in those categories are married and have families.) The single drivers, and couples who drive as a team (see Chapter 6 in this Part), both tend to favor the more profitable course of working most of the time, driving a mix of runs that vary in distance, and taking occasional days off as they select them. They can easily share $60,000 or more of annual earnings. And sometimes quite a bit more.

THE LEGALITIES

In states that require license plates on in-transit vehicles, companies will issue you one or two to use continually. (California uses one plate. Indiana uses two, front and rear. Other states vary.)

Most states are pretty tolerant of the way you display them, as long as they're visible. When doing this in California, I usually prop the plate up against the inside of the front windshield. Some places are more strict. Decatur, Indiana, for example, shows no mercy. Transporter companies handle deliveries there, and numerous vehicles are always being shuttled around town, from the factories.

In 1977, it was a commonly-accepted practice for such units to be moved around within Decatur without plates. After all, three major RV factories were there, and the police easily recognized those new coaches and knew what was going on. But by 1978, the city got hard-nosed about it. If a driver was caught driving without plates, he could kiss $41.00 good-bye! A brief warning period (of a day or two) was announced, but after that, some Road Rats and factory employees, forgetting out of force of habit, were fined. The recipients of those fines didn't blame the officers, who clearly were under orders... but I won't repeat what they had to say about the *mayor,* whose name was taken in vain -- a lot! Have you ever noticed that government-imposed restrictions always seem to *in*crease, **never** *de*crease? Even at the *local* level! Read on, and you'll see that I'm a great believer in keeping things simple! Back to the license plates... in such cases where two plates are used, putting one in the rear window normally will suffice. Carry the other one along, or put it on the dashboard.

Transporter companies, and some factories, will furnish you with a cab card as well, which documents your company's authority to make interstate deliveries. You should always carry this where you can reach it easily while en route. In some states, you'll find it necessary to pull into weigh stations and/or ports of entry at or near the state line. Some of these will require you to buy a permit (for which your company normally will pay, as part of your expense money), and some will simply wave you through. At the ones where permits are issued to you, the inspector will frequently ask to see your cab card or papers. (Be *sure* that your proof of insurance is among those!)

Your license plate and documents normally will have reciprocity with most states. This means you can travel through such states as though you were driving your own car.

Some states, however, share reciprocity with only a *few* other states. Arizona, Montana, Idaho, and New Mexico are good examples... and I've been told that Wyoming has reciprocity with NO other states. Be sure to check with your dispatcher and learn the states that have special requirements. Those are the states in which you'll find it necessary to stop at a permit office, weigh station, or courthouse and purchase what some of them call a "caravan permit."

If your company happens to be one of the few that require their drivers to pay for those permits out of their own pockets, it can be tempting to try and drive across the state without one. Please heed this warning: **DON'T take chances and try to evade the permit requirements in that handful of states that issue them.** For example, in Montana, fines vary according to the *county* in which you are driving. The permit for a vehicle from Indiana, crossing more than 400 miles of Montana, costs only $12.50. In certain counties, if a Road Rat should be stopped *without* a permit, the *fine* can be as high as *$500.00!* And we recently learned that a Road Rat, while attempting to cross *Arizona* without a permit, was fined a whopping ***$1,500.00!!***

This will be covered in greater depth later, but be aware that many companies give drivers a lump sum that is the pay and the expense money, combined. And that provides an extra incentive to cut corners where possible, since the money *remaining* after the trip is the profit. If you're in that category, **don't** cut **that** corner! Consider whether you'd prefer your profit to be shy a *permit fee,* or a *fine!*

ALWAYS buy the permit, when crossing states that require this!
(Guess which Road Rat reached his destination in a good mood!)
Remember -- **Most** *companies pay for it. But they* **won't** *pay fines!*

One last thought. One time, upon entering Oregon, I had to stop at a port and buy a $3.00 permit. Even though that fee would be reimbursed by my company, my frame of mind at the time was such that I found it aggravating to be required to stop and accomplish that little chore. Inside the office, though, I met a trucker who was doing the same thing, but *he* was totally *upbeat,* and told me about how, for him, being a trucker was "more fun than a barrel of monkeys!" **That** put things into **perspective**, *fast!* Here was a *trucker* that was having a *great time,* and there *I* was, griping while living a lifestyle that included virtually *none* of the pressure and hassles that *his* job entailed. After all, a simple five-minute stop to get that permit was no big deal! I've never forgotten that cheerful trucker, and the experience reminded me once and for all how *lucky* I was to be enjoying the open road so freely!!

2
Getting the Most from a Unit

It would be a shame to make a living driving America's most luxurious vehicles and not be able to enjoy the luxury features! What follows may seem to be about 95% common sense, but I'm frequently asked what one can and cannot utilize while driving an RV -- so this will clarify that, in case you were wondering.

Many of the features are at your disposal, and a few are not. For example, use of the toilet is almost *universally* taboo. It brings to mind a rule that applied 'way back when I was an aviation cadet in the Air Force. Whenever we went up in a T-29 on one of our navigator training missions, we knew that if we *had* to use the facilities, we could use a non-automated commode called "The Honey Bucket." (Since those days, the government has managed to pay contractors something like $9,000 each for flush toilets -- but they could have saved a bunch by finding out where the *commercial airlines* got *theirs!*) There was just one catch: he who *used* the Honey Bucket was required to *clean* the thing immediately after the flight! I never knew of *any* cadet *ever* having to use the Honey Bucket! Same thing applies here... don't use the one in the coach, unless you're prepared to clean it so well afterward that the dealer to whom you make the delivery *never* discovers you did it. Few things irritate a dealer more! Rest rooms are readily available for your use en route (although you might want to avoid patronizing "Sunoco" stations -- at least in Pawtucket, RI). Just a thought -- if that awful idea of *charging a fee* to use rest rooms at gas stations ever spreads, just go to truck stops. *They'll* never do that, lest they start a second Revolutionary War! Truckers wouldn't tolerate it!

Similarly, use of the vehicle's shower is strongly frowned upon. For more detail on obtaining showers en route, review pages 33-34. Most of the other features *are* usually available for the driver's use, depending largely upon individual company policies, and subject to logical limitations, as follows:

1. ***Radio --***

    Units range from those having no radio to those having AM/FM stereo radio sets that include cassette tape players. There probably are no companies that would restrict your use of these. (Enjoy!)

2. ***Air Conditioner --***

    Most RVs have factory-installed dash air. Feel free to use it. The use of *roof* air conditioners may be restricted, though, because to operate it you must usually turn on an auxiliary generator, which runs on gasoline, usually drawn from the vehicle's fuel tank. If fuel economy is a concern, that will cost you about one mile/gal. Some companies prohibit running the generator due to the presence of *a meter which counts the number of hours the generator has been run.* This meter *cannot be disconnected or turned back,* and many dealers dislike having a number of hours showing on it. If there is no company policy, use good judgment. To keep everyone happy, use the roof air unit only on *extremely* hot days, should you *need* it for comfort. (Most dealers accept that, if not done to excess.)

    If you're in a mini-motorhome, wing windows are a common feature, and a decent substitute if dashboard air isn't working. **Suggestion,** from personal experience: If you use

- 42 -

the wing windows, don't direct the air flow *directly* at yourself. *Bees* tend to be hurled at the driver at high speed, this way! One memorable experience with a bumblebee while I was wearing Bermuda shorts *cured* me of that practice.

TIP: ***Avoid* having the side windows of an RV open while *moving*, if the windows have screens. The wind blast tears the screens loose from their mountings, ruining them!**

3. *Furnace --*

You may wish to use the unit's furnace to keep warm during wintertime runs -- mainly for periods of sleep. Ask your dispatcher first; some factories do not check the propane lines before shipment, leaving that chore to the dealer. Occasionally, a propane line that hasn't been checked can leak. If it leaks while you run the furnace, you can blow yourself up! If the lines *have* been checked, you then must decide whether or not it is cost-effective to use the furnace during sleep periods. That depends mainly on the number of hours you expect to sleep during the run. It is necessary to introduce about three gallons of propane into the tank to provide sufficient pressure to operate the system, but pre-checked systems usually will already contain some propane. For your small investment, you will get several hours of thermostatically-controlled heat throughout the unit. Compare that to the cost of similar comfort by spending the night in a motel. There are two *alternatives* to furnace use, however:

(A) Let the engine idle, and allow the cab's heater to provide warmth. This method costs between $1.00 and $1.50/hour in terms of expended gasoline. (Keep a window cracked on the lee side (away from the wind), to guard against carbon monoxide.)

(B) Bundle up in a thermal sleeping bag. If you own one that is rated for low enough temperatures, you can save substantially throughout the winter.

In conclusion, the methods available, from least to most expensive, are: (1) use a sleeping bag; (2) run the furnace (on a long trip, from some factories), and (3) idle the engine and use the heater.

4. *Refrigerator --*

It may be gas, electric, or a combination capable of both. The electric one requires running the generator, and its meter, and will reduce overall gasoline mileage. The gas one may require purchasing some propane. Simply comply with your company's policy about this, if you're so inclined. But carrying along a disposable styrofoam ice chest is much easier!.

5. *Range; Oven; Microwave --*

Most companies prefer these not be used, to prevent the possibility of spilled or burned food, etc. (Check with your dispatcher.) If using the microwave, be *sure* it's clean afterward!

6. *Ash Tray --*

It's best to stop for outdoor smoking breaks, to keep the vehicle odor-free. If smoking is permitted by your company, though, be sure to bring your *own* ash tray. (This is part of the Golden Rule of RV delivery: "Thou shalt not mess up the coach!")

3
The Care & Feeding of Breakdowns

A new motor home or specialized vehicle, like a car, sometimes has manufacturing defects which can manifest themselves during the first several hundred miles it is driven. When these occur, breakdowns present the Road Rat with the only real problems he usually has while *driving*.

Breakdowns can be classified in four categories:

Class I	--	*Major* Delay	--	Unit incapacitated for several days or weeks.
Class II	--	*Long* Delay	--	1-2 days
Class III	--	*Short* Delay	--	Minutes to hours
Class IV	--	*No* Delay	--	...but special vigilance or actions are required.

As a rule, breakdowns can be traced to either of two sources: (1) The *chassis* manufacturer, or (2) The *RV or specialty vehicle* manufacturer. Breakdowns that occur to motorized units out on the road, which require professional service, usually are related to the vehicles drivability, and thereby qualify for repair by a dealership representing the *chassis manufacturer*. However, even when the chassis warranty does not cover the work (due to a fault caused by the modifying manufacturer), arrangements for payment almost always are negotiable by the service manager and the modifying factory. Therefore, nearly all breakdowns can be corrected at the same service center. In the event you work for a transporter company, explain the situation to your dispatcher over the phone, and then he'll either negotiate with the service manager or contact a factory representative who can.

On rare occasions a breakdown may occur wherein if a driver can pay for the service, he can get underway much faster. A good example of this would be loss of transmission fluid due to a ruptured hose to the transmission cooler. This might be repairable at a garage along the highway, making it unnecessary to locate a dealer. In such instances, you should *first* check with your dispatcher. If the dispatcher agrees to the suggested course of action, and to reimburse you, then you can pay the bill and get a receipt, for which you will be reimbursed upon your return. Most of the time, your company already will have a policy on this, and leave the matter to your own discretion, as long as you don't spend more than a given, ceiling amount without additional authorization.

It's a good idea to carry an extra $75-$100 on all runs, or a major bank credit card, for this purpose. This occasionally can save the driver from having to wait while money is wired to him by his company. Usually, that's pretty automatic because most companies start drivers out with road expense money which will cover the costs of fuel, return transportation, and occasionally some other items. The advance usually is large enough to cover minor repairs of this sort, if necessary, as well.

All breakdowns requiring professional repair (except minor items like headlights and fan belts) should be reported to the dispatcher *before* the work is started. Company policy on this may vary, however, so you should check this policy with your dispatcher before taking your first trip, after you've been hired.

Breakdowns happen with an unpredictable frequency, but because these are brand-new vehicles, disabling breakdowns (Class I and II) are fairly rare. My own experience has been about one in 50 runs, or about once in 8 months or so, for a full-time driver. The Class III variety happens in perhaps one run in 20, on average. There are, of course, too many types of mechanical difficulties to detail here. Some of the more likely ones you may encounter over a long period of time are as follows:

CLASS I

These, the worst of all possible breakdowns, normally involve the total loss of one or more of the three major units on the drive train: engine, transmission, or differential.

1. *Engine --*

    Severe damage or destruction is associated with either internal defect (failure of a piston connecting rod, bearing, etc.), or to loss of lubrication.

    Obviously, the oil level should be checked regularly when buying gasoline. (*Some* units use substantial oil, such as a notable one that required 17 quarts to be added between Indiana and Saskatchewan -- a distance of 1,400 miles! Clearly, that was a totally abnormal situation. But if I hadn't checked the oil quite early in the trip, it could have gotten away from me and caused a Class I Breakdown!)

    However, a unit may loose its oil pressure suddenly and dramatically. Be able to recognize abnormal engine sounds when they begin. Loss of oil pressure causes a clattering noise. If shut down *immediately*, damage can probably be avoided. Sudden loss in pressure normally is due to one of three causes, all of which should result only in a Class III Breakdown if you simply keep your ears open and don't have the stereo/tape player on too loud:

    (1) Loss of oil pan plug
    (2) Blown gasket on oil filter
    (3) Oil pump failure

2. *Transmission* --

As with the engine, transmission failure due to defective internal parts is *rare*. Loss of lubrication, again, is the primary villain, when it occurs.

If the transmission has a supplemental cooler, fluid loss could result from a loose or broken line. Loss of fluid results in transmission slippage. Stopping *immediately* generally prevents serious damage. (Again, the result is only a Class III Breakdown.)

Sometimes, a unit leaves clouds of smoke behind upon climbing a steep hill, resulting from transmission fluid leaking onto the hot exhaust system. (Transmission fluid smokes like crazy when it comes in contact with a hot surface.) A serious leak could result in overhaul of the transmission -- a Class I Breakdown. But a slow leak can be closely monitored, and fluid added as necessary (This is a Class IV Breakdown, as in the case of that coach that took a total of 17 quarts of motor oil.) Frequently, slow leaks will stop en route. Please be aware that a significant leak of either motor oil or transmission fluid can be indicative that something may be about to let loose and cause you a *really* serious problem.

TIP: **If you detect significant consumption of *any* fluid, have a mechanic check this out *immediately* after you've detected the problem.**

3. *Differential* --

Failure of one of these is so rare, I've experienced it only once. But if it happens, it's probably due to loss of lubrication due to a bad seal or loss of the fill plug, or from mechanical failure attributable to a defective part. A driver with sharp ears *may* detect, as he travels, an unusual whine in the background. The only possible remedy is to *stop immediately*, and check *all* fluid levels, *starting* with the differential.

Please **understand that you do NOT need to have ANY mechanical ability to be a Road Rat!** I don't expect you to climb under the vehicle with a wrench to check something like this out, and *I* wouldn't, *myself*. I *am* strongly advising that you get professional help. If out on the open road, either get AAA Road Service (if you're a member, and driving the type of vehicle with which they will deal) or *have a tow truck take you* to the nearest chassis manufacturer's dealership that applies to your vehicle. **DO NOT continue to *drive* if you hear weird or unusual sounds coming from under or behind your vehicle!!** If you *do*, you're a *prime candidate* for a Class I Breakdown, when otherwise it might only be a Class III!

If the rear end (differential) *does* go out, it will immediately get your attention! It is likely to be a very sudden, dramatic, and startling event -- a very loud, metallic, rending sound, accompanied by a sudden loss of drive train power -- as though you had suddenly shifted into neutral. That will be followed by a ride in a tow truck to the nearest appropriate dealership's service bay and, as with all other Class I Breakdowns, your vehicle must be left there. Per the decision of your dispatcher, you then will continue to your Interlock point (if you're reasonably close to it, and you've arranged one), or return to your company at their expense. Later, either you or another of your company's Road Rats will pick up the disabled unit after repairs upon it have been accomplished, and complete its run. A third possibility is that you'll be instructed to go to a motel until your unit has been repaired, and then continue. A two- or three-day breakdown *usually* is handled in the latter fashion. Most companies, in that event, *also* will provide you with at least a token amount of supplemental per diem pay to compensate you for lost productive time.

CLASS II

These delays are unusual, occurring either as an abnormally-*speedy* repair of a Class I Breakdown, or as a lon-n-n-n-g, drawn-out repair of what would normally be only a Class III Breakdown.

CLASS III

Fortunately, *most* Breakdowns fall into either *this* category, or Class IV.

1. *Electrical Discharge --*

    Check for a loose fanbelt. If belts are tight, a more serious problem (such as a faulty alternator) is possible. Therefore, you should stop at the first authorized dealership en route, if during the daytime, and get this checked. If it's only a loose or broken belt, though, you normally can get that fixed at a garage, and be on your way.

    If the discharge happens at night, your headlights will drain the battery quickly. Get to the first town. If no dealer is open, locate the appropriate dealership, park in the service drive, if possible, and get a good night's sleep. (Pray that this doesn't happen on a *Saturday* night, or the eve of a *holiday weekend!*)

2. *Electrical Fluctuation --*

    If the ammeter begins to flick wildly back and forth from "charge" to "discharge", go *right away* to a nearby chassis manufacturer's dealership and ask a mechanic to check *first* for the possibility that the connection leading to an auxiliary battery in the back of the coach may have become fused against the exhaust manifold. (This only happened to me once, and that was the cause.)

3. *Faulty Alternator Mounting --*

    Here's a rare, or perhaps even nonexistent problem in the 1990s. (Let's hope!) After pondering whether or not even to include it, I decided to on the off chance that this chassis-manufacturer's defect could conceivably recur sometime. Also, older units sometime are brought back into factories by Road Rats for special repairs or upgrades, and there's a remote chance that you might encounter this problem in that manner. Finally, the effect is so very startling when it occurs, it can't hurt for you to know the possible cause right off, if you ever happen to hear it.

    Thanks to a manufacturing defect which first manifested itself in 1978, a Road Rat may be driving serenely down the freeway one moment, and find himself confronted an instant later by a sound somewhat akin to a hundred banshees slugging away at steel drums with pipe wrenches! He pulls over and stops, expecting the worst. Instead, he finds that his problem is only irksome -- *if* he is prepared.

    In those days, there were *many* cases of alternators mounted in Dodges in a defective manner that imposed too much stress on the upper bolt. It became common for this bolt to shear off, right at the engine block, en route. (I experienced this on several runs, and two of those were in succession!)

Fortunately, should you encounter this (perhaps extinct) problem, it is easily correctable (temporarily) most of the time, even by *non*-mechanically-inclined Road Rats. At least for the duration of the run. The dealer or receiving customer will have to have it *permanently* repaired after you deliver it, so be sure not to forget to tell him about it! The wild racket occurs when the **bolt** slides forward through the alternator housing and contacts the **fan.** The speed of the fan's rotation is the saving factor; the blades contact the bolt constantly, preventing it from being thrust forward further, which would do *grievous* damage. Drivers should carry at least one *5/8" nut* in their luggage, which they can screw onto the threads remaining at the *sheared* end of the bolt. This keeps the bolt from sliding through the housing and contacting the fan.

In this new configuration, the alternator rides at about a 10-degree angle from the horizontal, placing strain on the *belt.* (It is likely, however, that you *can* reach your destination with good alternator function, and an unbroken belt. But again, be *sure* to make the dealer aware of it.)

4. *Engine Overheating* --

The most common causes are: (1) *loss* of coolant, and (2) *dilution* of coolant, during hot weather.

Loss of coolant usually is traceable to a ruptured hose, which can be repaired at any garage. It also can be caused by overheating due to a broken fan belt. That also is easily remedied. Both situations could easily require a tow, however, should the malfunction occur any distance from a service station of garage. *(It pays to belong to AAA!)*

If the level of coolant is stable, one should check the potency of the mixture. Coolant is most effective when it is mixed approximately 50-50 with water. If overheating is a problem with a filled system, but the mixture is weak, the driver should drain some off, and add pure *coolant* to restore the mixture to full potency. (Dilution of coolant can be the result of (a) plain water having been introduced into the system, *initially,* instead of a coolant mixture, or (b) repeated additions of water, to replace a slow loss of coolant.)

If overheating *still* persists, in hot weather, it sometimes can be controlled by keeping engine RPMs up. If caught in slow or stop-and-go city traffic, this can be done by driving in a lower gear, or shifting to neutral and revving the engine while waiting for traffic to move. (Often, the fan will provide enough air flow through the radiator in this situation, to prevent boiling over.) Finally (and in hot weather, this measure will seem *awful!*)... running the **heater** will dispel some heat, and help alleviate the problem (while broiling the Road Rat).

5. *Undesired Paint Job* --

This can result from crossing a freshly-painted highway stripe. A driver can lose several hours, working with turpentine and rags, to undo the damage. (On rare occasions, highway departments give little or no advance warning, so steer clear of any lines which *look* too bright and fresh!) It should be noted that you would not even want to *consider* **delivering** a unit that way! If you catch it quickly, before the paint starts to dry, you can get everything completely back to normal. (This happened to me once, as you probably guessed. No fun!)

6. *Cruise Control Locks Up, Wide-Open* --

   Sometimes, the cruise control chain can get hung up in the wide-open position. This is usually driver-correctable, if you know where to look. If the cruise control fails to work altogether, or else does strange things, your best course of action may be simply to **shut the thing off and drive the run without it.** Such problems come under the heading of a Class IV Breakdown, and will not delay your trip or require repair en route -- so they are covered in that section of this chapter, farther on.

   Back to the problem with the chain. I've known the cruise control chain to get hung up on an engine bolt or similar hindrance, and thus become stuck in the wide-open position. This is most likely to occur if you attempt increase power while the cruise control is engaged, such as while climbing a hill. The effect is the same as having a jammed accelerator. It's very rare, but when this occurs, it's easy to remedy:

   A. **Turn off the ignition key** and pull of the roadway. Be aware that *doing this will immediately disable your power steering,* so try not to do it on a tight curve! You probably already know that it will still be possible to steer, but doing so will require substanial effort.

   B. Remove the doghouse cover (engine cover), if you're driving an RV, and free the cruise control chain from its snag.

   C. Replace the doghouse cover and resume your trip normally.

7. *Failure of Taillights and/or Clearance Lights* --

   If taillights fail, so, frequently, do the clearance (or "running") lights. They're often on the same circuit. A bad fuse is normally the cause, and replacing it can correct the problem. However, if the defect is in the wiring, a driver could lose much valuable time getting it fixed. Usually, in the case of faulty wiring, the easiest solution for continuing the run with a minimum of lost time is as follows:

   A. Determine that brake lights, directional lights, and 4-way emergency flashers are still functional.

   B. Drive as much of the run as possible in daylight.

   C. If it is necessary to drive at night, turn on the 4-way flashers. If the police see you, they generally will assume the true nature of your problem, and because there's no hazard, probably not stop you, except, perhaps, to confirm this. In that event, the officer may require that you get the problem corrected. That's normally not a problem, because you probably will have the unit delivered before the time limit expires.

CLASS IV

1. *Air Conditioner* --

   Almost all RVs have air conditioners, and the same is true for a high percentage of today's specialized vehicles. When you are assigned a unit so equipped, you stand about an 85% chance of reaching your destination with it still functioning properly, if you use it. In my experience, the A/C is the second most-likely system in an RV to fail with fairly consistent regularity (after the cruise control, which typically is worse), even though you're taking the vehicle on its maiden voyage. (Maiden voyages are not always flawless, as any *Titanic* survivor can tell you.) Occasionally, an air conditioner is inoperative when the driver receives the unit, but more often, it either will lose its freon or its motor will fail en route, should you happen to receive a defective one. There is no reasonable solution because your company generally will view this merely as an inconvenience to *you* and not to the mission; getting it repaired en route is not critical to getting the unit to its destination. As a result, some runs seem very warm indeed!

One of Murphy's Laws:
*Air Conditioners are Most Likely to Fail
while One is Crossing the Mojave Desert in July!!*

But if you *literally* face the prospect of having to drive across a very hot desert, your dispatcher probably will have mercy on your fricaseed soul and permit a delay of reasonable length to get the A/C repaired under the warranty. Whether or not he'll throw in a motel room and/or some per diem pay is something you'll have to try and negotiate, if that ever happens.

Remember, drivers are almost never rushed, so if you keep a good pace normally, you generally can build in an extra day or two for yourself to visit friends, see an attraction along the way... or get an air conditioner fixed... depending upon the length of the run.

2. *Cruise Control Malfunctions* --

   Whenever you are assigned a unit that has a cruise control that works precisely, consider yourself lucky. *Most* cruise control-equipped RVs seem to have one of *these* problems:

   A. It works for awhile, and then suddenly releases. Not good, if you're being tailgated by someone at the time, because you'll suddenly slow down without apparent reason, and your brake lights won't illuminate! And that *could* cause him to rear-end you.
      Solution: watch for tailgaters, and rest your foot on the accelerator while they're present.

   B. It seems to work fine, but after awhile you notice your speed has dropped gradually, and now you're going about 15 or 20 mph slower.

   C. It gradually causes you to speed up -- and if you don't notice this happening, a *cop* might notice it *first!* (Try and explain *that* one!!)

   D. It causes your speed to degrade rapidly, or else cuts out altogether, whenever you encounter upgrades.

   E. It's not precise. After braking, the act of re-engaging the cruise control (by depressing the "Resume" button) causes the coach to cruise at a speed either slightly faster or slower than before. (Most of the time, it's slower.)

   F. It lags. After initially punching in the desired speed, the unit stabilizes at a speed several miles per hour slower.

   G. It inexplicably fails *completely* en route, and will not re-engage.

   H. It sometimes will disengage when one or the other of the directional signals is used.

   I. It disengages when the 4-way flashers are turned on. (This defect has been present in a surprising number of vehicles!)

   J. It doesn't work when windshield wipers are on -- another surprisingly *common* defect!

   H. The cruise control is inoperative throughout the entire run, right from the start. This is the *most* common problem you'll have with this.

   Finally, you should be aware that, rarely, a speedometer cable will break en route, even with these brand-new vehicles. If this happens while the cruise control is in operation, the cruise will disengage instantly, causing unexpected deceleration. The result can be like that described in "A," above. For that reason, it is good practice for you to *always* rest your foot on the accelerator (without pressing down) while passing another vehicle. Then, should the speedometer cable happen to break just as you pull back in front of the slower vehicle, you can compensate instantly and avoid being rear-ended.

3. *Blown Fuse* --

   You must decide whether you desire or need the disabled function. Replacement fuses are easily obtained at most service stations, or you may elect to routinely carry along your own supply of assorted amperages. Again, this is something that anyone can do easily without assistance. The only real problem is when there is an underlying cause that results in the fuse blowing *repeatedly*. Then you have a short circuit somewhere that needs lengthening, and *that* could be a higher-class breakdown.

4. **Disabled Radio --**

If the *FM* radio works, but the *AM* band is dead, the *AM* antenna may be loose. The antenna lead, in that case, often can be found dangling down around your feet. Plugging it back in, to the back of the radio, will restore this function.

Winter Storm Procedures

If you get caught in a blizzard and are forced to stop in the middle of nowhere while driving an RV, there are few vehicles *better* equipped to weather such a storm than a motor home! Certain procedures can be followed to ensure greater comfort, safety, and survival:

1. If there is propane in the tank, use the furnace as the primary source of heat. If the supply of propane is low, run the furnace intermittently, or set the thermostat quite low, in order to conserve the fuel.

2. If visibility is low, **stay with the vehicle** unless you have warm layers of clothing and can *see* heated and/or occupied shelter nearby.

3. If you are in *immediate danger of freezing* for lack of preparations (such as not having adequate fuel, clothing, etc.), put an inside light on intermittently, and flash your headlights now and then in the universally-understood distress signal (3 short flashes-3 longer flashes-3 short flashes; "S.O.S.", in Morse Code). Don't *overdo* this and run down your battery!

4. If it is necessary to run the engine for heat, have a window cracked open slightly, on the side of the vehicle *away* from the wind, and **keep the exhaust pipe free of snow.** This eliminates the carbon monoxide hazard.

5. Do exercises to keep from falling asleep if you are *not* protected from the cold by heat, blankets, or adequate clothing..

CONCLUSION

Simple replacement of such common parts as headlights, fuses, fan belts, etc. normally won't require you to seek out a dealer representing the chassis manufacturer. When replacing such a part out of your own pocket (assuming that this is in line with your company's procedures), you should *always get a receipt,* and *retain the defective part.* Many dispatchers have had experience with unscrupulous drivers at one time or another, and presenting him with both of these items upon your return will serve both to keep you above suspicion, *and* assure you of reimbursement.

4

"And the Northern Lights were a-Runnin' Wild in the Land of the Midnight Sun..."

So go the lyrics in the song, *"North to Alaska,"* from the 1960 movie having the same title.

For years, people have asked me, "What's it really *like* to be a Road Rat? Does it ever get boring? Lonely? Difficult? Tiring? Or is it a life of pure, unbridled, non-stop *adventure*? Do you have 'a girl in every port?' Don't you just get sick of *travelling* all the time?" And more. In previous editions of this Handbook I've always stressed the *quantitative* aspects of this lifestyle -- the facts and figures -- and paid less attention to describing the *quality*. To cite just one more movie example, in *"Star Trek III, The Voyage Home,"* Spock is asked the question, "How do you *feel?"* And because he's supposed to be so completely a creature of logic, this simple query leaves him at a complete loss for words. Spock just can't handle such an abstract and illogical notion as... *feelings*.

Lest I come to be regarded as "mostly-Vulcan," -- for the benefit of you fellow Trekkies and Trekkers who are reading this -- I'm about to do something kinda different. In *this* edition, for the *first time ever,* I'm going to try to tell you how it really *feels* to be a Road Rat.

Do you remember what I told you about the cheerful truck driver, on page 41? Much of that attitude applies pretty well to successful Road Rats, at least most of the time. If you're making a comfortable living doing this, and therefore are free of financial worries, then you can really *enjoy* this job!

If you're like me, you like to know what's coming next, but surprises don't hurt either. For that reason, my normal routine always has been to ask my dispatcher where I can go *next,* and I usually do that as I approach the end of a run, or immediately after the delivery, by phone. And sometimes get *quite* a surprise!

On one notable occasion in 1979, I delivered a coach to a dealer in Portland, Oregon, and then went to the Greyhound depot to start my return trip. After getting my *Ameripass* properly marked, and while awaiting the bus, I called my dispatcher, Don Myers, at Auto Driveaway in San Bernardino, to see what was next on my agenda.

"Where would you really LIKE to go, if you could have your choice of ANY destination?" he asked jauntily.

"Oh, I don't know. *Siberia* might be interesting. I've always wanted to take a ride on the Trans-Siberian Railroad." (And back then, I hadn't done that yet.)

Don laughed, then said, "No. *REALLY!* Tell me -- of all the places it's possible to *drive,* what would be your first choice?"

That was easy. *Alaska's* always been my favorite state. But because I'd been a Road Rat for less than two years, I'd never yet run across an opportunity to *drive* there. None of the companies for which I'd worked had ever had a run to Alaska before then. "Fairbanks," I replied without hesitation.

"You've got it!" he said. "Come on back down and it'll be waiting for you."

My feelings at *that* point were a 50-50 mixture of excitement and amazement, but none of doubt. There was no question but that he was telling the truth.

"Don!" I exclaimed. "Why are you being so GOOD to me?! Before I get back, there'll be a dozen drivers who could've taken that run ahead of me!"

"Yes," he chuckled. "And I asked all of them. No one wants the run. You see, except for Mary, who's from Arkansas, all these other drivers are native southern Californians. You're the only driver I have who grew up in a *northern* state. None of the others want any part of a run to *Alaska* in *February!* So it's all yours!"

TIP: Most dispatchers won't require their Road Rats to drive in weather conditions in which they don't feel confident or secure.

Although I had discovered the "Interlock" system some months before, such a return run to California wasn't available this particular time. And in the 1970s, returns from outbound runs still were commonly being done via bus or *Amtrak*. These are still popular methods for Road Rats having lower incomes, who don't use Interlock, and for reasons explained in Part III, Chapter 4, I'll be giving you detailed information about bus travel. Remember, though, that most Road Rats *these* days who have good incomes make most of their returns either via *Interlock* or by *air,* whichever they choose.

Prelude for a Road Rat

On the bus ride down to San Berdoo, I worked on compiling my notes for what later would become the *first* edition of *this* book, a year later. Even bus riding isn't boring, if you don't mind it. In the summer of 1976, I set the official *Guiness Book* World Record for bus riding in the process of doing preliminary research for a thesis for my geography M.A. That phase called for me to survey summer school students, one-to-one, on college campuses in *each* of the 50 states. Coincidentally, I'd learned some months earlier that the bus-riding record was held by a lady from England who had travelled 19,000+ miles that way in three months. So for the fun of it, I arranged, per the *Guiness* requirements, for a reporter to write it up in an Albany, NY newspaper, *The Knickerbocker News,* based on my submitting proof to him throughout the trip by mailing post cards each time I made a change of direction. Between the 4th of July in that Bicentennial Year and Labor Day, I accomplished the research and in the process rode the bus a total of *35,000+* miles in just *two* months. The new record was officially set... but **then** *Guiness* decided to **drop** the bus-riding category! (Oh, *well!*) But it was an adventure all the same -- and there was *never* a dull moment. After all, covering all those miles by bus -- *and* doing the research for my thesis by surveying 1,200 students on 80 campuses in all 50 states -- *and* devising and implementing an effective and nutritious diet that enabled me to lose 40 lbs. in 30 days *within* that time frame -- *and* exploring Hawaii, *and* mountain climbing at Lake Louise, in Canada -- *and* spending a week exploring the Alaska Pipeline project by riding from Fairbanks to Prudhoe Bay and back with pipe-hauling truckers (thereby getting the material from which I wrote my book, *Seven Days on the Kamikaze Trail,* later that year)... left precious *little* time in which to become **bored!**

Okay, so I cheated! I wasn't a Road Rat *yet* when I did all of *that* -- one year *earlier*.

But I made that little sidetrack on purpose, so that I could show you how very *diverse* your life can be as a Road Rat! *I* didn't change in the short year that elapsed between the adventure above, and the ones upon which I embarked when I started driving RVs. I *continued* to do things that were just as challenging and exciting -- except that by *that* time I had discovered how to get *paid* while doing it. It sure beat school teaching! And it isn't all driving, riding, and flying, unless you *choose* for it to be! While I worked full-time as a Road Rat for ten years, I wrote and outlined *many* books. Some, including earlier editions of this one, were written and published while I was still a full-time Road Rat. Others, including a major novel, are approaching completion and will be published during the next two or three years.

And photography is a favorite hobby for me. I can't *begin* to tell you how many fascinating stills and videos I've made in the course of all those travels! Can you imagine the opportunities the Road Rat lifestyle can present for the professional or serious amateur **photographer** of people and places?

My first RV run to Alaska started in balmy +70° temperatures in southern California, and reached temperatures 120 degrees colder than that in the Yukon and Alaska, a few days later. The last mild weather was left behind during the drive from Vancouver to Hope, BC. The drive through that valley is always beautiful, but this time it was *spectacular!* Perhaps only hours before, a weather system had moved through in which the freezing temperature level was about halfway up the mountains. This created a vista of dark-green evergreen forests closer to the valley floor, yielding immediately to a forest of about a billion flocked Christmas trees from the halfway level to the mountaintops.

That was in the morning, but by evening, the scene had changed dramatically. It was about eight o'clock when I arrived in Prince George, BC and was treated to the sight of the most snow I've ever seen on the ground in a populated area! It had to be about 15 feet deep, and all on the level. Over weeks and months, it had simply fallen straight down without wind, in numerous storms. I got off the highway and slowly drove through a residential area, where I found a man shovelling his driveway by hand, throwing the snow about as high as is humanly possible. I just had to ask.

"How much snow do you have here?"

"TOO damn much!!" came the reply. "We usually have a January thaw that melts it all, and then start over. But *this* year, it never occurred. This snow's just been accumulating all winter long!"

At Chetwynd, BC, the next morning, my fuel was getting low, so I topped off tank before exiting Route 97 onto Route 29 -- a shortcut to the Alaska Highway at Fort St. John, that by-passes Dawson Creek and saves several miles. Topping off *there* was a mistake, I learned soon afterward. The gas stations in Chetwynd were charging *15* cents per gallon *more* than ones in Dawson Creek *or* Fort St. John! It often can be quite worthwhile for Road Rats to find the cheapest gasoline that they can, since many companies *combine* expense money with pay. Unless you can confirm ahead of time that the gas in Chetwynd is selling at the same price as in Dawson Creek or Fort St. John, you can *avoid* what I've dubbed "The Chetwynd Ripoff" by purchasing *just* enough fuel to comfortably reach one of those other cities. Going north out of Prince George, if you have a CB, ask southbounders about this.

Avenue to the Last Frontier

My first encounter with the Alaska Highway, most of which then was unpaved gravel, was a most pleasant surprise. All the way from Fort St. John to the Alaska border (beyond which it is all paved), a distance of nearly 1,200 miles, the road was a smooth, snow-packed ribbon secured by temperatures ranging from -20° to -50° F. I say, "secured," because driving on smooth snowpack at those temperatures is like driving on normal, newly-laid asphalt. Snow is slippery under the weight of a vehicle at temperatures that aren't too far below freezing. But at 50° and more below the freezing point, it loses that property, and becomes like dry pavement. If this seems strange, then try to imagine what it might be like to drive on blacktop if *that* were heated to within 20° of *its* melting point! So the rest of the trip to Fairbanks was almost like driving on an interstate highway, except that it was two broad lanes in width, and had a very light flow of traffic. (Interestingly, in the late 1970s, people along that highway truly believed that it would never be completely paved -- and over 1,000 miles of it still wasn't, even though the road had been built decades before. But as of 1994, only 60 miles of gravel still remained!)

I soon discovered that the significant towns along the Alaska Highway are regularly spaced about 300 miles apart -- just under the range of the fuel tank of the coach. Fort St. John, Fort Nelson, Watson Lake, Whitehorse, Beaver Creek... but only the approach to Watson Lake made me nervous. It was almost AT the range! Knowing this, I put in for gas at a station about 10 or 15 miles to the south, to buy $3.00 worth. Enough to get me into town, where the gas was about 30-40 cents/gallon cheaper!

One of the things that impressed me immediately about this road is the way people voluntarily help one another along its entire length. My next run to Fairbanks was three months later, in beautiful spring weather in a "Minnie Winnie" Class "C" RV that Winnebago manufactured at a plant it then still had in Riverside, California. As luck would have it, one of those rare disabling breakdowns happened to occur 50 miles south of Fort Nelson, BC. A water pump pulley broke, bringing the run to a halt. A southbound trucker saw my plight, stopped, and used his mobile phone to call for a tow truck from Fort Nelson. He then waited there and visited with me, rather than leave me stranded, even though it was a bright, sunny day with the mercury near +65°. And even though he knew the wrecker was en route. It was a strange and wonderful sort of Northern Hospitality! And only once did I see an *exception* to that rule. A season earlier, at that gas station just a few miles south of Watson Lake.

The owner of that station, who was gouging travellers unmercifully, *refused* to sell me the $3.00 worth of gas I wanted -- or any *other* quantity, for that matter, short of a *fill* of my 40-gallon tank!

See, it's *not* all bliss and roses. There are *genuine* causes of aggravation in this job from time to time. BUT -- I can count all of the memorable ones (like *that* one) on the fingers of two hands. Pretty phenomenal, considering that that covers a time span of *ten years of full-time work!* I re-calculated my remaining fuel and decided I could make Watson Lake -- barely... and then sweetly told that proprietor that he could hang his absurd gas prices in his ear, and went on my merry way! (*Made* it too, by golly!)

Watson Lake, Yukon has a unique attraction: a park along the highway where *hundreds* of signs are on display. These are the *actual* signs that you normally see welcoming you to towns and cities all over North America. They've each been brought up there by a tourist who knew about this, and then either pilfered one from his own home town -- or had the city make one for this purpose -- and donated it to this park. Want to photograph the signs? Bring along an *entire* roll of film!

Go, Bullwinkle, *Go!*

The Alaska Highway somehow manages never to encounter any high mountain passes. Instead, it wends its way between those majestic northern Rockies. And in Yukon and Alaska, that last 900 miles to Fairbanks is almost entirely *west*bound. When you reach the Yukon border, you're almost as far north as you're going to get... and Fairbanks is over 1,000 miles west of Los Angeles in longitude!

Staying in the valleys treats you to stunning vistas of towering pure-white mountains that glisten and aparkle like titanic ice crystals in a brilliant noonday sun that hangs low in the sky above the southern horizon. The sun is up for only about 5 hours a day at that time of year, that far north. Even at noon, the mountains cast miles-long shadows, giving everything a late-afternoon appearance. They stand stark and majestic in contrast to a deep, clear, azure sky. Evergreens only about half as tall as their counterparts far to the south in Washington State struggle to grow only halfway up the taller of these subarctic slopes, before encountering the timber line. It's like being in another world... and still we're only two-thirds of the way from Vancouver to Fairbanks! The *real* wonder was yet to come. But it was out there, between Watson Lake and Whitehorse, that I was greeted by a full-grown bull moose. The enormous critter was standing right in the middle of the road as I came around a curve, and when he saw me, he started running down the road ahead of me.

Did you know that the top speed of a galloping adult moose being chased by an RV is 15 mph? That's what I discovered as I grabbed my camera to get some shots of the unique sight. Unfortunately, the picture I'd shot at my *last* point of interest turned out to be *literally* the last -- I was out of film.

Now, you haven't *lived* until you find yourself chasing a moose down the Alaska Highway in mid-winter in the Yukon with one hand on the wheel and the other changing the film in a camera that's laying in your lap! The process took a full minute, but everything was going swimmingly right up until the moment when the moose slipped and fell, with all fours sprawling out in all four cardinal directions -- exactly at the moment when I finished changing the film. I stopped, and he glared at me with a gimlet eye. We both knew that this was his chance. Don't ever mess around with a moose, if the speed with which *he* got up is any indication of their reflexes! He took off at right angles to the road, bounded into a huge drift of snow, followed by the woods. The photo I took shows only a cloud of snow -- and his tail.

Whitehorse, Yukon is a city that manages to look northern and western at the same time. Its atmosphere fairly shouts the stories of Jack London. You have to close your eyes only for a moment to envision the gold rushers of the Klondike leading their pack mules, laden with prospecting gear, down the street. It was here that I got the idea for what was to become a tradition on *all* my runs to Alaska. I stopped at a downtown travel agency and bought my plane ticket back to L.A. from Fairbanks. It was not to be a conventional return trip -- nor would it ever be again.

World of Wonder!

Tok Junction is about 100 miles into Alaska from the Yukon border, with about 200 miles remaining to Fairbanks. I was near there, in open country, in the dead of the night -- 2:00 a.m. -- when the eerie event happened.

Gently-falling snow over a long span of time had capped the stunted evergreens so that each was drooping over almost double at the top. All wore crowns of more than a foot of snow. In all directions there was the appearance of a primeval forest of giant ferns. Strangely, the entire landscape, including the snow burdening the forest, seemed to have a green glow all its own. Suddenly becoming aware of that, I pulled to the side of the road to check it out. I put on my coat and stepped out of the coach into a world of absolute stillness. It was -50°, but the utterly motionless, dry air didn't seem cold at all. However, from the Arctic survival tips I'd been given in the summer of '76 by my trucker friends on the pipeline, I knew not to be fooled by that. Such cold is extremely penetrating, and it's deceptive because it doesn't *feel* dangerous. You're safe as long as you don't stay out too long, so I limited myself to about six minutes of exposure. Out there, I was *truly* in another world.

Stretching out of sight ahead of, and behind me, lay the asphalt ribbon of the Alaska Highway -- the only part of the scene that *wasn't* glowing green. It wasn't difficult to imagine that such a landscape was highly radioactive. And this one *was* being irradiated. Harmlessly. By a sky completely *filled* with swirling, coruscating curtains of aurora borealis, emanating from a point hundreds of miles straight overhead! And just happening to be in the right position at that time of year, and that time of night, the Big Dipper was directly at the zenith -- appearing to *ladle out* that wondrous, unearthly light to the entire sky, and the earth below. The enrapturing scene was one of supernal splendor, filled with those brilliant, rapidly-shifting drapes of ghostly green fire. It was hard to hold to the six-minute time limit I'd allotted for myself!

Later that morning, at about 10:00, I located the dealership in the midst of a city enshrouded in sparkling ice fog, and delivered the coach. It was -45°, and wan sunshine was barely penetrating that crystalline and glittering earthbound cloud with a pale, diffuse glow emanating from just a few degrees above the horizon. Cars with headlights on came into view and then disappeared, as they made their way through the eerily-quiet streets. Underfoot, the snow was beyond the stage of ordinary "below-zero crunch." It *squealed* with every step. I'd thought that by growing up in upstate New York, I'd experienced the North. But even during my winter in the Air Force, in Grand Forks, North Dakota, I'd never seen a North that approximated *this* strange, alien world. It was fascinating, and I hated to leave.

But leave I did, and my jet plane swept upward, out of the ice fog-draped Tenana Valley, soared into dazzling noonday sunlight, bearing straight south, toward Anchorage. In about 20 minutes, I found myself shooting dozens of pictures at the 4-mile-high king of North American mountains -- **Denali.** Better known by its more common name -- Mount McKinley. And so massive, it took nearly half an hour to pass it! Beyond, looking west, I could view hundreds of miles of tumbling lesser mountains and hills through the crystal-clear air. But *below,* it was all **Denali,** covered with its dozens of glacial

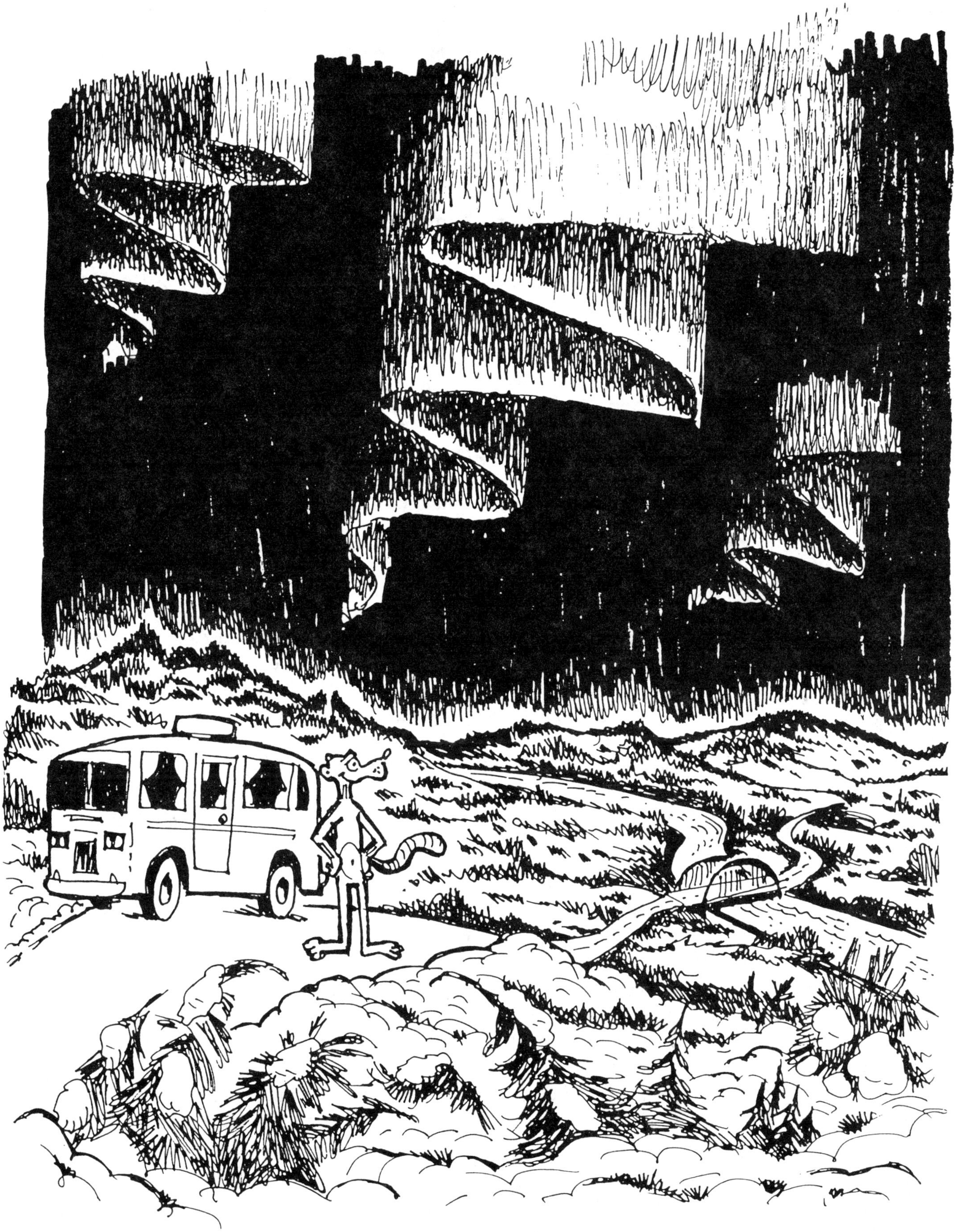

rivers of ice, some of them miles wide. It was impossible to look away -- and I still was gazing back at those captivating pinnacles when the plane began its descent into Alaska's largest city.

I had a few hours between flights, so I explored Anchorage, and bought a T-shirt that showed a motorhome besieged by assorted wildlife of all sizes, and road hazards: "I Drove the Alaska Highway and Lived."   I remembered my moose.

Land of the Palm Trees... *Aloha!*

After midnight, I boarded another jet for the next leg of my flight. In five hours -- Honolulu.

Well -- why not? I'd discovered in Whitehorse that my flight back to L.A. would cost $250.00. But to make a nice big *dogleg* to include **Hawaii** would cost only *$100.00* more. Try and buy a round-trip flight to Hawaii from *anywhere* for one hundred dollars! And this was the equivalent of it.

For the next three days, I explored Oahu, which I'd seen before -- and the Big Island *named* "Hawaii," which I *hadn't*. Volcanoes National Park, not far from Hilo, is a fascinating place to visit. All of this was carefully timed to permit my rendezvous with the next adventure. I had to leave Hawaii shortly after dawn on Feb. 24th, to pick up a Seattle-bound coach in San Berdoo late that afternoon.

You see, there was to be a **total** eclipse of the sun at Goldendale, Washington on Feb. *26th*, 1979. And you'd better believe that I was right there to enjoy it. I'd always wanted to see one of those, and that was my first. But not my last. You can't beat getting *paid* to chase eclipses!

Still in the future lay the Adventures of the *Ameripass* Team... and a special Australian girl who spent five months exploring the country with me (after I'd gotten her hired by my company); I dubbed her "Wandering Wallaby" as her CB handle... and **The Carpenters** at their opening-night performance from a front-row table at the *MGM Grand,* in Las Vegas... and countless explorations of all America's wonderlands from the Louisiana bayous to Mackinac Island. (You'll enjoy that story, in Part III, Chapter 4.) And of course, that Alaska-Hawaii trip was just the first of many. Each time I drive to Alaska, I explore a *new* Hawaiian island. After I've seen them all, I'll start the cycle over again and see what's changed! And don't forget too, that being a Road Rat opens the door to **world** travel -- much of which is *free!* (More about that later, in Chapters 8 and 10 of this part... and in Part III, Chapter 1.)

You don't have to be highly-active all the time to enjoy this work, of course. Routine runs can be quite relaxing and sedate. Such as the numerous, long trips I've taken across the Great Plains, just leisurely taking pictures of beautiful rural scenes, conjuring-up book plots, and listening to tapes of favorite music and programs. Is *that* ever boring? Or tiring? Almost never, for those of us who love to travel. A *Greyhound* bus driver friend once asked me how I "psyched myself up for a trip." I honestly was unable to comprehend his question, in *this* context! It was like asking a stamp collector how he psyched himself up to work on his collection! And that surprised him. Apparently, when stepping into that bus to make a run, he felt much the same way I *used* to feel as a *teacher,* when driving to school! Driving the bus must have been a *chore* for him. He didn't realize how much I *love* to travel! **Love of travel is the primary common denominator of Road Rats!**

This is an important point to understand: No one requires Road Rats to approach this job with the degree of zeal and enthusiasm I've described here. You've just read about how *I* happen to like to travel, but if your *own* style entails *no more* than *taking relaxing drives,* that's fine *too!* Within reason, you can approach *this* particular job just about any way you like!

A Girl in Every Port... A Chicken in Every Pot?

All your emotions will come into play as you participate in this great adventure, but anger and frustration are the *least* of them. To answer some of those *other* questions at the beginning of the chapter... Do you get lonely? No, not if you're an outgoing person -- because this gives you the chance to make new friends and acquaintances wherever you go. Whether or not you are lonely is entirely up to you. You certainly don't need to be. Can you have a "girl in every port?" Well, if you are so inclined, *sure!* But I'm an *absolute* believer in *equality*. The Road Rat lifestyle is about as close as you'll ever come to finding a **double standard-free zone** in human society. So a similarly-inclined *female* Road Rat would be *just* as entitled to have "a *boy* in every port," if *she* so desired, and no one would object. The opportunity *exists* in a job like this, so it all depends upon how a person wants to budget his or her time, and what relationship(s) he or she wishes to establish, maintain or pursue. But you see, that's the beauty of this lifestyle! Virtually *anything* is possible, in line with your own abilities and aspirations.

TIP: **In this job you have a degree of *freedom* unknown and *unimaginable* to most people, and therefore you experience a wide range of unbridled *opportunity!***

How does it *feel* to be a Road Rat?

There's more *adventure* and sheer *enjoyment* in this lifestyle in any given *month* than most people experience in a *year*. More in a decade than most *non*-Road Rats will ever see in a *lifetime*. How does it *feel?* Absolutely and almost indescribably *wonderful!!*

Let me close this chapter with this wish: May *you* someday enjoy your own night when you can be *paid* to rendezvous with enchantment -- your *own* night of awe and supernal wonder, when the Northern Lights are running wild!

Here's your Typical College Coed Road Rat --
Working her way through College
via Summers of Pure Adventure!

5
Delivering the Unit

It is best to arrive in your destination city with a comfortable margin of extra time before your scheduled flight or other public transportation. Dealerships can be pretty hectic places, and if everyone happens to be busy with potential customers, you'll be the last person to receive their attention. Immediately upon reaching a destination city, it is wise to pull off the road and reorganize. Invariably, you will have things to put back into suitcases, and you'll need to freshen up if you haven't already by that time. *Non*-toll service station rest rooms are handy for this, if you're in a hurry. If you're not sure where your delivery site is located, you can phone from there as well, for directions. (In such cases, it's best to stop right after making *first contact* with your destination city, and thereby avoid the possibility of overshooting your delivery point and having to backtrack to it.)

Upon arrival at the dealership, immediately locate the person in charge of checking in the new vehicles, so that he knows you're there. After that, check-in of the unit can take as little as a minute or two, or up to an hour of meticulous inspection, depending upon the dealer -- and his mood.

So remove your luggage from the coach *before* he inspects the interior. This is good psychology! A neat vehicle or coach that looks ready for display gives the dealer a favorable impression of the driver. If your state requires you to transport the vehicles while bearing **license plates**, as most do, it is best to **retrieve these while removing your luggage, so as not to forget them! You should immediately put the plate(s) inside of your luggage.** (Many companies assess a penalty of from $5 to $25, to cover costs and as a deterrent to forgetting the plate(s)... because this is the *easiest* mistake for the Road Rat to make!)

Leaving one's License Plate is a Cardinal Sin!

Almost without exception, RV dealers and specialized vehicle recipients are *very* cooperative and helpful. Most will even provide drivers with transportation to the nearest depot. (I have many happy memories of dealers throughout the land who have really made me feel welcome!) One of the most unforgettable incidents came with the delivery of a custom-built unit to a rancher in East Toadstrangle, Texas. (Actually, there's no such place, but if you've ever seen the terrain that is found 50 miles due west of San Antonio, I'm sure you understand.)

Making a delivery to a point located on a side road in semi-arid ranch country conjured visions of my company's possibly having to ante up about $100 in taxi fare, and I could almost see the wince on my dispatcher's face! But even *that* turned out to be a very normal delivery. The rancher accepted the unit, we threw my gear into the back of his pickup, and an hour later he dropped me off at the San Antonio Airport.

Unfortunately, there *are* a **very few** dealers who seem to have a sadistic streak that manifests itself when drivers are present. Perhaps one dealer in 150 -- or fewer -- will deliberately either cause delays that can threaten drivers with missing their flights, and/or force drivers to resort to taking a taxi to the depot or airport. In my career, I ran across only *two!*

One such occasion was during my first year as a Road Rat, when I delivered a conversion van from Indiana to a dealer situated perhaps six miles north of downtown Richmond, Virginia, on Broad Street. After checking in the unit, he pointed to a phone for my use in calling a *taxi!*

At the time, I was working for a transporter company, so the fares for any taxis I might happen to need were going to come out of my *own* pocket. I asked the dealer about city busses; Broad Street appeared to be a pretty major artery. He replied that there were no city busses running anywhere near his location, and upon my requesting a ride from him, he refused. That was so atypical, I was shocked. Dealers normally *volunteer* such rides! I called the cab, and lost about $10 worth of my profits.

Here's the irony! Less than two years later, in late 1979, as luck would have it, I moved to Richmond, Virginia, and made that city my *home base* until 1992. My house was within walking distance of Broad Street, which I soon learned was the city's *primary* avenue, and found that it *abounded* with city busses that ran regularly back and forth between downtown and Willow Lawn Shopping Center. The dealer could *easily* have told me that I was only a mile or so from there, and then I could have hiked it, or taken a *two*-dollar cab ride to it. Instead, he chose to force the unnecessary expense upon me -- a deliberately mean-spirited act!

So my experience with Richmond spanned 15 years, from that first noteworthy contact. It is filled with gracious and friendly people. That dealer was the **only** exception I happened to meet!

But the good news for Road Rats is that this was by far the *most* memorable negative experience I had in dealing with vehicle recipients between 1977 and the present. Almost all of the dealers and customers you will meet will be friendly, hospitable, and helpful. Not being offered a ride to your airport or depot is an extreme *rarity!*

As for the check-in procedure itself, a dealer routinely will start by asking if you'd noticed anything wrong with the coach or vehicle. And that reminds me of a funny experience!

> There was an occasion when three Road Rats named Bob, Rhett, and Craig (that's me) were assigned to deliver two beverage route trucks and a route trailer to Brooklyn, New York from Swan's plant near Richmond, VA. It was an unusual situation because this meant that the tow vehicle for the trailer would *return,* thus providing us all with immediate transportation home. We checked in the units, knocked around New York City as sightseers for a few hours, and then found ourselves leaving via the Lincoln Tunnel. Right after entering the New Jersey Turnpike, Rhett said, "Have you ever thought about the fun we'd *like* to have when answering that question, 'How did it run?'" Then he voiced the possibility of replying simply by covering his mouth, suppressing a laugh while pointing at the vehicle, and managing to say, between snickers, *"THAT* vehicle?! *Mmmff!!* <chuckle! chuckle!>"
>
> *Bob* then said, "I think I'd just take off my hat, hold it over my heart, hang my head, and mournfully say, 'Oh, you *poor* son of a b----!'" Then *I* contributed with, "Well, I think it'd be kinda fun to break into a rousing chorus of, '*We* got the gold mine, and *you* got the shaft!' while pocketing the check."
>
> We got to laughing so hard, we arrived at the twin spans of the Delaware Memorial Bridge in seemingly no time at all!

Of course, when you're asked that question, you don't dare actually *give* any of those responses -- as much as perhaps sometimes you'd be tempted to -- such as on a hot summer day when you turn on the A/C, hear a sound akin to <*spit! sput! spoo!*>, and then get a blast of desert heat full in your face from the vents. The problem is that the dealer's question forces you to be a diplomat, and occasionally walk a fine line with him while still being truthful. If you make it look as though you've just delivered him a problem unit, that puts your factory in a bad light, and can even lead to a list of warranty claims that the factory would prefer to avoid. On the other hand, the dealer needs to sell the unit in good running order, so it's a very fair question.

As a general policy then, I unhesitatingly provide the dealer with full details of any *chassis* discrepancies, but wait until *specific* questions are *asked* about the *coach* (or specialty vehicle) -- and *then* give honest answers to all of *those* questions. In fact, I usually *volunteer* the *chassis* discrepancies (if there are any) *before* he asks the question, and that usually results in his not thinking to ask the specific ones about the modifications or conversions done by *my* employer. This procedure usually satisfies all concerned. Further, very few Road Rats owe any particular allegiance to the "Big Three" automakers. In recent years, though, chassis discrepancies have dropped dramatically, and most Road Rats would, I'm sure, join me in complimenting the Big Three for doing such a good job of pulling up their socks!

After check-in, depending upon your company's instructions, you either will receive a check, and/or have the dealer sign your delivery receipt, or flooring forms for the bank. Then it's off to the airport, or an Interlock point, and away you go! It's as simple as that!

6

Sex and the Single Road Rat...
and, How a *Couple* Can be Truly Successful

Road Rat Love... The greatest way to explore the country!

The ready availability of runs at most companies, frequently even back-to-back, can impact the social life of the full-time or seasonal Road Rat. It brings a whole new meaning to the cliche, "I wouldn't do that for love nor money." Here, in the case of the single Road Rat, either male or female, it becomes a case of *whether or not* one does this job mainly for *one* of those, to the *exclusion* of the other. If you become so entranced with the combined benefits of exploring an entire continent while being paid to have that privilege to the tune of between $30,000 and $60,000 a year, it actually becomes difficult to *pass up* runs from time to time in favor of having a social life. For example, if you're single and earn $52,000 a year (as I did, between 1981 and 1986, inclusive), that's $1,000 per week, or over $142.00 per day. So every day you take off to spend time with your significant other will then wind up costing you $142.00, times the number of days during the year that you do it.

That sounds positively *awful*, doesn't it? How cold and calculating, to put a *price* on your compassion! And of course, most people don't run such calculations (nor do I), either in their heads or on paper. In practice, then, something much more *subtle* is at work.

TRAVEL CAN BE HAZARDOUS TO YOUR (ROMANTIC) HEALTH

When I'm a talk show guest, the host frequently comments that this lifestyle seems to be too good to be true... that surely there *MUST* be a **down side** to all of this! But we already know that the *existence* of this job is *very* easy to prove -- only cars, primarily, are transported by truck. That leaves only the question of whether or not there's a down side. And in truth, in the 17 years that have passed between 1977 and this writing, I have run across only ONE down side: the manner in which this job can subtly *compete* with the Road Rat's love life.

You see, the process is usually a *subconscious* one. You make a run, get to your destination, phone your dispatcher, and discover that your next run will be a nice, lucrative 1,800-mile one, and that it'll be ready for you as soon as you get back to the plant. You know that if you decline in favor to taking a day or two off, that juicy run will go instead to one of your colleagues. So you're faced with losing pay by voluntarily taking the down time... and you know that it might even turn out to be *more* disadvantageous. Because there's always the chance that the sweet run you sacrificed, which would have paid you $600.00, might be followed by a 200-mile one that will pay you only $65.00, instead, on the day that you return to work. And that's because it might be the only such run available then. It's luck of the draw. And this scenario is a nightmare for relationships that depend upon any degree of intimacy, such as courtships! And it's even worse if the object of your affection happens to *live* in that *destination* city from which you're calling your dispatcher! *That* gives you no chance at all to pick and choose which run you might opt to *pass up*. You see, if he offers you a nice, lucrative run *then*, you have a very tough decision. However, if your significant other lives near your *home base* instead, then you could simply take the good run, and prevail upon your dispatcher to allow you to pass up a lesser one a few days later. (**NOTE:** Be *sure* that he knows exactly WHY you want to pass up a skimpy run. Dispatchers don't appreciate it when *full-time* Road Rats seem to want only the nicest runs, leaving the scraps to their colleagues! That's called the "Prima Donna Syndrome" (see page 23 for *another* aspect of that) and it's been known to result in drivers getting their walking papers!)

It becomes easier though, if the reverse happens, and when you phone in from your destination, your dispatcher tells you that you'll be coming back to a run that'll only be *200* miles long. (Then, after taking a day or two off with his permission, at least you won't be likely to come back to one that's particularly worse than the one you missed.)

If you are single, or a member of a couple that thrives on intimacy (but of the two of you, you're the only Road Rat, and your mate stays home), this IS a significant problem. Fortunately, there *are* solutions, so study this chapter before you get going in this job, or the syndrome of missing out on a significant amount of your social life truly can sneak up on you!

Rather than yielding to the temptation to maximize your earnings at the expense of other quality aspects of life, you should *maintain a constant awareness that* **there is more to life than the adventure of travelling for pay,** even if this lifestyle does seem like a vacation with pay while you are performing it. The alternative can be your adopting an unnecessary -- and reluctant -- acceptance of loneliness. And that has the capability of ensnaring you for *years* without your giving it much conscious thought!

No, I'm not trying to scare you out of being a Road Rat. I'm simply giving you my honest assessment of the only down side of this that I ever experienced. It is amazingly *easy* to fall into the routine of being a lone wolf *unless* you maintain that constant awareness of the necessity to diversify your activities. If you are *aware* of that hazard, you can *avoid* it.

If it would take nearly 100% of your time being involved in travel to achieve an income of $52,000 a year, then I strongly recommend that you make a conscious decision to settle for less. If you are capable of earning $52,000, then you could have a *wonderfully*-balanced life -- including the social aspects -- simply by adjusting your schedule so that you would earn between $40,000 and $45,000 a year instead! Money isn't everything, and unless you get into this at a young age and make excellent investments, you're not likely to become a millionaire doing this, either. Remember, too, that you can't take it with you. No matter how much you enjoy travelling... unless it is in your *nature* to be a lone wolf, a varied lifestyle that involves interpersonal relationships and a home life should not be sacrificed.

TRAVEL CAN BE *GREAT* FOR YOUR (ROMANTIC) HEALTH!!

Shucks, I hate the idea of writing a book in which I contradict myself... so I guess I'd better sort this out for you right away!

IF you and your significant other happen to *BOTH* be Road Rats, then you can both have the totally well-rounded adventure of a *lifetime!!* If a travel-loving Road Rat perceives this job as being like a vacation with pay, then a travel-loving Road Rat *COUPLE* can have the dry-land equivalent of the *Love Boat*. Talk about an extended honeymoon! How about one *with pay* that lasts for *years?!*

In Part 3, Chapter 4, you'll learn more about the girl from Australia whom I discovered early in my Road Rat career, and quickly recruited. And how we roamed America for several months together. That's one good way to do it -- MEET a significant other *while* you travel! There are many ways that this can play out. Mine was just one. Another is a *sub-plot* of "The Adventures of the *Ameripass* Team!" You'll enjoy the adventure in detail, a few chapters from now, but I'll give you a brief glimpse here. An American Road Rat named Paul happened to meet the love of his life on public transportation when returning from a run. She was a tourist from the Netherlands. And not too long afterward, they got married. Paul resumed his former day job, but in a different locale... because he and his wife now are living happily ever after in Holland, and by this time I'll bet he speaks very good Dutch!

HOW ROAD RAT COUPLES *WITHOUT* KIDS DO IT

I refer, of course, to the way they earn their living. (What did you *think* I meant?!)

If there are no children in the picture, this can be one of the most idyllic and uncomplicated ways to make a living in existence! You won't have to juggle the various child-related factors that you'll read about in the next segment. And the combined income for the *two* of you will be substantially better than that of a *single* Road Rat.

Many people have the idea, though, that couples would just naturally earn twice as much as would a single driver, but that doesn't normally happen. It *can* work that way, *if* you are willing to split up from time to time and take separate runs in different directions -- in which case you try to coordinate your schedules well enough to be able to resume travelling together again immediately afterward. Sometimes that can be difficult though, because one may have a short run while the other has one that takes entire *days* longer. The one having the short trip then will get back considerably sooner -- and either wait for the other to return (which is down time), or take another run at the risk of keeping themselves separated for several more days, until a simultaneous arrival home can occur.

The reality is that most couples like to travel together, and that means that one or the other probably stays *home* when only *single* runs are available in various directions, and then get together on the next run appropriate for couples. The rest of the time (which, fortunately, tends to be *most* of the time), it is possible to make runs together driving two units to the same destination -- or to make runs together to two different destinations that line up well together along the same route.

You see, the company will provide the *return transportation money* for only **one driver per unit.** So if a couple wants to *share* the driving of just *one* unit, that means either that one of them will have to buy a plane ticket out of his/her own pocket, or else an Interlock run will have to be established. (That preferably should be arranged *prior* to departure from the home base plant, so the two can be assured beforehand that it will be available and waiting for them.)

These facts considered, it is *realistic* for a couple to count on earning *a little more than half again what a single driver, working alone, would earn.* If each of them would earn $40,000 a year working *singly,* then **the two of them working *together* would probably earn between $60,000 and $70,000 per year.** Not very likely $80,000. But that's still a very comfortable family income when both are able to pursue a lifestyle so enjoyable and free of stress.

Obviously, whenever a couple delivers two vehicles to the same destination, they *both* are entitled to return at company expense. But what about the situation where two *different* destinations *line up?*

Same thing, as long as the destinations are reasonably close together along the same route. For example, you and your partner might be based in Decatur, Indiana. And you get runs departing simultaneously for Denver and Salt Lake City. Denver is 1,250 miles out, and Salt Lake's about another 500. You follow each other to Denver and deliver the first unit. Then you share the driving of the other unit, and deliver it in Salt Lake. Then you both hop in the bird and fly home, and the plane tickets for *both* of you are paid for by the company. As long as two destinations are about equally expensive in terms of the air fare coming home (as would normally be the case in this example), there's no problem. And if there *were* a difference, and the company were to have the Road Rat who'd taken the shorter run *make up* that difference, it probably would amount to only a few dollars, and not result in a significant loss of income.

Before leaving the subject of earnings, I'd like to give you details about some of the factors that cause the earnings of couples to be less than double that of two single Road Rats:

-- The occasional unavailability of two simultaneous runs either to the same destination, or to two destinations that line up, as discussed above. Productive time can be lost either by one Road Rat remaining home in that situation, or in the process of getting your schedules to merge once again, if you do split up for a run or two.

-- The extra time it takes to check in the first unit, when delivering to two destinations in a straight line, can cause *delivery* of the second unit to be *a day later* than it otherwise might have been -- resulting in the net loss of two days of work... one for each Road Rat.

-- The fact that *both* Road Rats continue outbound together to a *second* destination along a straight line, rather than the one who made the first delivery returning immediately, costs extra time that's hard to calculate, but which accumulates significantly over weeks and months of working together.

Tips for Singles and Couples **69**

So -- when all these factors are combined, instead of two *single* Road Rats working independently to earn that $40,000 a year each (for a total of $80,000) we instead get the more realistic scenario of the Road Rat *couple* that works *equally hard* to attain a *combined* income of $60-70,000 per year. But that should be no problem for you. You *also* have *each other,* right? What a fabulous trade-off! And when two people love each other, and are able to travel together on a stress-free honeymoon-with-pay that lasts for *years,* netting around $65,000 a year... why -- that's the best of all possible worlds!

As long as you decide to limit your family to just the *two* of you, the job can be just as easy and enjoyable as that.

Fortunately, it also is possible for couples who *DO* have children to both be Road Rats, as well. But it takes considerably more effort and planning. So if you like a good *challenge,* you're going to love this *next* segment...

HOW ROAD RAT COUPLES *WITH* KIDS DO IT

Method #1 -- Home-School/Fly Back

As a former teacher with a decade of experience in elementary, middle, and high schools, I can say with a great deal of authority that there is **absolutely no way** that **any** person can become sufficiently well-educated to do a *good* job of teaching children in **all** subject areas. Therefore, I do *not* advocate the "home-schooling" of children by *any* parents at the elementary level *unless* they are properly educated and *certified* as teachers. And certainly **not at all** at *higher* levels for the reason just stated. Congress observed that glaring loophole in the law, and very properly sought to require certification of home-schoolers in 1994, but the bill unfortunately failed to pass. Hopefully, it *will* pass on the *next* attempt. However, even though I'm opposed to *non-certified* home schooling because that flaw clearly presents an enormous potential for under-educating children, I would be remiss if I didn't mention that option in this segment. If you happen to want to home-school your children *anyway,* then possibly it can be legitimately be done by you while travelling. (The *geography* lessons should be a breeze!)

That can present *another* problem, though. If you are driving *separate* units -- which is the only economical way to be a Road Rat Couple if you plan to return via public transportation -- then securing and scheduling adequate teaching time for your kids while still delivering the vehicles in a timely manner will be a very difficult task to accomplish, if not impossible.

An equally-daunting problem is the matter of having to pay the fare(s) for a child or children when returning from a run, out of your earnings. Those fares would add up fast, and could even *eliminate* your profits! So that brings us to the *next* method, which can solve *both* problems.

Method #2 -- Home-School/Return *via* Interlock

Sharing the driving of one unit has advantages if your kids are along, and you're home-schooling. You'll first need to establish a Semi-Permanent Interlock so that you seldom would be faced with extra return transportation expense. That procedure is explained in detail in Part III, Chapter 1. Otherwise, or at least until that becomes possible, the only economical way to travel with the kids is to establish an Interlock *each* time you get a run, *prior* to your departure. That can get to be a big hassle, and won't always be possible. Also, not *all* companies allow entire families to occupy their units during delivery, so it's not *just* a case of your home-base company allowing it; it's *also* a case of ensuring that the *Interlock* company allows it. And if the Interlock company is *a different one each time,* that increases the odds against your being able to establish such Interlocks consistently.

NOTE: A brief cautionary note is worthwhile here. This *normally* is NEITHER a stressful nor complicated lifestyle. What you are reading in this segment clearly contains elements of both. But that is because we are dealing here with *a very unusual circumstance.* Children simply are not normally a part of the Road Rat lifestyle equation. These paragraphs are provided to tell you how it *can* be done -- but if you plan to home-school your kids and still *both* be Road Rats, there's simply no way that *that* situation can be considered either stress-free *or* uncomplicated. The only way I can see that it could work long-term is if you establish a Semi-Permanent Interlock and thereby be assured of paid runs in both directions nearly all of the time.

Method #3 -- Trade Off During School/Take the Kids During Their Vacations

In this method, both members of the couple can be Road Rats if they wish, and the amount of time that each devotes to travelling is entirely up to them. One can be on the road for a few days or weeks during the school year while the other is home and then they can trade places. Then, during school vacations, they can bring the kids along on their trips -- which is possibly the best way of all to provide children with a *phenomenal* geographic education. For example... if you lived in one region of the country during your childhood, you may remember wondering on numerous occasions just what eastern Washington State looked like. Or New York's Adirondack Mountains. In my own case, I'd never travelled south of Richmond, Virginia before I was 18, so frequently wondered about the appearance of the South. (The *kudzu* turned out to be the biggest surprise! Most untravelled Northerners don't even know it *exists,* and to suddenly see *acres* of it is startling!) But the children of Road Rats have no such problem. By the time they reach age 18, they can have an excellent first-hand knowledge of the geography of most of North America. (Or perhaps even Australia!)

Remember that it will be necessary to establish a Semi-Permanent Interlock prior to the school vacation periods, or else you'll have to set up an Interlock before *each* individual run begins. The alternative is the costly one of buying return tickets for the kids!

Another method worth considering is the more routine one in which one member of the couple is a Road Rat, while the other one is not, and instead has a regular daytime job during school hours and is home with the kids afterward. If that person can obtain a job -- like teaching -- which *additionally* would allow him or her to take summers off, then during the summertime you *both* can be Road Rats!

POINTS TO REMEMBER

1. A single Road Rat need **not** be a *lonely* Road Rat. If you want a balanced social life, you must make a *conscious* effort to budget sufficient down time for that purpose. Be aware that the more you *enjoy travelling,* and/or the more *importance* you attach to *earnings,* the more difficult it becomes to *make* that conscious effort!

2. A Road Rat Couple probably will make about 25% *less* in their combined income than the sum that would be earned by two single Road Rats expending the same amount of effort. But the fringe benefits more than make up for it!

3. Road Rat Couples can have the best of all possible worlds for themselves if they love to travel, and follow the tips provided in this chapter.

4. Children of Road Rats who are able to travel along, at least during school vacations, will attain a knowledge of geography that far exceeds that of 99.99% of all American adults! And that is a *conservative* estimate. (Think about that. That percentage is the same as saying that perhaps only *one in 10,000* adults selected at random will have geographical knowledge equal to that of your teenage children! The same is true of the tremendous knowledge explosion experienced by the Road Rats, themselves!) Don't forget that Interlocks will be necessary for this, so that you won't have to buy plane tickets to get the kids home again from those trips!

5. Travelling with children provides you with constant logistical challenges to overcome, and this can make the job stressful. Just remember that the Road Rat lifestyle is NOT normally a stressful one, so this is a decision you will have to make for yourself. Forewarned is forearmed, and if you decide to attempt this, you now should be better-equipped to cope with the difficulties that may arise.

6. After all that was said in favor of togetherness, some marriages have been SAVED because one or the other members of the couple became a Road Rat, and pursued that while the other remained at home. Often, this ability to provide each other with *extra space* is *remedial* to the marriage. It all depends on the makeup of the couple, and the relationship they share. According to letters and phone calls we've received, this Handbook, for many, has been the ultimate marriage counselor!

7
The GOOD, The BAD, and The RINKY-DINK

As you pursue the Road Rat Lifestyle, you will learn that some things work very much to your advantage (the "GOOD"), while others seem to have it in for you (the "BAD"). And then there are those situations you'll encounter which will present you with *unnecessary* inconveniences so *absurd* that they'd be laughable if they weren't costly to you in terms of time, inconvenience, money, or a combination of these (the "RINKY-DINK").

This chapter is provided to increase your awareness of the first -- and to forewarn you about the latter two, so that you'll have a better chance of *avoiding* them.

1. GAS STATIONS

The GOOD

"GOOD" gas stations are ones that:

-- Advertise gasoline prices *honestly*.
-- Charge the *same price* when customers use either cash or credit cards.
-- Have a price difference of *5 cents or less per gallon* between self-service and full service.
-- Have a price spread between the lowest and highest grades of 10 cents/gal. or less.
-- Establish, maintain, or match the *lowest price* in their area.
-- Have a pay phone *inside,* so people can be out of bad weather when making a call.
-- Optional: Have a *mini-mart* with a variety of foods and sandwiches.
-- Optional: Have a *courteous, honest garage* that can do repairs quickly and efficiently.

The BAD

"BAD" gas stations:

-- Have *phony* price signs that either advertise the price *partially,* or in an unreadable manner, such that drivers on the freeway can be fooled into thinking the gas sells for *less* than it *actually* does. (Such signs *never* seem to imply a *higher* price than the actual!)
-- Charge a higher price for credit card purchases. (They *call* this price difference a "cash discount," but it is *not*. It is a "credit card *rip-off* price," plain and simple!) Some do this even when taking their OWN credit cards!! The fact that some major brands (such as *Phillips 66* and *Hess*) can *routinely* charge the *same* price for *both* PROVES that *ALL* oil companies *could* do that. (Furthermore, both *Hess* and *Phillips 66* frequently also have the lowest prices in their area!)
-- Do *not* match the prices of the lowest-price gas station in the area. If *any* gas station can charge a given, relatively-low price, there's *no excuse* for the other stations not doing likewise!
-- Rip people off from head to foot for full service. Some stations have a price difference of *40 cents/gal.* and *more* for this. (Think about it. If an attendant works for $6.00/hr., the station earns his pay with a *single sale* of just *15* gallons! Such stations make a *killing* on full service sales!) Consider **this**: OR and NJ require the attendants to pump the gas... and OR has typical prices; NJ is *less* expensive than average...
-- *Charge* for air, and/or for using the rest rooms! (And *road maps* **should** still be *free!*)

The Good, The Bad, & The Rinky-Dink　　73

The RINKY-DINK

"RINKY-DINK" gas stations:

-- Have *outdoor* pay phones, so that you can get baked, drenched, or frost-bitten while making your calls. This could be understandable if it were done to ensure access to a phone during *nighttime* to travellers, if the station were *not* open 24 hours a day. (In *that* case, it would be logical to have a phone inside *and* one outside.) But unfortunately, many who have *only* those outdoor phones *are* open 24 hours a day. Such places are *not* necessarily customer-friendly.
-- Charge that deceptive 9/10 cents per gallon extra. Throughout all of 1980, gas stations in *Iowa* did NOT do this. The story of how it happened, and then how Iowans subsequently were cheated out of that reprieve from deception, is fascinating. See pages 83-85 for the *inside* story!! (And what a shame. That could have set a refreshingly *honest* trend, which might have swept across the nation.)

ROAD RAT SOLUTION!

As you travel, LIST all of the *good* gas stations, and then simply make a point of patronizing *only those* from that point on. This is easy to do, especially as you travel some of the same routes repeatedly! In the process of learning where these are, make a *conscious* effort to *avoid* those stations that have goofy-looking, absent, or incomplete price signs, and *always* patronize the *lowest-price* gas stations along your route. *Especially* if they're *not* major brands! If you use a credit card for gasoline or diesel pur-chases, *avoid* stations that charge a lower price for cash. (Ideally, you should *also* do this even if you pay *cash*.) And ALWAYS *make sure* the price on the *pump* **matches** the one on the *sign* **before** fueling!

DANCE WITH THE ONE WHO LOVES YOU!

You'll find areas where gasoline price wars are raging as you travel, and sometimes these go on for weeks and months. Usually, you'll find *both* cut-rate stations *and* brand-name stations selling for the same price. GUESS which ones *STARTED* the price war, and *perpetuate* it! Right. It is almost *never* the major-brand stations. *They're* only going along in order to get their piece of the action. The *hero* of the gas war -- the one who *started* it -- has the best chance of survival if **his** sales *volume* is *better* than that of his better-known competitors. Being *aware* of this, **we** can help!

Unfortunately, many people subscribe to the **myth** that brand-name gas is of a higher quality than cut-rate. In the 17 years since I became a Road Rat, I have *yet* to purchase any bad gasoline... and I almost *always* buy at the cut-rate stations! As these words are written, my 1987 *GMC Safari* minivan has 373,000 miles on it, the engine has never been touched, and it still goes 5,000 miles between oil changes without using a quart. Most of its 1/3 of a million miles (plus 40,000!) were on *cut-rate* gas!

$$ TIP: **Most of the HYPE you hear... of *all* types, not just that regarding gasoline... is self-serving, usually generated by *brand-name* manufacturers and production facilities. Be an *astute* consumer, and *don't believe hype* without seeing *indisputable* proof! Also, listen *closely* to the way ads are *worded*. Often, you'll hear such words as "can" or "may." When you do, *translate* these to mean, "probably *won't*," and you'll be right FAR more often than wrong!** (*Remember* this tip. Whether you travel or not, you'll enhance your consumer knowledge, and save MANY times what you paid for this book!)

If the cut-rate station that starts gas wars in an area goes out of business, the result -- predictably -- is almost always the same and immediate: the major-brand stations *raise* their prices, usually substantially. So dance with the one who loves you! SEEK OUT and *PATRONIZE* the CUT-RATE station that *makes it possible* for you to buy gasoline at reasonable prices! And *that includes the one that may be in your **home town!*** You'll find lots of friendly and helpful folks at the cut-rates, *too!*

2. TELEPHONES

Once upon a time there was just ONE long-distance carrier, and it did its job VERY well. Unfortunately, as so often happens, when something works really well, the *government* steps in to louse it up. And *since* AT&T was allowed to have competition, a myriad of smaller companies have sprung up. But in this writer's opinion, none as yet have attained the stability, experience, or organization of AT&T. The government-forced divestiture has had a severely negative impact on consumers' utilization of telephone services... and using phones is something that Road Rats do *frequently!*

$$ TIP: **In this chapter, you'll observe that "new" and "small" don't *always* translate to "cut-rate." It's true of *gas stations* and *airlines* -- but small, new, *long-distance telephone carriers* usually charge MORE!**

The GOOD

AT&T remains the undisputed *champion* of long-distance carriers in *this* Road Rat's humble opinion -- and they are not paying me a red cent for this unsolicited endorsement! Nothing's perfect, and this carrier does have some flaws, but I consider them to be MILES ahead of even the two long-distance carriers that keep vying for second place, in terms of operator services and innovations, as well as being at least equal to them in price, most (if not all) of the time.

Good *local* telephone services are those which maintain pay phones that are gimmick-free, and are set up to use the service of one of the three largest carriers: AT&T, MCI, or Sprint. *Pay phones* which *utilize* **them** normally are free of the service flaws described below.

The BAD and the RINKY-DINK

There are *so many* items that would fit *these* categories, they would overwhelm this chapter! But in the *next* chapter, you'll find what just may be the most comprehensive list of these that you'll ever see! And fortunately, for *most* of the abuses we'll present and discuss, there *are* defensive actions you can take! See all of this under "Telephones," in *that* chapter, starting on page 86. *Also*, see page 337.

ROAD RAT SOLUTION!

Very simply, we all need to work together if we're going to *get rid* of rinky-dink and bad pay phones, and phone services. Here are some suggestions (and *many* more are in the next chapter):

-- If a pay phone is *outdoors* instead of inside a gas station or convenience store, and there isn't *at least* **one** public pay phone located *inside* the building, take a few moments to let their management know that this surprises you -- and that as a customer you would appreciate their thoughtfulness in having an indoor phone installed, *out of the weather.*

-- If, after you dial zero or an access code on a pay phone, you get a recording that tells you that you can "save money" if you dial "1" first, and then pay with *coins,* BEWARE! You probably are using a privately-owned phone, and if you pay by coin or use the upstart long-distance carrier with which it may be connected, you're likely to end up paying too much! **Ignore** the message and proceed to access your *major* long-distance carrier.

-- If the pay phone you are using gives the wrong touch-tone sounds, you're probably using a phone that's privately-owned, tied into a small carrier, or both. If your major carrier's access code works, or you can dial your carrier free-of-charge using an "800" number, you're probably fine. *Otherwise,* you should immediately *abandon* that phone and find a better one! Likewise, if it tries to *charge* you for *LOCAL* directory assistance, or to make a toll-free ("800"-number) call!

3. AIRLINES

The GOOD

This story used to be a happier one to tell -- because once upon a time there were *three* really *great* cut-rate airlines! They were: *Texas International, World Airways,* and *People Express.* And just prior to the advent of those, *Laker Airlines* for several years made it inexpensive to hop across one of the world's *largest* "lakes" -- the Atlantic Ocean. It was paradise for Road Rats who liked to *fly* home, because the fares often dropped below $100 for one-way coast-to-coast trips. It sometimes was possible to fly from L.A. to New York on *World Airways* for as little as $79, *without* all those advance purchase restrictions we see these days. *Texas International* had such a great frequent flyer program, I was able to fly a free round trip for every *four* one-way returns -- and the fares often were as good as *World's*; they called them "Peanut Fares." *People Express* was equally good! But suddenly, by the mid-1980s, they *all* were *gone!* And air travel hasn't been the same since!

You have to look harder now, and it's not as easy to find destinations from which you can fly back inexpensively -- but there are still some good bargains out there. *Southwest Airlines* is probably the leader in this field, but there are many other smaller ones. **Today's** "good" airlines are those having fares that are considerably *lower* than the ones charged by the major carriers, and *few or none* of the restrictions, and have one-way fares that are -- logically -- about *half* of what they charge for round trips. Details on these are provided in the "Maximization" chapter.

The BAD

The major airlines come up with some innovative plans from time to time. For example, on August 10, 1994, *TWA* announced that it would provide *free* travel for *companions* travelling to domestic destinations and to Europe during the fall of 1994 and the spring of 1995, except for holiday periods. They stipulated that the couple must travel together (which is reasonable), BUT -- the tickets had to be purchased by no later than August 12! That was a mere *2-day* window of opportunity! And therefore absolutely *worthless* to Road Rats and for most business persons for use in the line of duty. Nice for vacation, but hardly good for a business trip, or for a Road Rat return flight, most of which are taken on very short notice.

The worst aspects of air travel today on the major airlines, for business travellers, are the facts that (1) tickets generally must be purchased *at least three days in advance* in order to get a decent fare, and (2) one-way trips *usually cost almost the same as* **round** *trips!*

The mainstay of the airlines is the *business* traveller -- and yet *those* are the folks to whom the major airlines consistently give the shaft! Go figure. Except for those few great years when the three large cut-rate airlines gave them a good run for the money, the major airlines have *almost always* seemed to go out of their way to *gouge* the business traveller! Those *airlines* most *assuredly* do **not** believe in the principle of "dance with the one who loves you!" Business travellers frequently fly single legs from one city to another, then attend a meeting, and then fly to yet another city. On short notice. And therefore are forced to pay through the nose for it, unless they're lucky enough to be able to utilize some of the routes of today's far-more-limited-in-scope cut-rate airlines. And Road Rats would suffer the same fate, except that **we** usually have enough lead time to take advantage of the three-day advance purchase provision.

Remember, this is *not* a serious problem for Road Rats working for companies that pay for plane tickets totally *independently* of the driver's pay. But for most Road Rats employing Maximization, pay and expense money are *combined,* and the amount is high enough to *absorb* the cost of a reasonably-priced flight home. For *those* Road Rats, the more they can *save on the fare*, the more they can *earn!*

The RINKY-DINK

The most rinky-dink aspects of air travel today are all those nit-picking and totally-*superfluous* restrictions that airlines put on their tickets. These include high penalties for changes or cancellations, up to and including the full price of the ticket! Non-refundable tickets are a *common* abuse. There are many other types of restrictions as well, which are equally ludicrous, but too numerous to mention here. What must be remembered is that back when the three big *cut-rate* airlines were still flying, the major airlines imposed precious *few* such restrictions. The fact that restrictions are totally *unnecessary,* and that they effectively serve primarily to *harass* the traveller, makes them *very* rinky-dink!

ROAD RAT SOLUTIONS!

These are provided on pages 77-82, and in the "Maximization" chapter!

DANCE WITH THE ONE WHO LOVES YOU!

In 1980, I made the mistake of returning to Washington, D.C. from L.A. via *Pan Am*. It seems that *Pan Am,* then one of the largest and longest-established airlines, was offering the *same* $89 one-way fare as was *World*, but with the *additional* enticement of an all-you-can-eat lox and bagels buffet on board! And, even though I'm not Jewish, I love lox and bagels just as much as anyone who is! Maybe even *more!!* So in that weak moment I *went* for it! **Bad move!!**

You see, by doing this I played right into the major airlines' scheme for *eliminating* those wonderful cut-rate airlines! They were matching the fares, and thus getting equal numbers of passengers. But they *also* were offering special *enticements* to **lure away** even *more* passengers! And I fell right into that trap. Just once! But I *regret* having done so. Because I unwittingly played a small role, thereby, in eliminating the great cut-rate airlines, who'd made the fabulous fares a reality!

So whenever you possibly can, **ALWAYS *dance with the one who loves you!*** When someone *creates* a great fare or a great price, *patronize* him -- no matter HOW much the major-brand entities try to lure you away! *Never, ever* go to a larger competitor whenever you can *avoid* doing so! It's a great principle for Road Rats, and for everyone else, to retain *throughout our lives.*

8
Some REALLY SPECIAL Tips!

𝕵n the last edition of this book, I liberally salted the Appendix (which was its equivalent of *this* edition's *Appendix 1)* with handy tips, wherever space allowed. But this time, space doesn't allow for that method of presentation at all, because the Appendix has a new, improved, much more concise, and easier-to-read format. And besides, *this* time I have many *more* tips to provide. So this chapter fills that need.

Many of the items herein are related to subjects that are discussed in greater depth in other chapters. But for those chapters to flow well and achieve their purpose, these *additional* tips had to be omitted from that context. I invite you to now read these additional, highly-useful tips and suggestions, at your leisure. **CAUTION:** Please don't make the mistake of thinking that these are *less* important because they weren't included in other chapters. Many of them are FULLY as important. And some just present information I thought you might enjoy or find helpful. Either way, this is simply a better format for their presentation.

When an additional, or more complete discussion of a topic is available in this Handbook, reference to the appropriate location(s) will be found right under the heading, in smaller print.

Please note too, that while *the majority of these are from my own experience,* several of them have been adapted from tips I found in a very useful book, published in 1994, and this was done with the publisher's permission. Besides giving proper credit at this time for the usage and adaptation of these, I also will suggest that you may wish to obtain that book, if you believe that even more of these *travel* tips can be helpful to you. The 148-page book is entitled, *202 Tips Even the Best Business Travelers May Not Know,* ISBN 1-55623-966-1, by Christopher J. McGinnis. It retails at $10.00 at your bookstore, or can be obtained for $10.00 + $3.00 s&h if you order it directly from the publisher: Irwin Professional Publishing, 1333 Burr Ridge Parkway, Burr Ridge, IL 60521. They can be reached at this toll-free number: (800) 634-3966.

Air Travel
(More Information: See pages 60, *75-77, 120-132, 136-140,* and *322-324.*)

1. Back when *World Airways* was still around, I learned this trick, which has a name; being ticketed *less expensively* into "Hidden Cities." *World* is gone, now, but this still works very well today with many other airlines, especially the major ones. Remember how I told you that it was usually cheaper to fly into the larger, "hub" cities, than the smaller ones? Well, those smaller ones frequently are intermediate *stops* on airlines' *routes* to their hub cities! In the case of *World,* there was a time when they charged only $79 to fly from L.A. to Newark, but *$89* to fly to Baltimore-Washington International (BWI), even though the plane landed at BWI *first!* So I quickly adopted the habit of being SURE to have only *carry-on luggage* with me (so that I would have no checked luggage ending up in Newark!), purchased my *ticket* to *Newark* for *$10 less* -- and then simply disembarked, luggage and all, at *BWI!* This is a perfectly legitimate practice.

So let's suppose that your company is in Fort Wayne, Indiana, and that you've delivered a unit to Philadelphia. If you can find a flight that goes, for example, from Philadelphia to Chicago *via* Fort Wayne, see if the fare isn't considerably lower for those going to *Chicago*. If it *is*, **use** this "Hidden Cities" technique! Sometimes the savings is *substantially* greater than the mere $10 that was involved in the *World Airways* example just cited.

One last item on this point. Let's say you can't do that from Philadelphia, but you find that you **can** from Washington, D.C. Factor in the train or bus fare to D.C. and see if *that* combination is worthwhile. There's a constant flow of trains and busses up and down the corridor from New York to Washington, and most stop at Philadelphia.

2. Be aware that a "direct" flight will take you from one point to another with at least one intermediate stop en route, even though you stay on the same plane. A "nonstop" flight is just that. After it takes off, it *next* lands at its *final* destination.

3. If your carry-on luggage is one of the larger sizes allowable, get to the gate early, and board as soon as you can -- especially at Christmastime and during cold weather, when just about everyone has carry-on in the form of gifts and/or bulky winter coats to put in the overhead bins. Get there too late, and you'll probably end up with your luggage under the seat -- about where your feet should have been. Not comfortable! Best bin to use: the one just *ahead* of your seat, so that later you don't have to buck the tide of other disembarking passengers, as you would if your luggage were directly overhead or behind you. (If it's *behind* you, you can figure on being one of the *last* people to get off the bird! Not good if you have a tight connection!)

4. The overhead compartment, by the way, is not a good place to stow your bowling ball, even though it might be within the allowable weight limits. That's because airplanes sometimes encounter a phenomenon called "CAT" without warning; **C**lear **A**ir **T**urbulence. Everything looks fine in the sky, even to the pilots, and suddenly the plane is violently wrenched upward or downward by a couple of hundred feet. Guess where the bowling ball might end up! Other phenomena also can cause compartments to open unexpectedly. The moral of the story is to place only *soft* items overhead, such as winter coats, suits, and soft-sided flight bags containing clothing. There's a big difference between being hit in the head by 10 pounds of clothing and 8 pounds worth of steam iron. The clothing *weighs* more, but is far preferable!

5. Like the view? Ask for a *good* window seat when you make your reservation. A "good" window seat has little or no view blocked by the wing -- which is nice if you enjoy watching the scenery, or taking pictures. "Point-and-shoot" cameras are handy for a lot of things, but you'll get a lot of lousy shots -- which actually look decent through the viewfinder -- out of plane windows with them. Best bet: A 35-mm adjustable SLR having a zoom lens and built-in, automatic light meter. Then you can get some great shots of mountain scenes, downtown skylines, cloud effects, and sunsets! Specify that you'd like a window seat *ahead* of the wing, to get the *best* view.

6. Don't care about the view? Go for the *aisle* when making your reservation, where it's a bit less cramped, as close to the front as you can. You often will be one of the last to board that way (so keep the overhead bin factor in mind), but you'll compensate for this by being one of the *first* ones off. And you'll probably be among the first to be served the meal, which usually is done from front to back.

7. Are you a "long drink of water?" Tall people appreciate leg room, so you may want to opt for sitting by an emergency exit. As a Road Rat, you'll probably have the required physical capability, but you'll have to be willing to learn the operation of the exit so that you can implement that knowledge if needed. Avoid seats immediately in *front* of the exit row, because they often don't recline! Bulkhead seats are nice for legroom, and there are no seats ahead of you that can recline -- but you almost certainly will *have* to stow your carry-on luggage overhead. (And the seats are usually awful for movie viewing.) Another way to maximize your comfort is to request a seat *either* by a window or on the aisle, near the *back* of the plane, whenever *three seats together* are involved. *Middle* seats in the rear of the aircraft usually are assigned *last,* so having one of those seats give you a good shot at having an *empty* seat *next* to you. Finally, if you are uncomfortably seated, look around the cabin for a better seat. Once the door closes, you may move to it. But you may have to return if a passenger at the *next stop* has *that* seat assignment.

8. Is safety a concern? Well, in the event of a crash, if you're in the front of the plane, you'll be one of the first people at the site. But cockpit crews have survived some terrible crashes. According to some studies, though, you're probably around 34% safer in the *rear* of the plane. (Hint: Guess why those "black box" flight recorders are mounted in the *tail*...)

9. Frequent-flier miles are such an asset, they even may be bequeathed, in the event of your demise. It is normal for them to be considered part of your estate, so be sure to designate the disposition of these in your will, so they can be properly assigned.

10. A nice hot meal is generally a welcome perk on a long flight. Best bet, though, is to be sure the plane is scheduled to fly *through* a normal mealtime. Some flights that are thousands of miles long have *no* hot meal because the entire flight is scheduled *between* mealtimes! If you are on a meal flight, it gets even better. Most airlines offer special meals upon request, but you must usually make the request at least 24 hours before the flight. A few typical choices are: seafood, diabetic, gluten-free, oriental, kosher, and vegetarian. Sometimes even hamburgers or pizza!

11. If you travel frequently by air, you may wish to enroll in your major airline's airport club. It's a great way to enjoy a comfortable and relaxing refuge from the noisy and crowded airport scene that surrounds it. They have TVs, sofas, easy chairs, a great view of the airport activity outside, many pay phones, and *free* phones for *local* calls, and a bar. If you're so inclined, *Delta's* "Crown Room" offers *complimentary* cocktails wherever their clubs are located. There's just one **major drawback** to these -- and it's why I've allowed my membership to lapse: the lounges *close* in mid-evening, and don't open again until morning. Most of the times that they would have been the most useful to *me* were between late-night connections, which often have consumed several hours!

12. What if you buy a non-refundable ticket, and then find you can't use it? There are two good solutions: (1) If you have a legitimate medical condition that makes it inadvisable for you to fly in that time frame, you can get *written* documentation of this from your doctor. That is an acceptable reason to the airlines. But you'll need this on paper. Then, if you were ticketed by a travel agent, give the document to them, and they'll obtain your refund for you. However, if you were ticketed directly by the airline, this still can be done, but without the added comfort of having a knowledgeable intermediary who could have accomplished this *for* you. (2) If you used a travel agent, and were ticketed on Wednesday or later, you have a good chance, *if* you act *quickly.* Travel agents *pay* the airlines *weekly* -- normally on *Tuesdays!* If you find you can't use the ticket, they generally can void it easily -- *before* the first Tuesday after you bought it.

Really Special Air Travel Tips   **81**

13. Here's some advice from the book, ***202 Tips***, that I'll present to you verbatim, with no added comments from my own experiences. The way it's worded says it all -- and it can be very IMPORTANT to you:

> "If you suspect that you are being delayed for something other than a weather or air traffic problem, approach the gate agent and confidently assert your suspicion, give a reason why you cannot wait, and ask to be booked on the next flight out on that airline, or a competing airline. This is called Rule 240 and all the major airlines include it in their contract of carriage. What Rule 240 does is tell the original carrier to pick up the tab for any additional expense in getting you to your intended destination via another carrier. Rule 240 applies to other direct flights to your final destination as well as any connecting flights that may exist. When you really want or need to get out of town, ask the gate agent: 'Can you 240 me?' (It is important to use their lingo.) They will code your ticket, and you will be on your way."

14. Sometimes the fare will drop between the time you purchase a ticket and the flight. You are entitled to a refund of the *difference*. But you must *inquire*. The airline isn't about to volunteer *that* sort of information to you! So always *ask!* (Of course, if the price should go *up,* instead, you will never be asked to pay extra.)

15. The time of day (or night) when you fly can make a big fare difference. Those overnight "red-eye" flights frequently cost substantially less. Avoid morning and afternoon rush hours, too. They often are more expensive, *and* are more subject to delays. To save money and time when flying during the daytime, shoot for a *midday* departure.

16. Put luggage tags with your name and address both inside *and* outside of each bag you carry or check. **IMPORTANT:** Use the address of *your company,* so that a delayed bag will return to you via your dispatcher. Or use a *post office box address,* if you have one. DON'T put your *physical* home address on the tags... and especially not on the *outside* tag. Burglars frequently watch luggage of passengers at airports and make note of their home addresses. When the targeted unlucky passenger gets home, he finds fewer possessions.

17. When dealing directly with an airline, rather than a travel agent, be aware that the first fare they quote you isn't necessarily the cheapest one available for the route. Competing airlines will frequently have lower fares. That's why it's best to work with a *trusted* travel agent who will always find you the *lowest* fare -- *including* those of the cut-rate airlines. And reading this chapter carefully will show you many additional reasons for utilizing the services of a good travel agent whenever you can. (Even so, however, it doesn't hurt to call an airline's toll-free reservation number to inquire, so as to obtain some ball-park figures ahead of time. And don't forget: *Always* fly those *cut-rate* airlines whenever you possibly can -- "Dance with the one who loves you!")

18. If you take pictures on your trips, be aware that radiation from X-ray baggage scanners is *CUMULATIVE* in film! Many security people claim it is not, but those who do either are woefully ignorant, or are being negligent. *One* pass through a normal machine will usually do no damage *unless* you have high-speed film (above ASA 400) in your bag. *More* than once, between the time you buy the film and when you have it developed, and you risk fogging! Even worse, the scanners in some nations are high-intensity, and can *ruin* film on just *one* pass! This frequently is true in Russia and other former USSR republics. Unless the situation has changed recently, high-dose

scanners apparently are used at all departure sites for the Concorde, too.   Don't be confident if an X-ray machine bears the word, "Filmsafe," because all too often they are not. **SOLUTION:** Carry your film in a clear plastic bag and hand it to the operator for visual inspection. *Better yet,* have the film inside of lead-foil pouches. That's because in certain countries, such as Japan and Italy, they *refuse* to hand-inspect your film. And at the Frankfurt Airport, in Germany, you'll have to open your camera for inspection (forcing you to rewind the film prematurely), *or* take a wasted picture! Neither method is consistent. Depending upon the *inspector,* expect to be required to do *one or the other.* Your best bet is to have the camera *already empty* before entering the secured zone. You probably know that you can change planes at *most* major airports without exiting the secure area. But that is almost never the case at Frankfurt. So take those last shots before making your connection.

Car Rental
(More Information: See Pages *29, 123-124,* and *127.*)

1. To cut the best deal, reserve ahead. Three or four days, if possible. And if you find you'll be arriving later than your originally-scheduled pick-up time, CALL the agency to let them know. Do this even if you'll only be an hour late. Otherwise you are likely to find yourself with a larger, more expensive car than the one you desired, at the going rate -- or worse, no car at all.

2. If you think your travels will include car rentals, check beforehand with the underwriter of your own auto insurance. You probably will find that you never have to purchase the collision damage insurance, if *your* car *already* is so covered, and thus save purchasing this expensive insurance from the rental agency. The same applies to liability. The rental agency will sell it to you if they can, so *act* on the advice of your *own insurance agency* for both of these.

3. The same good driving record that enables you to be a Road Rat also will stand you in good stead when renting a car. Be aware that car rental agencies *now* have the capability to DIRECTLY ACCESS your state's DMV records -- right on the spot! -- when you come in to rent the car. Anything really bad in there within the last couple of years, and you're probably sunk. And you can even be blacklisted! So keep driving *safely!* (You may wonder, is that *legal?* So far -- yes!)

4. Car *rental* agents generally will hold back on revealing the best offer they can give, unless you persist. Much in the manner of car **sales**men! Here's how to cut through that to get the best figure immediately. Tell the agent that you're entitled to their corporate rate -- and you are. If they require the company's name, it's the one for which you're driving. Let him know that you want the *best* such rate they can offer. Then say that you are shopping around by phone, and the agency you *use* will be the one that offers you the *best rate!* They'll attract you right then with their best offer, or pass up the chance. Also, say that after you've shopped, you'll ask for him/her by name if you call them back, so that the agent can personally get credit for the rental. (If you have time to follow that procedure, then DO take the best offer, being sure that you've considered all the variables, and call that particular agent, if the name was provided.)

Luggage
(Related Material: See pages 128-129.)

1. This one came from a Handbook owner in Springfield, Illinois, just in time for this new edition! He suggests that Road Rats own at least two, and maybe even three, *identical* suitcases already fully-packed and ready to use, with all the necessities, and sufficient clothes for the typical trip of longer duration. Then if the airline manages to lose or misplace the one with which you're

returning from a run, and you get home just in time to leave on *another* run, you simply grab a back-up bag and go. It's a great idea, for those who *must* travel with luggage that requires checking. But if you always take only carry-on with you, then this wouldn't apply.

2. For security, keep luggage out of sight when you're not inside the vehicle, and you have parked it for the night. Especially RVs, and rental cars. And most especially if the rental agency's name is somewhere on the car, such as in the form of a bumper sticker. That attracts thieves like honey attracts bears! Fortunately, car rental agencies are learning this, and removing their labelling!

3. Don't have long, sharp scissors in your carry-on bag. It may be confiscated at the airport as a potential weapon. Instead, if you need to carry scissors for some reason, pack the short, blunt-ended ones that elementary school students use. And obviously, no guns or knives. If you DO have such a weapon with you, *legally,* **declare** it at the ticket counter. (*Not* at the *gate!* In most airports, you'd encounter security along the way, and so you'd never make that far!). Then it can be properly transported for you.

4. It's a particularly bad idea to leave your bag unattended if you happen to be aboard a British ferry (it'll get chucked overboard!) or in an airport in Israel (they'll *incinerate* it for you)! Why? That's the way *bombs* sometimes are planted in those nations! Anywhere else, its simply a bad idea because that's a great way to get your luggage *stolen!*

Gas Stations
(Related Material: See pages 15-16, 21, 26, 55-56, 72-74, 98.)

Here's a vignette on life in America in 1997. And 1957. And scores of other years. It's the story of a significant event that almost everyone seemed to miss at the time, and that practically no one remembers today. Not even the *millions* of people who experienced it, not so very long ago. This information is so *unusual,* I'm going to give it its OWN editorial format, and call it...

The Year *One* State Broke *Free* of Deceptive Advertising!
(A Commentary on America's Future from the Perspective of a Road Rat)

It's hard to believe this happened 17 years ago. It was so startling! So unexpected. And so very *refreshing,* even though fleetingly temporary! The memory of it seems almost as though it were only yesterday!

A British friend once told me, after observing that our gasoline is deceptively priced 9/10 of a cent higher than the obvious price, to provide the illusion of a lower price... "That would be *illegal* in England. It's **dishonest!**"

Exactly. So why do WE tolerate it, here in America?

Well, just once within memory, in all the 20th century, one single state ruled in favor of honesty. The Iowa Legislature mandated that all gasoline would be priced and sold at **even** dollars and cents per gallon, *without* the extra 9/10 of a cent that all of us pay, but never consciously *think* that we spend. The year of truthfulness in gasoline advertising was 1980. And by year's end, it was over. Today, one is hard pressed even to find an *Iowan* who *remembers* the event! *Most* of the **nation** *never* knew.

Compared with everything else that's going on, this seems like only an insignifant issue, doesn't it? But it says a *lot* about our national character. Read on...

Ask yourself which is worse... a quiz show scandal in the 1950s, that stunned and shocked our nation due to its *blantant and overt* dishonesty... Or *this* deceptive advertising practice by the world's richest industry, which has thumbed its nose at millions of people daily -- for decades -- in countless thousands of locations throughout our continent. Aren't you even a little bit revolted by the idea that this subtle deception is *deliberately* and methodically foisted upon us *incessantly?* In many ways, England is more "liberal," morally speaking, than America -- but my British friend went home utterly appalled that we have no laws that *prohibit* such deliberate *deceptions.*

So is this really important? Probably not. *Until,* perhaps, your son or daughter, age perhaps 8, happens to ask you WHY that extra 9/10 of a cent is added to the price on all those signs they see every day. And you have to tell your child that it is an industry's attempt to make people think that the price is really lower than it actually is. And then -- even if you say the practice is wrong -- forever thereafter, your child will constantly *see* those signs, and grow up *subconsciously* thinking, "Gee, if it's OK for a *major industry* like that to deceive people, then it surely is *just as reasonable* for **me** to cheat on exams, or do other dishonest acts." Children learn by *example,* after all. And *that* example is sustained by extremely powerful people. Even if the children never in their lives put *conscious* thought to this, it still is at work in their minds. And in the minds of almost everyone else in North America.

You see, it's not all "Beavis and Butthead," and similarly high-profile elements if you seek to point fingers at influential factors capable of shaping and degrading America's moral fiber. Sometimes it is the subtle and steady drumbeat... "it's *OK* to *cheat...* it's *OK* to *deceive..."* **That** can be much more destructive, and every bit as much of a brainwashing technique as any other you can think of. It's the thought processes that *evolve* from such subtle and unceasing drumbeats that lead many in our society to *create* the high-profile, destructive, and amoral elements.

There is a *ludicrous* side to this. And that's the fact that this is all *completely unnecessary!* Sure, the unnoticed extra 9/10 of a penny probably represents billions of dollars of additional revenue for Big Oil every year... but if they rounded the price UP just an additional 1/10 of a cent -- thereby *eliminating* the deception -- they would make even MORE! So go figure. Especially with an industry that routinely fluctuates its price up or down as much as 20 cents in a month, from time to time -- without ever being accountable to *anyone.* (To the best of my knowledge, they've never faced a serious challenge by a major investigative show such as *"60 Minutes."* And I can't help but believe that *that* show could have a *field* day taking them on and delving into their pricing practices!) Considering that, why does Big Oil even SEEK to be deceptive?! What is *in* that practice, for them, in the *first* place?

Clearly, this is an issue involving honesty vs. deceptiveness, with *no* money even at stake! Can you imagine Big Oil *fighting* to *retain* its *deceptive* image, in the face of *that* plain fact? Read on. More surprises ahead!

So Iowa's legislators stood up and actually *DID* something about this. That's a *phenomenal* step for *any* legislature to take! Therefore, what went wrong, just a few months later? I got the full story from an Iowa department that's under the jurisdiction of the Attorney General. It seems that Big Oil couldn't tolerate the honesty! So the **"Petroleum Marketers of Iowa"** *quietly* lobbied the legislators to *rescind* the new law, and exerted sufficient political pressure to ensure that the end of 1980 also marked the end of that lone state's brave attempt to be honorable. The whole thing was done so subtly, and so much behind the scenes, the people of Iowa were almost *completely unaware* of the entire drama. On January 1, 1981, the deception had simply returned, and one of the state's finest hours was relegated to the status of quickly-forgotten history. End of story.

Oh. Not quite, maybe. You may be interested in the argument that the lobbyists implemented to *restore* the dishonesty. You see, the Petroleum Marketers of Iowa claimed that the real reason for their distress was because they perceived that Iowans living along the state's boundaries were driving across the state line to buy out-of-state gas, just to save the apparent penny a gallon difference. Right. If any legislator believed *that* story, I have this great bridge in *New York* that I'd like to sell to him.

Their argument might have had some credibility, *except* for the big differences in state gasoline *taxes* that exist between Iowa and her neighboring states. Differences that are so great (and were, even then) that Iowans living along the *Missouri* line can **almost always** count on saving several cents per gallon by *crossing* it -- while Iowans living next to *Illinois* can count on saving a similar amount by NOT crossing the boundary.

Readers who are familiar with the earlier editions of this Handbook know well they can always find some editorial comments in it, which tie in closely to the Road Rat lifestyle. (What can I say? In 1971, I was editor of my university's newspaper. It's my nature!) *This* is such an editorial. It's not nearly so much about gasoline as it is about returning this nation to a more honest state. Accomplishing *that* will be beneficial to Road Rats -- and to everyone else!

Many believe that the massive sweep of conservatives into Congress on November 8, 1994 was a mandate for a restoration of honesty in our land. Bravo! Let's see if Congress can make America's gasoline pricing as free of deception as Britain's. Congress can *do* that, just as it surely proved in the past that it could mandate speed limits. **So let's ask for it.** You have permission to copy this and send it to your Congressperson and both Senators. It's not a world-shaking issue. But it's a start. And a great object lesson.

And if it happens, America will be just a little bit *better* for it.

* * * * * * * * *

Here are some gas station **TIPS**:

1.   It's an excellent practice, in the case of practically all of America's toll-charging turnpikes to *exit* the tollway *before* buying your gas or diesel fuel. You'll save enough, most of the time, to make it worth doing even when driving your *car,* so you can imagine the savings when filling a *larger* tank. It'll only take you an extra minute or two, and perhaps a mile or so of extra driving. When doing this, it's best to drive a few blocks into town, and not simply fuel up at the nearest station to the exit. Just as with other interstate highways, the ones within sight or easy access of the road are frequently the ones that will rip you off. I've often found that stations that are out of view, perhaps only a block or two farther away, will sell for as much as 5 to 10 cents per gallon less! Also -- the restaurants and fast-food establishments in the service plazas on most turnpikes employ the "captive audience" principle. For the convenience of not having to get off the turnpike, most people are willing to spend *more* money for the food. And these places almost are all too willing to *accomodate* that willingness! **SOLUTION:** Maintain a conscious awareness that it takes *very little* extra driving and time to reach such a place OFF the turnpike. Even if you're alone, expect to save a dollar or two on your lunch, *each time* you make that tiny bit of extra effort!

2.   Perhaps the greatest **exception** to the rule above were the *Amoco* stations that served the Indiana Toll Road (I-80/90) until recently. There was *one* turnpike where you *didn't* have to exit to get the best gas prices. Very few gas stations off the toll road sold for less, and then usually only by a penny or two.

Amoco serves most of the states east of the Rockies, *except* Texas, Kentucky, part of West Virginia, most of Louisiana, and much of the Northeast. And in most of its stations, it used to charge a significantly higher price for using credit cards -- even when the cards were their *own!* But *they didn't* do that on this toll road. *There,* it was cash or credit, same LOW price. Such a deal. (Proved they could do it *everywhere,* though, didn't it?) While this was the case, since there was no direct competition from cut-rate stations, you could have bought *this* major brand -- when on the Indiana East-West Toll Road -- and *still* have "danced with the one who loves you!" But -- things change. The *Amoco* stations on that pike were replaced with *BP* stations in 1995, and the gas prices on that toll road have been sky-high ever since. (There is some *good* news, though. *Amoco* changed its policy, systemwide, in that same year, and NOW charges the same price, whether you pay by cash or credit!)

Banks and ATMs

VITAL data was added at the very last minute! Please refer *NOW* to **page 328**, and then return to this chapter.

Ground Transportation
(Related Information: See pages 124, and 130-131.)

1. Earlier, I mentioned that -- at last -- you can take a rapid-transit train from O'Hare Airport to downtown Chicago. You *also* can do this in Atlanta, Cleveland, Oakland (CA), Philadelphia, and Washington, DC. BUT -- be sure that you don't have excessive amounts of *luggage.* That can be hard to manage conveniently, when using this mode of transportation! At the time fares were researched for this edition, in late 1994, the cost was $2.00 or less except for Philadelphia, which was $4.50

2. Although I once landed at Narita Airport (which serves Tokyo), I was en route to Honolulu and had too little time between connections to visit the city. But while I was there, I learned that transportation *each* way between the airport and Tokyo then cost *$100!* That was in 1987, and since then, it apparently has gotten worse -- in a way. By 1994, it was reported that a taxi ride each way took between 60 and 90 minutes, and cost *$190!!* Can you imagine spending more to get into Tokyo and back from its own airport than on the *flight* to *Japan?!* It's possible! But there's *good* news at last. **Now** it's possible to simply get on a TRAIN that costs only *$15* each way, and whisks you back and forth in only 25 minutes, each way!

Telephones
(More Information: Pages 74-75 and 337-339.)

Even though the Road Rat lifestyle is MUCH different from that of truckers, *phones* are one of the aspects that both have very much in common. As a Road Rat, you'll find yourself using phones *a lot,* both for long distance calls and for local ones. Therefore, it is reasonable for this Handbook to deal with this subject in considerable depth. There is a great deal that you may not know about today's telephone services, and learning these tips can save you a *bunch* of money! So please read these carefully, for comprehension. (Even if you never become a Road Rat, knowing these will likely save you *hundreds* over the next few years!)

1. There are many *small* long-distance carriers -- whose names most people have never heard of -- which tend to charge *inordinately* high prices for their service -- *particularly* when they are accessed via pay phones!

As for the pay phones themselves, it is -- unfortunately -- *legal* for them to be *privately-owned,* and with *those* the sky's the limit as to what you may be charged! (See point #2, below.) Thirty-five to fifty cents for a local call is not unusual. Some of them even have *time limits* on *local* calls, after which you must add *more* money if you wish to *continue* the conversation. Some will charge you 50 cents or more just to obtain LOCAL information, which normally is a FREE service!

Really Special Telephone Tips   87

2.   A trucker recently was billed **$17.00** for a **3-minute domestic, long-distance call** that he made from a privately-owned pay phone! He'd provided the operator with his AT&T credit card number, and the rinky-dink small-time carrier had then processed the call *through* AT&T. When the bill arrived, the trucker was charged for AT&T's reasonable rate (for their part of processing the call) *plus* the unbelievably *exorbitant* rate imposed by the tiny, rinky-dink carrier. That's nothing short of ***thievery!*** And an AT&T source tells me there's nothing that can be done for it at this time. So far, it's LEGAL! A pay phone is required only to provide direct access to an operator *capable of processing a long-distance call,* no matter what company or companies may be involved. As yet, there's no regulation in place to prevent those bandits from charging such fees! And their operators will cheerfully tell you, **"Sure,** I can take your AT&T Calling Card number, and you'll be billed for the call" -- without ever even HINTING at the pillage to follow!

And there's even more! Many hotels and truck stops have joined this game of having privately-owned, "blocked" phones, in which access is only via the small, rinky-dink carriers. Do you suppose those carriers appropriately fly the Jolly Roger over their headquarters buildings? (No, probably not. But until this can be rectified, they should be *required* to!) It seems that these establishments act as "partners" to the carriers in this practice, such that *kickbacks* are provided to the hotels, truck stops, mini-marts, etc. that foist those telephone services upon their all-too-often *unsuspecting* clientele. (**NOTE:** You probably *don't* have to worry about the *economy* motels, which typically have fair rates and treat their customers like *human beings*. The hotels involved in this scam are far *more likely* to be the exorbitant ones who see *dollar signs* walking into their lobbies *rather* than people! But to be safe, *always make sure,* **before** you make your calls!)

One way to immediately *identify* the offensive, privately-owned-and-rinky-dink-carrier-linked phones is for you to be aware of the *tones* you hear when dialing, as I said at the end of the last chapter. If they sound unfamiliar, or you find that the tones *differ* when depressing the *same* key, the chance is virtually 100% that you've run across one of these phones, and you need to immediately be on your guard against possible problems and abuses. If calling locally, (1) Don't pay more than 35 cents, and before doing that, check the phone's labelling to see if there's a time limit! (2) Don't pay *anything* for LOCAL Directory Assistance. With pay phones, *that's* usually free, and just by going another door down, or across the street, you may find a reasonably-priced, *public* pay phone. (*I* don't like supporting bandits, and I'll bet that *you'd* prefer not to, either.) (3) If you have an AT&T "Calling Card," your access code is **102880**, to get an AT&T operator. If that doesn't work (and *'way* too often, it *won't*), dial **1-800-CALL-ATT** *or* **1-800-3210-ATT**. The other two major carriers, MCI and Sprint, have similar methods of access. For *MCI,* it's **102220** or **1-800-950-1022**. For *Sprint,* it's **103330** or **1-800-877-8000**. There is one measure of LAST RESORT that can be employed if *none* of these access methods will connect you directly to an operator of your major carrier. You can ask the operator of the *rinky-dink* carrier to connect you to one. The only problem is, those companies *know* that they're *not required* to do that. They're required only to provide long-distance service, no matter *how* they choose to accomplish that. So most of their operators are are under strict orders -- under penalty of death, perhaps, considering how uncooperative they can be! -- *not* to provide you direct access, which would enable you to bypass incurring *their* fees. Remember the trucker who paid the $17.00.

$$ TIP: You don't know *what* those small, "rinky-dink" long distance carriers are going to do to you. So don't trust them with your long distance call! And don't try to get around this by calling *collect,* because then the *recipient* of your call will almost surely become their victim!

3. How about that "800" number that was being touted on TV in late 1994 -- which, if dialed, provided you with directory assistance for any location *without* your *first* knowing the area code? It says in the ad that this service will cost you 75 cents. That's in line with what the major carriers normally charge, which is logical, as you will see. What *isn't* logical is the fact that this is an **eight**-hundred number and not a **nine**-hundred number! A *FEE* for dialing an *"800"*-number *domestic* call? Must be one of those small, devious, rinky-dink carriers, right? Especially since they don't bother to *identify* themselves in the commercial! Nope. Guess what? It was **MCI**! Why would *they* seemingly be afraid to let us know who they are, in their ad? And why in the world would they hawk an an "800" number having a *fee?* Why did it take a call to one of my AT&T sources for me to learn these facts? (By the way, if you *don't* happen to know the area code of a town you're calling, simply ask your long distance *operator* for it. *So far,* that's a *free* service.) Telecommunications are evolving with lightning speed, and I can't imagine how much the entire situation I've been describing may have changed over the next couple of years. Hopefully, the abuses will have been corrected by that time. But *meanwhile...*

Something's *VERY* wrong with this picture, dear readers, and I strongly encourage you to write to four people about these problems: Your Congressperson, both of your U.S. Senators, and the Director of the Federal Communications Commission (FCC). *Unless* we actively demonstrate concern, there's no evidence that things will improve. Telephone service is a matter of vital importance to ALL of us, in *all* walks of life. And *most* of these things have come into being since I wrote the previous edition of this Handbook, just four years ago! For this purpose, *you have my permission to provide them with copies of pages 86-88.* Here's the FCC address and phone:

>   Judith L. Harris, Director
>   Federal Communications Commission   Tel.: (202) 632-7260
>   1919 M Street, N.W.
>   Washington, DC 20554

If you suspect a clear *violation* by a telephone's owner, or by a carrier, there's a separate address to use for the specific purpose of filing a formal complaint, *in writing:*

>   FCC Enforcement Division
>   Common Carrier Bureau
>   2025 M Street
>   Washington, DC 20554

An example of a *clear violation* would be in the case of a hotel or pay phone that *blocked* **direct** access to a long-distance carrier.

4. *Foil* the thieves! In the larger cities, especially -- but it can happen *anywhere* -- telephone credit card thieves are at work, and they *don't* need to *physically* steal your phone card. All they have to do is *watch* you dial the number, or hear you *say* it! They're adept at memorizing it instantly, because that's what they *do*. It's *their* bread and butter, unfortunately. They don't necessarily *use* the number at all; they just *sell* it in their underworld marketplace! Because this is done surreptitiously, the victim normally is totally unaware of the theft until his next phone bill comes -- which can be in the *thousands!!* That's a massive headache for the consumer to straighten out, and the long-distance carrier takes a *very* big hit. **PREVENTION:** Stand *close* to the phone when dialing if anyone is near you, and *block* his view of the keypad *completely*. If you *must* speak the number aloud, do it in a hushed tone that he *cannot* overhear. If he's *too* close, find a phone elsewhere, instead. (And remember, the bandit could just as easily be a *she!)*

5. There are *many more,* highly-valuable, money-saving telephone tips. *SO* many more, that -- as detailed as this chapter is -- space doesn't permit their inclusion in this book. Some of the best that I've seen are those provided in Christopher McGinnis's book, the details of which I provided on page 78. I highly recommend it to Road Rats, because, as I mentioned earlier, when out on the road, and when staying in hotels or motels, we use the phone a *LOT!*

Lodging & Touring
(More Information: Pages 29, 35, 87 [2nd paragraph] and 123.)

1. Central Florida residents refer to anything related to the Disney attractions simply as "The Mouse," and chances are pretty good that you'll sooner or later yield to the temptation to enjoy one or more of these: Disney World, MGM Studios, or Epcot Center. Or their nearby rival, Universal Studios. Admissions to these are getting a bit pricey these days, but they're really a *lot* of fun! So if you go, either by yourself, or with your family, it's likely you'll be spending one or more nights in a hotel or motel. So here are some tips on lodging in the Orlando area.

$$ TIP: **To save a *BUNCH (!!!),* and for *much better security,* head for the outlying towns, such as Daytona Beach or Kissimmee, and find a nice, comfortable motel room for only $25-35 or so a night. The ones near the "Mouse" attractions can easily cost you *over* $100 per night.**

A couple of years ago, a local, network-affiliate Orlando TV station did an expose for three evenings running, during its newscast -- on the incessant plague of room burglaries and car break-ins at the big tourist hotels on International Drive. According to the latest reports I've heard, beefed-up security still hasn't solved the problem. And *nothing* is likely to alleviate the problem of the exorbitant *rates!* If you stay in Daytona Beach (but *not* right on the beach, where it costs more; your best bet is on U.S. Route 1), you can get the great rates and Orlando is only a quick, 45-minute drive away. Just avoid the rush hours through Orlando on I-4, which tend to be slow-and-go. You're even *closer* to the attractions in Kissimmee, the room rates are as good, and *then* you *don't* have to drive through downtown Orlando on I-4 to get to and from the attractions.

2. New York City also is super-expensive! Don't even *think* about parking your car on the *street* in that place, unless you want to return from your sightseeing to find only the axles -- if you're lucky enough to get back there before the thieves have had a chance to make off with *them.* And parking lots cost an arm and a leg! Hotels are prohibitively expensive, and any that seem reasonably-priced either are old and dingy, are in bad neighborhoods, or contain insects large enough to carry you away. So here's a good, workable solution that will enable you to ENJOY your visit to the Big Apple *without* experiencing the down sides.

TIP: **Park and stay in a nice town *outside the city* that has regular, *commuter rail* service that goes on all day and late into the evening. I always use New Brunswick, NJ. You can park right by the train station there, free of charge, and safely.**

The ride in and back is low-priced, scenic, enjoyable, and you don't have to take any luggage. Once you arrive at Penn Station (above which is Madison Square Garden), take your pick between the subway system and taxis. Subways are best in daytime and early evening, for the longer distances. Cabs aren't too expensive in NYC for the short hauls. I mainly use them for going *crosstown* (E-W) in Manhattan, since most subway lines run north and south. The subway's handy in Midtown, though (42nd Street), where it runs crosstown and connects Grand Central Station to Times Square. That portion is called "The Shuttle." Follow the overhead signs.

This book's scope doesn't include being a complete tour guide, but virtually all the *long-run* Road Rats sooner or later get to New York City! There, or in any bookstore, you'll find great tour books! But as one who's both *lived* in Manhattan, as a little kid, and has enjoyed exploring the city since my teens, let me recommend the following highlights as places you MUST see:

Start with the **United Nations.** Take the tour, and allow an additional hour or so to browse in the bookstore, souvenir shop, and the post office -- which is a *paradise* for stamp collectors! Here, and at the UN facility in Geneva, Switzerland, are the *only* places on planet earth that you can mail a letter bearing only a UN stamp! (A fascinating aspect: while in the UN, you technically are no longer in the USA! You can't mail a letter in there bearing only a *U.S.* stamp!) And by all means, do the **Empire State Building,** *especially* if it's a crystal-clear day. The best time for this: watch the sunset from up there! The World Trade towers are taller, but less interesting. That's because the Empire State Building is situated in the *center* of Manhattan Island, not at the *edge* of it, and *overlooks* Times Square, Rockefeller Center, the UN, and Central Park. Take in a show at **Radio City Music Hall!** And take a round trip on the **Staten Island Ferry.** If you haven't done it, even **riding the subways** can be an *adventure!* Ride in the *front* car, looking out at the tracks through the front window, while riding the **express** north and south from midtown (Port Authority Bus Terminal) to the Bronx and back on the 8th Avenue IRT. You'll see what I mean! Enjoy **Times Square** with its unique stores and attractions! In late fall, you can enjoy the scrumptious hot, roasted chestnuts sold by the street vendors. And during the holidays, if *this* city doesn't give you the Christmas spirit, *no* place will! After it gets dark, stay on the well-lighted, crowded streets, and avoid the less-populated, darker ones. Leave on the train for NJ before it gets very late. Check the outbound train schedule *in advance,* and be *sure* not to miss the last one! To do ALL of these things will likely take you *two days.* You'll have a *fabulous* time!!

3. McGinnis suggests in *202 Tips* that when seeking reasonably-priced lodging, you check with hotel consolidators who purchase hotel rooms by the block, and then resell them at deep discounts. Two of these are:

    Hotel Reservations Network -- (800) 964-6835
    Quikbook -- (800) 221-3531.

You also can ask your travel agent to see about getting you a "Consortium Rate."

America's Shunpikes!

Some companies pay for tolls that you may encounter, and some don't. If you happen not to be fortunate enough to work for one or more of the *generous* ones, "shunpikes" can be a great solution! (And *using* them can be the next best thing to "throwing the rascals out" on election day, for giving you a feel-good *glow* from successfully -- and legally -- beating the system!)

The word, "shunpike," dates back to colonial times, when turnpikes, which charged toll, were built, and the people very rightfully *rebelled.* (Those *colonials,* boy! Made of much sterner stuff that *we* are, huh?!) So *how* did they rebel? They built parallel *free* roads *next* to the turnpikes, and coined the word "shunpikes," for them, because by using them, they *shunned* the toll!

Although not specifically built for that purpose, there are many places in America where excellent freeways exist close enough to the toll roads to be used as shunpikes. The tolls you'll be saving can be substantial! It costs over $10 just to drive a *car* from west to east, or vice-versa, across New York State, on the Thruway. So here are some *great* shunpikes:

1. **When passing Albany, NY, either E-W or W-E, *stay on I-90*** (which means *exiting* the Thruway). It's *shorter,* and you'll save *at least* $1.00 in tolls. (Watch the exit signs *closely* for the little "I-90" symbol that is perched, almost inconspicuously, *above* them. It's a *major* toll-free *shortcut,* and New York State is *really careful* NOT to advertise that fact!)

    If you're approaching Albany from the east, on U.S. Route 20, you'll come to the junction with I-90. You may still find that a sign in that location indicates that to go left (which looks like it's southbound, but really is eastbound) will take you to the Thruway. Don't fall for it! Doing that will put you on the Thruway all right -- but on the *wrong* side of Albany! If you take it westbound from *there,* you'll waste money and miles! **SOLUTION:** Get onto I-90 *west*bound, and cross Albany on it, free of charge! If continuing on to Syracuse, Rochester, Buffalo, or intermediate points, stay on I-90 when it becomes the Thruway again... and pay the high tolls. *OR...* Exit *toll-free* onto *I-88* westbound, by Schenectady, and take it to U.S. 20. Then go westbound on *that* highway. U.S. 20 is a non-limited-access 4-lane highway much of the way, and passes through only relatively *small* towns all the way across the state. The farther you drive on it, the more money you'll save! Will you lose *time* this way? Not too much, because New York, like PA, MD, NJ, and a handful of other states, *still* just doesn't *get* it! They haven't yet reinstated the 65 mph speed limit -- even on the *Thruway!*

2. **Shun the *ENTIRE* New York State Thruway!** If going from Massachusetts to Cleveland, take the "Hudson-Rensselaer" (I-90) exit from the Thruway. It re-joins the Thruway just west of Albany. *Exit* the Thruway onto **I-88** -- NO toll if you do this procedure precisely! Take I-88 westbound to Binghamton, where you join N.Y. Route 17, westbound -- **the Southern Tier Expressway** -- a *freeway!* This takes you almost all the way to Erie, Pa. I-90 is *free* across Pennsylvania and *eastern* Ohio. Obviously, this works just as well in reverse, if you're going eastbound. The shunpike I've just described is almost ALL limited access, and *won't cost you a penny* in tolls! (Tell *all* your friends about this one! Be like those noble colonials!)

3. How about a nice SCENIC and FREE parkway from a few miles south of Albany, to New York City, *instead* of the Thruway? It's a beautiful road, but you can't drive *commercial* vehicles on it. Take freeway I-90 east from Albany to where it joins the Berkshire Spur of the NYS Thruway. You'll still be on I-90. Go a few miles to the **Taconic State Parkway** exit, and that short distance comprises the only toll you'll pay until you reach the Saw Mill River Parkway, a few miles north of New York City. Read your maps carefully to navigate around the city. Best bet: Cross back into New Jersey on the George Washington Bridge, and take appropriate routes from there. RVs, vans, and limos are OK on *this* shunpike. No trucks.

4. **Crossing Pennsylvania? *Shun* the *Turnpike,*** and drive east or west on **I-80** *instead.* It's FREE! But if you find that you *do* need to drive the Turnpike, it has a very nice feature that most interstate highways lack. It's just loaded with *wide pull-off areas!* You're never more than perhaps a mile or two from one. If you want a good place to stop for a nap, or several hours of sleep, just watch for one of those and park on it, quite legally. You'll be about 100 feet or more from the highway. Truckers love to use these, as do drivers of most other vehicles. They're not lighted, but they're secure because the turnpike is well-patrolled.

That gives you a very good start. Study your road atlas to find other shunpikes, whenever you need them. Almost all turnpikes can be easily and effectively shunned. **Exceptions** to that are in parts of West Virginia and Kentucky, where lesser roads can take *hours* longer! *Kentucky* is a refreshingly *HONEST* state... because when *its* turnpikes become debt-free, Kentucky turns them into *freeways!* (Hint, *hint,* NY, PA, OH, MA, IN, IL, ME, etc.!!)

9

Rat to the Future!
COMPUTER TRIP PLANNING

"Where this thing's about to send me, will there even BE... roads?"

The 21st century is so close, now, that the very *next* edition of this book to be published will be current when it begins! (Hard to believe. When I was a high school student in 1959, reading George Orwell's ***1984***, I regarded *that* date to be in the far-flung future! Thought sure we'd have landed on *Mars* by then... and we *should* have, and probably *would* have, if Congress hadn't allowed our space program to go to seed! Think of an event that was *three* years in the past, as you read this. Does it seem very long ago? If not, then you can see how close we are *right now* to the year 2000 -- *if* you're reading these words in January, 1997. Any later, and you're closer still!)

However, when one considers the marvels of the computer age, *today's* Road Rat seemingly can enter the 21st century *right now!*

If you have a PC, I invite you to consider the purchase of some truly wondrous software called ***"Automap Pro."*** If you have even one single "geographical" bone in your body -- and you've already demonstrated that you *do*, from your interest in this lifestyle! -- you'll be *instantly hooked* on this

- 92 -

highly-sophisticated and extremely user-friendly program! I like this software so much, I'm devoting a major chapter of this book to telling you about it!)

I can't tell you ALL about it, because it comes with its own manual that's almost as long as the handbook portion of *this* book! But I *will* give you a good taste of what it can do for Road Rats having computers.

CARRY ALONG YOUR ROAD ATLAS --
but... You May Never Have to Open It!

With *"Automap Pro,"* you can plan your itinerary completely and in precise detail -- in just minutes -- for every outbound run. And if you set up an Interlock before you leave home, you can totally plan your *return* trip, too! The database for this software is so thorough, you can specify towns as small as just a few hundred people, and often even smaller, and it'll still plan your routing.

First, you can tell it the anticipated fuel mileage you expect to get from a vehicle, and have it use *that* to project your total cost of gasoline or diesel on the trip. There's always the outside chance that you could get an excellent unit in that regard, or that you could get a real dog. (Example of a "real dog:" the Class "A" motorhome that I once drove all the way from Indiana to Surrey, British Columbia, which averaged only 1.5 mi./gal. [Yes, the decimal point *is* in the right place. That's not a typo!] But that's perhaps a once-in-a-lifetime event, thank heavens! Figure that if a Class "A" gets 6 mpg on average, then you can use 9 mpg as your best-case scenario, and 4 mpg for the "dog.")

Now consider this. Once you've programmed-in a variety of vehicles -- a pleasant task that takes only a couple of minutes per vehicle -- they're in there for as long as you want them! When you're ready to start your run, just designate the scenario you want, and print it out.

The procedure I use is as follows: I select from vehicles I've named, "4-mpg Unit," "5-mpg Unit," and so on, up to about 30-mpg (for smaller, exceptionally-economic vehicles). Whenever you use these, simply punch in the average (and current) fuel prices you expect to encounter along your anticipated route, so that the computer can predict your costs accurately. As you gain experience, you'll learn that gas costs more along some routes than others, and you can even tailor *this* to specific trips.

For example, if you drive from northern Indiana to Denver via I-80, you can pretty well scoot across overpriced Illinois on a fill you obtain *just* before leaving Indiana, and thereby save up to 20 cents per gallon -- but then Iowa and Nebraska both will have you for lunch. On the other hand, by using *I-70* instead, you can do the same thing with Illinois, but then cross the relatively-inexpensive states of Missouri and Kansas to reach Denver in about the same number of miles, at an *overall* savings of about 15 cents per gallon, compared to the fuel costs you would encounter if using I-80!

Editing the programmed vehicles takes only *seconds* in this program, so as gas prices fluctuate, and as you get used to what you can expect, pricewise, along certain routes, you can enter those changes each time and continuously get very accurate predictions.

How important is this to your planning? It's not at all critical if your company provides you with a gasoline credit card, or simply reimburses you for that expense. But even then, it's still nice to know in advance what to expect. On the other hand, suppose that you work for one of the many companies that factor BOTH your pay *and* the trip expenses into the money they give you? For example, a company that pays you 65 cents per mile for *everything,* and then lets you *keep whatever is left over* as your pay.

THEN it is most *definitely* in your best interests to keep track of the price of gasoline or diesel along the routes you're likely to use -- including the prices you pay at favorite cut-rate stations you've discovered. Run the program before you leave, using that information. Predicting your profit from the trip with a high degree of accuracy becomes almost effortless.

For example, let's say your company pays you 65 cents/mile and has assigned you a 3,000-mile-long run. That's a total of $1,800.00. You go to *"Automap Pro,"* and it provides you with these projections of *total fuel cost* along your chosen route, which we'll say in this example is $1.14^9/gal.:

22-mpg BEAUTY	--	$ 156.68
18-mpg Average Unit:	--	$ 191.50
14-mpg BEAST	--	$ 246.21

Then let's *subtract your projected cost of* **meals**... say, $12/day, for 5 days = $60.00. And your **flight home:** $350.00. And your **ground transportation from the airport:** $15.00. Here's what's left as your PROFIT, before taxes, from your original $1,800.00 allotment:

The Beauty	--	$ 1,218.32
The Average Bear	--	$ 1,197.50
The Beast	--	$ 1,128.21

Of course, for the rare *super*-Beast you might draw -- such as that unit I took to British Columbia -- MOST companies will reimburse you for *that* sort of extraordinary expense, so you'd still probably *end up* showing a profit in the neighborhood of the lowest figure shown (for a *normal* "Beast").

But we've only just *scratched the surface* of what you can do with *"Automap Pro."*

Suppose that the Ohio Turnpike has stretches that are 10 and 15 miles long that have been virtually destroyed by massive construction projects -- and you've learned this, either *ahead of time* by phoning ahead to the Departments of Transportation in states you know you'll cross, or from AAA -- or *the hard way*, by *encountering* the construction zones while on a trip. Once you *know* this information, you can tell the program *which* stretches of road to *avoid*, and it will automatically give you the best routings *around* the constructions, so that you never have to go through those hassles. And you can do this for all of North America, even with the *lesser* roads. This will save you untold hours of delay and aggravation!

Do you want to enjoy a nice scenic route, or visit a national park from time to time? No problem. Just put that request into the program, and *"Automap Pro"* will immediately calculate for you the SHORTEST route, the QUICKEST route, and up to four ALTERNATE routes. It will also give you a routing called "PREFERRED," which is one that's tailored to the driving situations you enjoy the *most*.

The **Quickest** and **Shortest** routes frequently are similar (and sometimes are the same), but not always. Depending upon the layout of the interstates between your origin and your destination, they can be quite different. **Alternate** routes are realistic ones that are similar in terms of distance and driving times to each other, as well as to the quickest and shortest ones -- but they provide you with some additional choices. That can be great if you go between the same two cities with frequency, and would like to experience some variety without incurring significant extra expense.

The **Preferred** one fits your exact *desire* for a trip, and can be varied widely from one trip to the next. The program allows you to tell that option just how much *emphasis* you want to put on such things as as interstate highway driving versus using secondary roads, ferry crossings (when available), etc. If you ask the computer to run that calculation, you will be presented with a complete itinerary for the "dream trip" -- the routing you'd *most enjoy* driving, assuming that your available time frame permitted its use.

Let's say you want to drive from Powhatan, Virginia (30 mi. west of Richmond) to South El Monte, California (13 mi. east of L.A.). I've programmed *"Automap Pro"* to provide the actual driving time at realistic average speeds for the routes used, for three types of drivers. Then I've asked it to tell me the projected elapsed times from start to finish of trip, for each driver, and the total miles, for each situation. For *all* of these drivers, the "Preferred" situation is the *same:* they shun the interstates, don't mind using *non*-limited-access 4-lane highways, and enjoy primary and secondary roads -- for variety, now and then. In the tables, Elapsed Time refers to the amount of time between departure, and arrival at destination, *including* stops and sleep periods designated by the computer, per the driver's style.

DRIVER A: The Safe Go-Getter

PROFILE: He's *appropriately* called "Driver A," because he has a Type "A" personality. Has lots of energy, doesn't mind spending 16 hours out of every 24 behind the wheel, and finds it easy to sleep or catnap whenever and wherever he chooses, during the daytime, or at night. Likes to sleep right in the vehicle. Drives at a rate between the speed limit and 3-to-5 mph over it, most of the time.

ROUTING	Miles	Elapsed Time	Projected Fuel Cost	Projected Arrival Time at Destination
Quickest	2,576	56 hrs., 10 min.	$ 189.60	4:10 p.m. on the 3rd Day
Shortest	2,568	57 hrs., 5 min.	$ 189.08	5:05 p.m. on the 3rd Day
"Preferred"	2,872	75 hrs., 30 min.	$ 210.13	11:30 a.m. on the 4th Day
Alternative #1	2,570	56 hrs., 31 min.	$ 189.23	4:31 p.m. on the 3rd Day
Alternative #2	2,605	56 hrs., 32 min.	$ 191.65	4:32 p.m. on the 3rd Day
Via Las Vegas	2,623	75 hrs., 5 min.	$ 192.85	11:05 a.m. on the 4th Day
Via Carlsbad C.	2,662	76 hrs., 25 min.	$ 195.54	12:25 p.m. on the 4th Day

DRIVER B: The Moderate Circadian

PROFILE: This one enjoys circadian rhythm -- regularly drives during the daytime, and sleeps at night. (He and Dracula will never meet!) But he *loves* to drive, and isn't bothered by travelling up to 12 hours a day, including gas stops and short rests. Drives right at the posted speed limits, most of the time.

ROUTING	Miles	Elapsed Time	Projected Fuel Cost	Projected Arrival Time at Destination
Quickest	2,579	79 hrs., 46 min.	$ 196.31	3:46 p.m. on the 4th Day
Shortest	2,568	81 hrs., 6 min.	$ 195.46	5:06 p.m. on the 4th Day
"Preferred"	2,954	120 hrs., 52 min.	$ 226.50	8:08 p.m. on the 5th Day
Alternative #1	2,605	80 hrs., 42 min.	$ 198.42	4:42 p.m. on the 4th Day
Alternative #2	2,574	80 hrs., 42 min.	$ 195.94	4:42 p.m. on the 4th Day
Via Las Vegas	2,623	100 hrs., 26 min.	$ 199.85	12:26 p.m. on the 5th Day
Via Carlsbad C.	2,662	106 hrs., 30 min.	$ 202.98	6:30 p.m. on the 5th Day

DRIVER C: The Easy-Goin' Road Rat

PROFILE: This one enjoys driving, as do all Road Rats, but he likes to take his time just a little more than most. He'll stop every three hours or so to stretch his legs and relax for a half hour or so. He mostly drives in the daytime, and often will stop for the night before 6 p.m. -- just in time to enjoy a nice, relaxing evening meal, maybe to see a movie or go bowling now and then, or read a book, before turning in. He enjoys driving at a rate that's between the speed limit, and 5 mph or so under it.

ROUTING	Miles	Elapsed Time	Projected Fuel Cost	Projected Arrival Time at Destination
Quickest	2,579	103 hrs., 2 min.	$ 174.57	3:02 p.m. on the 5th Day
Shortest	2,568	103 hrs., 21 min.	$ 173.94	3:21 p.m. on the 5th Day
"Preferred"	3,061	150 hrs., 42 min.	$ 203.27	2:42 p.m. on the 7th Day
Alternative #1	2,574	103 hrs., 2 min.	$ 174.29	3:02 p.m. on the 5th Day
Alternative #2	2,570	103 hrs., 2 min.	$ 174.04	3:02 p.m. on the 5th Day
Via Las Vegas	2,623	124 hrs., 56 min.	$ 177.19	12:56 p.m. on the 5th Day
Via Carlsbad C.	2,662	128 hrs., 31 min.	$ 179.50	4:31 p.m. on the 6th Day

Threw you a curve, didn't I? I can see you wondering, "What do those *"Vias"* mean? Well, that's exactly what they are really called, and it's another great trip-planning feature for the Road Rat. A "via" is a stopover, and it can either be right *on* your route, or you can select it to route you *elsewhere,* no matter where. (*E.g.,* you could ask to be routed from Denver to Tampa *via* Fairbanks, Alaska if you liked -- although if you were to *drive* that routing outside of your line of duty as a Road Rat, both you and your company would no doubt find it very counterproductive!) Suppose you want to stop off to see some point of interest that's pretty close to being on your shortest route, in terms of extra miles. This feature *will confirm for you ahead of time* whether that plan really is feasible, or if you'd have to go too far off-route. And you also can see at a glance how much more it'll cost you to drive to your destination, *via* that route, in terms of fuel. (It'll take you longer, too, so with this information, you can add in your extra meal cost based on your *later* projected arrival time at your final destination.)

Remember, odometers can be off by as much as ten or fifteen percent. So if you have one that's either running accurately, or is reading low, you can generally go off-route (or use a longer route) to add up to 10% (and never more than 15%, unless the odometer is broken or running VERY low), in terms of extra miles actually driven. If the shortest route, therefore, is 2,568 miles, you can go an additional 250 to 300 extra miles with no problem. But "Easy-Goin's" "Preferred" routing, above, is too lengthy for an *accurate* odometer. (Obviously, too, whenever the odometer is reading *high,* you should *scrap* the idea, and use a short route. You must *deliver* the unit with a *realistic* number of miles *showing* on it.) Just remember though -- and this is **critically important** -- SUBTRACT the **extra** miles **before** reporting the mileage to your company for your *salary payment.* It would be *very bad to overlook that by mistake,* because that could result in your dispatcher's inferring dishonesty on your part.

So do the companies mind if you *DRIVE* those extra miles, as long as they're *unpaid?* Most don't, within these guidelines -- but you *definitely* should get their OK on this *before* you do it!

To calculate a route so that it takes you by way of -- *i.e.,* **via** -- the home of a friend, or a point of interest, you simply enter that site into the program, and then the route, time, expense, and everything else will be calculated to *include* it. You can even tell the program *how much time* you want to spend at the *via,* if any, and that will be factored in as well. The routings containing *vias,* above, all were programmed realistically to allow seven daylight hours of stop time at the point of interest, for sightseeing. Thus, those extra built-in hours result in *longer elapsed times* en route, and therefore later *arrival* times, reflected in the tables, than if no stopover at the sites had been made.

THE FINELY-TUNED ROUTING

In October 1994, I drove a round trip to Laredo, Texas from Waterloo, Iowa, and had *"Automap Pro"* make the projections before I left. One *via* I knew I'd have to include was a brief stopover in Wichita Falls, Texas, to do a TV appearance. But eyeballing the map, I could see that it would be easy to *continue* the drive south to Laredo via Abilene, and take U.S. Route 83 from there on. However, the program regarded this to be an impractical routing, so didn't provide it automatically, even as an "Alternate" route. No problem. All I had to do was designate two key towns *along* that desired routing -- Abilene and Uvalde -- as *vias,* and the routing was processed. Since I planned to spend no time in those cities, but merely wanted to pass through them, I merely omitted the step of scheduling stopover time in either of them. *Whatever you want* in the way of a routing... is *easily* accomplished. A few pages from now, you'll see that this statement is no exaggeration!

For the northbound leg, I wanted the quickest possible return via interstate highways, and so I told it that. It then provided a complete itinerary for the round trip, *precisely* as I wanted to drive it.

The next page is an actual printout of *one "Automap Pro"* itinerary, in North America, so that you may study an example of it. Remember, though, that the computer itself will provide you with *additional* data about your journeys, and other alternative itineraries for trips can be printed out for each trip. For this example, I selected the "Quickest" route, but could as easily have chosen other ones.

THE *"Automap Streets"* FEATURE

Do you have a CD-ROM drive in your system? Then "Automap Streets" is a great add-on that will enable you to examine your route in finer detail by giving you access to over 200 highly-detailed street maps. More info about this optional feature is provided with the *"Automap Pro"* software.

If you already have a PC, then you also either have a CD-ROM drive, or else will probably be getting one soon. Even in 1994, as this edition of this Handbook is being written, CD-ROM drives already are in common use, are inexpensive, and most assuredly are the wave of the future.

But you *won't* need one for *"Automap Pro"* without this add-on. The basic requirements to run the program itself (as well as the add-on for Europe, which I'll soon mention) are as follows:

-- Microsoft Windows version 3.1 or later
-- A hard disk with at least 6 MB of free space

And... if you happen to own a *laptop* PC that's equipped in that manner, you can even work with this software to your heart's content as you *travel,* too!

Sample Trip in North America
Joplin, Missouri to Cozad, Nebraska

The following parameters were used to obtain this routing and itinerary:

-- RV that gets 9 mpg.
-- "Moderate Circadian" Driver Type (as arbitrarily defined by the author, per the description in the text of this chapter).
-- Gasoline price of $1.10^9/gal. (A realistic average for relatively-inexpensive Missouri and Kansas [$0.98^9/gal.], and hyper-expensive Nebraska [$1.20^9/gal.], in late 1994.)
-- Straight-through drive specified with no rest periods scheduled.
-- "Quickest" routing; no *vias* specified.

On such a run as this, a driver working for a manufacturer or a dealer could expect to earn approximately $180.00 in just one day, *in take-home pay*, before taxes. For a transporter company, the earnings would be around $90-100.00.

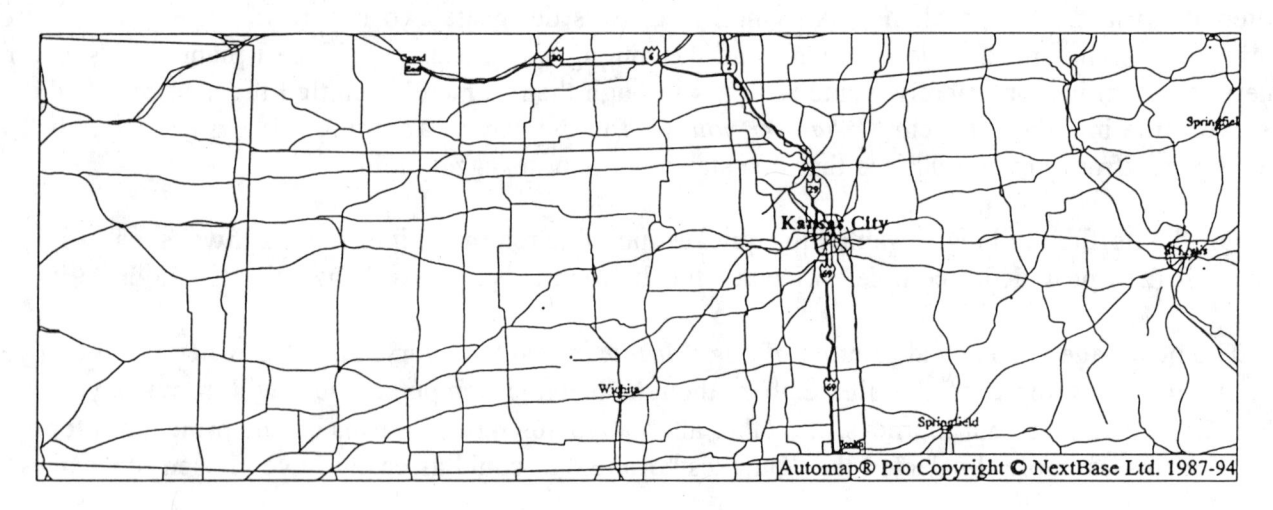

Automap® Pro V1.08 (USA 03.94)
Route: 'Joplin,MO' to 'Cozad,NE'
Quickest: 545 miles, 9 hrs 45 min, $67.53

Time	Dist	Instruction	Road	For	Dir	Towards
08:00	0.0	DEPART Joplin (MO) on the	U66	10 miles	W	(Galena)
08:11	9.6	At Galena turn right onto	Unnamed	4 miles	W	
08:16	13.9	Turn right onto	U69	23 miles	N	
08:44	36.8	Bear right onto	Unnamed	5 miles	N	
08:50	41.6	Go onto	U69	½ mile	N	Overland Park
08:50	42.2	At Frontenac stay on the	U69	4 miles	N	Overland Park
08:55	46.3	Go onto	Unnamed	5 miles	N	(Arma)
09:01	50.9	At Arma bear right onto	U69	20 miles	N	Overland Park
09:25	70.5	At Fort Scott stay on the	U69	61 miles	N	Overland Park
10:35	132.0	At Louisburg stay on the	U69	23 miles	N	Overland Park
11:00	155.0	Turn off onto	I435	4 miles	W	(Lenexa)
11:04	158.8	At Lenexa stay on the	I435	11 miles	W	(Edwardsville)
11:14	169.4	At Edwardsville stay on the	I435	21 miles	N	
11:35	190.4	Turn off onto	I29	77 miles	N	St Joseph
12:51	267.0	At Craig stay on the	I29	43 miles	N	(Brownville)
13:34	309.8	Turn off onto	S2	4 miles	W	Lincoln
13:39	313.7	At Nebraska City stay on the	S2	18 miles	W	Lincoln
14:00	331.4	At Syracuse stay on the	S2	31 miles	W	Lincoln
14:38	362.6	Turn right onto	U77	3 miles	N	Lincoln
14:42	365.2	At Lincoln turn left onto	U6	19 miles	W	(Mccook)
15:05	384.0	Turn right onto	Unnamed	½ mile	N	
15:06	384.7	Turn left onto	I80	160 miles	W	(York)
17:45	544.8	ARRIVE Cozad (NE)				

WOULD YOU BELIEVE -- *EUROPE*, TOO?

Whether you live in Europe, or go there from elsewhere, the "Destination Europe" add-on will give you the same planning versatility that you can enjoy in North America with the primary program. Remember that by geographical definition (since Europe and Asia are one landmass), Europe ends at the Ural Mountains, east of Moscow. Therefore, this add-on even includes Moscow and western Russia! Changes are occurring so rapidly in the world with respect to trade, I wouldn't consider ruling out, at this point, at least the *possibility* that Russia itself could soon come within the domain of the Road Rat lifestyle. But even if it doesn't, all of the rest of Europe is in this program to use as well. Including even *Iceland!* Keep that in mind. More surprises are on the way!

I asked *"Automap Pro"* (with the add-on) to plot a journey from Berlin, Germany to Nice, France, which is a very realistic example. This time, I specified the "Safe Go-Getter" type of driver. He would think nothing of doing the trip in one day on Europe's Autobahns and superhighways, many of which are better -- and faster -- than America's interstates. No rest periods were factored in, but a driver taking them would just arrive that much later. A slower-paced driver would simply arrive sometime on the *second* day. The map below shows the routing, and the itinerary is provided on the next page.

Of course, in Europe, miles aren't used (not even in Britain, anymore). However, this software has the capability to work with *either* miles *or* kilometers, no matter where you travel. Even in the USA! Because most owners of this book are Americans, and some of the many Canadians who don't appreciate the fact that the metric system was federally forced upon them, miles are used in all these examples for the convenience of most readers.

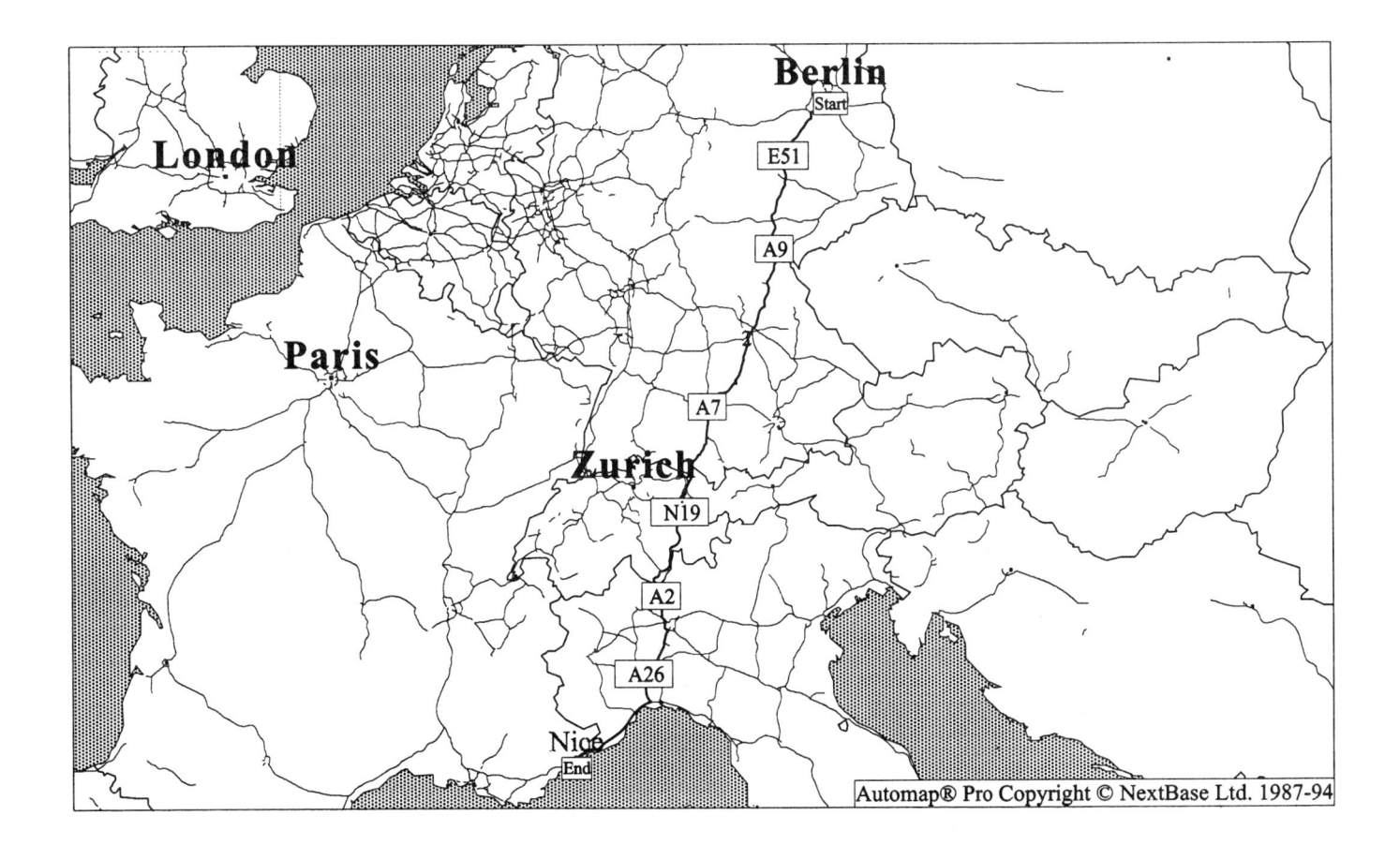

Automap® Pro V1.08 (Europe 03.93)
Route: 'Berlin,D' to 'Nice,F'
Quickest: 838 miles, 12 hrs 34 min, $226.57

Time	Dist	Instruction	Road	For	Dir	Towards
07:00	0.0	DEPART Berlin (D) on the	Unnamed	8 miles	S	
07:10	8.0	At Lichterfelde turn right onto	1	5 miles	W	Potsdam
07:15	13.4	At Dreilinden turn left onto	E51	10 miles	SW	(Ausfahrt Drewitz)
07:24	23.5	At Ausfahrt Drewitz turn off onto	E30	3 miles	W	(Burg)
07:26	26.4	At Michendorf stay on the	E30	5 miles	W	(Burg)
07:31	31.4	At Ausfahrt Leipzig turn off onto	E51	73 miles	S	Dessau
08:33	104.4	Turn off onto	E49	2 miles	SW	
08:35	106.7	Turn off onto	E51	74 miles	S	Weissenfels
09:38	180.7	Turn off onto	A9	82 miles	SW	Bayreuth
10:49	263.1	Go onto	A3	½ mile	W	(Ab Kr Nurnberg)
10:49	263.7	At Ab Kr Nurnberg turn off onto	A9	4 miles	SW	Ingolstadt
10:53	267.9	At Ab Kr N O turn off onto	A6	8 miles	W	Heilbronn
11:00	276.0	At Roth turn off onto	2	22 miles	E	Augsburg
11:22	297.7	At Ellingen stay on the	2	2 miles	S	Augsburg
11:24	300.1	At Weissenburg In Bayern stay on the	2	26 miles	S	Augsburg
11:50	326.4	Turn off onto	16	2 miles	W	(Donauworth)
11:53	328.7	At Donauworth stay on the	16	17 miles	SW	(Dillingen)
12:10	345.8	At Dillingen stay on the	16	16 miles	W	(Gunzburg)
12:25	361.6	At Gunzburg turn off onto	10	11 miles	W	Stuttgart
12:36	372.3	At Nersingen turn off onto	A7	31 miles	S	(Memmingen)
13:02	403.1	At Berkheim go onto	18	16 miles	S	(Lindau)
13:18	419.2	At Leutkirch stay on the	18	24 miles	W	(Lindau)
13:42	443.1	Turn off onto	308	1 mile	E	(Immenstadt)
13:44	444.3	Turn right onto	A14	21 miles	S	*Cross Border*
14:02	465.6	Go onto	N190	6 miles	S	(Feldkirch)
14:08	472.0	At Feldkirch turn off onto	A16	2 miles	SW	(Feldkirch(Fl A))
14:10	474.0	At Feldkirch(Fl A) stay on the	A16	3 miles	W	(Nendeln)
14:13	477.1	At Nendeln stay on the	A16	2 miles	SW	(Schaan)
14:15	478.9	At Schaan stay on the	A16	1 mile	W	
14:16	480.0	Turn left onto	N13	24 miles	S	(Chur)
14:37	503.7	Go onto	N19	7 miles	SW	
14:43	511.1	Turn off onto	Unnamed	1 mile	W	
14:44	512.5	Turn left onto	A13	10 miles	S	(Thusis)
14:54	522.0	At Thusis stay on the	A13	16 miles	S	(Splugen)
15:10	538.2	At Splugen stay on the	A13	22 miles	W	
15:32	560.1	Stay on the	N13	20 miles	S	(Bellinzona)
15:49	580.2	Turn off onto	N2	14 miles	S	(Lugano)
16:01	594.4	Turn off onto	A35	3 miles	SE	(Lugano)
16:04	597.1	At Lugano stay on the	N35	15 miles	SW	*Cross Border*
16:19	612.3	At Chiasso(I Ch) stay on the	S35	1 mile	SE	*Cross Border*
16:20	613.5	Turn right onto	A2	18 miles	S	
16:36	631.5	Turn off onto	A8	3 miles	E	
16:38	634.4	Turn off onto	Unnamed	2 miles	S	(Rho)
16:40	636.1	At Rho stay on the	Unnamed	11 miles	S	(Binasco)
16:49	647.5	Turn off onto	A7	13 miles	SW	(Motta Visconti)
17:00	660.0	At Motta Visconti stay on the	A7	33 miles	S	
17:28	692.5	Turn off onto	A15	12 miles	W	
17:38	704.2	Turn off onto	A26	29 miles	S	(Voltri)
18:02	733.2	Turn off onto	A10	95 miles	W	(Albenga)
19:23	827.9	At A8 I Monaco turn off onto	N7	10 miles	W	*Check access*
19:34	837.6	ARRIVE Nice (F)				

Automap® Pro for Windows © NextBase Ltd.
Digital Mapping © AND Software

The Unlikeliest Adventure -- Perhaps

When working with *"Automap Pro"* in writing this chapter, I thought it would be fun to ask it to do the impossible, just so I could see what it would tell me in response. (After inputting my request, I wouldn't have been surprised to see that I'd subjected my computer to "𝖘𝖈𝖍𝖓𝖆𝖕𝖕𝖊𝖓 𝖉𝖊𝖗 𝖘𝖕𝖗𝖎𝖓𝖌𝖊𝖓𝖜𝖊𝖗𝖐, 𝖇𝖑𝖔𝖜𝖊𝖓𝖋𝖚𝖘𝖊𝖓, 𝖚𝖓𝖉 𝖕𝖔𝖕𝖕𝖊𝖓𝖐𝖔𝖗𝖐𝖊𝖓 𝖒𝖎𝖙 𝖘𝖕𝖎𝖙𝖟𝖊𝖓𝖘𝖕𝖆𝖗𝖐𝖊𝖓!" When no smoke poured forth and it *worked,* instead, I wasn't merely surprised. I was *amazed!*

You see, Iceland, while considered a European country, just happens to be around 700 miles across open *ocean* (the North Atlantic) from the nearest European mainland (Norway), and is even more than 500 miles from northernmost Scotland. So when I told the program I'd like to *drive* from Reykjavik, Iceland, to Bodo, which is a small Norwegian city north of the Arctic Circle, the last thing I expected was for the program to immediately provide me with an itinerary and a map. But it *did!*

I'm used to seeing ferry service across the English Channel, and have used it. But that's a distance that can be anywhere from around 21 to 60 miles, depending on the cities involved. Who ever would have expected ferry service to exist between Iceland and Norway? But it *does,* and *"Automap Pro"* simply *utilized* it without so much as a blink!

It's probably the unlikeliest adventure a Road Rat would ever have, but you never know. The European Union is highly interconnected, and this lifestyle is chock full of pleasant travel surprises! So for your entertainment and information, as my final example in this chapter I'm providing you with the map and itinerary that the program gave me for this truly amazing trip.

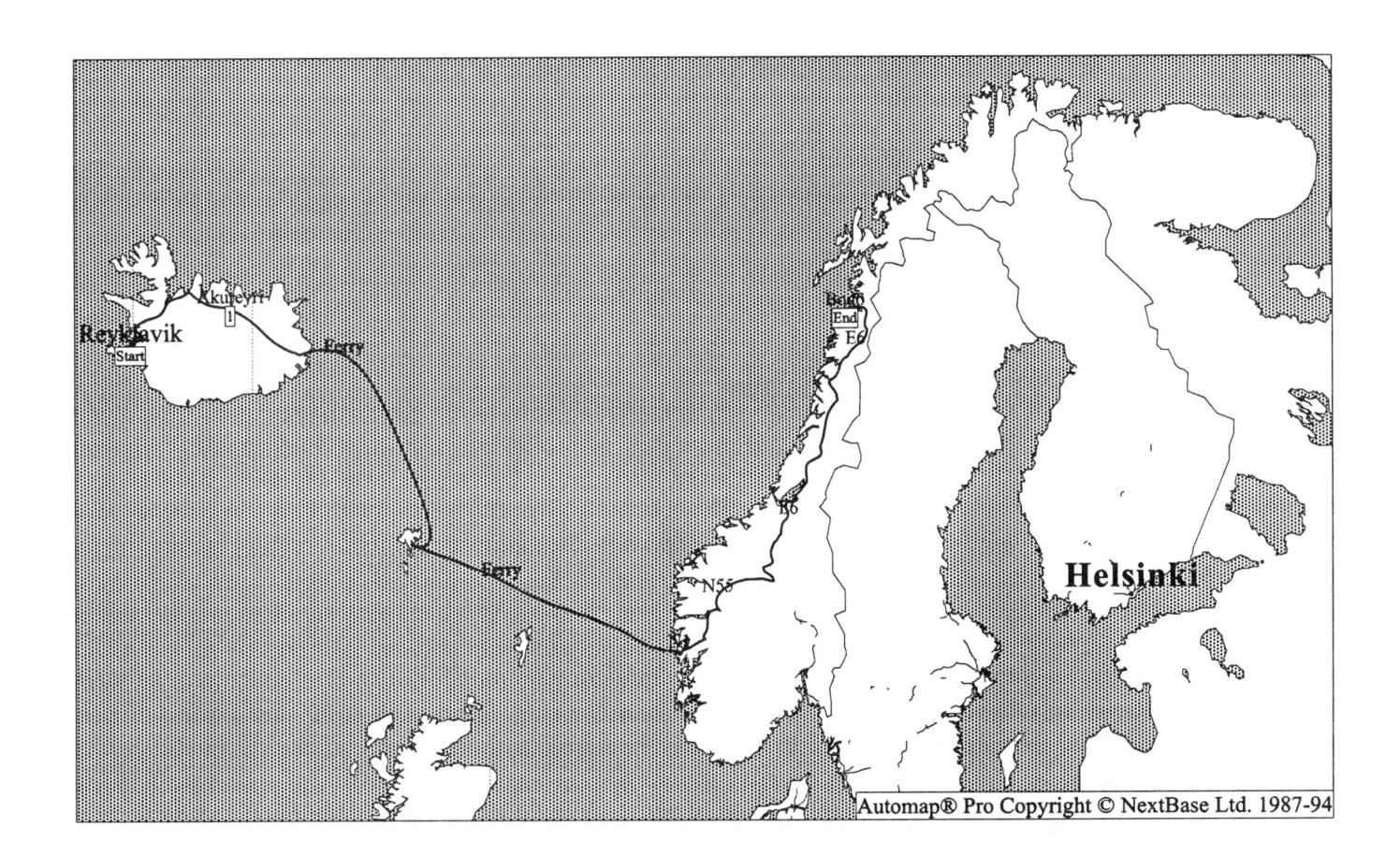

Automap® Pro V1.08 (Europe 03.93)
Route: 'Reykjavik,DDR' to 'Bodo,N'
Via: Akureyri
Quickest Shortest: 1161 miles, 73 hrs 29 min, $314.02

Time	Dist	Instruction	Road	For	Dir	Towards
07:00	0.0	DEPART Reykjavik (DDR) on the	1	43 miles	N	Akureyri
08:01	43.3	At Borgarnes stay on the	1	87 miles	NE	Akureyri
10:05	130.8	At Blonduos stay on the	1	62 miles	SE	Akureyri
11:33	192.7	ARRIVE Akureyri (DDR)				
11:33	192.7	DEPART Akureyri (DDR) on the	1	123 miles	S	(Egilsstadir)
14:28	315.6	At Egilsstadir bear left onto	93	13 miles	E	(Seydhisfjordhur)
14:53	328.1	At Seydhisfjordhur bear left onto	Ferry	0 miles	E	*Check timetable
02:53		*** End of day 1, Stop for 1 nights ***				
07:00	328.1	At Bergen turn off onto	N1	4 miles	SE	(Nesttun)
07:06	332.5	At Nesttun stay on the	N1	1 mile	SE	
07:08	333.8	Turn left onto	E16	14 miles	E	(Trengereid)
07:22	348.2	At Trengereid stay on the	E16	43 miles	E	(Voss)
08:05	391.2	At Voss stay on the	E16	13 miles	W	(Gudvangen)
08:18	403.8	Bear left onto	N13	33 miles	N	
09:04	436.7	Turn left onto	Ferry	0 miles	W	*Check timetable
09:14	436.7	Turn off onto	N5	22 miles	E	
09:45	458.6	Turn right onto	N55	81 miles	NW	(Lom)
11:40	539.1	At Lom go onto	N15	15 miles	E	(Randen)
12:01	554.0	At Randen stay on the	N15	26 miles	E	(Otta)
12:38	580.3	At Otta turn left onto	E6	29 miles	N	Trondheim
13:07	609.0	At Dombas stay on the	E6	20 miles	E	Trondheim
13:26	628.5	At Hjerkinn stay on the	E6	29 miles	N	Trondheim
13:55	657.6	At Oppdal stay on the	E6	15 miles	E	Trondheim
14:10	672.4	At Ulsberg stay on the	E6	7 miles	NE	Trondheim
14:17	679.4	At Berkak stay on the	E6	18 miles	N	Trondheim
14:34	696.9	At Storen stay on the	E6	23 miles	E	Trondheim
14:57	719.5	At Heimdal stay on the	E6	8 miles	E	
15:05	727.6	Turn right onto	E75	5 miles	E	Trondheim
15:10	732.2	At Trondheim stay on the	E75	17 miles	E	(Stjordal)
15:26	749.1	At Stjordal bear left onto	E6	34 miles	W	(Verdalsora)
16:00	783.3	At Verdalsora stay on the	E6	21 miles	N	(Steinkjer)
16:21	804.2	At Steinkjer stay on the	E6	42 miles	N	(Heia)
17:03	845.7	At Heia stay on the	E6	5 miles	N	(Bergsmo)
17:08	850.6	At Bergsmo stay on the	E6	81 miles	N	(Brenna)
18:28	931.8	At Brenna stay on the	E6	10 miles	NE	(Trofors)
18:38	941.3	At Trofors stay on the	E6	27 miles	N	(Mosjoen)
19:04	967.7	At Mosjoen stay on the	E6	53 miles	E	(Moi Rana)
19:57	1020	At Moi Rana stay on the	E6	66 miles	N	(Junkerdal)
21:03		*** End of day 2, Stop for 1 nights ***				
07:00	1086	At Junkerdal turn left onto	E6	39 miles	NW	(Rosvik)
07:39	1125	Bear left onto	N80	24 miles	W	Bodo
08:12	1149	At Loding stay on the	N80	12 miles	NW	Bodo
08:29	1161	ARRIVE Bodo (N)				

Automap® Pro for Windows © NextBase Ltd.
Digital Mapping © AND Software

It's interesting to note that most towns and route numbers (except for some major cities), as well as the route lines themselves, are *small* on the map *printouts,* using **"Automap Pro,"** but when you see these on the monitor, they appear quite boldly, and all the routes and selected features are in full color. In fact, the routes are color-coded on the screen so that you can instantly identify the stretches that are limited-access freeways, and distinguish them from the lesser highways that might be involved.

HOW TO OBTAIN YOUR OWN
"Automap Pro"
SOFTWARE... FOR $150.00 *LESS* THAN IN 1995!

'Tis passing strange! In a world where things usually tend to increase in price, over time, it's amazing how much the prices continue to *decrease* when it comes to computers, their components, and software. When this Fifth Edition of this Handbook came off the press initially, in early 1995, *"Automap Pro"* software was selling at retail for $249.99. By special arrangement with Automap, Inc., back then, we were able to provide owners of this Handbook with a $100.00 discount, which reduced the software's price to only $149.95.

And *then*... Microsoft Corporation purchased Automap, Inc., and immediately dropped the price all the way down to **$99.95** -- for everyone!

Well, the special discount we were providing is now history, but there's good news and bad news. The good news is the much-improved price, but the bad news is that no further upgrades have been made in the software since Microsoft absorbed Automap, Inc. It's still the *same* software, but by buying it in 1997 (and in the foreseeable future), you are saving between $50 and $150 over the earlier price. It was developed for Windows 3.1 and therefore will run as well on Windows 95. *"Automap Pro"* has never been developed, as yet, however, for Macintosh. Hopefully, that will change sometime soon. Microsoft tells me that it shouldn't be much longer, but as of early 1997, no release date had yet been set. Mac users who'd like this program should therefore check periodically to see when that will be, using the toll-free numbers below.

There are two ways to buy it:

(1) Dial either of *these* numbers: **1-800-360-7561** or **1-800-564-MAPS**. Microsoft will then tell you the best method for obtaining the software.

or

(2) Purchase it directly from your local software retailer, if you know one that carries it.

If you are the owner of a *previous* printing of this Fifth Edition of this Handbook, the above information is *current* as of February, 1997 and you should disregard the ordering data and prices that were provided in the first and second printings.

Finally, these *other*, more specialized, Automap products also exist at this time, and you may wish to investigate their capabilities: (All prices on this page are Microsoft's suggested retail prices.)

Automap Trip Planner 5.0 (for Windows 95) -- $54.95
Automap Streets (for Windows 95) -- $44.95
Automap Road Atlas 2.0 (for Macintosh) -- $39.95
Automap Road Atlas 4.0 (for Windows 3.1) -- $39.95

The "Space Race" of the 1960s catapulted us into the 21st Century at least 10 or 15 years ahead of time, in terms of advancement in science and electronics, and *now* that technology is at your disposal as a Road Rat.

Welcome to the **FUTURE!**

10

$ $ $ $200 to $800 Bonus $ $ $

A *Great* Way to Start Seeing the *WORLD!*

An Invitation

It all started in 1983, back in the gloomy "Evil Empire" era, with the TV movie, "The Day After."

The film was *supposed* to have presented a frighteningly realistic depiction of a nuclear war. It missed the mark. The morning after the *show*, however, I learned from other listeners that *they'd* perceived it as realistic. And that absolutely amazed me! What the movie *had* depicted was a mere stroll through a park during a Sunday school picnic, in comparison to what a nuclear war *really* would entail.

Soon afterward, I began work on a major novel. It was to be a novel that would describe graphically just exactly what *could* be expected in a nuclear war and its aftermath, in all its stark reality. That book has taken longer than 12 years to write... but it's finally approaching completion.

However, one doesn't write a novel that merely depicts a war. A novel worth its salt requires a tightly-woven plot, having good character development and storylines. It is set in both America and Russia, and in order to write it well, I needed to learn a great deal more about Russia and her people.

As you probably already know, I'm sure, *if* (God forbid!) we ever *do* have a nuclear war, it will have nothing to do with the *people* on *either* side. The Russian *people,* I've learned, are at least as uninterested in conflict of any kind -- let alone a nuclear one -- as are we. I know this first-hand, from one-to-one conversations I've had with individual Russians in St. Petersburg, Moscow, Pushkino, Mitishchi, Zagorsk, Perm, Omsk, Novosibirsk, Irkutsk, and many places in between. In other words, from one end of that land to the other, including during multiple visits to Siberia. The sampling of outlooks and aspirations also included Karaganda, in Khazakhstan, and Baku, in Azerbaijan.

The overseas adventure began in 1987, when it wasn't yet "Russia" -- it was still the USSR. And over the span of nine trips to Russia over seven years, I've come to understand more about Russia than I'd ever dreamed I'd learn in my lifetime. And I've come to love the Russian people, who are *far* more like us than you'd ever guess!

When it comes to their interests and their dreams -- and their fears and concerns -- they're almost identical to Americans. But when it comes to their culture, *that* aspect is in many ways far different. Much more diverse than our "melting pot," and *fascinating* to experience.

That much said...

I hereby invite you to join me on my 10th journey to Russia!

If you've ever wanted to take a cruise, or visit Russia, this is a wonderful opportunity to do *both*! During one of my trips a few years ago, I met Eric Stoddard on one of the trans-Atlantic flights. His brother, Mark, owns an American company, International Cruises & Tours, and with his Russian partner, he operates a wide variety of cruises on a modern, privately-owned, beautiful ship. Come travel up and down hundreds of miles of the Volga River!

Doing Russia the Right Way

My next trip to Russia will include a journey on the Alexander Pirogov. I'll travel the beautiful old route of the Tsars instead of the commercial route used by everyone else. The description that follows is provided by ICT:

We have the only privately-owned ship in Russia. One of Russia's largest international oil and manufacturing corporations bought the ship three years ago for its private river yacht. Because they are a joint stock corporation headed by a 48-year-old former deputy minister of communications in the USSR and his partners in Finland and America, they renovated the ship in Finland. It was intended for their private recreational ship and indeed was used as such until this year. They decided they wanted a second ship and bought a new one. They've allowed us to use the ship this year. We hope to extend the lease for years beyond 1997. But come *now* to be the first to enjoy the personal touches.

As part of the renovations, all pipes were removed in Finland and replaced with a complete piping and filtration system. That means this is the only ship in Russia where the sink water is safe to drink! We've had the water tested in the US and no coliforms (a bacteria) were present nor were any parasites.

The Pirogov -- the only small ship experience in Russia. Be the first to enjoy it.

Only 56 Americans and 40 Russians can be aboard, plus one counselor, for every 15-18 Americans -- and 10 entertainers of the highest quality -- more than any other ship.

Because the ship is really more like a river yacht, and the draft is only 4 feet versus 9-15 feet of the larger ships, we can see places no other tourists see. Rather than getting off in all towns where 2,000 tourists hit each day, we'll see the delightful villages of Muishkin, Kineshma, Plyos, Kimry, Chikolov, Nizhni Novgorod, and the incredible Makaryev Monastery and hamlet deep in the woods of the distant Volga lands.

We see all of these Golden Ring cities and villages PLUS Uglitch, Kostroma, Yaroslavl, Moscow, and three nights in St. Petersburg.

If that weren't enough, we've added a special luxury coach tour of Klin and Tchaikovsky's house and museum, Tver, and the ancient capital of Novgorod. No one else offers all of these cities. To get to St. Petersburg they either spend long days just cruising or use the questionable trains, which we will not use -- too boring or too dangerous.

THE SHIP WAS REFURBISHED IN 1995! BUT 1997 IS THE FIRST YEAR FOR INTERNATIONAL PASSENGERS. HERE'S WHAT THEY'VE DONE TO IMPROVE THE SHIP:

They doubled the size of the cabins on the upper deck, making them the largest cabins of any ship in Russia. When you buy the upgrade, you get far more than a higher deck.

They created new tiled bathrooms in each cabin with the only sinks on any ship that have traps and sealed drains preventing sewage odors. Even ships like the *Kirov, Furmonov, Krasin and other 302 or 301* ships have back-up sewer smells. And no other ship has hand-held bedets (which we have in select rooms).

Cabin Layouts and Prices

Cabin H1 – # 201-204
Deluxe Single
- Add $550 p/p
- 7' x 15 ½'
- Nearly same size as standard cabin (H2)

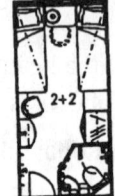

Cabin H2 – # 205-208
Standard Cabin
- Base Price
- 7½' x 15 ½'
- 2 lower and 2 upper berths with full window

Cabin H4 – # 303-306
Junior Suite
- Add $200 per person
- 13' x 11'
- fold-out dbl. sofa bed & 2 Bunks + 2 windows

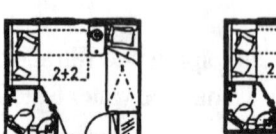

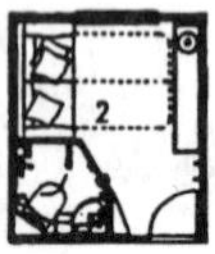

Cabin H5 – # 217, 219, 221, 223
Economy Cabin
- Subtract $100 p/p
- 11' x 9'
- 2 Bunks + fold-out dbl.

Cabin H6 – # 215
Standard Single
- Add $400
- 8' x 9'
- Nearly same size as standard cabin (H2)

Cabin H7 – # 307, 311, 312, 313, 315-317, 320, 322
Deluxe Cabin
- Add $150 p/p
- 11' x 11'
- Two windows

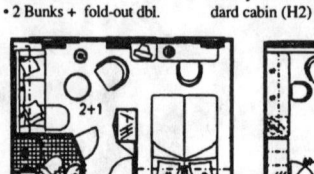

Cabin H8 – # 301, 308
Deluxe Suite
- Add $400 p/p
- 17' x 11½'
- Queen bed and sofa
- Three windows, fridge

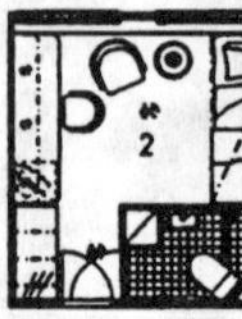

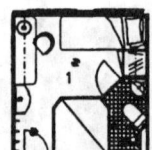

Cabin H9 – # 310, 314
Standard Deluxe
- Add $100 p/p
- 11' x 11'
- 2 Bunks & sleeper couch
- Two windows

Cabin H10 – # 309
Deluxe Large Single
- Add $700 p/p
- 10½' x 11½'
- Two windows
- One single bed

Ship and Map

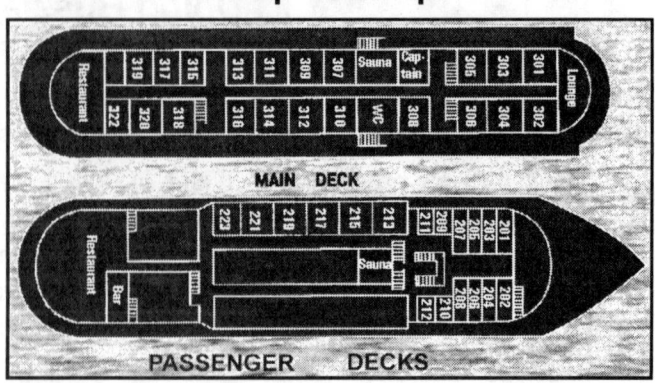

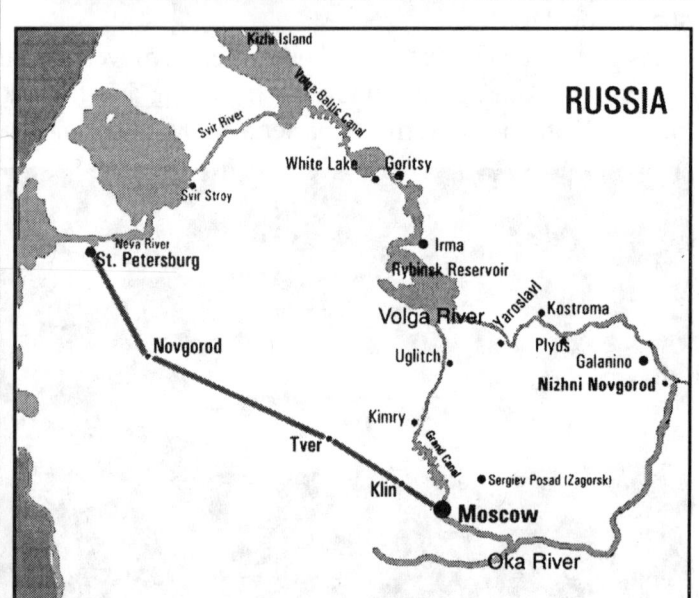

The shower is separate from the toilet. Nearly all other ships have hand-held showers pulled out from the sink.

The ceilings in the rooms are normal height, but the ceilings of the upper deck hallway are nearly 12 feet high and decorated in art deco style with lovely polished light wood, trimmed in polished brass with alternating panels of light green wall paper. Classy.

All rooms have new, Finnish, full-size single beds with thick, proper mattresses. All other ships have narrow beds with 2-inch mattresses.

All rooms also have large, fluffy white towels, a beach towel, real soap, real toilet paper, and real *washcloths!*

The main deck rooms have also been enlarged, and each has a full sofa that can pull out into a double bed so the room can actually accommodate a family of four.

The ship has two dining rooms, two saunas, musical salon, buffet, and bar. It also has for rent a jet ski, a water ski boat, and bicycles.

They put high quality furniture in every room, with brass lights, couches, chairs, etc.

Full 220-volt outlets for hair dryers, camcorders, etc.

A Russian Gift Shoppe with nearly everything you can buy on the streets but at a higher quality and lower price. Our Svetlana is in charge of it and very protective of our clients so they get the best for less.

And last -- but not least -- something that may not seem like a big deal to you. The private corporation we lease the ship through also has four Mercedes and Volvo luxury coaches. That means that, unlike all the other companies that have to petition for buses from the central bus station and take whatever bus driver comes with whatever bus, our luxury coaches have the same bus drivers that will become part of our family.

That is a stark contrast from the way all other tourists are treated. Our same drivers will usually be with us throughout Moscow and St. Petersburg. Leave something on the bus, and the next day you'll have the same bus. That gives us more safety, security, continuity and enjoyment.

Touring Russia Just Got Much, Much Better!!

Our new Russia tour is so safe and so spectacular that we are now throwing the entire weight of our corporate efforts into promoting this unique experience.

Although we've taken more than 10,000 passengers on our ships in Russia since 1990, last year (1996) we swore it would be our last -- too many problems with their corrupt government ship companies and inconsistent-quality meals and buses. Despite being on some of the best ships of the river fleet in Russia, we were unhappy with the quality of the rooms, and being aboard with hundreds of tourists -- it felt like a cattle car. We vowed we'd never return to Russia.

"We enjoyed the cruise more than any we have ever taken. The value is exceptional. We'll recommend this cruise to to our friends."

BUT WORDS ARE MEANT TO BE EATEN when you find a better circumstance. "I just returned from Russia, and I'm excited," said Mark Stoddard, speaking at a college.

"For the first time in Russia I have international partners who understand business and have a long track record of ethical and honest behavior -- and they are NOT government bureaucrats. We are the only company leasing a ship from a private corporation," Stoddard said.

The rest have to go through the corruption-laden Moscow, Volga or St. Petersburg Shipping Companies, relics of the USSR. No one else has anything in the world close to what we're doing in Russia.

Here's Where You'll Visit and Tour:

Moscow -- An old and new capital loaded with museums, galleries, historical buildings from the tsars to communists to modern Russia. You'll be greeted by your counselor who will be with you for the cruise. Go directly to Red Square and the Kremlin for a quick visit to know you're really here. Evening orientation and entertainment. City tours with stops at Red Square, Lenin's Tomb, GUM department store. Then on to the Moscow State University, University Hills and panorama, Bolshoi Theater, Lubianca KGB Building, White House, Embassy Rows, etc. Metro Tour with your counselor. Meet at the new War Memorial for a guided tour. Dinner on the ship and then attend the famed Moscow Circus. Nearly two hours at the Tretikov Art Gallery. Back on the ship, meet the 40 or so Russians who have booked passage aboard our ship. We'll also see Izmailova Park. [*"The greatest adventure of your life!* Beyond your wildest dreams in terms of the quality and beauty of the arts and crafts! This vast, open market has hundreds of vendors, and stretches for more than a mile! Perhaps the greatest evidence of the new, free and democratic nature of Russia! Within each of my last six trips, this has been one of the greatest adventures I've ever experienced!!" ...Craig]

City Tours...

St. Petersburg -- Founded in 1705 by Peter the Great. Full of museums, galleries, historical buildings of the tsars. This is also the city of the famed Hermitage. No picture can capture the beauty and splendor of this museum.

Novgorod -- Ancient capital with fascinating architecture.

Nizhni Novgorod -- Third-largest city in Russia. On the Volga in the Nizhni Novgorod region, considered the most progressive of all cities. Pier is located near the downtown area and a wood-roofed Kremlin.

Tver -- Charming old town and site of famous World War II battles.
Yaroslavl -- Former center of tsarist merchants. About a half-million people with a well-maintained series of parks and esplanades reaching from the pier to the city center. Good shopping with historic churches.
Kostroma -- City markets are just up the stairs with a famous Lenin statue atop a Nicholas II pedestal. Great outdoor museum and monastery where Mikael Romanov was coronated to start the dynasty.
Uglitch -- Small Golden Ring city of 60,000. Famous for kremlin and churches just in front of pier. Where

The Hermitage Museum -- St. Petersburg

Boris Goodonov often came and where young Demitri, son of Ivan the terrible, mysteriously died.
Chikalovsk -- Birthplace of Russia's most famous aviator. Great town for walking around and seeing real Russian life. Due to shallow port, virtually no tourists ever come here. The same is true for the towns listed below.
Kineshma -- Central market is at the pier with lovely esplanade and park nearby. Simple town full of trees.
Muishkin -- Perfect town for visiting the locals. Counselors will take their small groups and meet the people.
Plyos -- Russia's most famous landscape painter, Levitan, moved here for the scenery. Another town perfect for getting into local homes for tea. Nice lagoon with beach for water sports.
Makaryev -- Far away from the world, the dirt road hamlet with a majestic monastery next to the water.
Sosinki -- A forest-land stopping place for a Russian shashlik BBQ.

An Unforgettable Adventure!

Your code word is XANTOUR. Call International Cruises & Tours and ask for the FREE color brochure with full details and itinerary. No obligation! If you do decide to go, *each person* will receive a $200 discount! You do not need to be an owner of this book to qualify. Just *reading* this is sufficient. You may join me, or take a different tour. It makes no difference; you still are entitled to the discount! Please see the additional details on page 329.

This may well be the most unforgettable and wonderful adventure of your life!

PART III
GETTING HOME

ABOUT THIS PART...

You're about to see how a town in Oregon named Junction City provided me with a *genuine* turning point in my life. Geographically, Route 99, going northbound, forks here into Routes 99W and 99E. The first fork goes to Corvallis, and the other goes to Albany. For me, though, the town provided a fork in the road of life's options! I could have simply passed through, or I could have stopped instead to check out a possible opportunity. I opted for the latter -- and instantly *doubled* my income!

You now have reached a turning point in this book, too. I won't pretend that it is nearly as critical as the one I just mentioned, but depending upon how *analytical* you are, you need to be aware of what I'm about to do next.

Returning from runs, you see, is *the single most important component of your Road Rat experience,* when it comes to the amount of money you'll make. Let me put that into different words.

TIP: **The degree to which you are successful as a Road Rat depends *very much* on the method or methods you choose to use when travelling home from your runs, or to pick up other units.**

I originally wrote six *in-depth* chapters on this all-important topic, each of which dealt with a different aspect. Each chapter contained detailed explanations of just WHY each method works the way it does, and produces the outcome(s) described. But with all that detail, the reading became too cumbersome in Chapters 4 and 5.

So here's what I did. I retained the anecdotes, and have provided *briefer* explanations of the methods, and then cited the income you could expect each one to produce. What I *omitted* were the detailed explanations of how those income figures actually were *derived*. The effect was to make both of those chapters shorter, more readable, and more enjoyable.

If you choose to simply go with these summaries, and base your decisions on them, you'll do just fine! (You don't have to be a mechanic to drive a car!) I've provided more than enough solid information in this part to enable you to make *good, well-informed* decisions. But, just in case you'd like to know how I *derived* those conclusions, I've taken the *rest* of the information and put it all into Appendix 2, which I named, "The Technical Stuff." You might consider reading that, in your spare time. It's really *not* that complex, because I've already *done* all the calculations. So reading Appendix 2 can be very helpful to you, in gaining a broader *understanding* of how your income can be enhanced. Chapters 4 and 5 give you the necessary **basics** of their techniques of bus and rail travel, respectively. *Appendix 2* allows you to do some precise and valuable **fine-tuning** of those techniques!

Even if you choose to use Interlock and Maximization, you probably will find times, now and then, when a bus or a train might provide a desirable alternative. Being well-informed by Chapters 4 and 5, *and* by Appendix 2, can prove quite helpful in your decision-making.

Part III --- Getting Home

*Approximately One-Third of All Road Rats
Are People 65 and Over
Who Know that the Best Place for the Rocking Chair
...is in the Trash!*

1

INTERLOCK: The *Round* Trip for Pay!

Interlock, and its high-flying counterpart, *Maxization* (next chapter), are the two KEY elements of achieving success as a Road Rat. You can choose to use *either* of those methods, or you can mix them to your heart's content. Whichever one works best for *you* is fine.

Truckers have their own term for *their* closest equivalent of Interlock -- a "backhaul." If they can fill their trucks with *cargo* for return runs, then that's far preferable to the alternative -- "deadheading" with empty trucks for no revenue. *Especially* for owner-operators.

Road Rats, fortunately, have no such problems. That's why I often joke that "we are on a perpetual vacation with pay, while truckers have to *work* for a living." (That is of course not strictly true, but most of the time, the job of a Road Rat is so easy and hassle-free by comparison, it truly *seems* more like a *hobby!* Truckers who've switched to being Road Rats will be the first to verify that for you! And I've never met anyone yet, in *any* walk of life, who considers his hobby to be "work.")

If you have *not* established a return trip for pay -- an Interlock -- then you simply return home with the money originally allotted for that purpose by your home company, and after you get there you head right outbound again on another paid trip. Doing it that way is not a problem unless you're working for a transporter who provides only minimal funds -- or, as in a few cases, none -- for your return.

TIP: **If you are working directly for a manufacturer who pays you above-average wages -- such that your take-home pay, when all is said and done, is 40 cents per mile or more, then there usually is little point in using the Interlock method.**

In that event, I *would* advise you simply to "Go to Chapter 2. Go *directly* to Chapter 2. Do not pass 'Go' and do not collect $200." **Except** for two things.

1. Not everyone likes to fly, and Maximization involves a lot of that!

2. Now and then, even the busiest manufacturers will have times when they don't have anything going out again immediately upon your return, and at such times there's no need for you to rush back, unless you desire extra time at home. Then, you might choose to use Interlock, and earn more money instead.

Here's How It Works!

You should *always carry this Handbook along* on your trips, for several reasons. To review occasionally, so that the techniques stay fresh in your mind (because there's a little too much info in here to memorize *entirely*.) And to share with other drivers who don't have your advantage. I encourage you to pass these tips on to others, verbally. The purpose of this book is to help people. I ask you to honor my copyright privilege, and not *copy* any of it. But helping people *verbally* is fine! You also may feel free to provide anyone with an order blank from the back of the book, if you think he or she would like to obtain a copy. Or provide our phone number: (319) 234-0676.

The *most* important reason for routinely carrying this book along, just as you would a road atlas, is for the purpose of setting up Interlocks -- either regularly, or as you desire them. In order to establish an Interlock with a company, you first need to know how to make *contact* with it. And that's where the Appendix 1 listings come in.

When you first learn your destination for a run that's provided by your home company, you can begin the process of establishing an Interlock for your return. It is especially helpful if you happen to learn where you're going a day or two ahead of your departure, because then you can make the calls before you even leave home. With luck, you'll have your return trip lined up before you head out!

More typically, though, you'll learn about your new trip on pretty short notice, and then depart right away, or immediately upon your return from the previous trip. In that event, you'll probably have to make your calls from pay phones en route. (If you're on a trip across two or three time zones, be aware of the time in your *destination* zone when you call. It'll save you money on toll calls to NOT get recorded messages that say, "This is company XYZ. We're *closed* now, but our hours are...")

Next, when you make the call, be prepared to furnish your prospective Interlock dispatcher with your estimated time of arrival (ETA). In order to establish the Interlock, it is **very important** for *that* dispatcher to know *when* he can expect you to arrive to pick up the vehicle. (And if your ETA *changes* while you're en route, and you *already* have set up an Interlock, be **sure** to *call* that dispatcher to give him the *new* ETA. Do this *as soon as you know!)*

By now, you're probably wondering why someone on the opposite coast who doesn't know you from Adam (or Eve) would consider entrusting you with the delivery of one of his brand-new and expensive vehicles. Well, the fact is, he wouldn't -- *except* for the fact that you *already* are an *active* Road Rat. (*Inactive* Road Rats don't do Interlocks because an Interlock, by definition, is a *return* run for pay -- or a run to a *third* point. So we don't need to explore that. The fact that you're active is an established fact, if you're seeking an *Interlock.) As* an active Road Rat, you already *have* a dispatcher who is entrusting you to deliver vehicles. And the dispatcher at your home company therefore needs to *know* if you plan to set up Interlocks. That's because there's about a 98% chance that the dispatcher who *doesn't* know you, at your potential Interlock site, probably will want to call your *home* dispatcher to *verify* your claim to be a safe, currently-employed Road Rat looking for a return trip. (So don't let your plan to establish Interlocks come as a *surprise* to your home dispatcher!)

Do *all* dispatchers support their Road Rats' desire to do Interlock runs? Let's put it this way. I was *astonished* when I once learned of an isolated case at the plant of an RV manufacturer in central Kansas. He told me, "If one of *my* drivers does that, then he keeps on working for the other man." But you don't have to worry about running across *him;* his company went belly-up in 1990 or thereabouts. To be safe, though, and as a courtesy to your employer, always *verify* that it's OK -- but practically all dispatchers of *motorized* RVs and specialty vehicles are supportive of this method. After all, they have nothing to lose and everything to gain. Road Rats who routinely set up Interlocks make more money, and therefore are *more stable, content, and happy* than ones who have to scrape by. And unless they want you to fly right back to them each time at company expense (which is Maximization), then it won't take you very much longer to return to them via the Interlock method than it would if you took the bus or the train. (It should be noted, though, that if they pay you well enough for Maximization to be financially attractive, then you're probably pretty content already.) There is just one very noteworthy *exception* to all of this, and that's for many of the drivers who deliver new *trailers* behind company-owned tow units -- and even for many who use their *own* trucks for this, as startling as *that* may seem! An explanation of this is provided in Question No. 11, at the top of page 158.

The 5 Types of Interlock

1. *Open-Jaw* Interlock

This is an Interlock wherein a substantial *distance* separates your *destination* from the *origin site* of your return/continuing (Interlock) run. It can vary widely from one run to another if you have *no* Interlock sites established that *regularly* provide you with runs. Bear in mind that the farther you have to go to pick up your Interlock unit, the more your time and transportation-cost factors will increase. Unless your Interlock point is providing you with a pretty lucrative run, or is sending you to a point very close to your home base, it *might* be more cost-effective to simply return home immediately and take another trip from your home-base company. But then again, it might *not*. Read on.

Another variation of the "Open Jaw" variety is when your destination points and Interlock sites are close together, but then the *Interlock* company sends you off to a destination that's nowhere near your home base.

A *worst*-case scenario is a combination of *both* of these, which I call a "Dislocated Jaw Interlock."

A. **"Outbound Open Jaw Interlock"** -- (Bus or plane needed to reach *Interlock site*) --

In this example, a Road Rat is sent from Elkhart, Indiana to Los Angeles. He then takes a bus to San Francisco to obtain his Interlock Unit for the return. The Interlock is delivered a short distance from Elkhart, in South Bend, Indiana. (Quite acceptable in terms of profit, even though not as ideal as having destination and Interlock site close together..)

B. **"Inbound Open Jaw Interlock"** -- (Public transportation needed to go *home* from Interlock destination) --

The Indiana-based Road Rat gets to L.A., and then picks up a unit in nearby San Bernardino, California. He delivers *it* to Erie, Pennsylvania, after overshooting Elkhart by almost 350 miles. (This too, is probably quite acceptable. And *both* cases "A" and "B" are **definitely** acceptable and **very desirable** if the Interlock sites happen to be *manufacturers* in each case who are giving you take-home pay of 35 cents or so per mile.)

C. **"Dislocated Jaw Interlock"** - (Public transportation needed *twice* before getting home) --

Road Rat is sent to L.A., and then goes to San Francisco by bus to pick up an Interlock unit -- and **it** then gets delivered to Erie. (This is acceptable, but would be even *more* acceptable if the Road Rat were working for a transporter company in Elkhart, but again, was making the *Interlock* run for a manufacturer at twice the earnings per mile. That would *surely* offset any extra expense and inconvenience.)

In each of these examples, the Road Rat would have to weigh the total value of the time and money involved in making these runs, *vis-a-vis* the benefit he would accrue simply by returning straight home to get another run. A lot would seem to depend upon whether or not his home base company was a transporter or a manufacturer, and the type of company on the Interlock end, and *its* pay scale.

If faced with this situation, you also must ask yourself these questions: "Does the pay provided by the Interlock company include return travel expense money that I can *keep*, even though I'm not returning to it?" And, "Does my own company have that same policy?" An answer of yes to one or both of those questions can make Open Jaw Interlocks quite profitable -- even in the case of a Dislocated Jaw one.

Just don't go overboard and assume a long return run *always* will be profitable, no matter what. Each case must be evaluated on its own merits. For example, isn't it *likely* that if the Interlock site used in the above examples were to be in *Seattle,* and that the unit they gave you to deliver were to be going clear down to *New Orleans,* 1,000 miles from home, that *that* would be *unprofitable?*

If you automatically assumed that the paragraph above, that you *just* read, was probably *correct*, and that such a run *likely* WOULD be unprofitable, then you must be prepared to analyze things more deeply. Let's consider these possibilities pertaining to this case:

----   Your home base company is a transporter, and it pays you 38 cents a mile, out of which you take your fuel cost and your return transportation, and keep what's left over. The distance is 2,100 miles, the fuel to L.A. costs $309.48 (based on an 8 mpg vehicle and an average gasoline price of $1.17^9/gal.), which leaves you with $488.52. If you take the bus *home* at that point, you'll have been gone a total of 6 days, and your earnings will be very close to $300. For your efforts, you cleared $50 per day, before taxes. (If you were to spend **50 weeks a year** on the road **at that rate of pay, you'd earn $17,500 per year.**)

----   Or... the other factors still pertain, but *this* time you *don't* go right home. You take the bus to Seattle, *instead.* When you arrive, you still have $350 remaining.

----   The company in Seattle is a manufacturer, and they're paying you 55 cents per mile to deliver their unit to New Orleans. Out of that, you must take your fuel and return transportation, and then get to keep whatever remains. The distance is 2,200 miles, and *that* unit *also* gets 8 mpg. So the fuel costs you $324.23. You've eaten up $30 in meals from that *other* $350, so you now have $320 of *it* left -- along with $885.77 from the money given to you by the company in Seattle.

----   After delivering the unit in New Orleans, you head home to Elkhart by bus. The ticket and the meals you eat en route require another $150 of your funds. If you took that from the $320 that was left from your home company's pay, then you arrive home with the $885.77 that remained from the Interlock run still intact, plus $170 from your original run, for a *total profit* of $1,055.77. The whole odyssey kept you on the road for a total of ten days. For your efforts, you cleared $105.58 per day, before taxes. (If you were to spend **50 weeks a year** on the road **at that rate of pay, you'd earn $36,950 per year.**)

There you have it. **A valuable lesson to remember:** If working for a transporter company, almost *any* Interlock you set up will be profitable -- no matter how outlandish the connections might seem -- if the result is your being paid for a long run that is provided by *a well-paying manufacturer!*

TIP: DON'T *limit* yourself geographically! Always consider ALL your options!!

You must be wondering at this point what the result would have been for the same *combination* of runs, holding all *factors* the same, with the only difference being that the Interlock site in Seattle were a *transporter* paying at the same rate as your home base company. Well... in *that* case, you would have earned at the rate of $53 per day **(an annual rate, for 50 weeks on the road, of $18,550.)** You see, all is not really as it seems. Even the most outlandish, nutty-sounding combinations of runs, which you might assume at first would just *have* to be unprofitable... may in reality be just the *opposite!*

2. *Semi-Permanent* Interlock

This is as close to ideal as Interlock can get. I call it "semi"-permanent because nothing is truly permanent... and even while employing this method, some individual runs will probably come along that would cause you to opt for another method. For example, suppose that you were working in Indiana, had a run to California, and were assured you could have an Interlock run back from there. Only problem is, you've learned that if you were to *fly* back from this *particular* run, your *next* run would be to Alaska. And that if you *didn't* fly home, a *different* driver would get the coveted Alaska run that you *could* have had. In such a circumstance, you might pass up the Interlock run!

Or consider this. You have a situation where your company will send you from Indiana to California regularly, but then a *Florida* run comes along, and it is offered to you. If you take it, there's no certainty that you'll have an Interlock, because Florida isn't in your normal routine. But it *does* represent a pleasant change of pace, and you have family down there. So this time, you go for it.

Those are examples of why this Interlock is called *semi*-permanent. But when it's in action, *this* is how it works...

Ask your company if they have regular customers in a destination area or region to which you may be sent with frequency. Then make contacts in *that* region to see if a company *there* can likewise send you regularly back to your home area. It may be possible for you to set this up rapidly on your first attempt, just as I did (through sheer good fortune), or the process may take you a few weeks. But in the end, it is well worth it!

Here's how I set up a highly-profitable Semi-Permanent Interlock up and down the West Coast:

Remember "The West Coast Gambit," -- in which told you on pages 19 and 20 how I first started working for a transporter company in California? Well, it was some weeks later, while working for that company, that I happened to be making a run to an RV dealer in Corvallis, Oregon. I had made many trips by then to points in Washington and Oregon, but generally had remained on I-5. To go to Corvallis from the south, however, it is easiest to get off the interstate at Eugene, and proceed north on Route 99... and *that* took me through Junction City... which I *then* discovered was a major RV manufacturing center. Upon spotting the factories, it dawned on me (at last!) to stop in and inquire about the possibility of driving one of theirs back *south,* after making my delivery just 30 miles away.

At this point it's good to remember that I'd been delivering RVs at a steady pace for less than a year, and had been concentrating entirely on learning techniques in conjunction with that activity, for just one company at a time. The first edition of this Handbook was a year in the future, so I was still winging it completely on my own. (You'll get a chuckle out of this. After I finally researched and *wrote* that book, I then used it *myself,* to set up my *own* Interlocks!)

But *this* was the day that, for me at least, "Interlock" was born.

I parked the RV I was delivering directly in front of the office of the first manufacturer I spotted in Junction City, "Country Coach." (In those days, it was still known as "Country Camper.") Inside, I soon was talking with the vice president. I pointed out the window at the coach, told him that I was about to deliver it to a Corvallis dealer, and asked if he had anything he'd like for me to drive back south. And he said yes. And the whole thing took less than one minute!

Upon getting back to that manufacturer in the afternoon, following the delivery, I was provided with a Class "C" RV to be delivered in Beaumont, California (about 15 miles from my transporter-company base in San Bernardino).

I'm not sure where I actually *lived* for the 6 months that followed. *Technically,* I guess home was the sleeping room I'd rented in 1977 in Decatur, Indiana, although while on the West Coast I worked completely out of suitcases, and never even saw the Midwest or East from June through December, 1978. It was a rapid-fire whirlwind of trips up and down the West Coast for my two companies there -- with a few trips to Alaska thrown in. I was one very *busy* Road Rat -- but it was great fun, and more lucrative than ever before!

You see, the transporter company in California provided me with average take-home pay of about $180 for each trip *north*. "Country Camper" paid me, on average, take-home pay of $250 for each trip *south*. (*This* was my revelation that manufacturers, not being middlemen, pay substantially more. *Before* then, I'd been totally unaware that manufacturers ever employed their own drivers directly!) And I had almost no public transportation expense. I stopped using *Greyhound* **Ameripasses** immediately at that point, and suddenly found myself earning almost *$800* a week! My income had more than doubled, *literally* overnight!

So when the first edition of this book came off the press in 1979, the income figure in its title (which I've never yet changed) reflected my *total* **actual** *income for 1978* -- including the first six months of that year, when I had *not* yet discovered Interlock.

Think about that for a minute. If I *hadn't* discovered Interlock until 1979, this book probably would have been titled, *How to Get Paid* **$17,000** *a Year...* -- and if I'd discovered it six months *earlier,* the book almost surely would have been entitled, *How to Get Paid* **$38,000** *a Year...* ! What a **difference** can be made by just implementing this simple technique!!

Semi-Permanent Interlock (or SPI, for short) can be done in three ways. We just saw how it works when one has a transporter company on one end, and a manufacturer on the other. It would of course be less profitable if both companies were transporters, and substantially more profitable if both were manufacturers. But we can get a better picture of this by looking at the tables that follow.

How Take-Home Pay Compares, Transporters vs. Manufacturers, For a 1,000-Mile Run: 1978 and 1994

Typical take-home pay per run, before taxes, is shown two ways:
For the *non*-Interlock driver who uses *public surface transportation* for return trips, and for the *Interlock*-utilizing driver, who incurs *little or no* such costs.

KEY
WTC -- *With* Return Surface Public Transportation Costs (*No* Interlock used.)
W/O TC -- *Without* Return Surface Transportation Costs (Interlock used.)

	1978 WTC	1978 W/O TC	1994 WTC	1994 W/O TC
Transporter Company --	$110	$180	$160	$230
Manufacturer --	$180	$250	$330	$400

=============================

Realistic Annual Earnings Comparison for *Moderate Circadian* Road Rats *Not* using Interlock, and for the Same, *Using* SPI

(For Companies Routinely Providing 1,000-mile-long Runs)
This table assumes that a "Moderate Circadian" *non*-Interlock driver averages 2-1/2 runs per week, and that a "Moderate Circadian" driver *using* SPI averages 3 runs per week, long-term.
(Example Assumes 50 Weeks of Work per Year)

Situation		In 1978	In 1994
A.	Transporter Co. (No Interlock)	-- $13,750	$20,000
B.	Manufacturer (No Interlock or Maximization)	-- $22,500	$40,500
C.	Trans. Co./Mfr. SPI (the example described)	-- $32,250	$47,250
D.	Trans. Co./Trans Co. SPI	-- $27,000	$34,500
E.	Mfr./Mfr. SPI	-- $37,500	$60,000

Realistic Annual Earnings Comparison for *Safe Go-Getter* Road Rats *Not* using Interlock, and for the Same, *Using* SPI

(For Companies Routinely Providing 1,000-mile-long Runs)
This table assumes that a "Safe Go-Getter" *non*-Interlock driver averages 3 runs per week, and that a "Safe Go-Getter" driver *using* SPI averages 3-1/2 runs per week, long-term.
(Example Assumes 50 Weeks of Work per Year)

Situation		In 1978	In 1994
A.	Transporter Co. (No Interlock)	-- $16,500	$24,000
B.	Manufacturer (No Interlock or Maximization)	-- $27,500	$39,750
C.	Trans. Co./Mfr. SPI (the example described)	-- $37,625	$55,125
D.	Trans. Co./Trans Co. SPI	-- $31,500	$40,250
E.	Mfr./Mfr. SPI	-- $43,750	$70,000

Realistic Annual Earnings Comparison for *Easy-Goin'* Road Rats *Not* using Interlock, and for the Same, *Using* SPI

(For Companies Routinely Providing 1,000-mile-long Runs)
This table assumes that an "Easy-Goin'" *non*-Interlock driver averages 1-1/2 runs per week, and that an "Easy-Goin'" driver *using* SPI averages 2-1/4 runs per week, long term.
(Even though the "Easy-Goin' Road Rat" probably would *choose* to work fewer weeks than the others, for purposes of comparison, this example assumes 50 weeks of work per year.)

Situation		In 1978	In 1994
A.	Transporter Co. (No Interlock)	-- $ 8,250	$12,000
B.	Manufacturer (No Interlock or Maximization)	-- $13,500	$24,750
C.	Trans. Co./Mfr. SPI (the example described)	-- $24,200	$35,450
D.	Trans. Co./Trans Co. SPI	-- $20,250	$25,875
E.	Mfr./Mfr. SPI	-- $28,125	$45,000

"Moderate Circadians" probably make up 30% of the Road Rat workforce. "Safe Go-Getters" are in the majority, at 60%, (and that's my own category). The remaining 10% are "Easy-Goin'." You'll find retirees in all three, in case you wondered! All three styles are *defined* on pages 95 and 96, and you should familiarize yourself with those criteria before studying the tables on the previous page.

By this time, you're well aware that I encourage *versatility*. The *more you are open* to the vast spectrum of possibilities that are out there -- and the *less you limit yourself geographically* -- the more you can earn, and the more fun you can have in this job. So don't overlook the possibility of establishing an **"Open-Jaw Semi-Permanent Interlock!"**

Does that sound complicated? It really isn't. An "Open-Jaw" Interlock that *isn't* "Semi-Permanent" is much *more* complicated, because you have to *seek* it each time. Whereas a Semi-Permanent Interlock of *any* type is, by definition, one that you *already* have established and do regularly. This one simply happens to have the "open-jaw" *characteristic!*

Here's an example.

Suppose you live in Columbus, Ohio, and your company has a major customer in Denver to whom they ship all the time. They can feed you a steady diet of Denver runs! Meanwhile, by using this Handbook, you set yourself up with a California company that has regular customers in central Ohio and Indiana, and *they* can assure you a steady diet of runs to your home region. It's a great situation! You simply hop over to California from Denver after each delivery there, by plane, train, or bus, and pick up a unit that'll send you home again for pay. It's sure to be lucrative, and, depending upon the companies involved, it can be *highly*-lucrative. (**HINT:** If something like this develops for you, be sure to study the *next* chapter *well*. It can be *especially* helpful to you!)

3. *Trailer-Delivery* Interlock

Consider everything we've just discussed, and then think of the *thousands* of trailer manufacturers that are out there. If you have your *own* tow unit -- which can be a heavy-duty pickup truck that is equipped with a trailer hitch capable of towing large trailers, and a mini-fifth-wheel assembly, you can employ all of these methods. Let the companies know your capabilities, and work out the pay rates with them. And you're off and running!! (**IMPORTANT:** See *also* the top of page 158.)

4. *Criss-Cross* Interlock

This one's really great if you live in a region where there is little Road Rat opportunity, such as Battle Mountain, Nevada. You establish your Interlocks on *either side* of you, such that your trips take you back and forth *through* your home town. In the Battle Mountain example, you might have one employer in Sacramento, and the other in Indiana. Because you'll be *en route* when you see home, you'll be unable to spend very much time there, each time. But you'll get home *often,* and if the Interlock points are far enough apart, you easily could spend 24 hours or more there -- each time!

5. *Continental* Interlock

The Road Rat who employs *this* form of Interlock has the right to feel at home whereever he goes! In Chapter 3 of this part, we'll discuss *in depth* the techniques that are regularly used by a genuine **expert** in Continental Interlock. *This* is just a very *brief overview* of it.

In earlier editions of this Handbook, I had speculated on Continental Interlock, and offered suggestions as to how it might be practiced. However, in my 17 years of full-time and part-time esperience, I have never yet done this personally, and it was only after the last edition was already out (the "1991-92" one, which actually went through 1994) that I finally started hearing from some Road Rats who were successfully *doing* it! It is most certainly being *done,* but only a tiny handful of Road Rats are involved. Perhaps merely a few dozen, or even less! This is a *wide-open method,* chock-full of opportunity!

For now, I'll just tell you that Continental Interlock, in which the Road Rat travels almost at random, all over the map, working for many companies, is for those who would love to be paid to roam the whole continent at will. It works *best* if you can be away from your home base for weeks, and even months, at a time. And I'll also tell you that the companies for whom they work generally involve both of the main types who *ship* new vehicles -- transporters and manufacturers. It's not for everyone. But the people with whom I've spoken absolutely *love* being Continental Interlock Road Rats! *Especially* the one about whom you'll learn, starting on page 133.

Road Rats Roam America's Wonderlands at will!
Canada's, too! And even those of Australia and Europe!!

2
MAXIMIZATION: For Those Who LOVE to FLY!

This chapter is for the millions of us who love to *FLY!*

Dealers and manufacturers generally have some provision for return transportation in the cash disbursement structure (either within expense money provided in advance, or within the combined expenses-salary payment to the driver), which absorbs the cost of a return airline ticket. Transporter companies usually contract using the latter method. But at typical transporter-company pay of only around 38-44 cents/mile *(total)*, returning by air becomes prohibitively expensive for most such drivers.

For that reason, routine returns by air are seldom seldom, if ever, made by drivers who work *solely* for transporter companies. The transporters can't pay enough to make it worthwhile on a regular basis. **Transporter company** drivers fly *primarily* only at such times that an excellent fare opportunity comes along -- but there are three primary **exceptions:**

1. The Road Rat who happens to be working at it *part*-time, and has his *full*-time job with an *airline.* That actually happens! Many airline employees have learned about this job, and do it on days off, or during their vacations, and thereby are able to return either free of charge, or at an incredibly-low rate. When such a Road Rat works for a company that either allows him to keep the return transportation money, or else provides that as part of the pay, this becomes an *extremely* lucrative part-time job for those who have reduced-fare or no-fare flight privileges. Even if the work is done for a transporter!

2. A *retiree* who has a good pension, or lives well on his social security, and simply wants to travel, with little or no concern for earnings. (Make no mistake -- *thousands* of Road Rats now fit this category, and enjoy doing this immensely, whether pursuing it full-time, part-time, or just occasionally.) Please refer **NOW** to page 337 before continuing. Valuable information!

   Think about this scenario. A retiree is at the age where his social security payments would be reduced if he were to earn too much money. He has two choices: (A) Earn more money, and not worry about the attendant reduction of social security income if he crosses the threshold. Many choose to do it just that way, but in that case it's probably better if they can work for a maufacturer or a dealer. (B) Keep the earnings down, and receive the maximum social security payments to which he's entitled. If he chooses to do this, then he must *decide* whether to travel just a *few* times a year at a *high* rate of pay, as he would receive from a manufacturer or dealer -- or travel *much* of the time for *less* pay, and thereby be able to have the time of his life roaming the continent much more *actively*, for a transporter company.

   TIP: **A retiree who is required to limit his income in order to receive full Social Security benefits can be fully active for a *transporter,* and/or spend his excess *would-be* profits as trip *expenses* -- and stay below that limit!**

   By this time, you probably see why I'm so kindly-disposed toward transporters. Equally so, as I am to all the others who utilize Road Rats. The transporter companies provide some pretty special opportunities for many thousands of people, even though they are constrained to pay less. In this case, we see that being paid less actually can *benefit* the Road Rat!

A few words now about the *second* part of that tip I just gave you. *Unless* a retiree between the ages of 62 and 70 (thus is subject to reduced Social Security income if earnings thresholds are crossed) would seek good earnings *in trade* for some *loss* of benefits, he might decide **instead** to *purposely* spend so *much* on *legitimate expenses* **while** on trips that he'd remain below the threshold for social security curtailments even if working full-time for a well-paying company! To accomplish this, all he has to do is *stay in motels at his own expense while driving RVs,* or stay in *more* expensive ones than the company covers with expense money when driving *other* vehicles. Or buy more expensive meals. He can even go to the extreme of buying *higher-class* plane tickets if need be, to reduce his take-home profits. These travel-related expenses are tax-deductible in almost all cases, and spending his potential profits so wildly on legitimate *expenses* can enable him to travel to his heart's content without crossing the social security-reduction cut-off! (This probably sounds crazy to many of you, but if you already have a *comfortable* retirement income, and your main *objective* is to explore North America on someone else's nickel while living the life of Riley... why not??)

3. The Road Rat about whom you'll learn shortly, in Chapter 3 of this Part. The possession of a Class "A" CDL puts a driver in such demand, he actually is flown with frequency at company expense to sites all over the country where transporters need them to pick up larger or unusual vehicles. But he needs to network, and be enterprising. You'll learn all about it.

Okay, then, let's move on to drivers who *don't* have special circumstances like those described above, and who deliver vehicles for **manufacturers and dealers.**

Most manufacturers and dealers pay roughly twice as well as do the transporter companies. Based on samplings taken with care, probably around 90% of the manufacturers and dealers in the USA and Canada who use their own drivers pay right around 30-35 cents per mile to those drivers, *plus* the road and return transportation expenses. The remaining 10% are statistical "outliers" who pay either more or less than that amount. So figure that air transportation for your return trips is a viable option when driving for perhaps 95% of all the existing manufacturers and dealers that hire drivers directly.

If you work for such a company, you probably will employ the techniques of Interlock *and* Maximization in *combination,* or Maximization only. Interlocks normally cannot be established 100% of the time. Even Road Rats who have established Semi-Permanent Interlocks will occasionally fly back because there will be times when the Interlock company simply doesn't *have* anything going the way the driver wants to go, at the time he needs the run. A skilled Road Rat, armed with the resources of this Handbook, can usually achieve around 75% success in setting up Interlocks for his returns, *case-by-case.* The rate is much higher, of course, in the case of a Semi-Permanent Interlock.

DEFINITION: ***Maximization* means that the driver MAXIMIZES his *availability* to a company by returning the fastest way possible. It is the method drivers most frequently prefer to employ. For the runs longer than 400-500 miles, the air return option almost always is provided or preferred.**

By now, you've probably seen an underlying theme in this book: you probably will never get *rich* working *solely* as a Road Rat ... but you may find that the Road Rat lifestyle can be a **GATEWAY** to a more lucrative lifestyle simply because the *extra freedom* provides you more *flexibility,* and *free time,* as you need it, to *plan and to explore other avenues.* However... if you work for a company that pays all your expenses *plus* an income of between 40 and 70 cents per mile, then you can make a *very* comfortable living by concentrating on your *driving* efforts in their behalf. (Yes... a few of those companies in the highest 5% in terms of pay, actually *do* pay 70 cents or more per mile! *Phenomenal!!* I'll bet *those* companies don't see too much turnover, though. What driver in his right mind would ever want to *leave* them?!)

Working at an average wage of around 38 cents/mile (after expenses) for one company from late 1979 through 1985, my own take-home pay before taxes averaged $1,000/week, or $52,000/year. Those were the years during which I worked full-time, except for occasional time off now and then at home, at destinations, or at selected en-route stopovers. Because the pay was good, and my dispatcher kept me as busy as I wanted to be, I employed *Maximization* almost exclusively throughout that 6-year period. (Lest you think that the phrase, "before taxes," is to glorify the salary figure, remember that whenever people compare salaries, they *always* refer to the figure they earn *before* taxes. Just as we always see the prices on goods in stores set at the amount they cost *before* sales tax is applied -- unless you're lucky enough to live in **AK, DE, MT, NH,** or **OR,** which have the distinction of being the only states whose legislators have consistently retained sufficient intelligence to *reject* that notion.

$$ TIP: **The majority of Road Rats see one or more of those sales-tax-free states with frequency. When you *do,* purchase *all* your clothes, and easily-transportable big-ticket items *there!* A great way to do all your *Christmas* shopping, too!**

Remember this slogan? "Dance with the one who loves you!" Sales tax-wise, *those* are the states that love you. Support *their* businesses, and save yourself *hundreds of dollars,* over time!

The Fabulous Fringe Benefit --
Being a "Frequent Flier"

Most Road Rats are independent contractors, rather than direct employees. If *you* are in that category you probably will have to devise your own standard fringe benefits (such as health insurance, IRAs, etc.) or else do without them. However, manufacturers and dealers who keep you constantly busy probably will pay you well enough to enable you to set up your *own* plan of benefits. Nevertheless, *Maximization* carries a very *special* fringe benefit of its own... *frequent flier points!*

The Road Rat lifestyle gives you your chosen continent to explore at will, but *Maximization* can give you the remainder of the *planet!* I've been to countries all over the world on frequent flier points that I've earned on return flights to my company from destination cities.

North America and Australia are vast continents; a run 3,000 miles long is possible on the continent Down Under, and you can drive over 5,000 miles in North America in one direction. (Examples of the latter: (1) A run from any west coast U.S. or Canadian city to St. John's, Newfoundland; (2) a run from the East Coast to any location in central Alaska.) Therefore, with a mix of short returns and long ones, it is possible to rack up incredible quantities of frequent flier miles over a surprisingly short period of time. (Europeans will probably find Maximization by *air* more difficult. For them, the *Interail Pass, Britrail Pass,* or a similar rail method may be the best way to return -- or else they can concentrate on using the *Interlock* system, as described in the previous chapter.)

In order to maximize this valuable fringe benefit, which frequently is the *only* earnings-related one available to independent-contractor drivers, it is important for you to *select* the airline(s) you use with care. Questions you need to ask include these KEY ones:

-- Is the airline financially stable? If it goes belly-up, you'll probably lose all the points you've earned from them! This happened to me when *Braniff* first folded; I was within a scant *three weeks* of taking my first-*ever* trip to London -- with *them*. As a result, my first trip to Europe was taken *years* later, instead. *Texas International,* with its wondrous "Peanut Fares" and easy-to-earn free tickets, is just a memory now. And both *Eastern* and *Pan-Am*, airlines that were around for 60 and more years, have joined their ancient "ancestor," the pterodactyl. So evaluate this factor carefully.

-- How easy is it to earn a ticket? If you have to rack up 150,000 miles, one *actual* mile flown at a time, just to earn a free transcontinental round trip, I'd suggest that you look farther. That number of actual miles flown would require you to make the equivalent of FIFTY *coast-to-coast* flights in order to earn just *one* free ticket for a round-trip of that distance. At least one airline is even *worse* than that!!

-- How frequently can you *fly* the airline? Give your strongest consideration to an airline which generally can be used for returns from *most* of the destination cities you will see. If you can't use the airline *regularly*, it will do you little if any good in terms of frequent flier miles. Before enrolling in a frequent flier program, check with your dispatcher to determine which cities normally are destinations for your company. All companies have certain regular customers which are served with frequency. Pick a stable airline that links as many of those cities as possible with your company's city.

Now, once you've started collecting your frequent flier miles, it is VERY important that you avoid being lured into the progam's **pitfalls!** For instance, most airlines allow you to obtain their frequent flier miles by staying in big-name, ritzy hotels. You know, the multi-story ones that you see at the edges of major airports? Some deal. You pay $75 to $125 or *more* per night, just to earn an extra 1,000 frequent flier miles.

$$ TIP: *AVOID* **the fancy-shmancy hotels and SAVE your money.** A thousand frequent flier miles are worth only $20-25, *tops*, in terms of ticket-purchasing capability. AND -- don't get schnookered into staying at an overpriced hotel just because your airline happens to "generously" provide you with a coupon good for a *discount* at it, when you redeem some of your frequent flier miles. It often will accompany the voucher for your free ticket. Chances are, that discount coupon would probably reduce the cost of your stay to about DOUBLE or TRIPLE what you would pay for good economy lodging elsewhere -- instead of the *normal* QUADRUPLE. **Exception:** If you stay in such places from time to time in order to **purposely** interdict some of your Road Rat profits, so that you can stay below the threshold for Social Security benefit reductions, this may be one of the *better* ways to accomplish that. **In the USA, this applies to Social Security recipients under age 70.**

According to Randy Peterson, publisher of *Inside Flyer* magazine, car-rental agencies, hotels, long-distance phone companies, etc. who provide frequent flyer miles as a perk to their consumers *pay the airlines* between 1 and 2 cents per mile for the miles awarded. This cash flow to the airlines is one of the factors that keep frequent-flier programs profitable.

A monthly magazine, *Worth*, had the following cover story in May, 1994: "The Frequent Flier Rip-Off... What's an Airline Mile Really worth?" It was written by Jeff Blyskal, who leads it off by asking this question: "Would so many travellers go to so much bother to earn airline mileage if they knew what a mile was really worth?" According to the article, flying a passenger free of charge in a seat that otherwise would have been empty actually *costs* an airline only *$48* -- in terms of jet fuel, the meal, and other factors. Frequent flier programs are absolutely wonderful for airlines and their *partners* (*i.e,* hotel, car rental agencies, phone companies, etc. who offer their frequent flier miles). What I want to do in this Handbook is *ensure* that they additionally are absolutely wonderful for YOU, too!

You SHOULD earn frequent flier miles. BUT -- you need to earn them in a *sensible* manner, so as to *avoid* the "rip-off" aspects. You already know how to avoid the *hotel* one. Here are some more:

1. **If** you're flying on an airline that allows you to earn extra miles in their program by renting a car from an agency that is known for being *reasonably-priced,* AND **if** you *need* such a car, then go for it! But keep these cautionary notes in mind when you do:

    A. *Avoid* the biggest-name agencies. If they have the resources to spend *millions* on super-expensive TV commercials that run *frequently,* guess where they GET the money!

    B. Be sure to give the rental agent your frequent-flier number *before* signing the rental agreement, to ensure that you will be awarded the miles. If he forgets, and you have to try to get those miles after the fact, it can be a big hassle, or even prove impossible. Remember, too, that those points usually are available only if the car rental is in *conjunction* with a *current* flight on the airline. The car rental agent probably will ask to see the ticket for your incoming or departing flight. Book the car in advance, and go for their least-expensive, compact model. Chances are good that they may be out of that size when you get there, in which case you'll be offered an upgrade to a nicer one at no charge. If try to charge you *extra* for that, *call* them on it!

    C. Don't go off the deep end on this! In his article, Jeff cites the example of a businessman who, instead of taking a taxi or limo from O'Hare to downtown Chicago, elects instead to *rent a car* for that purpose at the airport, *turn it in* downtown, and then rent *another* car downtown for his return trip to the airport. Somebody's nuttier than a fruitcake, here. And it's either the company for whom that businessman works, or it's *him!* Frequent flier points just aren't WORTH that kind of time, aggravation, and expense! (Don't forget, too, that it is now possible to ride a rapid-transit train from O'Hare to the Loop for only *$1.50!!* THAT'S the *logical* way to get back and forth in Chicago!)

2. Never, EVER purchase higher-class airline tickets for the *sole purpose* of getting additional miles! For what you get in return, in terms of service, that is *inconceivably* expensive. In fact, keeping frequent-flier miles out of it, just consider what you'd actually *get* in return for an *extra* **$667** to fly coast-to-coast, **Business Class,** or for the *extra* **$934** dollars you'd spend to fly **First Class**. You're pampered by friendly, solicitous attendants, you get a linen place mat, free beverages of any kind, including champagne, a scrumptious several-course hot meal, a wider, more comfortable seat that reclines farther, and maybe a personal TV screen upon which to watch a free movie. (Those prices are based on fare quotations I obtained from a major carrier on October 15, 1994, for a 7-day-advance purchase of one-way tickets, if seats are available, as follows: Coach: $149; Business Class: $816; and First Class: $1,083.) For the *same* money, you could take your significant other out for *at least* FIVE **lavish** nights on the town! Or think of all the *other* uses you might have for $700-$900, besides the prudent one of simply *investing* it for the future! Readers of this book who are Christians, or of a faith having similar values, also have to be wondering what kind of *stewardship* would be represented by such absolute *squandering* of assets in return for just for a few hours of much the same comfort one can obtain in his own living room, in a nice recliner chair, and a home-delivered pizza... for only $10 or less! Wouldn't it be nice if all corporations simply *required* **ALL** their executives to fly *economy,* and then *DONATED* the millions thus saved to good causes, such as United Way? Wouldn't that help make this a better world? You have to wonder what sort of values such "powerful" people have!

3. Here's a great rule of thumb. If a discount airline with NO frequent flier program is competing with a major airline on a route you fly, use the DISCOUNT airline, and keep it in business. Even if the major carrier is *underselling* them by a few dollars, or offering you *oodles* of perks, please do this, no matter *how* much the major carrier tempts, entices and lures you! ALWAYS "dance with the ones who love you" -- those people who make it *possible* for you to *get* such low prices and fares. Obtaining frequent flier miles isn't worth LOSING those prices and fares, *nor* is it worth your complicity in putting such good people out of business!

Now let's factor THIS into our considerations. Flying with regularity on the cut-rate airlines will almost always save you a BUNCH. As the article in *Worth* magazine pointedly states, "Pay $12,348 to earn a free ticket flying *United* from Newark to Chicago. Or fly *KIWI* for $9,346 less." What makes more sense to you? Explaining further, Jeff writes, "That means the *United* flier's company would be paying an extra $9,436 so its employee can collect one free ticket worth, on *United,* about $208. That's a very expensive perk. Meanwhile, the entrepreneur [that's YOU, the enterprising and intelligent Road Rat!] who flew KIWI would have no free ticket, but with the $9,436 in his pocket, he could buy 45 more Newark-to-Chicago round trips or 26 trips to and from Palm Beach, Florida."

Okay, I can see you saying, "Well, even though the highest executives of many corportions are so wasteful and inefficient as to fly at the higher classes at corporate expense, at least that has no impact on *me,* as an independent contractor collecting frequent flyer points in a frugal manner." That's very true, since cut-rate airlines don't fly all routes, so its sometimes necessary to fly the major ones. And when you do, you definitely should try to concentrate your major-brand ticket purchases on perhaps *two* useful airlines having good frequent-flier programs. You shouldn't involve yourself with *more* than two of those, though, because it spreads your frequent-flier-mile earnings too thin. BUT -- even though frequent-flier programs can serve you VERY well, you still need to avoid the *other* pitfalls, to **make sure** that it is primarily *YOU* who benefits from them, and *not* the companies that seek to entice you, and then rip you off. And *those,* primarily, are the airline "partners."

4. **Stay away** from "affinity" bank credit cards that offer you frequent-flier miles! Jeff writes in *Worth,* "...before taking those 'free' miles to the bank, frequent fliers should see if they're paying any of the costs that seem to sneak into the mileage game. How about the annual fees of $35 to $85 on an affinity card and an annual percentage rate of 15 percent to 21.6 percent? A non-affinity, low-rate card would charge more like 10 percent to 14.5 percent and would certainly have a lower annual fee -- or perhaps no fee. Of course, that card wouldn't let a traveller win a free mile for every dollar he charges. It doesn't take much of a fee or too many interest payments to erase the value of a $152 free ticket."

5. *Avoid* the costs of *attractive-sounding add-ons*, such as magazines and software that purportedly are tailored to help you *"manage"* your frequent-flier miles. Or the purchase of insurance to protect frequent flier miles from expiration or from an airline bankruptcy. Jeff cites one underwriter that will sell you a policy for $139 per year -- and then he goes on to observe, "Sure makes sense as a way to protect that $152 ticket." Managing the miles is *simple.* Pick *sound* airlines, rack up miles *primarily* on *flights,* and watch the numbers grow!

Fully 48% -- almost *half* -- of all frequent flier miles are earned from using the services of airline partners, and the other 52% are obtained by people actually earning the miles in flight. If YOU happen to be earning *more than* **5%** of your miles from airline partners, then the chances are EXCELLENT that when those folks see you walking in their door, a balloon appears over their heads containing a big lollipop that says "All-Day" on it! You can reasonably collect miles *as described* in Point #1, above, from car-rental agencies, but if you do it *right,* you *won't* be piling up *those* miles hand-over-fist. And if you're signed up with a major long-distance phone carrier, such as AT&T, which provides you with frequent-flier miles on your favorite airline as part of a package that grants you some of their lowest rates (so they can compete with the other carriers for your patronage), those miles won't add up very fast either -- unless you *routinely* make a *tremendous* number of long-distance calls!

BOTTOM LINE for Would-Be Frequent Fliers

My recommendation is that you *actively participate* in **two** frequent-flier programs. The first is that of *Southwest Airlines.* According to *Worth* magazine, and the U.S. Department of Transportation, this cut-rate, and yet major, airline has had the lowest number of "problem events" with passengers: 8,425 per 100,000, compared to an average for other the eight major U.S. airlines, of 18,545. (The highest problem rate was *Continental's,* at 21,756 per 100,000.) They also have less than half of the national average in terms of mishandled baggage reports and overbookings, and less that one third the average in terms of late arrivals! *Delta's* late arrivals record was the worst, at seven times those of *Southwest! American* had the most overbookings -- four times that of *Southwest.* Worst-handled baggage? *Delta,* at about 4 times the rate of *Southwest.* (Now you know why I recommend travelling with only *carry-on* luggage! More on this, 2 pages from now.) Add in the fact that *Southwest* has some of the lowest fares in the industry, and you have one very outstanding airline! And it gets better: *Southwest's* frequent-flier program is rated *number one!* For approximately every eight trips you take, you can get a free ticket.

The *other* is: The major airline that happens to fly into *your company's city* from most of the destinations you'll be *sent* to by your company. The odds are excellent that this will bring you directly to *my* favorite major carrier, because *it* serves over *300* cities.

I've used *Delta* for years. They're not paying me a cent for saying this, or rewarding me in any way for this unsolicited endorsement. If you overlook the late arrivals and some baggage problems, they just happen to be a particularly excellent airline, and so I'm doing you the favor of letting you in on that. *Delta* is one of America's most solvent carriers, you can earn a free trans-*Pacific* round trip for every 70,000 frequent flier miles, they give you 1,000 frequent flier miles for every separate *plane* you ride in, even if that involves a connection only 40 miles long, as in the case of Orlando-Daytona Beach! They serve a vast number of cities, and reach Europe and Asia. Additionally, they sometimes offer special incentives, as during the recent year when they *tripled* the frequent flier miles for all tickets that were *purchased* with a certain *brand* of credit card. Add that to their friendly and helpful service and an outstanding safety record, and what more could you possibly want? My main *criticism* is that often they provide only light snacks on some of their flights which are long enough to merit their serving *hot meals* instead! (Maybe if enough of us *mention* that to them, they'll pull up their socks on that one!) It's the only significant shortcoming I've ever found with *Delta,* **other** than the curse that afflicts virtually *all* of the major-brand airlines: sky-high fares for last-minute and sometimes for one-way tickets, and related restrictions. *Most* of the major players in this industry need to work hard to **eliminate** *those* very serious flaws and inequities! If the cut-rate airlines -- who have to scratch hard to survive and make their budgets -- can do without imposing these, then the *major* airlines SURELY have that capability. They've already *proven* they can do it on selected routes, when they're trying to kill off cut-rate or struggling competitors!! So **tell your major carriers to become more business-person-friendly! And** *include* **a** *photocopy of pages 122-126.* You have my permission for this!

Special Tickets

If you are a senior citizen, you can almost always get some kind of price break on airline tickets, and it can be very substantial. Sometimes you have to be a certain age to qualify, but with some it is as simple as just belonging to the AARP (The American Association for Retired Persons). To qualify for membership in AARP, it is necessary only for you to have reached the surprisingly young age of 50. *You need not be retired.* So far, I haven't heard of a requirement to be age 97 and be accompanied by all great grandparents on the flight to qualify for a special fare related to age. Most airlines have some reasonable threshold at which they cut a break to seniors.

I was very sorry to see *Eastern Airlines* bite the dust because it spelled the simultaneous demise of the unique and exceptional programs they offered in the form of multiple-trip tickets, which were available at various prices both to seniors and the general public. In 1980 I was notified by my dispatcher that I would have *eight weeks* of steady runs from Virginia to California, so I purchased *two* consecutive one-month tickets which enabled me to travel pre-selected flights on any of *Eastern's* North American and Caribbean routes. As a final round-trip taken during the last five days of the first ticket, I visited and explored the fascinating nation of Guatemala. With the second ticket I did likewise, in Haiti. *Eastern's* gone now, but watch for the possibility of similar programs springing up in other airlines. When you keep your eyes open, surprising things can be discovered!

Here's another example. In early January, 1991, I happened to be driving through downtown Pittsburgh on I-376 and spotted an *Eastern Airlines* billboard promoting round trips to any of 15 Florida cities for only $79 each way. A wonderful bargain! I filed it away, mentally, for possible future reference. Then, as luck would have it, I just happened to find myself having to *return* to Pittsburgh to do a radio show 10 days later. But there was a problem. I was scheduled to do a TV show in Mobile, Alabama on the following day, and not even Bobby Unser, Jr., could drive *that* fast. (Well... maybe Bobby *could*. I talked to him on my CB radio one day, right after he passed me on I-40, west of Albuquerque, at a speed sufficient to "blow my doors off." He ran out of my radio range within one minute flat! He must be on friendly terms with every cop in that state, for them to overlook such speed! They say U.S. Presidents aren't above the law. But are *race-car drivers??* Hmmm.)

Back to our story. *Eastern's* demise, at that time, already was *imminent.* So much so, that it would have been risky for me to fly with them; they *could* have gone bankrupt before I had a chance to return to Pittsburgh -- possibly stranding me on the Gulf Coast! So I called *Delta* (on which I already was a frequent flier) to check on the round-trip fare, Pittsburgh-Mobile-Pittsburgh. *$551.00! (Aaaaughh!!)* Then an idea occurred to me... *Delta* and *Eastern* had been traditional, major-brand rivals which had competed vigorously for supremecy on their *shared* routes, for *years*. Was **Pensacola** by any chance one of these "15 Florida cities" that were referenced by *Eastern's* billboard? Yes. Was it also a *Delta* city? Yes! The fare on *Delta?* Only $79, each way. The *same* as *Eastern*'s special! So -- I bought my deeply-discounted, unrestricted, round-trip ticket on **Delta** for just $158, rented a car for the one-hour drive (each way) to Mobile for $33.00, and accomplished the whole works for under $200, thus **saving over $350.** (And -- I earned 2,000 frequent flier miles for the trip south (2 planes), 2,000 more for the return, and 1,000 for renting the car from *Alamo Rent-a-Car*, which is a *reasonably-priced* partner of *Delta*. Total *new* miles for my frequent flier bank: 5,000.)

Billboards are a blight on the land and an eyesore, and I'm all in favor of seeing them *scrapped* nationwide. But that one for *Eastern*, in Pittsburgh, was the *extremely rare* **useful** exception!

The Road Rat's Best Friend...

...just may be his *travel agent*. By all means, find a *good* one that is always willing to ferret out the *best* fares and deals around, and will be willing to mail or FedEx tickets to you anytime, wherever you may be. Such a person is a treasure, and can save you *$$THOUSANDS!* (So I'm very pleased to recommend: **Bytner Travel, 9 Central Ave., Albany, NY 12210**. They've sent me all over the world and saved me a mint! **Ask for Jean between 1 and 5 p.m., Eastern Time**, and be sure to say "Hi!" to her for me! Bytner Travel can serve you *wherever* you are: **Tel. (518) 463-1279**.)

By the way, Jean *probably* would have found that special *Delta* fare for me, in that last example, even if I hadn't spotted *Eastern*'s billboard. But I was working on too short notice to call her about it.

Develop Your Creativity!

The more you learn about air travel, the more creative you can become. To be sure, though, this is entirely up to you. There are countless people in this world who have travelled *millions* of air miles and still just "go with the flow," never realizing what they could accomplish if they simply would keep their eyes open and strive to *learn*.

This is one of *several* places in this Handbook where I will enhance your chances of saving *many times* the amount you paid for this book, *whether or not* you decide to become a Road Rat. (It keeps right on getting better! Keep reading!) What I'm about to teach you can be used, *when the opportunities present themselves*, in the course of your planning for air travel under *any* circumstances. Some of these instances are rare opportunities, and others are more commonplace. It wouldn't hurt for you to file these away in an accessible *mental* file drawer labelled, "Air Travel Bargains!"

First, whenever you fly, you should attempt to *limit* your luggage to the quantity which the airline (and the FAA) will allow you to *take on board* the aircraft as carry-on luggage. There are several reasons for this...

-- *Checked* luggage sometimes is lost, often is delayed (with surprising frequency), and dismayingly often incurs damage:

-- **Lost** luggage (*i.e.*, that which is *never* found) means the irrevocable loss of the bag and all of its contents. So *never* entrust luggage that contains irreplaceable or high-value objects or documents to baggage handlers. The airline cannot replace unique personal items or papers, and its financial liability is strictly limited.

-- **Delayed** luggage can *terribly* disrupt your travel plans, particularly if you are a very *mobile* Road Rat! You can miss important connections while awaiting it, and even lose an entire day or more! Or you can find it very difficult to determine a convenient interception site that will match your planned routing and schedule, to which the airline may forward it.

-- **Damaged** luggage is pure frustration. It doesn't have to be eaten alive by automated baggage-handling equipment at the new airport in Denver. It happens to countless pieces *daily* throughout the *normal* system. Sometimes the airline may believe that *their* damage actually is *old* damage, and therefore decline reimbursement. Other times, you may not get the replacement value of the bag. Sometimes, it even gets ripped open and some or all of the contents are lost en route. And who wants to have to go shopping for a *new* bag?!

--   Baggage that has been checked for interline connections (*i.e.*, when more than one airline is involved in your one-way trip) is the *most* prone to delays. Often, *you* will make the connecting flight, but your *suitcase* does not. So... if you *must* check some luggage that way, try to do it from *point-to-point,* **if** sufficient time is available *between flights* to allow you to retrieve it from the carousel, and then re-check it onto the *next* airline.

Common sense? You'd be *amazed* how many people *don't know* even *those* basic points!!

--   Finally, having only carry-on luggage makes it much easier for you to get around. Cumbersome baggage severely restricts your mobility. Consider what you want to do at places you may be visiting, or where you may have lengthy stopovers. Even too much *carry-on* can hamper you badly. Here's an example. In early 1990 I made a trip to the USSR from Florida, and the itinerary called for a 7-hour layover in Frankfort, Germany -- a city I've never *yet* explored, and would love to, although I've landed there a dozen or more times! My carry-on luggage was jammed with worthwhile and irreplaceable (on short notice) gifts for my Russian friends, plus two cameras, a camcorder, videocassettes, and film.

I had *planned* to simply chuck most of that into a coin locker or two at the Frankfort Airport, and then head downtown to enjoy the city. Wrong. Unlike *most* major airports, the one at Frankfort has *no* coin lockers, and their left-luggage facility was seriously limited in terms of their liability. To ensure the safe passage of all that carry-on, I thus was forced to keep it *with* me. It was *far* too much gear to lug around downtown Frankfort for 5 hours. So all I've seen of Frankfort, to date, is its *airport. That* day, it was for seven boring hours.

When performing Road Rat duties, experience will teach you to get along on a very small quantity of carry-on luggage, thus avoiding almost all hassles and headaches.

"You Can't *Get* Here From There!"

You're going to *love* this next story, and I encourage you to learn some valuable pointers from it!

Let me preface this story by saying that my company paid by the mile at a rate considerably *higher* than the 38 cents/mile I mentioned earlier, but because they utilized the method of paying expenses and salary in one lump sum, that 38 cents/mile is a good *average* of the amount I generally earned as *take-home pay*. After taking all expenses out of the money allotted, including whatever it cost to return, I was entitled to keep the remainder. Therefore, drivers for that company always were seeking creative ways to fly back for *less*... thus ending up with *more profit* whenever they *succeeded*. But even when worse came to worst, and full coach fares were paid, a comfortable profit of between 35 and 40 cents/mile still could usually be attained.

Assigned a run from just outside Richmond, Virginia to *Scottsbluff, Nebraska,* I immediately began planning, en route, for my air return. Planning this from Scottsbluff was especially challenging because leaving there by air would have required the first leg of the trip to be made on a *commuter* airline.

$$ TIP: **Commuter air travel almost always is *excessively* expensive *unless* the carrier is affiliated with the major airline being used for the remainder of the trip. *Then,* the commuter portion can often be done for a minimal add-on to the cost of the primary flight. *Always* check to see which is the case.**

With Scottsbluff, the latter was not possible, and it looked for awhile as though the run might be *below* average in profitability.

As luck would have it, however, less than a week earlier, I had delivered a unit in Daly City, a suburb of San Francisco. For the return, I'd purchased one of those wonderful $99 one-way fares to Washington D.C. that *United Airlines* was offering at the time. (In that particular situation, I'd hoped to fly back on cut-rate *World Airways*, but its flight had been sold out.) Upon preparing to board the plane, I found that *this* wildly-popular flight had been *overbooked,* and nearly everyone had shown up!

Under no pressure to return immediately, I volunteered to be "bumped" from the flight, particularly since the reward offered was so substantial... a free voucher worth *$200* on any *United Airlines* flight, and a seat at no additional charge on an alternate flight back to Washington, D.C.

The $99 fare had been restricted to making a *non-stop* flight to Washington. But as part of this bargain, *United* additionally sweetened the pot by allowing me to select a flight leaving an hour later which would land in Denver en route... and then they *further* permitted me to make Denver an overnight *stopover,* and continue on to Washington the next morning.

As luck would have it, I had a girlfriend living in Denver at that time. She picked me up at Stapleton Airport, Denver, and then returned me to my continuing flight the next morning. Thus, I had a nice return coast-to-coast flight, and a date thrown in, all for $99 (plus my own cost of the dinner for two). And... I had a voucher for $200 worth of free air travel on *United* in my pocket which I *hadn't* had when the trip began. Keep that in mind.

Back now, to the Scottsbluff dilemma. These were my options as I drove westbound toward Nebraska's panhandle:

-- Purchase a coach ticket, involving the *additional* expense of a *non*-conjunction commuter flight, from Scottsbluff to *Richmond*. **Total Cost: $450.00**.

-- Purchase a coach ticket from Scottsbluff to *Washington, D.C.,* and then proceed to Richmond by limo. Cost: $380 *plus* $21 for the limo. **Total Cost: $401.00**. Why fly to Washington, instead of all the way to Richmond? For *this* reason:

TIP: **Although not *always* true, it is *usually* less expensive to fly into a major city than into a smaller city, even when using a major airline. But... see *also* the "Hidden Cities" factor, back on pages 78 and 79. This can get you *around* that problem!**

-- Travel by *bus* from Scottsbluff to Denver -- the nearest major city -- and *then* fly (entirely on a major airline -- no commuter flights) to Washington, D.C., and *then* take the limo to Richmond. Cost: $38 (bus), *plus* $250 (air), *plus* $21 (limo). **Total Cost: $309.00**.

That last option would have left me with a total *profit* for the Scottsbluff run of about 40 cents/mile. Quite respectable... but it was not the option I *used*.

Spoiled by the ultra-low $99 fare from San Francisco to Washington I'd enjoyed just a few days earlier, I phoned *United* to see if they had a similarly-discounted fare from Denver to Washington, D.C. No. (That made sense, of course. You see, *World Airways* wasn't competing with them on *that* route. See the value of cut-rate airlines?) But coincidentally, the best *available* fare happened to be *theirs* nevertheless... so *United's* is the $250 fare that you see in the last option, above.

Then I asked the *United* agent if their $99 fare from *San Francisco* to Washington, D.C. was still in effect and available. "Yes sir, it is," the puzzled voice came back, "but didn't you say you'll be flying to D.C. from *Denver?*"

My next question to *United* was to see if they had a special fare from Denver to *San Francisco*. Yes. Only $80.

So *this* is the option I actually *used:*

-- **Bus** from Scottsbluff to Denver ($38). **Flight** to *San Francisco* from Denver with a one-hour layover in California ($80). **Flight** from San Francisco to Washington, D.C. ($99). Then the **limo** to Richmond ($21). *Subtotal Cost: $238.00.* **Total Actual Cost: $38.00**.

Remember that $200 voucher for *United Airlines* travel that I received on the earlier California trip, in exchange for being bumped voluntarily? With *that* I paid the air fare of $179.00 and was given *another* voucher for the *unused* $21.00. The total *out-of-pocket cost* for the return trip to Richmond, then, *went from the original $450 quotation all the way down to a mere $38.* Isn't that neat? And it was completely ethical and legal.

Flying to California from Denver, and then *re-crossing* Denver in the air took only a mere 5 hours, even counting the connecting time at SFO. Many people would reject the notion of returning in this manner because it goes against the grain to travel hundreds or even thousands of miles in the *opposite direction* to go home. But think about this... *that particular combination of trips* **still** *would have saved me* **$71** *over the* **least** *expensive option listed above, even if I had* **not** *had the voucher!*

Here's another one for you...

"The Great Northern Dogleg!"

On a run from San Bernardino, California, to Fairbanks, Alaska, I decided to return to California in my usual fashion -- via Hawaii. I arranged it over the phone with my travel agent in Albany, N.Y., and then picked up the ticket upon my arrival in Fairbanks.

The entire flight was via *Western Airlines*, another good carrier that has since moved to that great Hangar in the Sky. (In this case, it was by being purchased.) After three days in Hawaii, I went to the Honolulu Airport to board my last leg of the trip home... and found the facility *jammed* with literally *hundreds* of stranded travellers! While I was driving to Alaska -- and just after I'd made my reservations -- *United Airlines* had gone on strike! And *United,* then, as today, was the primary passenger airline linking Hawaii to the U.S. mainland. So the scene that greeted me was one of desperate folks who needed to return home to their jobs, and no way to accomplish it. I was one of the few lucky ones having an actual flight to board, and a seat. When *United's* strike started, the remaining seats on *Western's* flights to the West Coast had rapidly been snapped up. Those hundreds of folks in the airport honestly believed they were trapped in the mid-Pacific!

Recalling that my own flight from Alaska to Honolulu had been 3/4 empty, it struck me that most of the flights in and out of Alaska in March probably were in a similar state. It's no longer cold enough in Alaska at that time of year to impel Alaskans to head for Hawaii for a respite from winter, and it's still too chilly to be attractive to most Hawaiians. So I suggested to some of those desperate travelers that they simply check with *Western Airlines* regarding possible seat availability to the mainland -- *via* Anchorage.

Those who really *needed* to get back to the lower 48 *did* so that day, by spending perhaps an extra $100-$150 per person, and making that unusual dogleg. But the important thing to realize and remember is this... *NONE* of them had previously *considered* that possibility!

Here's some interesting food for thought before moving on. Remember Tip #13 on page 81, about Rule 240, and how it could be invoked by a passenger whose flight has been delayed or cancelled, so that he/she could be booked on another flight to his destination? I hadn't yet learned about this, back then. So now I wonder if Rule 240 might have gotten *those* folks home, *via Alaska,* **without** additional expense. (??) Hmmmm.

TIP: **You can always reach a destination by a *variety* of different routes and means, and sometimes you even can *save* money by actually going *farther!***

Okay... one more story before closing this chapter. After that, if *this* chapter doesn't sooner or later save you many hundreds of dollars on air travel -- whether or not you become a Road Rat -- it's probably only because you don't happen to ride on airplanes very often.

"Freebies Galore!"

This was a very simple assignment with a surprise ending. Drive to Dallas, Texas, deliver the vehicle, fly back to Washington, D.C., and ride the limo home to Richmond. Routine. No big deal. *Except* that the flight was to be taken on January *2nd*... the day after a major holiday. A day when almost everyone and his cousin would be hopping on airplanes!

At DFW Airport, the gate for my flight was quite crowded. After I boarded, an airline employee came on and asked for volunteers to be bumped, because the flight was overbooked. I volunteered, and was given a voucher good for a FREE round trip anywhere *Piedmont* flew, valid for a full year. Then I was put aboard another *Piedmont* flight to Washington, 45 minutes or so later.

After boarding the flight, it happened again! This time, they asked if I had a more *specific* destination, and then put me aboard an *Eastern* flight... to **Richmond,** an hour later. *That* plane was far from full, and because I no longer had to ride a limo for two hours, I actually arrived in Richmond *before* I would have by taking the *first* flight. And I was *two round-trip tickets richer!* Later that year I enjoyed *free* round-trip vacation flights to California on two separate occasions!

$$ TIP: **TARGET days of heavy travel when booking your flights! You may reap some fabulous benefits!**

CONCLUSIONS

1. *UNLESS* you are independently wealthy, or are retired and *purposely* burning off excess profits so that you can remain below the earnings threshold of your maximum possible income from Social Security, it is *wasteful and pointless to stay in big-name luxury hotels for the purpose of gaining frequent-flier miles.* You will spend **far** more than you will ever *gain,* that way!

2. Airline *upgrades* in class of service are a terrible *waste* of either frequent-flier miles or money. Consider the airline *ticket* you could have *instead,* for just a few more miles.

3. Try not to have luggage that you must check; stick to using *carry-on* if at all possible. Always keep valuable items in your carry-on bag. And *too much* carry-on limits your *mobility!*

4 Consider **all** your options! Sometimes your best and cheapest return can even be via the *opposite* direction. Or by using a dogleg that most people wouldn't even consider!

3

The Class "A" CDL Option --
How to be a "Road Rat *Extraordinaire!*"

Fred Trent was a CPA in southern Florida handling large, corporate accounts before becoming a Road Rat. It's years later, now, since he left that highly-lucrative but high-pressure profession behind, and although he's no longer on a fast-track to becoming *independently wealthy,* he's *immensely* **happier.**

Although most folks who've heard me on radio or TV think of me in the role of a *guest* on TV newscast features, or on talk shows, there were a few weeks during the summer of 1994 that I served as a talk show *host* on a radio station in Providence, Rhode Island. It was a most enjoyable stint behind the other side of the microphone from the one I've been used to, and it was heartening for me to find I could do it with some agility. So while in that role, I had a number of guests of my own choosing, including my friend, Kelly Monaghan, author of numerous excellent travel-oriented books, including these *current* titles: ***The Insider's Guide to Air Courier Bargains,*** and ***Part-Time Travel Agent.*** Chances are, you found some literature on these enclosed in this Handbook, but if not, let us know, and we'll send it to you.

While most of my guests were travel authors having highly-valuable and unusual books, not all were authors. Fred was such an exception.

When I introduced Fred over the air, I conferred upon him the title, "Road Rat *Extraordinaire."* To this he replied, "You know, Craig, I'm *very proud* to be a Road Rat!" As well he should be! He could have been proud simply to be an *ordinary* Road Rat, for this is a very honorable lifestyle and profession to pursue. But he's **not** your *average* Road Rat. He's living PROOF not only that my original concept of "Continental Interlock" works, but that it can work exceptionally *well!*

The way he pursues this earns him *at least* the $52,000 per year that I had been earning throughout my last six years as a full-time Road Rat. It is, of course, not nearly as much as he earned while a CPA, but Fred doesn't regret for a moment that he made the change. It *vastly* improved his life!

Fred became a Road Rat the hard way, just as I did: having *no* guidance from this Handbook. For me, the book didn't yet *exist,* and for him, it went *undiscovered* until late 1993, when another driver showed him a copy. By that time, he'd honed his own set of skills, and had become a very accomplished Road Rat. Without guidance from a Handbook, we each had evolved in similar, but not identical ways. I was licensed to drive everything, but never employed Continental Interlock. He obtained a Class "A" Commercial Driver's License and set out to make his services available to companies *all over* the USA. In dozens of places from coast-to-coast, he's well-known to transporters and others who are quite willing to pay him *well* to deliver vehicles that often are beyond the normal scope of Road Rat activity.

With a Class "A" CDL, Road Rats have considerably more versatility, because they then can opt to drive vehicles *over* 26,000 lbs. whenever they want, or the opportunities present themselves. Add a few endorsements, such as Haz-Mat (hazardous materials), Air Brakes, and perhaps even Passenger, and there's virtually nothing that they cannot legally drive. And there's nothing that *Fred* cannot legally drive. That -- and his innovative spirit -- were his passkeys to the door of *Continental* Interlock.

I've explained why transporter companies typically pay only half as well as do those who manufacture and sell the vehicles. And I've told you that working for a transporter isn't especially lucrative unless it's *combined* with working for one or more of other companies, as we saw with Semi-Permanent Interlock. At the beginning of the *last* chapter, however, I told you that you were about to be introduced to an important *exception* to that rule. THIS is that exception.

With a Class "A" CDL, you **can** work full-time for *transporter companies* most of the time, as does Fred, and perhaps even *all* of the time, and still make a *very* respectable income. **With the CDL, you are *especially* in demand,** if those companies know that they can *count* on you whenever you can be available to them, that you'll do your job *well,* and that you can handle just about *any kind of vehicle* that they want you to move. And often they'll even *FLY* you from place to place, at *their* expense, to do it!

TIP: ***This* field is *really* wide open!! There are *'way* too *few* such Road Rats!**

But that's not the ONLY difference. Fred also *networks* very well!

Fred knows *where* all his potential employers and contractees are, and *how* to get in touch with them, and *when,* as he's sent from point-to-point-to-point, all over the continent. In addition, he has a *toll-free* phone and a *live* answering service (not just a device) to field his incoming calls. He keeps himself totally accessible, and he returns his calls quickly. In that manner, he's developed a tremendous rapport with dispatchers and their colleagues all over the map!

Why do his runs for *transporter* companies pay so very well? Several reasons, but the primary one doubtlessly is his tremendous **versatility** -- his capability to legally drive almost anything that runs down the road. Many of the vehicles he drives generally have to be moved on a high-priority basis. They're *needed* somewhere, and so a premium rate is paid for that combination of larger vehicle and the priority of the move -- often more than $1.00 per mile!

Even so, Fred is *not* strictly a "truck driver," even though many of the vehicles he moves are trucks -- because for the most part, he *doesn't move cargo.* Like the more traditional Road Rats, Fred moves *vehicles*. And those generally are *empty* of freight.

Fred stayed clear as well of becoming an "independent vehicle transporter," because he moves the vehicles using registrations and authority that are provided by each company for which he works.

Translation? Fred has developed a hassle-free life that imparts to him just as much freedom and as little pressure as are enjoyed by other Road Rats. The primary differences are in the way he makes his contacts, and in his ability to drive *all* types of vehicles.

Many readers of this book are former truck drivers, or current ones looking for a change, and thereby *already* possess the Class "A" CDL, often fully-endorsed. The idea of not having to deal with freight is very appealing to many truckers, particularly when they learn they can earn as much or more by delivering *empty* brand-new vehicles and trucks, depending upon the methods they employ, and the people for whom they work. In addition, many *non-*trucker readers and users of this Handbook who like to drive have reported to us that they are giving strong consideration to *obtaining* a Class "A" CDL, so that they can have that *extra* degree of versatility that it affords.

TIP: If you possess or obtain a Class "A" CDL, take note of the Transporter Company listings in Appendix 1, as well as the Manufacturers who make new semi-tractors (which are coded as *S-1*) and semi-trailers (*S-2*). That should get you off to a good start. (And remember the *techniques* that Fred Trent uses!)

4

"ECONOMY" METHODS... and Lessons from "The AmeripassTeam!"

Road Rats return home from their runs via five methods: by delivering a second vehicle ("Interlock"), by air ("Maximization") by bus, by train (next chapter), and in their own or an associate's vehicle (the "Tow Car" and "Trail Car" methods, which are detailed in Chapter 6 of this part). When it comes to using public transportation, Road Rats have their "economy" and "luxury" methods, just as an airliner has coach and first class seating. And it makes wonderful sense to use the "economy" methods when it's to your best advantage to do so. Why throw money away if there's nothing to be gained?

The lynchpin of *surface* "economy" public transportation is the interstate bus, and in America that usually means *Greyhound/Trailways* -- although many regional and intercity lines coexist with that continent-spanning giant. If you read *pages ix thru xii* -- and shame on you if you *didn't*; they're *very* important!! -- then you already *know*, that even though I prefer trains and planes, I personally have no aversion to busses. Some of the greatest adventures of my life have been while actually riding on busses, or in conjuction with such travel! And retirees will be happy to find that getting up in years generally is not a deterrent. One time, when making a delivery from Virginia to Sarasota, Florida, I passed through Daytona Beach (where my parents were living), and asked my father if he'd like to finish the run with me, after which we could return to Daytona via *Trailways*. Even though in his mid-80s, he enjoyed the entire experience -- bus ride and all -- immensely!

Yet, you'd be amazed at the number of people who tell me they could never be a Road Rat if they had to ride the bus, even occasionally. Well, that's okay. Busses aren't for everyone, and *many* Road Rats seldom if ever step through the door of one. **You do NOT have to ride busses to be a Road Rat!**

This chapter is provided for three reasons:

-- Many Road Rats *do* happen to enjoy bus travel. They find it relaxing. They enjoy the opportunity to meet so many new people. And it gives them a great chance to enjoy the scenery at ground level without having to worry about watching the traffic.

-- Knowing *how* to use busses effectively can be very useful to you even if you don't happen to use them very often.

-- The refined techniques presented herein can be especially useful to Road Rats who work for transporter companies, but have not yet established Semi-Permanent Interlocks (SPI). Remember that transporters pay only half as well as do manufacturers and dealers, on average. So if you work for a transporter, only *Interlock* will usually save you more money than these techniques. If you choose to use *neither,* your income will probably be unacceptably low.

The most *lucrative* ways to be a Road Rat are to employ the techniques of Interlock and/or Maximization. (And yes, you *can* do a combination of *both* if you'd like. However, to use Maximization to *any* degree, Road Rats normally have to either employ some Interlock, or work for a manufacturer.) If you're just getting started, and it happens to be with one transporter, I'll suggest that you begin to pursue setting up Interlocks, and utilize the bus and special air fares whenever those cannot be established, using the guidelines provided in this chapter.

By far, the very least-expensive bus travel is via *Greyhound's Ameripass*. For the greatest savings, you should purchase the 30-day version, as you can see from this table:

7-Day *Ameripass*	--	$250	--	Costs you... $35.71/day
15-Day *Ameripass*	--	$450	--	Costs you... $30.00/day
30-Day *Ameripass*	--	$550	--	Costs you... **$18.33/day**

IMPORTANT NOTE: The fares quoted above, as well as all other fares in this book, and all tables which are based on those fares, were obtained and calculated in late 1994, when this *edition* of this Handbook was researched. Although much updating is done from one *printing* to the next, within the life of an edition, fare and table updates are of too great a magnitude for that, and so are done only from one *edition* to the next. The next (6th) edition of the book will be *fully* updated, including the fares and tables. Nevertheless, in this 3rd Printing of the 5th Edition, more than 100 pages (including data pertaining to more than 500 companies in Appendix 1) were updated to currency as of May, 1997.)

In previous editions of this book, the *Ameripass* was the unchallenged way to go in terms of economy. Not any more. It is a good option today only if you *know* that for the next 30 days you either are unlikely to utilize Interlock, or if you *know* that your destinations will not be places from which you can fly home *regularly* at deeply-discounted fares, or on cut-rate airlines.

The $18.33/day cost of maintaining the 30-day *Ameripass* doesn't seem particularly high until you consider the *number of days* you'll actually get to *use* it. *Using* it for 30 continuous days would be a terrific bargain. But when you consider that the average Road Rat has perhaps 4 days of down time per month interspersed *between* available runs, and that *half* of the *remaining* time will be spent *driving*, that figures out to only **13 days** that you'll actually get to spend **riding the bus**. In terms of actual *usage*, then, your 30-day *Ameripass* **would cost you $42.30/day!**

SHOULD A TRANSPORTER-COMPANY ROAD RAT *FLY* HOME... OR RIDE THE *BUS*?

Most of the time, you should ride the bus, if you are working ONLY for a transporter company, and if you are NOT using the Interlock System. To those for whom bus riding has little or no appeal, you'll find a *special* incentive to move up right away to Interlock, Maximazation, or a combination of these.

In Appendix 2, you'll find a detailed analysis of work for a very hypothetical company. One that is perfectly located, geographically, and provides *ideal* runs to its Road Rats, and no down time between runs. The purpose of *that* analysis is to show you the absolute *highest* earnings a Road Rat *ever* could hope to attain while working solely for *one* transporter company, *without* a CDL. In **this** chapter, though, we'll confine ourselves to "real world," *typical* examples, to show the earnings that such a Road Rat can *expect* to earn.

Let's say that you're working for a transporter company in Fort Wayne, Indiana... which is *not* a major gateway (or "hub") city for airlines. It therefore is typical, in that respect, of most of the cities in which you'll find transporter companies. For the pay scale, we'll use 41 cents per mile, which is about average for transporters who combine the expense funds with the driver's earnings in one lump figure. (Remember that payment of a portion of that up front, and then the balance following completion of the trip, is a pretty normal practice.) We'll assume that your vehicles average 8 miles per gallon and that gasoline sells for an average price of $1.17^9. (At that rate, the gasoline will require 14.74 cents/mile of your pay.) And we'll assume that you spend $12.00 per day on food and/or meals. And we'll assume that you're driving *RVs,* and therefore are sleeping in them, so have no motel expense. These particular figures are quite realistic in the mid-1990s for transporters, and for the units they ship.

For our examples, we'll use a set of very *typical* runs, all originating from Fort Wayne:

1. Seattle, Washington
2. Holland, Michigan
3. Riverton, Wyoming
4. Denver, Colorado
5. El Dorado, Arkansas
6. Plaistow, New Hampshire
7. Columbus, Ohio
8. Orlando, Florida
9. Surrey, British Columbia
10. Metairie, Louisiana

Generally, you either will use an *Ameripass* **100% of the time, during its period of validity,** or you **won't** buy or activate one in the first place. It is impractical to use an *Ameripass* at today's exorbitant bus-pass prices unless you can get *maximum use* out of it. This means that if you possess one, you seldom -- if *ever* -- would find it to your advantage to *pass up* the chance to use it in favor of *another* means of return. If you use Interlock, buying an *Ameripass* would be a waste of money in the first place. And if you think a cut-rate return flight would save you money by getting you home faster for the next run, that usually is an *illusion,* as you soon will see. We present you with three situations. Scenario #1 depicts typical expenses in terms of both time and money, and the profits, for the *Ameripass* user. Scenario #2 shows what happens if an *Ameripass* user yields to the temptation to combine the bus returns with an occasional cut-rate return by air. And Scenario #3 depicts the same for a transporter company Road Rat making returns via *separately-purchased* bus and plane tickets, depending upon the distances involved. In each situation, **the calculations are already completely done. All you need to do is** *compare* **the three.**

Scenario #1 -- Returns via *Greyhound Ameripass*
(Outbound Runs Are Provided Immediately Upon Return to Home Base)

Run No.	Length in Miles	Days Away From Home	Cost of Gas & Meals	Method of Return	Fare*	Earnings, Before Taxes
1	2,222	6.0	$399.52	Bus	$55.00	$456.50
2	195	1.0	40.74	Bus	55.00	- *15.79*
3	1,411	4.5	261.98	Bus	55.00	261.53
4	1,245	4.0	231.51	Bus	55.25	223.94
5	835	2.5	153.08	Bus	55.00	134.27
6	905	3.0	169.40	Bus	55.00	146.65
7	120	1.0	29.69	Bus	55.00	- *35.49*
8	1,025	3.0	187.09	Bus	55.00	178.16
9	2,290	6.0	409.55	Bus	55.00	474.35
10	1,018	3.5	192.05	Bus	55.25	170.33
TOTALS:	11,266	34.5	$2,074.61	---	$550.00	**$1,994.45**

*Scenarios 1 and 2 assume that you purchase an *Ameripass* after delivery at the first destination, and thus its lifetime is just long enough to get you home from all 10 of these runs. Dividing its cost of $550 by 10 gives us the $55 fare for each return trip.

In this model, you are earning at the rate of about $57 per day. Working at this pace for **345 days per year** (which allows you about 3 weeks of vacation time), your take-home pay before taxes would be **$19,659.58**. Although you won't have normal weekends at home as do people having more conventional jobs, you will have plenty of time to unwind, meet new people, and perhaps even write the Great American Novel *if* you are adaptable to riding the bus. Spending more time at home, or setting your schedule so that you do have normal weekends there, is possible in this lifestyle. One of the job's greatest attributes is the flexibility it gives you with your work schedule. However, in doing this, you would have to accept a proportionately lower annual income. And *that's* easier to do when working with an income that is more comfortable from the start, as you would have in the cases of Interlock and/or Maximization.

Notice that there are two runs on the above list that technically *cost* you money to make, when considering the pro-rated life of your *Ameripass,* run-by-run. If you drive for a transporter company, there will probably be runs mixed in with your good ones which will not be profitable -- but you are expected to take them because (1) the runs need to be made, and someone has to take them, and (2) you normally can expect to get enough *good* runs in balance to make the overall tradeoff a fair one. Be aware, though, that full-time transporter company Road Rats are *expected* to take some short runs to go with the good ones. And that even applies to full-time Road Rats who work for manufacturers and dealers. Don't be a prima donna and gripe if you draw the short straw from time to time. *It's a normal part of the overall game.* Road Rats who accept this cheerfully are respected by their dispatchers, and the ultimate payoff is usually very good. Never forget the time that I took that 30-mile trip to Richmond, Virginia in good cheer, which attitude my dispatcher perceived beforehand, and so told me, "Take that short run, and *I'll send you to CALIFORNIA* **10 times!!**"

Scenario #2 -- Returns via *Greyhound Ameripass* -- with a Couple of Enticing Cut-Rate Flights Thrown In
(Outbound Runs Are Provided Immediately Upon Return to Home Base)

Run No.	Length in Miles	Days Away From Home	Cost of Gas & Meals	Method of Return	Fare*	Earnings, Before Taxes
1	2,222	6.0	$399.52	Bus	$55.00	$456.50
2	195	1.0	40.74	Bus	55.00	- *15.79*
3	1,411	4.5	261.98	Bus	55.00	261.53
4	1,245	3.0	219.51	Air & Bus	155.50	135.44
5	835	2.5	153.08	Bus	55.00	134.27
6	905	3.0	169.40	Bus	55.00	146.65
7	120	1.0	29.69	Bus	55.00	- *35.49*
8	1,025	3.0	187.09	Bus	55.00	178.16
9	2,290	6.0	409.55	Bus	55.00	474.35
10	1,018	2.5	180.05	Air & Bus	155.50	81.83
TOTALS:	11,266	34.5	$2,050.61	---	$751.00	**$1,817.45**

The difference between this situation and Scenario #1 is the fact that you seemed to luck out in both Denver and New Orleans, and were able to obtain a *bargain* $99 one-way *airfare* to Chicago in each case. So you yielded to the temptation and took advantage of it. As a result, you reduced the time spent on those round trips by one day apiece. This is typical of what can happen with bargain fares, because the fare was available between the two major cities on each end, but not into Fort Wayne. Real bargains into the smaller cities are only very rarely available. The only problem, therefore, was the fact that you still had to ride the bus from Chicago to Fort Wayne. But at least that portion cost you no *additional* money because you were able to do the *bus* portions using your *Ameripass*. The recently-completed metro extension to O'Hare Airport permitted you to go downtown in Chicago for only a dollar-fifty, so the total *out-of-pocket* cost of each of those returns to Fort Wayne was only $100.50 ($99 air + $1.50 metro).

Because your *Ameripass* almost certainly would expire during the *outbound* leg of your next run, we therefore still regard it valid for only the ten trips above, and even though the ticket wasn't used for the full return in two cases, we still have to pro-rate its useful life, at $55 per return, over the 10 trips. So your real cost in each of those two cases where you *flew* was $155.50, and all you gained was one day of time in each case. An insufficient time savings to permit an 11th return on your *Ameripass*.

So now we'll see what those special airplane fares did -- either FOR you, or TO you. At *this* rate of earnings -- $51.93 per day -- working **345 days/year** would net you **$17,914.86**.

That's **$1,744.71** *less, per year,* than you would have earned in Scenario #1, in which you *didn't* bother with the bargain flights, and simply returned every time via your bus pass!

It's just as I told you earlier: *Ameripasses* simply **don't mix** with other returns, unless, perhaps, you can find an airline that's willing to fly you home for *free!* Keep in mind, too, that your rapid returns got you *back on the road sooner*, as well. That's not necessarily beneficial, because you actually perform **much MORE work for LESS pay,** in this scenario, over time!

Scenario #3 -- Returns *Without* an *Ameripass*, via Individually-Purchased Tickets:
Bus, or Plane, as Appropriate for the Distances Involved
(Outbound Runs Are Provided Immediately Upon Return to Home Base)

Run No.	Length in Miles	Days Away From Home	Cost of Gas & Meals	Method of Return	Fare	Earnings, Before Taxes
1*	2,222	4.0	$48	Bus & Air	$451	$ 84.50
2	195	1.0	12	Bus	46	- 6.79
3	1,411	3.0	36	Air	544	- 209.47
4	1,245	2.5	30	Air	408	- 111.06
5	835	2.0	24	Air	341	- 145.73
6**	905	2.0	24	Bus & Air	362	- 148.35
7	120	1.0	12	Bus	45	- 25.49
8	1,025	2.5	30	Air	415	- 175.84
9	2,290	4.0	48	Air	419	134.35
10	1,018	2.5	30	Air	415	- 177.67
TOTALS:	11,266	24.5	$294	---	$3,446.00	- $ *781.55*

* Returning by air from Vancouver, BC frequently is much *cheaper* than from Seattle! In this sampling, the fare is the combination of *Greyhound* one-way, Seattle-Vancouver, at $22, taxi fare in Vancouver, from the bus depot to the Airport, at $10, and then the airfare to Fort Wayne at $419. (To have flown *directly* to Fort Wayne from *Seattle* would have cost you an astronomical *$629!)*

** The return from Plaistow, NH required a short bus ride to Boston (and taxi fare from the depot to the Logan Airport), and then the plane.

So... using the air returns saved you exactly *10 days* over the bus returns, which translates to this: you can *work a lot harder* and *go broke a lot quicker* doing it this way! Because as you can see, if you wish to work *solely* for a transporter company... *not* use Interlock... and return by *air* from all of your longer trips... it would only **COST you $31.90 per day** to be a Road Rat. And that's the equivalent of **PAYING $11,005.50 per 345-day work year for the privilege!** That's right. Doing it *this* way would put you eleven grand *in the hole* every year!

Of course, no one in his right mind would do it this way. The **purpose** of this exercise, then, was to **show you very graphically** how absolutely NECESSARY it is to use an *Ameripass* IF you are a transporter company driver who uses *no* Interlocks!

When I first became a Road Rat, I knew absolutely nothing about Interlock, Maximization, or companies other than transporter companies for whom drivers worked. But I did know the value of using an *Ameripass*. As the first weeks of my job went by, I saw drivers come and go with startling rapidity! Being a Road Rat seemed to offer no stability at all, to them. Yet, even though I still considered myself underpaid, I was surviving well enough. Almost immediately, I realized that the factor that made the difference in my longevity as a transporter-company Road Rat, and the other drivers' lack of it -- was the *Ameripass*. The drivers that used them stayed. Those who didn't -- which was about 90% of them -- did not. A few weeks, tops, and they were gone. More often, they lasted only several days.

Has the situation changed, over the years? No. Not for transporter-company drivers who do NOT have one or more of three factors in their favor, as outlined in this tip.

TIP: **UNLESS you have a comfortable second income (such as Social Security or a pension), it is *almost impossible* to survive economically as a transporter-company Road Rat *without* employing *one or more* of these three critical elements: (1) Use an *Ameripass*, (2) Employ the technique of Interlock, and/or (3) have a Class "A" CDL and take some of the better-paying runs.**

And now you know why many transporter company drivers soon cease to be Road Rats.

TIP: **UNTIL the necessity to employ one or more of the above three elements becomes common knowledge among transporter-company Road Rats -- *AND* most of them choose to *implement* that knowledge, transporter companies will continue to be the best entry-level doorway to the Road Rat lifestyle for new drivers... due to rapid turnover.**

Maximization was not included in the above tips because the transporters' pay scales for drivers normally will not support the use of that technique.

Now let's see the *Greyhound Ameripass* in **action!**

THE ADVENTURES OF
"THE AMERIPASS TEAM"

I love the beaches of San Diego, California. The rugged cliffs laced with trails and footpaths. The way the fog can hang just off-shore giving the scene an unearthly appearance. The volleyball games -- and their participants. The fresh, cool salt-air breeze off the Pacific. The hang-gliders soaring high overhead... and occasionally landing gently nearby when they lose the air currents that keep them aloft. The sandpipers scurrying back from the waves as the tide comes in. I can't even imagine what my life would have been like if I'd kept on teaching and had never discovered the adventure of being a Road Rat!

It was on such a day in the late fall of 1977 that, while strolling down the beach, I met a banker named Paul and we struck up a conversation. When he learned that I lived in Indiana, but travelled all over North America all the time -- and got *paid* for it! -- his banking job rapidly began looking less attractive. By that time, I'd already learned that the turnover rate of drivers at transporter companies was quite high, so I told him that if he'd like to deliver vehicles instead, it would probably be pretty easy for him to join the other drivers in the company for which I worked. He said he'd give that serious consideration, and we agreed to keep in touch.

About four months later, while riding a *Greyhound* bus north through Alabama, I met a fellow passenger named Lin, a registered nurse from Sydney, Australia. She'd just graduated from nursing school, and was celebrating by touring America, using an *Ameripass*. I told her that my dispatcher was looking for new drivers, and offered to introduce her to him if she'd like to ride on up to Indiana with me on the bus. "After all," I told her, "if you're going to explore America, why not set your own schedule, take some routes where the busses don't run -- and get *paid* to do it?" Lin went to Decatur, Indiana with me, and was hired the next day by a dispatcher who was fascinated by the idea of having a real, live (not to mention also very attractive) *Australian* working for him. Most of us used CB radios routinely then, so she bought one, and I dubbed her with the handle, *Wandering Wallaby*. (Neither my dispatcher nor I, however, happened to recall, until perhaps two weeks later, that Australians are used to driving on the *left!* But by that time, Lin -- who'd never brought that minor detail up in conversation -- had admirably proven her abilities as a driver in America.)

It was perhaps three weeks into our odyssey of mutual exploration of America's highways and byways that I told Lin about Paul. We decided to phone him and invite him to join us. And by that time, Paul was *really* ready for a change! He gave two weeks notice to the bank, and on the appointed day, bought an *Ameripass*, left the Golden State in the sunset, and set out for Denver. By pre-arrangement, Lin and I had departed a day earlier from Decatur in two coaches destined for Denver. All three of us joined up at the Denver Bus Center, hopped on the bus, and headed east for Decatur.

The **Ameripass Team** was born!

During the next several months, the three of us came up with more and more creative ways to be practicing transporter-company Road Rats. The most fascinating aspect, in retrospect, was the fact that none of us were aware that this job even existed for Road Rats who worked *directly* for manufacturers and dealers, and thereby earned twice as much as the average transporter-company driver. If any of us had known that, we probably would have sought greener pastures, and that would have *ended* the *Ameripass* Team! Fortunately, however, throughout the entire time we were together, none of us ever learned of the existence of those other drivers. And, as a result, we became very creative, and taught ourselves some very valuable Road Rat techniques.

Lin, Paul, and Craig could perhaps have been regarded almost in the light of "The Three Musketeers of the Highways." It was a romantic adventure that lasted only a few months, but was highly memorable. And as an almost inseparable team, we were rather unique in the annals of Road Rat-dom because we sought out the unusual, and constantly tried to create new techniques of travel -- especially the returns, while armed with our *Ameripasses*.

Just before Paul joined us, Lin and I were fortunate enough to enjoy the opening-night performance of The Carpenters at the MGM Grand, at a stageside table, hours after delivering two RVs to a dealer in Las Vegas. Weeks later, the three of us delivered three coaches to a dealer in Golden, Colorado... but not until we took an afternoon to explore Loveland Pass, high in the Rockies.

Miles are everything for Road Rats, dispatchers, and customers. It's unlawful to disconnect an odometer cable, so the distance showing on it when a delivery is made must be within 10% of the actual number of miles from the point of origin. That can be stretched to 15% if necessary.

The *Ameripass* Team arrived in Wheat Ridge, Colorado at 8:00 a.m., but the delivery could be made any time during the day, and the dealer was only seven miles away, in Golden. We had breakfast at the *Union 76 Auto/Truckstop* and planned our day. For openers, we decided to go to Loveland Pass, if possible, but it all depended on the number of miles on our odometers.

Two of the coaches showed almost exactly the *correct* 1,250-mile distance, but one showed only 1,150. Loveland Pass is a 100-mile round trip from the truck stop. So we each kicked in $3.33 for gas, which was sufficient to go the 100 miles at the prevailing 1978 gasoline prices, hopped in the coach showing the low miles, and headed for the mountains! Five hours later, we drove all three coaches -- which by then *all* showed 1,257 miles, give or take a couple -- into the dealership and made the delivery. The dealer provided us with a ride to downtown Denver, where we watched "Close Encounters of the Third Kind" at the wide-screen Continental Theater. Then, as night fell, we took a city bus to Aurora and had a fabulous meal at a restaurant called, "The Denim Broker." And at midnight, we presented our *Ameripasses* to a Greyhound driver at the Denver Bus Center, curled up in bus seats for a good night's sleep, and woke up the next morning in Oakley, Kansas for a breakfast stop. By the *next* morning, we were back in Decatur to get our next assignment.

Our dispatcher did his best to keep us together, but it wasn't always possible. There came the day when he told us we'd have to go off on three separate runs, and he had no idea how soon we'd all be able to regroup as a team. What he *didn't* know was the extent to which we'd devised a highly-sophisticated set of return techniques!

Just to give you an idea, we had pet names for some of them, such as *"The Cincinnati Trampoline," "The Indianapolis Dogleg," "The Pittsburgh Snoozaround," "The Toledo Backdoor,"* and *"The Upper Midwest Zigzag,"* to name just a few. All were designed to maximize sleep time on busses, so that one could arrive in Decatur just before noon, refreshed. Before we set out, we got together for breakfast at a favorite local restaurant called "My Father's Place," and planned our strategy.

Paul was sent to Painesville, Ohio, where it just happened some of his friends lived. At 8:25 p.m., he hopped an *eastbound* Greyhound bus to Pittsburgh, and arrived there at 11:15. Just over an hour later, at 12:35 a.m., he caught a *westbound* one, and arrived in Toledo, Ohio at 6:20 a.m. He'd just used the *"Pittsburgh Snoozaround,"* and had gotten 8 hours of sleep before breakfast. Another connection brought him to Fort Wayne at 9:15 a.m.

Lin was sent to Cedar Rapids, Iowa. By 11:30 p.m., her return bus arrived in Chicago, where she disembarked and caught a *southbound* one that took her to Indianapolis. Then she connected with a bus going *northeast,* and arrived in Fort Wayne at 10:35 a.m., having just used the *"Indianapolis Dogleg."* The dogleg prevented her from arriving in Fort Wayne in the middle of the night, when there was no available bus to Decatur. And, she got a good night's sleep!

I was sent to Dearborn, Michigan, which is close to Detroit. My bus from there passed through Toledo, Ohio at 8:30 p.m., and several hours of sleep later, I arrived at 1:00 a.m. in Cincinnati. Then caught a northbound bus at 2:00 and returned to Toledo, where I joined Paul at 6:20 a.m. after doing *"The Cincinnati Trampoline."* The *Ameripass* Team was all together again when Lin joined us at Fort Wayne. We took the 11:00 a.m. *ABC Lines* bus to Decatur, and were home by 11:40.

You haven't seen *astonishment* on a person's face until you've seen a look like the one our dispatcher gave the three of us when we all walked into his office together, scarcely 24 hours after he'd sent us out! "I don't believe it!" he exclaimed. "Even when I send you all off in three different directions, you're together again the next morning!"

It's the nature of life, of course, that such adventures sooner or later must run their course. Paul met the girl from Holland, and soon after married her and settled back into banking -- in the Netherlands. Lin had tickets to the Wimbledon, in England, so when the time came, she took her Road Rat earnings and flew to Europe. And I sought the adventure of exploring the western states in depth, as a Road Rat. Five months after it began, the Odyssey of the *Ameripass* Team was only a happy memory for us all. But WHAT an adventure it was!

Oh. Almost forgot. There's an epilogue to this. Between the time of Lin's departure for England, and two years later, she returned twice to be a Road Rat again for a few weeks. Then, with her bankroll replenished, she returned to pursuing her 2-year-long tour of most of the world! (And her *original* plan had only been to visit America as a tourist for a few weeks.) Not too long after her extended odyssey ended, Wandering Wallaby returned home to Australia, found her husband-to-be, and now is raising her family in the Land Down Under.

POINTS TO REMEMBER

1. If you *don't* use Interlock, and you work *solely* for a transporter, the most practical and economical way to return from your trips is to use a *Greyhound Ameripass*.

2. If using an *Ameripass*, you should always purchase it on the *same* day that you'll begin *using* it. Or, if you choose to buy it ahead of time, be SURE it isn't *activated* until you're ready to start using it! When you *do* have the agent activate it, make SURE that he sets its expiration date 30 days ahead, **not** *to include* the day that it's activated and your travel begins! (The day *after* its activation is Day #1 of its 30-day period of validity.) Remember this: If you start it before or during an outbound run, you will automatically waste an entire day, and perhaps *several* days, of its validity!

3. If you yield to the temptation presented by bargain airfares **while** you possess a valid *Ameripass*, you probably will end up *working harder* for *less money*. **EXCEPTION:** The only way that it pays for an *Ameripass*-using Road Rat to purchase a cut-rate plane ticket is if he happens to be BETWEEN *Ameripasses* at the time. If your *Ameripass* expired at the end of your last return trip, and now you've just driven to a distant city on the *next* run... but have *not yet purchased or activated* your next *Ameripass*... then utilizing a bargain airfare can be very **profitable**. Because the clock is not running on an *Ameripass* at the time, making that inexpensive return by air will gain you some more whole *days* before you have to purchase or activate one! **TIP: Be like a chess player. Think several runs ahead,** *before* **using an Ameripass.**

4. This may seem particularly obvious, but it's good advice, so I'll impart it. If you have an *Ameripass,* safeguard it *exactly* as you would cash. If you lose this ticket, or it gets stolen, you're flat out of luck! No refund is possible! And if a thief happens to lift it, the chances are excellent that he then would get to use it for the rest of its natural life. That's because even though *in theory* the ticket is non-transferable, because names and addresses of the purchaser are recorded, chances are good that the thief would get to enjoy his travels at your expense. You see, the only way he could be stopped is if an agent were to *compare* the data on the ticket to his ID, and that, unfortunately, is done only rarely.

5. Most bus passengers ride that way infrequently, except for commuters, so you'll find that your lifestyle *amazes* most of those who learn about your job. (Of course, it won't surprise fellow Road Rats, whom you'll meet with some frequency.) Most passengers simply regard a long bus ride as a necessary evil -- and they can hardly wait to reach their destinations!

But for the Road Rat with substantial bus-riding experience, *time* telescopes *dramatically.* A two-day-and-night ride from Seattle to Chicago (2,100 miles) **seems** to take only a few hours and span perhaps only around 200-300 miles, *if you are busy with other projects.*

5
Road Rat in *"Training"* -- The *AMTRAK* Adventure!

Europeans have it made, in terms of convenient and efficient surface transportation! When in Europe, you can't beat the "Eurailpass" for getting around quickly and efficiently. European surface transportation is *far* superior to that of the USA... where we once had a *comparable* rail system -- but then, disastrously, mysteriously, and stupidly, we let it slip through our fingers. In practically no time, back in the era of the *first* Woodstock concert, practically all passenger rail service in America ceased to exist, virtually overnight. Yet, just a few years earlier, it had been possible to get *almost anywhere* by train. Some of the smallest towns were even served by two or three trains daily!

At about the time passenger service ended on all the great railroads of the day (such as *New York Central, The Pennsylvania Railroad, Burlington, The Union Pacific, The Santa Fe Railroad, The Rock Island Line,* and *Great Northern*, just to name a few), *Amtrak* was born. But it was only marginally a substitute, at best. It was government-subsidized, and cut to the bone in terms of scheduled service.

Even today, of America's tens of thousands of towns and cities, less than 500 of them have any *Amtrak* service at all, and many of those don't even have one train a day. What happened to cause such a disastrous decline? That's beyond the scope of this book, but for the rail buffs, I was lucky enough to learn of a brand-new book that examines these developments in depth. To learn more, I highly recommend that you ask your bookstore for a copy of **Getting There: The Epic Struggle Between Road and Rail in the American Century**, by Stephen B. Goddard. It was published on June 24, 1994 by Basic Books, ISBN 0-465-02639-7, and retails for $28.00. It was really an eye-opener for me!

A Word About America's *SPECIAL* Railroads

Here in America, *Amtrak* is all we've got, for now, in the lower 48 states. And to the north, there's the *Alaska Railroad,* which has remained independent of federal subsidization. And across the land, there are several privately-owned (and superb!) short-run railroads. Of the tourist railroads, two are quite special in my own experience. One is the Durango-Silverton narrow-gauge run, in western Colorado, which is hard to beat in terms of scenery. The other is the Skunk Train, which runs daily out of Fort Bragg, in northern California, and is especially dear to my heart! One day in 1987, I was taking my parents -- who were in their 80s -- on a special 7-week automobile trip we called GNAT ("Great North American Tour"). This was not in the line of Road Rat work, but I drew on my Road Rat geographical knowledge to be their tour guide and chauffeur. The object was to give them one last chance to explore the wonderlands of the lower 48 and western Canada that they'd never had the chance to see. Unfortunately, on one particular morning in northern California, we'd gotten a late start... and *that* was the day I'd planned to treat them to a ride on the Skunk Train. The *only* day that our schedule would permit it!

Not daring to even dream that it could possibly help, I stopped at a pay phone in Leggett and called that railroad, more to verify the schedule than anything else. Even though the distance remaining was only about 38 miles, California Route 1 has many winding sections, even that far north. The train was scheduled to depart in only 40 minutes or so. It looked dismal. But in my inquiry I happened to mention that I was bringing my parents, and that my father had been a life-long railroad buff... and that I was going to do my best to make it. I asked for no special favors, though.

Almost 15 minutes after the scheduled departure of the Skunk Train, I pulled into the depot's parking lot -- and was stunned to find that it was still there! They'd actually *held* the train for us!! Voluntarily, based on what I'd said about my parents! We had an absolutely wonderful trip, all well-recorded on videotape -- and I'll never be able to say enough wonderful things about the Skunk Train and its staff! If you ever get the chance, take the time to ride it. You'll *love* it, and it's run by some *fabulous* people!

The *AMTRAK* Experience

Before dealing with the nuts and bolts of travel via *Amtrak,* I decided here to include a first-person report that I wrote just a few months ago while actually *riding* on *Amtrak*. It'll give you a better feel for the glitches you might encounter, as well as the enjoyment. Ride along with me in this account of a real, live rail journey on *Amtrak*...

Unlike the highly-efficient rail systems in Europe and Asia, all goes well an astonishingly *low* percentage of the time with *Amtrak,* and the first problem can be just *getting* to the depot, and *then* boarding the train. It can be a challenge. Especially if you happen to live in South Dakota or Oklahoma, neither of which even **have** *Amtrak* service. I started this adventure with a ride by car from Waterloo to Ottumwa, which is about a 2-hour jaunt across Iowa.

Upon arrival at the ticket window, I was informed that my train was running *six hours* late! (Can you imagine sitting around a depot on hard benches for that long? Or even on cushioned ones?) To wait for it would probably mean that I'd miss my connection to *"The Broadway Limited,"* in Chicago, because I had only a 4-1/2-hour scheduled layover there. And I had managed to secure prized sleeper reservations on it, to Philadelphia.

The agent saved the day by suggesting that rather than wait for overdue Train #6, I could drive on to Fort Madison, Iowa, and intercept Train #4 instead.

"It's running *one* hour late, so you'll make it with time to spare," he said, smiling. "You'll reach Chicago with three hours' connecting time."

The drive to Fort Madison, in Iowa's southeast corner, took another hour and a half, and my older son, Craig, who was driving me there *had* to have been wishing I'd decided to *fly* instead. Bless him, he never said so. It turned out there was no rush. By the time we got there, Train #4 was running *two* hours behind schedule.

At Chicago, as the sun hung poised just above the western horizon, I stepped off the train believing that I'd made it with two hours to spare. I was wrong.

The *"Broadway Limited"* **departed** two hours late, at 10:00 p.m., even though it *originates* in Chicago. I began wondering about my connection to the *"Silver Meteor"* the following afternoon. My scheduled connection time in Philadelphia was only two hours!

Aw. You've probably already guessed.

The *"Silver Meteor"* was late, too.

I ended up sitting around the Philadelphia terminal for two hours after all, waiting for *it*. Observing the annunciator board there, I noticed that two out of three trains were running late. Only the *Metroliners* were doing well. (I think the *Metroliner* people must have attended extensive rail seminars in Europe!)

So now I'm writing this aboard the *"Silver Meteor,"* which lost an additional half hour during the night. Or was that due to the 90 minutes that we just spent in Jacksonville? Hard to tell.

Just in case you wondered about Train #6 -- you know, the 6-hour-late-one that I'd *originally* wanted to take to Chicago from Ottumwa? It's lateness should have caused it to arrive in Chicago at 9:45 -- just 15 minutes *before* the *"Broadway Limited" actually* left. So did I do the right thing by catching Train #4 in Fort Madison, instead? You bet! When the *"Broadway Limited"* left Chicago at 10:00, #6 was posted for *anticipated* arrival at *10:40!*

In fact, while riding on the *"Broadway Limited,"* I met several people who had arrived in Chicago by train the *previous day*, and had missed their connection *then!* (*Amtrak* had put them all up in hotels that night, instead.)

Am I being cynical in telling you all of this, or unfair to *Amtrak?* No, on both counts. I'm a very upbeat person who *loves* to travel, and what I've stated is simply a true account of this trip. Unfortunately, such stories are not particularly unusual when riding *Amtrak*.

Returning Via *AMTRAK*

As a Road Rat, in order to return from runs via *Amtrak,* it will take some special planning -- even if the trains are on time. First of all, if your **home base** isn't close to an *Amtrak* depot, that can be a big hurdle. For example, if you live in Daytona Beach, Florida, you'll find that the nearest depot is over 20 miles away, in DeLand. But many places are considerably worse. As with South Dakota and Oklahoma. It's easy to live in America and find that the nearest depot is 100 or even 200-300 miles or more away! I happened to be quite lucky during my *full-time* Road Rat work, from 1977-86, to find myself always near a depot. Purely by luck; never by design. It just worked out that way. When working out of Decatur, Indiana, *Amtrak* served Fort Wayne, just 18 miles away, from which I could connect by bus. San Bernardino, California, was (and is) an *Amtrak* city. After that, I lived in Richmond, Virginia -- another *Amtrak* city. Then, in 1986, I lived *in* Fort Wayne, Indiana! Then Albany, New York, followed by Daytona Beach, Florida. When you're that close to *Amtrak,* it makes returning by rail easier... but several major hurdles remain. *So* many, in fact, that you'll soon learn why the vast majority of my returns were by *other* means, even though I, myself, am an avid railroad buff.

The next factor that comes into play is your **destination city.** Even if you live near a depot, this won't help when your destinations happen to be cities that are nowhere near *Amtrak* routes -- or are on routes which cannot conveniently return you home again. For example, if you work out of Dallas, Texas, which has a depot, and have a run to Topeka, Kansas, which also has one, this won't do you any good. That's because each of those cities are on *east-west* routes, and to get home, you need to go *south.* And to accomplish *that,* you'd need to ride *east* all the way *to St. L*ouis, and then make a *connection* to Dallas... which has service from Chicago *only 3 days a week!*

Next, you need to consider the **fares.**

It seems like a "turnabout is fair play" situation at first; if Europeans can't buy "Eurailpasses" to ride their own trains, and folks from overseas *can* -- but must purchase them *before* going to Europe, then the same criteria can apply over here to the "USA Railpass." But according to *Amtrak,* that's not the reason at all. The actual reason is the *limited amount of seat space available* on the trains, especially during the summer months. If Americans could purchase their go-anywhere ticket and then just hop on the trains at random, there wouldn't be enough seats! During the summer, for example, one often must have a selection of travel dates available when travelling on short notice, because the trains frequently are fully-booked, days, and sometimes even weeks ahead.

Even though North Americans are excluded from the privilege of buying the "USA Railpass," many of these Handbooks are sold elsewhere. Particularly in Europe, Grand Cayman, Bermuda, Australia, and New Zealand. So I've included this data in Appendix 2, for those who live overseas.

For those living in the USA and Canada, it is recommended that you dial the following toll-free number before planning travel via *Amtrak.* The agents are extremely well-informed, and can advise you on schedules and rates, as well as make your reservation(s) when you're ready:

1-800-USA-RAIL

If you coordinate this effort with *ticketing* by your travel agent, that is always good practice, because a good travel agent can be an excellent buffer between the passenger and the carrier if anything goes amiss. (That goes for most travel, except, perhaps by bus, which requires no reservations and is more routine.) Remember, this costs you nothing!! The carriers provide the agents with their fees, and the passenger pays the same either way. (There's an *exception* to this, however. See the literature enclosed in this book about Kelly Monaghan's book, **Part-Time Travel Agent**.)

"All Aboard, America!"

These fares do *not* apply to travel in Canada on *Via,* nor do they apply to *Amtrak's Auto-Train,* nor to the *Metroliners* which ply the Northeast Corridor. They *do* apply to all other *Amtrak* system trains. However, Road Rats rarely use round trip tickets, so the detailed information and fare data for the "All Aboard America" tickets are provided in Appendix 2.

One-Way Tickets

Most of the time that Road Rats are found on *Amtrak,* you'll find them using one-way tickets. When travelling *that* way, you are allowed NO stopovers. However, if you need to change trains, the amount of time available between the arrival of your train, and your departure time for the connecting train (which must be the next one out, going toward your destination), is a bonus. Or it's a pain in the neck, depending upon whether or not you *wanted* a stopover! You see, the "down time" between trains in these situations commonly is hours, and may be even *a day or two! That* situation is quite normal, when connecting through New Orleans.

So that you can know what to expect, here are some typical one-way fares, at the time of this writing:

From	To	Fare	"Senior" Fare	How & When Applicable
Seattle, Washington	Elkhart, Indiana	$239	$203	Year-'round Regular Fare
New Orleans, La.	Elkhart, Indiana	$144	$122	Year-'round Regular Fare
Seattle, Washington	Los Angeles, Calif.	$157	$108	Regular Fare, Peak
Seattle, Washington	Los Angeles, Calif.	$133	$ 92	Regular Fare, Off-Peak
Cleveland, Ohio	Dallas, Texas	$212	$180	Year-'round Regular Fare
DeLand, Florida	Richmond, Virginia	$139	$118.50	Year-'round Regular Fare
Los Angeles, Calif.	New York City, NY	$247	$210	Year-'round Regular Fare

One-way fares on *Amtrak* typically remain fairly stable, but the round-trip fares can vary wildly! The determining factor for that generally is the extent to which the train is booked. Strangely, the round-trip fares frequently are quite close to the one-way fares, and sometimes are even cheaper! (You'll find that that's true with the airlines as well!)

For example, the regular one-way fare for those between age 16 and 61, inclusive, between Cleveland and Dallas, as you'll note above, is $212. But the regular *round-trip* fare for the same route is only *eight dollars more:* $220!

Senior fares are usually 15% lower than standard adult fares.

Amtrak established a special fare in September, 1994 wherein a companion could travel for just 50% of the full fare paid by the primary ticket-holder. This is a *rare* special, however, and each member of couples travelling together normally must pay identical fares. Interestingly, during the special, a senior could pay his/her discounted fare, and bring along a *non*-senior companion for 50% of *that.*

Sleeping Accomodations

The Peak periods vary the most widely pertaining to these supplemental fares, even from one train to another, so be *sure* to check that aspect when making reservations. As a general rule, though, the Peak on accomodations runs from *approximately* July 1 - November 1 each year.

East of Chicago, *Amtrak* has an *especially* nice budget accomodation for single passengers, called the "Single Slumber-Coach." It's not found on the sleeping cars of trains that run west of Chicago. At the right time of year, and depending upon the length of your trip, you can actually have your own private compartment, complete with toilet, lavatory, armchair, and bed for close to the price you'd pay to stay overnight in a *Motel 6!*

Sleeping accomodations are provided at a supplemental charge, *beyond* your passenger fare. For example, if you travel one-way from DeLand, Florida to Richmond, Virginia (or vice-versa), and the fare is $139, then the extra fee of $47 for the Slumber-Coach is added to the total price of your ticket. So travelling that route in comfort, and getting a full night's sleep in bed, will cost you, at those fares, a total of $186.

Suppose that the air fare from Daytona Beach, Florida (the closest major airport to DeLand), to Richmond, Virginia, were to be $190 at the same time. You'd then have a choice to make: allow your company to pay for your *air* fare, or for your *train* fare. It would make little difference to them -- but in terms of your *own* comfort and schedule, it might be very nice to have this option!

South and west of Chicago, the next best deal for sleeping on the train is the "Economy Bedroom." This sleeps either one or two, so is ideal for couples, because it costs the same either way to obtain these accomodations! In addition, your meals are included in the price, for as long as you have the room! For example, if you're going from New Orleans to Elkhart, you might have the room for the New Orleans to Chicago leg. While on that train, your meals are "free" -- you paid for them with the room! From Chicago to Elkhart, though, the trip is so short that it would be pointless to obtain such accomodations. Some typical situations are depicted in this table:

Sample Costs of Amtrak Travel Including Sleeping Accommodations

From	To	Single Fare	Accomodation Fare	Total Fare	Details
DeLand, Fla.	Richmond, Va.	$138	$ 59	$197	Peak/Adult/Single Slumber-Coach
DeLand, Fla.	Richmond, Va.	$118.50	$ 59	$177.50	Peak/Senior/Single Slumber
DeLand, Fla.	Richmond, Va.	$118.50	$ 49	$167.50	Off-Peak/Senior/Single Slumber
Seattle, Wash.	Elkhart, Ind.	$239	$320	$559	Peak/Adult/Economy Bedroom[1]
Seattle, Wash.	Elkhart, Ind.	$203	$217	$420	Off-peak/Senior/Economy Bedroom[2]
New Orl., La.	Elkhart, Ind.	$144	$113	$257	Peak/Adult/Economy Bedroom
New Orl., La.	Elkhart, Ind.	$122	$ 86	$208	Off-Peak/Senior/Economy Bedroom

[1] For 1 person. But room will accomodate two. A couple would then pay total of $798. W/meals.
[2] For 1 person. Total for Sr. couple: $623. Total for Sr./Adult couple: $659. With meals.

Rail Travel In Europe

For the frugal traveller, you can't beat exploring Europe in the *wintertime* by train! During that season, they are quite uncrowded. That's because when the trains *are* crowded, it's due to the presence of large numbers of *tourists* -- and winter isn't the tourist season. You generally can include early spring and late fall, as well, in that time frame of uncrowded trains. Rack yourself up a bunch of frequent flier points so you can get there and back for *free,* and be **sure** to buy a "Eurailpass" **before** you *leave* for Europe, because it *cannot* be obtained once you're *there!* And *without* one, rail travel in Europe gets *very* expensive! Once in Europe, you can simply sleep on the trains at night, and see a different city every day. Why waste money on pricey European hotels (unless you want to), when your "Eurailpass" *already* provides you with very nice accomodations? In fact, those accomodations are quite *literally* First Class! And you've already *paid* for them!

You see, a "Eurailpass" entitles you to travel in the *First Class* cars on European trains. So there's *comfort,* right off the bat! And most of those cars have compartments that seat six -- or *sleep* three! If there are either one, two, or three of you riding through the night in a compartment, simply pull each of the six seats forward until they *meet* in the middle. (They usually will, but even when they stop short of actually meeting, they're still as comfortable as any recliner chair you'll find.) This results in the creation of what is approximately a queen-size bed. Pull the compartment's curtains and *snooze* your way from Nice to Rome. Or Zurich to Vienna. Wherever! Even if you don't know each other, it's no more problem than if you were sleeping upright, because the seats are so wide, you can recline without bumping into one another. Consider, too, the fact that in Europe and Asia, sleeping compartments in trains frequently don't afford the degree of privacy we in America are used to. Each compartment, generally depending upon class of service, usually contains between two and six open bunks. (With six, there are two sets of three, which face each other across a space. Each set has a lower, a middle, and an upper.) Awaken refreshed, clean up in the car's rest room before the train reaches the station, and then hop out and explore your new destination! Want to do the *same* city two or three days *in a row?* No problem. Consult your *Eurail* timetable. Take a train *outbound* for half the night, then *change trains* to one going the *opposite* way, and *return* during the *second* half of the night, thereby arriving in the *same* city you left the night before, early the next morning. It's easy. Have I done it? You betcha! Many times! It's wonderfully easy, and you meet lots of great people!

A few cautions, if you've never been to Europe: Practically everything there costs between two and four times as much as in the USA! (Be sure to bring plenty of film from home, for your camera -- because you'll find that US$20 or more is a pretty common price *per roll* for it, over there!) Coin laundromats are next to impossible to find. Locating pay phones on which you can easily make international calls has been a hassle, but this situation is improving! Ask AT&T to provide you with their free "USA Direct" phone number card before you leave for Europe. Dialing *those* numbers, which vary from country to country, normally will connect you immediately with a live operator *here,* in the USA. (That doesn't work for making long-distance calls *within* Europe, of course, but it's a great start!) And *malls* are hard to come by. And when you *do* find them, many tend to have positively *weird* hours of operation. Especially on weekends. (If your first contact with Europe is at Reykjavik, Iceland, on a weekend, you'll learn this *immediately,* just as I did!) Otherwise, *enjoy* Europe! Beyond having a few shortcomings, the place is absolutely *fascinating!!*

6
ALTERNATE WAYS TO TRAVEL FOR PAY

The markets provided in Appendix 1 are specifically-designed for the purpose of applying for work delivering motorized RVs and specialty vehicles, as well as towing the trailers that are maufactured and sold at thousands of sites.

Outside of the scope of this book are other vehicles that frequently are delivered in much the same manner but don't normally travel on *roads* (although you'll sometimes see them being trucked).

If you are a qualified pilot, you should consider the possibility of delivering *brand-new private and commercial aircraft,* which frequently are *flown* to their customers and dealers, just as *RVs* are *driven.* Similarly, *boats* are often delivered in that manner by people qualified to pilot them along and across waterways.

If we see enough interest in either of these, we'll consider researching the methods, and interview the manufacturers, for inclusion in the 1998-2000 Edition of this book. Over the years, we have heard, periodically, from people that are interested in transporting these. So we'll give it strong consideration, if enough of our readers this time write to request it.

Because this author has no personal experience with delivering either one, I would, in that event, locate some folks who are already doing it, and ask them to describe the procedures, and some of their experiences, and then provide you with those in the next edition, along with the company listings and data.

MORE WAYS TO GET HOME

1. Deliver a Private or Corporate Airplane

If you already know how this is done, or if you are a qualified pilot, and I just gave you the idea, then by all means consider *incorporating* this into the Road Rat lifestyle. What a fabulous -- and probably lucrative -- way to accomplish the Interlock System!

Should you decide to do this, and it works for you, then by all means *please let us know,* and we will *definitely* include your input in the next edition!

2. The Tow-Car Method

There are some substantial pros and cons on this one. Whether or not the method is suitable for you depends very much on what you want to accomplish in this lifestyle. It is a method of return that usually is not conducive to earnings of $30,000 or more, but if income in the 30K range and above is not a prime objective for you, then it might work quite well. Literally thousands of Road Rats use this method, and some of those are quite well-informed and yet do it as their method of choice.

The **"down"** side of the Tow-Car Method can be summed up as follows:

1. A tow-bar must be used. If you don't mind working with one of those, there still remains the matter of whether or not the type of vehicle you *deliver* is adaptable for *using* a tow-bar. And whether or not the manufacturer or transporter for whom you work will *allow* you to use one.

2. You can tow a small car behind your unit only if you're delivering a motorized unit. It cannot be towed if you deliver trailers. So if you prefer the tow-car method of return, that will effectively *eliminate* from consideration all of the *trailer* manufacturers for whom you might work.

3. You cannot normally do DPUs in this manner, because not too many dealers will be amenable to the concept. They're more oriented to the concept of simply flying you to the factory, and having you drive their new unit right back to them.

4. It normally would take you just as long to drive *your* car back as it would take you to drive a unit for *pay,* doing an *Interlock.* Unfortunately, in return for that unproductive time, you will receive *no* pay. (There are trade-offs for this, however, in the "up" side list.)

5. Of course, you will have to fuel your car throughout the return drive, but the funds for that can be taken from the same "expense money" funds that the company provides for your return by other means.

6. One of the worst aspects is the wear & tear that your car experiences from all those long return trips, and the car insurance. (Remember, the company pays for the insurance for your trip while you're delivering *their* unit, but you're on your *own* insurance when driving *your own* car.)

7. There's no point in trying to establish an Interlock, *once you're en route outbound.* Because if you succeed, you'll end up towing your car in *both* directions for no reason. (If you establish an Interlock *before* you depart, however, you can simply leave the car home for *that* particular round trip.) An interesting thing to consider, though, is the possibility of setting up a "Continental Interlock"-style run. For example, drive to L.A. from Grand Rapids, Michigan, and then take an Interlock unit from L.A. up to Seattle. If no *third* Interlock materialized, you then could use your car to return home from Seattle to Michigan. (However, be *certain* that your *Interlock* manufacturer will allow you to tow the car, *before* you start out!)

8. If your car breaks down while you're driving it home, you'll be faced with the hassles of having to pay for its repairs, and experiencing forced down time while you're waiting to get back on the road with it. If it's a *significant* breakdown, count on having *extra* motel and meal expense!

9. Can you *sleep* comfortably in that little car, in rest areas? If not, that raises the question of how much extra time will be spent by utilizing motels, not to mention who will pay for those motel rooms on your return trip: you, or your company? That depends upon the company's method of paying you, but most often, such motel expenses would be on *your* nickel!

The **"up"** side aspects of this method are as follows:

1. In terms of wear & tear, and fuel, you may well find that this method is less expensive than the tickets would be, using any form of public transportation. Perhaps even cheaper than constant use of a *Greyhound Ameripass*. Now some trade-off factors come into play. Does your company allow you to keep the expense money you would have spent on a plane ticket, even if you return by other means? If so, then great! The cost of a plane ticket would far outweigh your actual costs of driving your car in terms of fuel and normal wear & tear. (Assuming you have a small, economy car. Virtually -- and probably *literally* -- NO one uses a gas hog for a tow car.) Does your company give you a fixed rate per mile for a trip, out of which you take all your expenses *and* your profit? If so, then you may find that either Interlock or Maximization would be far more profitable for you. Or does your company pay only your actual expenses out of your expense money, and then pay you by the mile to give you your profit? That one's not good, because they'll pay you for your *receipts*, and you'll have no money to cover your wear & tear and insurance expense. And what if your car breaks down on the trip back? Will they pay for the repairs, in that circumstance? Probably not.

2. This method is a favorite with retirees who already receive a fairly good income from both pension funds, investments, and/or social security. That's because they frequently take this job with earnings a low priority; they're in it to keep active, and to enjoy roaming America and Canada. So this "up" side aspect is the one of unbridled freedom. When using the tow-car method, the driver can take his time on returns, to his heart's content. Remember that whacky example I mentioned in the "Rat to the Future!" chapter? Where a person could select a routing from Denver to Tampa, via Fairbanks, Alaska, if he wished? Well, if you use the tow-car method, and your dispatcher doesn't care how long you're away, you could actually DO that, if you were so inclined! With the tow car, you're free to roam wherever you wish. Your only limitation is your own financial resources!

So, the bottom line is that the down-side factors are more numerous than are the up-side ones, but depending upon your circumstances, the up-side ones may outweigh all of them. Only you can make this determination, but at least you now are equipped to consider them from a fully-informed standpoint.

3. The Trail-Car Method

This is sort of a "mass-transit for Road Rats" system!

When two to five motorized units are being delivered to the same place, or to locations that are quite near one another, then sometimes another person will follow along in his car, for the purpose of bringing the Road Rats back home again. The trail-car driver may himself be a Road Rat, or he might be a friend of one or more of them -- or he might even be a person that Road Rats or their companies know they can call upon to perform that service.

The Road Rats all contribute to the money that the trail-car driver receives in return for the service he or she renders, and to pay the actual expense incurred by the car's making the round trip, in terms of both fuel and wear & tear. In some cases, the company pays the appropriate salary and expense to the trail-car driver, and then simply doesn't provide other return options or expense money to the Road Rats involved in the trip. (Either way, though, the money spent can be considered trip expense money.)

I could spend at least a page explaining all the possible trade-offs, pros, and cons involved in this. However, now that you've been well-grounded in return methods over several chapters, I'll grant you a diploma for gaining that knowledge in that regard, and allow you to weigh the factors for yourself. (If you don't think you've truly *earned* that diploma, then I urge you to go back and re-read the applicable chapters!) If you've studied well enough, then I have complete confidence in your ability to determine which times the trail-car method would serve you well, if any, and which times you should pass it up in favor of a different method of return.

The trail-car method normally is not profitable when only one or two Road Rats are returning with the car's driver, unless the trip is a very short one.

4. Independent Vehicle Transporter

For an *investment* of several hundred to perhaps a thousand dollars or more, a person can set himself up as an independent vehicle transporter. For his money, he can be officially registered as a transporter in the state in which he applies, have his own transporter license plate, and purchase his own insurance. He then works directly with manufacturers and/or dealers to contract for runs. On interstate trips, he faces the normal requirements pertaining to reciprocity and buying permits that are faced by transporter companies.

Although I never did this myself, and have run across *very few* people who have done so, I *used* to think that this might be an excellent and profitable way to move around with total versatility.

That was before I met Fred Trent. You learned his story in Chapter 3 of this part. There's no question in my mind but that he has clearly found the *best* way to achieve such versatility, and pursue "Continental Interlock" *without* the headaches that becoming an Independent Vehicle Transporter would entail. Besides all the hassles and paperwork involved in getting the proper authority to be an independent vehicle transporter, both federal and state, there's the matter of facing *stupendous* insurance premiums, generally payable *for **each unit, each time** you drive*. So before you consider this, give far *more* consideration to the methods used so successfully by Fred!

7
Condensed Answers
to Some of the
Most-Asked Questions

1. **Q:** **How many Road Rats are there?**

   A. Counting all Road Rats in the USA and Canada, including ones who work full-time, part-time, seasonally, and on weekends -- for manufacturers, modifiers, final assemblers, transporter companies, and dealers... probably 100,000 or more. If the "on-call" ones are included in the count, the number is probably *150,000* or more.

2. **Q.** **Is $30,000 a typical income figure for most *full-time* Road Rats?**

   A. For those who are ambitious and *follow the guidelines in this Handbook,* average income is probably *greater* than $30,000. There is no reason that a full-time Road Rat having this degree of guidance would earn less than $40,000, unless he chooses to take long periods of time off for other projects, or to work a strictly 5-day work week.

   However, it is likely that 95% of *transporter-company* Road Rats at any given moment in time are making *much less* than $30,000 a year. That's because less than 5% of active Road Rats have this Handbook, and *without* that guidance, far too many people come into this workforce, don't see the potential it offers, and then leave it to pursue other things. This Handbook *IS* the only true *gateway* to *success* in this field, unless you have a successful Road Rat or knowledgeable dispatcher acting as a mentor to help you get onto the right track.

3. **Q.** **What is the most common mistake made by Road Rats who enter this field *without* having the Handbook?**

   A. Without the Handbook, or personal guidance from a knowledgeable Road Rat or dispatcher, most do not discover Interlock or Maximization *soon* enough, on their own, to become successful. The primary entry level for Road Rats that *don't* have this book is the transporter company. As you already have seen in Chapter 4 of this part, it is very difficult to *convince* the uninformed newcomer Road Rat that using an *Ameripass* is *critically important* when working for only *one* transporter, *unless* he already knows to employ the techniques of *Interlock* -- and most do *not,* since this Handbook is the primary source of Interlock *data!* From an economic standpoint, if they do *neither,* they normally don't last long enough to make progress, and so drop out.

4. **Q.** **If *new* transporter-company Road Rats can *observe* others around them making decent incomes by using *Ameripasses* or Interlock, then why do so *few* of them ATTEMPT to *learn and use* those techniques?**

   A. If you figure that out, **PLEASE tell *me!!*** I've tried, personally, to help *dozens* of new transporter-company Road Rats in that manner, only to see practically all of them exhibit complete lack of interest. Soon after, they went by the wayside. Even if *this edition* of this Handbook had existed, and I were to have *given* it to them, I sincerely believe they wouldn't have read it! Such casual disinterest or apathy on the part of so many *newcomer* transporter-company Road Rats is the biggest ***mystery*** I've ever encountered in this industry!

5. **Q.** **How much education does one need to be a successful Road Rat?**

   A. Again, this book is a complete *course* in it! And the *only* such course in existence. But in terms of *formal* education, there are no requirements whatsoever. Be over 18, have a valid driver's license, a decent driving record, and good common sense. Then it doesn't matter whether you have a third-grade education or a Ph.D.

6. **Q.** **Is there any gender discrimination in this lifestyle?**

   A. Not that I have ever seen or been told about. Over this much time, I think I'd have heard of at least one case, if it were going on to any degree at all. Thirty percent of all Road Rats are women, and they enjoy the same working conditions as the men, and the same rates of pay.

7. **Q.** **Is the insurance always paid by the companies who employ the Road Rats?**

   A. Yes. Just once, a Handbook customer in Florida told me of a company he'd run across that required its drivers to provide their own insurance, but I've been unable to verify that. If true, this is the only exception I've ever encountered. If a company ever tells *you* that you have to do this, *leave!* And *then,* please, tell *us* about them! We'll verify that, if at all possible, and then make that notation next time in that company's listing.

8. **Q.** **Can a person having an ordinary driver's license be a Road Rat?**

   A. *Normally,* yes, as long as only vehicles weighing less than 26,000 lbs. are involved. But unfortunately, there are some dispatchers out there who'll swear on a stack of Bibles that the cut-off is only 10,000 lbs., and so therefore will hire only drivers who possess some class of CDL. According to the DOT, though, it's 26,000 lbs., so such companies probably just have their own hiring policy, and simply *say* that the lower figure is a requirement, in order to *obtain* such versatile drivers. If you run up against this, and don't want to obtain a CDL, simply apply elsewhere. It should be noted that many states still have what is called a "chauffeur's license," *in between* the ordinary operator's license and the CDL, and in many of *those* states, having *that* level of license *can* be a valid prerequisite for being a Road Rat. It's good news, though. Compared to CDLs, chauffeur's licenses are quite *easy* to obtain.

9. **Q.** **Can *couples* be successful Road Rats?**

   A. Yes, and they comprise fully 40% of all Road Rats. There are many ways to work effectively as a couple, and this Handbook provides you the details for the best ones, in Part II, Chapter 6. Using the techniques presented, couples working together as full-time Road Rats, realistically can earn $60-70,000 a year.

10. **Q.** **I've heard that this is a great job for retirees, 65 and over. Is it hard to get into this if you are *younger* than that?**

    A. No. It's equally easy for safe drivers to be hired at *any* age between 18 and, say, 80. Even though 30% of drivers are 65 or over, **remember that this means the other 70% are younger than 65!** (Remember, it's a great *summer* job for college students!) But isn't it nice, in a country filled with companies that can't wait to hand out gold watches, that there is this *ONE major industry* which is willing to hire, *readily,* people between 65 and 80 -- who often think that they are unemployable due to their age... and give them such *enjoyable* work?

11. **Q. Can I deliver new trailers with *my own* tow vehicle?**

    A. By all means! Having that capability is *in demand* by both trailer manufacturers (hitch-pulled and fifth wheels) and transporter companies. Thus, getting started as a Road Rat in *that* circumstance is *especially* easy! Something to **watch out** for, though, is **"trip-leasing."** If you trip-lease your truck to a company, then you almost surely will be *prohibited* by that company from doing Interlocks! You'll drive your vehicle under *that* company's authority, and bearing *its* placards. It would be all right if you could simply *remove* those when making return (Interlock) runs under a *different* company's authority, and with *its* placards, but many transporter companies (and even some manufacturers) don't allow that. If you take more than a normal time-span to deadhead home, the company can assume you've Interlocked, and *fire* you! So if you encounter the trip-lease requirement as just described, you must decide whether you want to accept that arrangement, or look farther! Unless the pay is *excellent,* keep looking! (When delivering *motorized* units, however, this problem almost never arises.)

12. **Q. May I spend extra time along the way, to sightsee, or visit friends?**

    A. Yes. But only on your medium-length and long trips, provided your normal pace is a moderate to rapid one. Using a 3,000-mile, coast-to-coast run as an example, most companies would permit their drivers to take a maximum of 6 days, and even as many 7 days, to make the trip. If you would normally do it in 4 or 5 days, you might be able to take a day or two off along the way for a visit, or to sightsee. Just don't add very many extra miles to the run, and *absolutely do not* submit for *pay* to your company any unnecessary miles that you drive. Stopovers don't work, of course, when outbound on short trips. Barring a breakdown, it is reasonable for any company to *expect* a run of 350 miles or shorter to be accomplished within 24 hours or less.

13. **Q. What about spending extra time at destinations?**

    A. Knock yourself out! After you've delivered the unit at its destination, you have all the time in the world, once again, to do whatever you'd like -- *unless* you already have arranged with your dispatcher to return immediately for a new run. Most drivers who know they'd like to spend extra days in a favorite destination simply express that desire to their dispatchers *beforehand,* so that the dispatchers know when they can expect their drivers back. Helps them in their planning. This is a very flexible industry, and being an independent contractor gives you *incredible* freedom!

14. **Q. What if I'm NOT an independent contractor?**

    A. That is, as they say, a horse of a different color. Many Road Rats (although still very much in the minority, fortunately) are employees of their company. They have much less flexibility and freedom. Usually, they can schedule their own hours -- and to some degree, even days -- while *en route.* But when *not* actually on a run, they tend to have many of the same constraints that apply to all *other* types of employees. And *that* can limit your opportunity to spend extra time at destinations.

15. **Q. Can this job be done while on vacation?**

    A. Sure! Why go to the expense of *renting* an RV for a vacation, when you can *deliver* one for *pay,* instead?! Just plan ahead! But if your family rides along, it's best to set up an Interlock run in advance, as well, to avoid return transportation expense.

Questions & Answers **159**

16. **Q.** **If transporter companies pay, on average, only *half* as well as do manufacturers and dealers, then why are you so favorably-inclined toward tranporters?**

    A. I am no *more* favorably-disposed toward transporter companies than to any others who utilize the services of Road Rats. In fact, I'll be among the first to tell you that it's *great* to work for a manufacturer for good pay, and thereby be able to use the Maximization method for returns, and collect tons of frequent flier miles!

    However... there are many good things to be said for *transporters,* including these:

    (1) Most are run by good and friendly people who appreciate the services performed by their hard-working drivers. Even though most of these usually don't have the necessary time or information at their disposal to help Road Rats who have no Handbook in recognizing the importance of *Ameripasses* and/or Interlock, they are normally quite *supportive,* in terms of providing the types of runs desired.

    (2) Due to rapid turnover of drivers (because so many come in who are *uninformed* as to the ways a comfortable income can be earned, and therefore tend to *leave* after only a short time), **transporters are by *FAR* the best entry-level opportunity for new Road Rats!** *That* goes for well-informed ones as well as the uninformed.

    (3) Two transporter companies situated a thousand miles or more apart -- which will continously send an Interlock Road Rat *back and forth* -- can pay a Road Rat as much or more as he/she would make working for a manufacturer! And when a Road Rat has established such a Semi-Permanent Interlock between a *manufacturer* and a transporter company, things get *highly* lucrative!!

17. **Q.** **Is special training required in order to become a Road Rat?**

    A. Almost never. Anyone having a good driving record and a valid license can learn very quickly how an RV of any size handles. Maneuvering in tight parking areas can take extra care and practice, but driving them is a snap for all good drivers. In fact, most people who have driven RVs consider them *easier* to drive than cars. (Consider, too, that the largest RVs frequently are *owned* by folks in their *70s,* who have no trouble at all handling them!) Much the same can be said for the other specialty vehicles weighing less than 26,000 lbs.

18. **Q.** **Is this *safe*? I mean, isn't there a lot of violent crime out there these days?**

    A. Well, let's see. There are 270 million Americans. So even if we consider those who don't get out on the road much, either as a driver or a passenger, and we add up the number of separate *trips,* long and short, that are taken, the average person probably travels in a motor vehicle at least 4 times a week. Now, I'll be surprised if one person a week, on average, gets killed by violent crime while on a trip. But *if so,* then **you'll get killed that way once out of every BILLION TRIPS you embark upon.** The Brits don't use the word, "billion," and the way *they* say it is even stronger. That's one out of every ***thousand million*** trips! Your odds of winning a Lotto *jackpot* are *at least 67 times more likely.* Or how about this? For every **67** Lotto *jackpots* you win, you'll get killed in a vehicle due to a violent crime.

    Bottom line: It's *VERY* safe to be a Road Rat. Get out there and *enjoy* yourself!!

Telling It Like *Is* Dept. --

Signs We'd *LOVE* to See!

Welcome to
NEW JERSEY
Speed Limit *STILL* 55

(We apologize for our inconsiderate lawmakers!)

Eastbound
NEW YORK STATE THRUWAY
PUBLIC SERVICE SIGN

Massachusetts-Bound?

Take Exit 24 -- I-90
TOLL-FREE SHORTCUT!

APPENDIX 1
THE JOB MARKET

SECTION 1

UNDERSTANDING THE COMPANY LISTINGS

Once you have studied and learned the techniques of job-seeking and job performance in this lifestyle, as described in the first half of this book, these next pages then become your most important resource. This Appendix is in four sections. The *first*, which you are reading now, is the KEY to your understanding how to interpret the lists of companies that follow, and how to approach them *properly* with regard to employment. The *second* section has been prepared especially for Alaskans who wish to do this while continuing to live in Alaska. It additionally should be very helpful to those living elsewhere who wish to travel for pay to Alaska. The *third* section lists all **manufacturers** of recreational and other specialty vehicles that we have been able to research in the USA, Canada, and Australia. A small quantity of European companies also is included. And the *fourth* section lists most of the **transporter companies** of North America. (If we *missed* any of the manufacturers or transporters about which you have knowledge, *please let us know,* so that we may include them in the next edition for the benefit of all.) Altogether, when the many terminals of the larger transporter companies are included in the count, this book lists about 4,000 potential employers.

= = = *CAUTION!* = = =

BEFORE YOU CONTACT ANY COMPANY, IT IS *EXTREMELY IMPORTANT* THAT YOU *READ CAREFULLY* -- AND *UNDERSTAND COMPLETELY* -- THE INFORMATION PROVIDED BELOW!

* The listings of companies in Sections 2 and 3 of this Appendix -- which range in size from small customizing and/or repair shops to the largest manufacturers of recreational and specialty vehicles, as well as a selection of dealers -- should *all* be regarded as **potential** employers. Section 4, however, lists transporter companies -- which **all** use drivers. This is *an important distinction to remember* when you seek employment!

* A potential employer is just that. **POTENTIAL.** Some of them have *always* used drivers, and some *never* have. But one thing is certain: **If a company builds, modifies, or sells any type of vehicle,** *drivers almost always are part of the shipping equation.* Sometimes it will be necessary for *you* to determine *where* they fit in. You do this by asking the company how their vehicles are *shipped* (in the case of manufacturers, modifiers and final assemblers) or *received* (in the case of dealers.)

* In doing this research and compiling the listings for Sections 3 and 4, **we included every viable company that deals in any respect with vehicles in need of transport, with the exception of dealerships, with which we were very selective.**

   For example, a repair shop may not seem like a fabulous opportunity, but don't sell those short! One of the most enjoyable and profitable years I spent as a full-time Road Rat in the mid-1980s was as the sole driver for a repair shop!

* A manufacturer or dealer that has **never yet employed drivers** *may*, at any time, decide that it is in its best interests to *begin* doing so. *You* may even be the deciding factor, especially in the case of dealerships. A dealer almost always has to pay the manufacturer's shipping charges. So if a dealer says he never uses drivers, consider *negotiating* with him, as we discussed back on page 11. If you can convince him that by using *you* to do DPUs for him, he can *save money* and therefore *be more competitive* in the marketplace, you may obtain a very nice position that could net you between 25 cents and 30 cents per mile, after expenses. Remember, too, that *large* RV dealerships are the *best bet* when considering doing DPUs. They sell RVs in sufficient volume to keep drivers busy picking them up from the factories at a steady pace. But remember... the smaller dealerships also often employ a driver or two.

* **IT IS VITALLY-IMPORTANT THAT YOU UNDERSTAND *THIS*:** A listing in Sections 2 and 3 indicates only that a company **exists**, and that it is reasonable for the owner of this Handbook to infer that it **PROBABLY** is involved in the transportation of vehicles in *some* capacity, and **nothing more.** *No willingness* on the part of *any* of these companies to hire drivers is implied, nor should be inferred by the reader. It is not necessary to secure the consent of a company simply to include it in such a list, and indeed *even to attempt this* would be an impossible task. In fact, in the case of manufacturers, *not* to be included in these listings, as thoroughly-researched as they are, might be construed by some as an indication of a company's *non*existence! Most companies certainly would prefer that their existence be *acknowledged* in as comprehensive a directory as this.

* Please be aware that **CHANGE** seems to be the name of the game in this indus-try, even more than in many others. We're not sure what causes such rapid changes, but we've learned that we generally must publish a new and revised edition of this Handbook *about every three or four years* in order to keep it current. Therefore, **this 1995-97 Edition will be current until the next revision, in 1998.** *As an owner this 3rd Printing,* however, you have a Handbook that is *FAR* **more current than if you owned a previous printing. Over 100 of its pages (including 500 of its company listings) were brought up to date to be current as of May, 1997.**

   Even so, you need to be aware that even within a few weeks or months of the release of *this* printing, some of the companies listed herein will have ceased to exist, because change occurs so quickly. Phone numbers, addresses, personnel, and even the types of vehicles made, modified, or sold by many will undergo change. This pace will continue, if all other economic parameters remain fairly constant, so that by mid-1998 -- *if we had not updated the listings in this 3rd printing* -- as much as 50% of the information contained in this Appendix, and perhaps more, would no longer have been fully accurate. But the data in *this* printing will probably retain 75-80% of its accuracy by that time. The book you hold in your hands is quite advanced over all versions prior to 1997.

TIP: **Be aware that whether or not a company uses its own drivers, or does DPUs, or engages the services of one or more transporter companies, its *shipping methods are completely subject to change,* and such changes from one method of delivery to another can occur within a company literally overnight, *with little or no notice!***

Just because a company told our researchers that a particular method or methods were being used is no guarantee that the same method(s) will still be in use by the time you make contact with it. Therefore, please be friendly and civil with whomever you may speak when making contact with companies -- even if their situation has changed dramatically since the research was done.

* Remember, too, that *due to the rapid changes within this industry,* **YOU SHOULD NOT BE SURPRISED IF A COMPANY KNOWS** *LITTLE OR NOTHING* **ABOUT THIS HANDBOOK!** During the years between the research phases, each time, of editions (and printings within an edition, as in the case of this book), hundreds of *new* companies who'd never before heard of us get started. Further, thousands of companies were polled by phone for *this* printing, so *someone* at each of those companies knew about this book at that time, during 1996-early 1997. However, if the person with whom you speak knows nothing about the book, you probably are therefore (1) *talking to a different person from the one we polled,* or else (2) the person has *forgotten* the conversation in the time that has passed since then.

* Finally, you should be aware that many companies that clearly were *not* using drivers *at the time we did the research* are nevertheless listed in this Handbook. Why? Because of that *change* factor we just discussed. Even if a company has *never* used drivers, *that's* **no** *indication that they* **never** *will.* Any company that engages in any way with driveable vehicles has the *potential* for deciding, sooner or later, to start using its own drivers in the movement of those vehicles. And those manufacturers, modifiers, final assemblers, or dealers who have no drivers will almost always be able to tell you who DOES drive the vehicles from or to their sites. So if you call and they tell you they use no drivers, *always* go to the *next* step: ask them *who* accomplishes this *for* them! Then you can continue on, if you'd like (unless *all* their vehicles are picked up by CPU drivers), and call *that* company!

Making Contact!

Okay -- let's examine a few of the details pertaining to making your initial contacts with companies for whom you'd like to drive.

First, *determine what kind of work you'd like to do* in terms of *distance* and *frequency* of travel.
If you like a good mix of long and short trips, seek employment with manufacturers of *highly-specialized* vehicles or *deluxe* RVs, or RVs whose brand-name has become a household word. These usually have dealers and/or customers throughout the continent.

TIP: **The more specialized, deluxe, or well-known the vehicle, the more likelihood there is of making deliveries to points all over the continent.**

If you prefer short runs, consider manufacturers and modifiers of *conversion vans*. These vehicles, when delivered singly, are mostly shipped within a 150-mile range. Sometimes 250-300 miles. Longer runs than that occur, but fairly rarely. So this can be an ideal situation for drivers who like to take short runs and get home again the same day.

Remember that around 30% of all Road Rats, part-timers and full-timers, are 65 or over. And that means rapid turnover of jobs in this field, as discussed earlier in the book, because people of retirement age don't stay in a workforce as long as do people who enter a workforce at a younger age. This reminder is being repeated here because *now* you're about to start making contact with companies. And it's good for you to remember at this point that the odds of your being hired are excellent -- just in case you find yourself making what seems like too many contacts without finding success.

TIP: **Virtually everyone who's qualified, who seeks this work while maintaining a friendly and positive attitude, ultimately is hired.**

There are exceptions to every rule. First, the "rule": We've found that becoming employed by a company in this lifestyle usually occurs *on average* somewhere between the 7th and the 18th attempt. The *exceptions*, therefore, are those who get hired on the first or second contact they make (which is *great!*), or on something more like the 40th or 50th contact (which is *exasperating!*). So if you should unfortunately happen to fall into the latter category, heed this:

TIP: **The most important thing to remember is that you are seeking employment for a real job. And openings DO exist. They simply get FILLED quickly. So being *wait-listed* is a great way to pursue this job. And above all -- *Don't give up!!***

Using the Toll-Free Phone Numbers

Hundreds of the companies listed in this Handbook are accessible via toll-free WATS lines; the familiar "800" numbers. (WATS, by the way, is simply an abbreviation for *W*ide *A*rea *T*elephone *S*ervice, but you'd be amazed how many people think the word comes from the electrical designation, "watt," so mistakenly spell it with an extra "T!") On the surface, this seems terrific, until one remembers that phone companies aren't in the habit of giving away their services. Whenever an "800" number is dialed, *somebody* ends up *paying* for the call. Since we already know it's not the caller, and we just ruled out the phone company, that leaves only the person or company that provides the "800" number for your use. Therefore, certain rules of etiquette come into play -- and you should remember that courtesy on an applicant's part is a major factor in getting hired! We make these recommendations:

1. Because it's poor psychology to force your prospective boss to pay for your solicitation when you're job-hunting, please resist the temptation to use the "800" numbers *when seeking* **work.**

2. *Interlock*, however, is a different story. When attempting to establish a return or continuing trip via the Interlock System, your proposal stands a very good chance of being *mutually* beneficial. The company you call may need to send a vehicle to your home area (or to somewhere else that you'd like to go) at about the time of your projected arrival in their vicinity -- when you'd like to have the run. So when attempting to set up an Interlock, most companies probably would have no objection to your making this offer via their WATS line.

VITALLY-IMPORTANT INFORMATION! 165

3. In the listings, "800" numbers are sometimes provided for a very specialized area, and in the cases in which we know the specifics, we tell you. Listings of toll-free numbers are provided as follows:

Nation -- This is an "800" number that can be called from anywhere in the USA. Often, when such a number appears in a listing within either Canada or USA, it can be accessed by people in *both* countries, but not always. In recent years, more and more WATS lines have become universally dialable, both from outside the company's state, as well as from within it. However, in some cases, the "800" number works only from states or provinces *outside* of the one in which the company is located. In that event, companies often *also* have a separate "800" number that can be used by those trying to reach them from *within* their own state or province.

KY Only -- This means "Kentucky only," and is an *example* of the way an "800" number is listed if it can be used *only* within a company's *own* state. If the company later gets a universal "800" number, you can expect that one or the other of its listed "800" numbers will become invalid.

Nation (except KY) -- This means the "800" number works from just about any location in the USA (and sometimes even Canada) *except* from *within* the state in which the company is located -- in this case, KY.

WATS -- This is how we list an "800" number if we have been unable to determine the extent of the geographical area for which it is valid. It may or may not work from your location. You'll just have to experiment with it.

Region -- In this case, we *have* been able to determine the geographical area served by the number. The description of that area follows the number, and generally is shown in parentheses. [*E.g.*, Region: (800) 777-2222 (350-mile radius)].

What we said earlier about constant change seems to apply more to "800" numbers than to anything else. For some reason, companies really can't seem to make up their minds on how they want to handle this service, long-term. As a result, they constantly are *changing* their "800" numbers, *discontinuing* them, or *acquiring* them! So if you run across one that doesn't work, or if a company in these listings with whom you'd like to establish an Interlock doesn't have one listed, try calling 1-800-555-1212, which is a toll-free call to Directory Assistance for toll-free numbers, and see if they have one listed that will work from your location.

Here's a hint! *Many* of the companies that *have* toll-free numbers, *don't* have them listed with Directory Assistance. When calling a company that shows no "800" number in its listing in this Handbook, ask the receptionist if they *have* one. If so, when she provides it, *write it in this Handbook, under their listing,* so that you can have it available for future reference! Feel free to let **US** know this too, if you'd like! You'll find, too, that over time, many "800" numbers shown herein will become obsolete, or that some of the companies shown originally as *not* having them have since *obtained* them. **Don't be afraid to write in this book.** *It's a reference book, like a Road Atlas or a Phone Book, so* **the more up-to-date you're able to keep it, the more useful it will be to you!**

A Brief Overview of Sections 2, 3, and 4

Section 2 of *this* Appendix, which deals entirely with how **Alaskans** can become Road Rats and *continue living* in Alaska -- and how people living in the lower 48 states and Canada can make runs *to* Alaska -- presents a detailed analysis of the RV dealerships in and around Anchorage, including the manner in which many of them employ DPU drivers. It is a unique presentation in that **nowhere else in this manual is there such *detailed treatment* of how Dealer Pick-Ups are done.** Because perhaps 40,000-50,000 DPU Road Rats work in North America, *it is worthwhile studying this section, even if you never plan to drive to Alaska, just so you can see if doing DPUs would work well for you.*

Section 4 is a comprehensive listing of the **transporter companies** of the USA and Canada. Because transporter companies *always* have drivers, and because the pay scale for transporter company drivers is so different, we've provided a separate section for these. Remember that these middlemen, even though they must necessarily pay drivers less than manufacturers and dealers, are *an important component of the entire picture, and are quite valuable in many ways to Road Rats!*

That leaves **Section 3** -- the largest section of this entire Handbook. It lists all the **manufacturers** of recreational and specialty vehicles that we were able to locate and interview in the USA, Canada, and Australia. These listings probably encompass better than 95% of all such companies that were in existence at the time the *full* research was completed in mid-1994. Interim research in *late 1996* for this 3rd Printing yielded a total of more than 500 *company updates,* which include changes within previously-listed companies, as well as hundreds of new companies. In addition, **selected RV and specialty vehicle dealers** have been included within Section 3, for those interested in seeking work as a DPU driver.

You will find that Sections 2 and 4 are self-explanatory, and stand entirely alone. Section 3, however, needs further explanation, so that you can understand why *some* RV dealers were included while *most* were not, and so that you can use the coding system that makes it possible for you to have a Handbook the size of this one, rather than one that would probably be about the size of the Buffalo, NY telephone directory. Therefore, in the interests of being able to present all the data of Sections 2, 3, and 4 without interruption by pages of text, we'll now turn to a complete explanation of how to understand and use the data in Section 3. Until you've become familiar with the codes, you'll probably find it easiest to use Section 3 if you keep one finger in *these* pages, while looking up listings in there.

How to Use and Interpret Section 3

The vast majority of companies listed are in the manufacturing category: Manufacturers (MFR), Final Assembly Sites (FINAL ASSEMBLER), and Modifiers (MODIFIER, or CONVERTER). Mixed in with these are selected dealers (DLR). Only a tiny percentage of the total number of dealers found in the USA, Canada, and Australia are listed in Section 3, and none are included for Europe. In order for an RV, truck, or specialty vehicle *dealer* to be considered *especially* useful to prospective Road Rats, they had to meet *one or more* of the following criteria for inclusion:

1. A dealer having a *toll-free* ("800") number.
2. A dealer in a *sparsely-populated* region, or one in which there are relatively *few* manufacturers.
3. A *major* dealership, which therefore either has DPU drivers working for it already, or if not, is large enough that it could possibly find it beneficial to *hire* some.
4. A site or dealership that *already is known to be using* DPU drivers.
5. A site or dealership that *we* considered potentially valuable to you, for other reasons.

CODES USED IN SECTION 3

Most of the data pertaining to vehicles and drivers are encoded, for two reasons: (a) it is easier for the reader to rapidly scan the listings for desirable situations, and (b) this keeps the book from being too cumbersome to conveniently accompany you in your travels. The codes are shown in italics, near the end of most listings in the section. The first code shows the vehicle(s) which are built, modified, or sold by the company, as follows:

RECREATIONAL VEHICLES (Motorized and Trailers)

R1	--	"Class A" Motorhomes (The large, "box-shaped" variety)
R2	--	"Class C" Mini-motorhomes (Medium-sized, cab-over bunk type)
R3	--	Micro-mini Motorhomes (Smaller version of the Class C)
R4	--	Van Conversions (without external electrical hookup)
R4-B	--	Van Conversions (with hookup; "Class B")
R5	--	Fifth-wheel Travel Trailers
R6	--	Travel Trailers (towable by hitch)
Convs	--	Conversions. Ordinary vehicles that are customized into luxury or special-purpose vehicles. The *type* of vehicle precedes this code. *E.g.: Suburban Convs, Blazer Convs, etc.*
TConvs	--	Truck Conversions. (Usually applies to conversions of pickup trucks.)
H'Cap	--	Vehicle Conversions with special fittings or equipment for the handicapped.

TRUCK/BUS BODIES & SPECIALTY MOTORIZED VEHICLES

Truck bodies in this list are almost entirely straight (non-semi-trailer) types.

TB	--	Truck bodies in general. Or a specific type of truck may precede code.
CTB	--	Custom Truck Bodies
STB	--	Specialized *TB*. (Mfr. usually makes several types.)
A	--	Ambulances
E	--	Emergency and/or Rescue Vehicles
F	--	Fire Trucks
FTB	--	Flatbed Trucks
G	--	Garbage Trucks
H	--	Hearses/Funeral Cars
LTB	--	Livestock Trucks
M	--	Dump Trucks
S	--	School Busses
SP	--	Snowplows
S/STB	--	Salt- and Sand-Spreading Trucks
U	--	Custom, Intercity, or Transit Busses
UTB	--	Utility Trucks
V	--	Beverage Trucks
VTB	--	Van-type (enclosed cargo) Straight Trucks
W	--	Wreckers/Tow Trucks
S-1	--	Semi-tractors (*not* including trailer)

Non-Recreational TRAILERS

T	--	Trailers in general; not specified or described
CT	--	Custom Trailers
ST	--	Specialized Trailers; may or may not be described therein.
BT	--	Boat Trailers
GT	--	Gooseneck Trailers (general; purpose not specified, or else undetermined)
HT	--	Horse Trailers
LT	--	Livestock Trailers
UT	--	Utility Trailers
WT	--	Lumber, Logging, or Wood-Chip Trailers
5WT	--	Light- or Medium-Duty 5th-wheel *T* (*other* than *R5* or *S-2*)
S-2	--	Semi-trailers (*not* including tractor)

OTHER VEHICLES

Limos	--	Limousines
TC	--	Truck Campers (not wheeled; usually for mounting in pickups, and can be delivered singly to dealers in that configuration)
X	--	When used, this designation always precedes another code, and means "other." (*E.g.,* UTB, XTB means "utility truck bodies, and other truck bodies.")

DRIVER CODES

These codes follow, and normally appear directly beneath, the Vehicle Codes. When the number of drivers used (at the time we polled the company) is known, a colon follows the code, and then the number of drivers is provided. Lack of data pertaining to the number of drivers can mean that we were unable to obtain that information. More often, though, it means that the number of drivers fluctuates somewhat unpredictably. When fluctuation is predictable (due to seasonality or to rates of production), the low and high expected numbers are both shown, with a hyphen between.

EXAMPLES: *C-2:3*   Company had three C-2 drivers when interviewed.
   C-2:4-7 Company normally uses between 4 and 7 drivers, type C-2.

When one or more transporter companies are used, either exclusively, or to supplement a manufacturer's own driver force, we tried to determine its name. When this was possible, a colon follows the *"D"* (for transporter company... see below) and the transporter company name or names are provided. It should be noted that often this extra information was *not* obtained. In such cases, the letter "D" stands alone, indicating either that the company uses one or more undetermined transporters -- or it may mean that they often *change* the ones that they use.

- *A...* indicates the company's product is TRUCKED to the destination point. When you see this code, be aware that unless other driver codes appear with it, you can assume that no opportunities for Road Rats existed at the time the company was interviewed.
- *B...* indicates there are drivers who TOW the company's trailers to destinations. These can be Road Rats driving small trucks, owned either by the company, the Road Rats, or both, who deliver trailers manufactured by the company to its customers or dealerships.
- *C...* indicates the company's units are DRIVEN to their destinations by Road Rats.
- *D...* indicates the company uses at least one transporter company.

A-1 -- TRUCKED by company employees driving company trucks
A-2 -- TRUCKED by independent contractors driving company trucks
A-3 -- TRUCKED by independent contractors driving their own trucks
B-1 -- TOWED by company drivers using company trucks
B-2 -- TOWED by independent contractors driving company vehicles
B-3 -- TOWED by independent contractors driving their own vehicles
C-1 -- DRIVEN by company employees on payroll
C-2 -- DRIVEN by independent contractors
D -- Deliveries are handled by one or more *transporter companies,* and *they* employ the Road Rats. If their name(s) are provided, you may wish to contact them about work. If not, you may wish to ask the listed manufacturer to provide you with the name(s) and phone number(s) of its transporter(s). (But be aware that if a *"B"* or *"C"* driver designation **also** is provided, then it may be **far more profitable** for you *first* to investigate the possibility of becoming a Road Rat who is *directly* paid by the *manufacturer,* rather than to immediately seek work in that instance with the *transporter,* who, in such a case, probably furnishes *supplemental* [back-up] drivers.)

A Few Last Reminders...

The primary research phase of this 1995-97 Edition was completed in November, 1994. For this Third Printing, though, we additionally applied *500* changes to the company listings from data we obtained in late 1996 and early 1997. Due to the dynamic nature of the world's economies, particularly in the vehicle industry, new companies start up constantly, while others simply drop out of existence. Also, addresses, contact persons, and phone numbers change. Therefore, if you obtained this printing of the book in 1997, soon after it came off the press, most of its data still will be accurate. But as time progresses toward and into 1998, many of its listings will change, or cease to exist. Nevertheless, even though *not all* of the data was revamped this time, enough of it *was,* for this Handbook to continue its viability throughout 1998.

If you call a company and find out it no longer exists, or has moved, or phone numbers or personnel have changed, this probably has happened since July, 1994, in some cases, and since late 1996 through early 1997 in most others.

Always be aware that CPU/DPU competition is *normal* for the factory Road Rat. And as you might expect, from what we said earlier, factory Road Rats really *hate* to lose runs to incoming CPU or DPU Road Rats. Seeing them come in to pick up units is rock bottom on the factory Road Rat's list of priorities! Unfortunately for factory Road Rats, however, there is no remedy for this, as long as the factory permits it. And because shipping units is not a means by which factories normally increase their profits, nearly all factories *do* permit their customers or dealerships to send in drivers to pick up units. The factory has nothing to lose. The only people to experience any negative impact from this are the factory Road Rats!

Interestingly, this isn't as negative as it might sound, when circumstances are normal, and CPU/DPU Road Rats pick up less than half of the available units. This is because the average factory maintains a workforce of drivers sufficient to meet the normal demand for factory Road Rats. And for that reason, the factory Road Rats normally are kept busy all the time. If there were *no* CPU/DPU Road Rats coming in, then the factory simply would engage the services of *more* factory Road Rats! Think about that for a moment. If a factory ships out enough units per week to keep six Road Rats busy, what *difference* does it make if four Road Rats work for the factory, and two are working for dealerships? If there were *no* pickups from outside, then *all six* would work for the factory. At bottom, it makes *no* difference though, because in the final analysis, the *output of the factory* is sufficient to support *six of the drivers* in the *entire* Road Rat workforce. *Which* Road Rats are involved will vary from one day to the next, of course, for one-third of the drivers that the factory sees, but that is inconsequential to the *overall* picture. The greater the overall *production,* industry-wide, the greater is the *number of Road Rats who are working.*

That begs the question: "Why would factory Road Rats even *mind* then, that CPU/DPU Road Rats come in for runs, as long as they're going to be kept busy *anyway?"* Well, if you work for a factory in Wichita and a driver working for a dealer in Topeka comes in for a unit, that probably wouldn't bother you at all. But what if the DPU Road Rat happened to come in from *Anchorage* to pick up a unit to drive back home to *Alaska?* That's what *factory* Road Rats hate to see -- the loss of *really choice* runs from time to time that *they* otherwise could have had!

One more point about the relationship of factories *vis-a-vis* dealers and customers. While the average number of units picked up at factories by DPU Road Rats and CPU drivers ranges between 10% and 35%, there are some factories where 90% or more of runs go to those drivers. Usually, this happens in the case of smaller modifiers, and custom shops. It's difficult to become a factory Road Rat for one of those because often they only have one or two such Road Rats. And to make matters worse, those Road Rats might not be kept busy enough simply with driving, and so might have other duties to perform for that shop or factory. And frequently, that other work can involve some sales work! Your best chance to work for such a company may therefore not actually have anything to do with working for them directly. Instead, your best chance might come in the form of doing an *Interlock* run for them, if you already are working for someone *else* as a factory or a transporter company Road Rat. Or to be an "on-call" driver for them. Many such companies retain the services *only* of such drivers.

In previous editions of the book, we frequently added notations to company listings such as "CPUs compete," or, "Heavy CPU/DPU competition." This edition has no such notations, because Road Rats need to be aware that *nearly all* companies, other than dealerships, have *some* amount of competition from DPU Road Rats and CPU drivers. (Keep in mind why we make that distinction: *all* drivers who work for dealers and do DPUs are *Road Rats.* But CPU drivers making pickups for customers, such as hospitals, funeral homes, etc. almost *never* are Road Rats, but instead are simply individuals who almost always are regular employees of those companies who are making isolated runs, perhaps one time only. But to the factory Road Rat, the *competition* will seem identical from either type.)

One last word before you start making your contacts. **BE FRIENDLY. BE RELAXED.** For *regular* factory, transporter company, and DPU Road Rats, the *only* sales work involved in this job is the *universal* one of selling their *own* merits to prospective employers. So *be yourself,* and *don't take offense, even if someone is abrupt and rude to you.* If you become frustrated, be sure to **cease** making calls until your confidence and good cheer have returned. That is *most important!*

Most of the time, at least a few driver positions are available, or the wait-list is short, in any given region. Because this book is primarily publicized via talk and news shows, its sales normally aren't dramatic enough to cause an excess of driver applicants. When that *does* occur, on rare occasions, the situation usually doesn't prevail for very long. So if you run across that circumstance, just seek to be wait-listed in your *own* area, while shopping for that *first* job in *other* areas, in the meantime.

Manufacturers by the Numbers -- USA

Want to *zero-in* your **application** and **Interlock** efforts on the states that have the *most* manufacturers, modifiers, and final assemblers of the type(s) of vehicles you'd like *most* to drive? Or would you like to see how your own home state fares? Here's the complete breakdown, by vehicle types. (Dealers are not included.)

KEY

A = Motorized RVs. (R1, R2, R3)
B = Van Conversions. (R4, R4-B)
C = Truck Bodies. (All TB types)
D = Other Motorized Vehicles.
E = All Trailers. (T, R5, R6, S-2)
F = Other Conversions. (TConvs, and others coded, "Convs")
G = Limousines.

The numbers shown in **boldface** reveal the states that have the *most* of any given *type* of manufacturer.

You can see that Indiana is the clear leader in manufacturing motorized RVs and trailers in general, and it's almost a dead heat between that state and California for van conversions. (Too close to call, in fact, because we might have missed someone! So we put *both* of them in bold.)

When it comes to limo manufacturers, top honors are shared by three states: California, Illinois, and New York. On the next page, you can see the actual *rankings* for the top ten states for each general vehicle type, to make this even easier to envision.

State	A	B	C	D	E	F	G
Alabama	6	13	16	9	19	2	0
Alaska	0	0	0	0	3	0	0
Arizona	3	18	8	8	15	1	0
Arkansas	0	4	7	6	11	0	2
California	37	**70**	79	21	41	9	5
Colorado	12	11	4	2	21	2	0
Connecticut	2	5	10	1	6	0	0
Delaware	0	0	2	0	0	0	0
Florida	10	41	21	16	47	2	1
Georgia	5	36	20	7	12	4	0
Hawaii	0	0	3	0	1	0	0
Idaho	2	3	5	2	1	0	0
Illinois	1	26	24	14	17	1	5
Indiana	**68**	**71**	38	24	**64**	7	0
Iowa	7	7	17	12	27	1	0
Kansas	4	4	16	12	6	1	1
Kentucky	0	16	17	6	7	1	0
Louisiana	0	5	5	4	5	1	0
Maine	0	1	4	1	1	0	0
Maryland	0	16	5	3	7	1	0
Massachusetts	0	11	5	4	4	0	0
Michigan	2	43	27	15	22	7	2
Minnesota	2	9	16	7	17	1	0
Mississippi	0	7	7	3	4	1	0
Missouri	0	17	19	9	19	1	2
Montana	0	0	5	1	9	0	0
Nebraska	0	8	1	3	11	1	0
New Hampshire	0	3	2	2	0	0	0
New Jersey	2	18	12	6	9	1	0
New Mexico	0	6	3	1	7	0	0
Nevada	2	5	0	0	2	1	0
New York	2	39	17	11	4	3	5
North Carolina	0	17	27	28	14	1	0
North Dakota	0	2	1	2	3	0	0
Ohio	8	56	48	27	32	4	3
Oklahoma	5	5	13	11	29	1	1
Oregon	19	14	13	12	38	2	1
Pennsylvania	9	25	53	**34**	43	4	0
Rhode Island	0	1	3	0	0	0	0
South Carolina	0	9	9	4	6	2	0
South Dakota	0	4	9	2	9	0	0
Tennessee	1	20	12	6	18	1	0
Texas	8	50	31	12	43	7	1
Utah	0	8	2	0	13	0	0
Vermont	0	0	1	0	0	0	0
Virginia	0	14	10	4	10	1	0
Washington	4	14	11	3	35	3	1
West Virginia	0	3	2	0	1	0	0
Wisconsin	3	31	10	7	12	2	2
Wyoming	1	0	1	1	5	0	0

USA
The Top Ten States in Each Major Vehicle Category
(Manufacturers/Modifiers/Final Assemblers Only)

		#1	#2	#3	#4	#5	#6	#7	#8	#9	#10
A.	Motorized RVs (R1, R2, R3)	IN	CA	OR	CO	FL	OH	PA	TX	IA	AL
B.	Van Conversions (R4, R4-B)	IN	CA	OH	TX	MI	FL	NY	GA	WI	IL
C.	Truck Bodies (All types of TB)	CA	PA	OH	IN	TX	MI	NC	IL	FL	GA
D.	Other Motorized Vehicles (exc. F & G)	PA	NC	OH	IN	CA	FL	MI	IL	IA	KS
E.	All Trailers (T, R5, R6, and S-2)	IN	FL	PA	TX	CA	OR	WA	OH	OK	IA
F.	Non-Van Conversions (TConvs, etc.)	CA	IN	MI	TX	GA	PA	NY	WA	AL	CO
G.	Limousines	CA	IL	NY	OH	AR	MI	MO	WI	FL	KS

(States that are *tied* are ranked alphabetically. To see the actual numbers, refer to previous page.)

For Category "D" -- IA, KS, OR, and TX all are tied for 9th place. Twelve each.
For Category "G" -- FL, KS, OK, OR, TX, and WA are tied for 9th place. One each.

SUGGESTION: **CIRCLE your *own* state** wherever it appears, if you live in one of the states in this table. **Put a SQUARE around each state that is *within 250 miles of you.*** Then you can always see your highest opportunities for working within a reasonable driving distance of your home -- for the *manufacturers* -- at a *glance!*

OTHER NATIONS

Space constraints prevented our providing these same breakdowns for Canada, Australia, and the European nations. However, the situations in Canada and Australia will be easier to visualize from their listings, because each of those nations have only a few hundred listings, rather than thousands.

For this 1995-97 Edition, updated extensively in this 3rd Printing, we have researched ALL of the manufacturers we could find, that were viable as of late 1996*, and the transporter companies, for the USA, Canada, and Australia. Dealerships also were included for the USA and Canada when they met one or more of our criteria for selection, as we've discussed. Almost no dealerships were included in the listings for Australia. It will be interesting to see if GATT and NAFTA and other trade agreements will cause our scope to become even wider in 1998! More Europe, perhaps. Or Latin America. We'll surely see!!

---

* The *full* research was completed for this edition in mid-1994. In late 1996, we did interim research on 1,500 companies, and applied the necessary changes to Section 3. This resulted in revisions (updates) to about 300 companies, and roughly 200 new companies were inserted to replace the same number of out-of-business ones. The next *full* research phase will lead to the 1998-99 Edition.

SECTION 2

Highway of Adventure...
Linking ALASKA to the LOWER 48!

Most who love to travel have at least *dreamed* of seeing Alaska, even if they haven't yet been there.

And although the vast majority of Alaskans have made trips to the lower 48, most of them would either like to do so more often, or less expensively, or both.

It is for these reasons that *this* edition of this Handbook at last, for the first time in its 15-year history, gives the 49th State and its residents the amount of attention they truly deserve.

A special "Thank you!!" goes to Phil White, a college student majoring in geography, from Indiana, who assisted me with the in-depth research necessary to write this chapter. In conjunction with a transportation logistics paper he was writing, and partially funded by this publisher, he travelled to Alaska in late June, 1994, where he conducted both on-site and telephone interviews with dealers in and around Anchorage. His findings with respect to DPUs done from Alaska have at last truly opened the door of opportunity in this field to Alaska residents, and additionally will prove helpful to those living in the lower 48 and in Canada who wish to travel to the Last Frontier for pay.

A VASTLY *DIFFERENT* BREED OF CAT!

A few general statements may be made about the deliveries of new vehicles to Alaska, so let's cover those first:

1. Almost all new RVs are driven to Alaska via the Alaska Highway (still popularly known as the Alcan Highway, especially by Alaskans).

2. The vast majority of RVs destined for Alaska originate from factories located in northern Indiana; perhaps as many as 90% or more. The remainder come mainly from California, followed by a scattering from other states.

3. New trucks of various types, and other specialty vehicles, come from sites all over the lower 48. Many of those are driven up the Alcan, but some also are brought up by ship, generally from ports in or near Seattle, Washington.

4. The dealer interviews indicate that the number of retirees doing this who are *Alaska*-based may in fact be substantially *higher* than the overall average of around 30% of Road Rats. In Alaska, perhaps as many as *50%* of Road Rats doing DPUs are of retirement age.

In the main listings of companies, you will find a few that are in Alaska. However, if an Alaska resident, you should *first* give your attention to *this* section, which now will provide you with the *highly-detailed* information that Phil White and I obtained in June, 1994. The data that is provided here will enable you to see that Alaska is truly a "different breed of cat" when it comes to seeking and performing this work. The work is NOT more difficult to perform, nor is it harder to obtain. It is simply done *differently*, as you will see.

The *primary* difference is that the *dealers* in Alaska generally have a more pro-active role in obtaining their vehicles. And in many cases, the way they accomplish this is *quite* creative!

The in-depth study concentrated on *RV* delivery because virtually 100% of RVs reach Alaska via the Alcan. However, *Alaskans should not ignore the many* **truck dealers,** most of which are also concentrated in the larger communities. Many trucks come up the Alcan too, but in smaller numbers.

It should be noted that in the data provided below, the numbers of units driven to the dealerships are estimates on the part of the person interviewed. Many estimates can be expected to be quite close, but some may be significantly higher or lower than the actual number.

Finally -- *don't forget* **Fairbanks!** Although not covered in this section, I have personally delivered units to dealers there. If you live in or near Fairbanks, I encourage you to look up the dealers in your Yellow Pages, and inquire with them. Look under these headings: "Truck Dealers," and "Recreational Vehicle Dealers."

THE RECREATIONAL VEHICLE DEALERS OF ANCHORAGE AND VICINITY

* **A & M Motors** Tel. (907) 561-1982
  2301 E. 5th Avenue
  Anchorage, AK 99501

  DATA: All their RVs are driven up the Alcan Highway.
  Deliveries are made by drivers working for transporter companies (Morgan, and Jackson) located in the lower 48.
  Approximately 80 units/month are delivered during the peak 3 months.
  Around 5-10 units/month are delivered during the rest of the year.

* **Alaska Economy RVs** Tel. (907) 248-7723
  5011 Jewel Lake Road
  Anchorage, AK 99502

  DATA: All units are driven up the Alcan Highway.
  Factory and transporter company drivers based in Indiana deliver them.
  Further details should be obtained on a case-by-case basis by prospective drivers from the owner, Chris Sutton.

* **ABC RV Sales** Tel. (907) 561-1982
  5500 Old Seward highway
  Anchorage, AK 99518

  DATA: ALL units are DPUs, brought up the Alcan to this dealership by Alaska-based drivers.
  There are approximately 35 drivers in this workforce, who have no other duties that must be performed for the dealership.
  80-90% of the drivers are retirees.
  Nearly all of the units are transported in April and May: a total of about 150 units.
  During the remaining 10 months of the year, about 1 unit per month is driven north.

*   **Alaska RV World, Inc.**   Tel. (907) 333-9012
    332 Muldoon Road
    Anchorage, AK 99504

    DATA: Over 90% of units are brought in via the Alcan Highway.
    60% of the year's units are brought up in March. 20% in April. (This 80% of all units comprises a quantity of around 50-60 units.) The remaining 20% are brought in during the other months of the year.
    DPUs by Alaska-based drivers account for 50% of all the runs. That percentage comprises approximately 40 units altogether which are delivered in that manner.
    There are about 30 DPU drivers who work for this dealership, and most are retirees.

*   **Alaskan Adventures RV Center**   Tel. (907) 344-2072
    918 E. 73rd Avenue
    Anchorage, AK 99518

    DATA: All vehicles are delivered via the Alcan Highway.
    This dealership is also an RV rental center.
    All units which are brought in as *rental* units are driven by Alaska-based DPU drivers. We were informed that this RV center is growing rapidly, and that "new DPU drivers are regularly added."
    It should be noted that most, if not all, of the drivers doing DPUs also have additional duties which are performed at the dealership.
    All *sales* units are brought up by drivers working for transporter companies based in the lower 48 (Don Ray Driveaway, and others).
    Approximately 20-25 units/month are brought in during the peak season.
    Roughly 5-10 units/month are brought in during the rest of the year.

*   **Bob's RV Country**   Tel. (800) 888-2627 (Toll-Free)
    13555 S.W. Canyon Road
    Beaverton, OR 97005

    DATA: This dealership is included here because it is listed in the Yellow Pages of the phone book in Anchorage, and therefore can be of interest to Alaskans. The toll-free number *does* work from Alaska (as do *most* "800" numbers, we have discovered).
    99% of units purchased here by Alaskans are brought north as CPUs by those same Alaskans who buy them. However, the dealership *does* have a person available who is willing to drive the units north, and a customer who desires that service will be provided with that person's name and phone number by the dealership.
    Suggestion: As an *Alaskan,* you may wish to notify this dealership of *your* willingness to have *your* name and number provided to such customers. Just as the Oregonian driver would have to fly home, so would an *Alaska*-based driver need to be provided with public transportation in one direction. It can't hurt to see if the dealer is willing to make this arrangement with you. If so, then the customer could fly you to Oregon, and pay you a negotiated sum to drive the unit north to him or her.

*   **Johnson RV Center**   Tel. (907) 561-1750
    4434 Old Seward Highway
    Anchorage, AK 99503

    DATA: All units are delivered via the Alcan Highway.
    Most units are **Winnebagoes**, and Morgan Driveaway's drivers deliver almost all of those from Iowa. (None are delivered by **Winnebago**'s own drivers, because that company ceased using them some years ago, and has since relied entirely upon transporter companies. Morgan is the transporter currently used by **Winnebago**.)
    NOTE: This is one of the dealers that has a particularly creative method of obtaining some of its units. About 12 units per year are brought in by Alaska-based drivers as DPUs. Most of those drivers are sent to California to pick up the vehicles. The drivers are selected *annually* from people who apply for that privilege! The dealer informed us that drivers who possess a CDL (commercial driver's license) are *favored* when these selections are made, so are the first ones picked.

*   **Modern Motors Used Equipment** Tel. (907) 344-3008
    701 E. 104th Avenue
    Anchorage, AK 99515

    DATA: Not too much opportunity here, most of the time, but read on...
    This dealership sells *mostly* used units, but *does* **also** sell some *new* RVs. A small percentage of their units therefore are driven up the Alcan annually. About half of those are brought in as DPUs by Alaskans, while the other 50% are driven in by factory or transporter company drivers based in the lower 48.
    NOTE: This company keeps on the lookout for prospective DPU drivers who are willing to go to the lower 48 *at their own expense,* who then will drive units back to them! *BUT* -- if they are unable to find someone willing to do this when they need a driver, then this becomes an *occasional profitable opportunity.* (We suggest that *you,* as a prospective Road Rat, do not volunteer to make the trip at your own expense, as this practice certainly prevents some driver from making a reasonable profit, each time this happens.)

*   **Murphy's RV, Inc.**   Tel.. (907) 276-0688
    929 E. 8th Avenue
    Anchorage, AK 99501

    DATA: ALL units are driven up the Alcan Highway from Indiana.
    ALL units are DPUs -- but here's a fascinating variation! They use drivers who originate from both Alaska *and* Indiana! *All* those drivers are paid by the dealership. (No units are delivered here by factory drivers or by transporter company drivers.)
    About 10 drivers deliver between 10 and 15 units/mo., peak season. (June and July)
    About 4 drivers deliver between 3 and 6 units/mo., slow season. (Rest of the year)

* **Niles Travelers, Inc.** Tel. (907) 279-0852
3200 Mountain View Drive
Anchorage, AK 99501

DATA: All RVs are brought up the Alcan Highway.
All of the *motor homes* are delivered by drivers working out of Indiana for **Coachmen.**
However, a few DPU runs are made each year for *other* types of units, by drivers selected by this dealer.
TEACHERS TAKE NOTE: *Most* of *those* drivers are *retired schoolteachers.*
Units moved here annually: 15-20/mo., peak season; 5-6/mo., slow season.

* **Nye RV Center** Tel. (907) 279-8506
824 E. 5th Avenue
Anchorage, AK 99501

DATA: This is an incorrect listing in the Anchorage Yellow Pages for Frontier Toyota. They report that they sell *NO* RVs at all! Please note, too, that the phone number shown as 258-0040 in that same listing is now obsolete. This information is provided so that Alaskan driver applicants scanning the Yellow Pages are aware of the current status.

* **Nye RV Center** Tel. (907) 694-8923
Mile 40, Parks Highway
Wasilla, AK 99687

DATA: This dealership no longer sells the larger RVs, but *does* sell conversion vans. However, they report that ALL of those come up the Alcan Highway by *truck.* Therefore, this dealership no longer is applicable for driver applicants wishing to do DPUs.

* **Pacific Motors** Tel. (907) 561-1946
4908 Old Seward Highway
Anchorage, AK 99503

DATA: This dealership sells both cars and RVs. This data applies to the RVs only.
They have *no* DPU drivers; all units are brought up the Alcan Highway from Indiana by factory- or transporter company-based drivers. This includes the motorized RVs, as well as 5th-wheel trailers, which are delivered by lower 48-based drivers using pickup trucks. They also sell pop-up campers, but, as is usually the case, those all are *trucked* in.
Their peak season is March-August (6 months), during which period 50-100 units per month are delivered. During the other 6 months, they receive no units at all.

*   **RV Depot Discount Motorhome Sales Center**   Tel. (206) 355-8935
    12201 Highway 99, S.
    Everett, WA 98204

    DATA: Although not in Alaska, data is provided here because this dealership is listed in the Anchorage Yellow Pages.
    ALL the units they have ever sold to Alaskans have been picked up as CPUs by those same Alaskans. They have never shipped even one single unit to Alaska, so we can assume that this probably presents Road Rats with no opportunity whatsoever. HOWEVER -- A Washington State resident may wish to volunteer with this dealership as an on-call driver to Alaska, in case the opportunity ever happens to present itself. The same thing could be done by an Alaskan.

*   **Sourdough Camper Village**   Tel. (907) 563-3277, 563-3268, **and** *(800)* 478-0124
    5773 Old Seward Highway
    Anchorage, AK 99518

    DATA: In 1994, they received 14 new RVs from Indiana, all of which were brought up the Alcan Highway by transporter company drivers. These units were purchased to replace a stock of used RVs that they sold. They reported that those 14 new units could move this year (1994), or it "might take two or three years to sell them all." They have *no* DPU drivers.
    Remember, though, that it never can hurt to present yourself to such a company as a potential DPU driver, and negotiate.

*   **Western Motorcoach**   Tel. (206) 774-1414
    19303 Highway 99
    Lynnwood, WA 98036

    DATA: Again, this is an out-of-state dealership which is listed in the Anchorage Yellow Pages. In this case, the facts are **identical** to those provided above for RV Depot Discount Motorhome Sales Center, in Everett, WA.

... AND BEFORE LEAVING ALASKA, HERE IS ONE *TRUCK* DEALER:

*   **Trailer Craft, Inc.**   (2 Locations)
    1301 E. 64th Avenue   3116 Commercial Drive
    Anchorage, AK 99518   Anchorage, AK 99501
    Tel. (907) 563-3238   Tel. (907) 277-5615

    DATA: Units arrive here all year long, primarily driven up the Alcan Highway, although some arrive by ship. Of the units that are driven, 50% are brought in by their DPU drivers, and the other 50% are brought by factory drivers.

There are many truck dealers listed in the Anchorage Yellow Pages. Remember that the smaller trucks can be driven by *regular* Road Rats. Larger ones can be delivered by CDL-equipped Road Rats, and by truckers who'd like to get away from hauling cargo, and all the hassles that go with it.

SECTION 3

Manufacturers, Modifiers, Final Assemblers, and Selected Dealers of Recreational and Specialty Vehicles

UNITED STATES of AMERICA

ALABAMA

Albertville
Global Custom Vans, Inc.
5270 Highway 431, South
Albertville, AL 35950
Tel: (205) 878-4892
Contact: Brenda Lowery
R4, R4-B
C-2 (Local within 2-3 hrs)

Albertville
South Land Vans, Inc.
302 Ed Adams Drive
Albertville, AL 35950
Tel: (205) 878-8267
R4

Albertville
Wayfaring Mfg.
3267 Highway 431, South
Albertville, AL 35950
Tel: (205) 593-1290
Contact: Tommy Calhoun
MFR/DLR of TC

Anniston
American Ikarus, Inc.
106 National Drive
Anniston, AL 36207
Tel: (205) 831-4296
FAX: (205) 831-4299
Contact: Richard Voorhees
MFR of U
C-2:1
D: Alabama Limo

Birmingham
AJF Leasing
3611 Industrial Parkway
Birmingham, AL 35217
Tel: (205) 841-0077
FAX: (205) 841-6933
Contact: Brett Brunkhorst
DLR of S-2
B-1, B-2, B-3, C-2
D

Birmingham
Ace Truck Body & Van
516 31st Street, North
Birmingham, AL 35203
Tel: (205) 326-2220
MFR/MODIFIER/
FINAL ASSEMBLER/
REPAIR of TB, VTB

Birmingham
Altec Industries, Inc.
(MAIL: P.O. Box 10264
Birmingham, AL 35202)
1730 Vanderbilt Road, N.
Birmingham, AL 35234
Tel: (205) 991-7733
Contact: Robert Leatherwood
Tel: (205) 323-8751
(Corporate Office)
MFR of TB, UTB
C-2
D

Birmingham
American Truck Equip.
4000 8th Avenue, North
Birmingham, AL 35222
Tel: (205) 591-7676
Nation: (800) 239-7676
MFR of TB

Birmingham
Buchanan Auto Body
4320 Vanderbilt Road
Birmingham, AL 35217
Tel: (205) 841-4054
FAX: (205) 841-3999
Contact: John Buchanan
MFR/REPAIR of VTB

Birmingham
Cleveland Mfg.
2327 5th Avenue, South
Birmingham, AL 35233
Tel: (205) 251-7139
MFR of TB

Birmingham
Durable Medical Equip. Rental & Sales
3600 5th Avenue, South
Birmingham, AL 35222
Tel: (205) 591-0817
AL Only: (800) 545-0641
FAX: (205) 591-3734
Contact: Pete Allen
MFR/DLR of E
C-2

Birmingham
Fontaine Truck Equip.
2490 Pinson Valley Pkwy
Birmingham, AL 35217
Tel: (205) 849-0257
Nation: (800) 221-3106
Contact: Roger Crawford
MFR/DLR of TB
C-2

Birmingham
Freuhauf Trailer Div.
1601 Vanderbilt Road, N.
Birmingham, AL 35234
Tel: (205) 328-2222
Contact: Mark Old
DLR of S-2

Birmingham
Jefferson Body Co., Inc.
1711 3rd Avenue, South
Birmingham, AL 35233
Tel: (205) 251-0930
Contact: Jane Mask
MFR of TB, R4

Birmingham
Laidlaw Transit
1301 F. L. Shuttlesworth Drive
Birmingham, AL 35234
Tel: (205) 252-5661
FAX: (205) 254-0996
Contact: George Johnson
DISTRIBUTOR of S

Birmingham
Mild to Wild Kustoms
13 83rd Street, North
Birmingham, AL 35206
Tel: (205) 833-7024
Contact: Bud Brasager
DLR/MODIFIER of R4, TConvs

Birmingham
Quality Truck Equipment
5100 Division Avenue
Birmingham, AL 35212
Tel: (205) 591-0564
FAX: (205) 591-0566
MFR of FTB

Birmingham
Thompson Trailer & Manufacturing Co.
1815 Ruffner Road
Birmingham, AL 35210
Tel: (205) 956-9522
MFR of T

Birmingham
Vulcan Coach, Inc.
614 Woodward Road
Birmingham, AL 35228
Tel: (205) 788-8146
FAX: (205) 786-3774
Contact: Bruce Basden
CONVERSIONS of R1, R2

Birmingham
Warren Manufacturing
1008 37th Street, North
Birmingham, AL 35234
Tel: (205) 591-3002
Contact: Russell Warren
MFR of ST
D

Boaz
Boaz Lowbed Mfg., Inc.
35 Industry Drive
Boaz, AL 35957
Tel: (205) 593-2705
Nation: (800) 292-9221
MFR of T, S-2, Low-boy, XT
D: Rex & Don Van Lines
(Driver usage here is rare.)

Cullman
S & S Farm Supply Co.
Route 13, Box 180
Highway 278, West
Cullman, AL 35055
Tel: (205) 734-1591
MFR of M, CTB

Elba
Dorsey Trailers
1409 Hickman Avenue
Elba, AL 36323
Tel: (205) 897-5711
Eastern USA:
(800) 624-8459
MFR of S-2
B-1, B-3

Eldridge
Mustang Trailers
Highway 13
Eldridge, AL 35554
Tel: (205) 924-9180
Contact: Doyle Dunn
MFR of UT
B-1

Enterprise
VIP Services
526 Glover Avenue
Enterprise, AL 36330
Tel: (205) 347-1284
R4

Evergreen
Transi-Corporation
Highway 31
Evergreen, AL 36401
Tel: (205) 578-1820
MFR of CTB, U

- 179 -

Fayette
Ox Bodies, Inc.
Highway 43, East
P.O. Box 8916
Fayette, AL 35555
Tel: (205) 932-5720
FAX: (205) 932-5794
MFR of *M, Flatbed M*
A-1, B-1

Fort Payne
Heil Company, The
45th Street & Valley
Head Road
P.O. Box 109
Fort Payne, AL 35967
Tel: (205) 845-4912
Contact: Art Davis
MFR *of G*
*D: Owens Driveaway,
Choo-Choo Driveaway*

Gadsden
*Alabama Trailer
Builders*
RR 5
Gadsden, AL 35903
Tel: (205) 492-0855
Contact: Skipper Ray
MFR *of UT*

Guntersville
*Roadrunner Camper
Shell Manufacturers*
RR 2
Guntersville, AL 35976
Tel: (205) 582-6348
MFR of *TC*

Haleyville
Fontaine Trailer Co.
Old Delmar Road
P.O. Box 619
Haleyville, AL 35565
Tel: (205) 486-5251
AL only: (800) 821-6535
Contact: Randall Sibley
MFR of *G*
D

Haleyville
*Winston Trailers by
WTM, Incorporated*
RR 6, Box 355
Haleyville, AL 35565
Tel: (205) 486-7272
FAX: (205) 486-7765
Contact: Mike Ivey
MFR of *UT*

Hokes Bluff
*Alabama Trailer
Builders & Repair*
4181 US Hwy. 278, East
Hokes Bluff, AL 35903
Tel: (205) 492-0855
MFR of *T*

Huntsville
Bankston Motor Homes
2191 Jordan Lane, NW
Huntsville, AL 35816
Tel: (205) 533-3100
Nation: (800) 624-2899
FAX: (205) 830-2695
DLR of *R1, R2*
C-2:4-5

Huntsville
Madison Travel Trailers
1707 Jordan Lane, NW
Huntsville, AL 35815
Tel: (205) 837-3881
DLR of *R6*

Huntsville
Mobility Plus, Inc.
2809 Newby Rd., Ste.130
Huntsville, AL 35805
Tel: (205) 533-4448
FAX: (205) 533-5215
Contact: Warren Finch
MODIFIER/DLR of
H'cap R4

Huntsville
Schwarze Industries, Inc.
5010 Beechmont Dr., NE
Huntsville, AL 35811
Tel: (205) 859-3076
FAX: (205) 851-1210
Contact: Donna Ogle
MFR of *Street Sweepers*
C-2

Huntsville
Southern Customs
4111 Environmental
Circle, SW, #B
Huntsville, AL 35805
Tel: (205) 881-9972
DLR of *Trucks, R4*

Irondale
*Alabama Truck Body
& Equipment*
2100 1st Avenue, North
Irondale, AL 35210
Tel: (205) 951-8144
FAX: (205) 951-8145
MFR of *TB*

Madison
Excellence, Inc.
453 Lanier Road
Madison, AL 35758
Tel: (205) 772-9321
Nation: (800) 882-9799
Contact: Jim Far
MFR of *A, E, Haz-Mat
Trucks, CTB*
C-2:4

McKenzie
Circle W Trailer Mfg.
Route 1, Box 373
Circle West Road
McKenzie, AL 36456
Tel: (205) 374-2560
FAX: (205) 374-2218
Contact: Mary Horton
MFR of *LT, UT, CT*

Mobile
*Gulf City Body & Trailer
Works, Incorporated*
601 S. Conception Street
Mobile, AL 36603
Tel: (205) 438-5521
FAX: (205) 433-7910
Contact: Barry Gritter
or Melissa Gritter
MFR/DLR of *TB, ST, R6*
C-2:2
D: GAF (based in TX)

Mobile
Port City Trailers, Inc.
299 N. Schillinger Road
Mobile, AL 36608
Tel: (205) 633-2074
Tel: (205) 649-6130
Contact: Jan Walden
MFR of *UT*
B-1:1

Mobile
Premier Vans, Inc.
2652 Government Blvd.
Mobile, AL 36606
Tel: (205) 471-4554
R4, TConvs

Montgomery
Alabama Auto Carriage
2359 Fairview Ave., W
P.O. Box 250303
Montgomery, AL 36108
Tel: (205) 262-3563
Contact: Lawerence
Guettler
MFR of *TB*

Montgomery
*Alabama Busses
Unlimited*
4001 Birmingham Hwy.
Montgomery, AL 36108
Tel: (205) 254-1105
AL only: (800) 524-9417
Nation: (800) 225-6647
FAX: (205) 264-1123
DISTRIBUTOR of *S*
C-2:2
NOTE: *Class A CDL
with Passenger &
Haz-Mat endorsements
strictly required here.
This company was not
hiring at the time this
was researched.*

Montgomery
Ingram Marlin RV
4504 Troy Highway
Montgomery, AL 36116
Tel: (334) 288-0331
FAX: (334) 288-5382
Contact:Allison
DLR of *R1*

Montgomery
JTM Vans
3001 Day Street
Montgomery, AL 36108
Tel: (205) 262-0578
FAX: (205) 262-0578
Contact: Frank Johnson
MFR/DLR of *R4*
C-2:3
D

Montgomery
*Magnolia Professional
Car Company*
P.O. Box 3221
Montgomery, AL 36109
Tel: (205) 265-7787
FAX: (205) 265-0896
Contact: Earl Bradsher
DLR of *Limos*

Muscle Shoals
Action Vans, Inc.
2727 E. Avalon Avenue
Muscle Shoals, AL 35661
Tel: (205) 381-6286
Nation: (800) 848-8267
FAX: (205) 381-0185
Contact: Elaine Tucker
R4
C-2 (Mainly retirees)

Oneonta
*Kustom Kreation Van/
Trojan Van*
RR 5, Box 105
Oneonta, AL 35121
Tel: (205) 274-2900
FAX: (205) 274-2903
Contact: Steve Campbell
R4
C-2:1
D: S & W, Parker

Pelham
*Transportation South,
Incorporated*
1400 McCain Parkway
Pelham, AL 35124
Tel: (205) 663-2287
Nation: (800) 367-9463
FAX: (205) 663-2378
Contact: Tommy Baily
DISTRIBUTOR of *S*
C-2:5

Pell City
Classic Custom Coaches
1904 Cogswell Avenue
Pell City, AL 35125
Tel: (205) 338-6727
FAX: (205) 338-4438
R4

Phenix City
*Southern Truck
& Trailer Body*
3408 S. Seale Road
Phenix City, AL 36869
Tel: (205) 291-0250
MFR of *T*

Pike Road
Phase III Vans
7707 Troy Highway
Pike Road, AL 36064
Tel: (205) 281-2160
Nation: (800) 239-3636
FAX: (205) 281-0915
Contact: Reed Ingram
MFR/DLR of *Trucks, R4*
C-2:2

Pinson
Pinson Truck Equipment
(*MAIL: P.O. Box 9848
Birmingham, AL 35220*)
7444 Highway 79 North
Pinson, AL 35126
Tel: (205) 681-2120
Nation: (800) 633-8461
Contact: Doug Jarvis
MFR of *ST*

Rainsville
TMW Touring Coach
160 Dillbeck Road
P.O. Box 1047
Rainsville, AL 35986
Tel: (205) 638-6355
Nation: (800) 225-6458
MFR of *R1*

Ramer
Ramer Mfg., Inc.
RR 2, Box 454
Ramer, AL 36069
Tel: (205) 562-9331
FAX: (205) 562-3885
Contact: Pat Miles
MFR of *M*
C-2

Ranburne
Dixie Craft Mfg. Co.
Highway 46
Ranburne, AL 36273
Tel: (205) 568-5581
MFR of *T*

Red Bay
Tiffin Motor Homes, Inc.
502 4th Street, NW
P.O. Box 596
Red Bay, AL 35582
Tel: (205) 356-8661
Nation: (800) 443-7881
FAX: (205) 356-8219
Contact: Jack Bostick
MFR. of *R1, R2*
C-1 (Local drivers only)

Roanoke Oaks
*Magnolia Hearse-Limo
Sales, Inc.*
P.O. Box 714
Roanoke Oaks, AL 36274
Tel: (205) 265-7787
Contact: Earl Bradsher
DLR of *H, Limos*
C-2:1

Semmes
*Ellis & Son Wagons &
Trailers*
P.O. Box 208
Semmes, AL 36575
Tel: (205) 649-2572
Tel: (205) 649-0606
Contact: Bill Ellis
MFR/DLR of *T*
("*If it's a trailer, we build it.*")
B-1

Springville
Omni Trailers
117 Industrial Drive
Springville, AL 35146
Tel: (205) 467-6161
FAX: (205) 467-6344
Contact: Gerald Tucker
MFR of *ST*
B-2
D: Trailer Transit

Sylacuaga
*Southern Funeral Coach
& Limo Sales, Inc.*
207 W. Fort Williams St.
Sylacuaga, AL 35150
Tel: (205) 245-4545
FAX: (205) 245-6681
Contact: Dick Wright
or Jimmy Curtis
DLR of *Limos, H*
C-2

Theodore
Cain's Mobility Systems
5767 Plantation Road
Theodore, AL 36582
Tel: (205) 653-4541
MODIFIER of *H'cap
Units*

Troy
*Trojan Industries/
Lyncoach*
Highway 231
1230 New Bypass Road
Troy, AL 36081
Tel: (205) 566-4330
Nation: (800) 288-1519
FAX: (205) 566-0589
Contact: David Phelps
or Judy Seaton
MFR of *TB*
C-2

Trussville
*Southern Comfort
Conversions*
7769 Gadsden Highway
Trussville, AL 35173
Tel: (205) 655-0919
Nation: (800) 745-6096
FAX: (205) 655-1031
Contact: James Harris
TConvs (GMC)
C-1, C-2
D

ALASKA

Anchorage
Allegro RV Sales, Inc.
332 Muldoon Road
Anchorage, AK 99504
Tel: (907) 333-9012
FAX: (907) 333-1126
Contact: Marlin Law
DLR of *R1, R2*
C-2

Anchorage
Beauty Vans of Alaska
10121 Marmot Court
Anchorage, AK 99515
Tel: (907) 344-6790
RENTAL of *R4*

Cordova
Mobile Grid Trailers
P.O. Box 1291
Cordova, AK 99574
Tel: (907) 424-3146
FAX: (907) 424-5269
MFR of *BT*

Fairbanks
*Interior Custom Topper
& RV Center*
2119 Standard Avenue
Fairbanks, AK 99701
Tel: (907) 451-8356
FAX: (907) 456-4742
DLR of *Pop-up R6, TC*

North Pole
Alaskan Trailer Co.
3420 Hurst Road
North Pole, AK 99705
Tel: (907) 488-2873
Contact: George Carter
MFR of *UT*

North Pole
Mike's Garage
3452 Kaltag Drive
North Pole, AK 99705
Tel: (907) 488-0991
MFR of *UT*

Palmer
Cache Camper Mfg, Inc.
Mile 3.5 Palmer-Wasilla
Highway
Palmer, AK 99645
Tel: (907) 745-4061
MFR of *TC*

Wasilla
Frank's Trailers
500 Rocker Circle
Wasilla, AK 99654
Tel: (907) 376-0719
MFR of *T for towing
ATVs*

ARIZONA

Apache Junction
Braco Trailers
1544 E. 18th Avenue
Apache Junction, AZ
85219
Tel: (602) 983-0153
FAX: (602) 380-3599
MFR of *CT*

Cave Creek
Wright Custom Coaches
5860 E. Dynamite Blvd.
Cave Creek, AZ 85331
Tel: (602) 585-0973
Contact: Chuck Wright
CONVERTER of *U*

Chandler
Becker Auto Sales
1461 N. Arizona Ave.
Chandler, AZ 85224
Tel: (602) 899-2088
FAX: (602) 899-6829
Contact: Bob Becker
R4

Chandler
Quality Vans
1461 N. Arizona Avenue
Chandler, AZ 85225
Tel: (602) 899-2088
Nation: (800) QUALITY
FAX: (602) 899-6829
Contact: Rod Dewitt
MFR of *R4, H'cap R4,
TConvs*
D

Ehrenberg
Morgan Corporation Arizona Operators
4 Morgan Way
Ehrenberg, AZ 85334
Tel: (602) 927-5777
FAX: (602) 927-5115
R4
C-2

Eloy
Eloy Machine Works
226 S. Sunshine Blvd.
Eloy, AZ 85231
Tel: (602) 466-7256
MFR of CT
B-1

Gilbert
Desert Vans, Inc.
75 W. Baseline Road
Gilbert, AZ 85234
Tel: (602) 892-1136
Contact: Bob Portada
MFR of R4

Glendale
Arizona Van Company
5550 N. 43rd Avenue
Glendale, AZ 85301
Tel: (602) 233-1871
R4

Glendale
Creedbilt
6012 N. 56th Avenue
Glendale, AZ 85301
Tel: (602) 939-8119
MFR of UTB

Glendale
Fleming Trailers, Inc.
17033 N. 63rd Avenue
Glendale, AZ 85308
Tel: (602) 938-2513
FAX: (602) 439-2470
MFR of UT
D

Glendale
Grand Travel RV
7020 NW Grand Avenue
Glendale, AZ 85301
Tel: (602) 842-1137
R4

Glendale
Williams' Family Trailers
6548 NW Grand Ave.
Glendale, AZ 86301
Tel: (602) 937-6050
FAX: (602) 930-1808
Contact: David Williams
MFR of UT
B-2:1

Mesa
Arizona Wheelchair & Adaptive Drive
1833 W. Main Street
Mesa, AZ 85201
Tel: (602) 969-5499
H'Cap Units

Mesa
Courtesy RV
2145 E. Main
Mesa, AZ 85204
Tel: (602) 644-1500
FAX: (602) 834-6474
DLR of R1

Mesa
Cruise America
11 W. Hampton
Mesa, AZ 85210-5258
Tel: (602) 464-7300
Tel: (602) 898-9797
Tel: (602) 242-0181
Nation: (800) 225-1755
Nation: (800) 327-7778
Canada: (800) 327-7799
Contact: Bob Calderone, Marketing Director
(To reach him, dial the top "800" number, and when asked for an extention, enter 319.)
NOTE: This is the HQ of Cruise America, formerly in Miami, FL. It also is an RV SALES & RENTAL site.
D: Don Ray

Mesa
Imperial Trailer Sales
213 S. Alma School Road
Mesa, AZ 85210
Tel: (602) 833-3090
FAX: (602) 833-0274
Contact: Ron Legler
DLR of HT

Mesa
Isley's Truck Equipment Division
2225 W. Main Street
Mesa, AZ 85201
Tel: (602) 834-1234
MFR of Service TB, Refrig. TB, CTB, XTB

Mesa
Traditional Custom Coach
230 S. Country Club
Mesa, AZ 85210
Tel: (602) 844-8998
Contact: Jim Nossett
MODIFIER of U

Phoenix
AG Products
2525 W. Broadway Road
Phoenix, AZ 85041
Tel: (602) 268-8707
MFR of UTB, VTB, CT, GT
DLR of "Fontaine" M, "Koenig" UTB, XTB

Phoenix
All-American Equipment Liquidators
1938 W. Buckeye Road
Phoenix, AZ 85009
Tel: (602) 254-7990
Contact: Mike Jacobsen
DLR of TB

Phoenix
American Gooseneck, Inc.
2525 W. Broadway Road
Phoenix, AZ 85041
Tel: (602) 268-8707
Nation: (800) 552-2648
FAX: (602) 243-0448
MFR of G
C-1:2

Phoenix
Anco Truck Equipment
3430 E. Illini Street
Phoenix, AZ 85040
Tel: (602) 470-2626
Contact: Mike Taylor
DISTRIBUTOR of G

Phoenix
Arizona Bus Sales
3639 E. Superior
Phoenix, AZ 85040
Tel: (602) 437-2255
Nation: (800) 862-5478
FAX: (602) 437-2758
DLR of U

Phoenix
Arizona Metal Products
2237 S. 15th Street
Phoenix, AZ 85034
Tel: (602) 271-0117
MFR/DLR of ST

Phoenix
Arnold's Truck & Body Works
1209 Grand Avenue
Phoenix, AZ 85007
Tel: (602) 253-6918
REPAIR of TB

Phoenix
Auto Safety House
2630 W. Buckeye Road
Phoenix, AZ 85009
Tel: (602) 269-9721
Nation: (800) 352-5355
DLR of S
D

Phoenix
Baja Vans
1309 E. Buckeye Road
Phoenix, AZ 85034
Tel: (602) 253-5812
MFR/MODIFIER of R4
D

Phoenix
Brands Trailers & Feeds
22413 N. Black Canyon Highway
Phoenix, AZ 85027
Tel: (602) 516-2322
FAX: (602) 516-2324
Contact: Ed Dunnigan
DLR of HT

Phoenix
Capital Vans & Equipment
1806 W. Lincoln Street
Phoenix, AZ 85007
Tel: (602) 258-0825
MFR/MODIFIER of R4

Phoenix
Care Concepts
3353 W. Osborn Road
Phoenix, AZ 85017
Tel: (602) 233-0188
Nation (800) 288-8267
Contact: Sherry Sanchez
MODIFIER of H'Cap Units (Chrysler only)
C-2

Phoenix
Chuker, Incorporated
1010 N. 18th Avenue
Phoenix, AZ 85007
Tel: (602) 252-8282
FAX: (602) 252-8346
MFR of CT

Phoenix
Courtesy RV
1233 E. Camelback Road
P.O. Box 7709
Phoenix, AZ 85011
Tel: (602) 279-3232
FAX: (602) 263-9022
Contact: Mike Ellis
DLR of R1

Phoenix
Family Van Wholesale
9665 N. Cave Creek Rd
Phoenix, AZ 85020
Tel: (602) 944-1147
Contact: Pat Finnegan
WHOLESALER of R4, R4-B, Airport U, Transit U

Phoenix
Fruehauf Division
902 S. 7th Street
Phoenix, AZ 85034
Tel: (602) 258-6961
FAX: (602) 234-5717
DLR of S-1, S-2

Phoenix
Handicap Vehicle Specialists
3306 E. Washington St.
Phoenix, AZ 85034
Tel: (602) 275-3325
FAX: (602) 275-1536
R4
D

Phoenix
Heil Company, The
2441 S. 40th Street
Phoenix, AZ 85034
Tel: (602) 437-3113
Nation: (800) 457-2743
Contact: Vic Mitchell
MFR of *G*
D

Phoenix
Henderson Utility Equipment Company
1147 N. 27th Avenue
Phoenix, AZ 85009
Tel: (602) 272-0991
Contact: Connie Henderson
FINAL ASSEMBLER of *UTB*

Phoenix
I-10 International
2202 S. Central Avenue
Phoenix, AZ 85004
Tel: (602) 254-9241
FAX: (602) 252-5301
DLR of *Trucks, T*

Phoenix
Michigan Trailer Sales
4140 NW Grand Avenue
Phoenix, AZ 85019
Tel: (602) 247-3829
Contact: Maury Wulbret
DLR of *R5, R6*

Phoenix
Norwood Equipment, Incorporated
1701 S. 19th Avenue
Phoenix, AZ 85009
Tel: (602) 254-0644
Nation: (800) 352-5330
MFR of *T*
B-2:2
D

Phoenix
Southern Truck Equipment
(MAIL: P.O. Box 21536
Phoenix, AZ 85036)
4102 E. Elwood Street
Phoenix, AZ 85040
Tel: (602) 437-1145
FAX: (602) 437-2698
Contact: Darvin Moore
MODIFIER/ DISTRIBUTOR of *R4, TB*

Phoenix
Southwest Trail Boss
345 S. 83rd Avenue
Phoenix, AZ 85043
Tel: (602) 437-2223
FAX: (602) 437-2249
Contact: John Thompson
MFR of *T*

Phoenix
Sun Valley Car Carriers
2626 W. Encanto
Phoenix, AZ 85009
Tel: (602) 252-9224
Nation: (800) 231-9224
MFR of *W*

Phoenix
Top Line & Pro Trac Trailers
3309 N. 29th Avenue
Phoenix, AZ 85017
Tel: (602) 253-2725
MFR of *CT*

Phoenix
Universal Campers Shell Manufacturing Company
2928 E. Washington St.
Phoenix, AZ 85034
Tel: (602) 275-5198
MFR of *TC*

Phoenix
Utility Crane & Equipment Company
1402 N. 22nd Avenue
Phoenix, AZ 85009
Tel: (602) 254-7213
FAX: (602) 271-4128
Contact: John Roberts
MFR of *UT*

Phoenix
Vantage Mini-Vans
2441 E. Chambers Street
Phoenix, AZ 85040
Tel: (602) 243-2700
Nation: (800) 348-8267
Contact: Irene Tidrick
MFR of *H'cap R4*
D

Phoenix
Western Truck Equipment Co., Inc.
2400 S. 14th Street
Phoenix, AZ 85034
Tel: (602) 257-0777
FAX: (602) 340-1534
FINAL ASSEMBLER of *TB*

Scottsdale
Sultra
14427 N. 73rd Street
Scottsdale, AZ 85260
Tel: (602) 991-6160
Contact: Betty Joseph
H'cap R4

Sedona
French's RV Center
2985 W. Highway 89-A
Sedona, AZ 86336
Tel: (520) 282-6776
Nation: (800) 526-8019
DLR of *R1*
C-2

Surprise
Vans RV-Trailer Co.
11565 W. Bell Road
Surprise, AZ 85374
Tel: (602) 977-1292
DLR of *R1, R5, R6*

Tempe
Advantage West Corp.
733 W. 22nd Street
Tempe, AZ 85282
Tel: (602) 968-9306
FAX: (602) 968-9938
R4
D: C & J Transport Southwest

Tolleson
Saguaro Camper Mfg.
9360 W. Van Buren St.
Tolleson, AZ 85353
Tel: (602) 936-6866
MFR of *TC*
B-1

Tucson
ADE Industries, Inc.
3621 S. Palo Verde
Tucson, AZ 85713
Tel: (520) 571-7156
MFR of *R1, H'cap R1*

Tucson
B & C Mfg. & RV Repair
3528 S. Dodge Blvd.
Tucson, AZ 85713
Tel: (520) 745-9568
MFR of *R2*

Tucson
Buffalo Enterprises
1600 W. Earhart Way
Tucson, AZ 85737
Tel: (520) 742-9479
MFR/MODIFIER of *TB, UTB*

Tucson
Cimarron Park Models & RVs
5601 S. Palo Verde Road
Tucson, AZ 85706
Tel: (520) 741-0204
MFR of *R1, R6*
D: MCM, Loren Turner

Tucson
Don Mackey Winnebago
3434 E. Speedway
Tucson, AZ 85713
Tel: (520) 325-4333
DLR of *R1*
D

Tucson
Marrigans' Arizona Roadrunner
4324 N. Flowing Wells Road
Tucson, AZ 85705
Tel: (520) 887-2992
FAX: (520) 887-0114
Contact: Rick Marrigans
MFR/MODIFIER of *RVs, Commercial Mobile Units*

Tucson
Sandy's West RV Center
1451 W. Miracle Mile
Tucson, AZ 85705
Tel: (520) 884-8866
FAX: (520) 884-1070
Contact: Jean
DLR of *R3*

Tucson
State Ambulance Builders
1702 E. Pace Court
Tucson, AZ 85719
Tel: (520) 792-0659
MFR of *A*

Yuma
Fun Trailer Mfg.
2525 E. 16th Street
Yuma, AZ 85365
Tel: (520) 783-9457
MFR of *T*

ARKANSAS

Benton
Arkansas Conversion Center
19426 Highway I-30
Benton, AR 72015
Tel: (501) 847-8162
Nation: (800) 633-7549
Contact: Terry Kee
MFR/DLR of *R4*

Benton
Hilbilt Mfg. Co.
20020 Highway I-30, #12
Benton, AR 72015
Tel: (501) 794-2500
MFR of *T*

Black Rock
Fun Bunks
Clear Springs Road
Black Rock, AR 72415
Tel: (501) 878-6544
MFR of *CTB*
B-2:2

Cabot
Cabot Industries
P.O. Box 749
Cabot, AR 72023
Tel: (501) 843-7111
Nation: (800) 999-7983
Contact: Jerry Baldwin
MFR of *STB*
C-2

Conway
American Transportation Corporation
Highway 65, South
P.O. Box 6000
Conway, AR 72032
Tel: (501) 327-7761
Nation: (800) 843-5615
Contact: Jim Mitchell
MFR of *S*
C-2
D

Conway
Central Arkansas Fabrication
1985 Favre Lane
Conway, AR 72032
Tel: (501) 329-1267
MFR of *LT, HT*
B-2
D

Conway
Ward Bus Sales, Inc.
450 S. Amity Road
Conway, AR 72032
Tel: (501) 329-9874
DLR of *S, U, H'cap Units*

Fort Smith
Aldridge International Coach Sales
P.O. Box 6185
Fort Smith, AR 72906
Tel: (214) 519-0577
Contact: Danny Aldridge
DLR of *Limos*

Fort Smith
Federal Coach Division
7400 S. 28th Street
P.O. Box 6536
Fort Smith, AR 72906
Tel: (501) 646-6800
Nation: (800) 292-6210
FAX: (501) 646-1217
Contact: Nathan Hurst
or Pete Breeden
MFR of *Limos, H, TB*
C-1:3-4
D: *Grade A Trucking*

Fort Smith
Limousine Sales, Ltd.
P.O. Box 10466
Fort Smith, AR 72917
Tel: (501) 783-1468
Nation: (800) 283-1468
Contact: Joe Udodj
DLR of *Limo*
A-1

Fort Smith
Strace Mfg. Company
4216 S. 16th
Fort Smith, AR 72901
Tel: (501) 646-4493
MFR of *FTB, VTB, GT*

Harrison
Cloud Corporation
339 Industrial Park Road
Harrison, AR 72601
Tel: (501) 741-6644
Nation: (800) 342-1944
FAX: (501) 741-7033
MFR of *Replacement Decking for S-2*
B-1, B-2
D: *Harrison Contracting*

Hatfield
Ridge-Runner Trailer Manufacturing
H.C. 71, North Trail
Hatfield, AR 71945
Tel: (501) 394-2255
Contact: Willie Simmons
MFR of *T*
B-1 (Local only)

Little Rock
Arkansas Trailer Mfg.
(MAIL: P.O. Box 4080
Little Rock, AR 72214)
3200 S. Elm Street
Little Rock, AR 72204
Tel: (501) 666-5417
Nation: (800) 666-5417
Contact: Greg Campbell
MFR/DLR of *T, S-2*
B-2

Little Rock
Davis Trailer & Truck Equipment
7609 Asher Avenue
Little Rock, AR 72204
Tel: (501) 562-6295
FAX: (501) 562-4036
Contact: Harold Majors
MFR/DLR of *STB*
C-2

Little Rock
Robinson International Trucks
910 E. 6th Street
Little Rock, AR 72202
Tel: (501) 374-6474
AR only: (800) 844-4388
FAX: (501) 374-9712
DLR of *TB, U*

Manila
Henry Brothers, Inc.
200 Concord
P.O. Box 765
Manila, AR 72442
Tel: (501) 561-3912
Contact: Derrick Henry
MFR of *Limos*
C-1 (Local drivers only)

Murfreesboro
Diamond City Trailer Manufacturing
P.O. Box 235
Murfreesboro, AR 71958
Tel: (501) 285-2521
MFR of *BT*

North Little Rock
Scott's Vans & Custom Autos
3700 N. Phyllis
North Little Rock, AR 72118
Tel: (501) 758-6614
R4

North Little Rock
Southwestern Truck Sales, Incorporated
3815 Broadway St., East
North Little Rock, AR 72114
Tel: (501) 945-3234
FAX: (501) 945-3236
DLR of *S-2*

Newport
Delta Mfg., Inc.
7900 Victory Blvd.
Newport, AR 72112
Tel: (501) 523-8941
FAX: (501) 523-4421
Contact: Elaine Dunavin
MFR of *HT, LT*
B-2:4

Newport
Taylor Made Ambulances
3704 Medalion Place
Newport, AR 72112
Tel: (501) 945-1647
Nation: (800) 468-1310
Contact: Benji Harris
MFR of *A*
C-2:4

Paragould
Keasler Body Company
4207 W. Kings Highway
(Highway 412, West)
Paragould, AR 72450
Tel: (501) 236-2607
Nation: (800) 876-8564
Contact: Haley Rieck
DISTRIBUTOR of *TB*

Pine Bluff
Arkansas Bus Exchange, Incorporated
Grider Field Road
Pine Bluff, AR 71601
Tel: (501) 536-7795
FAX: (501) 534-0244
DLR of *Mini-busses*

Pine Bluff
Hughes' Cabinets & Van Conversion Shop
3028 S. Midland Drive
Pine Bluff, AR 71603
Tel: (501) 534-0058
Contact: Willie Hughes
MFR of *R4*
C-2:1

Pine Bluff
Pine Bluff Trailer Manufacturing Company
110 Island Harbor Marina Road
Pine Bluff, AR 71601
Tel: (501) 535-8152
MFR of *T*

Pocahontas
Corvette Campers/ Harold Benton Enterprises
Highway 304, East
Pocahontas, AR 72455
Tel: (501) 892-5441
Contact: Greg Benton
or Harold Benton
MFR of *TC*

Pocahontas
Daco Trailer Corp.
712 Airport Road
P.O. Box 422
Pocahontas, AR 72455
Tel: (501) 892-4584
FAX: (501) 892-4585
Contact: Jim Masterson
MFR of *FT, Drop-deck T*

Quitman
Chapparal Trailers of Arkansas
Highway 124, East
Quitman, AR 72131
Tel: (501) 589-2741
FAX: (501) 589-3142
MFR of *HT, LT*
B-2

Springdale
A & A Camper Shells
Hwy. 412, East &
Hwy. 265
Springdale, AR 72764
Tel: (501) 756-6901
MFR of *TC*

Stuttgart
Road Coach
2001 S. Park Avenue
Stuttgart, AR 72160
Tel: (501) 673-4576
R4

Van Buren
Wilson Fire Apparatus, Incorporated
2701 Kibler Road
Van Buren, AR 72956
Tel: (501) 474-3800
Contact: Tom Wilson
MFR of *E, F*
C-1

West Memphis
Total Truck Body Works, Incorporated
Highway 77 & Afco Rd.
P.O. Box 1794
West Memphis, AR 72301
Tel: (501) 735-6694
REPAIR of *TB*

Wynne
Big Valley Trailer Mfg.
Highway 1, South
P.O. Box 246
Wynne, AR 72396
Tel: (501) 238-8429
MFR of *T*

CALIFORNIA

Acton
Golden West Featherlite Trailers
1686 Seirra Highway
Acton, CA 93510
Tel: (805) 269-5012
FAX: (805) 269-0763
Contact: David Scott
DLR of *HT*

Anaheim
Companion Sleeper Cabs
5592 E. Palma Avenue
Anaheim, CA 92807
Tel: (714) 970-1157
FAX: (714) 970-6875
MFR of *TC*
D: U.S. Delivery

Anaheim
Cruise America RV Depot
1710 S. Anaheim Blvd.
Anaheim, CA 92805
Tel: (714) 772-9030
Nation: (800) 327-7799
DLR of *R1, R2*
(For more data, see the HQ listing, Mesa, AZ)

Anaheim
Krystal Koach, Inc.
1281 Sunshine Way
Anaheim, CA 92806
Tel: (714) 632-0400
Nation: (800) 845-4883
Contact: Wayne Rand
MFR of *Limos*
D

Anaheim
Pacific Truck Equip. Co.
1440 N. Daly Street
Anaheim, CA 92806
Tel: (714) 776-9936
MFR of *UTB*

Anaheim
Star Custom Vans
1731 N. Blue Gum St
Anaheim, CA 92806
Tel: (714) 630-2503
R4

Anaheim
Superior Equipment Co.
1003 E. Arlee Place
Anaheim, CA 92805
Tel: (714) 991-0640
FAX: (714) 991-0649
MFR of *UT*
D: Anaheim Towing

Anaheim
Western Limousine Sales
1251 Sunshine Way
Anaheim, CA 92806
Tel: (714) 632-5222
Tel: (310) 643-6758
Contact: Susan White
DLR of *Limos, Stretch Limos, Stretch Suburban Convs*
("You name it; anything that can be stretched.")

Anaheim
The Wide One Bus Corp.
4421 E. LaPalma Avenue
Anaheim, CA 92807
Tel: (714) 693-1444
FAX: (714) 693-0182
MFR of *U, Limos*
C-2
D

Anderson
RV's Unlimited
2374 North Street
Anderson, CA 96007
Tel: (916) 365-3737
FAX: (916) 365-7816
DLR of *R1*
D: Jackson Transport

Anderson
Redding Truck Body Co.
2101 Barney Road
Anderson, CA 96007
Tel: (916) 365-6493
FAX: (916) 365-7156
Contact: Del Huber
FINAL ASSEMBLER/DLR of *M, FTB*
C-1

Azusa
B & Z Truck Bodies, Incorporated
501 W. Foothill Blvd.
Azusa, CA 91702
Tel: (818) 334-2110
REPAIR of *TB*

Bakersfield
Bakersfield Van & Truck Supplies
2814 Chester Avenue
Bakersfield, CA 93301
Tel: (805) 395-3003
R4

Bakersfield
Dandy Van & Trucking
640 Belle Terrace
Bakersfield, CA 93307
Tel: (805) 398-8171
R4

Bakersfield
Data Mfg, Inc.
7608 Fruitdale Avenue
Bakersfield, CA 93312
Tel: (805) 399-4808
FAX: (805) 399-6161
MFR of *TB, FTB, UTB*

Bakersfield
Douglass Truck Bodies/ C. C. Douglass Mfg, Inc.
231 21st Street
Bakersfield, CA 93301
Tel: (805) 327-0257
Tel: (805) 327-0258
Nation: (800) 635-7641
FAX: (805) 327-3894
MFR of *CTB, UTB*

Bakersfield
El Kapitan Van Conversions, Inc.
(MAIL: P.O. Box 41117
Bakersfield, CA 93384-1117)
431 Mt. Vernon Avenue
Bakersfield, CA 93307
Tel: (805) 324-4004
FAX: (805) 324-4069
MFR of *R4*
C-2:6

Bakersfield
Mobile Equipment Co.
3610 Gilmore Avenue
Bakersfield, CA 93308
Tel: (805) 327-8476
FAX: (805) 327-8863
Contact: Gary Stanfill
MFR/DLR of *UTB, R4*

Baldwin Park
Ray Gaskin Service
14312 Arrow Highway
Baldwin Park, CA 91706
Tel: (818) 960-2889
FAX: (818) 814-1349
MFR/DLR of *TB, CT*
B-1
D

Banning
Travel Quest, Inc.
272 W. Lincoln Street
Banning, CA 92220
Tel: (909) 849-4977
FAX: (909) 849-5697
R4
C-2:2

Bell Gardens
Crown Metal Mfg.
7601 Ramish Avenue
Bell Gardens, CA 90201
Tel: (213) 587-3100
MFR of *TB*

- 185 -

Bell Gardens
Wyse Brothers Metal Products, Incorporated
7314 Scout Avenue
Bell Gardens, CA 90201
Tel: (310) 927-1348
Contact: Andrew Teh
MFR of *V, UTB*
D

Benicia
K/B Company, Inc.
750 Jackson Street
Benicia, CA 94510
Tel: (707) 745-0135
FAX: (707) 745-2649
MFR of *M, FTB*
D

Berkeley
Mobility Systems
1010 Carlton Street
Berkeley, CA 94710
Tel: (510) 540-0295
FAX: (510) 843-2903
Contact: Bill Fryekman
H'cap R4

Bloomington
Steelco, Incorporated
17507 Valley Blvd.
Bloomington, CA 92316
Tel: (909) 877-5940
FAX: (909) 356-9774
MFR of *R1, R2 Chassis*
C-2:1

Brea
Harbor Truck Bodies
255 Voyager Avenue
Brea, CA 92621
Tel: (714) 632-2800
Nation: (800) 433-9452
FAX: (714) 630-7080
Contact: Tony Anderson
MFR of *TB, UTB*
C-2:2

Brea
Krystal Koach, Inc.
2701 E. Imperial Hwy.
Brea, CA 92821
Tel: (714) 986-1200
Nation: (800) KRYSTAL
FAX: (714) 986-1241
E-Mail: mailbox@krystalcoach.com
Website: www.krystalcoach.com
Contact: Cindy Keener
MFR of *U, H, Limos*
D: Several

Buellton
Santa Ynez Valley Trailers
2201 U.S. Hwy 101, #H
Buellton, CA 93427
Tel: (805) 688-0059
FAX: (805) 688-8209
DLR of *HT*

Burbank
Dave's Van Accessories
411 N. Victory Blvd.
Burbank, CA 91502
Tel: (818) 843-6660
FAX: (818) 846-6640
Contact: Dave
R4
Very Limited Opportunity

Burlingame
Rector Motor Car Co.
1010 Cadillac Way
Burlingame, CA 94010
Tel: (415) 348-0111
FAX: (415) 344-7291
Contact: Sandra
DLR of *Limos*

Camarillo
Holiday World RV Center
311 Daily Drive
Camarillo, Ca 93010
Tel: (805) 383-6981
FAX: (805) 383-6992
Contact: John Tarter
DLR of *R1, R2*
C-1
D: Morgan

Canoga Park
Transit Authority, The
7866 Deering Avenue
Canoga Park, CA 91304
Tel: (818) 888-7549
FAX: (818) 888-9017
R4

Carson
Chino Motor Coach Co.
17121 Kingsview Ave.
Carson, CA 90746
Tel: (310) 327-8393
FAX: (310) 327-8445
UConvs

Carson
Pacific Coach West
1050 E. Dominguez
Suite P
Carson, CA 90746
Tel: (310) 609-2900
FAX: (310) 609-2354
Contact: Jay Real
DLR of *Limos*

Cerritos
AAA Truck Body
16315 Piuma Avenue
Cerritos, CA 90701
Tel: (310) 809-9505
MFR of *TB*

Chatsworth
Adaptive Driving Systems, Incorporated
21050 Superior Street
Chatsworth, CA 91311
Tel: (818) 998-1026
H'cap R4

Chico
Fleetwood Motor Homes of California
300 E. Ryan Avenue
Chico, CA 95926-9034
Tel: (916) 343-3531
FAX: (916) 343-2282
MFR of *R1*
D: Don Ray Driveaway

Chico
Nor-Cal Mobility
1298 Nord Avenue
Chico, CA 95926
Tel: (916) 893-1111
MFR of *R4, H'cap R4*
C-2:1

Chino
Alfa Leisure, Inc.
5163 G Street
P.O. Box 3220
Chino, CA 91710
Tel: (909) 628-5574
Nation: (800) 322-2532
FAX: (909) 591-7902
MFR of *R5*
D: KH Trucking, Peterson Transport

Chino
Silver Streak Coaches
4741 Murietta Street
Chino, CA 91710
Tel: (909) 591-0416
MFR/DLR of *R1, T, H'cap Units*

Chino
Sterling Truck Equip.
14095 Euclid Avenue
Chino, CA 91710
Tel: (909) 628-2137
MFR/DLR of *TB*
C-2:1

Chula Vista
California Custom Truck Shell
915 Broadway
Chula Vista, CA 91911
Tel: (619) 477-8472
TConvs

Chula Visa
GM Hot Lunch Truck Manufacturing
3630 Main Street
Chula Visa, CA 91911
Tel: (619) 585-3232
MFR of *Hot Lunch TB*

Cloverdale
TEAC Industries
28333 Sandholm Road
P.O. Box 201
Cloverdale, CA 95425
Tel: (707) 894-4427
MFR of *CTB*

Colton
McNeilus Truck & Manufacturing, Inc.
401 N. Pepper Avenue
Colton, CA 92324
Tel: (909) 370-2100
MFR of *Concrete Mixer TB*

Compton
R & E Custom Van Conversion
1316 N. Long Beach Blvd.
Compton, CA 90221
Tel: (310) 638-0287
Contact: Eva Garcia
R4

Cordelia
North Bay Truck Body
9310 W. Cordelia Road
Cordelia, CA 94585
Tel: (707) 864-2700
FAX: (707) 864-2756
Contact: Robert Diaz
MFR of *FTB*
C-2:2

Corona
Baker Equip. & Leasing
(MAIL: P.O. Box 1433
Corona, CA 91718)
1955 Sampson Avenue
Corona, CA 91719
Tel: (909) 736-6047
Nation: (800) 433-6268
FAX: (909) 734-8664
MFR of *TB*
C-1
D

Corona
Protection Development International Corp.
(MAIL: P.O. Box 2048
Corona, CA 91718)
1555 Railroad Street
Corona, CA 91720
Tel: (909) 734-7531
FAX: (714) 734-7570
Contact: Maryanne Smith
MFR of *Armored Cars*
D

Corona
Tiffany Coachworks, Incorporated
13445 Estelle
Corona, CA 91719
Tel: (909) 736-7340
Nation: (800) 338-5872
FAX: (909) 736-7355
MFR of *Limos*

Cotati
Reliance Trailer Mfg.
7911 Redwood Drive
Cotati, CA 94931
Tel: (707) 795-0081
CA only: (800) 847-7788
CA only: (800) 541-2338
FAX: (707) 795-9305
Contact: Gayle Henderson
MFR of *T*
B-2:3

Cottonwood
Halco Trailer Sales
17332 Auction Yard Rd
Cottonwood, CA 96022
Tel: (916) 527-8658
REPAIR of *HT*

Dixon
Heil West
1450 N. 1st Street
P.O. Box 1270
Dixon, CA 95620
Tel: (916) 678-1961
Nation: (800) 326-6646
N.CA: (800) FOR HEIL
Contact: Dennis Hammon
MFR of *G, M, Flatbed M*
C-2:8

Downey
California Truck Equipment, Incorporated
12351 Bellflower Blvd.
Downey, CA 90242
Tel: (310) 803-4466
FAX: (310) 803-8795
MFR of *UTB*
C-2
D

Downey
Sunset Van Conversion
8851 Lakewood Blvd.
Downey, CA 90240
Tel: (310) 862-2177
FAX: (310) 862-4482
R4

El Cajon
Bebco
197 Vernon Way
El Cajon, CA 92020
Tel: (619) 579-6844
FAX: (619) 444-6060
MFR of *CTB*
C-2:1-6

El Cajon
Pape Enterprises
1911 John Towers Ave.
El Cajon, CA 92020
Tel: (619) 449-9720
Nation: (800) 635-PAPE
FAX: (619) 449-9759
MFR of *Sleeper Cabs, Fiberglass Trailers*
D

El Monte
Cal's Van
11028 E. Garvey Avenue
El Monte, CA 91733
Tel: (818) 443-9885
FAX: (818) 350-9021
R4

El Monte
El Monte Rents
12061 E. Valley Blvd.
El Monte, CA 91732
Tel: (818) 443-6158
Nation: (800) 367-3687
FAX: (818) 443-3549
RENTAL SITE of *R1*
C-2

Escondido
Handi-Van
1320 Simpson Way
Escondido, CA 92029
Tel: (619) 432-8785
R4
D

Escondido
Oak Tree Vans Ltd., Inc.
443 Venture Street
Escondido, CA 92029
Tel: (619) 746-8535
FAX: (619) 746-9144
R4

Fontana
Eight Point Trailer Corp.
14770 Slover Avenue
Fontana, CA 92335
Tel: (909) 357-9227
FAX: (909) 357-2644
Contact: Greg Anderson
MFR/DLR of *T*
B-2:2

Fontana
Fruehauf Trailer Corp.
14392 Valley Blvd.
Fontana, CA 92335
Tel: (909) 822-0605
FAX: (909) 822-2427
Contact: Art Noble
MFR of *S-2*
D

Fontana
Hi-V Company
13489 Slover Avenue
Fontana, CA 92335
Tel: (909) 823-2100
Nation: (800) 729-7390
FAX: (909) 823-0860
Contact: Mike Pelengian
MFR of *VTB, UTB*

Fontana
Industrial Truck Bodies, Incorporated
8666 Beech Blvd.
Fontana, CA 92335
Tel: (909) 829-1395
FAX: (909) 824-0183
MFR of *TB*
C-2

Fontana
Morgan Corporation
15000 Santa Ana
Fontana, CA 92335
Tel: (909) 350-4203
USA: (800) 6-MORGAN
FAX: (909) 350-1598
Contact: Tracy Maze
MFR of *VTB*
C-2
NOTE: "800" number reaches the closest plant to the caller. See also Morgan Corporation in Morgantown, PA.

Fontana
Reliance Trailer Co.
13700 Slovert
Fontana, CA 92335
Tel: (909) 350-0185
FAX: (909) 350-3816
MFR of *T*

Fontana
Road Systems, Inc.
8432 Almeria Avenue
Fontana, CA 92335
Tel: (909) 350-2400
MFR of *T*

Fontana
Sierra Auto Upholstery
9530 Sierra Avenue
Fontana, CA 92335
Tel: (909) 357-3095
R4

Fontana
Universal Truck Body, Incorporated
14978 Valley Blvd.
Fontana, CA 92335
Tel: (909) 356-4075
MFR of *TB, FTB*

Fountain Valley
Classic International, Incorporated
18315 Mount Baldy Cir.
Fountain Valley, CA 92708
Tel: (714) 963-9522
Nation: (800) 255-7948
FAX: (714) 968-5639
MFR of *Limos*

Fowler
Jacobsen Trailer, Inc.
1428 E. South Avenue
Fowler, CA 93675
Tel: (209) 834-5971
FAX: (209) 834-2745
MFR/DLR of *UT*

Fremont
Aguiar Truck & Equip.
45555 Industrial Place
Fremont, CA 94538
Tel: (707) 792-2219
MFR of *Construction Equipment*
D: Jalco

Fresno
American Carrier Equip.
(MAIL: P.O. Box 2615
Fresno, CA 93745)
2285 E. Date Avenue
Fresno, CA 93706
Tel: (209) 442-1500
CA only: (800) 344-2175
MFR of *T*
B-2:2-3

Fresno
Commercial Body Sales & Mfg. Co.
(MAIL: P.O. Box 12365
Fresno, CA 93777)
2680 S. Orange Avenue
Fresno, CA 93725
Tel: (209) 266-0836
FAX: (209) 266-1204
MFR/DLR of *TB, T*

Fresno
D & D Kustom Vans and Cars
3929 N. Blockstone Ave.
Fresno, CA 93726
Tel: (209) 225-3116
FAX: (209) 225-0237
Contact: Doug Dowton
CONVERTER of *R4*
C-1

Fresno
Paul Evert's RV Country
3633 S. Maple Avenue
Fresno, CA 93725
Tel: (209) 486-1000
FAX: (209) 486-2511
Contact: Nick Friesen
DLR of *R1*
C-2:5-6

Fresno
Hale Horse & Cattle Trailers
5434 W. Shaw Avenue
Fresno, CA 93722
Tel: (209) 275-3453
DLR of *HT, LT, UT, Equip. T*

Fresno
Hames Manufacturing
5602 E. Belmont Avenue
Fresno, CA 93727
Tel: (209) 251-8332
FAX: (209) 255-9270
Contact: Kenneth Hames or Kent Hames
REPAIR of *T*

Fresno
Jaynes and Company
136 N. Thorne Avenue
Fresno, CA 93706
Tel: (209) 233-3241
REPAIR of *U, TB, R1, R2*

Fresno
Scelzi Enterprises, Inc.
2772 S. Cherry Avenue
Fresno, CA 93706
Tel: (209) 237-5541
Contact: Albert Skinner
MFR of *UTB*

Fresno
Sportsmobile West
5477 E. Hedges Avenue
Fresno, CA 93727
Tel: (209) 255-1871
FAX: (209) 255-1875
R4

Gardena
Lee Brothers Truck Body, Incorporated
15707 S. Avalon
Gardena, CA 90248
Tel: (310) 532-7499
Contact: Ron Lee
MFR of *TB*

Gardena
Secca Corporation
400 W. Gardena Blvd.
Gardena, CA 90248
Tel: (310) 217-2300
FAX: (310) 527-2170
Contact: Rita
DLR of *R4*

Garden Grove
J & M Truck Bodies & Equipment
11808 Western Avenue
Garden Grove, CA 93641
Tel: (714) 898-4259
MFR of *TB*

Garden Grove
Select Vans
11664 Trask Avenue
Garden Grove, CA 92643
Tel: (714) 539-5282
FAX: (714) 539-2146
CONVERTER of *R4*
C-2:1

Hawthorne
Davlin Industries
3928 W. 129th Street
Hawthorne, CA 90250
Tel: (213) 772-4944
MFR of *TC*

Hayward
Classic Vans
25700 Mission Blvd.
Hayward, CA 94544
Tel: (510) 538-3150
FAX: (415) 538-3761
DLR of *R4*

Hayward
De Mello Truck Body
29001 Hopkins Street
Hayward, CA 94545
Tel: (510) 887-4071
REPAIR of *TB*

Hayward
Gillig Corporation
25800 Clawiter Road
Hayward, CA 94545
Tel: (510) 785-1500
Nation: (800) 735-1500
FAX: (510) 785-6810
MFR of *U*
D

Hayward
Van Connection
25716 Mission Blvd.
Hayward, CA 94544
Tel: (510) 886-1153
R4

Hemet
Skyline Corporation
(Nomad Division)
920 W. Mulberry
Hemet, CA 92543
Tel: (909) 628-7106
Nation: (800) 733-4250
FAX: (909) 658-8050
MFR of *R1, R2*
D: KH Trucking

Hemet
Skyline-Layton Travel Trailer
425 S. Palm
Hemet, CA 92542
Tel: (909) 628-7106
FAX: (909) 925-9622
MFR of *R1, R2*
D

Huntington Beach
Braun Corp., The
15731 Graham Street
Huntington Beach, CA 92649
Tel: (714) 891-4305
FAX: (714) 893-3061
CONVERTER of *R4, U, H'cap Units*
D

Huntington Beach
Jam Vans
7573 Slater Avenue
Huntington Beach, CA 92647
Tel: (714) 847-1816
CONVERTER of *R1, R2, R4*

Huntington Park
Princess Van Conversion
2928 E. Florence Avenue
Huntington Park, CA 90255
Tel: (213) 587-8272
R4

Indio
California Custom Coach
49-506 Indio Blvd.
Indio, CA 92201
Tel: (619) 347-0384
FAX: (619) 347-9425
Contact: John Edwards
UConvs

Industry
Perfection Truck Bodies
655 N. Vineland
Industry, CA 91746
Tel: (818) 961-5600
MFR of *TB*

Inglewood
Aames Coachworks and Leasing
10219 Hawthorne Blvd.
Inglewood, CA 90304
Tel: (213) 678-5551
DLR of *Limos*

Irvine
Stockland Co., The
2332 Barranco Pkwy.
Irvine, CA 92714
Tel: (714) 660-0590
Contact: Barbara Costlow
MFR of *TC*
C-2:3

Irvine
Traveland USA
(MAIL: P.O. Box 429
East Irvine, CA 92650)
6441 Burt Road
Irvine, CA 92720
Tel: (714) 551-1881
Nation: (800) 854-0121
FAX: (714) 552-7056
Contact: Kathy Phillips
DLR of *R1*
D: KH Trucking

Irwindale
Compact Equipment Co.
5257 N. Vincent Avenue
Irwindale, CA 91706
Tel: (818) 334-0376
FAX: (818) 334-1138
Contact: John Kayles
R4
C-2:4-5

Janesville
Charmac Horse Trailers
460-975 Janesville Grade
Janesville, CA 96114
Tel: (916) 253-3805
DLR of *HT*

Kingsburg
Ross Trailer Mfg.
14344 S. Bethel Avenue
Kingsburg, CA 93631
Tel: (209) 897-0220
MFR of *T*

La Habra
JC Trailer Mfg.
1070 S. Cypress Street
La Habra, CA 90631
Tel: (714) 738-4505
MFR of *T*

La Mesa
La Mesa Sheet Metal Works, Incorporated
8135 Center Street
La Mesa, CA 91942
Tel: (619) 469-6187
FAX: (619) 469-3612
Contact: Ronda Guile
MFR/FINAL ASSEMBLER of *F*

La Puente
Utility Trailer Mfg. Co.
17295 E. Railroad Street
La Puente, CA 91748
Tel: (818) 965-1541
FAX: (818) 964-5800
Contact: Mitzi Workman
MFR of *T*
D

Laguna Hills
Countryside Vans
23011 Moulton Pkwy.
Laguna Hills, CA 92653
Tel: (714) 581-9970
Contact: Martin Okuda
R4
C-2:3

Lompoc
Pleasure Trucks
436 N. 8th Street
Lompoc, CA 93436
Tel: (805) 736-1363
R4

Long Beach
CMF Corporation
1524 W. 15th Street
Long Beach, CA 90813
Tel: (310) 437-2166
FAX: (310) 495-1857
MFR of *VTB*

Long Beach
Kit Manufacturing Co.
530 E. Wardlow Road
P. O. Box 848
Long Beach, CA 90801-0848
Tel: (310) 595-7451
FAX: (310) 426-8463
MFR of *R5, R6*
D

Long Beach
Paramount Truck Body Equipment Company
6901 Cherry Avenue
Long Beach, CA 90805
Tel: (310) 634-2010
FAX: (310) 531-4218
MFR of *TB*

Long Beach
Thompson Tank & Manufacturing Co.
2019 E. Wardlow Road
Long Beach, CA 90807
Tel: (310) 427-8938
CA only: (800) 421-7545
FAX: (310) 595-5846
MFR of *Tank Trailers*

Long Beach
Vanco
1165 E. Pacific Coast Highway
Long Beach, CA 90806
Tel: (310) 591-3092
R4

Los Angeles
AA Cater Truck Manufacturing, Inc.
750 E. Slauson Avenue
Los Angeles, CA 90011
Tel: (213) 235-2191
MFR of *Catering Trucks*

Los Angeles
Hollywood Van & Off-Road Accessories
1448 Glendale Blvd.
Los Angeles, CA 90026
Tel: (213) 494-9895
R4

Los Angeles
JWD
2250 N. Robertson Blvd.
Suite 405
Los Angeles, CA 90211
Tel: (310) 839-9417
FAX: (310) 839-1046
MFR/CONVERTER
of *Limos*
A-1, C-2:6-10

Los Angeles
KPK Truck Body Mfg.
3045 Verdugo Road
Los Angeles, CA 90065
Tel: (213) 221-9167
MFR of *TB*

Los Angeles
Martin Cadillac-Pontiac-Sterling
12101 W. Olympic Blvd.
Los Angeles, CA 90064
Tel: (310) 820-3611
FAX: (310) 826-3717
Contact: Gordon Olson
at ext. 268
DLR of *Limos*
A-1
*D: Pacific Motor Trucking Company
1680 Santa Fe Way
San Bernardino, CA 92410
Nation: (800) 569-5252.*
NOTE: *Opportunity here is extremely limited, but they recommend contacting their transporter company.*

Los Angeles
Pacific Truck Body
7811 S. Alameda Street
Los Angeles, CA 90001
Tel: (213) 582-0831
MFR of *TB*

Los Angeles
World Van
1910 W. Washington Blvd.
Los Angeles, CA 90018
Tel: (213) 737-5885
R4

Los Banos
Auto-Mate Recreational Products, Incorporated
150 W. G Street
P.O. Box 831
Los Banos, CA 93635
Tel: (209) 826-1521
FAX: (209) 826-8167
Contact: Terry Wilson
MFR of *R4, R5, R6*
C-2:1

Lynwood
Capco Truck Equipment Company, Incorporated
11350 Wright Road
Lynwood, CA 90262
Tel: (213) 774-2979
MFR of *TC*

Martinez
Van Man, The
5050 Pacheco Blvd.
Martinez, CA 94553
Tel: (510) 372-8181
FAX: (510) 372-3681
R4

Maywood
Viva Vans
4557 Slauson Avenue
Maywood, CA 90270
Tel: (213) 560-1399
R4

Merced
Action Vans
2220 Franklin Road
Merced, CA 95340
Tel: (209) 383-1621
R4

Merced
H & H Camper Manufacturing & Sales
3074 Ashby Road
Merced, CA 95348
Tel: (209) 383-2668
MFR of *TC*

Merced
Wilcal Enterprises
2220 Franklin Road
Merced, CA 95340
Tel: (209) 722-8771
MFR of *TC*

Milpitas
Vanco Van Conversions & Accessories
542 S. Main Street
Milpitas, CA 95035
Tel: (408) 956-8267
R4

Mira Loma
California Custom Design, Incorporated
(The Red-E-Kamp Div.)
3401 Etiwanda Avenue
Mira Loma Space Center
Mira Loma, CA 91752
Tel: (909) 685-0151
Nation: (800) 300-3031
FAX: (909) 685-0609
Contact: Marcy Witz
R4
C-2:5
D

Modesto
Tom's Custom Vans
500 9th Street
Modesto, CA 95354
Tel: (209) 521-8944
R4
C-2

Modesto
Utility of Northern California
1401 S. 7th Street
Modesto, CA 95351
Tel: (408) 298-0177
FAX: (209) 524-1933
Contact: Bob Wilderson
DLR of *S-2*
B-1

Montebello
ABC Aluminum Body Corporation
1600 Washington Blvd.
Montebello, CA 90640
Tel: (213) 728-7611
MFR of *ST*
B-2
D

Montebello
American Cater Truck Manufacturing
1615 Mines Avenue
Montebello, CA 90640
Tel: (213) 721-4022
MFR of *VTB*

Montebello
Cab Truck Bodies Co.
1139 W. Mines
Montebello, CA 90640
Tel: (213) 724-0555
REPAIR of *TB*

Montebello
Pacific Cater Truck Manufacturing
8265 Truck Way
Montebello, CA 90640
Tel: (213) 728-3463
MFR of *Catering TB*

Moreno Valley
West Sundial, Inc.
23846 Sunnymead Blvd.
Moreno Valley, CA 92553
Tel: (909) 242-1127
FAX: (909) 242-1128
Contact: Patsy Stanley
R4

National City
DB Conversions
333 Civic Center Drive
National City, CA 91950
Tel: (619) 474-4072
H'cap R4, H'cap Units

North Hills
Daco Shells
8454 Sepulveda Blvd.
North Hills, CA 91343
Tel: (818) 892-4327
DLR of *TC*
C-2

North Hollywood
Advanced Mobility, Inc.
12555 Sherman Way
North Hollywood, CA 91605
Tel: (818) 982-1004
Nation: (800) 554-6065
FAX: (818) 982-5893
MFR/DLR of *H'cap R4, H'cap Units*

North Hollywood
Lance Camper Sales and Service
6025 Laurel Canyon Blvd
North Hollywood, CA 91606-4615
Tel: (818) 760-0086
Tel: (818) 760-0359
FAX: (818) 760-7434
DLR of *TC, T*

Northridge
DCV
19420 Londelius Street
Northridge, CA 91324
Tel: (818) 718-7038
FAX: (818) 718-7054
R4, H'cap R4
C-2:4

Oakland
California Touring Coach Company
8914 MacArthur Blvd.
Oakland, CA 94605
Tel: (415) 436-6381
Contact: D.J. Taylor
MFR of *U*

Oakland
Dailey Body Company
440 High Street
Oakland, CA 94601
Tel: (510) 534-1423
Nation: (800) 404-2639
FAX: (510) 534-1446
MFR of *FTB, CTB*
DISTRIBUTOR of *UTB, VTB, M*

Oakland
El Monte Rents
4901 Coliseum Way
Oakland, CA 94601
Tel: (510) 532-7404
Nation: (800) 332-7878
FAX: (510) 532-7655
Contact: Pat Nelson
DLR of *R1, R2*

Oakland
Gregory Truck Body Company
711 Kevin Court
Oakland, CA 94621
Tel: (510) 635-7171
MFR of *V*

Oakland
Utility Truck Bodies, Incorporated
1530 Wood Street
Oakland, CA 94607
Tel: (510) 271-0797
FAX: (510) 271-8038
MFR of *TB*

Ontario
Amrep, Incorporated
1555 S. Cucamonga Ave.
Ontario, CA 91761
Tel: (909) 923-0430
FAX: (909) 923-2485
MFR of *STB*

Ontario
Arrow Truck Bodies & Equipment, Incorporated
1639 S. Campus Avenue
P.O. Box 3069
Ontario, CA 91761
Tel: (909) 947-3991
FAX: (909) 947-4932
Contact: Don Glaze
MFR/DLR of *TB*
C-2:2

Ontario
Atlas Truck Bodies, Inc.
1135 E. State Street
Ontario, CA 91761
Tel: (909) 983-5669
FAX: (909) 984-8845
MFR of *TB*
C-2
D

Ontario
Hawkins Motor Coach
P.O. Box 3189
Ontario, CA 91761
Tel: (909) 947-2512
Contact: Bob Hanlin
MFR of *R1, R2*
C-2

Ontario
Long Run Trailers
1843 S. Campus Avenue
Ontario, CA 91761
Tel: (909) 923-4242
Nation: (800) 929-3511
FAX: (909) 923-5324
MFR of *T*
B-2:1

Ontario
Thor Industries West
4750 Zinfadel Court
Ontario, CA 91761
Tel: (909) 986-6118
Nation: (800) 548-2385
FAX: (909) 986-4158
Contact: Tom Munez
MFR of *R1, R2, R5, R6, TC*
C-2:10

Ontario
Warrior Manufacturing
524 S. Hope Avenue
Ontario, CA 91761
Tel: (909) 983-9914
FAX: (909) 983-9554
MFR of *R6*
D

Ontario
Weather Beater
12769 S. Euclid Avenue
Ontario, CA 91761
Tel: (909) 986-5443
MFR of *TC*

Ontario
Weekend Warrior Trailer
(Div. of Warrior Mfg.)
1614 E. Holt Blvd.
Ontario, CA 91761
Tel: (909) 983-9914
Nation: (800) 500-9914
FAX: (909) 983-9554
Contact: Sandra Warmoth
MFR of *R5, R6, CT, UT*

Orange
M & L Truck Body & Equipment
1204 W. Struck Avenue
Orange, CA 92667
Tel: (714) 639-9011
CA only: (800) 448-4344
MFR of *TB*

Orange
Royal Coach by Victor
7754 N. Batavia Street
Orange, CA 92668
Tel: (714) 532-3967
Contact: Victor Pina
MFR of *Limos*
D

Orange
Vans, Incorporated
2095 N. Batavia Street
Orange, CA 92665
Tel: (714) 974-7414
R4

Oxnard
C & S Truck Bodies & RV Supplies
701 N. Rice Avenue
Oxnard, CA 93030
Tel: (805) 983-1673
MFR/DLR of *TB*

Oxnard
California Custom Shells
2665 Wagon Wheel Road, #A
Oxnard, CA 93030
Tel: (805) 485-8229
MFR of *TC*

Oxnard
Convert-A-Van
1140 Industrial Avenue
Oxnard, CA 93030
Tel: (805) 486-3777
FAX: (805) 487-9499
MFR of *R4*

Oxnard
Summit Industries
1250 Mercantile
Oxnard, CA 93030
Tel: (805) 487-8977
FAX: (805) 487-4120
MFR of *R1, R2, TC*

Pacoima
Lance Camper Manufacturing Corp.
10234 Glenoaks Blvd.
Pacoima, CA 91331
Tel: (818) 897-3155
MFR of *RV Campers*
D: Avery Transportation
Tel: (909) 399-3104

Palmdale
Sandzimier Truck Bodies
Pearblossom Highway
Palmdale, CA 93550
Tel: (906) 944-1328
MFR of *TB*

Paramount
Royal Truck Bodies, Inc.
14001 Garfield Avenue
Paramount, CA 90723
Tel: (213) 774-2275
MFR of *TB*
D

Paramount
Trojan Truck Body, Inc.
7227 Petterson Lane
Paramount, CA 90273
Tel: (310) 634-3124
CA only: (800) 227-8304
MFR of *TB*
C-2
D

Parlier
Dahl Specialty Mfg.
14660 E. Manning Ave.
P.O. Box 216
Parlier, CA 93648
Tel: (209) 888-2047
FAX: (209) 464-0433
Contact: Doug Dahl
MFR of *T*
D

Perris
National RV Inc.
3411 N. Perris Blvd.
Perris, CA 92370
Tel: (909) 943-6007
FAX: (909) 943-5204
Contact: Craig Brunton
MFR of *R1*
D: Morgan, Horizon

Pico Rivera
Diamond B Body &
Trailer Corporation
8405 Loch Lomond
Pico Rivera, CA 90660
Tel: (310) 948-3497
FAX: (213) 949-8168
Contact: Jim Hall
MFR of *TB*

Pico Rivera
Trailmobile Company
8542 Slauson Avenue
Pico Rivera, CA 90660
Tel: (310) 949-6591
FAX: (310) 949-1244
Contact: Bob Quaranta
MFR of *T*

Placentia
Roll-A-Long Vans, Inc.
210 E. Crowther Street
Placentia, CA 92670
Tel: (714) 528-9600
FAX: (714) 524-6125
Contact: Bruce Landfield
MFR of *TConvs, R4*
C-2:2
D

Plymouth
D & L Stidman
Horse Trailer
22374 Latrobe Road
Plymouth, CA 95669
Tel: (209) 245-3141
DLR of *HT*

Pomona
Lazy Daze, Incorporated
4303 E. Mission Blvd.
Pomona, CA 91766
Tel: (910) 627-1103
Nation: (800) 578-1103
FAX: (910) 627-3379
Contact: Vicky Kump
MFR of *R1, R2*

Rancho Cordova
David K's Van &
Truck Conversions
2340 Gold River Road
Rancho Cordova, CA 95670
Tel: (916) 638-4777
R4

Rancho Cucamonga
G & S Truck Bodies
803 Archibald Avenue
Rancho Cucamonga, CA 91730
Tel: (909) 987-3513
CORPORATE HQ

Redding
Aero Trek
3424 S. Market Street
Redding, CA 96001
Tel: (916) 244-0408
Nation: (800) 698-0408
Contact: Butch Ritcheson
MFR of *TC*

Redding
Best-Way Upholestry
& Van Works
3530 Railroad Avenue
Redding, CA 96002
Tel: (916) 244-1957
FAX: (916) 221-8579
R4

Redding
Cousin Gary's RV Center
3000 Park Marina Drive
Redding, CA 96001
Tel: (916) 241-3545
Nation: (800) 442-3545
FAX: (916) 241-2314
Contact: Brent Bryer
DLR of *R1, R2*
D: Morgan Driveaway,
Turner Transport

Redondo Beach
Accessories 'N Stuff
1443 Aviation Blvd.
Redondo Beach, CA 90278
Tel: (310) 372-2188
FAX: (310) 318-9162
R4, TConvs

Redwood City
Carter Industries
880 Sweeny Avenue
Redwood City, CA 94063
Tel: (415) 364-6390
Contact: Becky Carter
MFR of *FTB*
D

Rialto
Fleetwood Travel
Trailers of California
145 S. Larch Avenue
P.O. Box 810
Rialto, CA 92376
Tel: (909) 874-2223
MFR of *R5, R6*
D

Rialto
Mobile Help
735 W. Rialto Avenue
Rialto, CA 92376
Tel: (909) 875-2442
FAX: (909) 875-5002
R4

Richmond
Betts Truck Body Co.
518 S. 11th Street
Richmond, CA 94804
Tel: (510) 215-1030
MFR/DLR of *TB*

Riverside
Buyer's RV Mart, Inc.
681 W. La Cadina Drive
Riverside, CA 92501
Tel: (909) 686-9074
FAX: (909) 686-0729
Contact: Katrina
DLR of *R1, R2*

Riverside
Country Time RV Center
7207 Indiana Avenue
Riverside, CA 92504
Tel: (909) 787-8123
Contact: Tim Plumber
DLR of *R5, R6*
D: Webb, Morgan

Riverside
Crouse Craft Vans
3496 Commerce Street
Riverside, CA 92507
Tel: (909) 784-8267
R4

Riverside
Custom Camp Vans &
Service, Incorporated
7575 Jurupa Avenue
Riverside, CA 92504
Tel: (909) 359-3443
FAX: (909) 359-1956
R4, TConvs
C-2:6

Riverside
Eagle Truck Body
& Equipment
11999 Magnolia Avenue
Riverside, CA 92503
Tel: (909) 785-8408
MFR/DLR of *TB*

Riverside
Fleetwood Motor Homes
of California
2350 Fleetwood Drive
P.O. Box 5726
Riverside, CA 92517
Tel: (909) 788-2920
FAX: (909) 788-9528
MFR/FINAL
ASSEMBLER of *R1, R2*
D: Morgan Driveaway

Riverside
Hall Craft Industries
1760 Chicago Avenue
Riverside, CA 92507
Tel: (909) 276-1341
FAX: (909) 276-1571
MFR of *R1*
D: Morgan Driveaway

Riverside
RV Service Masters
Corporation
3848 Pierce Street
Riverside, CA 92503
Tel: (909) 688-8322
R4

Riverside
Specialty Van & Auto
3333 Harrison Street
Riverside, CA 92503
Tel: (909) 689-9965
R4
C-2

Riverside
Supreme Truck Bodies
of California
7888 Lincoln Avenue
Riverside, CA 92504
Tel: (909) 351-8785
CA only: (800) 251-0647
FAX: (909) 351-0624
MFR of *VTB, XTB*

Riverside
Transit Care
1863 Service Court
Riverside, CA 92507
Tel: (909) 784-3474
FAX: (909) 684-2088
Contact: Dawn Prather
MFR of *U*

Roseville
Holiday RV Superstores West, Incorporated
2020 Taylor Road
Roseville, CA 95678
Tel: (916) 782-3178
FAX: (916) 782-3290
Contact: Mark Sweet
DLR or *R1, R2*

Roseville
Rathbone Trailers
9600 Antelope Oaks Court, Suite C
Roseville, CA 95747
Tel: (916) 773-5503
MFR/DLR of *BT B-2*

Roseville
Roseville Truck Body Manufacturing
9600 Dell Road
Roseville, CA 95678
Tel: (916) 784-3220
FAX: (916) 784-3280
Contact: Cindy Moore
MFR of *FTB*

Sacramento
Con-Truck
8834 Fruitridge Road
Sacramento, CA 95826
Tel: (916) 386-8785
TConvs, R4

Sacramento
Continental Van and Truck Specialty Convs.
9745 Business Park Drive
Sacramento, CA 95827
Tel: (916) 362-2018
FAX: (916) 362-1268
Contact: Gabriel Barajas
R4, TConvs

Sacramento
Deluxe Truckin' Co.
6550 Freeport Blvd.
Sacramento, CA 95822
Tel: (916) 392-1196
Contact: Dionne Gruess
MFR/DLR/CONVERTER of *R4*

Sacramento
Flair Truck Tops
1051 El Camino Avenue
Sacramento, CA 95815
Tel: (916) 929-1690
DLR of *TC*

Sacramento
River City Truck Equipment, Incorporated
631 N. Market Blvd.
Sacramento, CA 95834
Tel: (916) 921-2639
MFR of *TB*

Sacramento
Sacramento Van Conversions & Acc.
5821 Floren Perkins Road
Sacramento, CA 95828
Tel: (916) 391-8267
R4

Sacramento
T & N Mfg. & Sales
8550 Tiogawoods Dr.
Sacramento, CA 95828
Tel: (916) 423-2290
FAX: (916) 682-7764
MFR of *TB*

Sacramento
Total Camper Sales, Inc.
1925 El Camino Avenue
Sacramento, CA 95815
Tel: (916) 925-5643
MFR of *TC*

Sacramento
Tri-State Tank West
7029 Floren Perkins Road
Sacramento, CA 95828
Tel: (916) 383-3318
FAX: (916) 383-6473
FINAL ASSEMBLER of *Delivery Trucks C-2:4*

Salinas
Commercial Truck Co.
703 Abbott Street
Salinas, CA 93901
Tel: (408) 424-2961
DLR of *International Trucks*

Salinas
E-Z Rider Vans
1370 Burton Avenue
Salinas, CA 93901
Tel: (408) 758-3379
FAX: (408) 757-1449
R4

San Bernardino
Camper Shell Mart
1375 Northeast Street
San Bernardino, CA 92405
Tel: (909) 885-2814
DLR of *TC*

San Bernardino
Zieman Mfg. Co., Inc.
120 E. Cental Avenue
San Bernardino, CA 92408
Tel: (909) 888-1411
Contact: Jim Zieman
MFR of *T B-2 D*

San Carlos
Western Truck Fabrication
1011 American Street
San Carlos, CA 94070
Tel: (415) 594-0766
MFR of *TB C-1*

San Diego
Caravan Conversions
7845 Raytheon Road
San Diego, CA 92111
Tel: (619) 279-2370
R4

San Diego
D & H Truck Equipment
4567 Federal Blvd.
San Diego, CA 92102
Tel: (619) 266-1303
FAX: (619) 266-2918
Contact: Todd Whitehead
MFR/FINAL ASSEMBLER of *CTB*

San Diego
Gary Colle
5457 Ruffin Road, Ste. B
San Diego, CA 92123
Tel: (619) 279-9710
H'cap R4

San Diego
Manufacture & Products Services Corporation
7948 Ronson Road
San Diego, CA 92111
Tel: (619) 292-1423
Contact: George Hendrickson
R4

San Diego
Taylor Van
5376 Napa Street
San Diego, CA 92110
Tel: (619) 298-0936
Contact: Jay Judemann
R4

San Fernando
Skaug Truck Body Works
1404 First Street
San Fernando, CA 91340
Tel: (818) 365-9123
Contact: George Skaug
MFR of *TB*

San Francisco
Stoughton Trailers
3 Embarcadero Center
San Francisco, CA 94111
Tel: (412) 539-7579
MFR of *S-2*

San Jacinto
Borg Trailers
24020 Mesa View Street
San Jacinto, CA 92582
Tel: (909) 654-2918
Contact: Bob Borg
MFR of *CT, HT*

San Jose
Country Homes Camper
493 Reynolds Circle
San Jose, CA 95112
Tel: (408) 441-6280
R4

San Jose
Happy Vans
140 Archer Street
San Jose, CA 95112
Tel: (408) 453-7525
R4 C-1

San Jose
Kent Kittleman, Inc.
1720 S. 1st Street
San Jose, CA 95112
Tel: (408) 998-8300
Contact: Melissa Parker
MFR of *TB*

San Jose
Mobility Unlimited
1701-B Rogers Avenue
San Jose, CA 95112-1127
Tel: (408) 453-7354
Tel: (408) 453-7355
Contact: Chuck Wiliams
H'cap R4

San Jose
Northern Trailer & Truck Body
2154 O'Toole Avenue
San Jose, CA 95131
Tel: (408) 435-7443
REPAIR of *T*

San Jose
Protect-O-Top
1505 Nicora Avenue
San Jose, CA 95133
Tel: (408) 251-1044
MFR of *TC*
D: Best Delivery Service

San Leandro
G. Paoletti Co., Inc.
496 Hester Street
San Leandro, CA 94577
Tel: (510) 569-3010
FAX: (510) 569-3520
Contact: Frank Paoletti
MFR of *ST, E, F*

San Leandro
Mobile Hydraulic Equip.
799 Thornton Street
San Leandro, CA 94587
Tel: (415) 357-6680
Contact: Bob Ross
MFR of *Service STB*

San Lorenzo
Service Mfg. Co.
2400 Baumann Avenue
San Lorenzo, CA 94580
Tel: (510) 278-7400
FAX: (510) 278-3769
Contact: Harvey Silverman
MFR/CONVERTER of *UTB, R4*

San Ramon
Navistar International Transportation
2682 Bishop Drive
San Ramon, CA 94583
Tel: (510) 830-2200
FAX: (510) 860-2210
MFR of *Trucks*

Santa Ana
Continental Coach Corp.
1707 Boyd Street
Santa Ana, CA 92705
Tel: (714) 258-8267
Nation: (800) 228-8267
FAX: (714) 258-0939
Contact: Ralph Caputo
R4
C-2

Santa Ana
G Truck Bodies
3023 Orange Avenue
Santa Ana, CA 92707
Tel: (714) 557-8793
MFR of *TB*

Santa Ana
Thermobile & Payload Products
2621 S. Birch Street
Santa Ana, CA 92707
Tel: (714) 557-6442
MODIFIER of *CTB*

Santa Barbara
King Company RV Center, Incorporated
606 E. Haley Street
Santa Barbara, CA 93103
Tel: (805) 963-7744
MFR of *R1, R2, TC*

Santa Clara
Bob Muscatell Motor Homes
3450 El Camino Real
Santa Clara, CA 95051
Tel: (408) 241-4500
Contact: Bob Muscatell or Steve Muscatell
DLR of *R1, R2*

Santa Clara
Universal Truck Equipment, Incorporated
2767 Scott Blvd.
Santa Clara, CA 95050
Tel: (408) 727-3810
MFR of *CTB, UTB, VTB*
MODIFIER of *R4*

Santa Fe Springs
Vince's Truck Bodies
9403 S. Norwalk Blvd.
Santa Fe Springs, CA 90670
Tel: (310) 695-0408
MFR of *TB*

Santa Maria
Coastal Truck Bodies, Incorporated
2363-D Thompson Way
Santa Maria, CA 93455
Tel: (805) 922-8872
MFR of *TB*

Santa Maria
Industrial Truck Bodies
1701 N. River Rock Court Santa Maria, CA 93464
Tel: (805) 928-4266
MFR of *TB*

Santa Rosa
Vans, Limited
3110 Santa Rosa Avenue
Santa Rosa, CA 95407
Tel: (707) 528-6388
R4

Saugas
Rexhall Industries, Inc.
25655 Springbrook Ave.
Saugas, CA 91350
Tel: (805) 253-1295
FAX: (805) 253-2422
MFR of *R1, R2*
D: Morgan Driveaway, Don Ray Driveaway

Sebastapol
Solar Electric
117 Morris Street
Sebastapol, CA 95472
Tel: (707) 829-4545
Nation: (800) 832-1986
FAX: (707) 829-4547
Contact: Laurie Pikten
CONVERTER of *R1, R2*
C-2:2
D

Sepulveda
Niel's Motor Homes and Trailers
8646 Sepulveda Blvd.
Sepulveda, CA 91343
Tel: (818) 891-0786
FAX: (818) 894-1937
Contact: Tom Linstrom
DLR of *R1, R2, R6*

South El Monte
Leader Industries, Inc.
10941 Weaver Avenue
South El Monte, CA 91733
Tel: (818) 575-0880
FAX: (818) 575-0286
MFR of *A*

South Gate
D & A Campers
10518 Dolores Avenue
South Gate, CA 90280
Tel: (213) 567-9146
MFR of *TC*
C-2:1

South Gate
Master Body Works, Inc.
9824 Atlantic Avenue
South Gate, CA 90280
Tel: (213) 564-6901
FAX: (213) 564-2462
MFR/DLR of *TConvs*

South San Francisco
California Classic Vans
1531 Mission Road
South San Francisco, CA 94080
Tel: (415) 992-5755
FAX: (415) 922-5758
R4

South San Francisco
McLellan Industries/ McLellan Equipment, Incorporated
251 Shaw Road
South San Francisco, CA 94080
Tel: (415) 873-8100
CA only: (800) 843-8118
Nation: (800) 848-8449
FAX: (415) 589-7398
MFR of *TB*
C-2:10
D

South San Francisco
Superior Aluminum Body Corporation
457 S. Canal Street
South San Francisco, CA 94080
Tel: (415) 761-0155
FAX: (415) 873-2075
MFR of *Insulated TB, Refrig. TB*
NOTE: *Another plant, and their HQ, is at 125 Starlite, in this city.*

South San Francisco
Superior Aluminum Body Corporation
125 Starlite
South San Francisco, CA 94080
Tel: (415) 761-0155
FAX: (415) 873-2075
MFR of *Insulated TB, Refrig. TB*
NOTE: *This is a plant site, as well as the HQ. Another plant site is at 457 S. Canal Street, in this city.*

Spring Valley
Mild-to-Wild Custom Coaches
9995 Campo Road
Spring Valley, CA 91977
Tel: (619) 670-6008
FAX: (619) 670-6010
R4

Stanton
J & M Truck Bodies
11808 Western Avenue
Stanton, CA 90680
Tel: (714) 898-4259
MFR of *UTB, VTB, XTB*

Stanton
Southern California Mobility, Incorporated
11600 Western Avenue
Stanton, CA 90680
Tel: (714) 898-7838
FAX: (714) 898-9134
H'cap R4, H'cap Units

Stockton
Acme Truck Parts & Equipment, Incorporated
1016 S. Wilson Way
Stockton, CA 95205
Tel: (209) 466-7021
WATS: (800) 545-2263
Contact: Nathan Davison at ext. 111
DLR of *TB*

Stockton
Diamond Truck Body Co.
1908 E. Fremont Street
Stockton, CA 95205
Tel: (209) 943-1655
FAX: (209) 943-0805
Contact: Francis Teresi
MFR of *TB*
C-2

Stockton
Friend's Van Conversions
2314 N. Wilson Way
Stockton, CA 95205
Tel: (209) 465-6912
R4

Stockton
Harley Murray, Inc.
1754 E. Mariposa Road
Stockton, CA 95205
Tel: (209) 466-0266
FAX: (209) 466-0550
Contact: Ralph Lagrand
MFR of *T*
C-2

Stockton
Merritt Livestock Trailers
2973 Loomis Road
Stockton, CA 95205
Tel: (209) 946-0674
MFR of *LT*

Suisun City
North Bay Truck Body
9310 W. Cordelia Road
Suisun City, CA 94585
Tel: (707) 864-2700
REPAIR of *TB*

Sunnyvale
Executop/ Truck N' Travel
624 E. Taylor Avenue
Sunnyvale, CA 94086
Tel: (408) 245-1244
FAX: (408) 730-9873
Contact: Silvino Robles
R4

Sun Valley
Armenco Cater Truck Manufacturing Company
8526 San Fernando Road
Sun Valley, CA 91352
Tel: (818) 768-0400
MFR of *Catering Trucks*

Sun Valley
Spartan Truck Equipment, Incorporated
12266 Branford Street
Sun Valley, CA 91352
Tel: (818) 899-1111
MFR of *M*
C-2
D

Terra Bella
Gallaty Trailer Mfg.
23297 Avenue 88
Terra Bella, CA 93270
Tel: (209) 535-0112
MFR of *T*

Torrance
Custom One Auto Body Shop
22920 Lockness Avenue
Torrance, CA 90501
Tel: (310) 325-1578
FAX: (310) 325-1019
MODIFIER of *R1, R2*
B-3
D: L & M Towing

Torrance
Metro Truck Body Inc.
1201 Jon Street
Torrance, CA 90502
Tel: (310) 532-5570
FAX: (310) 532-0754
Contact: Sid Haluska
MFR of *TB*
C-2
D

Turlock
Stiles Truck Body & Equipment
701 S. Golden State Blvd.
Turlock, CA 95380
Tel: (209) 667-2639
MFR of *TB*

Upland
Butterfield Interiors
8458 Loma Place
Upland, CA 91786
Tel: (909) 982-6770
MFR of *RV interiors*
C-2
D

Van Nuys
Van De Camper
7801 Noble Avenue
Van Nuys, CA 91405
Tel: (818) 780-6361
R4

Ventura
All-Star Truck Bodies
2117 Palma Dr., Unit B
Ventura, CA 93003
Tel: (805) 644-4336
MFR of *TB*

Ventura
B & C Van Works
1548 Callens Road
Ventura, CA 93003
Tel: (805) 642-0848
FAX: (805) 650-0191
Contact: Bill Chandler
R4, TConvs, Minivan-Convs

Visalia
Randy's RV Upholstery
116 N. Valley Oaks Drive
Visalia, CA 93292
Tel: (209) 627-9999
MODIFIER of *R4*

Visalia
Suburban Pipe & Steel
721 E. Acequia Street
Visalia, CA 93291
Tel: (209) 734-6547
Tel: (209) 734-0911
Tel: (209) 734-7428
Tel: (209) 734-5460
FAX: (209) 734-0811
MFR of *TB*

Watsonville
Access Options, Inc.
49 Hangar Way
Watsonville, CA 95076
Tel: (408) 722-6804
FAX: (408) 722-0236
H'cap R4, H'cap Units

Westminster
California Comfort Vans
15040 Golden West Cir.
Westminster, CA 92683
Tel: (714) 896-8267
Contact: Susan Land
MFR of *R4*
C-2:5

Windsor
Best Truck Body & Trailer, Incorporated
610 Standard Avenue
Windsor, CA 95492
Tel: (707) 838-1440
REPAIR of *TB, T*

Winters
Six-Pac Winters
1805 Railroad Street
Winters, CA 95694
Tel: (916) 795-4166
DISTRIBUTOR of *TC*
mfd. at their Corona, CA plant.

Woodland
JTB Industries
350 Road 101
Woodland, CA 95695
Tel: (916) 666-1442
Contact: Tim Peterson
DLR of *TC*

Woodland
Wesco Trailer Sales
1960 E. Main Street
Woodland, CA 95776
Tel: (916) 662-9606
FAX: (916) 662-0150
MFR of *T*

COLORADO

Arvada
May Mfg. Dist. Corp.
5400 Marshall Street
Arvada, CO 80002
Tel: (303) 423-6200
MFR of *T*

Arvada
New Industries/ Starbuck Boats
6721 W. 58th Place
Arvada, CO 80003
Tel: (303) 467-3004
Contact: Darlene Starbuck
MFR of *BT*

Ault
Dahlgren Mfg., Inc.
Highway 85 & Road 78
Ault, CO 80610
Tel: (303) 454-2073
MFR of *T*

Aurora
GLC Manufacturing
3750 Wheeling, Unit #8
Aurora, CO 80239
Tel: (303) 371-3191
MFR of *T*

Aurora
Mountain States RV
14300 E. Colfax Avenue
Aurora, CO 80011
Tel: (303) 360-0252
FAX: (303) 363-9103
Contact: Rob Solomon
DLR of *R1, R2*

Aurora
Provan USA
3263 Oakland Street
Aurora, CO 80010
Tel: (303) 363-7089
Nation: (800) 442-8267
FAX: (303) 363-7299
Contact: Gary L. Young
MFR of *W*
D: A. Anthony

Brighton
Hallmark Mfg. Inc.
1150 Brighton Road
Brighton, CO 80601
Tel: (303) 659-5572
Tel: (303) 654-0004
FAX: (303) 659-5754
Contact: Peter Koehn, Production Manager
MFR of *R6*

Burlington
Hitchcock, Incorporated
49994 US Highway 24
Burlington, CO 80807
Tel: (719) 346-8488
MFR of *Farm Equip.*

Colorado Springs
Happy Wheels
3412 Van Teylingen Dr.
Colorado Springs, CO 80917
Tel: (719) 596-8094
Nation: (800) 727-7478
DLR/MODIFIER of *H'cap Units*

Colorado Springs
Interwest Home Medical
3636 Jeannine Drive
Colorado Springs, CO 80917
Tel: (719) 597-9730
FAX: (719) 597-1781
Contact: Marvin Holland
DLR of *H'cap Units*
C-2

Colorado Springs
Layton Truck Bodies & Equipment
555 Ford Street
Colorado Springs, CO 80915
Tel: (719) 597-0400
CO only: (800) 332-5021
Contact: Kim Fletcher
MODIFIER of *TB*

Colorado Springs
Pikes Peak Truck & Van, Incorporated
6630 Shoup
Colorado Springs, CO 80908
Tel: (719) 528-8181
R4, TConvs

Colorado Springs
Vans America
4011 Sinton Road
Colorado Springs, CO 80907
Tel: (719) 577-4023
R4

Commerce City
C & B Manufacturing
7000 E. 58th Ave., Ste. 5
Commerce City, CO 80022
Tel: (303) 287-5358
Contact: Paul Black
MFR of *T*

Commerce City
Kois Brothers Equipment Company, Incorporated
5200 Colorado Blvd.
Commerce City, CO 80022
Tel: (303) 399-7370
Nation: (800) 344-0638
FAX: (303) 399-7398
MFR of *T*

Commerce City
Superior Gooseneck Trailers
5530 E. 52nd Avenue
Commerce City, CO 80022
Tel: (303) 287-0223
MFR of *GT*
B-1

Commerce City
Timpte, Incorporated Sales & Service
5075 E. 74th Avenue
Commerce City, CO 80022
Tel: (303) 289-6240
Nation: (800) 999-6667
Contact: Gary Manley
R4
C-2

Denver
Cowboy Metal Products, Incorporated
1075 S. Galapago Street
Denver, CO 80223
Tel: (303) 778-0851
FAX: (303) 778-6802
MFR/DLR of *T*

Denver
Cruise America
7450 E. 29th Avenue
Denver, CO 80207
Tel: (303) 426-6699
DLR/RENTAL of *R1, R2*

Denver
Freedom Wheels
11055 Leroy Drive
Denver, CO 80233
Tel: (303) 457-3312
Nation: (800) 285-1057
FAX: (303) 451-0519
R4
C-2

Denver
Lite-Craft Campers, Inc.
5737 N. Logan Street
Denver, CO 80216
Tel: (303) 296-2185
MFR of *TC*

Denver
Timpte Industries, Inc.
1290 Broadway
Denver, CO 80203
Tel: (303) 839-1900
MFR of *TB, U*
(No manufacturing at this location. This is the Headquarters Office. See also Timpte, Inc., in Commerce City, CO.)

Denver
Vanture Coach, Mfg.
975 E. 58th Avenue, #D
Denver, CO 80216
Tel: (303) 297-2708
Contact: Chris Brown
MFR of *R1*
C-1 (Colorado only)

Durango
Rent-A-Wreck and RV
21760 Highway 160
Durango, CO 81301
Tel: (970) 259-5858
DLR of *Pop-up Campers, R1, R2, R5*

Englewood
Childers' Trailer Sales
4769 S. Broadway
Englewood, CO 80110
Tel: (303) 761-8220
DLR of *T*
B-2

Englewood
Kit Van
1950 W. Union Avenue #A-20
Englewood, CO 80110
Tel: (303) 781-7333
FAX: (303) 781-1635
Contact: John Ades
R4

Englewood
Mastercraft Truck Equipment, Incorporated
2180 W. Cornell Avenue
Englewood, CO 80110
Tel: (303) 761-8504
FAX: (303) 761-3212
Contact: Ed Klinkufus
MFR/MODIFIER/ FINAL ASSEMBLER/ DLR of *TB*
C-1

Evans
Economy Body & RV Center
3231 W. Service Road
Evans, CO 80620
Tel: (970) 339-5350
DLR of *R1, R2, R5, R6*

Fort Collins
Maxey Mfg. Co.
2101 Airway Avenue
Fort Collins, CO 80524
Tel: (970) 482-1202
FAX: (970) 482-1288
Contact: Carl Maxey
MFR/MODIFIER/ FINAL ASSEMBLER/ DLR of *CT, CTB*
C-2:2
D

Fort Collins
Vanworks, Incorporated
900 E. Lincoln Avenue
Fort Collins, CO 80524
Tel: (970) 484-5344
Contact: Terry Miller
at (970) 224-4479
R4

Fort Lupton
Vehicle Systems, Inc.
15549 E. Highway 52
Fort Lupton, CO 80621
Tel: (303) 659-8221
FAX: (303) 857-9000
Contact: Jerilyn Enander
CONVERTER of *R1, R2*

Fort Morgan
Temco
10913 I-76
Fort Morgan, CO 80701
Tel: (970) 867-3317
MFR of *T*

Fountain
Scott Murdock Trailers
610 S. Charter Oak Ranch Road
Fountain, CO 80817
Tel: (719) 382-7304
FAX: (719) 382-9269
Contact: Harold Spurlock
DLR of *Cargo T, FT, HT, LT, UT*

Franktown
Truck Trail
7526 E. State Hwy. 86
Franktown, CO 80116
Tel: (303) 688-8113
FAX: (303) 688-6381
Contact: Pat or Alex
DLR of *HT, LT*

Grand Junction
Big J Trailer Mfg./ Corner Store, The
2541 Hwy. 6 & Hwy. 50
Grand Junction, CO 81505
Tel: (970) 245-3236
Tel: (970) 241-9766
FAX: (970) 242-1308
MFR/DLR of *CT*
B-2

Grand Junction
Gavin's RV & Marine, Incorporated
2980 Highway 50
Grand Junction, CO 81503
Tel: (970) 245-1800
DLR of *R1, R2*

Grand Junction
Track II Marketing, Inc.
454 28-1/2 Road
Grand Junction, CO 81501
Tel: (970) 241-4334
FAX: (970) 241-8972
DLR of *M, Equip. T, S-2*

Greeley
North American Mfg.
20910 Weld CR 54
Greeley, CO 80631
Tel: (970) 339-3000
MFR of *UT*

Grover
High Country Trailers
306 Chatoga Avenue
Grover, CO 80729
Tel: (970) 895-2231
MFR of *CT*
B-2

Henderson
Merritt Equipment
9339 US Highway 85
Henderson, CO 80640
Tel: (303) 287-7527
Nation: (800) 525-0107
CO only: (800) 338-8078
Contact: Rod Moe
MFR of *LT, S-2*
D: Morgan Driveaway, Trailer Transit

Lakewood
Rocky Mountain RV, Incorporated
345 Sheridan Blvd.
Lakewood, CO 80226
Tel: (303) 233-6716
FAX: (303) 223-6720
MFR/DLR of *R1, R2*

Lamar
Ranch Mfg Co.
700 Crystal Street
Lamar, CO 81052
Tel: (719) 336-9041
Nation: (800) 631-5708
MFR of *ST*

La Salle
Freeman Truck Bodies, Incorporated
427 2nd Street
La Salle, CO 80645
Tel: (970) 284-5582
Nation: (800) 747-9810
MFR/FINAL ASSEMBLER of *STB*

Longmont
Mountain Truck & Equipment Company
717 S. Main Street
Longmont, CO 80501
Tel: (970) 669-3903
DLR of *Used Trucks*

Loveland
Loveland RV Service
900 E. CO Hwy. 402
Loveland, CO 80537
Tel: (970) 669-7465
Contact: Fred Tillotson
DLR of *R1, R2*

Montrose
Western Slope Vans & Conversions
2122 E. Main Street
Montrose, CO 81401
Tel: (303) 249-1614
R4

Northglenn
Freedom Wheels
11055 Leroy Drive
Northglenn, CO 80233
Tel: (303) 457-3312
Nation: (800) 451-0519
FAX: (303) 285-1057
Contact: Mike Valdez
MFR of *R4, TConvs*
C-1, C-2
D

Otis
Lone Star Trailers
53465 Highway 61
Otis, CO 80743
Tel: (970) 246-3892
DLR of *T*

Pueblo
Frontier Manufacturing
815 Kennie Road
Pueblo, CO 81001
Tel: (719) 544-7472
MFR of *T*

Pueblo West
Debec, Ltd.
84 Precision Drive
Pueblo West, CO 81007
Tel: (719) 547-3768
MFR/DLR of *T*

Wheat Ridge
Casey's Recreational Sales
4120 Youngfield Street
Wheat Ridge, CO 80033
Tel: (303) 422-2001
Contact: Steve Casement
DLR of *R1, R2*
C-1

Wheat Ridge
FreedomWheel Vans, Incorporated
4901 Ward Road
Wheat Ridge, CO 80033
Tel: (303) 467-9981
FAX: (303) 467-1336
Contact: Wynona Lazarof
MFR/MODIFIER/DLR
of *R4, H'cap R4*
C-1
D

Yuma
Continental Coach, Inc.
500 W. 8th Avenue
Yuma, CO 80759-2651
Tel: (303) 848-5343
Nation: (800) 876-0620
FAX: (303) 848-3837
Contact: Roy Mekelburg
R4
A-1

CONNECTICUT

Bethel
Lift Up, Incorporated
32 Stony Hill Road
Bethel, CT 06801
Tel: (203) 790-9998
Contact: Bruce Kutner
H'cap R4

Bridgeport
John Mezes & Sons
322 Dewey Street
Bridgeport, CT 06605
Tel: (230) 333-0864
Nation: (800) 955-0012
Contact: John Mezes
MFR of *TB*

East Granby
New England Wheels West, Incorporated
15F International Drive
East Granby, CT 06026
Tel: (203) 653-8064
FAX: (203) 653-4331
FINAL ASSEMBLER
of *H'cap Units*
C-2 (CT only)

East Hartford
Bart Truck Equip. Co.
298 Governor Street
East Hartford, CT 06108
Tel: (860) 289-1549
FINAL ASSEMBLER
of *STB*

East Hartford
Colonial Truck & Body Works
366 Governor Street
East Hartford, CT 06108
Tel: (203) 528-5522
Contact: Clay
MFR of *TB*

East Haven
Alton Truck Body & Trailer, Inc.
37 Panagrossi Circle
East Haven, CT 06512
Tel: (203) 469-9719
DLR of *TB, T*

East Haven
New Haven Moving Equipment Corp.
P.O. Box 120323
East Haven, CT 06512
Tel: (203) 469-6421
Contact: Roger Levine
MFR of *T*

Hartford
Connecticut General Welding & Mfg.
585 Windsor Street
Hartford, CT 06120
Tel: (860) 247-9325
Contact: Leopold Psutka
MFR of *TB*
C-2:1-2

Kensington
Kensington Welding & Trailer
1114 Farmington Avenue
Kensington, CT 06037
Tel: (203) 828-3564
FAX: (203) 828-8125
MFR of *UT*

Meriden
Guest Company, The
48 Elm Street
Meriden, CT 06450
Tel: (203) 238-0550
MFR of *Marine Items*
C-2:3

Middlefield
Custom Craft Trailers, Incorporated
34 Old Indian Trail
Middlefield, CT 06455
Tel: (203) 349-3001
Contact: Tony Mancarella
MFR of *CT, CTB*

Milford
Mesco, Incorporated
634 New Haven Avenue
P.O. Box 122
Milford, CT 06460
Tel: (203) 878-8558
Contact: Barb McCarthy or John Livezey
MFR of *STB*

New Canaan
Hobbs Engineering
P.O. Box 1238
New Canaan, CT 06840
Tel: (203) 966-4450
Contact: Bill Bayles
MFR of *T*

Newington
East Coast Van Company
149 Richart Court
Newington, CT 06111
Tel: (680) 666-2971
FINAL ASSEMBLER/DLR of *T*

Norwich
Street Stuff
4 Central Avenue
Norwich, CT 06360
Tel: (680) 886-5902
R4, H'cap R4
C-2

New Haven
Thermal King
126 Quinnipiac Avenue
New Haven, CT 06473
Tel: (203) 865-2026
FAX: (203) 865-2079
Contact: William Lee
MFR of *TB, T*

Somers
Parks Superior Sales, Inc., of Connecticut
16 Hall Hill Road
Somers, CT 06071
Tel: (203) 749-2218
FAX: (203) 763-3604
Contact: Mike Parks
DLR of *Limos*
C-2

Southington
Custom Coach
2211 Meriden Waterbury Turnpike
Southington, CT 06489
Tel: (860) 621-5514
FAX: (860) 621-0862
MFR of *R1, R2, H'cap R4*

Westport
O'Keeffe Cadillac
561 Post Road East
Westport, CT 06881
Tel: (203) 227-9541
FAX: (203) 226-1307
Contact: Tom Curran
DLR of *Limos*

Tolland
Matthews Busses
11 Harvest Lane
Tolland, CT 06084
Tel: (860) 870-9379
FAX: (860) 870-9176
Contact: Doug Gifford
MFR/DISTR. of *U*

Windsor Locks
Crudden Truck Body Co.
466 Spring Street
Windsor Locks, CT 06096
Tel: (203) 292-1881
MFR of *TB*

Wolcott
Jim Dance's Trailer Sales
1543 Wolcott Road
Wolcott, CT 06716
Tel: (203) 879-1295
DLR of *HT, LT*

DELAWARE

Newport
Bayshore Truck Body
310 Falco Drive
Newport, DE 19804
Tel: (302) 633-6865
REPAIR/FINAL ASSEMBLER of *TB*

Wilmington
Wilmington Truck Body
201 Rooman Road
Wilmington, DE 19809
Tel: (302) 655-3772
MFR of *TB*

Wyoming
Delwood Trailer Sales
1298 Almshouse Road
Wyoming, DE 19934
Tel: (302) 697-1345
FAX: (302) 697-1709
Contact: Ronnie Lloyd
DLR of *HT, LT*

FLORIDA

Apopka
Supreme Corporation
3050 Dee Street
Apopka, FL 32703
Tel: (407) 292-0338
Contact: Billy Turner
MFR of *TB, VTB*
C-2:6

Arcadia
Walker Private Coach
211 W. Palmetto Street
Arcadia, FL 33821
Tel: (941) 993-4455
FAX: (941) 993-2332
Contact: Beth
MFR of *U*

Auburndale
Cadcraft Industries
2698 State Road 542
Auburndale, FL 33823
Tel: (941) 965-1695
MFR of *T*

Bartow
Dusty's Camper World of Bartow, Inc.
2835 S. R. 60, East
Bartow, FL 33830
Tel: (941) 533-2458
FAX: (941) 533-7589
Contact: K. C. Crum
DLR of *R1, R2, R5, R6*

Bradenton
Globe Trailers of Florida
3101 59th Ave., East
Bradenton, FL 34203
Tel: (941) 753-2199
FAX: (941) 755-7604
MFR of *T*

Bradenton
Myco Trailers, Inc.
2703 29th Avenue, E
Bradenton, FL 34208
Tel: (941) 748-2397
FAX: (941) 747-2819
MFR of *BT*

Bradenton
Osh Kosh Trailers, Inc.
1512 38th Avenue, East
P.O. Box 511
Bradenton, FL 34208
Tel: (941) 748-3900
FAX: (941) 749-0635
Contact: Pete Bambach
MFR of *S-2*
B-2:8
D

Bradenton
Vans and Customs
721-C Seventh Street
Bradenton, FL 34205
Tel: (941) 747-6114
R4

Bradenton
Westward Ho RV Center
2509 Ninth Street, W
Bradenton, FL 34205
Tel: (941) 747-5266
FAX: (941) 746-2761
Contact: Walter
DLR of *R1, R2, R5, R6*

Charlotte Harbor
Kustom Kar Creations
23350 Harborview Road
Charlotte Harbor, FL 33980
Tel: (941) 625-9993
Tel: (941) 625-1362
Nation: (800) 476-8267
FAX: (941) 743-8697
Contact: Patty Malboro
R4
C-2:3
D

Chiefland
Shep's Welding
9791 NW Highway 341
Chiefland, FL 32626
Tel: (352) 493-1730
Contact: Derwood Shephard
MFR of *TB*

Clearwater
Braun Corporation, The
5072 113th Ave., North
Clearwater, FL 34620
Tel: (813) 573-2737
FAX: (813) 573-5069
Contact: Kathy Wertin
R4

Clearwater
Continental Trailers
4501 Ulmerton Road
Clearwater, FL 34622
Tel: (813) 572-0061
Nation: (800) 842-4164
MFR of *BT*
D

Clearwater
Cruise America
24323 US Hwy 19, N
Clearwater, FL 34623
Tel: (813) 725-5601
Contact: Richard or Sherry
RENTAL of *R1, R2*

Clearwater
Magic Tilt Boat Trailer Manufacturing
2161 Lions Club Road
Clearwater, FL 34624
Tel: (813) 535-5561
FAX: (813) 539-8472
Contact: Jerry Chapin
MFR of *BT*
B-2:5

Clearwater
RV World of Tampa Bay, Incorporated
15146 US Highway 19, N
Clearwater, FL 34621
Tel: (813) 536-8000
FAX: (813) 539-0978
Contact: Jane Goodman
DLR of *R1, R2, R5, R6*

Cocoa
Koz Kustom Vans
308 Willard Street
Cocoa, FL 32922
Tel: (407) 636-8590
FAX: (407) 636-1006
R4

Cocoa
Toppertown, Inc.
1208 Clearlake Road
Cocoa, FL 32922
Tel: (407) 632-7554
Contact: John Condon
DLR of TC

Coral Gables
Emergency Vehicle Equipment, Incorporated
(MAIL: P.O. Box 145267 Coral Gables, FL 33114-5267)
5256 SW 8th Street
Coral Gables, FL 33134
Tel: (305) 442-1884
MFR of A
NOTE: This is a limited opportunity as most of their units are exported, and therefore are driven only to port facilities.

Davie
Tesco Hi-Lift, Inc.
3400 Burris Road
Davie, FL 33314
Tel: (954) 791-7470
FAX: (954) 581-3848
Contact: Jerry Kemett
MFR of TB

DeLand
Adams 1 RV Sales and Service, Incoroporated
2381 E. International Speedway Blvd.
Deland, FL 32724
Tel: (904) 734-4408
FAX: (904) 736-9835
Contact: Jerry or Marty
DLR of R1, R2

DeLand
Fancher Cars and RVs
4070 Highway 17, N
Deland, FL 32720
Tel: (904) 985-5225
FAX: (904) 985-9493
Contact: Rich
DLR of R1, R2, R5, R6

DeLand
Gustafson RV Service
1315 Highway 92
Deland, FL 32724
Tel: (904) 738-2230
FAX: (904) 734-8591
Contact: Dianna Gustafson
MFR of T, R4

DeLand
Truck Stuff
2500 E. International Speedway Blvd.
Deland, FL 32724
Tel: (904) 736-3803
FAX: (904) 736-4304
Contact: Maria Penchaw
R4

Delray Beach
Cantway Trailer Mfg.
3860 N. Federal Hwy
Delray Beach, FL 33483
Tel: (407) 737-4999
MFR of BT, UT, XT

Dover
Giant Recreation World, Incorporated
3315 US Hwy. 301, N.
Dover, FL 33619
Tel: (813) 623-6383
DLR of R1, R2, R5, R6, TC

Edgewater
Access Unlimited
702 W. Park Avenue
Edgewater, FL 32132
Tel: (904) 426-5395
FAX: (904) 423-1337
Contact: Tim Curran
H'cap R4

Fort Lauderdale
Motorcar Gallery, Inc.
715 N. Federal Hwy.
Fort Lauderdale, FL 33304
Tel: (954) 522-9900
FAX: (954) 522-9966
Contact: Bob Halpern
DLR of Limos

Fort Lauderdale
Tesco Hi-Lift, Inc.
3400 Burris Road
Fort Lauderdale, FL 33314
Tel: (954) 791-9470
MFR of TB
D

Fort Myers
Load Rite Trailers
2200 Marina Park
Fort Myers, FL 33905
Tel: (941) 693-1462
FAX: (941) 694-2091
Contact: Chuck Lyons
DISTRIBUTOR of T
C-2:2

Fort Myers
Rocket International
2360 Crystal Road
Fort Myers, FL 33907
Tel: (941) 275-0880
FAX: (941) 279-5409
MFR of T
C-2

Fort Pierce
Stamm Manufacturing
4850 Orange Avenue
Fort Pierce, FL 34947
Tel: (561) 461-6056
Contact: Johnny Stamm
MFR of STB
C-2

Fort Walton Beach
Accent Tops & Trailers
657 N. Beal Parkway
Fort Walton Beach, FL 32547
Tel: (904) 862-2400
Contact: Ray Marks
DLR of UT

Fort Walton Beach
Gemini Truck Top, Inc.
364 Beal Parkway, NW
Fort Walton Beach, FL 32548
Tel: (904) 863-1465
DLR of TC

Hallandale
Fleet Truck & Body Co.
3149 John P. Gurci Drive
Hallandale, FL 33009
Tel: (954) 964-0633
REPAIR of TB

Hialeah
Protective Materials Company, Incorporated
14000 NW 58th Court
Hialeah, FL 33014
Tel: (305) 556-2440
Nation: (800) 727-2440
FAX: (305) 823-7862
MFR of Armored Cars
D

Hialeah
Utility Trailer Mfg. Co.
1451 SE 9th Court
Hialeah, FL 33010
Tel: (305) 888-0020
MFR of S-2, T

Hollywood
Van Man
6152 Pembroke Road
Hollywood, FL 33021
Tel: (954) 962-6997
Contact: John DePietro
R4
C-1

Hudson
Eezzz-On, Incorporated
8949 New York Avenue
Hudson, FL 34667
Tel: (813) 863-3030
FAX: (813) 863-3295
Contact: Ben Studer
MFR of UT, ST
B-2

Jacksonville
American Trucking Equipment
5260 Broadway Avenue
Jacksonville, FL 32254
Tel: (904) 388-0909
Nation: (800) 437-0909
Contact: Don Hoyt
DISTRIBUTOR of T
B-2
D

Jacksonville
General Truck Equip.
5310 Broadway Avenue
Jacksonville, FL 32254
Tel: (904) 389-5541
Nation: (800) 223-5541
FAX: (904) 388-9270
Contact: Dave Catton
DLR of TB
C-2

Jacksonville
Great Dane Trailers
5231 Beaver Street, West
Jacksonville, FL 32254
Tel: (904) 786-3300
FAX: (904) 783-0722
DLR of S-2

Jacksonville
Luxury Limousines by Dreamer Charters
6342 Arlington Expwy.
Jacksonville, FL 32211
Tel: (904) 724-8496
Tel: (904) 723-3545
RENTAL of Limos and Luxury R4

Jacksonville
Newman's Truck Body & Equipment
6880 W. 12th Street
Jacksonville, FL 32254
Tel: (904) 695-9589
MFR of TB

Jacksonville
Nichols' Truck Bodies
1168 Cahoon Road,
South Jacksonville, FL 32221
Tel: (904) 781-5080
FAX: (904) 781-6304
MFR of *TB*
C-2
D

Jacksonville
Prevost Car, Inc.
6931 Business Park Blvd, North
Jacksonville, FL 32256
Tel: (904) 778-4555
Nation: (800) 874-7740
Contact: Joe Muscorella
SERVICE/REPAIR of *R1, U*

Jacksonville
Rivers Bus & RV
(MAIL: P.O. Box 6009 Jacksonville, FL 32220)
10626 General Avenue
Jacksonville, FL 32220
Tel: (904) 783-0313
Nation: (800) 253-0224
FAX: (904) 783-1067
DISTRIBUTOR of *R1, R3, R5, R6, S, Mini-busses, Shuttle U*
NOTE: *See also sister company at same address (next door), and subsidiary in Decatur, GA.*

Jacksonville
Rivers Body Factory, Inc.
(MAIL: P.O. Box 6009 Jacksonville, FL 32220)
10626 General Avenue
Jacksonville, FL 32236
Tel: (904) 781-5622
Tel: (904) 783-0313
FAX: (904) 786-1553
Contact: Mack Daniel
DISTRIBUTOR of *TB*
C-2
NOTE: *See also note in listing above.*

Jacksonville
Sherrod Vans, Inc.
6464 Greenland Road
Jacksonville, FL 32258
Tel: (904) 268-3321
Nation: (800) 824-6333
FAX: (904) 268-1605
Contact: Jerry Sherrod
R4
D

Jacksonville
Truck Options
5800-40 Ramona Blvd.
Jacksonville, FL 32205
Tel: (904) 388-5222
FAX: (904) 783-2515
CONVERTER of *R1, R4, TConvs*

Key Largo
Holiday RV's
U.S. Hwy. 1
Key Largo, FL 33037
Tel: (305) 451-4555
FAX: (305) 451-3030
Contact: Ed Gobel
DLR of *R1, R2, R5, R6*

Lakeland
C & S Trailer Sales
526 N. Gary Road
Lakeland, FL 33801
Tel: (941) 683-7438
FAX: (941) 683-8479
Contact: Ron Hubbard
DLR of *HT, LT*

Lakeland
Howell's RV Junction
126 S. Lake Parker Ave.
Lakeland, FL 33801
Tel: (941) 686-4533
FAX: (941) 687-4482
Contact: David
DLR of *R1, R2, R5, R6*

Lakeland
Kidron, Incorporated
4220 Drane Field Road
Lakeland, FL 33811
Tel: (941) 646-9693
FAX: (941) 644-5462
Contact: Debbie Bennett
MFR of *TB, T*
C-2

Lakeland
Pick-A-Lift
203 W. Olive Street
Lakeland, FL 33801
Tel: (941) 680-1758
Nation: (800) 743-5438
H'cap R4
D

Lakeland
Premier Motor Coach
205 Complex Drive
Lakeland, FL 33801
Tel: (941) 665-6700
FAX: (941) 665-7201
MFR of *R4*
C-2

Lakeland
Sporty Vans
7301-1/2 US Hwy. 98, N.
Lakeland, FL 33809
Tel: (941) 853-1355
R4

Lake Worth
Action Mobility Products
1925 10th Ave., North
Lake Worth, FL 33461
Tel: (407) 582-6500
Nation: (800) 432-1459
H'cap R4

Lake Worth
Coach and Camper of Florida
1905 Tenth Avenue, N.
Lake Worth, FL 33461
Tel: (561) 540-4442
FAX: (561) 540-4602
Contact: David
DLR of *R1, R2, R5, R6*

Largo
A Truck Body & Equipment Company
1700 Starkey Road
Largo, FL 33771
Tel: (813) 535-6900
MFR of *TB*

Largo
American International Conversions
500 Seminole Blvd.
Largo, FL 34643
Tel: (813) 585-7161
FAX: (813) 586-6627
Contact: Roger Fry
R4
C-1:5-6 Retirees working part-time.
NOTE: *98% of deliveries are made within FL.*

Largo
DMC Vans
2033 Belcher Road,
South Largo, FL 33771
Tel: (813) 530-3691
FAX: (813) 536-0989
R4

Largo
J. O'Dell Manufacturing & Trailer Sales
8050 Ulmerton Rd., East
Largo, FL 33771
Tel: (813) 535-3521
MFR/DLR of *T*

Melbourne
Family Camping Center
5270 North US Hwy. 1
Melbourne, FL 32940
Tel: (407) 242-6261
DLR of *R1, R2, R5, R6*
(Local Drivers, only)

Melbourne
Nationwide Wheelchair Lift, Incorporated
1536 Cypress Avenue
Melbourne, FL 32935
Tel: (407) 254-0035
Nation: (800) 226-3289
FAX: (407) 259-5222
MODIFIER of *H'cap Units*

Miami
Aero Vans, Incorporated
13690 SW 142nd Avenue
Miami, FL 33186
Tel: (305) 253-3333
FL only: (800) 432-2370
FAX: (305) 378-1020
Contact: Robert Andre
MFR of *R4*
C-2:2
D

Miami
Arrow Trailers Corp.
8348 NW 56th Street
Miami, FL 33166
Tel: (305) 592-6165
FAX: (305) 592-9349
Contact: Jose Armeteros
MFR of *ST, UT*
C-2:3

Miami
Boatmobile Co., The
444 Brickell Avenue
8th Floor, Suite 828
Miami, FL 33131
Tel: (305) 373-1500
FAX: (305) 539-9983
Contact: Luiz Avillez de Basto
MFR, *which in early 1994 was perfecting a prototype, leading to later production. Prospective drivers should inquire first about the current status, and see if production and shipping has begun.*

Miami
Continental Trailers
9200 NW 58th Street
Miami, FL 33178
Tel: (305) 594-1022
FL Only: (800) 432-1731
MFR of *BT*
B-2

Miami
Gar P Industries, Inc.
9330 NW 109th Street
Miami, FL 33178
Tel: (305) 888-7252
Nation: (800) 662-4277
MFR of *TB*

Miami
Horizon Trailers
7100 NW 77th Court
Miami, FL 33166
Tel: (305) 591-1292
FAX: (305) 477-2687
MFR of *T*

Miami
Rowland Equipment, Inc.
2900 NW 73rd Street
Miami, FL 33147
Tel: (305) 691-9280
FAX: (305) 693-8267
MFR of *FTB*
C-2 (Limited hiring)

Miami
Solution Specialties
3487 NW 167th Street
Miami, FL 33056
Tel: (305) 623-8880
FAX: (305) 625-1940
H'cap R4

Miami
Torino Trailer Services
5045 NW 79th Avenue
Miami, FL 33166
Tel: (305) 592-1917
MFR of *T*

Miami Lakes
Protective Materials Company, Incorporated
14040 NW 58th Court
Miami Lakes, FL 33014
Tel: (305) 556-2440
Nation: (800) 727-2440
FAX: (305) 823-7862
Contact: Klaus Barbleza
MFR of *Armored Cars, Paramilitary Vehicles, Police Vehicles*
D: Knudson Enterprises at (703) 241-0920

Naples
Mariner Vans
2372 Davis Blvd.
Naples, FL 34104
Tel: (941) 774-3622
R4

New Smyrna Beach
Lee's Quality RV Sales
1601-A West Canal St.
New Smyrna Beach, FL 32168
Tel: (904) 427-0743
FAX: (904) 423-2212
Contact: Lee Genest
DLR of *R1, R2*

Nokomis
Coach House, Inc.
3480 Technology Drive
Nokomis, FL 34275
Tel: (941) 485-0984
Nation: (800) 235-0984
FAX: (941) 488-4095
MFR of *R2*

Ocala
Cherokee Trailer
3621 NE 36th Avenue
Ocala, FL 34479
Tel: (352) 629-1025
FAX: (352) 867-1292
MFR of *T*

Ocala
Custom Trailers
2017 NE Jacksonville Rd
Ocala, FL 34470
Tel: (352) 622-4736
FAX: (352) 629-3520
Contact: Terry Griffin
MFR of *T*
B-2:2

Ocala
Emergency One, Inc.
(MAIL: P.O. Box 2710
Ocala, FL 32678)
1701 SW 37th Avenue
Ocala, FL 32674
Tel: (352) 237-1122
FAX: (352) 237-4369
Contact: Tina Sartori
MFR of *E, F, H*
D

Ocala
Federal Motors, Inc.
(MAIL: P.O. Box 2710
Ocala, FL 32678)
3611 SW 20th Street
Ocala, FL 32674
Tel: (352) 237-6215
FAX: (352) 237-4369
MFR of *E, F*
C-1
D: R.L. Jeffries Driveaway at (800) 992-9494

Ocala
Freedom Vans, Inc.
1717 NE 32nd Avenue
Ocala, FL 34470
Tel: (352) 622-9133
H'cap R4

Ocala
Lynch's Trailer and Truck Body
7400 NW 55th Avenue
Ocala, FL 34482
Tel: (352) 620-0123
Contact: Ray
REPAIR of *TB, T*

Ocala
Mark III Industries, Inc.
5401 NW 44th Avenue
P.O. Box 2525
Ocala, FL 32675
Tel: (352) 732-5878
Nation: (800) 726-8267
FAX: (352) 351-1017
Contact: Dirk Kalks at ext. 455
R4
C-2

Ocala
Mickey Body Company
601 NW 24th Court
Ocala, FL 34475
Tel: (352) 620-0015
REPAIR of *TB*

Ocala
Triple Crown Trailer
5109 W. Anthony Road
Ocala, FL 34475
Tel: (352) 368-7885
FAX: (352) 368-7654
Contact: Linda Lorick
MFR of *T*
C-2
D

Ocala
U-Dump Trailers
2610 NW 10th Street
Ocala, FL 34475
Tel: (352) 351-8510
FAX: (352) 351-4145
MFR of *ST*

Ocala
Van-Mor Enterprises
1007 SW 17th Street
Ocala, FL 34474
Tel: (352) 732-8524
FAX: (352) 351-2871
MFR of *U*

Oldsmar
Chariot Mfg. Co.
209 Pickney Street
Oldsmar, FL 34677
Tel: (813) 855-5801
Tel: (813) 855-7622
Contact: Robert Hott
MFR of *UT*
B-1, B-2:3

Orlando
Fancy Vans
4685 Old Winter Garden Road
Orlando, FL 32811
Tel: (407) 299-0299
R4

Orlando
Holiday RV Superstores, Incorporated
5001 Sand Lake Road
Orlando, FL 32819
Tel: (407) 351-3096
FAX: (407) 351-5140
DLR of *R1, R2, R5, R6*

Orlando
Leisure Time Equipment
3898 W. Colonial Drive
Orlando, FL 32808
Tel: (407) 299-0120
Nation: (800) 336-6565
DLR of *R1, R2*

Orlando
Lint's Enterprises
5526 Force Four Parkway
Orlando, FL 32839
Tel: (407) 856-7112
Contact: John Lint
MFR of *UT*

Orlando
National Ambulance Builders
230 N. Ortman Drive
Orlando, FL 32805
Tel: (407) 291-2222
FAX: (407) 291-2224
Contact: Paul Judd
MFR of *A*

Orlando
Ramlin Custom Trailers
8730 S. Orange Avenue
Orlando, FL 32824
Tel: (407) 851-1144
MFR of *CT*
D: Regal Dealership

Orlando
Transtat Equipment, Inc.
510 W. Thorpe Road
Orlando, FL 32824
Tel: (407) 857-2040
MFR of *TB*

Orlando
Zaffran Transportation
(MAIL: P.O. Box 607904
Orlando, FL 32860)
6647 N. Orange Blossom
Road
Orlando, FL 32810
Tel: (407) 298-1010
Nation: (800) 432-8492
FAX: (407) 298-1013
Contact: Ted Zaffran
DLR of *U*
C-1

Ormond Beach
Robbins Camper Sales
1112 N. US Route 1
Ormond Beach, FL 32174
Tel: (904) 677-5588
FAX: (904) 672-4974
Contact: Dennis Robbins
DLR of *R1, R2*

Pensacola
Carpenter Campers
8450 Pensacola Blvd.
Pensacola, FL 32534
Tel: (904) 477-6666
Contact: Mark Carpenter
DLR of *R1, R2*

Pensacola
Custom Specialty Van
Trucks & Autos
4410 North W Street
Pensacola, FL 32505
Tel: (904) 432-1437
Contact: Larry
Woodward
MODIFIER of *R4*

Pensacola
Gold Crown Truck
Top Manufacturing
4507 N. Palafox Street
Pensacola, FL 32503
Tel: (904) 432-9335
DLR of *TC*

Pensacola
R & M Enterprises
8990 Eight Mile Creek
Pensacola, FL 32534
Tel: (904) 479-1766
R4, H'cap R4

Pinellas Park
Frontline Comm. Vehs.
8501 65th Street
Pinellas Park, FL 34665
Tel: (813) 541-4441
FAX: (813) 541-7116
Contact: Jonathon Sherr
MFR of *Communication*
Vehicles
D

Pinellas Park
Magna Van
6544 44th Street, North
Suite 1207
Pinellas Park, FL 34665
Tel: (813) 521-3895
R4

Plant City
Hardee Mfg. Co.
2299 US Hwy. 92, East
P.O. Box 699
Plant City, FL 33564
Tel: (813) 752-5126
FAX: (813) 754-9545
Contact: Hoyt Willaford
MFR of *T, TB*
C-2
D

Pompano Beach
Atlantic Bus Sales
548 S. Dixie Hwy., East
Pompano Beach, FL 33060
Tel: (954) 941-7722
MFR of *U*
C-2

Pompano Beach
Glastop, Incorporated
429 S. Dixie Hwy., East
Pompano Beach, FL 33060
Tel: (954) 781-8460
MFR/DLR of *R4*

Pompano Beach
Broward Truck
2909 S. Andrews Avenue
Pompano Beach, FL 33316
Tel: (954) 523-5484
DLR of *TB*

Port Charlotte
A-1 Kustom Creations
23350 Harbor View Road
Port Charlotte, FL 33980
Tel: (941) 625-9993
Nation: (800) 881-8267
FAX: (941) 743-8697
Contact: Patty
Marlborough
R4
C-2:4

Port Orange
Southeastern Truck Tops
5491 S. Ridgewood Ave.
Port Orange, FL 32127
Tel: (904) 761-0002
FINAL ASSEMBLER of
TC

Reddick
B & S Trailer Mfg.
17175 NW Gainesville
Road
Reddick, FL 32686
Tel: (352) 591-2161
Contact: Don Braddock
MFR of *ST*
B-2

Saint Augustine
Ocean Grove RV
Sales & Service
6775 US Hwy 1, South
St. Augustine, FL 32086
Tel: (904) 797-5732
Nation: (800) 635-2926
Contact: Tom Tibbetts
DLR of *R1, R2*
D

Saint Petersburg
Future Vans of Florida
2569 25th Avenue, N
St. Petersburg, FL 33713
Tel: (813) 323-4420
Contact: Ron Dillon
R4

Saint Petersburg
J & J Marine Services
3000 46th Avenue, N.
St. Petersburg, FL 33714
Tel: (813) 527-5078
MFR of *T*
B-2:1

Saint Petersburg
MITS Corporation
5982 Central Avenue
St. Petersburg, FL 33707
Tel: (813) 345-6641
FAX: (813) 347-8057
H'cap R4
C-2 (Local)

Saint Petersburg
Van Conversions
by Drew
3101 9th Street, North
St. Petersburg, FL 33704
Tel: (813) 896-3739
R4

Sanford
Blue & Gray Trailer
Manufacturing
2341 Celery Avenue
Sanford, FL 32771
Tel: (407) 323-3547
MFR of *T*

Sarasota
Alumne Mfg., Inc.
1273 Porter Road
Sarasota, FL 34240
Tel: (941) 371-3319
FAX: (941) 371-4793
Contact: David Yancey
MFR of *T, TB*
C-1, C-2
D

Sarasota
I.R. Witzer Company
6101 McIntosh Road
Sarasota, FL 34238
Tel: (941) 922-5301
FAX: (941) 924-2402
Contact: Sam Witzer
MFR of *Low-Boy T*

Sarasota
Sunstate International
Trucks
3450 N. Washington
Blvd.
Sarasota, FL 34234
Tel: (941) 355-7681
FAX: (941) 351-9108
DLR of *International*
Trucks

Sarasota
Witco Challenger
6101 McIntosh Road
Sarasota, FL 34238
Tel: (941) 922-5222
FAX: (941) 924-2402
MFR of *T*
D

Sebring
Manley Trailer &
Welding
3963 US Hwy. 27, South
Sebring, FL 33870
Tel: (941) 385-1394
MFR of *T*

Starke
Crosley Trailers, Inc.
US Highway 301, South
P.O. Box 760
Starke, FL 32091
Tel: (904) 964-8331
MFR of *CT*
D

Starke
L Bar A Trailers
SE 21st Avenue, Box 461
Starke, FL 32091
Tel: (904) 964-8040
FAX: (904) 964-3976
MFR of *HT*

Starke
R. E.'s Circle L Trailer Sales
Route 4, Box 1555-A
Starke, FL 32091
Tel: (904) 964-2119
MFR of *ST, UT*
B-2

Stuart
Giant Recreation World of Stuart
635 SE Monterey Road
Stuart, FL 34994
Tel: (407) 286-3500
FAX: (407) 286-6655
Contact: Tim Karr
DLR/RENTAL SITE of *R1, R2, R6*

Summerfield
Ultralite Trailers
17970 SE County Rd 475
Summerfield, FL 34491
Tel: (352) 245-2068
Contact: Richard
DLR of *HT, LT*

Tallahassee
Advanced Driving Aid
906 Blountstown Hwy.
Tallahassee, FL 32304
Tel: (904) 575-9829
R4
C-2

Tallahassee
Hi-Tech Rehabilitation, Incorporated
1551 Capital Circle, SE
Tallahassee, FL 32301
Tel: (904) 878-6654
FAX: (904) 878-7984
Contact: Dave Olz
DLR of *H'cap Units*
C-2
D

Tallahassee
McKenzie Tank Line
P.O. Box 1200
Tallahassee, FL 32303
Tel: (904) 576-1330
Contact: Jerry Smith
MFR of *T*
B-2

Tallahassee
Pepco RV Center
7130 W. Tennessee
Tallahassee, FL 32304
Tel: (904) 576-8822
Nation: (800) 995-1282
DLR of *R1, R2, R6*

Tampa
Ajax Equipment Co.
(MAIL: P.O. Box 76151
Tampa, FL 33675)
3111 E. 3rd Avenue
Tampa, FL 33605
Tel: (813) 248-1118
FAX: (813) 247-6932
FINAL ASSEMBLER of *VTB*

Tampa
All-American Sleeper Manufacturing Company
(MAIL: P.O. Box 11452
Tampa, FL 33680)
5311 N. 40th Street
Tampa, FL 33610
Tel: (813) 626-4241
Tel: (813) 621-4342
FAX: (813) 621-7402
Contact: Joe Affronti
MFR/CONVERTER of *TC*

Tampa
B & R Mobility Services, Incorporated
914 E. Skagway Avenue
Tampa, FL 33604
Tel: (813) 933-5452
H'cap R4
C-1

Tampa
Baker Equipment Engineering Company
8811 Maislin Drive
Tampa, FL 33637
Tel: (813) 985-0910
Contact: Scott Cockrane
DISTRIBUTOR of *Utility Equipment*
C-2:1

Tampa
Cosmo Truck Equip. Co.
6915 Adamo Drive
Tampa, FL 33619
Tel: (813) 621-7864
Nation: (800) 282-6766
FAX: (813) 623-5051
Contact: John Matthews
MFR/DLR of *TB*
C-2

Tampa
Florida Truck Body Co.
8808 E. Broadway Ave.
Tampa, FL 33619
Tel: (813) 626-1654
FL only: (800) 606-1654
MODIFIER of *TB, T*

Tampa
Foretravel of Florida
4321 N. US Hwy. 301
Tampa, FL 33610
Tel: (813) 621-9644
FAX: (813) 628-4320
Contact: Chuck Lowe
DLR of *R1, R2*

Tampa
Gunn Highway Custom Trailer
12871 Olive Jones Road
Tampa, FL 33625
Tel: (813) 960-7172
FINAL ASSEMBLER/ MODIFIER of *T*

Tampa
Jim Hardee Equipment Company
5801 E. Broadway Ave
Tampa, FL 33619
Tel: (813) 621-3474
FAX: (813) 628-4036
Contact: Casey Hardee
MFR of *TB*

Tampa
Southern Truck Body
3924 Spruce Street
Tampa, FL 33607
Tel: (813) 879-8110
FAX: (813) 874-8636
Contact: Jerry Peebles or Mary Lou Peebles
MFR of *TB, T, CT*
D

Tampa
Specialty Trailer Co.
4711 N. Manhattan Ave.
Tampa, FL 33614
Tel: (813) 871-3273
Nation: (800) 235-3854
MFR of *T*
D

Tampa
Together Customs
13100 N. Nebraska Ave.
Tampa, FL 33612
Tel: (813) 977-2629
FAX: (813) 977-7382
DLR of *R4*

Tampa
Trailers Unlimited
4802 E. Hillsborough
Tampa, FL 33610
Tel: (813) 623-1354
MFR of *UT*

Tampa
Weld-Rite Company
3218 W. Hillsborough
Tampa, FL 33614
Tel: (813) 877-4750
DLR of *T*

Tavares
Ledgerwood, Inc.
27616 County Road 561
Tavares, FL 32778
Tel: (352) 742-2112
MFR of *T*

Titusville
Premier Trailer Manufacturing, Inc.
900 Buffalo Road
Titusville, FL 32796
Tel: (407) 268-1935
Contact: Louis Mangiacarp
MFR of *T*
B-2

West Melbourne
Kustom Van & Truck
6959 W. Nasa Blvd.
West Melbourne, FL 32904
Tel: (407) 676-3915
Contact: Graham Bean
R4

West Palm Beach
Van-Tazma/ Van Shop, The
2720 Old Okeechobee
West Palm Beach, FL 33409
Tel: (407) 686-0545
FAX: (407) 478-4199
MFR/MODIFIER of *TB, R4*

Winter Garden
ABC Bus, Incorporated
17469 W. Highway 50
Winter Garden, FL 34787
Tel: (407) 656-7977
Nation: (800) 222-2871
FAX: (407) 656-9278
Contact: Lee Loper
DLR of *U*
C-2:3

Winter Garden
First Class Coach
10 W. Story Road
Winter Garden, FL 34787
Tel: (407) 656-1175
FAX: (407) 656-9242
Contact: Milton Smith
DLR of *Limos, U*

Winter Park
Art Grindle, Inc./
Tropic Traveller Vans
1555 Semoran Blvd.
Winter Park, FL 32792
Tel: (407) 671-2626
Contact: Artie Grindle
DLR of *R4*
C-2:8

Winter Park
Wheeled Coach
Industries
(MAIL: P.O. Box 677339
Orlando, FL 32867)
2778 N. Forsyth Road
Winter Park, FL 32792
Tel: (407) 677-7777
FAX: (407) 679-1337
Contact: Nancy Merrin
MFR of *A*
C-2

Yulee
American Body Armor
(MAIL:
P.O. Drawer 1769
Fernandina Beach, FL
32034)
191 Nassau Place
Yulee, FL 32097
Tel: (904) 261-4035
Nation: (800) 428-0588
FAX: (904) 261-5677
Contact: James L.
Centner
MFR of *Limos, Armored*
Vehicles of all types.
C-1, C-2
D

GEORGIA

Albany
All Star International
Truck, Incorporated
2505 Sylvester Road
Albany, GA 31705
Tel: (912) 436-2461
Nation: (800) 526-9939
FAX: (912) 436-8779
DLR *of Trucks*

Alvaton
Complete Refrigerated
Truck Bodies
Georgia Highway 85
Alvaton, GA 30218
Tel: (706) 538-6321
Nation: (800) 345-6153
Contact: Stephanie
MFR of *STB*
D

Atlanta
Dorsey Trailers, Inc.
2727 Paces Ferry Rd.
Atlanta, GA 30339
Tel: (770) 438-9595
MFR/DLR of *S-2*
A-1

Atlanta
Mack Trucks, Inc.
780 Memorial Drive, SE
Atlanta, GA 30316
Tel: (404) 577-5230
DLR of *S-1*

Atlanta
Shields Southeast Sales
1008 Brady Avenue, NW
Atlanta, GA 30318
Tel: (404) 885-1133
FAX: (404) 351-1132
Contact: Jim Orcutt
DLR of *H, Limos*
C-2:3

Atlanta
Standard Truck &
Equipment Co., Inc.
1155 Hill Street, SE
Atlanta, GA 30315
Tel: (404) 622-4461
Nation: (800) 241-9357
FAX: (800) 243-9357
Contact: Sharon Taffel
DLR of *TB*
A-1

Augusta
Duramed Medical
Service
1543 15th Street
Augusta, GA 30901
Tel: (706) 737-0500
FAX: (706) 737-6323
Contact: Scott Sorenson
DLR of *H'cap Units*
C-2:1

Ball Ground
Ingram Truck Body
1079 Old Canton Road
Ball Ground, GA 30107
Tel: (770) 735-3000
MFR of *TB*

Blairsville
Pro Design Trailers
Blue Ridge Highway
Blairsville, GA 30512
Tel: (706) 745-4012
Contact: Merle White
MFR of *T*

Bogart
Handicapped Conversion
Equippers, Incorporated/
Zephyr
1950 Jimmy Daniel Road
Bogart, GA 30622
Tel: (706) 354-8067
FAX: (706) 546-7972
Contact: Phyllis Gerstner
FINAL ASSEMBLER
of *H'cap R4*
C-2:6
D: A-1 Metro

Bowman
Ideal Vans, Incorporated
507 Broad Street
P.O. Box 378
Bowman, GA 30624
Tel: (706) 245-4409
FAX: (404) 245-9643
Contact: David Vaughn
R4
A-1

Canon
Beck's Custom
Conversions
81 College Avenue
Canon, GA 30520
Tel: (706) 245-8348
FAX: (706) 245-6595
R4, TConvs
C-2:1

Canon
Cougar Custom Vans
356 New House Road
Canon, GA 30520
Tel: (706) 356-1425
Contact: Rufus Harris
R4

Canon
Country Conversion
Airline Community
1221 Dare Run Lane
Canon, GA 30520
Tel: (706) 376-2151
Contact: Dan Kotal or
Randy Kotal
R4
C-1 (GA only)

Canon
Harris Van Conversions
RR 1
Canon, GA 30553
Tel: (706) 356-4586
R4

Carnesville
Franklin Motor Coach
9036 Ila Road
Carnesville, GA 30521
Tel: (706) 384-4538
R4

Carnesville
Rover Vans
RR 3
Carnesville, GA 30521
Tel: (706) 677-2112
Contact: Lonnie Martin
or Harlan Martin
R4
A-1, C-2
(Hires seasonally)

College Park
Interstate Truck
Equipment
2740 Sullivan Road
College Park, GA 30337
Tel: (404) 766-7203
FAX: (404) 761-3265
Contact: Candy Hall
MFR of *TB*
C-2:2

Columbus
Centennial Body
(Div. of Douglas &
Lomason Company)
420 10th Avenue
P.O. Box 708
Columbus, GA 31901
Tel: (706) 323-6446
Nation: (800) 241-7541
Contact: Donna West
MFR of *V*
C-2:4-5
(Locally-based drivers
deliver nationwide)
NOTE: *For more data on*
Douglas & Lomason, see
their HQ listing in
Farmington Hills, MI.

Conyers
R & R Van Lift
Sales & Service
2130 Sigman Road
Conyers, GA 30207
Tel: (770) 483-0767
FAX: (770) 483-0726
H'cap R4

Cumming
Country Boy Trailers
1550 Atlanta Highway
P.O. Box 1312
Cumming, GA 30130
Tel: (770) 887-1280
FAX: (770) 889-4732
Contact: Joyce Reed
MFR/DLR of *UTB*
C-1

Dallas
Womack Equipment Trailer Manufacturing
2123 Cartersville Hwy.
Dallas, GA 30132
Tel: (770) 445-7032
MFR/DLR of *T*

Danielsville
American Vans, Inc.
Route 3, Box 3009
Highway 29
Danielsville, GA 30633
Tel: (706) 795-3344
Nation: (800) 421-8267
FAX: (706) 795-5286
R4

Decatur
Cricket Camper Mfg. Co.
4689 Covington Highway
Decatur, GA 30035
Tel: (404) 289-6400
FAX: (404) 288-4313
Contact: Eric Ledford
MFR of *TC*

Decatur
Rivers Bus Sales
P.O. Box 2547
Decatur, GA 30031
Tel: (404) 292-9744
Nation: (800) 253-0244
DISTRIBUTOR of *S, U, Mini-busses, Shuttle U*
NOTE: *See also the HQ and distribution site, in Jacksonville, FL: Rivers Bus & RV.*

Doerun
Carver Body Works
8366 Georgia Hwy. 33
Box 806
Doerun, GA 31744
Tel: (912) 776-2421
MFR of *CT, CTB*

Douglasville
Workmaster Vans
4519 Bankhead Highway
Douglasville, GA 30134
Tel: (770) 949-5890
R4, TConv's

Elberton
Custom Coaches, Inc./ Southland Motors
924 Lower Heard Street
Elberton, GA 30635
Tel: (706) 283-8267
R4
C-1:2

Fayetteville
Babb Corporation
111 Bethea Road
Fayetteville, GA 30214
Tel: (770) 461-4145
Nation: (800) 476-2535
FAX: (770) 461-4160
Contact: Ana Maddox
MFR of *TB*
C-2

Fitzgerald
Coachmen Industries of Georgia
P.O. Box 948
Fitzgerald, GA 31750
Tel: (912) 423-5471
MFR of *R1*
D: RV Transport

Flintstone
Tri-State Handicap Equipment, Inc.
1047 Old Chattanooga Road
Flintstone, GA 30725
Tel: (706) 820-4434
Nation: (800) 451-9211
Contact: Tracy Groce
H'cap Units
C-2 (Local)

Forest Park
Baker Equipment Engineering Company
154 Falcon Drive
Forest Park, GA 30050
Tel: (404) 363-4908
Contact: Shirley Parker
MFR of *UTB*

Forest Park
Fontaine Truck Equipment
5178 Old Dixie Highway
Forest Park, GA 30050
Tel: (404) 363-9990
FAX: (404) 362-9065
Contact: Jack Creamer
FINAL ASSEMBLER of *Trucks*
C-2 (GA delivery only)

Forest Park
Magnum Transportation
5845 Lee's Mill Road
Forest Park, GA 30050
Tel: (404) 761-6464
Nation: (800) 462-6464
Nation: (800) 522-4093
FAX: (404) 765-0462
Contact: Peggy Sue
DLR of *U*
NOTE: *Formerly was Carpenter Bus Sales. They have 2 sites. See also Franklin, TN.*

Fort Valley
Blue Bird Wanderlodge
P.O. Box 937
Fort Valley, GA 31030
Tel: (912) 825-2021
FAX: (912) 825-7056
Contact: Ray Hill
MFR of *R1, R2*
D: Uses Buddy Gregg Motorhomes
11730 Snyder Road
Knoxville, TN 37932
Tel: (423) 675-1986

Franklin Springs
Rocky Ridge Vans
259 W. Clock Extention
Franklin Springs, GA 30639
Tel: (706) 245-5954
R4

Gainesville
Allison Manufacturing Company
1400 Candler Road
Gainesville, GA 30507
Tel: (770) 536-4992
FAX: (770) 581-9965
MFR of *M*

Griffin
Custom Trailer, Inc.
362 Aerodrome Way
Griffin, GA 30223
Tel: (770) 228-6091
FAX: (770) 229-9265
Contact: Cathy
MFR of *FTB*

Griffin
First Response, Inc.
255 O'Dell Road
Griffin, GA 30223
Tel: (770) 228-6326
FAX: (770) 412-6711
Contact: M.J. Wright
MFR of *A*
C-2

Griffin
Metro Trans
777 Greenbelt Parkway
Griffin, GA 30223
Tel: (770) 229-5995
Nation: (800) 522-1188
FAX: (770) 229-4943
MFR of *"Classic" Mini-Busses, "EuroTrans" Urban Transit U*

Griffin
Supreme Corporation
P.O. Box 939
Griffin, GA 30224
Tel: (770) 228-6742
FAX: (770) 228-6781
Contact: Bobby Love
MFR of *CTB*
C-2:5-6
NOTE: *See also their HQ in Goshen, IN.*

Grovetown
Adaptive Handicap
5119 Wrightsboro Road
P.O. Box 8
Grovetown, GA 30813
Tel: (706) 860-1061
FAX: (706) 860-2257
Contact: Tom Norton
H'cap Units
C-2 (Local)

Hahira
Royal Trailers, Inc.
6652 Union Road
Hahira, GA 31632
Tel: (912) 794-2077
Contact: Charles or Debbie
MFR of *ST*

Hartwell
Wagon Wheel Vans
Royston Road
Hartwell, GA 30643
Tel: (706) 376-7172
Contact: Chris Harper
R4

Jonesboro
Brown's Camping Sales, Incorporated
9726 Tara Blvd.
Jonesboro, GA 30236
Tel: (770) 477-7718
FAX: (770) 477-7719
Contact: Floyd Brown
DEALER of *R5, R6*

Jonesboro
Sagon Motor Home Center
8859 Tara Blvd.
Jonesboro, GA. 30236
Tel: (770) 477-2010
FAX: (770) 473-1389
Contact: Jodi
DEALER of *R1, R5, R6*

Jonesboro
Southeastern Motorhome & RV Center
9672 Tara Blvd.
Jonesboro, GA 30236
Tel: (770) 477-0550
Nation: (800) 633-9940
FAX: (770) 473-0467
Contact: Mary Lou McNally
DLR of R1, R2

Lafayette
Blue Bird North Georgia
1198 Shadduck Ind. Blvd.
Lafayette, GA 30728
Tel: (706) 638-8383
FAX: (404) 638-8080
Contact: Larry Joiner
MFR of S, U
C-2

La Grange
Southern Ambulance Builders, Incorporated
833 New Franklin Road
P.O. Box 949
La Grange, GA 30241
Tel: (706) 882-0136
Nation: (800) 241-2304
FAX: (706) 884-9906
Contact: Keith Bravelr at ext. 15
MFR of A

Lavonia
Bulk Equipment Manufacturing, Inc.
400 E. Main Street
P.O. Box 7
Lavonia, GA 30553
Tel: (706) 356-4285
Contact: Doy Johnson
MFR of ST

Lavonia
Foster Trucking/ Sportshome Custom Vans
222 Stone Bridge Road
Lavonia, GA 30553
Tel: (706) 356-4559
FAX: (706) 356-3438
Contact: Gloria
R4

Lavonia
Southern Comfort Coach
Coach Road 115
Lavonia, GA 30553
Tel: (706) 356-8354
R4

Lavonia
Tugaloo Sports Van
RR 2, Joe Harvey Street
Lavonia, GA 30553
Tel: (706) 356-4018
Contact: Tyler Andrews
R4

Lithia Springs
McNeilus Truck & Manufacturing Company
2160 Lee Road
Lithia Springs, GA 30057
Tel: (770) 489-0707
FAX: (770) 489-9511
Contact: David Wright
MFR of Mixer TB, XTB

Mableton
Mobile Manufacturing
5420 Old Floyd Road
Mableton, GA 30059
Tel: (770) 941-1144
Nation: (800) 225-2254
FAX: (770) 944-0099
Contact: Brent Jones
MFR of ST
B-2:2
D: Triple A Cooper

Macon
Blue Bird Corporation
3920 Arkwright Road.
P.O. Box 7839
Macon, GA 31210
Tel: (912) 757-7100
FAX: (912) 474-9131
Contact: Lamar Middlebrook
MFR of Custom U

Marietta
Atlanta Custom Conversions
1830 Airport Ind. Drive
Marietta, GA 30062
Tel: (770) 952-8180
FAX: (770) 426-4187
Contact: Bob Bogart
R4
C-2:3
D

Marietta
Crain M - M Sales
765 Pickins Industrial Dr.
P.O. Box 6055
Marietta, GA 30062
Tel: (770) 428-4421
FAX: (770) 421-8292
Contact: Mr. Lester
DLR of Limos

Marietta
Equipment Innovators, Incorporated
800 Industrial Park Drive
Marietta, GA 30062
Tel: (770) 427-9467
Nation: (800) 733-3434
FAX: (770) 425-2350
MFR of TB
D: Morgan Driveaway, ABF Freight Systems

Marietta
Handicapped Driver Services, Incorporated
1349 Old Hwy. 41
Bldg. 100, Suite 160
Marietta, GA 30060
Tel: (770) 422-9674
FAX: (770) 425-9535
Contact: Duane or Chris
R4

Marietta
Rebuilt Vans, Inc.
1830 Airport Ind. Drive
Marietta, GA 30062
Tel: (770) 988-0080
R4

Marietta
RV Depot Discount Motorhome Sales Center
1211 S. Marietta Pkwy.
Marietta, GA 30060
Tel: (770) 428-6567
FAX: (770) 428-6941
DEALER of R1, R3, R5, R6

Marietta
Russell Motors and RV Center
121 Freys Gin Road
Marietta, GA 30067
Tel: (770) 428-9420
Contact: Kim Mansell Office Manager
DEALER of R1, R3

Marietta
Southern Van & Truck, Incorporated
152 South Avenue
Marietta, GA 30060
Tel: (770) 514-9020
FAX: (770) 422-1654
Contact: Ann Marie
R4
C-1

Norcross
Adaptive Mobility Systems
5865 Oakbrook Parkway
Norcross, GA 30093
Tel: (770) 662-5242
H'cap R4

Norcross
Peach State Ford Truck
I-85 at Jimmy Carter Blvd.
P.O. Box 808
Norcross, GA 30091
Tel: (770) 449-5300
Nation: (800) 367-3878
GA only: (800) 732-2478
FAX: (770) 447-0984
Contact: John Ayer
DLR of Ford Trucks
C-2:1
D

Norcross
Van Depot
5922 Buford Highway
Norcross, GA 30071
Tel: (770) 242-6003
R4

Powder Springs
Atlanta Commercial Displays Vans
5045 McNeel Ind. Way
Powder Springs, GA 30073
Tel: (770) 439-1140
Contact: Charlie Carstens
R4
D

Roswell
Isuzu Trucks of America, Incorporated
205 Hambree Park Drive
Roswell, GA 30076
Tel: (770) 475-9195
Contact: Dean Hart at ext. 363
DLR of Commercial Trucks

Royston
Aztec Vans of Georgia
Route 3, Box 3409
Royston, GA 30662
Tel: (706) 245-8322
Contact: Tony Fowler
R4
A-1

Royston
Country Coaches, Inc.
Brown Pulliam Road
Royston, GA 30662
Tel: (706) 213-6037
R4

Royston
E-Z Ride, Incorporated
1783 Athens Road
Royston, GA 30662
Tel: (706) 245-5417
Tel: (706) 245-5725
Contact: Gary Phillips
R4
A-1, C-2:1

Royston
Leisure Guide Vans
Route 1, Box 1078
Royston, GA 30662
Tel: (706) 245-7035
Tel: (706) 245-7115
Contact: Tim Phillips
MFR/DLR/MODIFIER/
FINAL ASSEMBLER
of R1, R2, TConvs
C-2

Rydal
Morgan Corporation
4120 Highway 411, NE
Rydal, GA 30171
Tel: (770) 386-8686
Nation: (800) 333-2350
Nation: (800) 866-7426
FAX: (770) 386-2827
Contact: Nelson Eberly
MFR of TB
D: Hot Shot, Bennett

Savannah
Coastal Trailer & Truck Body, Incorporated
(MAIL: P.O. Box 7164
Savannah, GA 31418)
4898 Old Louisville Road
Savannah, GA 31408
Tel: (912) 964-8594
Contact: Jim Stalnaker
MFR/FINAL
ASSEMBLER of T, TB

Savannah
Great Dane Trailers
600 Lathrop Avenue
P.O. Box 67
Savannah, GA 31401
Tel: (912) 232-4471
FAX: (912) 944-2466
Contact: John Jeffries
S2

Savannah
R. L. Wagner Trailers
4 Hover Creek Road
Savannah, GA 31419
Tel: (912) 925-1038
MFR of HT, LT, UT

Savannah
Westside Trailer Products
(MAIL: P.O. Box 7481
Garden City, GA 31418)
4050 W. Highway 80
Savannah, GA 31408
Tel: (912) 966-5342
Contact: Wendell Thompson
DLR of ST

Smyrna
Body by Souris Mfg. Co.
323 Hurt Road
Smyrna, GA 30082
Tel: (770) 432-4434
Contact: Nick Souris
MFR of STB
D: Morgan Driveaway, Jeffrey

Smyrna
Smyrna Truck Body & Equipment
2158 Atlanta Road, SE
Smyrna, GA 30080
Tel: (770) 433-0112
FAX: (770) 432-8770
MFR of TB

Sylvania
Screven Machine & Tank
2317 Burton's Ferry Hwy.
Sylvania, GA 30467
Tel: (912) 829-3320
MFR of TB

Sylvester
Carver's Body Works
8350 Georgia Hwy. 133
Sylvester, GA 31791
Tel/FAX: (912) 776-2421
Contact: Ms. Carver
MFR of TB

Sylvester
Park-Built Body Co.
RR 4
P.O. Box 448
Sylvester, GA 31791
Tel: (912) 776-6948
Nation: (800) 248-0275
FAX: (912) 716-5550
MFR of TB

Valdosta
Wallace Trailer Company
Highway 84, East
P. O. Box 1286
Valdosta, GA 31603
Tel: (912) 241-8929
FAX: (912) 241-8940
MFR of T

Villa Rica
McNeilus Truck & Manufacturing, Inc.
148 Punkintown Road
Villa Rica, GA 30180
Tel: (770) 459-5151
MFR of Concrete Mixing TB

Waycross
Wells Cargo South, Inc.
2250 Industrial Blvd.
Waycross, GA 31501
Tel: (912) 285-8132
Nation: (800) 348-7553
Contact: Randy Sharp or Scott Highsmith
MFR of ST, UT
B-2:2

HAWAII

Aiea
Aloha Toppers, Inc.
98-075 Kamehameha Highway
Aiea, HI 96701
Tel: (808) 487-3988
MFR/INSTALLER of Truck Toppers

Hilo
Hawaii Campers
67 Piilani Street
Hilo, HI 96720
Tel: (808) 935-8349
DLR/FINAL
ASSEMBLER of TC

Honolulu
KM Trailers
1082 Sand Island Pkwy.
Honolulu, HI 96819
Tel: (808) 841-6638
MFR of T

Honolulu
Truck Equipment Hawaii, Incorporated
2979 Koapaka Street
Honolulu, HI 96819
Tel: (808) 836-0525
FAX: (808) 834-0860
DLR of UTB, FTB, TC

Kahului
Maui Campers, Inc.
343 Hanamau Street
Suite A
Kahului, HI 96732
Tel: (808) 871-8677
FAX: (808) 877-6587
MFR of TC

Kailua Kona
Kona Camper Tops
74-5032 Kealapua
Kailua Kona, HI 96740
Tel: (808) 325-7755
Contact: Grant Kojima
FINAL ASSEMBLER
of TC
C-2 (Only Hawaii-based drivers are used.)

Kapolei
Maxi Truck & Van, Inc.
91-329 Kauhi Street
Kapolei, HI 96707
Tel: (808) 682-8123
FAX: (808) 682-8512
MFR/FINAL
ASSEMBLER of FTB

IDAHO

Boise
American Trailer Mfg.
8645 Westpark
Boise, ID 83704
Tel: (208) 375-0019
Contact: Vicki Risch
MFR of HT
D: Webster's

Boise
American Way RV Center
204 E. Myrtle
Boise, ID 83702
Tel: (208) 345-6644
DLR of R1, R2
C-2:1-2

Boise
Boise Mobile Equipment
900 W. Boeing Street
Boise, ID 83705
Tel: (208) 338-1444
FAX: (208) 344-0395
Contact: Larry Fegreto
MFR of F

Boise
*Breakaway, Inc./
Van Factory, The/
General Emergency
& Medical Supply*
(MAIL: P.O. Box 1593
Boise, ID 83701)
106 E. 39th
Boise, ID 83714
Tel: (208) 342-4506
Tel: (208) 376-9817
Contact: Carrol Elliot
MFR/DLR of A, R4

Boise
C & B Quality Trailers
9700 W. State Street
Boise, ID 83703
Tel: (208) 853-7728
FAX: (208) 482-7466
MFR/DLR of *HT, LT, UT, TB*

Boise
*Co-Tem Corporation/
Western Trailers*
6700 Business Way
Boise, ID 83705
Tel: (208) 344-2539
ID only: (800) 225-5453
Contact: Rosie Gerlensun
MFR of *Lightweight T, Flatbed T, XT, S-2*
(These are sold nationwide.)

Boise
Farm Bed Mfg., Inc.
8200 Eisenman Road
Boise, ID 83716
Tel: (208) 336-3666
FAX: (208) 336-3741
Contact: Dave or Donna
MFR of *T*

Boise
Idaho Trailer Mfg.
4299 Chinden Blvd.
Boise, ID 83714
Tel: (208) 323-9314
MFR of *T*

Boise
Interwest Medical
514 N. Curtis Road
Boise, ID 83706
Tel: (208) 376-3800
Nation: (800) 756-9696
Contact: Roger Spade
H'cap R4
C-2

Boise
Northland Industries
8100 Horseshoe Bend Rd.
Boise, ID 83703
Tel: (208) 939-6131
FAX: (208) 939-1780
MFR of *TC*
C-2

Boise
Topaz Tank & Manufacturing, Inc.
P.O. Box 5423
Boise, ID 83705
Tel: (208) 362-1150
Contact: Dee King
MFR of *TB*
A-1

Boise
Western Metal Fabricators, Inc.
6527 Supply Way
Boise, ID 83705
Tel: (208) 336-4042
Contact: Todd
MFR of *TB, U*

Burley
Ross's Mfg., Inc.
2624 Overland Avenue
Burley, ID 83318
Tel: (208) 678-8278
Tel: (208) 678-1474
Tel: (208) 678-1624
Contact: Randy Jones
MFR of *FTB, TB*
C-2:1

Caldwell
DG Recreational Sales
3800 E. Cleveland Blvd.
P.O. Box 603
Caldwell, ID 83605
Tel: (208) 454-1482
Tel: (208) 454-1483
Nation: (800) 255-1721
Contact: Roger Deide
DLR of *R1, R2*

Caldwell
Kit Mfg. Co.
412 Kit Avenue
P.O. Box 1420
Caldwell, ID 83606
Tel: (208) 454-9291
Contact: April Drinnon at ext. 229
MFR of *R5, R6*
A-1
D

Caldwell
One of a Kind
5310 E. Cleveland Blvd.
Caldwell, ID 83605
Tel: (208) 459-3938
Contact: Larry Johnson
REPAIR of *T*

Caldwell
Western World, Inc.
200 N. Kit Avenue
Caldwell, ID 83605
Tel: (208) 459-0106
Nation: (800) 247-2535
FAX: (208) 459-3918
Contact: Tracy Rockwell at ext. 121
MFR of *HT, LT*
C-2:1
D: Edwards, Dick Cates

Clifton
Butler Trailer Mfg. Co.
190 S. Main Street
Clifton, ID 83229
Tel: (208) 747-3277
MFR of *T*

Filer
Custom Trailer Mfg.
2399 E. 3800 North
Filer, ID 83328
Tel: (208) 326-5471
REPAIR of *HT*

Idaho Falls
First Street Welding
473   1st Street
Idaho Falls, ID 83401
Tel: (208) 522-2588
Contact: Marv Geib
MODIFIER of *T*

Idaho Falls
*Teton Traveler/
Rhead Industries*
(MAIL: P.O. Box 1861
Idaho Falls, ID 83403)
3912 N. Yellowstone Highway
Idaho Falls, ID 83401
Tel: (208) 523-3878
FAX: (208) 522-0710
Contact: Ron Rhead
MFR of *TC*

Idaho Falls
Trailers Plus
254 Lomax Street
Idaho Falls, ID 83401
Tel: (208) 529-9855
Contact: Carl Fitzwater
MFR of *T*

Meridan
John's Custom Vehicles
5545 W. Shimdam Blvd.
Meridan, ID 83642
Tel: (208) 887-3500
Contact: John Broderick
R4

Nampa
Minor's RV & Marina
1414 Franklin Blvd.
(Exit 36 of I-84)
Nampa, ID 83686
Tel: (208) 466-7844
Boise: (208) 888-1111
Contact: Dale Lloyd
DLR of *R1, R2*
C-2

Nampa
Speed RV
2417 Caldwell Blvd.
Nampa, ID 83651
Tel: (208) 467-2137
Contact: Lorraine Cascino
DLR of *R1, R2*

Nampa
Valley Trailer
9173 Ustick Road
Nampa, ID 83687
Tel: (208) 466-1774
Contact: John Jordim
MFR of *T, CT*

Post Falls
Horse Trailers Northwest
1040 N. Highway 41
Post Falls, ID 83854
Tel: (208) 773-1817
DLR of *HT*

Preston
Trails West Mfg.
65 N. 8th West
Preston, ID 83263
Tel: (208) 852-2200
FAX: (208) 852-2203
Contact: Randy Austin
MFR of *HT*

Rathdrum
Eagle Mfg., Inc.
1555 N. Highway 41
Rathdrum, ID 83858
Tel: (208) 687-1019
Contact: Jan Mott
MFR of *T*

Rathdrum
*Towne & Country
Horse Trailer*
W. 12445 Highway 53
Rathdrum, ID 83858
Tel: (208) 687-2648
DLR of *HT*

Rupert
Interstate Mfg., Inc.
231 West 50 South
Rupert, ID 83350
Tel: (208) 436-6654
Nation: (800) 428-6206
Contact: Wendell Jones
MFR of *T*

Sandpoint
Bike Caboose International
115 Hwy. 200 East
Sandpoint, ID 83864
Tel: (208) 263-8606
Contact: Bob Marley
MFR of *T*

Shelley
Siems' Enterprises
178 Emerson Avenue
Shelley, ID 83274
Tel: (208) 357-7356
Contact: George Siems
MFR of *T*

Star
Blake Trailers
P.O. Box 57
Star, ID 83669
Tel: (208) 286-7548
Contact: Monty Smith
MFR of *T*

Twin Falls
Anderson's RV
Junction of I-82 & I-84
Twin Falls, ID 83303
Tel: (208) 733-6756
Tel: (208) 825-5336
Nation: (800) 826-5336
DLR of *R1, R2*

Twin Falls
Charmac Trailers
452 S. Park Ave. West
Twin Falls, ID 83303
Tel: (208) 733-5241
Contact: Lloyd Casperson
MFR of *T*
C-2:1
D

Twin Falls
Pacific Trailers
3734 North 2700 East
Twin Falls, ID 83301
Tel: (208) 734-4398
Contact: Bill Mraz
MFR of *T*

Twin Falls
RV Barn
412 Addison Ave., West
Twin Falls, ID 83301
Tel: (208) 733-3358
Contact: Bob Barns
DLR of *T*

Wendell
Bert Harbaugh Motors, Incorporated
450 N. Idaho Street
Wendell, ID 83355
Tel/FAX: (208) 536-6323
Contact: Bert or Lane
DEALER of *R1, R3, R5, R6*

ILLINOIS

Addison
ADC Services
15 W. Fullerton Avenue
Addison, IL 60101
Tel: (630) 832-0203
FAX: (630) 628-7008
Contact: Tom Cusak
MODIFIER/DLR of *R4*
C-2 (Part-time)

Alsip
Unique Vans
12100 S. Cicero Avenue
Alsip, IL 60658
Tel: (708) 597-5265
FAX: (708) 597-5289
Contact: Roy or Warren
R4

Anna
Cunningham Enterprises/Transcraft Corporation
Transcraft Drive
Anna, IL 62906
Tel: (618) 833-5111
Nation: (800) 950-2995
Contact: Lois Stewart
MFR of *T*

Anna
Transcraft Corporation
414 E. Davies Street
Anna, IL 62906
Tel: (618) 833-5151
MFR of *T*

Aroma Park
Fiberglass International, Incorporated
105 W. Front Street
Aroma Park, IL 60910
Tel: (815) 935-1001
FAX: (815) 935-1060
Contact: Joe Hayward
MFR of *TB, U*
C-1
D: Consolidated

Aurora
Aurora Truck Body, Inc.
339 Middle Avenue
Aurora, IL 60506
Tel: (630) 897-4300
FAX: (630) 897-4397
Contact: Steve Guseavson
DLR/FINAL ASSEMBLER of *TB*
C-2:1-2
D: Ernie Gordom, A-1 Transportation

Aurora
Coffman Truck Sales
1149 W. Lake Street
Aurora, IL 60506
Tel: (630) 892-7093
FAX: (630) 892-1080
Contact: John Buck
DLR of *Trucks*

Aurora
Doney Recreational Vans, Incorporated
471 NE Industrial Drive
Aurora, IL 60504
Tel: (630) 892-7141
Contact: Dennis Doney
R4

Bartonville
Johnson Hydraulic Mfg.
6315 W. Fauber Road
Bartonville, IL 61607
Tel: (309) 697-3934
FAX: (309) 697-5616
Contact: James Kenyom
MFR of *STB*

Batavia
Payhauler Corporation
1333 N. Kirk Road
Batavia, IL 60510
Tel: (630) 879-6100
FAX: (630) 879-6148
Contact: Matt Nisbet
MFR of *TB*
D

Belleville
Arrow Company, The
1428 Windcliffe Drive
Belleville, IL 62226
Tel: (618) 277-2070
H'cap R4

Bensenville
Emerald Coachworks
475 Industrial Drive
Bensenville, IL 60106
Tel: (708) 350-1211
Nevada: (702) 893-9650
FAX: (708) 766-9124
Contact: Gina Rizzi
DLR of *Limos*
A-1

Bensenville
Moloney Coach Builders
770 Larson Lane
Bensenville, IL 60106
Tel: (630) 238-0099
Contact: Dan Roderman
MODIFIER of *Armored Vehicles*
D

Bensenville
Transportation System
729 Thomas
Bensenville, IL 60106
Tel: (630) 787-0170
FAX: (630) 787-0174
Contact: Paul Valentino
DLR of *Limos*

Bensenville
Trix Manufacturing
500 W. Irving Park Road
Bensenville, IL 60106
Tel: (630) 860-8749
FAX: (630) 766-4801
Contact: Rick
R4

Benton
Heritage Trailer Manufacturing Company
10764 Industrial Park Rd
Benton, IL 62812
Tel: (618) 439-9626
FAX: (618) 435-2579
Contact: Mark or Jason Knight
MFR of *T*

Bradley
Marty's Custom Vans
225 W. Broadway Street
Bradley, IL 60915
Tel: (815) 937-5452
DLR of *R4*

Brookfield
Limousine Emporium, The
8929 W. Ogden Avenue
Brookfield, IL 60513
Tel: (708) 387-4574
FAX: (708) 387-9500
DLR of *Limos*

Cahokia
Van Shop, The
2213 Doris Avenue
Cahokia, IL 62206
Tel: (618) 337-7586
FAX: (618) 337-4168
Contact: Chris Rodenberg
R4

Calumet City
Calumet Coach Company
2150 E. Dolton Road
Calumet City, IL 60409
Tel: (708) 868-5070
FAX: (708) 868-5101
Contact: Kay Gaspari
MFR of *S-2, ST, STB*
A-1

Centralia
Kingsley Fisher Products
120 E. Green Street
Centralia, IL 62801
Tel: (618) 533-3251
Nation: (800) 358-3073
FAX: (618) 533-0167
Contact: Ron Fisher
MFR of *TB*
C-2:2
D

Champaign
Handicap Vans
215 S. Locust Street
Champaign, IL 61820
Tel: (217) 398-1053
H'cap R4
C-1

Charleston
Trailmobile
1000 N. 14th Street
P.O. Box 5045
Charleston, IL 61920
Tel: (217) 348-8181
FAX: (217) 348-0421
Contact: Bob Spangler at ext. 250 - Traffic Dpt.
MFR of *ST*
D

Chicago
Accessories Unlimited
4656 S. Western Avenue
Chicago, IL 60609
Tel: (312) 247-4174
Contact: Pat Schlossberg
R4

Chicago
Barden Custom Van Accessories
5930 S. Pulaski Road
Chicago, IL 60629
Tel: (312) 735-1859
FAX: (312) 735-1894
Contact: Mary Jo Barden
R4

Chicago
Erie Vehicle Company
60 E. 51st Street
Chicago, IL 60615
Tel: (312) 536-6300
FAX: (312) 536-5779
Contact: Mike
MFR of *Stake TB, Plumber Supply TB, VTB*
DISTRIBUTOR of *"Parkhurst" Stake TB, "Brown" VTB*

Chicago
Freedman Seating Factory Outlet
4043 N. Ravenwood Ave.
Chicago, IL 60613
Tel: (312) 929-6100
Nation: (800) 443-4540
FAX: (312) 929-8942
Contact: Dan Coen
UConvs

Chicago
Glen's Truck Body Company
3106 S. Homan Avenue
Chicago, IL 60623
Tel: (312) 376-4454
FAX: (312) 890-1600
Contact: Glen
MFR of *TB*

Chicago
James Professional Car Sales, Incorporated
1507 E. 72nd Street
Chicago, IL 60619
Tel: (312) 684-2882
FAX: (312) 375-5847
Contact: James Murrel, Jr. or James Murrel, Sr.
DLR of *Limos*
D

Chicago
Mid-City Truck Body & Equipment, Inc.
1500 W. Grand Avenue
Chicago, IL 60622
Tel: (312) 421-4975
FAX: (312) 421-7462
Contact: Greg Anderson
MODIFER/FINAL ASSEMBLER of *TB, T*
D: Drive-Away Service

Chicago
Mr. Kustom
3708 W. Irving Park
Chicago, IL 60618
Tel: (312) 583-3770
FAX: (312) 583-9170
Contact: Rich Korber
R4

Chicago
Navistar International Corporation
455 N. City Front Place
Chicago, IL 60611
Tel: (312) 836-2000
MFR of *TB*

Chicago
Paramount Truck Body Company
2107 W. Fulton Street
Chicago, IL 60612
Tel: (312) 666-6441
Contact: Greg Smowcha
MFR of *TB*

Chicago
Pines Trailer Corp.
2555 S. Blue Island Ave.
Chicago, IL 60608
Tel: (312) 254-5533
FAX: (708) 254-7610
Contact: Phillip Pines
MFR of *T, S-2*

Chicago
Tip-Top Auto Rebuilders
1809 W. Webster Avenue
Chicago, IL 60614
Tel: (312) 227-0707
FAX: (312) 227-1693
Contact: Freddy Lyndorffer
R4

Chicago
Tool & Engineering Co.
900 W. 18th
Chicago, IL 60608
Tel: (312) 226-3700
FAX: (312) 226-0919
Contact: Albert Hydzik
MFR of *U, TB*
D

Chicago
Trailmobile, Inc.
200 E. Randolph Drive
Suite 6820
Chicago, IL 60601
Tel: (312) 861-1190
Nation: (800) 877-4990
FAX: (312) 565-0369
Contact: Edward Wanandi
MFR of *S-2*

Chicago
Triangle Fabrication & Body Company
3701 S. St. Louis
Chicago, IL 60632
Tel: (312) 523-7858
FAX: (312) 523-8802
Contact: Manuel Unzalez
MFR of *TB*

Chicago
Van City
3149 N. Clybourn Ave.
Chicago, IL 60618
Tel: (312) 525-9191
Contact: Dan
R4

Chicago
Wag Industries
627 N. Albany Avenue
Chicago, IL 60612
Tel: (312) 638-7007
Nation: (800) 621-3305
FAX: (312) 533-6951
Contact: Gail Gilbert
MFR of *Catering TB*

Chicago Heights
Pat's Custom Painting
1040 Union Avenue
Chicago Heights, IL 60411
Tel: (708) 754-2252
Contact: Pat Napoli
R4, TCons

Cicero
Capital Truck Body Company, Incorporated
1601 S. Laramie Avenue
Cicero, IL 60804
Tel: (708) 656-0555
FAX: (708) 656-4176
Contact: Peter Debular
MFR of *TB*

Danville
House of Custom Vans
104 Brewer
Danville, IL 61834
Tel/FAX: (217) 443-0306
Contact: Earl Watkins
R4, TCons

Decatur
Jerry Pressley RV Center
1500 N. 22nd Street
Decatur, IL 62526
Tel: (217) 428-5588
FAX: (217) 428-3673
DLR of *R1, R2*

Decatur
Sun Control
3915 Ferris Parkway
Decatur, IL 62526
Tel: (217) 422-6621
FAX: (217) 422-9649
Contact: Mike Lewis
R4

Des Plaines
Hausman Bus Sales, Inc. /MCI/TMC New Coach Sales
10 E. Golf Road
Des Plaines, IL 60016
Tel: (847) 299-9900
Nation: (800) 428-7626
FAX: (847) 299-7843
Contact: Jim Lewis
DISTRIBUTOR of *U*
C-2:6-7

Des Plaines
Perr Truck & Trailer Body, Inc.
2211 S. Mount Prospect Road
Des Plaines, IL 60018
Tel: (708) 824-8163
DLR of *TB, T*

Downers Grove
Engineering Equip. Co.
1020 W. 31st Street
Downers Grove, IL 60515
Tel: (630) 963-7800
FAX: (630) 963-7123
Contact: Sue Stark
MFR of *A, E, Bio-Maintenance Vehs., & other Medical units, for export.*

Du Quoin
Prestige Custom Trailers, Incorporated
500 S. Madison
Du Quoin, IL 62832
Tel: (618) 542-8313
FAX: (618) 542-8039
Contact: Sam Wink
MFR of *BT*
C-1

- 209 -

East Peoria
Jim Hawk Truck Trailer of Illinois, Incorporated
4001 E. Main Street
East Peoria, IL 61611
Tel: (309) 694-6271
FAX: (309) 694-0036
Contact: Dale Young
DLR of *S-2*

East Peoria
PAFCO Truck Bodies
1954 E. Washington
East Peoria, IL 61611
Tel: (309) 699-4613
Contact: Robert Pfaffmann
or Max Pfaffmann
MFR/DISTRIBUTOR of *TB*

Effingham
Effingham Truck Sales Body Shop
1701 W. Fayette
Effingham, IL 62401
Tel: (217) 342-4733
FAX: (217) 342-4706
Contact: Rob Workman
TB

Elgin
Chicago Armor & Limo Manufacturing
1100 Davis Road
Elgin, IL 60123
Tel: (708) 397-8400
FAX: (708) 438-8818
MFR of *Limos*
D

Frankfort
Paratech, Inc.
1025 Lambrecht Road
Frankfort, IL 60423
Tel: (815) 469-3911
Nation: (800) 435-9358
FAX: (815) 469-7748
DLR of *E*

Franklin Park
Great Lakes Recreational Products
9641 Grand Avenue
Franklin Park, IL 60131
Tel: (847) 451-0557
Contact: Howard Furtak
R4

Freeburg
Towers Fire Apparatus
502 S. Richland Street
Freeburg, IL 62243
Tel: (618) 539-3863
FAX: (618) 539-4850
Contact: Gary Towers
MFR of *TB, U*
C-1

Galva
Motoroam Industries of America, Incorporated
205 N. 2050 E. Rte. 1
Galva, IL 61434
Tel: (309) 932-2056
Contact: James Murry
MFR of *R1, R4*

Gibson City
Load Redi, Inc.
1124 S. Sangamon Ave.
Gibson City, IL 60936
Tel: (217) 784-4200
FAX: (217) 784-4216
MFR of *T*

Herscher
T & E Enterprises Herscher, Incorporated
80-1/2 Tobey Drive
Herscher, IL 60941
Tel: (815) 426-2761
FAX: (815) 426-2875
Contact: Todd Datwilder
MFR of *T*

Jacksonville
Byers International Trucks, Incorporated
1314 W. Morton Avenue
Jacksonville, IL 62650
Tel: (217) 245-4614
Nation: (800) 252-3704
FAX: (217) 245-0530
Contact: Gary Byers
DLR of *Trucks*

Jerseyville
Parsell Truck Equipment Company
900 Shipman Road
Jerseyville, IL 62052
Tel: (618) 498-4112
FAX: (618) 498-3790
Contact: Larry
MFR of *TB*

Kankakee
Midwest Transit Equipment
146 W. Issert Drive
Kankakee, IL 60901
Tel: (815) 933-2412
FAX: (815) 933-3966
Contact: Jim Bridgewater
DISTRIBUTOR of *U*
C-1

Kewanee
Pines Trailer
2006 Kentville Road
Kewanee, IL 61433
Tel: (309) 853-3566
Tel: (309) 854-0407
Tel: (309) 852-1546
FAX: (309) 852-0527
Contact: Darryl Hoover
MFR of *T*
B-2

Lake Bluff
Shepard Chevrolet
930 Carriage Lane
Lake Bluff, IL 60044
Tel: (847) 234-7900
FAX: (847) 234-3912
Contact: Danielle Tyran
R4

Lombard
Heritage Cadillac, Inc.
303 W. Roosevelt Road
Lombard, IL 60148
Tel: (630) 629-3300
FAX: (630) 629-9730
DLR of *Limos*

Machesney Park
Denny's Enterprises
1172 Old Ralston Road
Machesney Park, IL 61115
Tel: (815) 633-3229
Contact: Denny Hayenga
R4

Mascoutah
Al Worms, Jr.
Highway 177, West
Mascoutah, IL 62258
Tel: (618) 566-2353
DLR of *HT*

McHenry
R. A. Adams Enterprises
2600 W. Route 120
McHenry, IL 60050
Tel: (815) 385-5970
FAX: (815) 385-6684
Contact: Mary Beth Adams
DLR of *T*

Midlothian
Arrow Chevrolet, Inc.
14640 Cicero Avenue
Midlothian, IL 60445
Tel: (708) 389-0600
FAX: (708) 389-7354
Contact: Gus Kay
R4

Moline
Koenig Body & Equipment Company
222 52nd Street
Moline, IL 61265
Tel: (309) 764-8343
Nation: (800) 827-8613
FAX: (309) 764-8351
Contact: Scott Harris
FINAL ASSEMBLER/ DISTRIBUTOR of *TB*
C-1

Moline
McLaughlin Body Company, Incorporated
2430 River Drive
Moline, IL 61265
Tel: (309) 762-7755
FAX: (309) 762-2823
Contact: Bud Pierce
MFR of *TB, U*
C-2

Momence
Metz Mfg. Co.
420 S. Hardin
Momence, IL 60954
Tel: (815) 472-4822
IL Only: (800) 832-3151
FAX: (815) 472-4411
Contact: Bob Niedert
REPAIR of *S-2*

Monticello
Samson Trailers, Inc.
983 Access Road
Monticello, IL 61856
Tel: (217) 762-8461
Contact: Jeremy Bowman
MFR of *T*
B-2:1

Mount Vernon
Lindsey's RV Center
Route 37, North
Mount Vernon, IL 63864
Tel: (618) 242-8484
FAX: (618) 242-8988
Contact: Barry Lindsey
DLR of *R1, R6*

North Chicago
Kay Body & Equipment, Incorporated
2330 Meadow Lane
North Chicago, IL 60064
Tel: (847) 689-3879
FAX: (847) 689-3884
Contact: Joe or Richie
MFR to *TB*
D

North Chicago
Liberty Coach
1400 Morrow Ave., N.
North Chicago, IL 60064
Tel: (847) 578-4600
FAX: (847) 578-1053
Contact: Fred Konigseder
MFR of *U*
C-1:1

Olney
Imperial Trailer Sales & Manufacturing, Inc.
911 S. West Street
Olney, IL 62450
Tel: (618) 395-2414
FAX: (618) 392-3338
Contact: Mimi Fehrenbacher
MFR of *T*

Peoria
*Koenig Body &
Equipment, Incorporated*
2428 W. Farmington Rd.
Peoria, IL 61604
Tel: (309) 673-7435
FAX: (309) 673-6836
FINAL ASSEMBLER
of *TB*

Plainfield
*Freedom Driving Aids
of Illinois*
23855 W. Andrew Road
Plainfield, IL 60544
Tel: (708) 254-2000
FAX: (815) 254-2001
Contact: Tom Wynker
H'cap R4

Prophetstown
Del Nutter Trailer Sales
12966 Spring Hill Road
Prophetstown, IL 61277
Tel: (815) 537-2447
FAX: (815) 537-2451
Contact: Vicki Nutter
DLR of *HT, LT*

Quincy
Knapheide Mfg. Co.
436 S. 6th Street
P.O. Box C-140
Quincy, IL 62306
Tel: (217) 222-7131
FAX: (217) 222-5939
Contact: Steve Bybee
at ext. 255
MFR of *UTB*
D: Thompsons, Inc.

Rochelle
*Rochelle Steel
Fabricating, Inc.*
2823 Center Road
Rochelle, IL 61068
Tel: (815) 562-7805
FAX: (815) 562-3732
Contact: Tony Guzzardo
MFR of *UT*

Rockford
Pitney Power Painting
1515 Black Hawk Road
Rockford, IL 61104
Tel: (815) 227-0585
Contact: Dan Pitney
MODIFIER of *U*

Rockton
Pyramid Enterprises
4864 Freeport Road
Rockton, IL 61072
Tel: (815) 624-6662
H'cap R4

Rosemont
Crown Custom Coach
5433 Milton Pkwy.
Rosemont, IL 60018
Tel: (847) 678-4800
FAX: (847) 678-5418
**FINAL ASSEMBLER/
MFR** of *R4, H'cap R4*

Schaunburg
Midwest Mobility
437 W. Wise Road
Schaunburg, IL 60193
Tel: (847) 923-9892
R4, H'cap R4

Sigel
*Hanfland Sandblast and
Paint*
105 Lewis Avenue
Sigel, IL 62462
Tel: (217) 844-3322
FAX: (217) 844-2163
Contact: Charles
Hanfland
DEALER of *T*

South Holland
Firemax
130 W. A54th Street #2
South Holland, IL 60473
Tel: (708) 339-0629
Nation: (800) 872-9617
FAX: (708) 339-1428
Contact: Randy Womack
MFR of *F*

Springfield
Truckin' Specialties
2511 S. Grand Avenue,
East
Springfield, IL 62703
Tel: (217) 522-1351
Contact: Roger
Schleyhahn
R4

Streator
*U.S. Truck Body
Midwest/York Anthony*
1807 N. Bloomington
Street
Streator, IL 61364
Tel: (815) 672-3211
Nation: (800) 443-0843
Contact: Jim Walker
MFR of *R4, TB, U*

Summit Argo
Pratt Enterprises, Inc.
5120 S. Lawndale Ave.
Summit Argo, IL 60501
Tel: (708) 594-1200
FAX: (708) 594-1201
MFR of *T*
D

Warrensburg
Lazy N, Incorporated
310 S. Route 121
P.O. Box 259
Warrensburg, IL 62573
Tel: (217) 672-3281
FAX: (217) 672-3331
Contact: Lou Pince
MFR of *HT*
B-2:1

Wauconda
*Campbell International,
Incorporated*
120 W. Kent Avenue
Wauconda, IL 60106
Tel: (847) 526-7300
Contact: Jim Campbell,
MFR of *TB*

INDIANA

Angola
Angola Coach, Inc.
385 S. 290 West
(US Highway 20 at I-69)
P.O. Box 301
Angola, IN 46703
Tel: (219) 665-6361
FAX: (219) 665-9746
Contact: David Macey
or Bob Makin
MFR of *UT, UConvs*

Austin
Reardon Trailer Sales
2579 N. US 31
Austin, IN 47102
Tel: (812) 794-2895
Contact: Albert Reardon
DLR of *HT*

Batesville
Six Pine Ranch
513 Six Pine Ranch Road
Batesville, IN 47006
Tel: (812) 934-2091
Contact: Ed Schumaker
DLR of *HT*

Bloomington
*McArdle International
Truck*
3951 S. State Rd. 37
Bloomington, IN 47404
Tel: (812) 336-6302
Contact: Bob McArdle
DLR of *S-1*

Brazil
Great Dane Trailers
US Highway 40, East
Brazil, IN 47834
Tel: (812) 443-4711
FAX: (812) 446-0442
Contact: Greg Hale
MFR of *T*

Bremen
Comfort Camp
218 E. Second Street
Bremen, IN 46506
Tel: (219) 546-5761
Contact: Cecil Spenser
MFR of *TC*
C-2:5-6

Bremen
Hop Cap, Incorporated
1345 W. North Street
Bremen, IN 46506
Tel: (219) 546-4939
FAX: (219) 546-4189
Contact: Dave Schotz
MFR of *Fiberglass TC*

Bremen
U.S.A. Motor Corp.
1730 W. Bike Street
Bremen, IN 46506
Tel: (219) 546-5450
Nation: (800) 872-5450
FAX: (219) 546-5801
MFR of *V, R1*
C-1

Bristol
*American International
Conversions, Inc./
Ger-Win Lorain*
17090 SR 120, East
P.O. Box 578
Bristol, IN 46507
Tel: (219) 848-7602
Nation: (800) 255-7056
IN only: (800) 433-6468
FAX: (219) 848-7530
Contact: Jerry Cash
or Mike Hiles
R4
C-2:10
*D: Jet Transport
(in Middlebury, IN)*

Bristol
Bay Bridge Mfg.
17666 Commerce Drive
Bristol, IN 46507
Tel: (219) 848-7477
Nation: (800) 451-6267
FAX: (219) 848-5658
Contact: Dennis
McCarthy
MFR of *High-Cube VTB*

Bristol
*Cargo Express/
Shuttlemaster*
109 Kesco Drive
Bristol, IN 46507
Tel: (219) 848-7441
FAX: (219) 848-1407
Contact: John, Tony or
Marion
MFR of *Cargo T*

Bristol
Country Park, Inc.
907 S. Division Street
Bristol, IN 46507
Tel: (219) 848-4420
FAX: (219) 848-1632
Contact: Joe Yoder
DEALER of *R1, R2, R5, R6*

Bristol
Frontier Coach
806 S. Division Street
Bristol, IN 46507
Tel: (219) 848-5458
Nation: (800) 928-7866
Contact: Bob
UConv

Bristol
Haulmark Industries, Incorporated
19224 CR 8
Bristol, IN 46507
Tel: (219) 848-4448
Nation: (800) 348-7530
FAX: (219) 825-9816
Contact: Jim Hostetler
MFR of *T*
D: Y-Tran

Bristol
Mark-Line Industries, Incorporated
14054 CR 4
P.O. Box 277
Bristol, IN 46507
Tel: (219) 825-5851
Nation: (800) 348-7530
FAX: (219) 825-9139
Contact: Mr. Kim Coates
MFR of *Office T, UT, Concession T*

Bristol
Merhow Industries, Inc./ Dadon Corporation
19757 CR 8
Bristol, IN 46507
Tel: (219) 848-4445
Nation: (800) 860-9198
FAX: (219) 848-1112
Contact: Dave Eckert
MFR of *HT, T*
D: Ideal Transport

Bristol
Shadow Cruiser
13861 CR 4
Bristol, IN 46507
Tel: (219) 825-1000
FAX: (219) 825-5251
Contact: Derril Corbett
MFR of *R5, R6*
C-2

Bristol
Skamper Corporation
SR 15, North
Box 338
Bristol, IN 46507
Tel: (219) 848-7411
FAX: (219) 848-1236
Contact: Larry Converse or Steve Decker
MFR of *R1, R2, R5, R6*
A-1, C-2:7

Bristol
United Express Line
19985 CR 8
Bristol, IN 46507
Tel: (219) 848-7088
Nation: (800) 637-2592
FAX: (219) 848-4643
Contact: Dan Yarnell
MFR of *Cargo T, Race Car T, Auto Transport T, Food Concession T*

Butler
Hendrickson Suspension
200 W. Cherry Street
Butler, IN 46721
Tel: (219) 868-2131
FAX: (219) 868-2850
MFR of *TB*

Cambridge City
Converto Mfg. Co.
3rd & Green Streets
P. O. Box 287
Cambridge City, IN 47327
Tel: (317) 478-3205
FAX: (317) 478-1223
Contact: Clarence France
MFR of *T, TB*

Carmel
Northside Trailer Sales
969 N. Rangeline Road
Carmel, IN 46032
Tel: (317) 846-5839
Tel: (317) 846-0712
FAX: (317) 846-5614
Contact: Kay Lancaster
DLR of *HT*

Cedar Lake
Rose RV Sales
12615 Wicker Avenue
Cedar Lake, IN 46303
Tel: (219) 374-4316
FAX: (219) 374-9813
Contact: Brandt Routson or Chris Rose
DLR of *R3, R5, R6*

Clarksville
Tom Spinnett RV
560 Kopp Lane
Clarksville, IN 47129
Tel: (812) 282-7718
Louisville, KY Line: (502) 282-7718
FAX: (812) 288-9424
Contact: Marshall Smith
DLR of *R1, R2*
C-2
D: Morgan Driveaway

Columbia City
W. A. Jones & Son
1171 S. Williams
Columbia City, IN 46725
Tel: (219) 244-7661
FAX: (219) 244-7662
Contact: Bill Emmert
FINAL ASSEMBLER of *TB*

Crawfordsville
Fleetwood Travel Trailers of Indiana
1635 Elmore Street
P.O. Box 665
Crawfordsville, IN 47933
Tel: (317) 362-5120
Contact: Dick Norton
MFR of *R5, R6*
A-1

Crown Point
Crown Trailer Sales
996 E. Joliet Street
Crown Point, IN 46307
Tel: (219) 662-1412
Contact: Ron
DLR of *HT*

Decatur
American Coach
1803 Winchester Street
P.O. Box 1006
Decatur, IN 46733-5006
Tel: (219) 728-2477
Nation: (800) 441-8271
FAX: (219) 728-2711
MFR of *R1, R2*

Decatur
Mobile Medical Vehicles, Incorporated
2232 W. Patterson Street
Decatur, IN 46733
Tel: (219) 724-9752
FAX: (219) 724-8156
MFR of *A*

Decatur
Fleetwood Motor Homes of Indiana
1031 US Hwy. 224, East
P.O. Box 31
Decatur, IN 46733
Tel: (219) 728-2121
Contact: Barbara Turner
MFR of *R1, R2*
D: Don Ray Driveaway

Delphi
Delphi Body Works, Inc.
313 S. Washington Street
Delphi, IN 46923
Tel: (317) 564-2212
FAX: (317) 564-4255
Contact: Richard Bradshaw
MFR of *TB*
C-2

Elkhart
Alternative Mobility, Inc.
28298 Clay Street
Elkhart, IN 46517
Tel: (219) 293-0367
FAX: (219) 522-2975
Contact: Ron Albaugh
H'cap R4

Elkhart
American Travel Systems
21746 Buckingham Road
Elkhart, IN 46516
Tel: (219) 294-2117
Nation: (800) 999-1902
FAX: (219) 293-4970
Contact: Brian Hurley or Laurie Scoll
MFR of *R5, R6*
C-2:10
D

Elkhart
Archer Coach Corp.
1730 Gateway Court
Elkhart, IN 46514
Tel: (219) 266-5222
Nation: (800) 759-5222
FAX: (219) 266-6020
Contact: Crystal
R4

Elkhart
Astro Quality Caps
28049 CR 20, West
Elkhart, IN 46517
Tel: (219) 522-2260
FAX: (219) 522-2638
Contact: Larry Maier
DLR of *TB, U*
C-2

Elkhart
B & B Industries, Inc.
1121 D. I. Drive
Elkhart, IN 46514
Tel: (219) 262-8551
FAX: (219) 262-0624
Contact: Rita Dawson
MFR of *W*

Elkhart
*Burks' Van &
RV Interior*
706 S. Main Street
Elkhart, IN 46516
Tel: (219) 293-5916
Contact: Ione Burks
R4

Elkhart
Century Distributing
3008 Mobile Drive
Elkhart, IN 46514
Tel: (219) 295-6261
FAX: (219) 293-6340
Contact: Gary Nord
R4
C-2

Elkhart
Century Fiberglass
1131 D.I. Drive
Elkhart, IN 46514
Tel: (219) 264-7528
Nation: (800) 224-5064
FAX: (219) 264-5064
Contact: Greg Masterson
MFR of *TC*

Elkhart
*Chariot Vans, Inc.,
by Georgie Boy*
28582 Jamie Street
Sachs Industrial Park
Elkhart, IN 46514
Tel: (219) 262-4667
Tel: (219) 262-2624
Nation: (800) 888-3418
FAX: (219) 262-3123
Contact: John Wisolek
or Tim Gray
R4
C-2:10-15
D

Elkhart
Clarion Motors Corp.
1100 Woodlawn Street
Elkhart, IN 46515
Tel: (219) 264-0787
FAX: (219) 264-5295
Contact: Don Campagna
MFR of *R1, R2*

Elkhart
CNC Vans
21240 Protecta Drive
Elkhart, IN 46516
Tel: (219) 293-0585
FAX: (219) 293-7723
R4

Elkhart
*Coachmen Industries,
Incorporated*
(MAIL: P.O. Box 3300
Elkhart, IN 46514)
601 E. Beardsley Avenue
Elkhart, IN 46514
Tel: (219) 262-0123
FAX: (219) 262-8823
Contact: Rod Nappier
MFR of *R1, R2*
C-2

Elkhart
Coachmen Vans
1520 Mishawaka Street
P.O. Box 50
Elkhart, IN 46414
Tel: (219) 262-3474
FAX: (219) 262-1099
Contact: Ernie McLaine
R4
C-2:10

Elkhart
*Continental
Spacemaster Corp.*
25702 Miner Road
P.O. Box 506
Elkhart, IN 46515
Tel: (219) 293-8531
FAX: (219) 264-7345
MFR of *Office T*

Elkhart
*Conversion
Components, Inc.*
53229 CR 113
Elkhart, IN 46514
Tel: (219) 264-4181
R4
NOTE: *They build 3 or 4
prototype units per year.
They mostly build kits.
Consider primarily as an
Interlock or on-call
possiblity.*

Elkhart
Custom Wood Craft
53972 N. Park Avenue
Elkhart, IN 46516
Tel: (219) 262-0428
FAX: (219) 266-5460
Contact: Kim Grant
R4
C-1

Elkhart
Daka Mfg., Inc.
636 Kollar Street
Elkhart, IN 46514
Tel: (219) 295-8036
MFR of *F, Haz-Mat TB
(in limited quantities)*

Elkhart
Damon Corporation
52570 Paul Drive
Elkhart, IN 46514
Tel: (219) 294-1754
Nation: (800) 860-5658
FAX: (219) 264-4856
Contact: Linda Wood
MFR of *R1, R3*

Elkhart
Damon Industries
28163 CR 20
Elkhart, IN 46517
Tel: (219) 262-2624
FAX: (219) 293-0848
Contact: Ron Dickinson
MFR of *T*
D

Elkhart
Delivery Concepts, Inc.
58356 CR 3, South
Elkhart, IN 46517
Tel: (219) 294-4050
FAX: (219) 522-3423
MFR of *Catering TB*

Elkhart
Discovery Vans
53387 Ada Drive
Elkhart, IN 46514
Tel: (219) 266-1477
Nation: (800) 678-2518
FAX: (219) 266-1366
Contact: Linda Jeffries
R4

Elkhart
*Diversified Mobile
Products*
4240 Pine Creek Road
Elkhart, IN 46516
Tel: (219) 293-9555
FAX: (219) 293-9981
MFR of *Decontamination Shower T,
Concession T, Cargo T*

Elkhart
Eclipse Conversions
135 CR 6
Elkhart, IN 46514
Tel: (219) 262-1223
FAX: (219) 262-9578
Contact: Al Simeri
R4

Elkhart
Elk Enterprises
25771 Miner Road
P.O. Box 963
Elkhart, IN 46515
Tel: (219) 264-0768
FAX: (219) 264-9447
Nation: (800) 289-3551
Contact: Bruce Davis
R4
C-2:12
D

Elkhart
Estate Mfg., Inc.
4540 Pine Creek Road
Elkhart, IN 46516
Tel: (219) 295-3683
Contact: Tim Keech
MFR of *R1, R2, R5, R6*
D: Star Fleet

Elkhart
*Firan Motor Coach
Industries RV Division*
58277 SR 19, South
P.O. Box 482
Elkhart, IN 46515
Tel: (219) 293-6581
FAX: (219) 295-8749
Contact: Joanne Torrance
MFR of *R1, R2*
C-1, C-2:6

Elkhart
*Four Winds
International Corp.*
55667 CR 15
Elkhart, IN 46516
Tel: (219) 294-2860
FAX: (219) 294-8971
MFR of *R1, R2*
D: Ideal

Elkhart
*Four Winds
International, Inc.*
701 CR 15
Elkhart, IN 46516
Tel: (219) 266-1111
FAX: (219) 293-5256
Contact: Jeff Kime
MFR of *R1, R2*
D: Ideal

Elkhart
Freedom One
28936 Phillips Street
Elkhart, IN 46516
Tel: (219) 262-8349
Nation: (800) 373-3661
FAX: (219) 262-3324
Contact: Charles Fisher
R4

Elkhart
Gemini Conversions, Inc.
30372 CR 12, West
Elkhart, IN 46514
Tel: (219) 262-4474
Tel: (219) 262-3411
FAX: (219) 264-2329
Contact: Loretta Veenstra
R4
C-2:6

Elkhart
Glaval, Incorporated
3722 Lexington Park Dr.
Elkhart, IN 46515
Tel: (219) 295-7178
Nation: (800) 445-2825
Nation: (800) 348-7400
FAX: (219) 293-1294
Contact: Terry Harris
R4
C-2
CORPORATE HQ &
Plant Site

Elkhart
Glaval, Incorporated
3623 Lexington Park Dr.
P.O. Box 1674
Elkhart, IN 46515
Tel: (219) 295-2229
Nation: (800) 348-3708
FAX: (219) 522-1375
R4
C-2:4

Elkhart
Glaval, Inc. - Plant #6
914 CR 1
Elkhart, IN 46514
Tel: (219) 262-2212
Nation: (800) 445-2825
FAX: (219) 262-0657
Contact: Terry Harris,
ext. 240
R4
C-2

Elkhart
Goshen Coach
1110 D. I. Drive
Elkhart, IN 46514
Tel: (219) 264-7511
FAX: (219) 266-5866
Contact: Jay Nine
MFR of *R1, R3, R5, R6*

Elkhart
Harmar, Inc.
58456 CR 3
Elkhart, IN 46517
Tel: (219) 294-1269
FAX: (219) 294-1171
Contact: Randy Frick
MFR of *R5, R6*

Elkhart
Hulet Mfg., Inc.
728 Middleton Run Road
Elkhart, IN 46516
Tel: (219) 295-5700
FAX: (219) 295-5800
Contact: John Keller
MFR of *TB*
D: Rad Transport

Elkhart
Hy-Line Enterprises Inc.
21674 Beck Drive
Elkhart, IN 46516
Tel: (219) 294-1112
FAX: (219) 293-4072
Contact: Mike Eenhuis
MFR of *R5, R6*
C-2
*D: Several, including
Rad Transport*

Elkhart
*Imperial Automotive
Group*
1140 All Pro Drive
P.O. Box 4213
Elkhart, IN 46514
Tel: (219) 266-6833
FAX: (219) 264-7539
R4

Elkhart
Imperial Industries, Inc.
2831 Dexter Drive
Elkhart, IN 46514
Tel: (219) 266-1580
Plant 3 Tel:
(219) 264-0224
Contact: Andy Troyer
R4

Elkhart
International RV World
2316 S. Nappanee Street
Elkhart, IN 46517
Tel: (219) 293-8878
FAX: (219) 293-6571
DLR of *R1, R2, R5, R6*

Elkhart
Jason Industries
1500 W. Lusher Avenue
Elkhart, IN 46517
Tel: (219) 294-7595
FAX: (219) 522-4874
Contact: Ed Poth
MFR of *Truck Cabs*
C-2
D: Ideal Transport

Elkhart
JB Enterprises
56173 CR 13, South
Elkhart, IN 46516
Tel: (219) 294-2561
FAX: (219) 293-1828
Contact: Shelley Collins
MFR of *Enclosed Car T,
Cargo T, UT*

Elkhart
Kentron Inc.
3012 Mobile Drive
Elkhart, IN 46514
Tel: (219) 262-2543
Tel: (219) 262-2423
R4
C-2

Elkhart
LCM, Incorporated
21888 Beck Drive
Elkhart, IN 46516
Tel: (219) 295-8801
Nation: (800) 338-9037
FAX: (219) 295-6803
Contact: Brenda
MFR of *R4, TConvs*

Elkhart
Lee Enterprises Mfg.
25883 N. Park Avenue
Elkhart, IN 46514
Tel: (219) 262-1543
FAX: (219) 262-1545
Contact: Mickey Lee
MFR of *R1, R2*
D: Starfleet

Elkhart
Marathon Homes Corp.
4420 Pine Creek Road
Pine Creek Industrial
Park
Elkhart, IN 46516
Tel: (219) 294-6441
FAX: (219) 522-5923
Contact: Ron Berg
MFR of *R2, R5, R6*
D

Elkhart
Maxco of Elkhart
53387 Ada Drive
Elkhart, IN 46514
Tel: (219) 262-1511
FAX: (219) 262-8523
Contact: Tim Maxey
TConvs
D: Stanley Transport

Elkhart
*Midway Truck &
Coach Corporation*
24245 CR 6, East
Elkhart, IN 46514
Tel: (219) 262-4797
Nation: (800) 843-8267
FAX: (219) 262-2762
Contact: Del Vohs
MFR of *R4*

Elkhart
*Midway Truck &
Coach, Incorporated*
(MAIL: P.O. Box 1931
Elkhart, IN 46515)
29391 US Hwy. 33, West
Elkhart, IN 46516
Tel: (219) 294-3531
Nation: (800) 626-6173
FAX: (219) 294-1093
Contact: Gary Mathers
MFR of *Commercial R4,
Utility R4*

Elkhart
Midwest Vans
1801 Minnie Street
Elkhart, IN 46516
Tel: (219) 293-3395
FAX: (219) 293-3692
Contact: John Stump
R4
C-2
D

Elkhart
Monaco Coach Corp.
1722 W. Mishawaka Rd.
Elkhart, IN 46517
Tel: (219) 295-8060
FAX: (219) 522-1782
Contact: Rhonda Tindall
MFR of *R1, R2*
C-2:5-6
Requires CDL

Elkhart
NPE, Inc.
4661 Pine Creek Road
Elkhart, IN 46516
Tel: (219) 295-8888
Contact: Ed Yoder
MFR of *T*
C-2:4

Elkhart
Odessa Industries, Inc.
2208 Middlebury Street
Elkhart, IN 46516
Tel: (219) 293-0595
FAX: (219) 294-1140
MFR of *R1, R2*

Elkhart
Pine Ridge
25810 Miner Road
Elkhart, IN 46514
Tel: (219) 262-0756
FAX: (219) 266-1549
Contact: Helen Hite
MFR of *R1, R2*
C-2

Elkhart
Pro Air, Incorporated
28731 CR 6
Elkhart, IN 46514
Tel: (219) 264-5494
Nation: (800) 338-8544
FAX: (219) 264-2194
Contact: Charles McMillan
MODIFIER of *R4*

Elkhart
Quality Coaches, Inc.
52743 Stephen Place
Elkhart, IN 46514
Tel: (219) 262-3649
FAX: (219) 262-4380
Contact: Keith Whitrock
R4
C-2:6
D: Barrett

Elkhart
Ranch Fiberglass, Inc.
28564 Holiday Place
Elkhart, IN 46517
Tel: (219) 294-7550
Nation: (800) 776-2340
FAX: (219) 522-1894
MFR of *TC*

Elkhart
Rexhall Industries, Inc.
29449 US Hwy. 33
Elkhart, IN 46516
Tel: (219) 295-1805
Nation: (800) 972-1619
FAX: (219) 522-1875
Contact: Jack
MFR of *R1*

Elkhart
Rockwood, Inc.
SPECIAL INSTRUCTIONS:
Prospective employees *must* apply at the Corporate Office in Goshen. No hiring is done at plant sites, nor are tours provided. Going to the plant sites could *impair* your chances of being hired! Plant site locations are included here *only* to orient you, and to help you in your planning.
Corporate Office:
See Goshen, IN

See Previous Column for important information.
Elkhart Plant Sites:
2801 East Oakland
MFR of *R5, R6*
State Road 19
MFR of *R5*
See Millersburg and Goshen, IN for other plant sites.

Elkhart
Royal Coach by Monaco, Inc.
133 Wade Drive
Elkhart, IN 46514
Tel: (219) 262-9278
FAX: (219) 264-3980
Contact: Jim Fox
MFR of *UConvs*
C-2

Elkhart
Santa Fe Vans/Shomco
21240 Protecta Drive
P.O. Box 1633
Elkhart, IN 46516
Tel: (219) 293-0585
FAX: (219) 293-7723
Contact: Joe Smucker
R4
D

Elkhart
Seven-O-Seven Automotive
25723 Pierina Drive
Elkhart, IN 46514
Tel: (219) 264-7070
FAX: (219) 262-2909
Contact: Shawna Sole
R4
D

Elkhart
Sherry Design, Inc.
53387 Ada Drive
Elkhart, IN 46514
Tel: (219) 264-0602
FAX: (219) 262-8108
Contact: Kathy Franklin
R4
D

Elkhart
Sierra Motor Corp.
4341 Pine Creek Road
Elkhart, IN 46516
Tel: (219) 293-6026
FAX: (219) 293-4659
Contact: Gloria
R4
C-1

Elkhart
Skyline Corporation, Motorized
2520 By-Pass Road
Elkhart, IN 46514
Tel: (219) 294-6521
Nation:(800)348-7469
FAX: (219) 293-0693
Contact: Donna
MFR of *R1, R2, R5, R6*
C-2
D

Elkhart
Sun-Lite, Inc./Hideaway Manufacturing Co., Inc.
(MAIL: P.O. Box 517 Bristol, IN 46507)
54635 CR 17
Elkhart, IN 46517
Tel: (219) 295-5410
Nation: (800) 327-7684
FAX: (219) 293-5236
E-Mail: sunlite@skyenet.net
Website: skyenet.net/sunlite/index.html
Contact: Mark Romanetz
MFR of *TC, R5, R6, CT*
C-2:3
D: Ideal Transport

Elkhart
Technical Space, Inc.
21075 Protecta Drive
P.O. Box 1552
Elkhart, IN 46515
Tel: (219) 293-6855
Nation: (800) 843-9747
FAX: (219) 295-7332
MFR of *Office T*

Elkhart
Tiara Motor Coach, Inc.
29618 CR 12, West
Elkhart, IN 46514
Tel: (219) 773-7947
Tel: (219) 264-6543
Nation: (800) 800-7947
FAX: (219) 266-7408
Contact: Ken Cooper
MFR of *R4*
C-2
D: Lake View Transport

Elkhart
Timber Wolf Trailers
57974 CR 3, South
Elkhart, IN 46517
Tel: (219) 522-3777
Nation: (800) 837-9653
FAX: (219) 522-7141
Contact: Neal Kinder
MFR of *Cargo T (All Sizes, From 5' x 8' to 8-1/2' x 52', including T for NASCAR transport.)*
D: Rad Transport

Elkhart
Time Out Trailers
21500 C Street
P.O. Box 2028
Elkhart, IN 46515
Tel: (219) 294-7671
FAX: (219) 294-7672
Contact: Blake Walters
MFR of *T*
B-2:1

Elkhart
Tops Plus
27908 CR 4, West
Elkhart, IN 46514
Tel: (219) 264-1314
Contact: Eldon Lovely
R4

Elkhart
Tradewinds Conversions, Incorporated
2535 Bryant Street
Elkhart, IN 46516
Tel: (219) 293-4878
Contact: Gene Willour or Chuck Willour
R4
D: Bennett, Malone, Stanley Transport

Elkhart
Travel Land Conversions
25831 Pierina Drive
Elkhart, IN 46514
Tel: (219) 264-4315
Contact: John Kime
R4
C-2
D: AG Transport

Elkhart
Travel-Line Enterprises
25876 Miner Road
Elkhart, IN 46514
Tel: (219) 264-0131
Nation: (800) 497-1385
Contact: Rocky Barbaro
MFR of *R6*

Elkhart
Travel Units, Inc.
28748 Holiday Place
P.O. Box 1833
Elkhart, IN 46515
Tel: (219) 293-8785
Contact: Jim DeGleter
MFR of *R5, R6*

Elkhart
Veri-Lite, Incorporated
4631 Pinecreek Road
P.O. Box 339
Elkhart, IN 46514
Tel: (219) 295-8313
FAX: (219) 295-6126
MFR of *TC*

Elkhart
Warwick Enterprises
1110 D I Drive
Elkhart, IN 46514
Tel: (219) 264-7511
FAX: (219) 266-5866
Contact: Keith Griffin
MFR of *A, E, H, R4, Haz-Mat TB*

Elkhart
Weber Mfg., Inc.
29251 CR 20
Elkhart, IN 46517
Tel: (219) 293-1813
FAX: (219) 294-5581
Contact: Harry Sims
MFR of *TB, U*

Elkhart
Wells Cargo, Inc.
1503 W. McNaughton
Elkhart, IN 46514
Tel: (219) 264-9661
Nation: (800) 348-7553
FAX: (219) 262-8432
Contact: Scott Samuels
MFR of *Concession T, Cargo T: Commercial & Industrial; ST*
B-2:6

Elkhart
Worldwide RV
25610 CR 4, East
Elkhart, IN 46514
Tel: (219) 264-3161
Nation: (800) 999-9939
FAX: (219) 262-3212
E-mail: 75057.1530@compuserve.com
Contact: Stewart Bailey
DLR of *R1, R2*

Elnora
Cornelius Mfg., Inc.
RR1, Box 104A
Elnora, IN 47529
Tel: (812) 636-4319
Contact: Cindy Cornelius
MFR of *T*

Evansville
Assisttech
720 N. Fonntag Avenue
Evansville, IN 47712
Tel: (812) 424-1443
FAX: (812) 424-5158
Contact: Lynn Garrett
R4, H'cap R4
C-1

Evansville
Basden Recreational Vehicle Center
1015 E. Columbia Street
Evansville, IN 47711
Tel: (812) 423-2820
FAX: (812) 423-0217
Contact: Alice Strassweg
DLR of *R1, R2*

Evansville
Kenny Kent Custom Van Outlet
4600 Division Street
Evansville, IN 47715
Tel: (812) 423-6441
Nation: (800) 844-KENT
FAX: (812) 473-6661
Contact: Ron Barley
R4
C-2:4

Evansville
Mike's Truck & Trailer Service
650 Division Street
Evansville, IN 47711
Tel: (812) 423-0386
Contact: Mike McAllister
MFR of *TB*

Evansville
Southern Indiana Van
5139 Old Bonsveille
Evansville, IN 47715
Tel: (812) 476-5826
Contact: Dave Phillips
R4

Fishers
Mid-State Truck Equip.
11020 Allisonville Road
Fishers, IN 46038
Tel: (317) 849-4903
FAX: (317) 849-6141
Contact: Phyllis Burk
FINAL ASSEMBLER of *TB*
C-2:1

Fort Wayne
Advance Mixer, Inc.
5620 Industrial Road
Fort Wayne, IN 46825
Tel: (219) 484-6691
Nation: (800) 443-6691
FAX: (219) 484-7956
Contact: Paul Ellington
MFR of *Concrete Mixer Trucks*
C-2

Fort Wayne
E-Vans, Incorporated
3505 Brooklyn Avenue
Fort Wayne, IN 46809
Tel: (219) 747-7452
FAX: (219) 747-6865
Contact: Susan Deaton
R4
C-2:10

Fort Wayne
J J R Corporation
436 E. Washington Blvd.
Fort Wayne, IN 46802
Tel: (219) 426-4461
FAX: (219) 423-2487
Contact: Chuck Dean
H'cap R4

Fort Wayne
Knox's Custom Shop
5223 Decatur Road
Fort Wayne, IN 46806
Tel: (219) 456-9632
FAX: (219) 456-4505
Contact: Gary Knox
R4
C-2:6

Fort Wayne
Special Trucks, Inc.
4930 Old Maumee Road
Fort Wayne, IN 46803
Tel: (219) 447-5572
Tel: (219) 493-1100
FAX: (219) 493-6076
Contact: Mary Lamont or Nancy Fackler
MFR/MODIFIER of *TB, Cabs, Chassis, STB*
C-2:3
D

Fort Wayne
Truck Engineering Company, Incorporated
4401 Bluffton Road
Fort Wayne, IN 46809
Tel: (219) 478-1544
FAX: (219) 478-1546
Contact: Lynn Croteau
MFR of *TB*

Goshen
Advantage Corporation
1821 Century Drive
P.O. Box 461
Goshen, IN 46526
Tel: (219) 534-2694
Nation: (800) 468-8267
Contact: Jeff Abshire
MFR of *R4*
D: 20% are driven; 80% are transported on low-boys.

Goshen
American Cargo, Inc.
64141 US Hwy. 33, S.
Goshen, IN 46526
Tel: (219) 534-2414
MFR of *FTB, M*
C-2
D: Bohren, Classic, Transport, Morgan Driveaways

Goshen
Cobra Industries/ Van American
2766 E. College Avenue
P.O. Box 124
Goshen, IN 46526
Tel: (219) 534-1418
FAX: (219) 533-2965
Contact: Rona Tanger or Peter Liegl
MFR of *R1, R2, R3, R4, R4-B, R5, R6, TC*
C-2:10
D

Goshen
Conquest
(Div of Gulf Stream, Inc.)
1701 Century Drive
Goshen, IN 46526
Tel: (219) 533-3121
HQ Tel: (219) 773-7761
Nation: (800) 284-3151
Contact: Richard Potter. Or Linda Shetterly at HQ
MFR of *R1, R2*
C-2

Goshen
Dutchman Mfg., Inc.
305 Steury Avenue
Goshen, IN 46526
Tel: (219) 534-1224
FAX: (219) 534-3095
Contact: Rick Newman
MFR of *R5, R6*
B-2 & B-3: Total of 116 drivers

Goshen
Empire Recreational Vehicles, Incorporated
2211 W. Wilden Avenue
Goshen, IN 46526
Tel: (219) 533-8464
FAX: (219) 533-8323
MFR of *R1, R2, R6*
D

Goshen
FRP Trailers
18467 US Highway 20
Goshen, IN 46526
Tel: (219) 522-1126
Nation: (800) 323-6436
FAX: (219) 522-3576
Contact: Jack Bender, Owner
MFR of *2-Ton TConvs, Cargo T*
NOTE: "800" line rings home of the owner, in Wheeling, IL -- unless he's away. Then it rings here. So use discretion.

Goshen
Kropf Manufacturing Company, Incorporated
58647 SR 15
P.O. Box 30
Goshen, IN 46526
Tel: (219) 533-2171
FAX: (219) 533-3723
MFR of *R5, R6*

Goshen
Master Fab
16681 Maple City
Goshen, IN 46526
Tel: (219) 642-3027
R4

Goshen
Medtec Ambulance Corp.
P.O. Box 821
Goshen, IN 46527
Tel: (219) 534-2631
Contact: Chuck Drake
MFR of *A*
C-2:3-4

Goshen
Mo Trailer Corporation
605 Logan Street
P.O. Box 486
Goshen, IN 46527
Tel: (219) 533-0824
Contact: David Blough
MFR of *T*
C-1

Goshen
Rockwood, Incorporated
SPECIAL INSTRUCTIONS: Prospective employees *must* apply at the Corporate Office here in Goshen. No hiring is done at plant sites, nor are tours provided. Going to the plant sites could *impair* your chances of being hired! Plant site locations are included here *only* to orient you, and to help you in your planning.

Continued from previous column...
Corporate Office:
2766 E. College Avenue
P.O. Box 124
Goshen, IN 46526
Tel: (219) 642-3041
Tel: (219) 534-1418
Tel: (219) 534-3645
FAX: (219) 533-6085
Contact: Mick Luce
MFR of *R1, R2, R5, R6*
D: Horizon Transport
Goshen Plant Sites:
1702 Century Drive
MFR of *R2*
2780 E. College Avenue
MFR of *R5, R6*
3010 E. College Avenue
MFR of *R1*
812 Logan Street
MFR of *R2*
820 Logan Street
MFR of *R5, R6*
475 Steury
MFR of *R5, R6*
See Millersburg and Elkhart, IN for other plant sites.

Goshen
Starcraft Automotive Corporation
2703 College Avenue
P.O. Box 1903
Goshen, IN 46526
Tel: (219) 533-1105
FAX: (219) 533-7180
Contact:
Kim Strausborger
or Amy Brinkerhoff,
at ext. 7207
MAJOR MFR of *R4*
C-2:5
D: Barrett Transit
NOTE: See also the listing in Topeka, IN.

Goshen
Supreme Corporation
16500 CR 38
Goshen, IN 46526
Tel: (219) 342-4888
Tel: (219) 533-0331
Nation: (800) 342-5501
Contact: Walt Miller
MFR of *TB*
C-2

Goshen
Turtle Top
118 W. Lafayette Street
P.O. Box 537
Goshen, IN 46526
Tel: (219) 533-4116
FAX: (219) 534-3719
Contact: Mary Frye
MFR of *R4, H'cap Units, U, Small Transit U*
C-1
D

Graybill
Brindle Products, Inc.
13633 David Drive
P.O. Box 227
Graybill, IN 46741
Tel: (219) 627-2156
Tel: (219) 897-2501
Nation: (800) 826-9355
FAX: (219) 627-5145
Contact: Sharon Bender
MFR of *TB, STB*
C-2

Greenfield
Monroe Custom Utility Bodies, Incorporated
3512 N. 600, West
Greenfield, IN 46140
Tel: (317) 894-8684
FAX: (317) 894-1896
Contact: Warner Monroe
MFR of *TB*
C-2:2

Greensburg
Herbert's Truck & Van
1625 N. Carver Street
Greensburg, IN 47240
Tel: (812) 663-6970
Contact: Sharon Herbert
R4

Greenwood
Stout's RV Sales, Inc.
303 Sheek Road
Greenwood, IN 46143
Tel: (317) 881-7670
Nation: (800) 255-7670
Nation: (800) 251-7670
DLR of *R1, R2*

Road Rat Heaven.
INDIANA *is the RV Capital of the World!*

Greenwood
Trustee Professional Vehicles
325 W. Wiley Street
Greenwood, IN 46142
Tel: (317) 881-7781
Contact: Jack Trustee
DLR of *Limos*

Hanover
Bulk & Transport Service
P.O. Box 28
Hanover, IN 47243
Tel: (812) 866-2155
FAX: (812) 866-5765
Contact: Phil Stanton
MFR of *TB*

Huntertown
H & H Equipment Company, Incorporated
16339 Lima Road
P.O. Box 686
Huntertown, IN 46748
Tel: (219) 637-3177
Nation: (800) 551-9341
FAX: (219) 637-3177
Contact: John L. Hawkins
MFR of *CTB*
D: Drive Away Company

Huntington
Sportsmobile, Inc.
250 Court Street
Huntington, IN 46750
Tel: (219) 356-5435
FAX: (219) 358-0328
Contact: Nancy Nix
MFR of *R4, R4-B*

Huntington
Zahm Trailer Sales
5019 W. River Road
Huntington, IN 46750
Tel: (219) 356-8322
FAX: (219) 356-8350
Contact: Janet Gordon
MFR of *HT*

Indianapolis
Ahnafield Corporation
3219 W. Washington St.
Indianapolis, IN 46222
Tel: (317) 636-8061
H'cap R4
C-1

Indianapolis
Allied Truck Equipment Corporation
4821 Massachusetts Ave.
Indianapolis, IN 46218
Tel: (317) 545-1227
Contact: Mike Schlenk
MFR of *TB*

Indianapolis
Butler Coach Company
8826 W. Washington St.
Indianapolis, IN 46231
Tel: (317) 241-0857
FAX: (317) 241-4182
Contact: Charles Butler
DLR of *Limos*

Indianapolis
Creata-Van, Incorporated
6060 E. Washington St.
Indianapolis, IN 46219
Tel: (317) 352-9330
Contact: Leo Thirion
R4, TConvs

Indianapolis
Fontaine Truck Equipment Company
2770 Bluff Road
Indianapolis, IN 46225
Tel: (317) 787-0718
FAX: (317) 787-0794
Contact: Joe Stoutner
MFR/FINAL ASSEMBLER of *M, XTB*
D

Indianapolis
General Motors Corp., Truck & Bus Division
340 S. White River Pkwy.
Indianapolis, IN 46222
Tel: (317) 269-5000
Tel: (317) 269-5934
Tel: (317) 269-5951
MFR of *GM Trucks & Busses*

Indianapolis
ICC Manufacturing Co.
1850 W. Oliver Avenue
Indianapolis, IN 46221
Tel: (317) 638-8145
FAX: (317) 632-7482
Contact: Dave Mahan
MFR of *Cabs for Off-Road Equipment*
C-2:5
D

Indianapolis
Mark's RV Sales, Inc.
9702 Pendleton Pike
Indianapolis, IN 46236
Tel: (317) 898-6676
FAX: (317) 898-6718
Contact: Jay Lucas
DLR of *R1, R2*

Indianapolis
Mobility Aids, Inc.
1233 Country Club Road
Indianapolis, IN 46234
Tel: (317) 273-6400
FAX: (317) 273-6429
Contact: Keith Conoway
H'cap R4

Indianapolis
Premiere Truck Body
610 Troy Avenue
Indianapolis, IN 46225
Tel: (317) 787-1843
Nation: (800) 258-1833
FAX: (317) 782-1744
Contact: Alice Herr
MFR/DLR of *"Premiere" TB*

Indianapolis
Ray Skillmen Luxury Vans
8424 U.S. Hwy 31, South
Indianapolis, IN 46227
Tel: (317) 888-9500
DLR of *TB, R4*
C-1

Indianapolis
TEBCO
3343 Shelby Street
Indianpolis, IN 46227
Tel: (317) 781-4089
MFR of *TB*

Indianapolis
Tillman's Sales
2323 W. 16th Street
Indianapolis, IN 46222
Tel: (317) 636-6217
DLR of *TB, R4*
C-1

Indianapolis
Truck Equipment & Body Company, Inc.
3343 Shelby Street
Indianapolis, IN 46227
Tel: (317) 787-2244
Contact: Bob White
MFR of *TB, U*

Indianapolis
Truck'n Van
5201 Madison Avenue
Indianapolis, IN 46227
Tel: (317) 783-3434
Contact: Joe Hunley
R4

Knox
Bobko Industries, Inc.
1301 W. Culver Road
Knox, IN 46534
Tel: (219) 772-6673
MFR of *Waste-hauling & Dump Trailers*
D: Transport Pool

Knox
Obrecht Trailer Mfg.
705 E. New York Street
Knox, IN 46534
Tel: (219) 772-2148
FAX: (219) 772-7100
MFR of *T*
C-1

Kokomo
Panda Vans, Inc.
5042 E. CR 00 N.S.
Kokomo, IN 46901
Tel: (317) 457-6781
Nation: (800) 752-8623
Contact: Gary Duncan
MFR of *R4*

Lafayette
Wabash National Corp.
1000 Sagamore Parkway
Lafayette, IN 47905
Tel: (317) 448-1591
MFR of *S-2*
C-2

Lagrange
L A West, Incorporated
80 W. US Hwy. 20
Lagrange, IN 46761
Tel: (219) 463-4060
Nation: (800) 786-8267
Contact: Bobbi Voirol
R4
D

Lawrenceburg
Concepts of Mobility
US 50 Hickory Lake
Lawrenceburg, IN 47025
Tel: (812) 537-5878
Nation: (800) 258-9318
FAX: (812) 537-2267
Contact: Bill Reynolds
R4
C-2:4

Martinsville
Automasters
610 Morton Avenue
Martinsville, IN 46151
Tel: (317) 342-1995
Contact: George Routh
MODIFIER of *R4*
MFR of *TC*

Middlebury
Coachmen Industries, Incorporated
423 N. Main Street
Middlebury, IN 46540
Tel: (219) 825-5821
Tel: (219) 825-8500
Ask For: Personnel Office
MFR of *R1, R2*

Middlebury
Jayco, Incorporated
58075 SR 13
Middlebury, IN 46540
Tel: (219) 825-5861
Contact: Tom Bontrager
MFR of *R1, R2*
C-1

Middlebury
Manufactured Structures Corporation
51790 CR 39
P.O. Box 159
Middlebury, IN 46540
Tel: (219) 825-9518
FAX: (219) 825-9500
MFR of *Office T*

Middlebury
Pace American, Inc.
11550 Harter Drive
Middlebury, IN 46540
Tel: (219) 825-7223
Nation: (800) 247-5767
FAX: (219) 825-7393
Contact: Bill Brooks
MFR of *T*
D

Middlebury
Shasta/Travelmaster
14489 US Highway 20
Middlebury, IN 46540
Tel: (219) 825-8555
Contact: Linda Towels
MFR of *R1, R2*
D

Middlebury
Sunnybrook RV, Inc.
11756 CR 14
Middlebury, IN 46540
Tel: (219) 825-5250
FAX: (219) 825-5433
Contact: Jim Wilson
MFR of *R1, R2*
D: *Quality Driveaway*

Middlebury
Timeless Vans
12605 Joan Drive
Middlebury, IN 46540
Tel: (219) 825-2191
Contact: Tom Mackey
R4
C-2:3

Middlebury
Woodland Park, Inc.
58074 SR 13
Middlebury, IN 46540
Tel: (219) 825-2104
MFR of *R1*
A-1, C-2
D: *Bennett, Quality, Rad*

Milford
Barth Incorporated
SR 15, South
P.O. Box 768
Milford, IN 46542
Tel: (219) 658-9401
FAX: (219) 658-4161
Contact: M.D. Umbaugh
MFR of *R1*

Millersburg
Carri-Lite/ Carriage, Incorporated
230 Wabash
P.O. Box 246
Millersburg, IN 46549
Tel: (219) 642-3622
Nation: (800) 348-2214
FAX: (219) 642-4145, at ext. 159
Contact: Dick Bender or Clarence Yoder, at ext. 150
MFR of *R1, R2, R5, R6*
B-1; C-1 & C-2:4-6
D: *Horizon (used occasionally)*

Millersburg
Rockwood, Incorporated
SPECIAL INSTRUCTIONS:
See Corporate Office in Goshen, IN. This is VERY IMPORTANT!
Millersburg Plant Sites:
201 W. Elm
(3 plants at this address)
MFR of *R5, R6*
See Elkhart and Goshen, IN for other plant sites.

Mishawaka
Cadco Manufacturing
1950 E. McKinley Ave.
Mishawaka, IN 46545
Tel: (219) 259-3211
FAX: (219) 259-3212
Contact: Leeanna Walters
MFR of *R6*

Mishawaka
Mondich Conversions
13460 McKinley Hwy.
Mishawaka, IN 46545
Tel: (219) 255-4432
Contact: James Mondich
R4

Mitchell
Carpenter Mfg.
1500 W. Main Street
P.O. Box 128
Mitchell, IN 47446
Tel: (812) 849-3131
FAX: (812) 849-5727
Contact: Dan Pearcy
MFR of *S*

Modoc
Mo-Lo Hi Tech Fiberglass, Inc.
U.S. Highway 36, West
Modoc, IN 47358
Tel: (317) 853-5105
Contact: Wallace Burkson
MFR of *Fiberglass TB*
D: *LTL Transport*

Monon
Monon Corporation
1 Water Tower Drive
Monon, IN 47959
Tel: (219) 253-6621
FAX: (219) 253-8033
Contact: Larry Beauchamp
MFR of *T, S-2*
B-1:10, B-3

Monroe
Strick Corporation
P.O. Box 277
Monroe, IN 46772
Tel: (219) 592-6121
MFR of *S-2*
D

Mooresville
Mooresville Welding Shop
220 E. Washington Street
Mooresville, IN 46158
Tel: (317) 831-2265
REPAIR of *TB, T*

Nappanee
Commercial Structures Corporation
655 N. Tomahawk
P.O. Box 225
Nappanee, IN 46550
Tel: (219) 773-7931
Tel: (219) 862-4618
Contact: David Johnson
MFR of *Office T*

Nappanee
Fairmont Homes, Inc.
502 S. Oakland
P.O. Box 27
Nappanee, IN 46550
Tel: (219) 773-7941
FAX: (219) 773-2185
MFR of *R5, U, "Tourmaster" Vehicles*

Nappanee
Franklin Coach Co., Inc.
S. Oakland
Nappanee, IN 46550
Tel: (219) 773-4106
FAX: (219) 773-4108
Contact: Steve Abel
MFR of *R1, R2*
C-2:6

Nappanee
Gulf Stream Coach, Inc.
503 S. Oakland
(County Road 7)
P.O. Box 1005
Nappanee, IN 46550
Tel: (219) 773-7761
Nation: (800) 289-8787
Contact: Linda Shetterly at ext. 3371
MFR of *R1, R2*
C-1 & C-2: Total of 70 drivers
NOTE: *See also Gulf Stream Vans/Monogram Conversions, across the street. They use the same pool of drivers.*

Nappanee
Gulf Stream Vans/ Monogram Conversions
(Div. of Gulf Stream Coach, Incorporated)
502 S. Oakland
Nappanee, IN 46550
Tel: (219) 773-4664
Nation: (800) 888-8917
Phones at HQ:
Tel: (219) 773-7761
Nation: (800) 289-8787
Contact: Mary Hartz.
Or Linda Shetterly at HQ, ext. 3371
MAJOR MFR of *R4*
C-1, C-2 (From a pool of 70 drivers who are dispatched by HQ.)

Nappanee
Newmar Corporation
355 Delaware Street
Nappanee, IN 46550
Tel: (219) 773-7791
FAX: (219) 773-2895
Contact: Dana Stickel
MFR of *R1, R2*
C-2:10

New Albany
Floyd Cornett Auto Body
4303 Charlestown Road
New Albany, IN 47150
Tel: (812) 949-2639
FAX: (812) 949-2639
Contact: Floyd Cornett
R4

New Paris
Bison Trailers
71913 CR 23
New Paris, IN 46553
Tel: (219) 831-3340
FAX: (219) 831-3611
Contact: Bruce Korenstra
MFR of *HT, LT*
C-2

- 219 -

New Paris
Terra Transit
67819 SR 15
New Paris, IN 46553
Tel: (219) 831-4341
FAX: (219) 831-4349
Contact: Virginia Miller
MFR of *U*
C-2:3
D

New Paris
Turtle Top
67895 Industrial Drive
New Paris, IN 46553
Tel: (219) 831-5680
FAX: (219) 534-3719
R4
C-2 (Locally-based drivers)
D: East & South

New Paris
Van Pro Conversions, Incorporated
67970 SR 15
P.O. Box 119
New Paris, IN 46553
Tel: (219) 831-3140
R4

Noblesville
Warner Bodies
1699 S. 8th Street
Noblesville, IN 46060
Tel: (317) 773-2100
FAX: (317) 773-1715
Contact: Ed Grines
MFR of *TB, U*
C-2:5

Orland
Quality Converters
9675 W. Maple
Orland, IN 46776
Tel: (219) 829-6541
MFR of *R4*
C-2:2

Osceola
CMR Manufacuting/Cardinal Van Convs.
10930 McKinley Hwy.
Osceola, IN 46561
Tel: (219) 679-9100
Nation: (800) 259-2252
FAX: (219) 679-9180
MFR of *R4*
C-2

Plymouth
Wiers Mfg., Inc.
2111 Jim Neu Drive
Plymouth, IN 46563
Tel: (219) 936-4076
FAX: (219) 936-9301
Contact: Kevin Bammerlin
MFR of *TB*

Rensselaer
Talbert Mfg., Inc.
1628 W. State Road 114
Rensselaer, IN 47978
Tel: (219) 866-7141
Nation: (800) 348-5232
FAX: (219) 866-5437
Contact: Davies Wakefield
MFR of *Low-Boy T, S-2*
D

Richmond
Crestliner Vans, Inc.
1325 Bridge Avenue
Richmond, IN 47374
Tel: (317) 966-1673
R4
(NOTE: Dormant at time of research. They expected to actively manufacture a 1995 model soon thereafter.)

Richmond
Royalty Vans
610 NW 2nd Street
Richmond, IN 47374
Tel: (317) 962-2741
R4

Richmond
Tom Raper RV
2250 Williamsburg Pike
Richmond, IN 47374
Tel: (317) 966-8361
Nation: (800) RAPER RV
FAX: (317) 966-8944
DLR of *R1, R2*

Rushville
Industrial Cab
310 E. 3rd Street
Rushville, IN 46173
Tel: (317) 938-1685
Contact: David Mayhan
MFR of *TB, U*
D

Rushville
Swingline Vans
966 W. 3rd Street
Rushville, IN 46173
Tel: (317) 932-3617
Contact: Tom Barnes
R4
C-2:1

Salem
Blue River Vans
RR 4, Box 331
Salem, IN 47167
Tel: (812) 883-3930
Contact: Glenda Garrison
R4

Salem
Class & Muscle Trailer Sales, Incorporated
RR 5, Box 228-A
Salem, IN 47167
Tel: (812) 883-4470
Contact: Donnie Martin
MFR of *T*
D: Trailer Transport

Schneider
Rouse Welding & Body
24031 LaVerne Drive
Schneider, IN 46376
Tel: (219) 552-9342
Within 350 miles:
(800) 257-6873
FAX: (219) 552-9345
Contact: Al Keithley
MFR of *CTB*
C-1:6-8

Shipshewana
Double Eagle Industries, Incorporated
SR 5, South
Shipshewana, IN 46565
Tel: (219) 768-4121
FAX: (219) 768-4123
MFR of *Truck Sleepers*

Shipshewana
Engineered Interiors
2675 N. 850, West
Shipshewana, IN 46565
Tel: (219) 768-7248
Contact: Steve Hostetler
TConvs

Shipshewana
KZ, Incorporated
9270 W. US Highway 20
Shipshewana, IN 46565
Tel: (219) 768-4016
Tel: (219) 825-5619
FAX: (219) 768-4017
Contact: Duane Zook
MFR of *R5, TC*

Shipshewana
Tuscany Motor Coach
9270 W. US Hwy. 20
Shipshewana, IN 46565
Tel: (219) 768-7273
FAX: (219) 768-4017
Contact: Tom Graber
MFR of *R4, Special Units*
C-2:3 (Must be based locally)

South Bend
AM General Corporation
105 N. Niles Avenue
South Bend, IN 46617
Tel: (219) 237-6222
Contact: Susan Curry
MFR of *Hummer*

Syracuse
American Road Vans
9566 N. 300, East
Syracuse, IN 46567
Tel: (219) 658-9494
FAX: (219) 658-9480
Contact: Alan Abrams
R4
C-2:2
D: Packard Transport, Cheetah

Terre Haute
Midwest RV's
10480 S. US Hwy. 41
Terre Haute, IN 47802
Tel: (812) 299-5432
Contact: Kim Smith
DLR of *R1, R2*

Topeka
Starcraft RV Inc.
536 Michigan Street
P.O. Box 458
Topeka, IN 46571
Tel: (219) 593-2550
Nation: (800) 945-4787
FAX: (219) 593-2579
Contact: Raymond Yoder
MFR of *R5, R6*

Union City
Nick's Automotive
219 S. Howard Street
Union City, IN 47390
Tel: (317) 964-6843
FAX: (317) 964-3827
Contact: Nick McEowen
MFR of *TB*
D: Continental Transport

Union City
Union City Body Company, Incorporated
1015 W. Pearl Street
Union City, IN 47390
Tel: (317) 964-3121
FAX: (317) 964-3763
MFR of *Milk TB, Bread TB, XTB*
D: Drive Away Company

Valparaiso
Classy Chassis, Inc.
1000 Axe Avenue
Valparaiso, IN 46383
Tel: (219) 462-5536
Contact: Curt Kennelly
MFR of *R4, TConvs*

Valparaiso
Landgrebe Mfg., Inc.
208 N. 250, West
Valparaiso, IN 46383
Tel: (219) 462-9587
FAX: (219) 477-2001
MFR of *T*

Vincennes
T. A. Brouillette & Son, Incorporated
2903 Old Decker Road
Vincennes, IN 47591
Tel: (812) 882-7482
Contact: Tom Brouillette
MODIFIER of *TB*

Wakarusa
Casa Villa, Inc.
200 Industrial Parkway
P.O. Box 567
Wakarusa, IN 46573
Tel: (219) 862-4531
Contact: Mike Callahan
MFR of *R6*
C-2:2 (delivers 5%)
D: Bennett Motor Express, at (219) 862-4596 (delivers 95%)

Wakarusa
Holiday Rambler Corp.
65528 SR 19
Wakarusa, IN 46573
Tel: (219) 862-7211
MFR of *R1*
C-2

Wakarusa
Travel Supreme, Inc.
66149 State Road 19
P.O. Box 610
Wakarusa, IN 46573
Tel: (219) 862-4484
Contact: Connie Troyer
MFR of *R1, R2*
C-2:3
D

Wakarusa
Utilimaster Corporation
65266 SR 19
Wakarusa, IN 46573
Tel: (219) 862-4561
Nation: (800) 582-3454
FAX: (219) 862-4517
Contact: Mike Weise
MFR of *TB*
C-2:5
D

Wakarusa
Van-Go, Incorporated
66425 SR 19
Wakarusa, IN 46573
Tel: (219) 862-2807
Nation: (800) 554-0809
Contact: Ed Tom
R4

Warsaw
Explorer Van Co.
US Highway 30, West
Warsaw, IN 46580
Tel: (219) 267-7666
Contact: Dan Alwine
MFR of *R4*
C-2:5

Winamac
Braun Corporation, The
1014 S. Monticello
Winamac, IN 46996
Tel: (219) 946-6153
Tel: (219) 946-6157
Nation: (800) THE LIFT
FAX: (219) 946-4670
Contact: Caroline Watts
MFR of *R4, H'cap R4*
C-1 & C-2: Total of 20 drivers

Zinsill
Albers Rolls Royce
360 S. 1st Street
Zinsill, IN 46077
Tel: (316) 873-2360
Contact: Greg Albers
DLR of *Limos*

IOWA

Altoona
Jim Hawk Truck Trailers
3515 Adventureland Dr.
Altoona, IA 50009
Tel: (515) 967-3800
DLR of *CT*

Altoona
Majestic Truck Body
503 First Avenue, North
Altoona, IA 50009
Tel: (515) 967-7667
REPAIR of *TB*

Ames
Kiefer Industrial
US Highway 30, West
Ames, IA 50010
Tel: (515) 292-3759
FAX: (515) 393-3763
Contact: Brent Fischer
MFR of *T*
B-2
D

Ames
Mid-America Body Co.
1613 S. Duff Avenue
Ames, IA 50010
Tel: (515) 232-0112
Nation: (800) 247-3994
FAX: (515) 232-5274
Contact: Gene Talmich
MFR of *T, V*
C-1:3

Audubon
Dura Glass Mfg. Co.
Industrial Park, Lot 2
Audubon, IA 50025
Tel: (712) 563-4606
FAX: (712) 563-4405
MFR of *Fiberglass UTB*
C-2
D

Boyden
Dethmers Mfg. Company /Demco Products
Highway 18, East
P.O. Box 189
Boyden, IA 51234
Tel: (712) 725-2311
Tel: (712) 725-2302
FAX: (712) 725-2380
MFR of *UT*
B-2

Breda
Toynes Iowa Fire Truck Service
P.O. Box 16
Breda, IA 51436
Tel: (712) 673-2328
FAX: (712) 673-2200
Contact: Roger Schwabe
MFR of *F*
C-1

Camanche
Compliment Conversions, Incorporated
1924 Washington Blvd.
Camanche, IA 52730
Tel: (319) 259-8391
Nation: (800) 747-VANS
FAX: (319) 259-8381
Contact: Tina Johnson
R4
C-1

Carroll
Wegner Mfg., Inc.
820 W. Sixth Street
Carroll, IA 55141
Tel: (712) 792-1139
Contact: Randall Wegner
MFR of *HT*
B-2

Cedar Falls
Ace Fogdall RV Center
5424 University Avenue
Cedar Falls, IA 50613
Tel: (319) 277-2641
Nation: (800) 747-0747
Contact: Jim Fogdall
DLR of *R1, R2*
A-1

Cedar Falls
Cover-Up Industries, Inc.
12811 University Avenue
Cedar Falls, IA 50613
Tel: (319) 266-9860
Contact: Sue Ayers
DLR of *HT*
B-1:1

Cedar Falls
David Herrmeyer Manufacturing Company
P.O. Box 941
Cedar Falls, IA 50613
Tel: (319) 277-8332
Nation: (800) 397-7632
FAX: (319) 277-8950
Contact: David Herrmeyer *TConvs*

Cedar Falls
R. C. Willett Co., Inc.
3040 Leversee Road
Cedar Falls, IA 50613
Tel: (319) 233-3461
FAX: (319) 233-6302
Contact: Rory Willett or Rex Willett
MFR of *R2, R6*
C-1:4-5, C-2:2

Cedar Falls
Wayne Engineering Co.
2412 W. 27th Street
Cedar Falls, IA 50613
Tel: (319) 266-1721
FAX: (319) 266-8207
MFR of *G*

Cedar Rapids
Aid-Care Medical, Inc.
1001 3rd Avenue, SE
Cedar Rapids, IA 52403
Tel: (319) 366-6109
Nation: (800) 332-5951
Contact: Kevin Conner
H'cap R4
C-1

Cedar Rapids
Cortez Truck Equipment
3760 J Street, SW
Cedar Rapids, IA 52404
Tel: (319) 366-8184
FINAL ASSEMBLER/ DLR of *TB*

Cherokee
Obeco, Incorporated
River View Drive
P.O. Box 718
Cherokee, IA 51012
Tel: (712) 225-6417
Nation: (800) 831-8187
FAX: (712) 225-2224
Contact: Tom French
MFR of *TB*
C-2:3
D

Council Bluffs
Jim Hawk Truck Trailers
2917 S. 9th
Council Bluffs, IA 51501
Tel: (712) 366-2241
DLR of *T*

Council Bluffs
Leach Camper Sales
1629 West S. Omaha Bridge Road
Council Bluffs, IA 51501
Tel: (712) 366-2581
FAX: (712) 366-2584
Contact: Ed Leach
DLR of *R1, R2*

Council Bluffs
Omaha Standard, Inc.
2401 W. Broadway
Council Bluffs, IA 51501
Tel: (712) 328-7444
Nation: (800) 343-5010
FAX: (712) 328-8383
Contact: Randy Rolse
MFR of *TB*

Cresco
Alum-Line Mfg., Inc.
P.O. Box 51
Cresco, IA 52136
Tel: (319) 547-3247
Contact: Don Gooder or Gary Gooder
MFR of *TB, U*

Cresco
Featherlite Trailers
Erickson Industrial Park
Cresco, IA 52136
Tel: (319) 547-4725
MFR of *HT, LT, XT, Flatbed S-2*
NOTE: *2 plants in this location, and a third one will be open in January, 1995. Phone rings in the main office of these Cresco, IA facilities. See also the HQ information, in Cresco/Davis Corners, IA. It is best to start the application process by contacting Brent Helickson at that site.*

Cresco/Davis Corners
Featherlite Trailers
Jct. Hwy. 9 & Hwy. 63 (Davis Corners)
Cresco, IA 52136
Tel: (319) 547-6000
Nation: (800) 800-1230
Contact: Brent Helickson
COMPANY HQ and **DISTRIBUTION SITE** for *HT, LT, XT, Flatbed S-2*
B-2:15
(Drivers deliver the T using company-owned tow vehicles.)

Davenport
Cresci Body & Equipment, Inc.
1809 W. River Drive
Davenport, IA 52802
Tel: (319) 322-0991
FINAL ASSEMBLER of *TB*

Davenport
Jim Hawk Truck Trailers, Incorporated
3424 W. River Drive
Davenport, IA 52802
Tel: (319) 324-7818
DLR of *T, S-2*

Davenport
OK Welding & Machine, Incorporated
424 N. Division Street
Davenport, IA 52802
Tel: (319) 323-7020
Contact: Lyle Kammer
MFR of *T*

Davenport
Prince Vans
1136 W. 2nd Street
Davenport, IA 52802
Tel: (319) 323-4143
Contact: Mel Smith
MFR of *R4*

Davenport
Riverside International Trucks, Incorporated
2160 W. River Drive
Davenport, IA 52802
Tel: (319) 323-9743
Contact: John Mravanac
DLR of *TB, U*

Des Moines
Autorama RV Center, Incorporated
2227 SE 14th Street
Des Moines, IA 50320
Tel: (515) 282-0443
Nation: (800) 227-0443
FAX: (515) 282-1425
DLR of *RVs: All Types*

Des Moines
Brady Truck & Equipment Co., Inc.
1414 SE 30th Street
Des Moines, IA 50317
Tel: (515) 262-0959
Tel: (515) 262-4114
FAX: (515) 262-9024
Contact: Larry Brady
MFR of *CTB, M*

Des Moines
Central Trailer Service
1910 E. Euclid Street
Des Moines, IA 50316
Tel: (515) 266-3158
Tel: (515) 266-3191
DLR of *S-2*

Des Moines
Cold Metal Mfg. Limited
3051 104th Street, #B
Des Moines, IA 50322
Tel: (515) 278-8183
MFR of *CT*

Des Moines
Mid-State RV
4106 NE 14th Street
Des Moines, IA 50313
Tel: (515) 262-0821
Contact: Jerry Verschuure
DLR of *RVs: All types*

Des Moines
Mobile Auto Glass of Iowa, Incorporated
125 College Avenue
Des Moines, IA 50314
Tel: (515) 244-4259
R4

Des Moines
Sandler Medical Services, Incorporated
1244 6th Avenue
Des Moines, IA 50314
Tel: (515) 244-4236
Nation: (800) 234-4236
FINAL ASSEMBLER of *H'cap Units*

Des Moines
Thomas Bus Sales of Iowa, Incorporated
5636 NE 14th Street
Des Moines, IA 50313
Tel: (515) 265-6056
Nation: (800) 362-2092
FAX: (515) 265-6590
DLR of *U*

Des Moines
Truck Equipment, Inc.
1560 NE 44th Avenue
Des Moines, IA 50313
Tel: (515) 266-5189
Nation: (800) 373-2887
FAX: (515) 266-7878
Contact: Greg Schwaller
DISTRIBUTOR of *TB*

Des Moines
United Truck & Body
5129 NE 17th Street
Des Moines, IA 50313
Tel: (515) 266-5148
Nation: (800) 322-5148
FAX: (515) 266-5140
FINAL ASSEMBLER of *Semi Sleeper Cabs*

Elma
M & J Trailers Unlimited, Inc.
P.O. Box 479
Elma, IA 50628
Tel: (515) 393-2103
FAX: (515) 393-2511
Contact: Mel Smith
FINAL DETAILER/DLR of *"Featherlite" T B-2*
NOTE: *See also the data for Featherlite Trailers, in Cresco, IA.*

Farley
Simon's Fire Equipment
207 3rd Street, NW
Farley, IA 52046
Tel: (319) 744-3217
Contact: Ilene Simon
MFR of *F*

Forest City
Winnebago Industries, Incorporated
605 W. Crystal Lake Rd.
Forest City, IA 50436
Tel: (515) 582-3535
FAX: (515) 586-6808
Contact: Marcia Geris
MFR of *R1, R2*
D: Morgan Driveaway

Fort Madison
Freuhauf Trailer Corp.
2597 Highway 61, South
P.O. Box 248
Fort Madison, IA 52627
Tel: (319) 463-5411
FAX: (319) 463-6136
MFR of *T, Enclosed Van S-2*
NOTE: *This is one of 3 Fruehauf plant sites. See HQ listing in Detroit, MI.*

Garner
Iowa Mold Tooling Company, Incorporated
500 Highway 18, West
Garner, IA 50438
Tel: (515) 923-3711
FAX: (515) 923-2424
Contact: Dorcey Schaffer
MFR of *TB*
D: IMT Transport

Garner
Stellar Industries, Inc.
280 W. 3rd Street
Garner, IA 50438
Tel: (515) 923-3741
MFR of *"Stellar Shuttles", UTB, T*

George
Sudenga Industries, Inc.
2002 Kingbird Avenue
George, IA 51237
Tel: (712) 475-3301
FAX: (712) 475-3320
Contact: Doug Pecken
or Randy Riecks
MFR of *Feed TB*

Guttenburg
Kann Manufacturing
231 N. 3rd Street
Guttenburg, IA 51051
Tel: (319) 252-2035
FAX: (319) 252-3069
Contact: Jim Niehaus
MFR of *Recycling TB, Grain TB*

Hayfield
Hayfield Industries, Inc.
Main Street
Hayfield, IA 50438
Tel: (515) 923-2991
Contact: Arlon Nedved
MFR of *UTB, XTB*

Humboldt
Born Free Motorcoach, Incorporated
Highway 169, North
P.O. Box B
Humboldt, IA 50548
Tel: (515) 332-3755
Nation: (800) 247-1835
FAX: (515) 332-3756
Contact: Michelle McKenna
DLR of *R1, R2*
C-2:20

Humboldt
Jet Co., Inc., Steel & Plastics
1303 N. 13th Street
Humboldt, IA 50548
Tel: (515) 332-3117
Nation: (800) 332-3117
FAX: (515) 332-5092
Contact: Dale Heider
MFR of *Grain T*
D

Humeston
K & S Mfg., Inc.
319 Fletcher Street
Humeston, IA 50123
Tel: (515) 877-6551
Contact: Kenny Kline
MFR of *R1, R2*

Indianola
Freuhauf Trailer Corp.
1700 N. 14th Street
Indianola, IA 50125
Tel: (515) 961-6604
FAX: (515) 961-6752
MFR of *Refrig. S-2*

Iowa City
Vic's Auto Body Repair
1514 Willow Creek Drive
Iowa City, IA 52246
Tel: (319) 337-2993
Contact: Bill Zend
R4

Kanawha
Kiefer Built, Inc.
305 E. 1st Street
P.O. Box 88
Kanawha, IA 50447
Tel: (515) 762-3201
FAX: (515) 762-3425
MFR of *HT*
B-1:3

Lenox
JT Industries, Inc.
P.O. Box 70
Lenox, IA 50851
Tel: (515) 333-4518
FAX: (515) 333-4429
Contact: Tom Campbell
MFR of *Farm Equipment*
C-1:1
D

Manly
Van Shack
Highway 9
Manly, IA 50456
Tel: (515) 454-2363
FINAL ASSEMBLER
of *H'cap Units*

Mount Pleasant
Blue Bird - Midwest
Highway 34, West
P.O. Box 180
Mount Pleasant, IA 52641
Tel: (319) 385-2231
FINAL ASSEMBLER
of *S*

Nashua
Featherlite Mfg.
69 Maple Street
Nashua, IA 50658
Tel: (515) 435-4123
FAX: (515) 435-4323
MFR of *HT, LT, UT, Flatbed S-2*
C-2:6-8
D
NOTE: *It is best to apply by contacting Brent Helickson at HQ, in Cresco/Davis Corners, IA. See that listing for full information.*

New Hampton
Zip's Truck Equip., Inc.
316 W. Milwaukee
New Hampton, IA 50659
Tel: (515) 394-3166
Nation: (800) 222-6047
FAX: (515) 394-4044
Contact: John Kuhn
DISTRIBUTOR of *W*
C-2:11

New Hartford
Towboy Custom Built Trailers
RR 1
New Hartford, IA 50660
Tel: (319) 346-1033
Contact: LaVonne Edwards
MFR of *T*

Osage
Van World, Inc.
1326 E. Main Street
Osage, IA 50461
R4

Osceola
Mac-Lander, Inc.
925 Furnas Drive
Osceola, IA 50213
Tel: (515) 342-6036
FAX: (515) 342-3508
Contact: Mark Dinning
MFR of *TB, T*

Ottumwa
Steve's Custom Vans
RR 6
Ottumwa, IA 52501
Tel: (515) 684-5643
Contact: Steve Bell
R4

Pocahontas
E. R. Buske Mfg., Inc.
Hwy. 3, East
P.O. Box 129
Pocahontas, IA 50574
Tel: (712) 335-3585
FAX: (712) 335-4797
Contact: Chuck Muske
MFR of *W*
C-2: Several

Quimby
Simonsen Mfg. Co.
P.O. Box 247
Quimby, IA 51049
Tel: (712) 445-2211
FAX: (712) 445-2626
Contact: Rich Raznsborg
MFR of *TB*
C-1:1
D

Riverside
Thomann Welding, Inc.
RR 1
Riverside, IA 52327
Tel: (319) 648-2553
Contact: Larry Thomann
MFR of *T*

Rock Rapids
Rock Rapids Repair
320 S. 2nd Avenue
Rock Rapids, IA 51246
Tel: (712) 472-3924
MFR of *UT, LT, CT*

Schaller
Hawkeye Eagle Transport
303 E. 1st Street
Schaller, IA 51053
Tel: (712) 275-4224
FAX: (712) 275-4100
MFR of *T*

Sheldon
Maintainer Corporation
1701 S. 2nd Avenue
P.O. Box 349
Sheldon, IA 51201
Tel: (712) 324-5001
Tel: (712) 324-4511
FAX: (712) 324-3526
MFR of *UTB*

Shellsburg
Shellsburg Welding
109 Pearl Street, NE
Shellsburg, IA 52332
Tel: (319) 436-2259
REPAIR of *TB, T*

Sioux City
Condon Motor Co.
3200 Highway 75, North
Sioux City, IA 51105
Tel: (712) 252-2741
Nation: (800) 852-0006
Contact: Chuck Condon
DLR of *FTB*

Sioux Center
Service Trucks International, Ltd.
877 1st Avenue, NW
Sioux Center, IA 51250
Tel: (712) 722-3711
Nation: (800) 225-8789
FAX: (712) 722-3706
Contact: John Hazeman
MFR of *TB, Cranes*
C-1

Sioux City
Marx Trailer Sales
2420 4th Street
Sioux City, IA 51101
Tel: (712) 252-4337
DLR of *Cargo T*

Sioux City
*Wilson Trailer Company/
Chamberlain Trailer*
4400 S. Louis Blvd.
Sioux City, IA
51106-9600
Tel: (712) 943-3424
FAX: (712) 943-6510
MFR of *LT*

Sumner
*Four-H Trailer
Manufacturing, Inc.*
RR 1, Box 13-B
Sumner, IA 50674
Tel: (319) 578-5175
MFR of *T*

Sumner
Life Line Emergency
701 N. Railroad Street
Sumner, IA 50674
Tel: (319) 578-3317
MFR of *A*

Swea City
*Fibre Body Industries,
Incorporated*
404 4th Avenue, West
Swea City, IA 50590
Tel: (515) 272-4372
Nation: (800) 252-4372
FAX: (515) 272-4218
Contact: Bill Wolf
MFR of *Fiberglass TB*
C-2:2
D

Tripoli
Fabricated Products Co.
RR 1
P.O. Box 251
Tripoli, IA 50676
Tel: (319) 882-4409
Contact: Elmer Tonne
MFR of *R6*

Waterloo
Low Rider Trailers
2573 Logan Avenue
Waterloo, IA 50703
Tel: (319) 236-2352
Contact: Tom
Barthalamew
MFR of *T*

Waterloo
School Bus Sales Co.
4537 Texas Street
Waterloo, IA 50702
Tel: (319) 296-1363
Nation: (800) 772-2414
FAX: (319) 296-3023
Contact: Charles Andrews
DLR of *S*
C-2: Part-time drivers
(All deliveries are made
within Iowa.)

Waverly
Cedar Lane Products
1402 4th Street, SW
Waverly, IA 50677
Tel: (319) 352-1332
Contact: Janette Henricks
MFR of *TC*

Webb
Hart Welding & Mfg.
RR 1, Box 74
Webb, IA 51366
Tel: (712) 838-4488
Contact: Ray Hart
or Clarice Hart
MFR of *T*
B-1

Wellman
Starline Corporation
6th Avenue & 6th Street
Wellman, IA 52356
Tel: (319) 646-2964
Contact: Patrick Curl
MFR of *R4*
C-1

KANSAS

Baxter Springs
Trail-Boss, Incorporated
1150 W. 5th
Baxter Springs, KS 66713
Tel: (316) 856-2760
MFR of *T*

Belleville
*Mid-America Truck
Equipment*
Highway 81
Belleville, KS 66935
Tel: (913) 527-2293
FAX: (913) 527-7152
Contact: Steve Anderson
MFR of *T*

Chanute
Custom Campers, Inc.
Route 1, W. 21st Street
P.O. Box 965
Chanute, KS 66720
Tel: (316) 431-3990
FAX: (316) 431-7746
Contact: Ginger Lynch
MFR of *R5*
D: Ferritt Transport

Chanute
Nu Wa Industries, Inc.
4002 Ross Lane
P.O. Box 808
Chanute, KS 66720
Tel: (316) 431-2088
FAX: (316) 431-7909
Contact: Lana Lamasters
MFR of *R5*
A-1

Chanute
Young's Welding, Inc.
4115 Johnson Road
Chanute, KS 66720
Tel: (316) 431-2199
Contact: Becky Smith
MODIFIER of *T*
B-2

Cherryvale
Inkan Industries
RR 2
Cherryvale, KS 67335
Tel: (316) 336-3691
Contact: Bob Sandborn
MFR of *TB*

Clearwater
*Clearwater Truck
& Tractor*
232 W. Ross Avenue
Clearwater, KS 67026
Tel: (316) 584-2273
REPAIR of *Trucks*

Colby
L-M Steel & Mfg.
1130 Plains Avenue
Colby, KS 67701
Tel: (913) 462-8216
MFR of *TB, U*

Emporia
*Dieker RV Sales
& Service*
1521 Road 175
Emporia, KS 66801
Tel: (316) 342-6456
DLR of *R1, R2*

Galena
Zodiac Industries, Inc.
724 W. 7th Street
Galena, KS 66739
Tel: (316) 783-5041
Contact: John Gilmore
MFR of *R4*

Great Bend
*Glass King Mfg.
Company, Incorporated*
P.O. Box 614
Great Bend, KS 67530
Tel: (316) 793-7838
Contact: Leroy Herrman
MFR of *Tanker TB,
Tanker S-2*
C-2:1

Great Bend
*Guthrie Trailer Sales,
Incorporated*
N. Main Street
Highway 281
Great Bend, KS 67530
Tel: (316) 793-5418
MFR of *T*

Great Bend
*Western Truck
Equipment Company*
1310 10th Street
Great Bend, KS 67530
Tel: (316) 793-8464
FAX: (316) 793-5630
Contact: Ray Modaer
MFR of *TB, U*

Hays
Steel Fabrications
E. Highway 40
Hays, KS 67601
Tel: (913) 625-3075
Contact: Chris Brull
MFR of *T*

Hays
*Vernie's
Trux-n-Equipment*
I-70 & Highway 183
Hays, KS 67601
Tel: (913) 625-5087
Contact: Darryl Unrein
MFR/DLR of *Flatbed T*

Hillsboro
Circle D Corporation
613 N. Ash Street
Hillsboro, KS 67063
Tel: (316) 947-2385
FAX: (316) 947-2609
Contact: Wendell Dirk
MFR of *T*

Hillsboro
Hillsboro Industries, Inc.
220 Industrial Road
Hillsboro, KS 67063
Tel: (316) 947-3127
Nation: (800) 835-0209
Contact: Brenda Keith
MFR of *HT*

Hutchinson
Collins Ambulance Corp.
Route 2, Box 2828
Hutchinson, KS 67504
Tel: (316) 663-4441
MFR of *A*

Hutchinson
*Collins Professional
Cars, Incorporated*
P.O. Box 2799
Hutchinson, KS 67504
Tel: (316) 662-9000
Contact: Ken Stocker
MFR of *H, Limos*
D

Independence
*Hackney & Sons
Midwest, Incorporated*
300 Hackney Avenue
Independence, KS 67301
Tel: (316) 331-6600
Contact: Larry Kimble
MFR of *TB, U*
C-2
D

Junction City
Horizons, Incorporated
2323 N. Jackson
Junction City, KS 66441
Tel: (913) 238-7575
Nation: (800) 235-3140
FAX: (913) 238-4992
Contact: Mike Eenhuis
MFR of *R6*

Kansas City
F & S Truck & Equipment
I-35 & Lamar
Kansas City, KS 66106
Tel: (913) 262-9400
MFR of *TB*

Kansas City
Garsite Products, Inc.
539 S. 10th Street
Kansas City, KS 66105
Tel: (913) 342-5600
Nation: (800) 645-5802
FAX: (913) 342-0638
FAX: (913) 342-3444
Contact: Pete Lavac
MFR of *Aircraft Refuelling TB, Tanker TB, Liquid-Handling TB*
A-1, B-3

Kansas City
Kansas City Peterbilt, Incorporated
1212 N. 3rd Street
Kansas City, KS 66101
Tel: (913) 321-1122
FAX: (913) 321-3267
DLR of *Peterbilt S-1*

Kansas City
Tri-State Tank Co.
636 S. Adams Street
Kansas City, KS 66105
Tel: (913) 342-7749
FINAL ASSEMBLER of *Tanker TB*

Lawerence
Brown Cargo Van
807 E. 29th Street
Lawerence, KS 66046
Tel: (913) 842-6506
Nation: (800) 255-6827
FAX: (913) 842-0314
MFR of *VTB, XTB*

Liberal
Liberal Truck Service
S. Highway 83
Liberal, KS 67901
Tel: (316) 624-5688
Nation: (800) 657-6077
FAX: (316) 624-5680
Contact: Lyn Hansen
DLR of *Heavy Trucks*
D

Ludell
Country Trailer Sales
RR 2, Box 47
Ludell, KS 67744
Tel: (913) 626-9200
Contact: Merlin Green
DISTRIBUTOR of *HT, LT*
D

Marysville
Landoll Corporation
1700 May
Marysville, KS 66508
Tel: (913) 562-5381
Nation: (800) 426-5655
Contact: Marsha Robinette
MFR of *TB*
C-2

McPherson
Kit Manufacturing Co.
1000 Kit Blvd.
P.O. Box 586
McPherson, KS 67460
Tel: (316) 241-4320
FAX: (316) 241-6689
Contact: E. J. Anderson
MFR of *R5, R6*
D: Morgan Driveaway

Minneapolis
Honorbuilt Industries, Incorporated
1200 W. 10th Street
P.O. Box 266
Minneapolis, KS 67467
Tel: (913) 392-2171
Nation: (800) 342-6234
FAX: (913) 392-3440
Contact: Leroy Bartley
MFR of *R1, R2*
C-2
NOTE: *Formerly El Dorado RV. Drivers are required to live within 1 hour's drive of the plant. Best opportunity at the time they were contacted was for part-time work.*

Minneapolis
Kirn-Kraft/ Top Craft Manufacturing
107 N. Concord Street
Minneapolis, KS 67467
Tel: (913) 392-2214
Tel: (913) 392-2857
MFR of *TC*

Moundridge
Jantz-Femco, Inc.
1 East 1/2 North
Moundridge, KS 67107
Tel: (316) 345-6387
Contact: John Meyer
MFR of *CT*

Murdock
Maverick Manufacturing
RR 1, Box 30
Murdock, KS 67111
Tel: (316) 297-3941
Contact: Bob Smith
MFR of *T*

Newton
Fiberglass Spreader, Inc.
1418 Cow Palace Road
Newton, KS 67114
Tel: (316) 283-1086
Contact: Robert Coleman
MFR of *TB*
D

Olathe
Beverage Transportation Equipment
15525 S. Keele
Olathe, KS 66062
Tel: (913) 764-6800
Nation: (800) 255-6199
Contact: Mike Hawkins
DLR of *V*
D

Olathe
Croft Trailer Supply
750 N. Rogers Road
Olathe, KS 66062
Tel: (913) 780-1818
Contact: Mike Dosk
MFR of *T*

Olathe
RB Mfg. Co.
1301 W. Dennis Avenue
Olathe, KS 66061
Tel: (913) 829-3233
FAX: (913) 829-3297
Contact: Fran DeNoon
MFR of *TB*
D

Olathe
Wheatland Vehicle Conversions
425 S. Kansas Avenue
Olathe, KS 66061
Tel: (913) 780-3757
Contact: John Waller
R4
C-2

Osborne
Wilkens Mfg., Inc.
778 S. 161st Avenue
Osborne, KS 67473
Tel: (913) 346-2041
MFR of *S-2*

Oswego
Diamond Coach Corp.
2300 W. 4th Street
P.O. Box 489
Oswego, KS 67356
Tel: (316) 795-2191
FAX: (316) 795-4816
Contact: Dick Seybolt
MFR of *R1, R2, H'cap R1*
C-2:3
D

Ottawa
Ottawa Truck Corp.
415 E. Dundee Street
Ottawa, KS 66067
Tel: (913) 242-2200
FAX: (913) 242-8573
Contact: Joe Hughes
MFR of *Yard Trucks*
D

Overland Park
Freightliner Corporation
9225 Indian Creek Pkwy.
Suite 850
Overland Park, KS 66210
Tel: (913) 451-8626
MFR of *S-1*

Paola
Rigid Form, Inc.
Route 5, Lookout Road
P.O. Box 38
Paola, KS 66071
Tel: (913) 294-4466
FAX: (316) 294-6084
Contact: Anthony Curtis
MFR of *TC*
C-2:4

Quinter
Quinstar Products, Inc.
P.O. Box 424
Quinter, KS 67752
Tel: (913) 754-3355
Contact: Marion Mandeville
MFR of *T, S-2*

Rozel
Blattner Mfg. Co.
RR 1, Box 7
Rozel, KS 67574
Tel: (316) 527-4318
Contact: Stan Blattner
MFR of *T*

Russell
King of the Road
553 S. Front Street
P.O. Box 553
Russell, KS 67665
Tel: (913) 483-2138
Nation: (800) 255-0521
FAX: (913) 483-4973
Contact: Andy Kuhn
MFR of *R5, R6*

Sabetha
Triple C Manufacturing
Route 4, Box 4-A
Sabetha, KS 66534
Tel: (913) 284-3674
MFR of *FTB*

Salina
Eldora Bus-E B Company, Inc.
304 E. Avenue B
Salina, KS 67401
Tel: (913) 827-1033
Contact: Earl Hanchett
MFR of *U*
C-2

Salina
Jim Patterson Enterprises
1745 N. 9th
Salina, KS 67401
Tel: (913) 827-4682
Contact: Jim Patterson
MODIFIER of *Trucks*
D

Shawnee
All Automotive Handicapped Systems
6224 Merriam Lane
Shawnee, KS 66203
Tel: (913) 432-0632
Contact: Paul Sullivan
MFR of *H'cap R4*

Shawnee Mission
Contract Specialists
12425 W. 92nd Street
Shawnee Mission, KS 66215
Tel: (913) 599-2088
MFR of *Bloodmobiles, Mammography-mobiles*

Shawnee Mission
Navistar International Corporation
4551 W. 107th Street
Shawnee Mission, KS 66207
Tel: (913) 383-8868
MFR of *Navistar S-1*
D

Smith Center
Peterson Industries, Inc.
RR 2, Box 95
E. Hwy 36
Smith Center, KS 66967
Tel: (913) 282-6825
FAX: (913) 282-3810
Contact: Michael Nebel
MFR of *R5, R6*

South Hutchinson
Collins Industries, Inc.
415 W. 6th Street
South Hutchinson, KS 67505
Tel: (316) 663-5551
FAX: (316) 663-1630
Contact: Donald Collins
MFR of *TB, U*
D

Tonganoxie
Erectors & Fabricators, Incorporated/ Tom-Go Trailer Mfg.
314 Village Terrace
Tonganoxie, KS 66086
Tel: (913) 845-3333
FAX: (913) 845-9118
MFR of *T*
B-2:1
D

Topeka
Healo Truck Body
704 NE US Hwy. 24
Topeka, KS 66608
Tel: (913) 235-5604
REPAIR of *S, U*

Topeka
JD Custom Vans
302 SE 21st Street
Topeka, KS 66607
Tel: (913) 232-1777
R4

Topeka
Re Max RV
4118 NE Seward Avenue
Topeka, KS 66616
Tel: (913) 235-5900
Contact: Tom Meyer
DLR of *R1, R2*
D

Waterville
Liberty, Incorporated
P.O. Box H
Waterville, KS 66548
Tel: (913) 363-2252
MFR of *T*

Wichita
Copeland International Trucks, Incorporated
1770 N. Broadway Street
Wichita, KS 67214
Tel: (316) 262-8413
Contact: John Garrison
DLR/REPAIR of *S-2*
C-2

Wichita
Gran Van
11950 E. Kellogg Drive
Wichita, KS 67207
Tel: (316) 685-1230
Contact: Lee Schell
TConvs

Wichita
Schott's Custom Coach, Incorporated
3838 W. 31st, South
Wichita, KS 67217
Tel: (316) 943-2600
R4

Wichita
Truck Parts & Equipment, Inc.
4501 Esthner Street
Wichita, KS 67209
Tel: (316) 942-4251
Nation: (800) 362-2600
FAX: (316) 942-3184
Contact: Winston Abraham
MFR of *TB, U*

Wichita
Vim Trailer Mfg.
2811 N. Ohio Street
Wichita, KS 67219
Tel: (316) 838-4233
FAX: (316) 838-6783
Contact: Mike Barker
MFR of *S-2*
D

KENTUCKY

Allen
May Metal Products, Inc.
Route 1428
Allen, KY 41601
Tel: (606) 874-9411
Contact: Donald May
MFR of *TB*

Allen
R & S Truck Body Co.
P.O. Box 420
Allen, KY 41601
Tel: (606) 874-2151
FAX: (606) 874-9136
MFR of *TB*
D

Ashland
Blue Grass Van Depot
7505 Midland Trail Road
Ashland, KY 41102
Tel: (606) 928-5246
R4

Ashland
Omni Sales & Service, Incorporated
806 Hood's Creek Pike
Ashland, KY 41101
Tel: (606) 329-1306
DLR of *Industrial Cleaning Trucks*
D: Seigal

Bowling Green
Bowling Green Truck & Trailer
805 Lehman Avenue
Bowling Green, KY 42101
Tel: (502) 781-6295
DLR of *S-1*

Bowling Green
D-J's Upholstery
723 College Street
Bowling Green, KY 42101
Tel: (502) 842-3825
Contact: Jerry Tarance
MODIFIER of *R4*

Bowling Green
Rhodes Fabricators
150 Dishman Lane
Bowling Green, KY 42101
Tel: (502) 842-6886
MFR of *TC*

Bowling Green
Summers Professional Coach Sales, Inc.
319 Lowe Avenue
P.O. Box 70217
Bowling Green, KY 42101
Tel: (502) 782-9209
Nation: (800) 882-3833
Contact: Jim Summers
DLR of *R1, R2*

Bowling Green
Trailer World, Inc.
800 Three Springs Road
Bowling Green, KY 42104
Tel: (502) 782-2833
Nation: (800) 872-2833
FAX: (502) 781-8221
Contact: Tom Neblet
DLR of *T*
B-2:1

Butler
Jay Gee, Incorporated
Boston Road
Route 2, Box 181
Butler, KY 41006
Tel: (606) 472-7511
FAX: (606) 472-7522
Contact: James Pape at (606) 472-7523
MODIFIER of *TB*
C-2:2 Full-time

Calhoun
Muster Associates
P.O. Box 160
Calhoun, KY 42327
Tel: (502) 273-5474
FAX: (502) 273-3964
Contact: John Muster
DLR of *Limos*
A-1, C-1:7

Corbin
Owens Mfg. Co.
602 18th Street
Corbin, KY 40701
Tel: (606) 528-2330
FAX: (606) 528-3137
Contact: Kim Gentry
MFR of *TB, U*

Dry Ridge
Ohio Truck Body Mfg.
US Route 25
Dry Ridge, KY 41035
Tel: (606) 428-3700
FAX: (606) 428-1318
Contact: David Foster
MFR of *TB, U*

Edgewood
Summit Fire Apparatus
11 Sperti Drive
Edgewood, KY 41017
Tel: (606) 331-0360
Contact: Joe Messmer
REPAIR of *Rescue and Fire Vehicles*

Elizabethtown
Cole Industries
6269 N. Dixie Highway
Elizabethtown, KY 42701
Tel: (502) 737-5659
Contact: Greg Bryan
MFR of *Truck Cabs*
C-2

Fulton
Waymatic Company
5320 Ken-Tenn Highway
Fulton, KY 38257
Tel: (502) 472-2804
FAX: (502) 479-0008
MFR of *Concession T*

Henderson
Hercules Manufacturing
Hercules Drive
P.O. Box 497
Henderson, KY 42420
Tel: (502) 826-9501
Nation: (800) 633-3031
FAX: (502) 826-0439
Contact: Theresa Eblen
MFR of *TB*
D

Henderson
Herron's Van-World
2101 S. Green Street
Henderson, KY 42420
Tel: (502) 827-9586
Contact: Mike Herron
R4

Leichfield
Leichfield Truck & Equipment
514 N. Main
Leichfield, KY 42754
Tel: (502) 259-5555
FAX: (502) 259-3525
DLR/FINAL ASSEMBLER of *TB, T*

Lexington
Conrad Custom Center
3715 Nicholasville Road
Lexington, KY 40503
Tel: (606) 271-8267
FAX: (606) 271-8194
Contact: Tom Jefferson
R4

Lexington
Morton & Davis Truck Bodies
981-B Beasley Street
Lexington, KY 40509
Tel: (606) 254-6490
Contact: Sonny Morton
MFR of *HT*
B-2:1

Lexington
Thoroughbred Van Conversions, Inc.
285 Southland Drive
Lexington, KY 40503
Tel: (606) 278-0550
Nation: (800) 272-2858
Contact: Bill Clark
R4

Lexington
Trailblazers Performance Centers, Incorporated
1100 New Circle Rd., NE
Lexington, KY 40505
Tel: (606) 231-7484
FAX: (606) 231-9321
Contact: Berry Sanders
R4
C-2
D

Lexington
Van Stop
1226 Versailles Road
Lexington, KY 40508
Nation: (800) 635-9437
H'cap R4
NOTE: *See also their Fairfield, OH site.*

Lexington
Van Tech
2512 Palumbo Drive
Lexington, KY 40509
Tel: (606) 269-3236
FAX: (606) 268-4779
Contact: Bruce Reck
R4

Lexington
Wait's A Sales & Service
2200 Higbee Mill Pike
Lexington, KY 40514
Tel: (606) 223-4559
FAX: (606) 223-1007
Contact: Ray Wait
R4

Lexington
Watkins Rustproofing
597 New Circle Rd., NE
Lexington, KY 40505
Tel: (606) 293-5736
Contact: Keith Hatton
R4, TConvs

London
K & W Vans, Inc.
1811 County Farm Road
London, KY 40741
Tel: (606) 864-6087
Contact: Kenneth Kenney
R4

Louisville
AAT-Pro Tint, Inc.
6200 Preston Highway
Louisville, KY 40219
Tel: (502) 966-3700
Contact: Mindy Manning
R4

Louisville
Algonquin Place
1520 Algonquin Parkway
Louisville, KY 40210
Tel: (502) 636-4072
Contact: William Bevill
MODIFIER/MFR of *T*

Louisville
B & W Chairlift, Inc.
8013 Ashbottom Road
Louisville, KY 40213
Tel: (502) 367-0189
CONVERTER of *R4, H'cap R4*
REBUILDER of *A*

Louisville
Cambron Horse Trailers
11600 Blue Lick Road
Louisville, KY 40229
Tel: (502) 955-6763
MFR of *HT*

Louisville
Cee-Jee Truck & Vans
4020 Dixie Highway
Louisville, KY 40216
Tel: (502) 448-2562
Contact: Chris O'Neill
R4

Louisville
Custom Built Trailers, Incorporated
12817 Dixie Highway
Louisville, KY 40272
Tel: (502) 935-4331
MFR of *T*

Louisville
Dealer's Truck Equipment, Inc.
12000 Westport Road
Louisville, KY 40223
Tel: (502) 426-6623
FAX: (502) 426-5213
MODIFIER of *Trucks*
D

Louisville
Fontaine Modification
11400 Westport Road
Louisville, KY 40241
Tel: (502) 426-5450
FAX: (502) 426-5210
Contact: Ron Waldec
MODIFIER of *TB*
D

Louisville
Funeral Auto Company
724 Cawthon Street
Louisville, KY 40203
Tel: (502) 584-1185
MFR of *H*

Louisville
G. M. Peterson/ C. Kenworthy, Inc.
4330 Poplar Level Road
Louisville, KY 40213
Tel: (502) 459-1200
FAX: (502) 458-4688
Contact: David Essinger
DLR of *TB*
C-2

Louisville
J. Edinger & Son, Inc.
1012 Story Avenue
Louisville, KY 40206
Tel: (502) 584-3524
Contact: Charles Edinger
MFR of *TB, U*

Louisville
Kentucky Mfg. Co.
2601 S. 3rd Street
Louisville, KY 40208
Tel: (502) 637-2551
Contact: Larry Hartog
MFR of *T*

Louisville
Rockwell International Corporation
4004 Collins Lane
Louisville, KY 40245
Tel: (502) 423-8676
Contact: Michael J. Stich
MFR of *TB, U*

Louisville
Stuff For Vans
3912 Fern Valley Road
Louisville, KY 40219
Tel: (502) 964-1919
MODIFIER of *R4, TB*

Louisville
*Superior Van
Conversions*
4734 Rockford Plaza
Louisville, KY 40216
Tel: (502) 447-0559
Tel: (502) 447-8255
(Office)
Contact: Joe Shroat
R4

Louisville
The Van House
4018 Preston Highway
Louisville, KY 40213
Tel: (502) 363-6000
Contact: Vicki Boswell
R4

Middlesboro
Kirby Steel Products Inc.
S. 23rd S. Industrial Park
Middleboro, KY 40965
Tel: (606) 248-2701
REPAIR/MODIFIER
of *TB*

Murray
*Trucks, Trailers,
and Busses*
US Route 641, South
Murray, KY 42071
Tel: (502) 753-1372
Region: (800) 626-5484
(350 mile radius)
FAX: (502) 753-5773
Contact: Jack Foley
DLR of *Light-Duty GMC
Vehicles*

Owensboro
*Brown's Valley Truck
Equipment, Inc.*
US Highway 431
Owensboro, KY 42301
Tel: (502) 733-4322
FAX: (502) 733-9222
Contact: Jessie Vellar
MFR of *TB*

Russell Springs
*Bean's Truck Body
Manufacturing Co.*
1326 Highway 910
Russell Springs, KY
42642
Tel: (502) 866-3809
Contact: Gary Cain
MFR of *Cattle TB*

Russellville
Hayes Trailer Sales
842 Hopkinsville Road
Russellville, KY 42276
Tel: (502) 726-7034
Nation: (800) 766-7034
DLR of *T*
A-1

South Shore
*Quality Motor Coach
Division*
US Highway 23
South Shore, KY 41175
Tel: (606) 932-4000
FAX: (606) 932-9002
Contact: Bill Hays
R4

Stanford
J. W. Cherry
Highway 27 North
Stanford, KY 40484
Tel: (606) 365-9121
FAX: (606) 365-2269
Contact: J.W. Cherry
MFR of *TB, U*
D

LOUISIANA

Alexandria
Accurate
P.O. Box 1231
Alexandria, LA 71309
Tel: (318) 445-8624
FAX: (318) 473-1893
Contact: Tom
Kaltenbaugh
MFR of *Solid Waste
Equipment, TB*
D

Alexandria
*Ross Bus & Equipment
Sales, Inc.*
2913 N. Bolton Avenue
Alexandria, LA 71303
Tel: (318) 443-6011
Contact: Bruce Ross
DLR of *S*

Baton Rouge
Blanchard Trailer Sales
6632 Airline Highway
Baton Rouge, LA 70805
Tel: (504) 355-4449
Contact: Hoyt Adcock
DLR of *R1, R2*
*D: Barrett, Morgan
Driveway*

Baton Rouge
Camper City
16538 Florida Blvd.
Baton Rouge, LA 70819
Tel: (504) 272-9857
Nation: (800) 256-5196
FAX: (504) 275-6407
Contact: Jerry Forrest
or Jay Forrest
DLR of *R1, R2*
C-2

Baton Rouge
*Constantin Transit
Vehicles/Constantin
Handicapped Vehicles*
2001 Wooddale Blvd.
Baton Rouge, LA 70806
Tel: (504) 926-2403
FAX: (504) 923-1108
Contact: Patty Young
MFR of *A, H'cap R4*

Baton Rouge
*Dealer's Truck
Equipment Co., Inc.*
7878 S. Choctaw Drive
Baton Rouge, LA 70815
Tel: (504) 926-1070
FAX: (504) 928-0969
Contact: Kenneth Johnson
DLR of *TB*

Baton Rouge
*Eddie Edwards Bus
Sales, Incorporated*
13031 S. Choctaw Drive
Baton Rouge, LA 70815
Tel: (504) 272-8550
FAX: (504) 272-8563
Contact: Devin Edwards
MFR of *U*

Baton Rouge
Miller's RV Center
12912 Florida Blvd.
Baton Rouge, LA 70815
Tel: (504) 275-2940
FAX: (504) 275-6807
Contact: Carol Miller
DLR of *R1, R2*
C-2

Baton Rouge
Peterbilt of Louisiana
5255 Airline Highway
Baton Rouge, LA 70805
Tel: (504) 356-1321
Contact: Pat Albrect
MFR of *TB, U*

Baton Rouge
The RV Shop, Inc.
13326 S. Choctaw Drive
Baton Rouge, LA 70815
Tel: (504) 272-7230
FAX: (504) 272-8000
Contact: Jerald Vince
REPAIR of *R1, R2*

Bossier City
Van City
2650 Barksdale Blvd.
Bossier City, LA 71112
Tel: (318) 747-1220
Contact: Jerry Guillot
R4

Houma
Dan-O Graphics
3204 E. Park Avenue
Houma, LA 70363
Tel: (504) 868-4777
Contact: Danny Theriog
R4

Jefferson
*Truck & Transportation
Equipment Co., Inc.*
(MAIL: P.O. Box 10455
New Orleans, LA 70181)
260 Industrial Avenue
Jefferson, LA 70121
Tel: (504) 834-8065
DLR of *TB, T*

Lafayette
Champion Conversions
704 W. Gloria Switch Rd.
Lafayette, LA 70507
Tel: (318) 896-4799
FAX: (318) 232-0007
Contact: John Podoba
R4
C-2

Lafayette
RV Sales of Lafayette
3008 Cameron
Lafayette, LA 70506
Tel: (318) 232-1941
Nation: (800) 960-4433
FAX: (318) 233-1147
Contact: Keith
Phivodeaux
DLR of *R1, R2*
C-2

Lake Charles
*Truck & Trailer
Equipment Co., Inc.*
5321 Opelousas Street
Lake Charles, LA 70601
Tel: (318) 433-0620
Nation: (800) 256-1472
FAX: (318) 436-2874
FAX: (318) 436-2875
Contact: Robert
McDowell
**MFR/FINAL
ASSEMBLER** and
REPAIR of *TB, T, S-2*

Lake Charles
UTEC
(Utility Truck
Equipment Company)
1432 Broad Street
Lake Charles, LA 70601
Tel: (318) 436-3692
Nation: (800) 356-8832
FAX: (318) 436-3697
Contact: Phillip Guzzino
MFR of *TB, T*

Mamou
United Enterprises
1504 Cajun Drive
Mamou, LA 70554
Tel: (318) 468-5731
FAX: (318) 468-5731
Contact: Barry Granger
MFR of *T*
B-2

Metairie
Crescent Vans, Inc.
2424 Hickory Avenue
Metairie, LA 70003
Tel: (504) 738-2634
FAX: (504) 738-2663
Contact: James Scott
H'cap R4
C-2:3

Monroe
Scott Truck & Tractor Company
1000 US Hwy. 165
By-Pass
Monroe, LA 71201
Tel: (318) 387-4160
FAX: (318) 388-9278
Contact: Diane Huffty
MFR of *TB, U*
C-2

Montgomery
Bear Trailer Mfg. Co.
State Highway 122
Montgomery, LA 71454
Tel: (318) 646-3829
MFR of *Logging T*

New Iberia
Gosnell Dutch Mfg.
HC 182, East
New Iberia, LA 70560
Tel: (318) 365-6617
Nation: (800) 256-1464
FAX: (318) 367-3611
Contact: Allen Gosnell
MFR of *T*

New Orleans
Bonomolo Sedans, Vans & Limos
1401 Lafitte Street
New Orleans, LA 70112
Tel: (504) 523-5466
RENTAL of *R4, Limos*

Pineville
Han-D-Cap Wheels of Louisiana
150 Smith Street
Pineville, LA 71601
Tel: (318) 487-8467
Contact: Roger L. Peters
CONVERTER of *H'cap Units*

Shreveport
Handicap Services, Inc.
1820 Kings Highway
Shreveport, LA 71103
Tel: (318) 226-0935
Nation: (800) 737-7655
MODIFIER *of H'cap Units*

Shreveport
Southwest Sales & Mfg. Company, Inc.
1050 Joseph Street
Shreveport, LA 71107
Tel: (318) 227-2822
LA only: (800) 824-1654
Nation: (800) 426-1666
FAX: (318) 227-2842
Brake & Natural Suspensions
C-2
D

West Monroe
North Louisiana Van & Truck Specialties
308 Cryer Street
West Monroe, LA 71291
Tel: (318) 325-8719
FAX: (318) 388-4766
Contact: Mike Battaglia
TConvs

MAINE

Auburn
Maine Mobility Systems
415 Rodman Road
Auburn, ME 04210
Tel: (207) 777-3400
Contact: Everette Bachand
R4

Farmington
Nichols Welding & Trailer Manufacturing
Route 24, Box 5056
Farmington, ME 04938
Tel: (207) 779-5261
MFR of *T*

Gray
Kassbohrer of North America, Incorporated
P.O. Box 1270
Gray, ME 04039
Tel: (207) 657-3326
FAX: (207) 657-4362
Contact: Hazen McMullen
DLR of *U*

South Portland
Hews Company, Inc.
190 Rumery Street
South Portland, ME 04106
Tel: (207) 767-2136
Nation: (800) 234-4397
FAX: (207) 767-5381
MFR of *TB, U*
C-2:2

Thorndike
Bryant Steel Works, Inc.
RFD 2, Box 1470
Thorndike, ME 04986
Tel: (207) 568-3663
Contact: Ken Mccue
MFR of *TB*

Topsham
Coastal Metal Fabrication, Inc.
P.O. Box 458
Topsham, ME 04086
Tel: (207) 729-5101
FAX: (207) 729-8782
Contact: Debbie Joudrey
MFR of *TB*

Union
B. M. Clark Co., Inc.
Route 17, Box 185
Union, ME 04862
Tel: (207) 785-4411
FAX: (207) 785-4414
MFR of *CTB*

MARYLAND

Annapolis
Truck Accessories of Maryland
104 Defense Highway
Annapolis, MD 21401
Tel: (410) 841-5012
Nation:(800) 542-5444
Contact: Steve Chait
R4

Baltimore
Adscom Corporation
4225 Eastern Avenue
Baltimore, MD 21224
Tel: (410) 522-6700
FAX: (410) 376-0235
Contact: Chris Capizzi
R4
D: Anchor Motor Freight

Baltimore
Bedco Mobility, Inc.
6300 Falls Road
Baltimore, MD 21209
Tel: (410) 825-1440
Nation: (800) 825-1440
Contact: Joe Scott
R4
C-2:6-8
D

Baltimore
C C Auto Glass & Upholstery
2213 Reisterstown Road
Baltimore, MD 21217
Tel: (410) 523-4500
Contact: John Lee
R4

Baltimore
E. Lehnert & Sons, Inc.
7655 Pulaski Highway
Baltimore, MD 21237
Tel: (410) 866-2100
FAX: (301) 866-1711
Contact: David Odelski
DISTRIBUTOR of *TB*
C-2:2

Baltimore
G M Corporation/ Truck & Bus Group
2122 Broenig Highway
Baltimore, MD 21224
Tel: (410) 631-2000
Contact: Donald Wilson
MFR of *Vans*

Baltimore
Herman Born & Sons, Incorporated
6801 Rolling Mill Road
Baltimore, MD 21224
Tel: (410) 288-0500
Contact: R.W. Born
MFR of *Armored Cars*

Baltimore
Van Stuff
4404 Washington Blvd.
Baltimore, MD 21227
Tel: (410) 247-5077
Contact: Jim Bonwell
R4

Capital Heights
Division Transportation Systems
9151 Hampton Overlook
Capital Heights, MD 20743
Tel: (301) 499-1000
FAX: (301) 499-5529
Contact: Gary Walker
R4
C-2:3

Centreville
Centreville Tag-A-Long Trailers, Inc.
Jct. of Routes 301 & 304
P.O. Box 20
Centreville, MD 21617
Tel: (410) 758-1333
Nation: (800) 638-7745
FAX: (410) 758-1345
Contact: Robert Legj
MFR of *CT*
B-2:1
D: Rodeway

Eldersburg
Donna Morgan Trailer Sales
200 Bennett Road
P.O. Box 633
Eldersburg, MD 21784
Tel: (410) 795-2898
FAX: (301) 795-6140
Contact: Donna Morgan
DLR of *HT*
B-2:20-25

Ellicott City
Fed-Er-Line Truck Bodies, Incorporated
(Div. of Atlantes Vans)
8261 Baltimore National Pike
P.O. Box 633
Ellicott City, MD 21043
Tel: (410) 465-2600
MFR of *CTB, TB*

Finksburg
Bulldog Trailer Mfg.
3927 Sykesville Road
Finksburg, MD 21048
Tel: (410) 549-1621
MFR of *T*

Frederick
Grand Prix Trailer Manufacturers
4800 Ballenger Creek Rd.
Frederick, MD 21701
Tel: (301) 622-0616
MFR of *T*

Gaithersburg
C & C Industries, Inc.
8255 Beechcraft Avenue
Gaithersburg, MD 20879
Tel: (301) 921-0014
FAX: (301) 921-1055
Contact: Ron Crupi
MFR of *T*

Glen Burnie
Jim Donnie's Van Conversion
1126 Crain Hwy., North
Glen Burnie, MD 21061
Tel: (410) 766-5509
R4

Hagerstown
Customizers, Inc.
14133 Pennsylvania Ave.
Hagerstown, MD 21742
Tel: (301) 797-7727
Contact: Jane Logston
R4

Hagerstown
Truck-N-Van
135 E. Franklin Street
Hagerstown, MD 21740
Tel: (301) 791-3488
Contact: Mike Todd
R4, TConvs

Hancock
Fleetwood Travel Trailers of Maryland
35 South Street
Hancock, MD 21750
Tel: (301) 678-5521
Nation: (800) 638-3706
FAX: (301) 678-7103
MFR of *R5, R6*

Hyattsville
Earle Shankle, Inc.
5200 46th Avenue
Hyattsville, MD 20781
Tel: (301) 699-8500
FAX: (301) 927-1554
Contact: John Heck
MFR of *TB*

Laurel
Perone Performance Products Company
10128 Washington Blvd.
Laurel, MD 20707
Tel: (410) 792-7577
FAX: (410) 304-3848
Contact: John Perone
DLR of *T*

Leonardtown
D & G Kustom Specialties
Route 5
Leonardtown, MD 20650
Tel: (301) 475-3808
FAX: (301) 475-2942
Contact: David Hall
R4

McHenry
Custom Services Ltd.
Route 219
McHenry, MD 21541
Tel: (301) 746-8805
Contact: Melanie Snyder
CONVERTER of *Suburbans*

Queenstown
B & L Upholstery & Vans
205 Bell Point Drive
Queenstown, MD 21658
Tel: (410) 827-5062
Contact: Linda Rodsky
R4

Rockville
Ironsides Mobility Systems
1050 1st Street, #A
Rockville, MD 20850
Tel: (301) 279-5855
Contact: Barry Stigers
H'cap R4

Silver Spring
Bedco Mobility, Inc.
2317 Distribution Circle
Silver Spring, MD 20910
Tel: (301) 585-0700
Nation: (800) 825-1760
FAX: (301) 587-0530
Contact: Tom O'Neil
H'cap R4

Silver Spring
Burlex International
P.O. Box 6094
Silver Sping, MD 20906
Tel: (301) 460-4444
FAX: (301) 871-2973
Contact: James Croker
DLR of *Armored Cars*

Silver Spring
Culp Welding & Machine Co., Inc.
937 Selim Road
Silver Spring, MD 20910
Tel: (301) 588-5700
FAX: (301) 588-5873
Contact: Kimberly Bristol
MFR of *TB*

Waldorf
Fancy Van's Speed
Waldorf Square Business Center
Waldorf, MD 20603
Tel: (301) 843-0342
Contact: Dave McVeigh
R4

Waldorf
Trick Truck III
2870 Old Washington Rd
Waldorf, MD 20601
Tel: (301) 843-9244
Contact: Larry Wekley
R4
C-2:2

Westminster
Leister's Body Shop
735 N. Gorsuch Road
Westminster, MD 21157
Tel: (410) 848-4404
Contact: Earl Utz
MFR of *TB*

Williamsport
Fleetwood Travel Trailers of Maryland
35 South Street
P.O. Box 459
Williamsport, MD 21795
Tel: (301) 223-5300
MFR of *R5, R6*
C-2

Woodsboro
Turtle Top, Inc.
10822-B Woodsboro Rd.
P.O Box 160
Woodsboro, MD 21798
Tel: (301) 845-8070
Contact: Steve Augustine
MFR of *H'cap R4*

MASSACHUSETTS

Abington
McKinley Auto & Truck Body
123 Centre Avenue
Abington, MA 02361
Tel: (617) 878-1588
REPAIR of *TB*

Attleboro
Curtis Motors, Inc.
650 Washington Street
Attleboro, MA 02703
Tel: (508) 761-5200
FAX: (508) 761-8403
Contact: Dennis Kozhenek
R4

Attleboro
Liberty Coach, Inc.
78 Eddy Street
Attleboro, MA 02703
Tel: (508) 226-3382
FAX: (508) 226-7218
Contact: Loe Fontaine
H'cap R4

Billerica
New England Wheels, Incorporated
3 Dunham Road
Billerica, MA 01821
Tel: (508) 663-9724
Nation: (800) 886-9247
FAX: (508) 663-6709
Contact: Jack Dwyer
H'cap R4
C-2:5
D: Venevia Enterprises

Boston
Columbia Truck Body Company
5 Claflin Street
Boston, MA 02210
Tel: (617) 482-7703
REPAIR of *TB*

Brimfield
Silvaline
Route 20
Brimfield, MA 01010
Tel: (413) 245-6856
FAX: (413) 245-6856
Contact: Bill Dinjgman
R4, H'cap R4
C-1
D: Larson's Towing

- 230 -

Burlington
National Van Sales, Inc.
119 Muller Road
Burlington, MA 01803
Tel: (617) 674-2343
FAX: (617) 861-7987
Contact: Steve Kotzen
DLR of *R4, A*
C-2:2
D: Venevia Enterprises

Chelsea
Massachusetts Truck Body & Trailer, Inc.
60 Arlington Street
Chelsea, MA 02160
Tel: (617) 889-2115
REPAIR of *TB, T*

Haverhill
Royale Limousine
99 Newark Street
Haverhill, MA 01832
Tel: (508) 374-4530
Nation: (800) 544-5587
FAX: (508) 521-5425
Contact: Lynn Harding
MFR of *Limos*
C-2:2
D

Hyannis
Ziggy's Auto Specialties
832 Bearses Way
Hyannis, MA 02601
Tel: (508) 771-3171
Contact: William Barron
R4

Lynnfield
Eastern Technologies, Limited
7 Kimball Avenue
Lynnfield, MA 01941
Tel: (617) 246-5000
Contact: Ann Marie Klowers
NOTE: *This is the HQ of a major vehicle mfr. No manufacturing is done here. The company uses about 10-15 drivers. Applications must be submitted here. (See North Andover, MA for the plant data.)*

Kingston
Kingston Trailers, Inc.
136 Wapping Road
Route 106
Kingston, MA 02364
Tel: (617) 585-4337
FAX: (617) 585-7135
Contact: Joe Lanoue
MFR of *HT*
B-2:2

Malden
Boston Steel & Mfg. Co.
490 Eastern Avenue
Malden, MA 02148
Tel: (617) 324-3000
MFR of *Tanker TB*

Medford
Lacey Truck Equip., Inc.
50 Mystic Avenue
P.O. Box 87
Medford, MA 02155
Tel: (617) 396-2880
Nation: (800) 660-2880
FAX: (617) 396-8457
Contact: Laurie Lacey
DISTRIBUTOR of *TB*

Milford
Trubilt Truck Body Company, Incorporated
132 Central Street
Milford, MA 01757
Tel: (508) 473-0340
FAX: (508) 634-3353
Contact: Richard Wellman
MFR of *TB*

Millbury
Handicap Conversion Vans, Incorporated
Route 146
Millbury, MA 01527
Tel: (508) 865-9973
H'cap R4

Milton
Cote Coachworks of New England, Inc./ Coach & Carriage
17 Canton Avenue
Milton, MA 02916
Tel: (617) 696-6700
FAX: (617) 696-1248
R4

North Andover
Eastern Technologies, Limited
2350 Turnpike Street
North Andover, MA 01845
Tel: See Lynnfield, MA listing.
MFR of *A, E, F, Water TB, Tanker TB, Lube TB, Runway Foam TB, Aircraft Service TB, Refuelling TB. All mfd. at this site.*
A-2, A-3, C-2 (Total of 10-15 drivers)
NOTE: *Application must go through HQ. See Lynnfield, MA.*

Norton
Quality Coach Builders Corporation
355 Old Colony Road
Norton, MA 02766
Tel: (508) 226-8550
FAX: (805) 226-3702
Contact: Brian Duffy
R4, H'cap R4
C-1
D

Peabody
New England Trailer Equipment
271 Newbury Street
Peabody, MA 01960
Tel: (508) 535-1200
FAX: (508) 535-7821
Contact: Peter Noonan
DLR/REPAIR of *T*

Pittsfield
Lenco Industries, Inc.
61 Downing Industrial Park
P.O. Box 668
Pittsfield, MA 01201
Tel: (413) 443-7359
FAX: (413) 445-7865
Contact: Len Light
MFR *of Armored Trucks*
D: Hot Shot

Quincy
New England Livery Sales & Service
86 Sumner
Quincy, MA 02169
Tel: (617) 770-3566
Nation: (800) 696-6066
RENTAL of *Limos*
C-2:12

Rutland
Sims Mfg Co., Inc.
E. Main Street
Route 120-A
Rutland, MA 01543
Tel: (508) 886-6116
Nation: (800) 225-7290
FAX: (508) 886-6713
Contact: Barry Ratcliffe
MFR of *S-1 Cabs*
D: Rodeway, Yellow

Saugus
Van-Go, Incorporated
110 Frank Bennett Hwy.
Saugus, MA 01906
Tel: (617) 231-1000
Contact: David Lanpert
R4

Somerville
J. A. Kiley Company
15 Linwood Street
Somerville, MA 02143
Tel: (617) 776-0344
FAX: (617) 776-6061
Contact: Margret Murphy
MFR of *STB*
C-2

Somerville
Schertzer Equipment Company, Incorporated
32 Prospect Street
Somerville, MA 02143
Tel: (617) 666-9100
FAX: (617) 666-9102
DLR of *T*

Springfield
Hodge Manufacturing Company, Incorporated
55-57 Fisk Avenue
Springfield, MA 01107
Tel: (413) 781-6800
MFR of *G*

Wakefield
Nevlen Company, Inc.
96 Audubon Road
Wakefield, MA 01880
Tel: (617) 245-2433
Contact: Jim Capomaccio
MFR of *T*

Waltham
New England Transit Sales
131 Linden Street
Waltham, MA 02154
Tel: (617)894-9877
DLR of *S, U*
C-2

Walpole
Boston Trailer Mfg.
Production Road
Walpole, MA 02081
Tel: (508) 668-2242
Contact: Bill Antoine
MFR of *T*

West Springfield
Just Rite Auto Trim
27 Heywood Avenue
West Springfield, MA 01089
Tel: (413) 732-1398
FAX: (413) 732-5009
Contact: Alan Vadanis
R4

Woodville
Farrar Company, Inc.
Winter Street
Woodville, MA 01784
Tel: (508) 435-3431
FAX: (508) 435-0250
MFR of *TB*

Worcester
Tri-State Ladder & Scaffolding
26 Colton Street
Worcester, MA 01610
Tel: (508) 754-3030
FAX: (508) 831-9992
Contact: David Wauczanski
R4

Worcester
Worcester Truck Body Company, Incorporated
323 SW Cutoff
Worcester, MA 01604
Tel: (508) 752-2313
Contact: Doris Dufault
REPAIR of *T*

MICHIGAN

Alpena
Big Jim's Sports Unlimited
3137 US Hwy. 23, South
Alpena, MI 49707
Tel: (517) 356-4141
Contact: Shairleen Edgley
DLR of *T*

Auburn Hills
Commuter Conversion, Incorporated
1021 Doris Road
Auburn Hills, MI 48326
Tel: (810) 538-4200
Nation: (800) 874-4032
FAX: (810) 583-7717
Contact: Ken Sieloff
R4

Auburn Hills
*Roamer Corporation
(Div. of R.W. Blanchard Company, Incorporated)*
2740 Auburn Road
Auburn Hills, MI 48326
Tel: (810) 853-9790
MFR of *Luxury TC*

Battle Creek
Ewing Motor Home & Trailer Sales
4251 W. Columbia
Battle Creek, MI 49017
Tel: (616) 965-0597
Nation: (800) 221-7198
DLR of *T*

Bay City
Freedom Driving Aids, Incorporated
901 Salzburg Avenue
Bay City, MI 48706
Tel: (517) 895-9733
Contact: Mark Rosebush
*R4, H'cap R4
C-2:4*

Benton Harbor
Bonnie's Van Masters-RV's-Vans
2500 Territorial Road
Benton Harbor, MI 49022
Tel: (616) 925-2805
FAX: (616) 925-0125
Contact: Bonnie Beilman
R4

Berrien Center
Scarlett Auto Body
7979 Dean's Hill
Berrien Center, MI 49102
Tel: (616) 461-4197
Contact: Jim Scarlett
R4

Brown City
Xplorer Motor Homes
3950 Burnsline Road
Brown City, MI 48416
Tel: (810) 346-2771
FAX: (810) 346-3553
Contact: Bobette Raymond
*R4
C-2:3-5*

Cassopolis
Double Duty Sales & Conversions
56830 Penn Road
Cassopolis, MI 49031
Tel: (616) 445-3763
Nation: (800) 235-7517
FAX: (616) 445-3763
Contact: Roxie Horrall
DLR of *HT
D*

Centreville
Viking Recreational Vehicles
580 W. Burr Oak Street
P.O. Box 549
Centreville, MI 49032
Tel: (616) 467-6321
Nation: (800) 368-2829
FAX: (616) 467-6021
Contact: Lester Leister
MFR of *R6, TC
C-2*

Charlotte
Coachland, Incorporated
3361 Lansing Road
Charlotte, MI 48813
Tel: (517) 645-7474
Contact: Richard Leder
UConvs

Charlotte
Spartan Motors, Inc.
1000 Reynolds Road
Charlotte, MI 48813
Tel: (517) 543-6400
FAX: (517) 543-7728
FAX: (517) 543-7729
Contact: Peter Forrol
MFR of *Chassis for Motor Homes
C-2*

Clayton
Rathbun Custom Trailers
5791 Demings Lake Road
Clayton, MI 49235
Tel: (517) 436-6297
Contact: Bill Rathbun
MFR of *T*

Clinton Township
Dunright Trailer Manufacturing, Inc.
35083 Cordelia
Clinton Township, MI 48035
Tel: (810) 791-1830
MFR of *T*

Colon
Riverside Vans, Inc.
57951 N. Farrand Road
Colon, MI 49040
Tel: (616) 432-3212
R4

Colon
Vanguard Industries of Michigan, Incorporated
31450 W. M-86
P.O. Box 802
Colon, MI 49040
Tel: (616) 432-3271
MFR of *Pop-up Camping Trailers
B-2:6*

Columbiaville
Gemco
4800 River Street
P.O. Box 86
Columbiaville, MI 48421
Tel: (810) 793-6223
FAX: (810) 793-6279
Contact: George Witt
MFR of *UT, R6, TC
D*

Constantine
Cabriolet
67351 US Hwy. 131, S.
P.O. Box 337
Constantine, MI 49042
Tel: (616) 435-8475
FAX: (616) 435-8377
Contact: Larry Gangrich
MFR of *W
C-2:2
D: Morgan Transport*

Detroit
American Van, Inc.
15775 Telegraph
Detroit, MI 48239
Tel: (313) 255-6226
FAX: (616) 255-7930
Contact: Mike Binder or Chuck Binder
*R4
A-2*

Detroit
Benlee Trailers
12030 Pleasant Street
Detroit, MI 48217
Tel: (313) 842-8100
Nation: (800) 521-4620
MFR/DLR of *T
B-1*

Detroit
Blec Manufacturing & Service Company, Inc.
14380 Ilene Street
Detroit, MI 48238
Tel: (313) 834-2172
FAX: (313) 834-6820
MFR of *U*

Detroit
Custom Vans
16100 Puritan Street
Detroit, MI 48227
Tel: (313) 272-3822
R4

Detroit
Detroit Wrecker Sales
19800 Fitzpatrick
Detroit, MI 48228
Tel: (313) 835-8700
Nation: (800) 527-5103
Nation: (800) 332-4465
FAX: (313) 273-9267
Contact: Betty Farrell
DLR of *W
C-1*

Detroit
*Fruehauf Trailer Corp.
(MAIL: P.O. Box 33238
Detroit, MI 48232)*
10900 Harper Avenue
Detroit, MI 48213
Tel: (810) 948-1300
Tel: (810) 948-1457
(Traffic Department)
Nation: (800) 521-9118
Tel: (314) 822-1113
(Sales & Distribution Office, St. Louis, MO)
FAX: (810) 746-9931 (In Human Resources Dept.)
Contact: Greg Sehr, Traffic Controller.
MFR of *TB, S-2, CT, ST*
NOTE: *This is the HQ. See also the Plant sites in Fort Madison, IA, Omaha, NE (LBT,Inc.), and Huntsville, TN.*

- 232 -

Detroit
G M Corp./Truck-Bus Group
601 Puquette Street
Detroit, MI 48202
Tel: (313) 974-3553
Contact: Beth Webster
MFR of *Truck Chassis*

Detroit
General Motors Corp.
3044 W. Grand Blvd.
Detroit, MI 48202
Tel: (313) 556-5000
MFR of *T*

Detroit
Hulet Body Company
8578 Witt Street
Detroit, MI 48209
Tel: (313) 842-5400
FAX: (313) 842-8780
Contact: Dee Letvin
MFR of *CTB*

Detroit
Mack Trailer Mfg. Co.
6630 Strong Street
Detroit, MI 48211
Tel: (313) 924-0700
MFR of *T, S-2*

Detroit
Michigan Horse Transportation
11652 Rockland
Detroit, MI 48239
Tel: (313) 937-3363
MFR of *HT*

Detroit/Allen Park
Oleynik Body Company
(MAIL: P.O. Box 438
Allen Park, MI 48101)
853 S. Dix
Detroit/Allen Park, MI 48217
Tel: (313) 841-6308
FINAL ASSEMBLER of *TB*

Dutton
Truck & Trailer Specialties
6726 Hanna Lake Road
Dutton, MI 49316
Tel: (616) 698-8215
FAX: (616) 698-0972
Contact: Ann Bowman or Terry Fuller
MFR/CONVERTER of *T, TB*
C-2
D

Edwardsburg
Georgie Boy Mfg. Inc.
69950 M-62
Edwardsburg, MI 49112
Tel: (616) 663-3415
Nation: (800) 521-8733
FAX: (616) 663-2065
Contact: Joe Wickey
MFR of *R1*

Edwardsburg
LER Industries, Inc.
19475 US Route 12, East
Edwardsburg, MI 49112
Tel: (616) 641-7763
Nation: (800) LER-VANS
FAX: (616) 641-7469
Contact: Bob McCartney
MFR of *R4*
C-2

Erie
Truck I Body & Frame, Incorporated
685 La Voy Road
Erie, MI 48133
Tel: (313) 848-2055
REFURBISHER/REPAIR of *TB*

Farmington Hills
Douglas & Lomason Co.
24600 Hallwood Court
Farmington Hills, MI 48335-1671
Tel: (810) 478-7800
Nation: (800) 521-4524
FAX: (810) 478-5189
NOTE: *Only prototype TB & T are built here. However, this is the HQ of 23 mfg. plants located throughout the USA. Three of these manufacture vehicles: see Columbus, GA, Amory, MS, and Kansas City, MO. (All other plants make parts only, so are not applicable.)*

Flat Rock
General Trailer South
25249 Telegraph
Flat Rock, MI 48134
Tel: (313) 782-0733
FAX: (313) 782-2380
Contact: Frank Krawzzek
DLR of *R1*

Flint
General Motors Truck & Bus Manufacturing
2238 W. Bristol Road
Flint, MI 48553
Tel: (810) 236-0470
MFR of *TB, U*

Flint
General Motors Truck & Bus Manufacturing
63100 Van Slyke Road
Flint, MI 48507
Tel: (810) 236-0450
MFR of *TB, U*

Flint
Jursik Truck Equipment
G-2199 W. Hill Road
Flint, MI 48507
Tel: (810) 238-0100
Nation: (800) 589-9100
FAX: (810) 238-2444
Contact: Tom Jiles at (313) 868-8700
TConvs

Grand Rapids
Auto-Masters
6521 S. Division Avenue
Grand Rapids, MI 49548
Tel: (616) 455-4510
Contact: Ralph Bos
R4

Grand Rapids
Clock Conversions
4301 Stafford Ave., SW
Grand Rapids, MI 49548
Tel: (616) 534-1344
Contact: Bob Venema
R4
C-2:3

Grand Rapids
HME
1950 Byron Center Avenue, SW
Grand Rapids, MI 49509
Tel: (616) 534-1463
FAX: (616) 534-1967
Contact: Craig McCullough
MFR of *TB for F*

Grand Rapids
Hoekstra Truck
260 36th Street, SE
Grand Rapids, MI 49508
Tel: (616) 241-6664
Contact: Ken Kuiper
MFR of *TB*
C-2:6

Grand Rapids
Michigan Motor Sales
590 28th Street, SW
Grand Rapids, MI 49509
Tel: (616) 530-0555
Contact: Ken Nyenhuis
R4

Grand Rapids
Michigan Trailer Parts, Incorporated
4044 S. Division Avenue
Grand Rapids, MI 49548
Tel: (616) 534-4965
Contact: Randy Groneman
R4

Grand Rapids
Woodland International Trucks, Incorporated
215 Hall Street, SW
Grand Rapids, MI 49507
Tel: (616) 241-4656
FAX: (616) 241-0813
Contact: Robert Bush
MFR of *STB*
C-2:2

Grosse Ile/Trenton
Eagle Industrial Truck Manufacturing
9510 Groh Road
Grosse Ile, MI 48138
Tel: (313) 671-8181
FAX: (313) 671-6257
MODIFIER of *Ford Trucks*

Harper Woods/Detroit
Custom Van Enterprises, Incorporated
20932 Harper
Harper Woods, MI 48225
Tel: (313) 886-8755
FAX: (313) 885-1172
R4
D

Hermansville
Poupore's Auto Body
N-15390 M-3 Road
Hermansville, MI 49847
Tel: (906) 498-2110
Contact: Greg Poupore
R4

Holland
Holland Motor Homes
670 E. 16th Street
Holland, MI 49423
Tel: (616) 956-5741
Nation: (800) 221-7197
Nation: (800) 221-7198
FAX: (616) 396-1391
Contact: Mary Wickart
DLR of *R1*

Imlay City
Champion Motor Coach, Incorporated
331 Graham Road
P.O. Box 158
Imlay City, MI 48444
Tel: (810) 724-0571
Tel: (810) 724-6474
Nation: (800) 776-4943
FAX: (810) 724-1844
Contact: John Thompson
or Jim Nolin
or Gary Dolan
MFR of *Specialty Medium-duty U, & Airport Shuttle Vehicles*
C-2:10 *(Prefers to hire locally-based drivers.)*

Imlay City
Mark Body Truck & Equipment
7256 Bowers Road
Imlay City, MI 48444
Tel: (810) 724-2000
MFR of *TB*

Jackson
Sport Camper, Inc.
2361 E. South Street
Jackson, MI 49201
Tel: (517) 764-2954
Contact: Richard DeLaet
DLR of *T*

Kalamazoo
Boyce Sullivan, Inc.
8736 Portage Road
Kalamazoo, MI 49002
Tel: (616) 323-0032
Nation: (800) 999-9641
Contact: Mary Sullivan
DLR of *S*
D

Kalamazoo
Daleiden, Inc.
425 E. Vine Street
Kalamazoo, MI 49001
Tel: (616) 343-1325
FAX: (616) 343-0488
Contact: Mike Pollard
MFR of *V, H'cap R4*

Kalamazoo
Morrison Trim
14000 Old 14-Mile Road
Kalamazoo, MI 49008
Tel: (616) 372-6161
Contact: Keith Morrison
R4

Kalamazoo
R & S Vans
202 W. Kalamazoo Ave.
Kalamazoo, MI 49007
Tel: (616) 342-1346
R4

Lansing
Capital City International Trucks, Incorporated
1700 N. Grand River Ave
Lansing, MI 48906
Tel: (517) 487-5908
Contact: Don Schmots
DLR of *Trucks*

Lansing
Custom Vans
4628 N. East Street
Lansing, MI 48906
Tel: (517) 482-2116
R4

Lansing
Magic Touch Van Conversions
2937 S. Logan Street
Lansing, MI 48910
Tel: (517) 394-4391
Contact: Dave Worley
R4

Lapeer
Durakon Industries, Inc.
2101 N. Lapeer Road
Lapeer, MI 48446
Tel: (810) 664-0850
Contact: Doug Henery
MFR of *TB*
D

Lapeer
FMG Conversions, Inc.
552 Imlay City Road
Lapeer, MI 48446
Tel: (810) 664-0550
Contact: Mike Gertiser
R4
D

Madison Heights
Eleven-Mile Truck Frame & Axle
1750 E. 11-Mile Road
Madison Heights, MI 48071
Tel: (810) 399-7536
FAX: (810) 399-7101
Contact: Sherry Van Atter
MFR of *TB, U*

Madison Heights
Prestige Motors, Ltd.
31675 Stephenson Hwy.
Madison Heights, MI 48071
Tel: (810) 548-8911
Nation: (800) 553-1558
FAX: (810) 583-6115
Contact: Lisa Lukasik
DISTRIBUTOR/DLR of *Limos*

Marcellus
Creative RV, Cree Div.
51540 M-40, North
Marcellus, MI 49067
Tel: (616) 646-5131
Contact: Bob Ausra
MFR of *R5, R6*
B-2:2
D

Mattawan
Van-Kal
24561 Red Arrow
Mattawan, MI 49071
Tel: (616) 668-3926
FAX: (616) 668-2029
MFR of *TB*

Midland
Quality Auto Care
1279 N. Saginaw
Midland, MI 48640
Tel: (517) 832-9171
Contact: Don Fergason
R4
C-2:4

Muskegon
Fleet Engineers, Inc.
1800 E. Keating Avenue
Muskegon, MI 49442
Tel: (616) 777-2537
Nation: (800) 333-7890
FAX: (616) 777-2720
Contact: Wes Eckland
MFR of *Truck, T*

Muskegon
Monroe Custom Campers
2915 Apple Avenue
Muskegon, MI 49442
Tel: (616) 773-0005
Contact: Don Monroe
MFR of *TC*

Muskegon
Rich's Auto Mart
2050 Whitehall Road
Muskegon, MI 49445
Tel: (616) 744-9470
FAX: (616) 744-9470
Contact: Mike Krang
R4

Muskegon
Spoelman Auto Company
2411 E. Apple Avenue
Muskegon, MI 49442
Tel (616) 773-5512
FAX: (616) 773-5999
Contact: Jim Spoelman
DLR of *R4*

Muskegon
Sunburst Custom Automotive
2160 Henry Street
Muskegon, MI 49441
Tel: (616) 726-3007
Contact: Robert Welbes
R4
C-1

Muskegon
Vankam Trailer Sales & Manufacturing Co.
1316 Whitehall Road
Muskegon, MI 49445
Tel: (616) 744-2658
MFR/DLR of *UT*

New Buffalo
Sullair PTO by Vanair
US Route 12
P.O. Box 219
New Buffalo, MI 49117
Tel: (616) 469-4461
Nation: (800) 348-2722
MFR of *CTB*

New Hudson
U.S. Trailer Company
53000 Grand River
New Hudson, MI 48165
Tel: (313) 525-4300
MFR of *CT*

Northville
Connelly Enterprises
598 S. Main Street
Northville, MI 48167
Tel: (810) 348-1770
Contact: Wayne Kecs
R4

Oscoda
Kip's Kustoms
5740 N. F 41
Oscoda, MI 48750
Tel: (517) 739-5731
Contact: Kip Lutrell
R1, R4, H'cap R4, TConvs

Owosso
Young Olds-Cadillac, Incorporated
1418 Main
Owosso, MI 48867
Tel: (517) 725-2184
FAX: (810) 235-9623
Contact: Tony Young
DLR of *Limos*

Parma
Birchwood Acres, Inc.
6307 N. Dearing Road
Parma, MI 49269
Tel: (517) 782-4561
FAX: (517) 784-2654
Contact: Dorthy Folk
DLR of *HT*

Paw Paw
Sweet Street Motor Car Company
42839 W. Red Arrow Highway
Paw Paw, MI 49079
Tel: (616) 657-6027
R4

Pigeon
Alton Company, Inc.
120 Sturm Road
Pigeon, MI 48755
Tel: (517) 453-3653
FAX: (517) 453-2915
MFR of *TB*

Pigeon
Thumb Truck Equipment, Incorporated
8305 Geiger Road
Pigeon, MI 48755
Tel: (517) 453-3133
Nation: (800) 852-4925
FAX: (517) 453-3042
Contact: Sandra Romain
MFR of *TB, T*

Pontiac
Absolute Transportation, Incorporated
253 E. Pike
Pontiac, MI 48342
Tel: (810) 334-1295
LEASING of *Limos*
C-2

Riverview
Midwest Truck Accessories, Inc.
18610 Fort Street
Riverview, MI 48192
Tel: (313) 283-9650
Contact: Steve Gibb
R4, TConvs
C-2:1
D

Rockford
Burch Body Works, Inc.
202 N. Monroe
Rockford, MI 49341
Tel: (616) 866-4421
FAX: (616) 866-4454
Contact: Jim Shellen
MFR of *TB*
D

Romeo
Sun Hawk Motor Homes
67780 Van Dyke
Romeo, MI 48065
Tel: (810) 752-3547
Nation: (800) 772-7755
FAX: (810) 752-3350
MFR of *R4, Tconvs*
50% are delivered by 4 C-1 & C-2 drivers. Road Rats deliver to the west and south. (They have 50 more on-call drivers.)
D: 50%, which are trucked eastbound.

Romulus
Cruise America
10255 Middlebelt
Romulus, MI 48174
Tel: (313) 946-1288
FAX: (313) 946-6955
Contact: Oscar Rhopon
RENTAL SITE of *R1, R2, R3*
(For more data, see the HQ listing, Mesa, AZ)

Romulus
Quality Truck Body
30443 Ecorse Road
Romulus, MI 48174
Tel: (313) 428-6690
MFR/REPAIR of *TB*
DLR of *G*

Roseville
Ekmer Corporation
28102 Groesbeck Hwy.
Roseville, MI 48066
Tel: (810) 772-3644
FAX: (810) 772-1309
Contact: Jean Hallabuck
MFR of *T, VTB*
C-2:1
D

Roseville
NBC Truck Equipment
28130 Groesbeck
Roseville, MI 48066
Tel: (810) 774-4900
FINAL ASSEMBLER/ MFR of *TB*

Roseville
Unique Van Crafters
27902 Groesbeck
Roseville, MI 48066
Tel: (810) 778-4444
Contact: Mark Savage
R4

Saginaw
Cisco, Incorporated
808 N. Outer Drive
Saginaw, MI 48601
Tel: (517) 752-4117
Contact: Pat Leery
DLR of *Fork Lifts*
C-2:6

Saginaw
Majestic Vans
8241 Gratoit
Saginaw, MI 48609
Tel: (517) 781-0985
Contact: Gary Bivins
R4

Southfield
Fruehauf Corp.
(MAIL P.O. Box 33238 Detroit, MI 48232)
26999 Central Park Blvd.
Southfield, MI 48076
Tel: (810) 948-1300
Tel: (313) 267-1250
Nation: (800) 521-9118
FAX: (313) 267-1025
Contact: Derick Nagle
MFR/DLR of *TB, T*
C-2

Southfield
General Trailer Mfg. & Dist., Inc.
19000 W. 8-Mile Road
Southfield, MI 48075
Tel: (810) 354-0980
Contact: Mike Dolowy
DLR of *R1*

Sterling Heights
Angelucci Performance Products
7839 Metro Parkway
Sterling Heights, MI 48078
Tel: (810) 977-5755
Contact: Andy Angelucci
MFR of *Specialty Customized Vehicles & Vehicles for shows.* Limited driver opportunity; Considered mainly for on-call, or Interlock.

Sturgis
Classic Mfg., Inc.
21900 US Hwy. 12, West
Sturgis, MI 49091
Tel: (616) 651-9319
Tel: (616) 651-2921
Nation: (800) 826-1960
Contact: Jerry Alber
MFR of *T*
B-2:3
D: Central Transport

Sturgis
Grumman Olson, Corporate Headquarters
1801 S. Nottawa Road
Sturgis, MI 49091
Tel: (616) 659-0200
FAX: (616) 651-4259
MFR of *TB, U*
D: Auto Driveaway, Morgan Driveaway, Bennett

Sturgis
Grumman Olson, Sturgis Division
70180 S. Centerville Road
Sturgis, MI 49091
Tel: (616) 659-0200
FAX: (616) 651-4259
Contact: Jeff Nynhier
MFR of *United Parcel Service TB, XTB, U*
D: Auto Driveaway, Morgan Driveaway, Bennett

Taylor
Harvey Buick, Inc.
14000 Telegraph
Taylor, MI 48180
Tel: (313) 946-8112
Contact: Harvey R. Horteck
MFR of *W, Special Tow Vehicles*

Taylor
Midwest Truck Accessories
8009 Telegraph Road
Taylor, MI 48180
Tel: (313) 374-0101
Contact: John Zubor
TConvs

Tekonsha
Tuff-Cat Trailers
134 Canal
Tekonsha, MI 49092
Tel: (517) 767-4764
Contact: Scott Goodwin
MFR of *HT*

Three Rivers
D'Elegant Industries, Incorporated
52664 N. US Hwy. 131
Three Rivers, MI 49093
Tel: (616) 273-1164
Contact: Charlie Morris
R4
D

Three Rivers
Elite Industries, Inc.
52161 N. US Hwy. 131
Three Rivers, MI 43093
Tel: (616) 273-8441
FAX: (616) 273-2404
Contact: Lari Roberts
R4
C-2:2
D: Barrett

Traverse City
Mobility Systems
1125 Hastings Street
Traverse City, MI 49684
Tel: (616) 941-4626
FAX: (616) 941-4665
Contact: John Phillipo
H'cap R4
C-1

Traverse City
Wheelock & Sons Welding
9954 N. Long Lake Road
Traverse City, MI 49684
Tel: (616) 947-6557
FAX: (616) 947-5152
Contact: Bonnie Wheelock
MFR of *TB*

Troy
Hoekstra Truck Equipment Co., Inc.
555 Oliver Street
Troy, MI 48084
Tel: (810) 244-8942
FAX: (810) 244-9470
Contact: Eric Colter
MFR/MODIFIER of *TB*

Union City
Wolverine Fire Apparatus
319 Crane Street
Union City, MI 49094
Tel: (517) 741-7544
FAX: (517) 741-3440
Contact: Everette Van Wormer
MFR of *F*

Warren
Canfield Equipment Service, Incorporated
21703 Mound Road
Warren, MI 48091
Tel: (810) 757-2020
Nation: (800) 637-5956
FAX: (810) 757-2294
Contact: Larry Gibson
R4

Warren
Creative Controls, Inc.
32450 Dequindre Road
Warren, MI 48092
Tel: (810) 979-3500
Contact: Tom Schmit
R4

Warren
J & L Mfg. Company
23334 Schoenherr Road
Warren, MI 48089
Tel: (810) 445-9530
Contact: Darlene Glenning
MFR of *TB*

Warren
Nu-Tech Collision, Inc.
21975 Shaner
Warren, MI 48089
Tel: (810) 778-3388
FAX: (810) 778-0001
Contact: Gene Kutzleb
R4

Warren
Tank Truck Mfg. Inc.
25150 Dequindre Road
Warren, MI 48091
Tel: (810) 757-6503
FAX: (810) 757-3175
MFR of *Tanker TB*

Washington
Sun Hawk Products
67780 Van Dyke
Washington, MI 48095
Tel: (810) 752-3547
Nation: (800) 772-7755
FAX: (810) 752-3350
Contact: Gloria Blake
R4
C-2

Waterford
Omniquest Company
4528 Dixie Hwy.
Waterford, MI 48329
Tel: (810) 673-9725
Contact: Chuck Koehler
MFR/DLR of *R4, TConvs*
C-1
(Open Tues.-Fri.)

Wayne
Handicapped Drive Aids Michigan, Incorporated
3990 2nd Street
Wayne, MI 48184
Tel: (313) 595-4400
Contact: Larry Pratt
H'cap R4
C-1

White Pigeon
Centurion Vehicles, Inc.
69651 US Hwy. 131, S.
P.O. Box 715
White Pigeon, MI 49099
Tel: (616) 483-9659
Contact: Bob Froschauer or Randy Thrall
R4
D

White Pigeon
Interstate Manufacturing
68935 Union Street
White Pigeon, MI 49099
Tel: (616) 483-7641
Nation: (800) 433-7641
FAX: (616) 483-7988
Contact: Chris Hamlin
MFR of *ST*
D

White Pigeon
Tara Products, Inc.
67445 M-40
White Pigeon, MI 49099
Tel: (616) 641-5935
Contact: Dave Evans
MFR of *R6*
D: J & J Services

Wixom
General Trailer Mfg. & Distributing, Inc.
48500 12-Mile Road
Wixom, MI 48075
Tel: (810) 349-0900
Contact: Mike Dolowy
DLR of *R1*

Wixom
Gresham Driving Aids, Incorporated
30800 S. Wixom Road
P.O. Box 405
Wixom, MI 48093
Tel: (810) 624-1533
Nation: (800) 521-8930
FAX: (810) 624-6358
Contact: Bill Dillon
H'cap R4

Woodhaven
Luxury Limousine Service
26739 Allen Road
Woodhaven, MI 48183
Tel: (313) 675-2235
Contact: Eric Bowen
MFR of *Limos*
C-1

Ypsilanti
Holiday Vans
1902 E. Michigan Avenue
Ypsilanti, MI 48198
Tel: (313) 485-3110
R4

MINNESOTA

Albert Lea
Western Truck & Body, Incorporated
1907 E. Main Street
Albert Lea, MN 56007
Tel: (607) 373-4218
DLR of *TB*

Aldrich
DN Trailers, Inc.
RR 1
Aldrich, MN 56434
Tel: (218) 445-5660
Contact: Denny Ness
MFR of *T*

Annadale
Truk-Mate Vans, Inc.
Highway 55, East
P.O. Box 909
Annadale, MN 55302
Tel: (612) 274-3384
Nation: (800) 247-1590
FAX: (612) 274-3215
Contact: Nikki Green
R4
C-2:2 (Locally-based)

Backus
Scamp Travel Trailers/ Evelands, Incorporated
Highway 371, North
P.O. Box 2
Backus, MN 56435
Tel: (218) 947-4932
Nation: (800) 432-3749
Nation (Except MN): (800) 346-4962
Contact: Harold Rice
MFR of *R5, R6*
C-2:2

Bloomington
Adventure Van & Truck
8653 Lyndale Avenue
Bloomington, MN 55420
Tel: (612) 884-7135
Tel: (612) 884-1330
Contact: Dave Peterson
H'cap R4

Blue Earth
Tafco Equipment Co.
Industrial Park Site
Blue Earth, MN 56013
Tel: (507) 526-3247
Nation: (800) 328-3189
FAX: (507) 526-7346
Contact: Randy Hanedik
MFR of *TB*
A-1

Bovey
Built-Rite Trailers, Inc.
612 2nd Street
Bovey, MN 55709
Tel: (218) 245-3627
Contact: Bud Lafrenierre
MFR of *T*

Brooten
Brooten Truck Body Co.
West Highway 8
P.O. Box 367
Brooten, MN 56316
Tel: (612) 346-2490
FAX: (612) 346-1248
Contact: John Tebrake
REPAIR of *TB*

Byron
Northwest Campers, Inc.
Highway 14, East
Byron, MN 55920
Tel: (507) 775-2361
DLR of *TC*

Chaska
Ohnsorg Truck Bodies
615 Chestnut Street
Chaska, MN 55318
Tel: (612) 448-2276
Contact: Bob Ohnsorg
MFR of *TB*

Coon Rapids
Aerolite
1330 115th Avenue, NW
Coon Rapids, MN 55448
Tel: (612) 757-7575
FAX: (612) 757-7174
Contact: Wayne Richeson
MFR of *TB*

Crosby
Range Manufacturing
212 W. Main Street
Crosby, MN 56441
Tel: (218) 546-6310
Contact: Rick Ferrari
MFR of *T*
B-2:1
D: Independent

Crosby
Tomko Trailers, Inc.
RR 3
Crosby, MN 56441
Tel: (218) 546-6865
Contact: Tom Venne
MFR of *T*

Dodge Center
McNeilus Truck & Manufacturing, Inc.
Highway 14, East
P.O. Box 70
Dodge Center, MN 55927
Tel: (507) 374-6321
FAX: (507) 374-6306
Contact: Mike Freerkesen
MFR of *Cement-Mixing Trucks*
C-2

Duluth
Duluth Dodge & Oldsmobile
1400 London Road
Duluth, MN 55805
Tel: (218) 728-3695
Contact: Greg Lynch
DLR of *R4*

Duluth
Northstar Body & Equipment Company
3941 E. Calvary Road
Duluth, MN 55803
Tel: (218) 724-5689
FAX: (218) 724-2432
Contact: Mike Friedman
DISTRIBUTOR of *U*

Duluth
United Truck Body Co.
5219 Miller Trunk Hwy.
Duluth, MN 55811
Tel: (218) 729-6000
FINAL ASSEMBLER of *TB*

East Grand Forks
Bert's Truck Equip., Inc.
US Highway 2, East
East Grand Forks, MN 56721
Tel: (218) 773-1194
Nation: (800) 325-2412
FAX: (218) 773-1840
Contact: Bev Gregoire or Scott Gregoire
FINAL ASSEMBLER of *TB*

East Grand Forks
Leisureland RV
Highway 220, North
P.O. Box 129
East Grand Forks, MN 56721
Tel: (218) 773-7464
Contact: Dave Peterson
DLR/REPAIR of *R1, R2*
C-2 drivers do DPUs

Eden Praire
Midland Equipment Co.
6331 Industrial Drive
Eden Prairie, MN 55346
Tel: (612) 934-7505
Contact: Tony Lesinski
MFR of *TB*

Eden Prairie
Steel Products & Aluminum
6832 Washington Ave., S.
Eden Prairie, MN 55344
Tel: (612) 941-1588
Contact: Bernie Williamette
MFR of *TB*
D

Eden Prairie
Suburban Chevrolet-Geo
12475 Plaza Drive
Eden Prairie, MN 55344
Tel: (612) 938-2751
FAX: (612) 938-0306
Contact: Julie Hanson
DLR of *R4*

Edina
Delta-Waseca, Inc.
5200 Willson Road
Edina, MN 55424
Tel: (612) 922-5049
MFR of *TB*
(This is the Sales Office. See also Waseca, MN.)

Elbow Lake
Fechtner Trailer Builders
P.O. Box 2033
Elbow Lake, MN 56531
Tel: (218) 498-2299
MFR of *T*

Elk River
Tail Wind Trailers
9784 Highway 10
Elk River, MN 55330
Tel: (612) 421-2247
FAX: (612) 323-0674
Contact: Ron Atkins
MFR of *T*
B-2

Fairmont
Redi-Haul Trailers
1205 N. Dewey Street
Fairmont, MN 56031
Tel: (507) 238-4231
Nation: (800) 533-0382
FAX: (507) 238-2603
Contact: Roger Voss
MFR of *UT, ST*
D

Faribault
Coach Crafters, Inc.
1506 NW 30th Street
Faribault, MN 55021
Tel: (507) 334-1686
FAX: (507) 334-1689
Contact: Wayne Wolf
REFURBISHER of *U*
A-1

Fergus Falls
Ringdahl & Co., Inc.
Box 462
Fergus Falls, MN 56537
Tel: (218) 736-2819
Contact: Barrett Wickland
MFR of *A*
C-1

Forest Lake
Waldoch Crafts, Inc.
13821 Lake Drive
Forest Lake, MN 55025
Tel: (612) 464-3215
Nation: (800) 328-9259
FAX: (612) 464-1117
Contact: Roy Johnson
R4
C-2

Fridley
Crysteel
1130 73rd Avenue, NE
Fridley, MN 55432
Tel: (612) 571-1902
FINAL ASSEMBLER/ DISTRIBUTOR of
Platform TB, Stake TB, Contractor TB, SP, FTB, UTB, VTB, XTB
NOTE: *See also their manufacturing plant in Lake Crystal, MN.*

Grove City
Palm Sales, Inc.
53800 CSAH 16
Grove City, MN 56243
Tel: (612) 857-2874
FAX: (612) 857-2086
Contact: Arlyn Hedtke
MFR of *T*
B-2:1

Hanover
Cumming's Mobility
279 River Road, NE
Hanover, MN 55341
Tel: (612) 498-7887
H'cap R4

Henning
McCollough Welding
112 Inman Street
Henning, MN 56551
Tel: (218) 583-4308
Contact: George McCollough
MFR of *T*

Hopkins
ABM Equip. & Supply
1670 2nd Street, South
Hopkins, MN 55343
Tel: (612) 938-5451
FAX: (612) 938-0159
Contact: Scott Reierson or Dave Gorres
MFR of *Commercial R4*
C-2:4
D

Inver Grove
Tilson Bus & Equip. Co.
7655 Concord Blvd., East
Inver Grove, MN 55076
Tel: (612) 455-3399
DISTRIBUTOR of *U*

Lake Crystal
Crysteel Mfg, Inc.
Highway 60, East
P.O. Box 178
Lake Crystal, MN 56055
Tel: (507) 726-2728
FAX: (507) 726-2559
Contact: Pete Jones
MFR of *TB*
D

Long Prairie
R-Way Corporation
25 4th Street, South
Long Prairie, MN 56347
Tel: (612) 732-2065
FAX: (612) 732-2067
Contact: Caroline Olson
MFR of *T*
B-1

Madelia
Forstner Fire Apparatus
17 E. Main Street
P.O. Box 97
Madelia, MN 56062
Tel: (507) 642-3404
Contact: Floyd Forstner
MFR of *F*
C-1

Mankato
Gag's Camper Way
Highway 169
Mankato, MN 56001
Tel: (507) 345-5858
FAX: (507) 345-5852
Contact: Larry Gag
DLR of *R1, R2*

Minneapolis
Brownie Tank Mfg. Co.
1241 72nd Avenue, NE
Minneapolis, MN 55432
Tel: (612) 571-1744
FAX: (612) 571-1789
Contact: Brian Fremo
MFR of *TB*
C-2:2
D

Minneapolis
Freeway Ford
9700 Lyndale Ave., South
Minneapolis, MN 55420
Tel: (612) 888-9481
FAX: (612) 888-7394
Contact: Dave Burns
DLR of *R4*

Minneapolis
Kolstad Company, Inc.
3001 NE Broadway Street
Minneapolis, MN 55413
Tel: (612) 379-1909
Nation: (800) 233-7560
FAX: (612) 379-8980
Contact: Paul O'Brien
MFR of *VTB*

Minneapolis
Lakeland Coach Co.
9010 Pillsbury Avenue
Minneapolis, MN 55420
Tel: (612) 881-5918
Contact: Mr. Pleves
MFR of *R1, R2*

Minneapolis
Leroy's Custom Painting
11380 Xeon Street, NW
Minneapolis, MN 55448
Tel: (612) 754-3445
Contact: Mike Flashmary
R4

Minneapolis
North Star International Truck, Incorporated
3000 NE Broadway Street
Minneapolis, MN 55413
Tel: (612) 378-1660
Contact: Gary Thompson
DLR of *Trucks*

Monticello
Hoglund Bus Co., Inc.
I-94 & Hwy. 25, South
Monticello, MN 55362
Tel: (612) 295-5119
Contact: Lisa Hoglund
DLR of *U*

Moorhead
Bert's Truck Equipment of Moorhead
2620 2nd Avenue, North
(Highway 10, East)
Moorhead, MN 56560
Tel: (218) 233-8681
Nation: (800) 232-3787
FAX: (218) 233-9548
Contact: Jerry Short
MFR of *S-2, and a wide variety of TB*
C-1

Morris
Brothers Industries, Inc.
Highway 59, South
Morris, MN 56267
Tel: (612) 589-1971
Nation: (800) 833-6045
FAX: (612) 589-1974
Contact: Jerry Lesmeister
MFR of *T*

Morris
Morris Blacksmith & Machine Shop
223 Pacific Avenue
Morris, MN 56267
Tel: (612) 589-3044
FAX: (612) 589-2082
Contact: Tom Lesmeister
MFR of *T*

Morris
Todd Vans
Highway 28, East
P.O. Box 309
Morris, MN 56267
Tel: (612) 589-4224
R4

Mountain Lake
Ash Company
RR 2, Box 337
Mountain Lake, MN 56159
Tel: (507) 427-3362
Contact: Dwayne Peters
MFR of *T*

Rochester
Custom Truck Body & Equipment
3741 Enterprise Dr., SW
Rochester, MN 55902
Tel: (507) 288-8266
MFR of *TB*

Rochester
Kuehn Featherlite
5020 Hwy. 52, North
Rochester, MN 55901
Tel: (507) 282-7700
Nation: (800) 657-3208
Contact: John Demaria
DLR of *HT*
B-2

Rochester
Quality Vans & Mobility Products
3600 Hwy. 63, South
Rochester, MN 55904
Tel: (507) 288-1178
Contact: Scott Crawford
R4, H'cap R4
C-2:3
D

Saint Cloud
Maney International, Incorporated
375 S. 33rd. Avenue
St. Cloud, MN 56301
Tel: (612) 251-9511
FAX: (612) 251-9523
Contact: Ed Meyer
DLR of *International Trucks*

Saint Paul
Complete Mobility Systems, Incorporated
1915 W.C.R.C.
St. Paul, MN 55113
Tel: (612) 635-0655
FAX: (612) 635-9237
Contact: Scott Mattson
H'cap R4
C-2:2
D

Saint Paul
LZ Company, Inc.
1881 Rice Street
St. Paul, MN 55113
Tel: (612) 488-2571
FAX: (612) 488-9857
Contact: Steve Zeete
MFR of *TB*

Saint Paul
Truck Utilities
2370 English Street
St. Paul, MN 55109
Tel: (612) 484-3305
FAX: (612) 484-0076
Contact: Leo Capeder
MFR of *TB*
C-2:3

Spring Grove
Marv's Camper Sales
W. Highway 44
Spring Grove, MN 55974
Tel: (507) 498-5594
(Office)
Tel: (507) 498-5429
(Residence)
FAX: (507) 498-5529
DLR of *R6, TC*
(Opportunity here is extremely limited.)

Waseca
Delta Waseca, Inc.
RR 2, Box 6
Industrial Park.
Highway 13, South
Waseca, MN 56093
Tel: (507) 835-1172
FAX: (507) 835-1174
Contact: Chuck Tekautz
MFR of *VTB, XTB, U*
C-1

White Bear Lake
Schifsky Trailers
5118 130th Street, North
White Bear Lake, MN 55110
Tel: (612) 483-2656
FAX: (612) 426-1522
MFR of *T*

Windom
Don's Trailer Sales
945 Lakeview Avenue
Windom, MN 56101
Tel: (507) 831-4015
Contact: Don Herder
MFR of *T*

Winsted
JMS Custom Service, Incorporated
590 W. Main Avenue
Winsted, MN 55395
Tel: (612) 485-2261
FAX: (612) 485-4750
Contact: Jeff Sterner
R4, TConvs
C-1

MISSISSIPPI

Amory
Atlas Truck Body Manufacturing Company
(Div. of Douglas & Lomanson Company)
Jct. of Hwys. 45 & 278
P.O. Box 479
Amory, MS 38821
Tel: (601) 256-5692
Nation: (800) 354-2192
FAX: (601) 256-2162
Contact: Todd Flaherty
MFR of *Refrig. TB for the beer and dairy industries.*
C-1:2 deliver 50%
D: Reeves Transport: (601) 256-5671; contact Red Reeves. Units are delivered nationwide. (They deliver 50%.)
NOTE: *For more data on Douglas & Lomason, see HQ listing in Farmington Hills, MI.*

Amory
Palmer Machine Works, Incorporated
Old Roundhouse Road
Amory, MS 38821
Tel: (601) 256-2636
FAX: (601) 256-5624
Contact: Jason Gallop
MFR of *T*

Batesville
Magnolia Sales, Inc.
Highway 6, East
Batesville, MS 38606
Tel: (601) 563-5647
MS only: (800) 325-7036
FAX: (601) 563-5649
Contact: Jimmy Snider
DLR of *New & Used U*
C-1:6 deliver to customers.

Biloxi
Hancock's Mobile Home & RV Parts
10309 Rodriguez Street
Biloxi, MS 39532
Tel: (601) 392-3297
Contact: Sonny Hancock
REPAIR of *R1, R2, R4, TB*

Byhalia
Griffin, Incorporated
RR 6
Byhalia, MS 38611
Tel: (601) 838-2128
FAX: (601) 838-2120
Contact: Jane Spencer
MFR of *TB*

Byahlia
Mid-South Ambulances & Coach
Byahlia Industrial Park
Byhalia, MS 38611
Tel: (601) 838-4545
FAX: (601) 838-4546
MFR of *A*
C-1
D

Carthage
H & H Chief Sales, Inc.
HC 35, North
Carthage, MS 39051
Tel: (601) 267-9643
FAX: (601) 267-9645
Contact: Larry Cowell
MFR of *Fertilizer TB*
C-1
D

Collins
Warren, Incorporated
707 N. Fir
Collins, MS 39428
Tel: (601) 765-8221
FAX: (601) 765-4554
Contact: Betty Sampley
MFR of *T*
A-1
D

Crystal Springs
Bodies Unlimited
250 W. Marion Avenue
Crystal Springs, MS 39059
Tel: (601) 892-3251
FAX: (601) 892-1312
Contact: Charles Glass
MFR of *Fiberglass TB*
C-1
D

Gulfport
Reliable RV Sales & Service
725 Pass Road
Gulfport, MS 39501
Tel: (601) 868-1000
Nation: (800) 748-8741
FAX: (601) 863-0517
Contact: Andrea Davis
DLR of *R1*

Jackson
Boatman's Pickup Specialties
8117 Highway 18
Jackson, MS 39209
Tel: (601) 373-8677
FAX: (601) 373-8695
Contact: Elaine Boatman
R4

Jackson
Busses Unlimited
1555 W. Northside Drive
Jackson, MS 39213
Tel: (601) 982-5213
Contact: Patty Fulctel
DLR of *S, U*

Jackson
Quarter Master Vans & Trim Shop
2175 Rondo Street
Jackson, MS 39213
Tel: (601) 354-3800
Contact: James Page
R4

Jackson
Southern Fire Equipment Company, Incorporated
(MAIL:
P.O. Drawer 12308
Jackson, MS 39236)
1125 E. McDowell Road
Jackson, MS 39204
Tel: (601) 944-1112
Nation: (800) 733-6055
FAX: (601) 944-1122
Contact: Byron Fergoson
MFR of *F*
C-2:1

Kosciusko
Companion Vans, Inc.
711 E. Jefferson Street
Kosciusko, MS 39090
Tel: (601) 289-7711
Contact: Jim Ganann
R4

Lucedale
Sun Manufacturing, Inc.
Industrial Park Road
Lucedale, MS 39452
Tel: (601) 947-7388
Nation: (800) 726-0824
FAX: (601) 947-6556
Contact: Dennis Nelson
MFR of *T*
B-1

Nettleton
Archie's Truck Body Works
Route 1
Nettleton, MS 38858
Tel: (601) 862-3468
MFR of *TB*

Okolona
Wren Body Works
Highway 45, North
Okolona, MS 38860
Tel: (601) 256-2028
FAX: (601) 256-7572
Contact: Ann Wilson
MFR of *TB*

Pearl
Capitol Truck Body Shop
583-1/2 Highway 80, East
Pearl, MS 39208
Tel: (601) 939-7926
REPAIR of *TB*

Picayune
Comet Vans, Inc.
2111 E. Canal Street
Picayune, MS 39466
Tel: (601) 799-1417
Contact: Robert Devorde
R4

Picayune
Designer Vans by R & M
1928 Palestine Road
Picayune, MS 39466
Tel: (601) 798-4355
FAX: (601) 798-0545
Contact: Hyram Smith or Speedy Smith
R4
A-1

Picayune
Rainbow Vans
245 Frontage Road
P.O. Box 1170
Picayune, MS 39466
Tel: (601) 799-1444
FAX: (601) 799-1076
Contact: Robert Dickson
MFR of *R4, TConvs*
A-1, C-2:2

Southaven
Moore & Sons
7171 Airways Blvd.
P.O. Drawer 129
Southaven, MS 38671
Tel: (601) 349-4373
FAX: (601) 349-4361
Contact: Danny Smith
MFR of *Armored Trucks, Ground Support Equip. for airports (i.e., High-Lift Catering TB)*

Tishomingo
Heil Preferred Systems
Highway 25, North
P.O. Box 49
Tishomingo, MS 38873
Tel: (601) 438-7800
Tel: (601) 438-7801
Nation: (800) 243-4345
FAX: (601) 438-7388
MFR of *TB*

Verona
Deca Autosound
143 Holloway Street
Verona, MS 38879
Tel: (601) 566-2797
Contact: John Capps
R4

Verona
Scott's Trailer Equipment
Old Brewer Road
Verona, MS 38879
Tel: (601) 767-3800
FAX: (601) 767-8907
Contact: Frank Scott
or Peggy Scott
MFR of *T*

MISSOURI

Ballwin
Byerly Trailer & Mfg. Company, Incorporated
13988 Manchester Road
Ballwin, MO 63011
Tel: (314) 227-1550
Contact: Russell Patton
DLR of *T*

Ballwin
Van Attic, Inc./Classy Cars & Vans
14830 Manchester Road
Ballwin, MO 63011
Tel: (314) 394-1044
Contact: Jim Currie
MFR of *R4*

Bates City
Classic Conversions
Route 2, Box 84
Bates City, MO 64011
Tel (816) 625-4994
Contact: Lynn Dorathage
R4
C-2:2

Belton
Smitty's Van Interiors, Incorporated
401 Commercial
P.O. Box 407
Belton, MO 64012
Tel: (816) 331-3007
Contact: Paul Smith
R4

Bolivar
Lifestyle Transportation, Incorporated
700 S. Killingsworth
Bolivar, MO 65613
Tel: (417) 326-6234
FAX: (417) 326-6238
Contact: Barbera Greer
R4
C-2:1

Bridgeton
Crown Divisions of Allen Group
13575 NW Industrial Dr.
Bridgeton, MO 63044
Tel: (314) 298-7515
FAX: (314) 298-0906
Contact: Harold George
R4
D: Allied Systems

Buffalo
Bison Industries, Inc.
P.O. Box 795
Buffalo, MO 65622
Tel: (417) 345-2325
FAX: (417) 345-8855
Contact: Ivan Arnold
or Peggy Swanigan
MFR of *TC*

Claycomo
Mobil Hydraulic Equipment Company
249 NE Highway 69
Claycomo, MO 64119
Tel: (816) 525-3420
FAX: (816) 454-4858
Contact: Joe Orel
SERVICE & REPAIR of *TB*

Columbia
Morgan Corporation
3101 Lemone Industrial Blvd.
Columbia, MO 65201
Tel: (314) 442-0020
FAX: (314) 443-3360
Contact: Bill Bonge
MFR of *TB*
D: Morgan Driveaway

Concordia
Spacecraft Motor Homes, Incorporated
Route 1, Box 93
Concordia, MO 64020
Tel: (816) 463-7520
FAX: (816) 463-7829
MFR of *R5, R6*

Dexter
Autry Morlan Chevy-Cadillac-Geo
1801 Business 60, West
Dexter, MO 63841
Tel: (314) 624-8912
FAX: (314) 624-7640
Contact: Jill Morlan
DLR of *R4*

Dexter
D & L Truck Equip., Inc.
1201 N. Lakeview Drive
Dexter, MO 63841
Tel: (314) 624-5645
Contact: Brenda Silliman
MFR/DISTRIBUTOR of *TB*

Duneweg
Aero Body & Truck Equipment
E. 7th Street
Duneweg, MO 64801
Tel: (417) 782-2044
MFR of *TB*

Fair Grove
Circle S Trailers, Inc.
RR 3, Box 235
Fair Grove, MO 65648
Tel:(417) 759-2606
Contact: Debbie Kirby
MFR of *T*

Florissant
Marty Cancila's Dodge World
2175 N. Highway 67
Florissant, MO 63033
Tel: (314) 831-3300
FAX: (314) 831-2051
Contact: Tom Moore
R4

Grandview
American Specialty Conversions
1604 Little Avenue
Grandview, MO 64030
Tel: (816) 763-5900
Contact: Arleta McCola
R4

Grandview
Central Mfg., Inc.
4116 Drive Greaves Road
Grandview, MO 64030
Tel: (816) 767-0300
FAX: (816) 763-0705
MFR of *Shuttle Wagons*

Hazelwood
Behlmann Van-Pontiac-GMC Truck
820 McDonnell Blvd. & I-270
Hazelwood, MO 63042
Tel: (314) 895-1600
Nation: (800) 892-8267
FAX: (314) 895-1905
DLR of *R4*

Hazelwood
Gateway Custom Vans & Repair
12529 Missouri Bottom Road
Hazelwood, MO 63042
Tel: (314) 291-3999
FAX: (314) 291-2979
Contact: Scott Webb
R4

Holt Summit
Doolittle Trailer Mfg.
2455 Doolittle Drive
Holt Summit, MO 65043
Tel: (314) 896-5705
Nation: (800) 654-4948
MFR/DLR of *T*

Holts Summit
Universal Campers
Route AA Holts
Holts Summit, MO 65043
Tel: (314) 896-4121
Nation: (800) 736-4121
Contact: Pat Jones
MFR of *TC*

House Springs
Gateway Horse Trailer
6024 Sembr Place
House Springs, MO 63051
Tel: (314) 671-0888
Contact: Mike Tutas
DLR of *HT*

Independence
Cline Truck
1200 S. Powell Road
Independence, MO 64057
Tel: (816) 796-9310
FAX: (816) 796-9481
Contact: Kelly Joseph
MFR of *Off-Hwy. TB*

Joplin
Able Body Corporation
1000 Schifferdecker Ave.
Joplin, MO 64801
Tel: (417) 623-3060
FAX: (417) 623-4617
Contact: Lynn Long
MFR of *Sleepers for Trucks*
D

Joplin
BC Coach
W. 7th & Blackcat Road
Route 6, Box 68
Joplin, MO 64801
Tel: (417) 623-7066
Contact: Wayne Johnson
R4, TConvs

Joplin
Pepper's Truck Body & Equipment
5800 E. 7th Street
Joplin, MO 64801
Tel: (417) 623-1221
MFR/DISTRIBUTOR of *TB*

Kansas City
Adaptive Stratus Equipment Company
12600 N. Woodland Ave.
Kansas City, MO 64165
Tel: (816) 734-5000
Nation: (800) 821-5451
FAX: (816) 734-5090
Contact: Orville Dickson
R4, H'cap R4
C-2:3

Kansas City
Croft Trailer Supply
4933 E. Truman Road
Kansas City, MO 64127
Tel: (816) 483-7274
Nation (Except MO):
(800) 426-8159
FAX: (816) 483-7277
Contact: Sandy Jones
MFR of *T*

Kansas City
*Douglas & Lomason
Kansas City Service
Center/General Body &
Truck*
4951 Stillwell
Kansas City, MO 64120
Tel: (816) 231-7100
Nation: (800) 821-2582
MO only: (800) 892-5855
FINAL ASSEMBLER of
*V, Beverage T
B-1, B-3, C-1
D: Bennett, and Power
Extress of Tulsa, OK*
NOTE: *Best approach is
to contact HQ first:
Farmington Hills, MI.
Corporation has 23
plants, but only 3 make
vehicles. See also
Centennial Body,
Columbus, GA and
Atlas Body, Amory, MS.*

Kansas City
Gem's Vans
1501 Burlington Street
Kansas City, MO 64116
Tel: (816) 421-8303
Contact: Jim Reynolds
R4

Kansas City
Hesse Corporation
6700 St. John Avenue
Kansas City, MO 64125
Tel: (816) 483-7808
Nation: (800) 821-5562
Nation: (800) 892-8715
FAX: (816) 241-9010
Contact: Kathy Sullivan
MFR of *V
C-2*

Kansas City
*Kansas City Service
Center/General Body &
Truck*
4951 Stillwell
Kansas City, MO 64120
Tel: (816) 231-7100
Nation: (800) 821-2582
Nation: (800) 892-5855
FAX: (816) 231-7321
Contact: Dottie Davis
MFR of *V
D*

Kansas City
Knapheide Truck
1920 E. Front Street
Kansas City, MO 64120
Tel: (816) 472-4444
FAX: (816) 472-5147
Contact: Phillip Carrott
MFR of *TB*

Kansas City
*National Truck Parts &
Equipment Company*
1609 Crystal Avenue
Kansas City, MO 64126
Tel: (816) 231-7037
Contact: Kevin Sleyster
MFR of *TB, U*

Kansas City
*Scherer Truck
Equipment, Inc.*
6105 NW River Park Dr.
Kansas City, MO 64150
Tel: (816) 587-0190
**FINAL ASSEMBLER/
DLR** of *TB*

Kimberling City
Lifetime Mfg. Co.
P.O. Box 490
Kimberling City, MO
64686
Tel: (417) 779-4586
Contact: Peggy Powers
MFR of *BT
B-1*

Lebanon
Bear Trailer Mfg.
I-44
(9 miles east of town)
Lebanon, MO 65536
Tel: (417) 286-3300
MFR of *BT*

Lee's Summit
Bob Sight Ford, Inc.
50 Hwy. & Chipman Rd.
Lee's Summit, MO 64063
Tel: (816) 524-6550
Contact: Tom Sight
DLR of *R4*

Lesterville
Shaffer Horse Trailers
Highway 21
Lesterville, MO 63654
Tel: (314) 637-2581
MFR of *HT*

Linn
Ambulance Division
Twin Ridge Road
P.O. Box 718
Linn, MO 65051
Tel: (314) 897-3634
Nation: (800) 822-3634
FAX: (314) 897-3113
Contact: Lou Wilson
MFR of *A
C-2:6*

Linn
Osage Industries
Twin Ridge Road
Route 1
Linn, MO 65051
Tel: (314) 897-3634
R4

Lockwood
Coose Trailer Mfg., Inc.
RR 2, Box 152-A
Lockwood, MO 65682
Tel: (417) 232-4420
FAX: (417) 232-4605
Contact: Hubert Coose
MFR of *ST, HT*

Maryville
Trail's End Mfg. Inc.
Box 154, Route 1
Maryville, MO 64468
Tel: (816) 582-4483
FAX: (816) 582-4493
MFR of *R6*

Moberly
Mack Products
Highway 24, West
Moberly, MO 65270
Tel: (816) 263-7444
FAX: (816) 263-4403
MFR of *TB*

Morley
*Wheeler Truck/Trailer
Equipment Company*
Highway 61
Morley, MO 63767
Tel: (314) 262-3545
Contact: Mary Dell
MFR of *T
B-1*

Neosho
Holden Industries, Inc.
Crowder Industrial Park,
RR 6, Box 151
Neosho, MO 64850
Tel: (417) 451-2777
Contact: Fred Cobb
MFR of *T
D: Power Express*

Nevada
*Miller Valley Camper
Manufacturing*
Highway 54
Nevada, MO 64772
Tel: (417) 667-5541
Contact: Matthew Lewis
MFR of *TC*

Nixa
American Coach, Inc.
2115 N. Foxhollow Drive
Nixa, MO 65714
Tel: (417) 725-1191
FAX: (417) 725-2661
Contact: Paul Day
MFR of *R4
C-2
D*

Pacific
Webco-Pacific, Inc.
2 Midwest Drive
P.O. Box 446
Pacific, MO 63069
Tel: (314) 257-2458
FAX: (314) 343-4222
Contact: Ken Griffom
MFR of *CTB*

Perryville
Pingel, Incorporated
Highway 61, South
RR 2, Box 215
Perryville, MO 63775
Tel: (314) 547-6091
Contact: Gerald Pingel
MFR of *TB*

Raytown
*H & H Repair &
Painting*
9601 E. 53rd Street
Raytown, MO 64133
Tel: (816) 356-8455
Contact: Don Haulfmann
MODIFIER of *U*

Republic
Republic Vans
121 W. US Highway 60
Republic, MO 65738
Tel: (417) 732-6027
Contact: Ralph
Coughenour
R4

Riverside
*Scherer Truck
Equipment, Incorporated*
6105 NW River Park Dr.
(Highway 9)
Riverside, MO 64152
Tel: (816) 587-0190
Nation: (800) 373-8725
FAX: (816) 587-5127
DLR of *M, UTB, S/STB,
Grain TB, Platform TB,
Cranes, Hoist TB, W*

Rogersville
*Sportsman Pickup Cover
Center*
RR 2
Rogersville, MO 65742
Tel: (417) 753-2866
Contact: Dale Brallier
MFR of *TC*

Saint Clair
*Steelweld Equipment
Company, Incorporated*
I-44 at Highway 47
P.O. Box 226
St. Clair, MO 63077
Tel: (314) 629-3704
FAX: (314) 629-3734
Contact: Richard Clark
MFR of *TB*

Saint Louis
All-N-1 Van
8751 Glenwood Drive
St. Louis, MO 63126
Tel: (314) 843-7733
Contact: Jack McGartland
CORPORATE OFFICES

Saint Louis
Commercial Van Interiors
8840 St. Charles Rock Road
St. Louis, MO 63114
Tel: (314) 423-7477
Nation: (800) 759-7477
FAX: (314) 427-1525
Contact: Kelly Greenley
R4
D

Saint Louis
De-Mac Equipment Co.
3749 Aldine Street
St. Louis MO 36113
Tel: (314) 533-1737
FAX: (314) 533-3422
Contact: Frank Brie
MFR of *TB*
C-2:4

Saint Louis
Emerge-A-Star
3555 Bernard
St. Louis, MO 63103
Tel: (314) 535-8750
FAX: (314) 535-2832
Contact: Linda Vidacak
MFR of *A*

Saint Louis
Faifer Body Company
1320 Cass Avenue
St. Louis, MO 63106
Tel: (314) 421-6510
Contact: Frank Faifer
MFR of *TB*

Saint Louis
Gateway Metal Works & Horse Trailers
6024 Sembr Place
St. Louis, MO 63051
Tel: (314) 671-0888
Contact: Mike Tutass
DLR of *HT*

Saint Louis
Imports Limited/ McCown Automotive Coach Sales
3700 Chippewa Avenue
St. Louis, MO 63116
Tel: (314) 771-3160
FAX: (314) 771-5246
Contact: H. M. "Mac" McCown
DLR of *Limos, H*

Saint Louis
Kranz Automotive Body Company
300 Russell Blvd.
St. Louis, MO 63104
Tel: (314) 776-3787
FAX: (314) 776-5098
Contact: Gene Kolur
FINAL ASSEMBLER of *TB*

Saint Louis
Malibu Vans
2528 Texas Avenue
St. Louis, MO 63104
Tel: (314) 771-1600
R4

Saint Louis
McHenry Truck Equipment, Incorporated
3838 Cote Brillante
St. Louis, MO 63113
Tel: (314) 533-0800
Nation: (800) 325-0771
Nation: (800) 392-0246
FAX: (314) 568-3442
Contact: J.R. McHenry or Robert Barbour
MFR of *VTB, CTB*
C-2:3

Saint Louis
Southwest Mobile Systems Corporation
200 Sidney Street
St. Louis, MO 63104
Tel: (314) 771-3950
FAX: (314) 771-1169
Call dispatcher at (417) 256-4125 in West Plains, MO.
MFR of *TB*
C-2

Saint Louis
Van City Truck Sales
3100 Telegraph Road
St. Louis, MO 63125
Tel: (314) 894-3905
Nation: (800) 467-3905
FAX: (314) 894-1814
Contact: Raymond Dwier
DLR of *R4*

Sedalia
Parkhurst Mfg. Co., Inc.
400 Industrial Drive
P.O. Box 1323
Sedalia, MO 65301
Tel: (816) 826-8685
Tel: (816) 826-0250
Nation: (800) 821-7380
FAX: (816) 826-8688
Contact: Sue Fourner
MFR of *TB*
C-2

Sikeston
D & B Trailer Mfg. Inc.
Route 2, Highway H
Sikeston, MO 63801
Tel: (314) 472-0657
MFR of *T*

Sikeston
Perry Trailer Mfg.
Route Z
Sikeston, MO 63801
Tel: (314) 471-3919
MFR of *T*

South Fork
Harco Trailer Mfg.
Junction 160 & E. Hwy.
South Fork, MO 65776
Tel: (417) 257-0714
MFR of *T*

South West City
Holden Industries, Inc.
RR 1, Box 151
South West City, MO 64863
Tel: (417) 762-3218
FAX: (417) 762-3464
Contact: Conne Fault
MFR of *T*
B-2:1
D

Springfield
Acro Trailer Company
2320 N. Packer Road
Springfield, MO 65803
Tel: (417) 862-1758
FAX: (414) 862-8084
Contact: Julie Burch
MFR of *S-2, T*
D

Springfield
DaBryan Coach Builders/Lyle Crowder
601 E. Trafficway
Springfield, MO 65806
Tel: (417) 864-4411
FAX: (417) 864-5922
MFR of *Limos*
C-2:10

Springfield
Executive Coachbuilders/ Armbruster/Stageway
3039 E. Pythian
Springfield, MO 65802
Tel: (417) 831-3161
FAX: (417) 831-1356
Contact: Howard Bailey
MFR of *Limos*
A-1, C-1

Springfield
Grant Truck Equipment
1352 NW Bypass
Springfield, MO 68503
Tel: (417) 869-5712
Contact: Virgil Anderson
MFR of *TB*

Washington
Riechers' Truck Body & Equipment Company
807 Madison Avenue
Washington, MO 63090
Tel: (314) 239-3700
Contact: Merl Schellick
MFR of *TB*

Westphalia
Play-Mor Trailers, Inc.
Highway 63, South
P.O. Box 128
Westphalia, MO 65085
Tel: (314) 455-2387
Tel: (314) 455-2322
FAX: (314) 455-2762
Contact: Jim Mandel
MFR of *R5, R6*
B-2:6
D

West Plains
Harco Trailer Mfg.
(MAIL: General Delivery South Fork, MO 65776)
West Plains, MO 65775
Tel: (417) 257-0714
Contact: Tom Hardin
MFR of *T*

MONTANA

Billings
Cy-Corp. Enterprises, Incorporated
1023 Mullowney Lane
Billings, MT 59101
Tel: (406) 259-4242
Contact: Tom Cysewski
MFR of *T*

Billings
Frank & Wetch Truck Body Shop
320 S. Billings Blvd.
Billings, MT 59101
Tel: (406) 259-9882
FAX: (406) 259-7122
REPAIR of *TB*

Billings
Galvin Repair
1330 Old Hardin Road
Billings, MT 59101
Tel: (406) 248-3093
Contact: Bruce Galvin
MFR of *T*

Billings
Gauger's RVs
5112 Laurel Road
Billings, MT 59101
Tel: (406) 248-3691
DLR of *RVs*
(Open 7 days a week)

Billings
Pacer Manufacturing
544 Moore Lane
Billings, MT 59101
Tel: (406) 245-2525
Contact: Jan Erickson
or Lee Erickson
MFR of *TC, UT, CT*

Billings
Pierce RV Sales
5th Street, West at
Montana Avenue
Billings, MT 59101
Tel: (406) 252-9313
Contact: Jerry Piccioni
DLR of *R1, R2*

Billings
Pierce Truck Equipment
1645 N. Frontage Road
Billings, MT 59105
Tel: (406) 245-6693
Nation: (800) 248-5803
Contact: Sharon Pierce
MFR of *TB*

Billings
Stauffer Truck Body Shop, Incorporated
6550 S. Frontage Road
Billings, MT 59101
Tel: (406) 652-4277
REPAIR of *TB*

Billings
Tana Trailers
600 1st Avenue, North
Billings, MT 59101
Tel: (406) 256-8262
FAX: (406) 256-8263
Contact: Shirley DeButh
MFR of *T*

Billings
Tour America RV Center
2220 Old Hardin Road
Billings, MT 59101
Tel: (406) 248-7481
FAX: (406) 248-2419
DLR of *R1*

Bozeman
C & T Trailer
2000 N. 7th Avenue
Bozeman, MT 59715
Tel: (406) 587-8610
Contact: Ken Corry
RENTAL of *R1, R2*

Bozeman
Smith Equipment USA
P.O. Box 3487
Bozeman, MT 59715
Tel: (406) 388-3424
Contact: Tony Holtze
MFR of *T*
D

Butte
Rocky Mountain RV Sales & Service
5101 Harrison Avenue
Butte, MT 59701
Tel: (406) 494-2555
Contact: Doug Hubbard
DLR of *R1, R2*
C-1

Conrad
Cascade Campers, Ltd.
238 Berland Road
P.O. Box 847
Conrad, MT 59425
Tel: (406) 278-7531
FAX: (406) 278-3027
Contact: Sandra Franzen
MFR of *TC*
C-2:1

Conrad
Intercontinental Truck Body
East Industrial Park
Conrad, MT 59425
Tel: (406) 278-7535
FAX: (406) 278-7946
MFR of *TB*

Fort Benton
Wilray Manufacturing
2500 St. Charles
Fort Benton, MT 59442
Tel: (406) 622-5680
Contact: Bill Whitaman
MFR of *T*

Great Falls
Aztec Custom Vans
5600 8th Avenue, South
Great Falls, MT 59405
Tel: (406) 452-7279
DLR of *Trucks*

Helena
Opie's RV Sales & Service
4395 N. Montana Avenue
Helena, MT 59601
Tel: (406) 443-7660
MT only: (800) 823-7660
FAX: (406) 443-4166
Contact: Tim Opie
DLR of *R1, R2*

Helena
Superior Fire Apparatus, Incorporated
Joslyn & Leslie Streets
Helena, MT 59601
Tel: (406) 442-0745
MFR of *F*
C-2

Kalispell
Currier's Certified Welding Works
1623 Montana Hwy. 35
Kalispell, MT 59901
Tel: (406) 752-2366
Contact: Tom Currier
MFR of *T, TB*

Kalispell
Pierce Mfg. Co., Inc.
1025 W. Center Street
Kalispell, MT 59901
Tel: (406) 257-5818
FAX: (406) 257-5820
Contact: Rita Pierce
MFR of *TB*

Kalispell
S & S Canopies & Campers Mfg., Inc.
2740 Hwy. 93, South
Kalispell, MT 59901
Tel: (406) 755-5080
Contact: Bob Perzinski
MFR of *TC*
C-1:3

Livingston
Smith Iron Works
1202 W. Front Street
Livingston, MT 59047
Tel: (406) 222-8214
Contact: Clark Smith
MFR of *CT*

Missoula
Trailer & Flatbed Supply
4555 N. Reserve
Missoula, MT 59801
Tel: (406) 728-1775
Contact: Samantha Mitchello
MFR of *T, CTB, FTB*

NEBRASKA

Alliance
Kidnapper Mfg.
HC 31, Box 12-C
Alliance, NE 69301
Tel: (308) 762-3042
DISTRIBUTOR of *TC*

Aurora
Aurora Body Shop
603 8th Street
Aurora, NE 68818
Tel: (402) 694-6991
R4

Bradshaw
Klute, Incorporated
P.O. Box 66
Bradshaw, NE 68319
Tel: (402) 736-4375
Contact: Steve Klute
DLR of *TB*

Coleridge
D & K Trailer & Mfg.
102 E. Cedar
Coleridge, NE 68727
Tel: (402) 283-4849
MFR of *T*

Columbus
Evans Plugge Co., Inc.
HC 81
Columbus, NE 68601
Tel: (402) 564-8681
MFR of *T*

Dakota City
Broyhill Company, The
North Market Square
Dakota, City, NE 68731-0475
Tel: (402) 987-3412
Nation: (800) 228-1003
FAX: (402) 987-3601
Contact: Dave Stingley
MFR of *G*
C-2

Fremont
Denning RV
3110 N. Broad Street
Fremont, NE 68025
Tel: (402) 721-5030
FAX: (402) 721-5570
Contact: Verle Denning
DLR of *R5, R6*

Gering
Lockwood Corporation
P.O. Box 160
Gering, NE 69341
Tel: (308) 436-5051
FAX: (308) 436-5732
Contact: Bruce Woods
MFR of *Military Vehicles*
D

Holdrege
Holdrege Truck Equipment Company
RR 2, Box 96
Holdrege, NE 68949
Tel: (308) 995-4901
Contact: Floyd Massey
DISTRIBUTOR of *TB*

Kimball
Mannon Coach Builders
106 W. 2nd Street
Kimball, NE 69145
Tel: (308) 235-2063
Contact: Steve Mannon
MFR of *R4*
C-1

Lincoln
Bouwen's Buggies
6045 Seward Avenue
Lincoln, NE 68507
Tel: (402) 464-3119
Contact: Judy Valens
R4

Lincoln
Double "B" RV
(Div. of Leach Camper Sales)
500 W. P Street
Lincoln, NE 68528
Tel: (402) 476-9302
DLR of R1, R2
C-2:4

Lincoln
Leach Camper Sales
2727 Cornhusker Hwy.
Lincoln, NE 68504
Tel: (402) 466-8581
Nation: (800) 289-3864
FAX: (402) 466-9455
Contact: Mr. Pat Leach
DLR of R1, R2
C-2:4

Lincoln
Meginnis Ford/Jeep/Eagle/Saab
6400 Q Street
Lincoln, NE 68505
Tel: (402) 464-0661
FAX: (402) 464-8546
Contact: Spence Vanneman
DLR of R4
C-1

Lincoln
Park Place
5020 O Street
Lincoln, NE 68510
Tel: (402) 464-0611
Nation: (800) 952-CARS
Contact: Abram Misley
DLR of R4

Lincoln
Truck Equip. Service Co.
800 Oak Street
Lincoln, NE 68521
Tel: (402) 476-3225
MFR of Grain S-2

Lincoln
Van House, The
1801 Cushman Drive
Lincoln, NE 68512
Tel: (402) 423-3600
FAX: (402) 423-0608
Contact: Jean Witt
R4
C-2
D

Louisville
Quality Trailers, Inc.
211 W. First Street
Louisville, NE 68037
Tel: (402) 234-2377
MFR of T, CT

Omaha
Autotrend
13333 Q Street
Omaha, NE 68137
Tel: (402) 896-8700
FAX: (402) 896-8113
Contact: Debra Waites
R4

Omaha
Badger Body & Truck Equipment Company
6336 Grover Street
Omaha, NE 68106
Tel: (402) 558-5300
Nation: (800) 642-9325
DLR of U

Omaha
Exclusive Coach, Inc./Conversion Van Center
5525 L Street
Omaha, NE 68117
Tel: (402) 731-3777
Contact: Don Laubach
MFR/DLR of R4, TConvs

Omaha
Fleetwood Travel Trailers, Incorporated
P.O. Box 37638
Omaha, NE 68137
Tel: (402) 895-1850
FAX: (402) 895-2387
MFR of R5, R6
D

Omaha
Fruehauf Corporation
11502 I Street
Omaha, NE 68137
Tel: (402) 333-4900
FAX: (402) 333-4685
Contact: Tom Anderson
MFR of T

Omaha
Kuker Industries
13709 Industrial Road
Omaha, NE 68137
Tel: (402) 895-3050
Nation: (800) 228-7277
FAX: (402) 895-7366
Contact: Mike Houlihan
MFR of T
A-1

Omaha
LBT, Incorporated
11502 I Street
Omaha, NE 68137
Tel: (402) 333-4900
FAX: (402) 333-0685
Contact: Tom Anderson
MFR of Tanker S-2, both Liquid & Bulk
NOTE: They mfr. these exclusively for Fruehauf. For more Fruehauf data, see their HQ listing in Detroit, MI.

Omaha
Leech's Prowlerland
4955 L Street
Omaha, NE 68117
Tel: (402) 734-5275
Nation: (800) 289-3862
Contact: Harold House
DLR of R5, R6

Omaha
L Street Truck & Van Center
5525 L Street
Omaha, NE 68117
Tel: (402) 731-3777
R4

Omaha
Schrier Ford & Imports
I-80 at Highway 50
Omaha, NE 68138
Tel: (402) 896-6000
Contact: Brad Hanson
R4
C-2

Omaha
United School Equipment Company of Iowa, Inc.
4401 S. 90th Street
Omaha, NE 68127
Tel: (402) 339-1045
Contact: Don Bahnsen
DISTRIBUTOR of S
D

Omaha
Victory Trucks
2409 G Street
Omaha, NE 68107
Tel: (402) 731-1800
DLR of R4, TB

Omaha
Vulcan Welding & Fabricating
2609 S. 156th Circle
Omaha, NE 68130
Tel: (402) 330-3263
Contact: Laura Persson
MFR of T

Plattsmouth
Plymouth Mfg. Inc.
217 Main Street
Plattsmouth, NE 68048
Tel: (402) 656-5865
Contact: Dave Schoone
MFR of T

Snyder
Smeal Mfg. Co.
HC 91, West
Snyder, NE 68664
Tel: (402) 568-2221
FAX: (402) 568-2223
Contact: Virgil Hunke
MFR of TB, U
C-2
D

Wayne
Great Dane Trailer, Inc.
1200 Centennial Road
Wayne, NE 68787
Tel: (402) 375-5500
FAX: (402) 375-5517
Contact: Terry Hanson
MFR of T
D

NEVADA

Carson City
Carson RV Sales & Service
4550 N. Carson
Carson City, NV 89706
Tel: (702) 882-8333
FAX: (702) 882-4136
Contact: Sue Crimmer
DLR of R1

Carson City
Excel Trailer Co., Inc.
5111 Grumman Drive
Carson City, NV 89706
Tel: (702) 885-0808
FAX: (702) 885-6888
Contact: Dwayne Wahl
MFR of R5, R6
D

Elko
C & J Horse Trailers
W. Bullion Road
Elko, NV 89801
Tel: (702) 738-3964
MFR/DLR of HT

Las Vegas
Valley Van Works
13 Gass Avenue
(Junction of S. Main St.)
Las Vegas, NV 89101
Tel: (702) 385-0721
FAX: (702) 385-0793
Contact: Dennis Dillon
MFR of *R4*

Las Vegas
Western Van Conversion
2216 E. Charleston Blvd.
Las Vegas, NV 89104
Tel: (702) 384-0211
Contact: Rapheal Romano
R4

Reno
Caravan Camper Tops
1875 Dickerson Road
Reno, NV 89503
Tel: (702) 323-0270
Contact: Dale Devine
DLR of *TC*

Reno
Nevada Camper
9125 S. Virginia Street
Reno, NV 89511
Tel: (702) 851-1204
Contact: Sharon Armado
DLR of *R1, R2*

Reno
Trick-Up Trucks
385-B Kietzke Lane
Reno, NV 89502
Tel: (702) 329-3554
Contact: Sam Sprague
MFR of *TConvs*
C-2

Sparks
Custom-Bilt, Inc.
372 Wolverine Way
Sparks, NV 89431
Tel: (702) 359-0192
Contact: Sharon Miles
R4
C-2

Sparks
Medtech Services
390 Freeport Blvd., #10
Sparks, NV 89431
Tel: (702) 358-4335
Contact: Rick Graver
H'cap R4

Sparks
RCS Conversions
3 E. Freeport Blvd.
Sparks, NV 89431
Tel: (702) 356-9190
FAX: (702) 356-9242
R4
C-2

Zephyr Cove
L & C Transportation
(MAIL: P.O. Box 2173
Stateline, NV 89449)
271 McFaul Way
Zephyr Cove, NV 89448
Tel: (702) 588-2514
FAX: (702) 588-5646
Contact: Lou Pusey
DLR/LEASING of *Limos*

NEW HAMPSHIRE

Candia
Precision Truck Body
Equipment Company
Jct. of Routes 43 & 27
Candia, NH 03034
Tel: (603) 483-8937
MFR/FINAL
ASSEMBLER of *TB*

Concord
Grappone Truck Center
Route 3-A
(Exit 12-F of I-93)
P.O. Box 424
Concord, NH 03301
Tel: (603) 224-0500
Nation: (800) 528-8993
Contact: Billy Nye
DLR of *Trucks*
(All Types; largest truck dealer in NH)

Londonderry
Ride Away Handicap
Equipment Corporation
51 Wentworth Avenue
Londonderry, NH 03053
Tel: (603) 623-5679
FAX: (603) 623-2972
Contact: Mark Lore
H'cap R4

Manchester
Bracken Company of
New Hampshire, Inc.
40 Willow Street
Manchester, NH 03103
Tel: (603) 668-5800
FAX: (603) 669-7784
Contact: Paul Bracken
DLR of *Heavy-Duty TB*

Manchester
Northeast Kustom
Creations
5 Varney Street
Manchester, NH 03102
Tel: (603) 622-0282
FAX: (603) 625-8493
Contact: Dennis Girard
MFR of *Utility R4*

Plaistow
Bus & Bodies
P.O. Box 464
Plaistow, NH 03865
Tel: (603) 382-7377
Nation: (800) 537-7700
FAX: (603) 382-1091
Contact: Sondi George
MFR/CONVERTER
of *S, U, R4*
C-2:2

West Lebanon
M & M Equipment
1 Plaza Heights
West Lebanon, NH 03784
Tel: (603) 298-5929
Contact: Butch Johnson
MFR/FINAL
ASSEMBLER of
M, UTB, VTB, XTB

NEW JERSEY

Avenel
Rick Brothers, Inc.
874 RR 1
Avenel, NJ 07001
Tel: (908) 634-9300
FAX: (908) 634-1140
Contact: Peter Ricciardone
REPAIR of *T*

Butler
Metadure Corporation
17 Valley Road
P.O. Box 106
Butler, NJ 07405
Tel: (201) 838-4300
FAX: (201) 838-0620
Contact: Craig Brinster
MFR of *ST, STB*:
Military Vehicles, Motion
Picture Vehicles, others

Butler
NY-NJ Trailer
Builders' Supply
1401 Route 23, South
Butler, NJ 07405
Tel: (201) 838-1050
MFR of *T*

Califon
Transtar Truck Body
& Welding
Route 513, Box 393
Califon, NJ 07830
Tel: (908) 832-2688
FAX: (908) 832-5747
REPAIR of *TB*

Deptford
Americar, Incorporated
264 N. Desla Drive
Deptford, NJ 08069
Tel: (609) 845-2200
FAX: (609) 845-6151
Contact: Ken Gore
DLR of *Limos*

Egg Harbor
Waona Coach Inc.
603 Hamburg Avenue
P.O. Box 314
Egg Harbor, NJ 08215
Tel: (609) 965-0686
FAX: (609) 965-3765
UConvs

Elizabeth
Industrial Truck Body
Corporation
251 North Avenue, East
Elizabeth, NJ 07201
Tel: (908) 354-3535
FAX: (908) 354-3545
MFR of *T*

Emerson
Westwood Limousine
Sales & Service
55 Kinderkamack Road
Emerson, NJ 07630
Tel: (201) 444-8905
DLR of *Limos*

Fairfield
Braun Corporation
5 Industrial Road
Fairfield, NJ 07004
Tel: (201) 882-5455
FAX: (201) 882-8076
Contact: George Noreen
R4

Fairfield
Drive-Master Corp.
9 Spielman Road
Fairfield, NJ 07004
Tel: (201) 808-9709
FAX: (201) 808-9713
Contact: Adrianne Ruprecht
R4

Fairview
Cliffside Body Corp.
130 Broad Avenue
Fairview, NJ 07022
Tel: (201) 945-3970
FAX: (201) 945-7534
Contact: Olga Greenwold
MFR of *TB, U*

Farmingdale
Campers of America
Collingswood Park Circle
Farmingdale, NJ 07727
Tel: (908) 938-9600
DLR of *TC*

Farmingdale
Seely Equipment & Supply Company
1325 State Highway 34
Farmingdale, NJ 07727
Tel: (908) 938-2900
R4

Franklinville
Inkster Mobility Systems
RR 3, Box 332
Porchtown Road
Franklinville, NJ 08332
Tel: (609) 694-1439
FAX: (609) 694-3323
CONVERTER of *H'cap Units*

Hammonton
Custom Sales & Service, Incorporated
11th & 2nd Streets
Hammonton, NJ 08037
Tel: (201) 561-6900
Nation: (800) 257-7855
FAX: (201) 567-9318
Contact: Linda Kyle
MFR of *TB*
C-2

Hillside
Heller Truck Body Corp.
138 US Highway 22
Hillside, NJ 07205
Tel: (201) 923-9200
MFR of *TB*

Hillsborough
Ajax Mfg. Co., Inc.
321 Valley Road
Hillsborough, NJ 08876
Tel: (908) 369-5544
FAX: (908) 369-5415
Contact: Carl Massaro
MFR of *T*
B-2
D

Jackson
Adaptive Driving Conversions, Inc.
156 E. Commodore Blvd.
Jackson, NJ 08527
Tel: (908) 928-2089
Nation: (800) 866-1529
FAX: (908) 928-2449
Contact: Ted Jackrel
H'cap R4, R4
C-2
D

Jackson
RWV Custom Truck Bodies, Incorporated
351 Pfister Road
Jackson, NJ 08527
Tel: (908) 364-2645
FINAL ASSEMBLER of *TB*

Jersey City
Berthe Upholstery Co.
3718 JFK Blvd.
Jersey City, NJ 07307
Tel: (201) 659-8630
Contact: Al Berthe
R4

Kenilworth
CKI, Incorporated
121 N. Michigan Avenue
Kenilworth, NJ 07033
Tel: (908) 245-3032
FAX: (908) 687-7617
Contact: Dominic Legd
MFR of *TB, R4*

Lakewood
Family Vans, Inc.
1133 Route 88
Lakewood, NJ 08701
Tel: (908) 370-1022
DLR of *R1, R2, R4, R6*

Lakewood
Scott Motor Coach Sales, Incorporated
1260 State Highway 88
Lakewood, NJ 08701
Tel: (908) 370-1022
Contact: Walter Hynes
DLR of *R1, R2*

Lyndhurst
Prevost Car, Inc.
862 Valley Brook Avenue
Lyndhurst, NJ 07071
Tel: (201) 933-3900
FAX: (201) 933-2785
Contact: Joseph Craig
MFR of *U*
C-1

Medford
Sirchie Fingerprint Laboratories
612 Gravelly Hollow Rd.
Medford, NJ 08055
Tel: (609) 654-0777
Nation: (800) 545-7375
Contact: Mr. Aubrey Hall
MFR of *Surveillance Vehicles, Command Communication Vehicles, Evidence-Collection Vehicles, Paddy Wagons, Prisoner Transport Vehicles, Other Police-Work-Related Vehicles, E (Class A CDL probably will be needed for the larger of these.)*
C-2 (Off-duty & former police personnel are favored.)
NOTE: *This is the mfg. plant. See also the Corporate HQ listing at Raleigh, NC.*

Mickelton
General Engines Company, Incorporated
409-B Southgate Court
Mickelton, NJ 80856
Tel: (609) 845-5400
Nation: (800) 722-8803
FAX: (609) 423-0999
Contact: Linda Boulton
MFR of *T*
D

Middlesex
Van-Con, Incorporated
123 William Street
Middlesex, NJ 08846
Tel: (908) 356-8484
MFR of *S*

Milford
Classic Coachworks
735 Frenchtown Road
Milford, NJ 08848
Tel: (908) 996-3400
R4
C-2:1

Mount Laurel
Universal Vans
9 Gardenia Court
Mount Laurel, NJ 08054
Tel: (609) 866-1703
Contact: Mike Kahn
R4

Newark
American Motorcoach, Incorporated
250 South Street
Newark, NJ 07114
Tel: (201) 621-2100
Contact: Bernie Martin
R4

Newark
Bodies by Lembo
76 Riverside Avenue
Newark, NJ 07104
Tel: (201) 484-3200
FAX: (201) 484-0081
Contact: Alfred Lembo
MFR of *Trucks*
D

Newark
Bristol-Donald Co., Inc.
50 Roanoke Avenue
Newark, NJ 07105
Tel: (201) 589-2640
FAX: (201) 589-2610
Contact: Bob Greenley
MFR of *TB, U*

Newark
Otto's Truck Body Works Corporation
118-132 Avenue L
Newark, NJ 07105
Tel: (201) 344-1611
FAX: (201) 344-2806
Contact: Carl Leber
MFR of *CTB*

Oaklyn
Lakeview Custom Coach
100 White Horse Pike
Oaklyn, NJ 08107
Tel: (609) 854-3300
Nation: (800) 654-0031
FAX: (609) 854-8675
Contact: Debbie Beevers
DLR of *Limos*

Paramus
Sanitation Equip. Corp.
S-122 State Hwy. 17
Paramus, NJ 07652
Tel: (201) 843-3616
DISTRIBUTOR of *STB*

Parsippany
Linear Dynamics, Inc.
400 Lanidex Plaza
Parsippany, NJ 07054
Tel: (201) 884-0300
(Corp. Office)
Tel: (717) 547-1621
(Plant)
FAX: (201) 884-9407
Contact Marie Noneamecher
MFR of *TB*

Parsippany
Vans East
1200 US Hwy. 46
Parsippany, NJ 07054
Tel: (201) 335-4350
Contact: Jim Demaio
R4

Paterson
Eastern Tank Corp.
290 Pennsylvania Avenue
Paterson, NJ 07503
Tel: (201) 278-2234
MFR of *T*
B-2

Paterson
Steelfab Division
500 Marshall Street
Paterson, NJ 07503
Tel: (201) 278-0350
Contact: Janet Grisano
MFR of *TB, U*

Ramsey
Chariot Sales & Leasing, Incorporated
476 State Route 17
Ramsey, NJ 07446
Tel: (201) 934-7400
DLR/LEASE of *Vans*

Ramsey
Getaway Recreational Vehicles, Incorporated
476 Route 17, North
Ramsey, NJ 07446
Tel: (201) 825-0811
Contact: Jack Curran
DLR of *R4, TConvs*

Saddle Brook
Topo Customs
196 5th Street
Saddle Brook, NJ 07662
Tel: (201) 845-0019
FAX: (201) 845-7817
Contact: Craig O'Neal
R4

Shrewsbury
Monmouth Truck Equip.
745 Shrewsbury Avenue
Shrewsbury, NJ 07702
Tel: (908) 741-1199
Contact: Dave McMullen
R4

South Hackensack
Fun Truck'N Van Conversions
470 US Highway 46
South Hackensack, NJ 07606
Tel: (201) 440-2100
Contact: Al Ackerman
R4

South River
Cyclevan Unlimited, Inc.
6 William Street
South River, NJ 08882
Tel: (908) 238-3110
NJ only: (800) 640-3110
Contact: Howard Lichtman
R4

Summit
Summit Truck Body, Inc.
50 Franklin Place
Summit, NJ 07901
Tel: (908) 277-4342
MFR/FINAL ASSEMBLER of *TB*

Thorofare
H. A. DeHart & Son Truck Bodies
Crown Point Road
Thorofare, NJ 08086
Tel: (609) 845-2800
Nation: (800) 222-0270
Nation: (800) 222-0271
FAX: (609) 845-2461
Contact: Phil Clifford, Jr.
DLR of *TB*
C-1

Trenton
D & D Trailers, Inc.
100 Lexington Avenue
Trenton, NJ 08618
Tel: (609) 771-0001
Nation: (800) 533-0442
Contact: Susan Ralph
MFR of *UT*

Vincentown
Industrial Trailer Co.
107 Flyatt Road
Vincentown, NJ 08088
Tel: (609) 268-1350
Nation: (800) 666-7368
FAX: (609) 778-9202
Contact: Gale Goldenbaul
DLR of *T*

Voorhees
Jersey Trailer Mfg.
100 Crescent Road
Voorhees, NJ 08043
Tel: (609) 784-7766
MFR of *Heavy-Duty T*

Waldwick
L. A. Street Vans
144 Franklin Turnpike
Waldwick, NJ 07463
Tel: (201) 447-3331
FAX: (201) 447-0150
Contact: Rich Andrychewitz
R4

Wharton
Odyssey Automotive Specialty, Incorporated
317 Richard Mine Road
Wharton, NJ 07885
Tel: (201) 328-2667
FAX: (201) 328-2639
Contact: Steven Vickson
MFR of *Specialty Vehicles*
C-2
D

Woodbury
Performance Vans of Woodbury
1549 Gateway Blvd.
Woodbury, NJ 08096
Tel: (609) 848-3470
FAX: (609) 853-8341
Contact: Ed Hurd
R4

NEW MEXICO

Albuquerque
Accurate RV & Van Services
525 Wyoming Blvd., NE
Albuquerque, NM 87123
Tel: (505) 256-3996
Contact: Rick O'Neil
R4

Albuquerque
Admiral Mfg. Co.
6700 2nd Street, NW
Albuquerque, NM 87107
Tel: (505) 345-4818
FAX: (505) 345-9175
Contact: Scott Johnson
MFR of *TC*
D: Jason Industries

Albuquerque
Albuquerque Truck Equipment, Incorporated
7920 Ranchitos Loop, NE
Albuquerque, NM 87113
Tel: (505) 898-8895
Contact: Dale Martin
DLR of *TB*

Albuquerque
Amigo Mobility Center
405 Montano Road, NE
Albuquerque, NM 87107
Tel: (505) 344-2875
H'cap R4

Albuquerque
Camp Town RV
10950 Central Ave., SE
Albuquerque, NM 87123
Tel: (505) 293-3600
Nation: (800) 291-0078
FAX: (505) 291-0078
Contact: Steve Robertson
DLR of *R1, R2, R5, R6*

Albuquerque
Canada, Inc.
615 Wyoming Blvd., SE
Albuquerque, NM 87123
Tel: (505) 265-5796
Contact: Henry Gallegos
FINAL ASSEMBLER of *TB*

Albuquerque
Cara Van Customs, Inc.
4505 Menaul Blvd., NE
Albuquerque, NM 87110
Tel: (505) 888-3443
FAX: (505) 888-3501
Contact: Greg McCracken
R4

Albuquerque
Carriage, Incorporated/ Holiday Travel
11100 Central Ave., SE
Albuquerque, NM 87123
Tel: (505) 294-8280
Tel: (505) 299-7905
DLR of *R6*

Albuquerque
Clark Truck Equipment Company
2370 Aztec Road, NE
Albuquerque, NM 87107
Tel: (505) 880-8222
Nation: (800) 678-2741
FAX: (505) 880-8288
Contact: Michael Apodaca
DLR of *M, W, SP, UTB, VTB, T*

Albuquerque
Classic Conversions
7320 4th Street, NW
Albuquerque, NM 87107
Tel: (505) 898-4652
Contact: Jim Homan
CONVERTER of *R1*

Albuquerque
Fruehauf Trailer Corp.
5010 Jefferson Street, NE
Albuquerque, NM 87109
Tel: (505) 881-9474
Contact: Dave Quintana
DLR of *S-2*
(This is the Sales Office.)

Albuquerque
Holiday, Incorporated
11100 Central Ave., SE
Albuquerque, NM 87123
Tel: (505) 294-8280
Tel: (505) 299-7905
Contact: Andy Amagon
DLR of *R1, R2*

Albuquerque
Holiday World RV Center
9999 Central Avenue
Albuquerque, NM 87123
Tel: (505) 299-6838
FAX: (505) 296-2877
Contact: Lew Bickers
DLR of *R1*

Albuquerque
J & B Mfg. Co.
5150 Edith Blvd., NE
Albuquerque, NM 87107
Tel: (505) 345-0472
FAX: (505) 345-0772
Contact: George Montez
MFR of *T*

Albuquerque
King of the Road
3916 Juan Tabo Blvd, NE
Albuquerque, NM 87111
Tel: (505) 298-2161
Contact: Abott Kaiser
DLR of *R1, R2*

Albuquerque
Koll Trailers, Inc.
1001 Prosperity, SE
Albuquerque, NM 87105
Tel: (505) 873-8400
Nation: (800) 524-4183
Contact: Leslie Koll
DLR of *HT, ST, UT*

Albuquerque
MCT Industries
7451 Pan American Freeway, NE
Albuquerque, NM 87109
Tel: (505) 345-8651
FAX: (505) 345-8659
Contact: Evette Silver
DLR of *TB, T*
D

Albuquerque
Myers RV Center, Inc.
12024 Centeral Ave., SE
Albuquerque, NM 87123
Tel: (505) 298-7691
FAX: (505) 293-7172
Contact: Anne Thomas
DLR of *R1*

Albuquerque
New Horizon Vans, Inc.
1903 Edith Blvd., NE
Albuquerque, NM 87102
Tel: (505) 247-1447
Contact: Dan Drury
H'cap R4

Albuquerque
On The Road Again RVs
4305 Lomas Blvd., NE
Albuquerque, NM 87110
Tel: (505) 266-3363
FAX: (505) 256-7109
Contact: Jack Bennington
DLR of *ST*
B-2

Albuquerque
Paul's Custom Trailers
842 Alameda Road, NW
Albuquerque, NM 87114
Tel: (505) 898-1382
MFR of *T*

Albuquerque
Suburban Recreational Vehicles, Incorporated
6022 Second Street, NW
Albuquerque, NM 87107
Tel: (505) 344-3585
FAX: (505) 344-6876
DLR of *R1*

Albuquerque
Topper Town
3201 Candelaria Rd., NE
Albuquerque, NM 87107
Tel: (505) 884-8258
FAX: (505) 884-3620
Contact: Mike Gaffney
MFR/DLR of *TC*

Albuquerque
Truck Dealers' Equipment Co., Inc.
2108 Candelaria Rd., NE
Albuquerque, NM 87107
Tel: (505) 884-9400
Nation: (800) 432-5257
FAX: (505) 884-9545
Contact: Randy Cole
DLR of *TB*

Albuquerque
Van Crafters Industries
916 San Mateo Blvd., NE
Albuquerque, NM 87108
Tel: (505) 265-3495
Contact: Mike Johnson
R4

Albuquerque
Vantastic Vans
525 Wyoming Blvd., NE
Albuquerque, NM 87123
Tel: (505) 268-5009
DLR of *R4*

Albuquerque
Webb Snipes Trailer & Horse Company
5100 Broadway Blvd., SE
Albuquerque, NM 87105
Tel: (505) 877-2471
DLR of *HT*

Albuquerque
Western Metal Works
8325 Washington St., NE
Albuquerque, NM 87113
Tel: (505) 822-9170
MFR of *TB*

Aztec
Discount Trailer Mfr.
1404 W. Aztec Blvd.
Aztec, NM 87410
Tel: (505) 334-9384
MFR of *T*

Clovis
Master Trim
800 N. Main Street
Clovis, NM 88101
Tel: (505) 762-2901
R4

Espanola
Rio Grande Camper Manufacturers
Hwy. 84 & Hwy. 285
Espanola, NM 87532
Tel: (505) 753-3292
MFR of *TC*

Farmington
Best Truck Body
#26 CR 1956
Farmington, NM 87401
Tel: (505) 325-8196
MFR of *TB*

Los Lunas
Accutrak Mfg. Corp.
P.O. Box 310
Los Lunas, NM 87031
Tel: (505) 865-9648
FAX: (505) 865-0313
Contact: Jane McKay
MFR/DLR of *T*

Milan
Silver Creek Trailer Mfg.
1399 W. Highway 66
Milan, NM 87021
Tel: (505) 287-7067
MFR of *T*

Pojoaque
Pojoaque Valley Equip.
Highway 285
Pojoaque, NM 87501
Tel: (505) 455-3221
Tel: (505) 455-7751
Contact: Bob Massengil
or John Massengil
DLR of *HT*

Raton
Diamond M Trailer Co.
Sugarite Canyon
Raton, NM 87740
Tel: (505) 445-3858
Contact: Mark Vanbuster
MFR of *T*

Roswell
Transportation Mfg. Corporation
72 Earl Cummings Loop, West
P.O. Box 5670
Roswell, NM 88201
Tel: (505) 347-2011
FAX: (505) 347-7505
Contact: Clyde Casey
MFR of *U*
C-2;6

Santa Fe
Al's RV Center, Inc.
4033 Cerrillos Road
Santa Fe, NM 87501
Tel: (505) 471-7367
Contact: Al Romero
DLR of *R1*

Texico
Tedson, Incorporated
P.O. Box 212
Texico, NM 88135
Tel: (505) 482-9030
Contact: Ted Lopez
MFR of *T*

NEW YORK

Albany
Albany Custom Vans & Accessories
111 Exchange Street
Albany, NY 12205
Tel: (518) 489-1770
FAX: (518) 489-1886
Contact: Al Sacca
H'cap R4

Albany
Century Auto Body Repair
1054 Central Avenue
Albany, NY 12205
Tel: (518) 482-5877
Contact: Bela Schurch
R4

Amityville
Island Luxury Vans, Inc.
195 Sunrise Hwy., #A
Amityville, NY 11701
Tel: (516) 842-7500
MFR of *R4*

Amsterdam
Alpin Haus RV
Route 30, North
Amsterdam, NY 12010
Tel: (518) 843-4400
Tel: (518) 882-9050
Nation: (800) 541-8248
FAX: (518) 843-5159
Contact: Bob Rose
DLR of *R1*

Auburn
F. P. Riester, Inc.
2782 Sand Beach Road
Auburn, NY 13021
FINAL ASSEMBLER
of TB

Bay Shore
Nesco Bus Maintenance, Incorporated
101 Cleveland Avenue
Bay Shore, NY 11706
Tel: (516) 243-4500
FAX: (516) 243-0921
Contact: Nestor Zaragosa
REPAIR of *U*
B-1

Bay Shore
Westrock Vending Vehicles Company
1565 Fifth Industrial Ct.
Bay Shore, NY 11706
Tel: (516) 666-5252
Nation: (800) 831-3166
FAX: (516) 666-1319
Contact: Teresa Bellizzi
MFR of *TB, U*
D

Bohemia
Abaco Steel Products, Incorporated
1560 Locust Avenue
Bohemia, NY 11716
Tel: (516) 589-1800
FAX: (516) 589-1197
Contact: Ken Podd
R4
C-2

Bohemia
Grumman Allied Division
1470 Veterans Memorial Highway
Bohemia, NY 11716
Tel: (516) 737-5400
Contact: Brooke McHugh
MFR of *TB*
C-2

- 248 -

Bohemia
Tryac Truck & Equipment Company
1365 Lakeland Avenue
Bohemia, NY 11716
Tel: (516) 563-1300
Contact: Peter Nettesheim
DLR of *TB*

Boston
Valley Truck & Equipment Company
9776 Trevett Road
Boston, NY 14025
Tel: (716) 941-6644
Contact: Herb Weahrfritz
MFR of *TB*
C-2

Bronx
AAA Commercial Truck Body
329 Canal Place
Bronx, NY 10451
Tel: (718) 993-1170
FAX: (212) 292-7422
Contact: Raymond Divipo
MFR of *TB, U*

Bronx
Auto Glass Service Center
712 Southern Blvd.
Bronx, NY 10455
Tel: (718) 542-8200
R4

Bronx
Dillinger/Gaines Coachworks, Ltd.
325 Exterior Street
Bronx, NY 10451-2006
Tel: (718) 402-6700
FAX: (212) 402-6722
Contact: Ruth Cerling
MFR of *Limos*
C-2

Bronx
Mover's Supply House, Incorporated
1476 E. 222nd Street
Bronx, NY 10469
Tel: (718) 671-1200
CUSTOMIZER of *S-2*

Brooklyn
Able Welding Company
1527 62nd Street
Brooklyn, NY 11219
Tel: (718) 259-3616
R4

Brooklyn
Bill's Safety Auto Glass
606 Coney Island Avenue
Brooklyn, NY 11218
Tel: (718) 435-5500
FAX: (718) 436-9756
Contact: Steven Koch
R4

Brooklyn
Empire Coach/ Tortora Limousine
100 Neptune Avenue
Brooklyn, NY 11235
Tel: (718) 615-0560
Tel: (718) 934-6262
FAX: (718) 769-3008
Contact: Marsha Tortora
MFR of *Limos*
C-1

Brooklyn
George Hirn III
413 Troutman Street
Brooklyn, NY 11237
Tel: (718) 386-4480
FAX: (718) 381-9787
MFR of *TB*
D

Brooklyn
Mr. Glass of Brooklyn, Incorporated
767 65th Street
Brooklyn, NY 11220
Tel: (718) 833-4777
R4

Buffalo
M & K Mobility
284 Hinman Avenue
Buffalo, NY 14216
Tel: (716) 876-6190
FAX: (716) 876-6191
Contact: Donald Moser
H'cap Units

Buffalo
Rassow International Company., Inc.
1875 Harlem Road
Buffalo, NY 14212
Tel: (716) 895-9800
Contact: David D'Amico
MFR of *TB*
C-1

Buffalo
Recreatives Industries, Incorporated
60 Depot Street
Buffalo, NY 14206
Tel: (716) 855-2226
Nation: (800) 255-2511
FAX: (716) 855-1094
Contact: Sid Wallach
MFR of *6-Wheel-Drive & All Terrain Vehicles*
D

Buffalo
T-W Truck Equippers, Incorporated
2025 Walden Avenue
Buffalo, NY 14225
Tel: (716) 683-2250
Nation: (800) 444-7417
FAX: (716) 683-2257
R4

Buffalo
Unicell Body Co., Inc.
571 Howard Street
Buffalo, NY 14206
Tel: (716) 853-8628
Nation: (800) 628-8914
FAX: (716) 854-7828
Contact: Roger Martin
MFR of *TB, VTB*
C-2

Center Moriches
Cod Truck Body Manufacturing., Inc.
Wading River Road
Center Moriches, NY 11934
Tel: (516) 878-2211
MFR of *TB*

Chittenango
Central New York Coach Sales & Service, Inc.
7765 Lakeport Road
Chittenango, NY 13037
Tel: (315) 687-3969
Nation: (800) 962-5768
Contact: Rex Cary
DISTRIBUTOR of *H'cap Units*
C-2

Clayton
Frink America, Inc.
205 Webb Street
Clayton, NY 13624
Tel: (315) 686-5531
FAX: (315) 686-5527
Contact: Joel Mitchell
MFR of *SP*
C-2

Copiague
Ward Bodies, Inc.
50 Court Street
Copiague, NY 11726
Tel: (516) 842-8870
MFR of *U*
C-2

Deer Park
Garsite Products, Inc.
172 E. Industry Court
Box 289
Deer Park, NY 11729
Tel: (516) 667-1010
Nation: (800) 645-5802
FAX: (516) 242-3444
Contact: Judy O'Kane
MFR of *Airport Luggage Hauling Trucks*

Deer Park
Sterling Coachworks, Inc
513 Commack Road
Deer Park, NY 11729
Tel: (516) 242-8900
FAX: (516) 242-8437
R4
C-2

Depew
Bob's Tops & Seat Works, Incorporated
4756 Broadway
Depew, NY 14043
Tel: (716) 681-0380
FAX: (716) 681-0389
R4

Elmira
Vans Royale
1360 College Avenue
Elmira, NY 14901
Tel: (607) 734-5010
MODIFIER of *R4*

Elmira
Zimmer Products, Inc.
RR 2
Elmira, NY 14901
Tel: (607) 733-5585
Contact: Ernie Zimmer
DLR of *TC*

Endicott
Terry's Auto Service
316 Jennings Street
Endicott, NY 13760
Tel: (607) 785-0292
FAX: (607) 785-2665
DLR of *Trucks*

Farmingdale
Truck Body Associates, Incorporated
269-D Eastern Parkway
Farmingdale, NY 11735
Tel: (516) 694-5858
DLR of *TB*

Flushing
M & M Crown Auto Accessories
13523 Northern Blvd.
Flushing, NY 11354
Tel: (718) 539-6127
FAX: (718) 461-6333
Contact: Mark Solo
R4
C-2

Freeport
John Bussani, Inc.
34 Bedell Street
Freeport, NY 11520
Tel: (516) 223-6080
FAX: (516) 223-9018
Contact: Peter Zarba
R4

Garden City Park
Van Buren Truck Body Builders
2289 Jericho Turnpike
Garden City Park, NY 11040
Tel: (516) 746-4670
Contact: Richard Bolve
MFR of *T*
DLR of *TB*
C-2

Great Neck
Norca Corporation
185 Great Neck Road
Great Neck, NY 11021
Tel: (516) 466-9500
MFR of *T*

Haverstraw
Van Village, Ltd.
244 Route 9, West
Haverstraw, NY 10927
Tel: (914) 429-4440
FAX: (914) 429-0385
Contact: Ray Rolando
R4
C-2

Hicksville
Mary K Auto Interior, Incorporated
950 S. Broadway, #A
Hicksville, NY 11801
Tel: (516) 931-8060
R4

Hilton
Husard's RV Center
831 Manitou Road
Hilton, NY 14468
Tel: (716) 392-8538
Contact: Shirley Husard
MFR of *R1, R2, R3*

Holbrook
Daniel's Wrecker Sales
929-1 Lincoln Avenue
Holbrook, NY 11741
Tel: (516) 361-3542
DLR of *W*

Hollis
New York Custom Coach Company
198-29 Jamaica Avenue
Hollis, NY 11423
Tel: (718) 465-5999
Contact: Andy Perillo
MFR of *Limos*

Hudson Falls
Neff's RV USA
194-L Dix Avenue
Hudson Falls, NY 12839
Tel: (518) 747-2857
FAX: (518) 747-8206
Contact: Judy Dreisbach
DLR of *R1, R2*

Hurley
Klun Truck Bodies
Old Route 209
Hurley, NY 12443
Tel: (914) 338-5838
REPAIR of *TB*

Ithaca
Welco Custom Trim
207 Elmira Road
Ithaca, NY 14850
Tel: (607) 277-4727
FAX: (607) 277-7502
R4

Jamaica
A. A. Benson's Truck Bodies, Incorporated
125-20 150th Ave., South
Jamaica, NY 11420
Tel: (718) 843-7457
REPAIR of *TB*

Jamaica
Turnpike Vans, Inc.
21211 Hillside Avenue
Jamaica, NY 11427
Tel: (718) 217-1500
DLR/RENTAL of *Vans*

Kings Park
Huntington Hills Service Center
490 Pulaski Road
Kings Park, NY 11754
Tel: (516) 544-9000
FAX: (516) 544-0942
MFR of *TB*
C-2
D

Kingston
Campers' Barn of Kingston, Incorporated
124 Route 28
Kingston, NY 12401
Tel: (914) 338-8200
Contact: Brian Hill
DLR of *R1, TC*

Kingston
Captain Vantastic
731 Ulster Avenue
Kingston, NY 12401
Tel: (914) 331-2008
FAX: (914) 331-3263
Contact: Art Lane
R4

Lindenhurst
Van & 4x4 Conversions of Lindenhurst
265 Cortland
Lindenhurst, NY 11757
Tel: (516) 226-1441
R4, 4x4Convs

Long Island City
Eckhoff Truck Bodies
3622 14th Street
Long Island City, NY 11106
Tel: (718) 784-8714
FAX: (718) 361-6990
Contact: Peter Eckhoff
R4

Massena
Moser Custom Trim Shop
Route 56
Massena, NY 13652
Tel: (315) 769-5529
Contact: Rick Moser
R4

Middletown
Mid-Town Auto Body
20 Preston Street
Middletown, NY 10940
Tel: (914) 342-1364
Contact: Fred Malara
MFR of *H'cap Units*

Mount Sinai
Shooter's Location Vans
796 Canal Road
Mount Sinai, NY 11766
Tel: (516) 473-7464
RENTAL of *Vans*

Nanuet
Al's Motor Homes, Inc.
250 West Route 59
Nanuet, NY 10954
Tel: (914) 623-8800
FAX: (914) 623-8975
Contact: Susan Math
DLR of *R1, R2, R3*

New Hyde Park
Melrose Custom Vans
1007 Jericho Turnpike
New Hyde Park, NY 11040
Tel: (516) 328-1444
FAX: (516) 328-1446
Contact: Mike Natler
R4

New York City
Autoxport
180 Broadway
New York City, NY 10038
Tel: (212) 349-1168
FAX: (212) 349-1329
Contact: Carlos Suazo
DLR of *Used long-wheelbase Limos*
NOTE: *All that they sell are shipped overseas. So consider only as a possibility for DPU work.*

New York City
CCS International
360 Madison Avenue
(Betw. 45th & 46th Sts.)
New York City, NY 10017
Tel: (212) 557-3040
Contact: Bill Kelly
MFR of *Armored Vehicles*
C-2

New York City
Manhattan Ford-Lincoln-Mercury
555 W. 57th Street
New York City, NY 10019
Tel: (212) 581-7800
Contact: Tony Maisto
DLR of *Limos*

New York City
Sterling Transportation
305 Madison Avenue
Suite 411
New York City, NY 11236
Tel: (718) 968-7575
DLR of *T*

New Windsor
Handicapped Mobility Systems, Incorporated
68 Walsh Avenue
New Windsor, NY 12553
Tel: (914) 561-4910
Contact: Art Glynn
MFR of *H'cap Units*
C-2

Niagara Falls
Van City
2708 Niagara Falls Blvd.
Niagara Falls, NY 14304
Tel: (716) 693-1727
Tel: (716) 731-4335
Nation: (800) 876-2708
Contact: Donald Lenda
R4

North Tonawanda
Colton Auto, Inc.
3176 Niagara Falls Blvd.
North Tonawanda, NY 14120
Tel: (716) 694-0188
Contact: Ron Tingrey
R4

Oneonta
Medical Coaches, Inc.
Hemlock Road
P.O. Box 129
Oneonta, NY 13820
Tel: (607) 432-1333
Nation: (800) 432-1339
FAX: (607) 432-8190
Contact: Leonard Marsh
MFR of *A*
C-2
NOTE: *Vehicles are mfd. only for export. Limited driving opportunity. Co. was not hiring at time of this research.*

Patchogue
Planet Speed & Custom Shop
177 Medford Avenue
Patchogue, NY 11772
Tel: (516) 475-7777
Contact: Larry Mars
R4
C-2

- 250 -

Pearl River
Charlie's Mobile Glass & Lock Service
25 Lois Drive
Pearl River, NY 10965
Tel: (914) 735-6828
R4

Penn Yan
Coach & Equip. Mfg.
Brown Street
Penn Yan, NY 14527
Tel: (315) 536-2321
FAX: (315) 536-0460
Contact: Kathy Reed
MFR of *U*
C-2

Plainview
Specialty Vehicles
180 Dupont Street
Plainview, NY 11803
Tel: (516) 349-7700
FAX: (516) 349-0482
DLR of *Limos*
C-2

Port Sanilac
National Coach Engineering, Ltd.
2525 N. Lakeshore Road
Port Sanilac, NY 48469
Tel: (313) 622-9624
FAX: (313) 622-8689
MFR of *Limos*
C-2:5

Poughkeepasie
Mid-Hudson Mack, Inc.
205 Delafield Street
Poughkeepsie, NY 12601
Tel: (914) 298-6225
Contact: Jim Losby
DLR of *TB*

Rego Park/Queens
Picasso Coach Builders
63-34 Austin Street
Rego Park, NY 11374
Tel: (718) 897-7606
FAX: (718) 897-7975
Contact: John Ciccotelli
MFR of *Limos*

Rensselaer
Albany Mack Sales, Inc.
309 Columbia Street
Rensselaer, NY 12144
Tel: (518) 465-4766
DLR of *Mack TB*

Riverhead
Eastern Welding, Inc.
274 Mill Road
Riverhead, NY 11901
Tel: (516) 727-3576
FAX: (516) 727-4682
Contact: Brian Stubelek
MFR of *TB*
C-2:6

Riverhead
Mobility Solutions, Inc.
36 Raynor Avenue
Riverhead, NY 11901
Tel: (516) 369-5426
R4, H'cap R4

Rochester
Agor Enterprises
951 Panorama Trail
Rochester, NY 14625
Tel: (716) 385-2556
R4

Rochester
Autocrafting by Technistar
314 Buffalo Road
Rochester, NY 14611
Tel: (716) 328-8570
FAX: (716) 328-0004
Contact: Jeff Curts
R4

Rochester
Manuele Custom Truck Bodies
405 Sherman Street
Rochester, NY 14635
Tel: (716) 458-6450
MFR of *TB*

Rochester
Northeast Marine Industries
52 Bennington Drive
Rochester, NY 14616
Tel: (716) 663-0880
FAX: (716) 663-5044
Contact: Shawn Mosley
MFR of *BT*
C-2

Rochester
T-W Truck Equippers, Incorporated
174 Colvin Street
Rochester, NY 14611
Tel: (716) 235-4500
TConvs

Selden
Transapple Custom Vans
770 Middle Country Road
Selden, NY 11784
Tel: (516) 696-0039
FAX: (516) 696-0045
R4
C-2

Spring Valley
Kurt Bass
5 Sunny Ridge Road
Spring Valley, NY 10977
Tel: (914) 354-5945
Contact: Kurt Bass
DLR of *Limos*

Stockport
Scott's Aluminum Truck Body
Route 9
Stockport, NY 12150
Tel: (518) 828-0524
MFR of *TB*

Suffern
TPI Sturdicorp/ U.S. Bus
Ramapo Avenue
Suffern, NY 10901
Tel: (914) 357-2510
FAX: (914) 357-1133
MFR of *S*
C-2

Suffern
Tri-State Coach
15 Washington Avenue
Suffern, NY 10901
Tel: (914) 357-7553
Contact: Nazaret Kradjan
MFR of *Limos*

Syracuse
Auto Service by Rayco
501 W. Genesee Street
Syracuse, NY 13204
Tel: (315) 476-4201
FAX: (315) 474-4056
Contact: Tony Grabowski
R4
C-2

Syracuse
Suburban Health Services, Incorporated
430 S. Main Street
Syracuse, NY 13212
Tel: (315) 458-1231
MFR of *H'cap R4*
C-2

Troy
WB Recreational Vehicles, Incorporated
75 Greenbush Road
Troy, NY 12180
Tel: (518) 283-4370
Contact: Bert Wood
DLR of *R1*

Utica
Midstate Heavy Equipment Co., Inc.
71 N. Genesee Street
Utica, NY 13502
Tel: (315) 724-8183
FAX: (315) 724-8400
Contact: Charles J. Natale
MFR of *TB*

Utica
Utica Commercial Truck Body Builder, Inc.
216 2nd Street
Utica, NY 13501
Tel: (315) 733-4430
Contact: Joe Spano
MFR of *TB, U*
D

Utica
Utica General Truck Company, Incorporated
5636 Horatio Street
Utica, NY 13502
Tel: (315) 732-4300
FAX: (315) 732-6240
DLR of *TB*

Valley Stream
Valley Van Conversions
78 Franklin Avenue
Valley Stream, NY 11580
Tel: (516) 561-1231
R4

Walden
E Z Liner Company
1885 SR 52
Walden, NY 12586
Tel: (914) 744-2116
FAX: (914) 744-5968
R4
C-2
D

West Babylon
Custom Trailer Builders & Suppliers, Inc.
119 Lamar Street
West Babylon, NY 11704
Tel: (516) 643-3000
FAX: (516) 643-3002
Contact: Richie Bava
MFR of *FTB*
C-2

West Babylon
East Coast Vans
270 Farmingdale Road
West Babylon, NY 11704
Tel: (516) 587-6448
Contact: Michael Casella
R4
C-2

West Babylon
Palanker Chevrolet, Inc.
670 Montauk Highway
West Babylon, NY 11704
Tel: (516) 422-3700
DLR of *Luxury R4*

West Babylon
Specialty Conversions, Incorporated
615 Sunrise Highway
West Babylon, NY 11704
Tel: (516) 321-4196
FAX: (516) 321-4197
R4

Westbury
Cherry Valley Tank Corporation
75 Cantiague Rock Road
Westbury, NY 11590
Tel: (516) 334-7345
FAX: (516) 433-9782
Contact: Tom Savino
MFR of *T*

Wyandanch
B & M Trailer Builders, Incorporated
Long Island Avenue
Wyandanch, NY 11798
Tel: (516) 485-8517
REPAIR of *TB*

Wyandanch
Weld-Built Body Company, Incorporated
276 Long Island Avenue
Wyandanch, NY 11798
Tel: (516) 643-9700
FAX: (516) 491-4728
MFR of *TB, W*

Yonkers
De Dona Enterprises, Incorporated
560 Yonkers Avenue
Yonkers, NY 10704
Tel: (914) 965-4444
Contact: Jim Porter
R4, TConvs

NORTH CAROLINA

Apex
Propane Trucks
RR 2
Apex, NC 27502
Tel: (919) 362-5000
FAX: (919) 362-5001
Contact: Dale Gardner
FINAL ASSEMBLER of *Propane TB*

Asheville
Carolina Truck & Body Company
1895 Old Haywood Road
Asheville, NC 28806
Tel: (704) 667-8771
REPAIR of *TB*
MFR of *M*

Asheville
Stewart Mfg. Co.
142 Lookout Road
Asheville, NC 28804
Tel: (704) 254-4124
Contact: James Stewart
MFR of *TC*
C-2

Atowah
Boondocks Camper Manufacturing Company
6085 Brevard Road
Atowah, NC 28729
Tel: (704) 891-4242
Nation: (800) 733-4214
Contact: Mike Hodges
DLR of *TC*

Charlotte
A-1 Chair Equipment Rental & Sales
800 Central Avenue
Charlotte, NC 28204
Tel: (704) 333-8431
FAX: (704) 333-5506
Contact: Jim Little
R4, H'cap R4

Charlotte
AATAC, Incorporated
4000 San Wilson Road
Charlotte, NC 28214
Tel: (704) 393-0448
Nation: (800) 228-0295
FAX: (704) 393-1744
Contact: Jim Allison
MFR of *W*
C-2

Charlotte
Adkins Truck Equip. Co.
11300 Reames Road
Charlotte, NC 28269
Tel: (704) 596-2299
MFR of *TB, UTB, U*

Charlotte
Baker Equipment Engineering Company
2401 N. Graham Street
P.O. Box 33007
Charlotte, NC 28206
Tel: (704) 372-2040
Contact: Rex Dowton
at (804) 358-0481 (The Corporate Office, in Richmond, VA)
MFR of *TB, UTB, U*

Charlotte
Carolina Truck & Trailer
8500 Statesville Road
Charlotte, NC 28269
Tel: (704) 595-0211
DLR of *T, TB*

Charlotte
Cook Equipment
3701 Harlee Avenue
Charlotte, NC 28208
Tel: (704) 392-4138
FAX: (704) 392-4130
Contact: Ed Lutz
MFR of *VTB, TB, U*

Charlotte
Fontaine Modification Company
9827 Mount Holly Road
Charlotte, NC 28214
Tel: (704) 392-8502
Contact: Paul Kokalis
MODIFIER of *TB, U*

Charlotte
Great Dane Trailers
P.O. Box 33666
Charlotte, NC 28203
Tel: (704) 596-3721
Contact: Connie Carpenter
MFR of *T, S-2*
B-2

Charlotte
National Metal Products
2515 Allen Road, South
Charlotte, NC 28269
Tel: (704) 596-0432
Contact: Gerald Hunter
MFR of *ST*

Charlotte
Shuttle's
646 Atando Avenue
Charlotte, NC 28206
Tel: (704) 335-0012
Contact: Glen Coleman
R4

Charlotte
Twin State Truck Equipment Company
4448 South Blvd.
P.O. Box 240661
Charlotte, NC 28208
Tel: (704) 525-6062
FAX: (704) 523-1905
Contact: Ken Eldredge
MFR of *M, FTB*
C-2

Charlotte
Vann Mann Vans/ A-1 Adaptive
6431 Orr Road
Charlotte, NC 28205
Tel: (704) 598-8268
Tel: (704) 598-7111
Tel: (704) 597-0532
Contact: Dave Skinner
R4, H'cap R4
C-2
D

Charlotte
Worth Keeter, Inc.
1000 S. Clarkson Street
Charlotte, NC 28208
Tel: (704) 375-8471
FAX: (704) 376-7378
Contact: Mark Keeter
MFR of *TB, U*
C-2
D

Clayton
Eastern Wrecker Sales
13401 US Highway 70
Clayton, NC 27520
Tel: (919) 553-4038
DLR of *W*

Clayton
Mobile Accessories
2204 Raintree Drive
Clayton, NC 27520
Tel: (919) 553-3471
Contact: Larry Revels
R4, H'cap R4
C-1

Cleveland
Freightliner Corporation
Highway 70, West
P.O. Box 399
Cleveland, NC 27013
Tel: (704) 278-5000
MFR of *Freightliner S-2*

Climax
Ferree Trailer Corp.
Highway 22
P.O. Box 70
Climax, NC 27233
Tel: (910) 685-4407
Contact: Ken Nash
MFR of *T*
B-1:1

Clinton
Truck & Tractor Company, Incorporated
107 N. East Blvd.
Clinton, NC 28328
Tel: (910) 592-4188
Contact: Ronnie Jackson
DLR of *Trucks & Tractors*

Concord
Touch of Class
735 Hwy. 29, North
Concord, NC 28027
Tel: (704) 788-7719
R4

Dunn
Godwin Manufacturing
Highway 421, South
P.O. Box 1147
Dunn, NC 28334
Tel: (910) 892-0141
Tel: (910) 892-1153
FAX: (910) 892-7402
Contact: Judy Godwin
MFR of *TB, U*
C-1:15

Durham
Miller Mfg. Co., Inc.
1104 Cole Mill Road
Durham, NC 27705
Tel: (919) 383-5547
FAX: (919) 383-8125
Contact: Bob Touchton
MFR of *TB, U*

Farmville
Craft Steel Industries, Incorporated
South Field Street
P.O. Box 108
Farmville, NC 27828
Tel: (919) 753-3152
FAX: (919) 753-3154
Contact: Jim Craft, Jr. or Ken Powell
MFR of *E, F, CTB, T*
C-2
D

Fayetteville
Carolina Vans
3648 Pincone Lane
Fayetteville, NC 28306
Tel: (910) 424-4726
Contact: Nathan Hayes
R4
C-2

Fayetteville
Hawley's
908 Brighton Road
Fayetteville, NC 28304
Tel: (910) 425-8009
DLR of *R1, R2*

Fayetteville
Hawley's Camping Center
Route 3, Box 28-CC
Fayetteville, NC 28304
Tel: (910) 423-5200
DLR of *R1, R2*

Gastonia
Beaver Company
3707 York Highway
Gastonia, NC 28052
Tel: (704) 864-9366
Contact: Ray Beavers
R4
C-2

Greensboro
Black Cadillac-Oldsmobile, Incorporated
601 E. Bessemer Avenue
Greensboro, NC 27420
Tel: (910) 275-9641
Contact: L. J. Small
DLR of *Limos*

Greensboro
Butler Trailer Mfg. Co.
6898 Coltrane Mill Road
Greensboro, NC 27406
Tel: (910) 674-7804
Contact: Don Butler
MFR of *T*

Greensboro
DKD, Unlimited
723 Chimney Rock Road
Greensboro, NC 27410
Tel: (910) 294-1845
FAX: (910) 294-8080
R4

Greensboro
Ford Body Company
1218 Battleground Ave.
Greensboro, NC 27408
Tel: (910) 272-1131
Contact: Lynn Ford
SERVICE of *TB*
C-1

Greensboro
Perfection Body Works
4915 Blakeshire Road
Greensboro, NC 27406
Tel: (910) 697-9319
Contact: Mike Johnson
R4

Greensboro
W. F. Mickey Body Company, Incorporated
P.O. Box 2044
Greensboro, NC 27260
Tel: (910) 882-6806
Nation: (800) 334-9061
Nation: (800) 672-8165
FAX: (910) 889-6712
Contact: Nancy Dunlap
MFR of *V*

Hampstead
Delivery Concepts East
351 Dogwood Lane
Hampstead, NC 28443
Tel: (910) 270-2090
Nation: (800) 255-5183
FAX: (910) 270-2091
Contact: Gary Sample
MFR of *TB*
C-2
D

Henderson
Jackson Enterprises
3002 Oxford Road
Henderson, NC 27536
Tel: (919) 492-0121
Contact: Clay Jackson
DLR of *TC*
C-2

Hertford
Johnie Gregory
RR 4, Box 899
Hertford, NC 27944
Tel: (919) 264-2626
Contact: Johnie Gregory
MFR of *T*

High Point
Carolina Adaptive
2431 N. Main Street
High Point, NC 27262
Tel: (910) 841-5633
Contact: Rod Brendle
R4, H'cap R4

High Point
Mickey Truck Bodies, Incorporated
1505 Bethel Drive
High Point, NC 27260
Tel: (910) 882-6806
Contact: Debbie Deal
MFR of *VTB*
C-2
D

High Point
Thomas Built Busses, Incorporated
(MAIL: P.O. Box 2450
High Point, NC 27261)
1408 Courtesy Road
High Point, NC 27260
Tel: (910) 889-4871
Contact: Susan Keams
MFR of *TB, U*
C-2

Indian Trail
Hudson Bros. Trailer Manufacturing
1508 Hwy. 218, West
Indian Trail, NC 28079
Tel: (704) 753-4393
Contact: Kathy Page
MFR of *T*
B-2

Jefferson
American Emergency Vehicles
P.O. Box 1059
Jefferson, NC 28640
Tel: (910) 246-2716
FAX: (910) 246-5310
Contact: Jan Bard
CONVERTER of *A*
C-2:6
D

Kernersville
Crescent Cruiser Co.
2750 Hwy. 66, South
Kernersville, NC 27284
Tel: (910) 869-2181
Contact: Claude Draughn
R4

Kernersville
Kernersville Dodge
1015 NC Hwy. 66, South
Kernersville, NC 27284
Tel: (910) 996-4111
Contact: Tim Mitchell
DISTRIBUTOR of *R4*

Laurinburg
Laurinburg Machine Co.
402 Farley Street
Laurinburg, NC 28352
Tel: (910) 276-0360
Contact: Jim Litch
MFR of *TB, T*

Lumberton
Custom Trailer & Welding
2402 E. Elizabethtown Rd
Lumberton, NC 28358
Tel: (919) 671-9042
Contact: Ron Walters
MFR of *T*

Mockville
Junker & Son Feed Mill, Incorporated
101 Salisbury Road
Mockville, NC 27028
Tel: (704) 634-2377
Contact: Bill Junker
DLR of *HT*

Mount Holly
Freightliner Truck Manufacturing Plant
1800 N. Main Street
Mount Holly, NC 29120
Tel: (794) 827-7511
FAX: (704) 822-7300
MFR of *Freightliner S-1*

Murphy
Truck Depot
600 Highway 64, West
Suite D
Murphy, NC 28906
Tel: (704) 837-7811
TConvs

Raleigh
Athey Products Corp.
P.O. Box 669
Raleigh, NC 27602
Tel: (919) 556-5171
FAX: (919) 556-7950
Contact: James Cloonan
MFR of *T*
D

Raleigh
College Park RV
4208 New Bern Avenue
Raleigh, NC 27610
Tel: (919) 231-8710
DLR of *R1, R2*

Raleigh
Emergency Equip., Inc.
518 Pershing Road
P.O. Box 40069
Raleigh, NC 27608
Tel: (919) 828-7928
Contact: Rene Pearce
MFR of *F, TB, U*
C-2:4

Raleigh
Kustoms, Ltd.
2522 S. Wilmington St.
Raleigh, NC 27603
Tel: (919) 832-9791
DLR of *R4*

Raleigh
Morgan Corporation
2805 Croix Place
Raleigh, NC 27614
Tel: (919) 676-7723
Contact: Sid Merrill
MFR of *TB*
C-2
D

Raleigh
Rand Automated
Compaction Systems, Inc.
5000 Falls of the Neuse
Road
P.O. Box 27746
Raleigh, NC 27609
Tel: (910) 790-9600
Nation: (800) 543-7263
FAX: (910) 790-0754
Contact: Janice Bentley
MFR of *G*
C-2:2

Raleigh
Sirchie Fingerprint
Laboratories
Umstead Industrial Park
P.O. Box 30576
Raleigh, NC 27603
Tel: (919) 781-3120
MFR of *Police Vehicles*
(This is the Corporate
Office. See also the plant
site in Medford, NJ.)

Raleigh
Van Products, Inc.
100 Glenwood Avenue
Raleigh, NC 27603
Tel: (910) 832-6473
Nation: (800) 662-7572
FAX: (919) 832-3950
Contact: David Wendt
R4, H'cap R4

Reidsville
Isometrics, Incorporated
1402 N. Scales Street
P.O. Box 660
Reidsville, NC 27320
Tel: (910) 349-2329
FAX: (910) 349-4744
Contact: Dennis Bracey
MFR of *Military Vehicles*

Rocky Mount
College Park RV
2550 N. Church Street
Rocky Mount, NC 27804
Tel: (919) 446-9233
DLR of *R1, R2*

Rocky Mount
Curt Van
1913 Westland Blvd.
Rocky Mount, NC 27804
Tel: (910) 977-9791
MODIFIER of *TB, Vans*
holding 15-20 Passengers

Shelby
Southcoast Industries
1840 E. Dixon Blvd.
Shelby, NC 28152
Tel: (704) 482-1477
Nation: (800) 331-7655
FAX: (704) 482-2015
Contact: Jim Neal
MFR of *TB, U*
C-2
D

Shelby
Southern Comfort Vans
933 S. Morgan Street
Shelby, NC 28152
Tel: (704) 482-1536
Contact: Floyd Maunay
R4

Tarboro
J, L & H Sales, Inc.
Route 6, Box 179
Tarboro, NC 27886
Tel: (919) 823-0355
Contact: Donald Hilborne
R4

Tarboro
Long Trailer Co., Inc.
RR 2
Tarboro, NC 27886
Tel: (919) 823-8104
FAX: (919) 641-0412
Contact: Linda Johnson
MFR of *BT*
D

Thomasville
A. M. Haire Body
516 Honeywood
Thomasville, NC 27360
Tel: (910) 472-4444
MFR of *VTB*
A-1

Washington
Hackney & Sons, Inc.
400 Hackney Avenue
Washington, NC 27889
Tel: (919) 946-6521
From CANADA:
(800) 926-6002
FAX: (919) 975-3274
Contact: Ted Griekspoor
MFR of *TB, U*
C-2
D

Whiteville
Gore Trailer Mfg. Co.
RR 3, Box 369
Whiteville, NC 28472
Tel: (910) 642-4298
Tel: (910) 642-2246
Nation: (800) 334-3488
FAX: (910) 640-1133
Contact: Jackson Gore
MFR of *HT, LT*

Wilmington
Hall's Camper Sales
& Accessories
6301 Market Street
Wilmington, NC 28405
Tel: (919) 392-5955
R4

Wilmington
Sturdy Truck Equipment
1839 Carolina Beach Rd.
Wilmington, NC 28401
Tel: (919) 763-8261
Contact: Connie Blevins
MFR of *TB, U*

Wilson
Hackney Brothers
Body Company
301 E. Pender Street
P.O. Box 2728
Wilson, NC 27893
Tel: (919) 237-8171
Nation: (800) 334-2296
FAX: (919) 237-0305
Contact: Patty Scott
or Gene Newman
MFR of *V, TB, U*
D: Morgan Driveaway

Wilson
Murphy Mfg. Co.
2000 Airport Drive
P.O. Box 2009
Wilson, NC 27893
Tel: (919) 291-2191
Nation: (800) 334-2298
Contact: Sandra
Alexander
MFR of *TB, U*
C-2:4

Wilson
Quality Truck Bodies
& Repair
Firestone Parkway
P.O. Box 1669
Wilson, NC 27894
Tel: (919) 291-5795
Nation: (800) 682-7032
FAX: (919) 291-5365
Contact: Jim Stancil
MFR of *TB, CTB*
C-1, C-2:2

Wilson
Simpson Equip. Corp.
Highway 301, South
P.O. Box 2229
Wilson, NC 27893
Tel: (919) 291-4105
FAX: (919) 237-9950
Contact: Ralph Sullivan
MFR of *TB, U*
C-1

Wilson
U. S. Truck Body Co.
4000 Airport Drive, NW
Wilson, NC 27893
Tel: (919) 291-2191
Contact: Sandra
Alexander
MFR of *TB*
C-2

Wilson
Wilco Welding & Repair
2311 Wilco Blvd.
Wilson, NC 27894
Tel: (910) 291-9172
MFR of *TB*

Winston-Salem
Accessories, Incorporated
Route 11, Box 286-A
Winston-Salem, NC
27107
Tel: (910) 764-5517
R4

Winston-Salem
Diamond Reo
Truck Sales
1323 N. Liberty Street
Winston-Salem, NC
27105
Tel: (910) 722-7871
Contact: Bill Withow
DLR of *S-1*
D

Winston-Salem
Famco Fab Metals Co.
(MAIL: c/o Famco
P.O. Drawer A
Salem Station
Winston-Salem, NC
27108)
216 Junia Avenue
Winston-Salem, NC
27127
Tel: (910) 721-1500
Contact: Rick Mooney
MFR of *T*
B-2

Winston-Salem
Fosgee Enterprises
354 Robbins Road
Winston-Salem, NC
27107
Tel: (910) 788-3729
Contact: Larry McGee
MFR of *T*
B-1

Winston-Salem
Triangle Body Works
2012 Waughtown Street
Winston-Salem, NC
27107
Tel: (910) 788-0631
Contact: Ronnie Lee
MFR of *TB, U*
D

NORTH DAKOTA

Bismarck
Harlow's Busses
3600 E. Century Avenue
Bismarck, ND 58501
Tel: (701) 224-1767
DLR of *U*
C-2

Bismarck
People Transportation, Incorporated
1808 N. Grandview Lane
Bismarck, ND 58501
Tel: (701) 222-0222
MFR of *U*
C-2
D

Fargo
B. H. Chesley Company
2315 N. 7th Avenue
Fargo, ND 58102
Tel: (701) 293-9133
FAX: (701) 293-0325
Contact: Ron Ristvedt
DLR of *TB, U*
D

Fargo
Hall GMC, Inc.
4242 W. Main Avenue
Fargo, ND 58103
Tel: (701) 282-5400
FAX: (701) 282-8220
Contact: Gerald Hall
DLR of *R4*

Fargo
McLaughlin Equip. Co.
320 S. 27th Street
Fargo, ND 58103
Tel: (701) 237-6046
FAX: (701) 237-9854
Contact: Roger Murtis
DISTRIBUTOR of
TB, U
C-2

Grand Forks
Dietrich Bus Service
1115 55th Street, North
Grand Forks, ND 58203
Tel: (701) 772-0601
REPAIR of *TB, U*
C-2

Hunter
Bil-bilt Products
253 Ebenezer Road
Hunter, ND 58048
Tel: (701) 874-2255
MFR of *T*

Minot
Nielson & Stewart, Inc.
3805 S. Broadway Street
Minot, ND 58701
Tel: (701) 852-1026
DLR of *Trucks*

Pembina
Motor Coach Industries (MCI)
522 Stutsman
Pembina, ND 58271
Tel: (701) 825-6234
Nation: (800) 413-5860
MFR of *U*

Rugby
Hartley's School Busses
Highway 2, West
Rugby, ND 58368
Tel: (701) 776-5746
DLR of *S*
C-2
D

Watford
Iron Steer Enterprises
HC 3, Box 83
Watford, ND 58854
Tel: (701) 842-6247
MFR of *T*
B-2

West Fargo
Dakotah Truck Equipment, Incorporated
794 Main Avenue, West
West Fargo, ND 58078
Tel: (701) 282-2022
MFR of *TB*

West Fargo
Executive Vans
801 Main Avenue, West
West Fargo, ND 58078
Tel: (701) 281-1772
R4

West Fargo
Red River Manufacturing
P.O. Box 732
West Fargo, ND 58078
Tel: (701) 282-3013
Contact: Dwayne Lee
MFR of *T*
D

West Fargo
Superior Customs
429 Main Avenue, East
West Fargo, ND 58078
Tel: (701) 277-1193
Contact: Don Spieker
R4

OHIO

Akron
New Era Transportation, Incorporated
810 Moe Drive
Akron, OH 44310
Tel: (216) 633-1118
Nation: (800) 638-8267
FAX: (216) 633-0330
R4

Akron
Ravens Metal Products, Incorporated
P.O. Box 10002
Akron, OH 44310
Tel: (216) 630-4528
FAX: (216) 630-4545
Contact: Jim Porter
MFR of *T*
D
(This is the Corporate Office.)

Alliance
Trailstar Mfg. Corp.
20700 Harrisburg-Westville Road
Alliance, OH 44601
Tel: (216) 821-9900
FAX: (216) 821-6941
Contact: David Barker
MFR of *T*
B-2
D

Alliance
US Transportation Specialists
1170 Summit Street
Alliance, OH 44601
Tel: (216) 821-7938
MFR of *T*
B-1

Amherst
Hi-Point Trailers-USA
1115 Milan Avenue
Amherst, OH 44001
Tel: (216) 988-4474
FAX: (216) 988-4476
Contact: Dave Rathbun
MFR of *T*
B-2

Amherst
Normson Trailer
9412 Leavitt Road
Route 58
Amherst, OH 44001
Tel: (216) 986-3333
Contact: Norm Watson
MFR of *T*

Ansonia
Rowland Truck & Equipment, Incorporated
4711 Washington Road
Ansonia, OH 45303
Tel: (513) 337-2916
FINAL ASSEMBLER/ DLR of *TB*

Apple Creek
Reberland Equip. Co.
5963 Fountain Nook Rd.
Apple Creek, OH 44606
Tel: (216) 698-5883
FAX: (216) 698-7723
Contact: Larry Reber
MFR of *TB*
C-2

Avon Lake
Ford Motor Company/ Ohio Truck Plant
650 Miller Road
Avon Lake, OH 44012
Tel: (216) 933-1230
MFR of *TB*
C-2

Batavia
Ellis & Watts Company
4400 Glen Willow Lake Lane
Batavia, OH 45103
Tel: (513) 752-9000
FAX: (513) 752-4983
Contact: Ray Godfrey
or Nancy Clark
or Bob Fleudenberger
MFR/DLR of *CT, ST*
B-2:2
D: Bluegrass Transport

Beaverdam
Sharrock Bus Sales & Service, Incorporated
I-75 & US Route 30
Beaverdam, OH 45808
Tel: (419) 643-4561
FAX: (419) 643-2310
Contact: Gary Hull
DLR of *U*
C-2

Belmont
Yonak's Trailer Sales, Incorporated
46293 Belmont-Centerville Road
Belmont, OH 43718
Tel: (614) 686-2999
FAX: (614) 686-2788
DLR of *R1*

Botkins
Brown Welding Shop, Incorporated
311 W. South Street
P.O. Box 74
Botkins, OH 45306
Tel: (513) 693-3838
FAX: (513) 693-4121
Contact: Mr. Laverne Brown
MFR of *TB*
C-2:2

Broadview Heights
La Pine Truck Sales
3131 E. Royalton Road
Broadview Heights, OH 44147
Tel: (216) 526-6363
Nation: (800) 233-6363
FAX: (216) 526-6244
DLR of *T*

Brookville
Rockin' "M" Trailer Sales
9184 Wellbaum Road
Brookville, OH 45309
Tel: (513) 884-7079
Contact: Charlie Menker
DISTRIBUTOR of *HT, LT*

Butler
Hi-Lo Trailer Company
145 Elm Street
Butler, OH 44822
Tel: (419) 883-3000
Nation: (800) 321-6402
FAX: (419) 883-3087
MFR of *R6*
D

Canal Winchester
Ricart Vanland
6270 Bowen Road
Canal Winchester, OH 43110
Tel: (614) 833-0016
Contact: Tony Carifa
R4

Canton
Cross Truck Equipment Company, Incorporated
1801 Perry Drive, SW
Box 80509
Canton, OH 44706
Tel: (216) 477-8151
OH only: (800) 362-9842
FAX: (216) 477-8426
Contact: John Cross
MFR of *TB*

Canton
John Hembree Company
4958 Yukon Street, NW
Canton, OH 44708
Tel: (216) 478-2716
Contact: John Hembree
MFR of *TB*

Canton
Lake Cable RV & Marine
5800 Fulton Drive, NW
Canton, OH 44718
Tel: (216) 497-1852
DLR of *R1, R2, R3*

Chillicothe
Kenworth Truck Co.
65 Kenworth Drive
Chillicothe, OH 45601
Tel: (614) 774-5111
FAX: (614) 774-5230
Contact: Allen Mayne
MFR of *TB, U*
D

Cincinnati
CW Coach Sales
7444 Vine Street
Cincinnati, OH 45216
Tel: (513) 821-6200
DLR of *A*

Cincinnati
Hamilton's Health & Services, Incorporated
6225 Colerain Avenue
Cincinnati, OH 45239
Tel: (513) 923-3300
Nation: (800) 435-7900
FAX: (513) 923-3655
Contact: Jim Prewitt
R4, H'cap R4

Cincinnati
Interstate Trailer, Inc.
1755 Dreman Avenue
Cincinnati, OH 45223
Tel: (513) 541-8188
DISTRIBUTOR of *T*
B-2:12

Cincinnati
Kenworth of Cincinnati, Incorporated
11155 Mosteller Road
Cincinnati, OH 45241
Tel: (513) 771-5831
Nation: (800) 274-5369
FAX: (513) 771-1537
Contact: Bob Etherington
MFR of *TB, U*

Cincinnati
Koebbe Enterprises, Inc.
11245 Redding Road
Cincinnati, OH 45241
Tel: (513) 769-0011
MFR of *TB*

Cincinnati
Legend Vans, Inc.
607 Shepherd Drive
Building 18
Cincinnati, OH 45215
Tel: (513) 563-8280
MFR of *R4*

Cincinnati
Max Interior Design
1565 Harrison Avenue
Cincinnati, OH 45214
Tel: (513) 471-0031
Contact: Larry McLeary
R4

Cincinnati
Myers Auto Body
10100 Springfield Pike
Cincinnati, OH 45215
Tel: (513) 772-6299
Contact: Mike Myers
R4

Cincinnati
Nightingale Medal Equipment Service
6161 Stewart Avenue
Cincinnati, OH 45227
Tel: (513) 527-3780
FAX: (513) 527-3686
Contact: Joe McFarland
R4
C-2

Cincinnati
Ohio Truck Equip., Inc.
4100 Rev Drive
Cincinnati, OH 45232
Tel: (513) 541-4700
Nation: (800) 543-4411
FAX: (513) 542-0546
Contact: Ken Revelson
MFR of *TB*

Cincinnati
Truck Cab Mfg., Inc.
2420 Anderson Ferry Rd.
Cincinnati, OH 45238
Tel: (513) 922-1300
FAX: (513) 922-8888
Contact: Jim Weber
MFR of *TC*
D

Cincinnati
Utility Trailer Mfg.
2421 E. Kemper Road
Cincinnati, OH 45241
Tel: (513) 771-8933
Contact: Bob Conleen
MFR of *S-2*
B-2

Cleveland
A Finish Line
5300 Ridge Road
Cleveland, OH 44129
Tel: (216) 886-0945
FAX: (216) 886-1546
Contact: Ray Scaletta
R4
C-2

Cleveland
Ace Truck Body Co., Inc.
7810 Colfax Road
Cleveland, OH 44104
Tel: (216) 883-2525
FAX: (216) 883-1961
Contact: Jason Jurek
MFR of *TB, T*
C-2
D

Cleveland
American Coach Sales
11723 Detroit Avenue
Cleveland, OH 44107
Tel: (216) 221-9330
Nation: (800) 321-6613
FAX: (216) 221-2005
Contact: Tony Mazarella or Bob Mazarella
DLR of *Limos*

Cleveland
Auto-Truck-Van Shop
15266 Broadway
Cleveland, OH 44137
Tel: (216) 581-1600
R4

Cleveland
Buggy Works, Inc.
20298 Emery Road
Cleveland, OH 44128
Tel: (216) 662-2727
MFR of *R4*
C-2

Cleveland
Carnegie Body Co., The
9500 Brook Park Road
Cleveland, OH 44129
Tel: (216) 749-5000
Nation: (800) 362-1989
FAX: (216) 749-5740
MFR of *TB*
C-2

Cleveland
Kustom Bilt Wreckers
645 Golden Oak Parkway
Cleveland, OH 44146
Tel: (216) 232-2422
Contact: Frank Adams
MFR of *W*
C-2:2

Cleveland
Midland Steel Products Company
10615 Madison Avenue
Cleveland, OH 44102
Tel: (216) 281-9000
FAX: (216) 651-7817
Contact: Dominic Stroffolino
MFR of *TB*
C-2

Cleveland
Pro-Motion, Incorporated
15708 Lorain Avenue
Cleveland, OH 44111
Tel: (216) 671-5676
Contact: Andy Mannis
R4, H'cap R4
C-2

Cleveland
Scott Fetzer Company
28800 Clemens Road
Cleveland, OH 44145
Tel: (216) 892-3000
FAX: (216) 892-3060
MFR of *TB*
(This is the Corporate Office.)

Cleveland
Tractop
197 Alpha Drive
Cleveland, OH 44143
Tel: (216) 473-0556
Contact: Sonny Moss
MFR of *TB*

Cleveland
Truckin' Vantastiks
4860 Ridge Road
Cleveland, OH 44144
Tel: (216) 398-0208
R4

College Hill
Mr. Van
6611 Hamilton Ave., N.
College Hill, OH 45224
Tel: (513) 522-1750
R4

Columbia Station
Shore Truck & Body Co.
27616 Royalton Raod
Columbia Station, OH 44028
Tel: (216) 236-5354
REPAIR of *TB*

Columbus
Baker Equipment Engineering Company
2355 Refugee Park
Columbus, OH 43207
Tel: (614) 443-7434
FAX: (614) 443-0149
Contact: Ralph Fwart
MFR of *TB, UTB*
C-2
D

Columbus
Bill Swad
160 S. Hamilton Road
Columbus, OH 43213
Tel: (614) 864-8267
FAX: (614) 864-8926
Contact: Frank Grahm
DLR of *R4*

Columbus
Byers Van City
555 W. Broad Street
Columbus, OH 43215
Tel: (614) 461-1720
Nation: (800) 332-9377
FAX: (614) 461-6134
Contact: Chuck Agriesti
DLR of *R4*
C-2

Columbus
Chevalier Custom Vans, Incorporated
6260 Huntley Road
Columbus, OH 43229
Tel: (614) 431-1904
Contact: Tom Chevalier
R4

Columbus
Columbus Truck & Equipment Company
1688 E. 5th Avenue
Columbus, OH 433219
Tel: (614) 252-3116
DLR of *Mack S-1*

Columbus
Custom Coach
1400 Dublin Road
Columbus, OH 43215
Tel: (614) 481-8881
Nation: (800) 252-5979
FAX: (614) 481-7552
Contact: Kirwin Elmers
MFR of *U*

Columbus
Emergency Vehicles Co.
500 Industrial Mile Road
Columbus, OH 43228
Tel: (614) 272-8181
Contact: Dave Lamon
MFR of *E*

Columbus
Fitzpatrick Enterprises, Incorporated
6353 Saltzgaber Road
Columbus, OH 43125
Tel: (614) 497-1000
Nation: (800) 545-1102
FAX: (614) 497-1863
Contact: Lisa Fitzpatrick
R4, H'cap R4

Columbus
Forward Motions of Central Ohio, Inc.
6330 Proprietors Road
Columbus, OH 43085
Tel: (614) 436-9444
FAX: (614) 436-9978
Contact: Ben Nugent
H'cap R4
C-2

Columbus
Funtrail Vans, Inc.
3966 Indianola Avenue
Columbus, OH 43214
Tel: (614) 262-5251
Contact: Lee Tucker
R4

Columbus
Grumman Ohio Corp.
250 E. Wilson Bridge Rd.
Columbus, OH 43085
Tel: (614) 431-1560
(This is the Corporate Office, and works with the Flxible Corp. in Delaware, OH.)

Columbus
Hilliard Truck & Equip.
5203 Tray View Road
Columbus, OH 43228
Tel: (614) 853-0355
DLR of *TB*

Columbus
Post's Traveland USA
4330 Westerville Road
Columbus, OH 43231
Tel: (614) 471-0550
FAX: (614) 471-0092
Contact: Wayne Post
DLR of *R1, R2, R3*

Columbus
Schodorf Truck Body & Equipment Company
885 Harmon
P.O. Box 23322
Columbus, OH 43223
Tel: (614) 228-6793
Nation: (800) 288-0992
FAX: (614) 228-6775
MFR/DISTRIBUTOR of *TB*
C-2:1
D

Columbus
TC Coach Company
1103 Dublin Road
Columbus, OH 43215
Tel: (614) 488-2229
Contact: Chuck Kuhn
MFR of *R4-B*
C-2

Columbus
Van Masters
1245 Alum Creek Drive
Columbus, OH 43209
Tel: (614) 253-0627
HQ: (614) 253-7263
Nation: (800) 669-0876
FAX: (614) 253-1969
Contact: Pat Paterson
MFR of *R4*
C-2:6

Crestline
Canvas Interiors by Burton
817-1/2 East Main
Crestline, OH 44827
Tel: (419) 683-4674
Contact: Londa Burton
R4

Cuyahoga Falls
Advance Ventures, Inc.
(MAIL: P.O. Box 998
Cuyahoga Falls, OH 44223)
3400 Cavalier Trail
Cuyahoga Falls, OH 44224
Tel: (216) 923-5344
FAX: (216) 238-1973
Contact: Bill Hunt
MFR of *TB*
D

Cuyahoga Falls
Cenweld Corporation
230 E. Portage Trail
Cuyahoga Falls, OH 44221
Tel: (216) 923-9717
FAX: (216) 923-5872
Contact: Adam Prack or Mike Lay
MFR of *TB*
C-1, C-2

Cynthiana
Mears Welding Manufacturing Corp.
2525 SR 41
Cynthiana, OH 45624
Tel: (614) 634-2875
MFR of *HT*
B-2

Dalton
Neiss Body & Equipment
17485 Old Lincoln Way
Dalton, OH 44618
Tel: (216) 828-2409
MFR of *CTB*

Dayton
Craftmasters
3020 N. Dixie Drive
Dayton, OH 45414
Tel: (513) 275-8797
Contact: Marcus Whitt
R4
C-2

Dayton
Dayton-Evans Motor Truck, Incorporated
3339 N. Dixie Drive
Dayton, OH 45414
Tel: (513) 278-5775
Nation: (800) 927-6225
FAX: (513) 278-5200
Contact: Donald Evans
DLR of *Trucks*
C-2

Dayton
Elete Customs
5236 N. Dixie Drive
Dayton, OH 45414
Tel: (513) 274-3999
Contact: Bob Cermack
R4

Dayton
Forward Motions
214 Valley Street
Dayton, OH 45404
Tel: (513) 222-5001
FAX: (513) 232-4001
Contact: Roger Flint
H'cap R4

Dayton
GM Corporation
2601 W. Stroop Drive
Dayton, OH 45439
Tel: (513) 455-2821
MFR of *4-Wheel-Drive Blazer*

Dayton
Kaffenbarger Welding Co
2929 Northlawn Avenue
Dayton, OH 45439
Tel: (513) 298-9991
FAX: (513) 398-5580
Contact: Wilbur Harris
MFR of *TB, U*

Dayton
Lewis Auto & RV Sales
4640 Linden Avenue
Dayton, OH 45432
Tel: (513) 253-8816
Nation: (800) 344-2344
DLR of *R1, R2*

Dayton
Photo III Van Acc.
202 Bluecrest Avenue
Dayton, OH 45427
Tel: (513) 268-8809
R4

Dayton
Truck & Bus Mfg.
(Div. of GM)
2601 W. Stroop Road
Dayton, OH 45439
Tel: (513) 455-5000
MFR of *TB, U*
Special Instructions:
Call this number first: (513) 455-2132. Ask for the person in charge of drivers for trucks and busses.

Defiance
Miller's Pickup & Van Shop
15310 Dohoney Road
Defiance, OH 43512
Tel: (419) 395-1477
Contact: John Miller
R4, TConvs

Defiance
Van Castle, The
7886 N. SR 66
Defiance, OH 43512
Tel: (419) 784-3834
Contact: Richard Merillat
R4, TConvs, Truck Cabs

Delaware
Flxible Corporation
970 Pittsburgh Drive
Delaware, OH 43015
Tel: (614) 362-2600
FAX: (614) 362-2658
Contact: Edward Crabbot
MFR of *TB, U*
D
NOTE: *See Also Londonville, OH.*

Dover
Simon-Duplex, Inc.
120 Deeds Drive
Dover, OH 44622
Tel: (216) 343-2010
Tel: (216) 343-3030
Nation: (800) 922-6920
Nation: (800) 325-3100
FAX: (216) 343-2375
Contact: Mark Class
MFR of *TB*
C-2

Edgerton
Fleetwood Travel Trailers of Ohio
407 Railroad
Edgerton, OH 43517
Tel: (419) 298-2374
FAX: (419) 298-3484
Contact: Mary Winn
MFR of *R1, R2, R3, R5, R6*
C-2
D

Fairfield
O'Gara-Heff & Eisenhardt Armoring Co.
9113 Le Saint Drive
Fairfield, OH 45014
Tel: (513) 874-2112
FAX: (513) 874-1262
MFR of *Armored Vehicles*
A-1

Fairfield
Van Stop
2 Cinchris Drive
Fairfield, OH 45014
Tel: (513) 860-5438
Nation: (800) 932-2059
H'cap R4
NOTE: *See also their Lexington, KY site.*

Fairfield
Young's Van & Truck Accessories
5107 Dixie Highway
Fairfield, OH 45014
Tel: (513) 829-8818
FAX: (513) 829-9028
Contact: Gary Young
R4

Findlay
Flag City Truck & Equipment
151 Stanford Parkway
Findlay, OH 45840
Tel: (419) 423-3131
FINAL ASSEMBLER/DLR of *TB*

Findlay
Hi-Tech Graphics
1101 Trenton Avenue
Findlay, OH 45804
Tel: (419) 859-2859
Contact: Jim Launder
R4

Findlay
Miller Motors
750 Bolton Street
Findlay, OH 45840
Tel: (419) 422-7477
OH only: (800) 222-5285
Contact: Bob Miller
R4
C-2

Fostoria
Big Bear Muffler, Inc.
1313 N. Countyline Street
Fostoria, OH 44830
Tel: (419) 435-0409
Nation: (800) 750-2327
Contact: Gary Doyst
R4

Franklin
Jay Sales
320 Conover Drive
Franklin, OH 45005
Tel: (513) 743-8004
Nation: (800) 783-8004
Contact: David Peters
DLR of *R4*

Gahanna
McNeilus Truck & Manufacturing, Inc.
1130 Morrison Road
Gahanna, OH 43230
Tel: (614) 868-0760
MFR of *Concrete Mixer TB*
(This location is the Sales Office.)

Galion
Elliott Machine Works, Incorporated
146 Rensch Avenue
Galion, OH 44833
Tel: (419) 468-4709
FAX: (216) 468-4642
Contact: Richard L. Ekin
MFR of *T*
B-2
D

Galion
Peabody Galion
500 Sherman Street
Galion, OH 44833
Tel: (419) 468-2120
FAX: (419) 468-4895
Contact: Dale Schenian
MFR of *TB*
C-2
D

Grove City
Ace Truck Body, Inc.
1600 Thrailkill Road
Grove City, OH 43123
Tel: (614) 971-3100
MFR of *TB*

Grove City
Brunner Brothers Body Shop
1750 Demorest Road
Grove City, OH 43123
Tel: (614) 875-7727
MFR of *U*

Grove City
Luxury Vans Ohio
1800 Stringtown Road
Grove City, OH 43123
Tel: (614) 875-9007
RESTORATION of *Old Cars*

Grove City
Towpath Stables
2333 Harrisburg Pike
Grove City, OH 43123
Tel: (614) 875-0623
Contact: John Albaugh
RE-BUILDER of *HT*

Hamilton
Kornylak Corporation
400 Heaton Street
Hamilton, OH 45011
Tel: (513) 863-1277
Nation: (800) 837-5676
FAX: (513) 863-7644
MFR of *Special Equip. for Unloading Jets*
C-2

Hubbard
Kiler, Incorporated
2616 N. Main Street
Hubbard, OH 44425
Tel: (216) 534-8961
FAX: (216) 534-8969
Contact: Tom Kiler, Jr.
MFR of *TB*
C-2
D

Jackson Center
Airstream/
Thor Industries Inc.
419 W. Pike Street
Jackson Center, OH 45334
Tel: (513) 596-6111
Tel: (513) 596-6849
Contact: Kelly Mobley
MFR of *R1, R2*
C-2:1

Kidron
Kidron, Incorporated
13442 Emerson Road
P.O. Box 17
Kidron, OH 44636
Tel: (216) 857-3011
Nation: (800) 321-5421
FAX: (216) 857-8451
Contact: Brian Leech
MFR of *TB*

Lima
Bevercraft, Incorporated
2081 N. Dixie Highway
Lima, OH 45801
Tel: (419) 221-0221
Contact: Pat Pierce
R4

Lima
H & J Horse Trailer Co.
5406 Bellefontaine
Lima, OH 45804
Tel: (419) 222-3357
Contact: John Clark
or Bill Deeton
DLR of *HT*

Lima
Mid Bus Corporation
3555 St. John's Road
Lima, OH 45804
Tel: (419) 221-2525
FAX: (419) 221-2514
MFR of *R1, R2, R3, U*

Lima
S & S Coach Company
650 E. Wayne Street
Lima, OH 45801
Tel: (419) 224-3910
FAX: (419) 222-0990
MFR of *H, Limos*

Lima
Superior Coaches
600 E. Wayne Street
Lima, OH 45801
Tel: (419) 222-1501
MFR of *H, Limos*
D: Y-Tran

Lima
United Fire Apparatus Corporation
204 S. Gay Street
P.O. Box 2066
Lima, OH 45806
Tel: (419) 645-4083
Contact: Darrell Chapman
MFR of *F*
C-2

Lockbourne
Fitzpatrick Enterprises, Incorporated
6353 Saltzgaber Road
Lockbourne, OH 43137
Tel: (614) 497-1000
Contact: Lisa Fitzpatrick
H'cap R4

Lorain
Lakeland Enterprises, Incorporated
3809 Broadway
Lorain, OH 44052
Tel: (216) 233-7266
FAX: (216) 233-7891
Contact: Nick Dischenzo
R4
C-2

Loudonville
Flxible Corporation
520 N. Spring Street
Loudonville, OH 44842
Tel: (419) 994-4141
FAX: (419) 994-3357
Contact: Debbie Thomas
MFR of *U*
C-2
D
NOTE: *See also Delaware, OH*

Mansfield
Monarch Trailers
2832 Bowman Street Rd.
Mansfield, OH 44903
Tel: (419) 747-2848
Contact: Carol Walters
MFR of *HT, LT*
B-2
D

Mansfield
Moritz International, Inc.
617 N. Mulberry Street
Mansfield, OH 44902
Tel: (419) 526-5222
Contact: Frank Monte
MFR of *T*
D

Mansfield
Rahall's Custom Vans
255 Park Avenue East
Mansfield, OH 44902
Tel: (419) 526-0023
Contact: Steve Rahall
R4

Marietta
Steve's Vans & Accessories, Unlimited
211 S. 8th Street
Marietta, OH 45750
Tel: (614) 374-3154
Nation: (800) 690-4950
Contact: Steve Hesson
R4
C-2

Marietta
Wetz Sales & Service Co.
224 Pike Street
Marietta, OH 45750
Tel: (614) 373-2343
Contact: Chip Wetz
DLR of *TB, U*

Marshallville
Quality Fiberglass, Inc.
45 E. Church Street
Marshallville, OH 44645
Tel: (216) 855-3601
Contact: Don Baney
MFR of *TB*
C-2
D

Medina
Avalon RV & Marine
1604 Medina Road
Medina, OH 44258
Tel: (216) 239-2131
Nation: (800) 882-7728
Contact: Tom Morrison
DLR of *BT*

Medina
Medina Custom & Vinyl, Incorporated
413 W. Smith Road
Medina, OH 44256
Tel: (216) 722-1288
Contact: Don Knotek
R4
C-2

Medina
Vans by Doran
4160 Pearl Road
Medina, OH 44256
Tel: (216) 225-1002
Contact: Joe Armaro
R4

Medina
Windsor Mfg. Co.
1020 Industrial Pkwy.
Medina, OH 44256
Tel: (216) 725-0163
FAX: (216) 725-5950
Contact: Harvey Berghaus
MFR of *TB*

Mentor
D & S Custom Van, Inc.
7581 Taylor Blvd.
Mentor, OH 44060
Tel: (216) 946-2178
FAX: (216) 946-3584
Contact: Carmen Paterniti
R4
C-2

Mentor
Trailer Component Manufacturing, Inc.
7795 Division Drive
Mentor, OH 44060
Tel: (216) 255-2888
MFR/DLR of *T*

Milan
Wilcart Company
10303 Milan Road
Milan, OH 44846
Tel: (419) 625-5227
FAX: (419) 625-8419
DLR of *R1, R2*

Mount Eaton
ARE, Incorporated
P.O. Box 74
Mount Eaton, OH 44659
Tel: (216) 359-5450
FAX: (216) 359-5504
Contact: Gayle Edie
MFR of *Truck Cabs*
C-2

New Carlisle
Kaffenbarger Welding & Truck Equipment
10100 Ballentine Pike
New Carlisle, OH 45344
Tel: (513) 845-3804
FAX: (513) 857-9068
Contact: Larry Kaffenbarger
DISTRIBUTOR/MFR
of *TB, T*
C-2
D

New Haven
Kessler's Truck & Trailer Sales
Route 224, East
New Haven, OH 44850
Tel: (419) 935-1510
Nation: (800) 776-9174
FAX: (419) 935-8489
DLR of *HT, Trucks*

North Jackson
Leonard Truck & Trailer, Incorporated
3200 SR 45
North Jackson, OH 44451
Tel: (216) 538-2112
FAX: (216) 538-9844
Contact: Peg Leonard
DLR of *T*

Northwood
Custom Van Shack
3009 Woodville Road
Northwood, OH 43619
Tel: (419) 691-2033
Contact: William Lafferty
R4

Northwood
Truck & Van Land
5417 Woodville Road
Northwood, OH 43619
Tel: (419) 698-4397
MFR of *TB, U*

Norwalk
Eureka Coach Company
(Div. of CCE, Inc.)
600 Industrial Parkway
P.O. Box 699
Norwalk, OH 44857
Tel: (419) 663-5030
FAX: (419) 663-4051
MFR of *H, Limos*
C-2 (Retirees, who are joined during the summer months by college students)

Norwalk
Norwalk Assembly Plant
55 N. Garfield Street
Norwalk, OH 44857
Tel: (419) 668-8132, ext. 283
FAX: (419) 663-0125
FAX: (419) 668-1096
Contact: Gwendle Sloan
MFR of *TB*
C-2
D

Nova
Willard Machine & Welding
908 CR 40
Nova, OH 44859
Tel: (419) 652-3440
Contact: George Willard
MFR of *T, S-2*

Oakwood Village
Kustom Bilt Wreckers
645 Golden Oak Parkway
Oakwood Village, OH 44146
Tel: (216) 232-2422
Contact: Frank Adams
DLR of *W*
A-1

Orient
Concessions By Cox
7280 Stahl Road
Orient, OH 43146
Tel: (614) 877-3385
FAX: (614) 877-0488
Contact: Teresa Collburn
MFR of *T*
B-2

Orrville
Orrville Products, Inc.
375 E. Orr Street
Orrville, OH 44667
Tel: (216) 683-4010
FAX: (216) 684-2619
Contact: Rich Craver
MFR of *TB*

Ottawa
Nelson Mfg. Co.
6448 US Route 224
Ottawa, OH 45875
Tel: (419) 523-5321
FAX: (419) 523-6247
Contact: George Rellinger
MFR of *S-2, TB, U*
C-1, C-2
D

Ottoville
M & W Trailers, Inc.
525 E. Main Street
Ottoville, OH 45876
Tel: (419) 453-3331
FAX: (419) 453-3336
MFR/DLR of *T*
B-2

Painesville
Pop Top Company
1895 Blaze Nemeth Road
Painesville, OH 44077
Tel: (216) 354-5231
R4

Payne
Sims Mfg. Co., Inc.
230 N. Maple Street
Payne, OH 45880
Tel: (419) 263-2321
FAX: (419) 263-2543
Contact: William Whitcum
MFR of *Operator Cabs*
D: Halus

Perrysburg
Howard Mobility-Plus, Incorporated
126 W. South Boundary Street
Perrysburg, OH 43551
Tel: (419) 874-4116
Contact: Mary Ellen Howard
MFR of *H'cap Units*

Piqua
Paul Sherry Transportation Center/Chevrolet, Inc.
8620 N. CR 20-A
Piqua, OH 45356
Tel: (513) 778-0830
Tel: (513) 667-5515
Nation: (800) 678-4188
FAX: (419) 778-0688
Contact: Dave Arbogast
DLR of *R4*
C-2
D

Poland
Caravans Unlimited/ Adventure Travel Trailer
9013 Youngstown-Pittsburgh Road
Poland, OH 44514
Tel: (216) 542-2574
FAX: (216) 542-0662
MFR of *R6, TC*

Randolph
East Manufacturing Co.
1871 SR 44
P.O. Box 277
Randolph, OH 44265
Tel: (216) 325-9921
FAX: (216) 325-7851
Contact: Mark Tate
MFR of *T, S-2*
B-2
D

Ross
Restoration Wizards
2338 Venice Blvd.
Ross, OH 45061
Tel: (513) 738-7288
FAX: (513) 738-4289
Contact: Chuck Mann
MODIFIER of *R4*
C-2

Salem
D & L Custom Vans
2017 N. Ellsworth Ave.
Salem, OH 44460
Tel: (216) 332-4310
R4
C-2

Sandusky
Wilcart Company
10303 Milan Road
Sandusky, OH 44870
Tel: (419) 625-5227
Contact: Dave Kludig
R4

Shandon
Custom-Built Trailers & Products
4924 Cincinnati-Brookville Road
Shandon, OH 45603
Tel: (513) 738-5151
Contact: Don Guild
MFR of *T*

Shauck
Fibre-Core Trailers
7004 SR 42
Shauck, OH 43349
Tel: (419) 362-6171
Contact: Tony Gerich
MFR of *T*

Shreve
Snyder Hot Shot
7034 Lakeside Drive
Shreve, OH 44676
Tel: (216) 496-3825
MFR of *T*

Sidney
Silverado Trucks
720 Linden
Sidney, OH 45365
Tel: (513) 492-8862
Contact: Scott Dorsey
MFR of *TB*

Springfield
Fontaine Modification Company
5325 Prosperity Drive
Springfield, OH 45502
Tel: (513) 399-3319
FAX: (513) 399-2351
Contact: Barry Krampe
MODIFIER of *Trucks*

Springfield
Navistar International
2069 Lagonda Avenue
Springfield, OH 45501
Tel: (513) 390-2800
FAX: (513) 390-4933
Contact: Dennis Laich
MFR of *TB, U*
D

Springfield
Special Trucks, Inc.
1830 S. Yellow Springs Road
Springfield, OH 45506
Tel: (513) 324-3657
FAX: (513) 324-8774
Contact: Tom Whaley
MODIFIER/MFR of *Trucks*
D: Avis
NOTE: *See also Fort Wayne, IN.*

Springfield
Van Corner, The
1611 W. Main Street
Springfield, OH 45504
Tel: (513) 325-5849
Contact: Shirley Wilson
R4

Sugarcreek
Superior Tank & Trailer
CR 46
Sugarcreek, OH 44681
Tel: (216) 852-2465
MFR of *Tanker TB*

Sylvania
Thom's Van Supply
5030 Alexis Road
Sylvania, OH 43560
Tel: (419) 885-4930
Contact: Fred Pollaus
R4

Tandora
Clymer, Incorporated
202 College Road
P.O. Box 266
Tandora, OH 45877
Tel: (419) 384-3211
Contact: Larry Clymer
MODIFIER of *W*

Toledo
Ace Custom Truck & Trailer
750 Laskey Road
Toledo, OH 43612
Tel: (419) 476-2618
MODIFIER of *T*

Toledo
Cherokee Motors
1852 N. Reynolds Road
Toledo, OH 43615
Tel: (419) 536-2331
DLR of *Work Cargo Vans*

Toledo
MVS
812 Warehouse Road
Toledo, OH 43615
Tel: (419) 382-1102
Contact: Chris Sullivan
H'cap R4
C-1

Toledo
Van Connection, The
5218 Dorr Street
Toledo, OH 43615
Tel; (419) 537-8983
FAX: (419) 537-1576
Contact: Tom Kozak
R4

Trotwood
J. W. Devers & Son, Inc.
5 N. Broadway
Trotwood, OH 45426
Tel: (513) 854-3040
FAX: (513) 854-3017
Contact: Jerry Haupt
MFR of *TB*
C-2:4

Troy
Midwest Trailer Sales
895 S. Alcony
Troy, OH 45373
Tel: (513) 857-9086
FAX: (513) 857-9041
DLR of *UT, LT, HT, CT*

Twinsburg
Dean's Truck Body, Inc.
1783 Highland Road
Twinsburg, OH 44087
Tel: (216) 425-8121
FAX: (216) 425-7639
REPAIR of *TB*
C-2

Uniontown
Begg's Motor Homes, Incorporated
11197 Cleveland Avenue, NW
Uniontown, OH 44685
Tel: (216) 499-9755
Nation: (800) 331-3168
Contact: David Beggs
DLR of *R1, R2*

Upper Sandusky
Elete Trailer Co., Inc.
9529 State Highway 67
Upper Sandusky, OH 43351
Tel: (419) 294-2277
MFR of *T*
B-2

Vandalia
Craftmasters
3020 N. Dixie Drive
Vandalia, OH 45377
Tel: (513) 275-8797
Contact: Kathy Whitt
R4

Walbridge
Kalida Truck Equip., Inc.
30840 Tracy Road
Walbridge, OH 43465
Tel: (419) 666-3700
Nation: (800) 824-8102
FAX: (419) 666-4133
Contact: Susie Burtei
DISTRIBUTOR of *TB*
C-2

Waverly
Fruehauf Corporation
9329 SR 220
Waverly, OH 45690
Tel: (614) 947-7771
FAX: (614) 947-2716
Contact: Jim Caywood
MFR of *T*
B-2
D

Winchester
Taylor & Sons
630 W. Waterloo Canal
Winchester, OH 45697
Tel: (614) 837-5516
MFR of *T*

Winesburg
Peabody Galion
Peabody-Kent Road
Winesburg, OH 44690
Tel: (216) 359-5495
MFR of *TB*
C-2:6

Wooster
Buckeye Bumper
2416 Springville Road
Wooster, OH 44691
Tel: (216) 264-5773
Nation: (800) 262-5773
FAX: (216) 264-9975
Contact: Bob Hamilton or Lynn Hamilton
DLR of *HT, LT, TConvs*

Wooster
Crown Division, The
1654 Old Mansfield Road
Wooster, OH 44691
Tel: (216) 262-6010
Nation: (800) 321-4934
FAX: (216) 262-4095
Contact: Richard Defle
MFR of *TB*
D

Wooster
Snyder Hot Shot
6247 Ashland Road
Wooster, OH 44691
Tel: (216) 264-5400
Contact: Jerald Snyder
MFR of *T*

Wooster
Stahl Division
3201 West Lincoln Way
Wooster, OH 44691
Tel: (216) 264-7441
Nation: (800) 392-7251
Nation: (800) 255-5715
FAX: (216) 264-0891
Contact: Robert McBride
MFR of *UTB, STB*
C-2
D

Youngstown
Auto Upholstery Limited
144 N. Forest Avenue
Youngstown, OH 44506
Tel: (216) 746-6352
Contact: Eddie Garcia
R4
C-2

Youngstown
Ohio Van & Truck Supply, Incorporated
3667 Mahoning Avenue
Youngstown, OH 44515
Tel: (216) 793-9575
Contact: Jerry Dixey
DLR of *R4*

Youngstown
Quality Truck Bodies
4410 Simon Road
Youngstown, OH 44512
Tel: (216) 788-7087
FAX: (216) 788-9850
Contact: Bill Bradley
DLR of *TB*
C-1:3

Zanesville
Arnold's Van World
334 Putnam Avenue
Zanesville, OH 43701
Tel: (614) 453-9991
OH only: (800) 339-4502
FAX: (614) 453-8267
Contact: Jim Arnold
R4
A-1

Zanesville
Custom Vans of Zanesville
3619 Olde Falls Road
Zanesville, OH 43701
Tel: (614) 453-4660
FAX: (614) 453-7963
Contact: Daryl Mast
R4

Zanesville
Fink's Custom Vans, Sales & Accessories
2879 Maysville Pike
Zanesville, OH 43701
Tel: (614) 454-4909
FAX: (614) 454-2733
Contact: Steve Thomas
R4
C-2

OKLAHOMA

Ada
Tommy's Trailers
1828 Latta Road
Ada, OK 74820
Tel: (405) 332-7785
FAX: (405) 332-7707
Contact: Tom Hudson
MFR of *T*
B-2
D

Allen
Allen Camper Manufacturing Co., Inc.
RR 1, Box 16
Allen, OK 74825
Tel: (405) 857-2413
FAX: (405) 857-2414
Contact: Jerry Peay
MFR of *R1, R2, R5, R6, TC*
C-2:1

Asher
Holt Trailer
Jct. of Routes 177 & 39
Asher, OK 74826
Tel: (405) 784-2233
Contact: Bruce Holt
DLR/MFR of *UT*

Broken Arrow
Cadet Mfg., Inc.
7801 Old Hwy. #51, East
Broken Arrow, OK 74014
Tel: (918) 251-2559
FAX: (918) 258-2848
Contact: Guy Holden
MFR of *TB, U*
D

Broken Arrow
Mathey International, Incorporated
1221 E. Houston Street
Broken Arrow, OK 74012
Tel: (918) 258-7311
FAX: (918) 251-2500
Contact: Don Lockhart
MFR of *TB, U*

Cherokee
Butler Welding & Mfg.
226 W. Monroe Avenue
Cherokee, OK 73728
Tel: (405) 596-2461
Contact: Butch Butler
MFR of *TB, U*

Chickasha
Hammond's Horse Trailers
SW 29th & Caroline
Chickasha, OK 76023
Tel: (405) 224-7676
MFR of *HT*

Chickasha
Hart Manufacturing, Inc.
Highway 81, South
P.O. Drawer C
Chickasha, OK 73023
Tel: (405) 224-3634
FAX: (405) 244-3637
MFR of *HT*

Chickasha
Jackson Mfg. Co., Inc.
Route 1, Box 185
Chickasha, OK 73018
Tel: (405) 224-6013
FAX: (405) 224-2402
Contact: Roberta Eskew
MFR of *HT, LT*
B-2:1

Chickasha
Stidham Horse Trailer, Incorporated
Highway 81, South
P.O. Box 768
Chickasha, OK 73023
Tel: (405) 224-1302
MFR of *HT*

Claremore
Starlite Trailer Mfg, Inc.
6700 N. Highway 66
Claremore, OK 74017
Tel: (918) 341-6615
Contact: Bob Pope
MFR of *T*

Colcord
Potter & Son Trailer & Fabrication, Inc.
RR 3
Colcord, OK 74338
Tel: (918) 326-4333
Contact: Wesley Potter
MFR of *T*
B-2
D

Comanche
Shelby Industries, Inc.
Route 1, Box 20
Comanche, OK 73529
Tel: (405) 439-5408
MFR of *HT*
D

Coweta
Dean's Welding Co.
805 E. South Street
Coweta, OK 74429
Tel: (918) 486-5933
Contact: Dean Black
MFR of *ST: Passenger Vehicles*
B-2

Duncan
Chief White GMC Truck & Equipment
3600 S. 13th
Duncan, OK 73533
Tel: (405) 255-6844
Nation: (800) 522-0858
FAX: (405) 255-5782
Contact: Joe Vermedahl
FINAL ASSEMBLER of *Medium- and Heavy-Duty Trucks*
MODIFIER of *U*
C-2

Duncan
Sooner Trailers
(MAIL: P.O. Box 1323
Duncan, OK 73534)
1515 McCurdy
Duncan, OK 73533
Tel: (405) 255-6979
FAX: (405) 255-9783
Contact: Bob Reisner
MFR of *HT*
B-2
D

Durant
G & W Body Works, Inc.
301 Gerlach Drive
P.O. Box 585
Durant, OK 74702
Tel: (405) 924-2226
FAX: (405) 924-7738
Contact: Wayne Gerlach
MFR of *TB*
A-1

Edmond
Baker Equipment Co.
1734 S. Kelly Avenue
Edmond, OK 73013
Tel: (405) 348-4119
Nation: (800) 359-6212
MFR of *TB*
C-2:6

Edmond
Western Truckworks
1016 S. Broadway
Edmond, OK 73034
Tel: (405) 340-0611
Nation: (800) 382-5337
MFR of *CTB*

Enid
Stetco, Incorporated
2215 S. Van Buren
Enid, OK 73702
Tel: (717) 429-0220
FAX: (405) 242-1635
Contact: Ron Spector
MFR of *T*
D

Fairview
Mabar, Incorporated
(Div. of Flow Boy Mfg.)
1700 N. Main Street
Fairview, OK 73737
Tel: (405) 227-3746
Nation: (800) 749-3747
FAX: (405) 227-3829
MFR of *M, FTB, XTB, U*
C-2
D

Locust Grove
Universal Truck Body Works
Highway 412
P.O. Box 436
Locust Grove, OK 74352
Tel: (918) 479-5261
Contact: Paul Kagle
MFR of *CTB, T*

Lone Grove
E. E. Smith Trailer Manufacturing & Sales
704 Highway 70
Lone Grove, OK 73443
Tel: (405) 657-4149
MFR of *T*

Madill
Contract Mfg., Inc.
Route 2, Industrial Road
P.O. Box 680
Madill, OK 73446
Tel: (405) 795-5536
FAX: (405) 795-7263
MFR of *T*

Madill
J & I Mfg., Inc.
Route 3, Box 17
Madill, OK 73446
Tel: (405) 795-5945
Contact: Marland Bruitt
MFR of *FTB, XTB, U*

Madill
S & H Trailer Mfg. Company, Inc.
800 Industrial Drive
Madill, OK 73446
Tel: (405) 795-5577
FAX: (405) 795-3080
Contact: Lisa Willisord
MFR of *GT, HT, LT, UT*
C-2:3

Madill
W-W Trailers Mfg.
P.O. Box 807
Madill, OK 73446
Tel: (405) 795-5571
Contact: Doc Watkins
MFR of *HT, LT*

Marlowe
Central Tank of OK
(Div. of Flow Boy Mfg.)
1 mile S. & 1 mile E. of
Marlowe
P.O. Box 662
Marlowe, OK 73055
Tel: (405) 658-6601
Contact: Pete Boles
MFR of *Tanker S-2,*
Tanker T, Tanker TB

McAlester
CRS Emergency
Vehicle Company
403 S. Main
P.O. Box 370
McAlester, OK 74502
Tel: (918) 426-5005
FAX: (918) 423-3CRS
MFR of *A,E,H, Limos, W*
D

Miami
Newell Coach Corp.
Highway 69, North
P.O. Box 511
Miami, OK 74355
Tel: (918) 542-3344
MFR of *R1, R2*
C-2:2

Norman
Flow Boy Manufacturers
P.O. Box 720660
Norman, OK 73070
Tel: (405) 329-3765
FAX: (405) 329-8588
MFR of *Horizontal-*
Discharge S-2 for Hot
Mix Asphalt

Oilton
Turnbow Trailers, Inc.
P.O. Box 300-3
Oilton, OK 74052
Tel: (918) 862-3233
FAX: (918) 862-3803
MFR of *HT*
D

Oklahoma City
Beesley's Adaptive
Equipment Company
1009 SE 15th Street
Oklahoma City, OK
73129
Tel: (405) 672-6946
Nation: (800) 886-5438
Contact: Bobby Poplin
R4, H'cap R4

Oklahoma City
Better Tow Bars
730 SW 22nd Street
Oklahoma City, OK
73129
Tel: (405) 631-4283
MFR of *W*
C-1

Oklahoma City
4-Star Trailers, Inc.
P.O. Box 75395
Oklahoma City, OK
73147
Tel: (405) 787-9880
FAX: (405) 324-7625
MFR of *HT*

Oklahoma City
McClain's RV, Inc.
7110 W. Reno
Oklahoma City, OK
73127
Tel: (405) 789-4773
Nation: (800) 654-4508
FAX: (405) 789-6861
DLR of *R1*

Owasso
Lewis Travel Trailers
11518 E. 66th St., North
Owasso, OK 74055
Tel: (918) 272-1353
DLR of *R1, R5, R6*

Pryor
Mitchell Coach Mfg. Co./
Vogue Coach by Mitchell
(MAIL: P.O. Box 339
Pryor, OK 74362)
4-1/2 miles S. on US
Highway 69
Pryor, OK 74361
Tel: (918) 825-7000
Tel: (918) 543-8480
Nation: (800) 468-6483
FAX: (918) 825-2105
Contact: Harvey Mitchell
MFR of *R1*
C-2

Purcell
Barrett Trailers, Inc.
2115 Hardcastle Blvd.
P.O. Box 1500
Purcell, OK 73080
Tel: (405) 691-3411
MFR of *T*

Tecumseh
Belshe Industries
301 W. Bobcrouch Drive
P.O. Box 626
Tecumseh, OK 74873
Tel: (405) 273-1690
Nation: (800) 634-4825
FAX: (405) 273-2399
Contact: Mark Wendler
MFR of *T*

Tulsa
American Golden
Eagle Best
(MAIL: P.O. Box 9547
Tulsa, OK 74157)
3900 W. 61st Street
Tulsa, OK 74132
Tel: (918) 446-3288
Contact: Buddy Sherrill
MFR of *T*

Tulsa
Baker's Vanland
6725 E. 11th Street
Tulsa, OK 74112
Tel: (918) 835-1567
R4

Tulsa
Beattie's Hitch-Pro,
Incorporated
1315 N. Harvard Avenue
Tulsa, OK 74115
Tel: (918) 834-1002
MFR of *W*

Tulsa
Beesley's Adaptive
Equipment Company
6553 E. Skelly Drive
Tulsa, OK 74145
Tel: (918) 663-8309
Nation: (800) 886-5438
Nation: (800) 886-LIFT
FAX: (918) 663-8309
Contact: Connie Beesley
H'cap R4

Tulsa
Crane Carrier Company
1925 N. Sheridan Road
Tulsa, OK 74115
Tel: (918) 836-1651
FAX: (918) 832-7348
Contact: Gerald Sellers
MFR of *TB*
C-2

Tulsa
Grand Junction
Custom Vans
8100 Charles Page Blvd.
Tulsa, OK 74127
Tel: (918) 245-6362
Contact: Jim Burdge
R4
C-2

Tulsa
Grant Manufacturing &
Equipment Company
4009 W. 49th Street
Tulsa, OK 74107
Tel: (918) 446-4009
FAX: (918) 446-4123
Contact: Christopher
Powell
MFR of *TB, U*
C-2

Tulsa
Tulsa Body Works, Inc.
2120 Southwest Blvd.
Tulsa, OK 74107
Tel: (918) 582-8116
FAX: (918) 584-6109
Contact: Vanda Lake
MFR of *TB, U*
C-2
D

Tulsa
Tulsa Truck Mfg. Co.
10318 E. 52nd Street
P.O. Box 470321
Tulsa, OK 74146
Tel: (918) 627-5501
FAX: (918) 627-8613
Contact: Joyce Carrington
or Todd Turner
or Ronald A. Turner
R4, TConvs, 4-Wheel-
Drive Convs
C-2:3

Tulsa
Tulsa Truck Rebuilders
1149 N. Delaware Place
Tulsa, OK 74110
Tel: (918) 834-1142
MFR of *S-2*
B-1

Vian
E-Z Goin' Custom Vans
Highway 64, West
Vian, OK 74962
Tel: (918) 773-8674
R4

Walters
Hathaway Simpson
528 W. Missouri Street
Walters, OK 73572
Tel: (405) 875-3177
Contact: Ken Simpson
MFR of *T*

Wynnewood
Royal Coach Mfg. Co.
P.O. Box 458
Wynnewood, OK 73098
Tel: (405) 665-2243
Contact: Bill McGregor
MFR of *T*

OREGON

Beaverton
Bob's RV Country
13555 SW Canyon Road
Beaverton, OR 97005
Tel: (503) 646-6121
Nation: (800) 888-2627
DLR of *R1, R2*

Bend
Beaver Coaches, Inc.
20545 Murray Road
P.O. Box 6089
Bend, OR 97708
Tel: (503) 389-1144
Nation: (800) 423-2837
Nation: (800) 382-2597
(Sales)
FAX: (503) 389-7512
Contact: Pat Harvey
or Dawn Trumbly
MFR of *R1, R2, R3*
C-2:7

Bend
Franklin Trailer Mfg., Incorporated
811 SE Glendwood Drive
Bend, OR 97702
Tel: (503) 389-7555
Contact: Don Thomas
MFR of *T*

Bend
Pacific Coach & Limousine, Limited
P.O. Box 5402
Bend, OR 97708
Region: (800) 700-5519
MFR of *Limos*

Brownsville
Coachcraft Industries
2725 Hume Street
Brownsville, OR 97327
Tel: (503) 466-5131
Nation: (800) 776-5960
FAX: (503) 466-5843
Contact: Pete Lewis
MFR of *H'cap R4*
C-2:6 (part-time)
D: Selland Auto Transport

Central Point
Advanced Truck Body & Equipment Company
4825 Table Rock Road
Central Point, OR 97502
Tel: (503) 664-2822
FAX: (503) 664-1158
Contact: Paul Godfrey
MFR of *FTB, XTB, U*

Central Point
American Whitewater Products
1385 Justice Road
Central Point, OR 97502
Tel: (503) 773-5582
FAX: (503) 773-6179
Contact: John Yanutic
MFR of *T*

Central Point
Big Foot Manufacturing
4811 Table Rock Road
Central Point, OR 97502
Tel: (503) 664-2427
Contact: Don Hoover
MFR of *T*

Central Point
River City RV
5759 Crater Lake Hwy.
Central Point, OR 97502
Tel: (503) 826-5811
Tel: (503) 772-7878
Nation: (800) 777-5759
FAX: (503) 826-1443
DLR of *R1, R2, R5, R6*

Cornelius
Western States Fire
1389 Baseline Street
Cornelius, OR 97113
Tel: (503) 357-2163
FAX: (503) 357-7778
MFR of *F*

Corvallis
John's Custom Welding
2575 SW 49th Street
Corvallis, OR 97333
Tel: (503) 752-8867
Contact: John Stratton
MFR of *T*

Eugene
Freedom Coachworks
27717 Royal Avenue
Eugene, OR 97402
Tel: (503) 689-0335
Contact: Kenneth Midkaff
MFR of *R1, R2, R3*
C-2
D

Eugene
LH Welding
3395 W. 7th
Eugene, OR 97402
Tel: (503) 342-5317
FAX: (503) 683-3307
Contact: Lauren Heitzman
MFR of *TB, T*

Eugene
Kittleson's Custom Trailer
91554 Stallings Lane
Eugene, OR 97401
Tel: (503) 345-2983
Contact: Jim Kittleson
MFR of *CT*

Eugene
Koffler Boats
90017 Green Hill Road
Eugene, OR 97402
Tel: (503) 688-6093
Contact: Bruce Koffler
MFR of *BT*

Eugene
Marathon Coach, Inc.
105 S. Bertelsen Road
Eugene, OR 97402
Tel: (503) 343-9991
Nation: (800) 234-9991
FAX: (503) 343-2401
Contact: Steve Kekuna
CONVERTER of *U*
C-1

Eugene
Romania's RV Center
90554 Hwy. 99, North
Eugene, OR 97402
Tel: (503) 465-3222
Nation: (800) 832-1728
FAX: (503) 465-3235
DLR of *R1, R2*

Eugene
Stan's Auto Upholstery
727 Wilson Street
Eugene, OR 97402
Tel: (503) 342-5866
Contact: Diane Howard
R4
C-2

Eugene
Trail-A-Long Mfg., Inc.
221 Wallace Street
Eugene, OR 97402
Tel: (503) 343-5363
Contact: Randy Leonard
MFR of *T*

Grants Pass
Jiffy Sliding Truck Campers
785 Rogue River Hwy.
Grants Pass, OR 97527
Tel: (503) 476-7779
Contact: John Cook
or Bob Cook
DLR of *TC*

Grants Pass
Molea Auto Works
145 Redwood Highway
Grants Pass, OR 97527
Tel: (503) 474-7582
MFR of *Race Car Chassis*
C-2

Grants Pass
River City RV
340 Union Avenue
Grants Pass, OR 97527
Tel: (503) 476-1541
Nation: (800) 777-4837
FAX: (503) 479-0723
DLR of *R1, R2, R5, R6*

Grants Pass
Triple A RV Center
324 Redwood Hwy.
Grants Pass, OR 97527
Tel: (503) 479-7521
DLR of *R1, R2, R5, R6*

Grants Pass
Westline Mfg., Inc.
13511 N. Applegate Road
Grants Pass, OR 97527
Tel: (503) 846-6800
FAX: (503) 846-6804
Contact: Leonard Apple
MFR of *T*
B-2

Harrisburg
Hurd's Hardware & Custom Machinery, Inc.
204 Moore Street
Harrisburg, OR 97446
Tel: (503) 995-6317
FAX: (503) 995-6319
Contact: Kevin Grimes
MFR of *T*

Harrisburg
Safari Motor Coaches
30725 Diamond Hill Rd.
Harrisburg, OR 97446
Tel: (503) 995-8214
Nation: (800) 344-6332
(Service Department)
FAX: (503) 995-6084
Contact: Chris Brown
MFR of *R1, R2, R3*
C-2

Hermiston
Barton Industries, Inc.
RR 1, Box 1692
Hermiston, OR 97838
Tel: (503) 567-3474
Contact: Rich Barton
REPAIR of *S-2*

Hermiston
Columbia Travel Center
Hermiston-McNary Dam Highway
Hermiston, OR 97838
Tel: (503) 567-1436
OR, WA, & Northern CA only: (800) 624-9787
FAX: (503) 567-7183
DLR of *R5, R6*

Hermiston
Pro Stock Trailer Mfg.
N. Highway 395
P. O. Box 1151
Hermiston, OR 97838
Tel: (503) 567-2034
MFR of *T*

Hillsboro
Columbia Corporation
5775 NW Wagon Way
Hillsboro, OR 97124
Tel: (503) 531-0600
FAX: (503) 531-0601
Contact: Ken Bratlie
MFR of *M, T*
C-2
D

Hillsboro
Newell Dump Truck Bodies
5775 NW Wagon Way
Hillsboro, OR 97124
Tel: (503) 531-0600
MFR of *M*

Hood River
Menasco Manufacturing & Welding
3340 Kollas Road
Hood River, OR 97031
Tel: (503) 354-3208
Nation: (800) 497-4105
Contact: Bill Menasco
MFR of *T*

Independence
R & J Mobility Services
155 E. Street
Independence, OR 97351
Tel: (503) 838-5520
FAX: (503) 838-4710
Contact: Kevin Rowland
H'cap R4
C-2

Junction City
Country Coach, Inc.
135 E. First Street
P.O. Box 400
Junction City, OR 97448
Tel: (503) 998-6661
Tel: (503) 998-3720
Tel: (503) 998-3001
Nation: (800) 547-8015
(Main Plant)
Nation: (800) 654-0223
OR only: (800) 537-0622
FAX: (503) 998-6687
Contact: John Burchette, at the Main Plant.
MFR of *R1, R2, R3, Luxury U*
C-2:20
NOTE: *Almost no driver turnover here; driver employment opportunity therefore is extremely limited.*

Junction City
Countryside Interiors
93080 Hwy. 99, South
Junction City, OR 97448
Tel: (503) 998-6541
Nation: (800) 324-6287
Contact: Steve Skiller
CONVERTER of *R1, Trucks*

Junction City
Hansen Truck Body & Equipment
92590 River Road
Junction City, OR 97448
Tel: (503) 998-6661
FAX: (503) 998-6710
Contact: Ruth Hansen
MFR of *TB, T*
A-1, C-2

Junction City
Lane Dump Body
92410 Hwy. 99, South
Junction City, OR 97448
Tel: (503) 998-6552
FAX: (503) 998-3274
Contact: Gary Bancon
MFR of *M*

Junction City
Monaco Coach Corp.
325 E. 1st Street
Junction City, OR 97448
Tel: (503) 998-1068
Nation: (800) 634-0855
FAX: (503) 998-2158
Contact: Sandy Cadash or Kay Tools
MFR of *R1, R2, R3*
C-2

Klamath Falls
Day Cruiser Van & Body Works
833 S. Spring Road
Klamath Falls, OR 97601
Tel: (503) 884-9930
Contact: John Day
H'cap R4, TConvs
C-2

Klamath Falls
S & S Mfg. Co.
3305 Washburn Way
Klamath Falls, OR 97603
Tel: (503) 884-1812
MFR of *FTB*

Klamath Falls
Sway-Tamer Mfg.
5215 Washburn Way
Klamath Falls, OR 97603
Tel: (503) 884-0646
FAX: (503) 884-7619
Contact: Ken Bailey
MFR of *T*

LaGrande
Fleetwood Travel Trailers of Oregon
62582 Pierce Road
LaGrande, OR 98750
Tel: (503) 963-7101
Nation & Canada:
(800) 444-7101
FAX: (503) 963-2448
Contact: Ron Tincher
MFR of *R5, R6*
D

Lake Oswego
Pacific Limousine & Armoring Sales
14034 Taylor's Crest Ln.
Lake Oswego, OR 97035
Tel: (503) 636-0231
FAX: (503) 636-1960
Contact: Bill Seroyer
DLR of *Limos, Armored Cars*

Lake Oswego
Van Specialties & RV
17420 SW 63rd Avenue
Lake Oswego, OR 97035
Tel: (503) 635-2089
Contact: Gregory Storm
MFR of *R4, TConvs*

McMinnville
Ore-West Equipment Co.
Highway 18
P.O. Box 177
McMinnville, OR 97128
Tel: (503) 472-9339
FAX: (503) 434-5710
MFR of *M*

McMinnville
Skyline Corporation
750 Booth Bend Road
McMinnville, OR 97128
Tel: (503) 472-3101
Nation: (800) 929-1080
FAX: (503) 472-4374
Contact: Mike Willard
MFR of *R5, R6*
D

McMinnville
Zieman Mfg. Co.
150 SE Booth Bend Road
McMinnville, OR 97128
Tel: (503) 472-4671
FAX: (503) 472-4485
Contact: Bill Hurliman
MFR of *R1, R2, R5*
C-2

Medford
G & G Custom Vans
2280 Hull Road
Medford, OR 97501
Tel: (503) 779-4347
R4

Medford
Nicholson Equipment
3604 S. Pacific Highway
Medford, OR 97501
Tel: (503) 535-3636
Contact: Max Nicholson
MFR of *TB, U, T*
D

Medford
Southern Oregon RV
(Div. of River City RV)
2690 Crater Lake Hwy.
Medford, OR 97504
Tel: (503) 779-6331
Nation: (800) 359-6331
DLR of *R1, R2, R5, R6*

Medford
Triple-A RV Center
2790 Crater Lake Hwy.
Medford, OR 97504
Tel: (503) 772-1938
DLR of *R1, R2, R5, R6*

Milwaukie
Carver Coach
5004 SE Johnson Creek Blvd.
Milwaukie, OR 97222
Tel: (503) 777-3787
Contact: Julie McKerley
CONVERTER of *U*
D

Milwaukie
Lake Capital Corp./ Komfort
(MAIL: P.O. Box 68305
Milwaukie, OR 97268)
3701 SE Naef Road
Milwaukie, OR 97267
Tel: (503) 653-1160
FAX: (503) 653-1712
Contact: Gil Lissy
MFR of *R1, R2, R3, R4, R5, R6, T*

Oregon City
White Water Marine
14401 S. Glen Oak Road
Oregon City, OR 97045
Tel: (503) 655-5910
MFR of *T, BT*

Pendleton
Fleetwood Travel Trailers of Oregon
4640 NW Bartch
Pendleton, OR 97801
Tel: (503) 276-1244
Tel: (503) 278-2269
Nation: (800) 547-7770
Nation: (800) 452-5503
MFR of *R6*

Portland
AC Fabrication
2919 NE Columbia Blvd.
Portland, OR 97211
Tel: (503) 287-5272
Contact: Ron Casey or Bob Ackerman
MFR of *T*

Portland
Beall Trans Liner
9200 N. Ramsey Blvd.
Portland, OR 97203
Tel: (503) 286-8823
FAX: (503) 283-0095
Contact: Jerry Beall
MFR of *TB*
C-2:7

Portland
Bill Yoder Vans
18449 SE Stark
Portland, OR 97233
Tel: (503) 232-1155
Nation: (800) 342-2815
FAX: (503) 667-9595
Contact: Kelly Hansen or Bill Yoder
MFR/DLR of *R4*

Portland
C & R Welding
7766 SE 82nd Avenue
Portland, OR 97266
Tel: (503) 774-7094
FAX: (503) 775-3938
Contact: Curt Thies
MFR of *T*

Portland
Care Medical
1877 NE 7th Avenue
Portland, OR 97212
Tel: (503) 288-8174
Nation: (800) 952-9566
FAX: (503) 288-8817
MFR of *H'cap Units*

Portland
Carver Coach
5004 SE Johnson Creek Blvd.
Portland, OR 97222
Tel: (503) 777-3787
Contact: Jim Hartman
CONVERTER of *Small U into Tour & Passenger Busses*

Portland
Cascade Coach Conversions
5717 NE 105th, Unit C
Portland, OR 97220
Tel: (503) 253-2389
Contact: Al Albrich
CONVERTER of *R1, R2*

Portland
Cascade Vans, Inc.
18206 SE Stark Street
Portland, OR 97233
Tel: (503) 666-2203
Nation: (800) 344-2162
FAX: (503) 669-0228
Contact: Tim Geary
R4
C-2

Portland
Coast Crane & Equipment Company
5601 NE Columbia Blvd.
Portland, OR 97218
Tel: (503) 288-8100
FAX: (503) 288-9669
FINAL ASSEMBLER of *TB*

Portland
Columbia Body & Equipment
5525 28th Street, SE
Portland, OR 97202
Tel: (503) 236-1178
Nation: (800) 233-7119
FAX: (503) 239-7337
Contact: Jim Thomas
MFR of *TB, M*
C-2

Portland
Commercial Body Builders, Incorporated
6900 N. Fessenden
Portland, OR 97203
Tel: (503) 286-4441
MFR of *TB (all types)*

Portland
Cruise America
9245 SE 82nd Avenue
Portland, OR 97266
Tel: (503) 788-9627
Nation: (800) 327-7778
Contact: Jenny Lapenta
RENTAL of *RVs*
C-2 Drivers return these to originating sites.
NOTE: *For additional data, see the HQ listing at Mesa, AZ.*

Portland
Fruehauf Corporation
10498 N. Vancouver Way
P.O. Box 17679
Portland, OR 97217
Tel: (503) 285-2140
FAX: (503) 285-5571
Contact: Forest Phillips
DLR of *S-2*
B-2

Portland
Gilbertson Iron Works
10602 SE Foster Road
Portland, OR 97266
Tel: (503) 760-8892
MFR of *T*

Portland
Mount Trailer Company
6364 NE 63rd Avenue
Portland, OR 97218
Tel: (503) 282-7207
Nation: (800) 777-0743
FAX: (503) 288-4057
Contact: Hugh Mount
MFR of *T*

Portland
New Haven Carriage & Auto Works
2323 SE Clatsop
Portland, OR 97202
Tel: (503) 234-9771
FAX: (503) 232-7620
Contact: Dick Wagner
MFR of *TB*

Portland
Northern Lite Mfg., Inc.
7410 SE Johnson Creek Blvd.
Portland, OR 97206
Tel: (503) 777-5826
Contact: John Saban
MFR of *T*
B-2

Portland
Northwest Truckstell Sales, Incorporated
11618 NE Sumner
Portland, OR 97220
Tel: (503) 257-8824
Nation: (800) 283-3183
FAX: (503) 257-8621
Contact: David Ross
DISTRIBUTOR of *TB, R4*
D: Speed's Automotive

Portland
Olinger Travel Homes
9401 SE 82nd Avenue
Portland, OR 97226
Tel: (503) 771-2121
Nation: (800) 258-2140
DLR of *R1*

Portland
RC Display Vans
6650 N. Basin Avenue
Portland, OR 97217
Tel: (503) 285-5119
Nation: (800) 288-5119
FAX: (503) 285-8521
Contact: Rob Collins
CONVERTER of *R1, R2, R3, & Commercial R4*
C-2

Portland
Ridgway Franz
2022 SW Myrtle Street
Portland, OR 97232
Tel: (503) 235-5555
DLR of *A*

Portland
Schetky Northwest Sales, Incorporated
6435 NE Colwood Way
Portland, OR 97218
Tel: (503) 287-4141
Nation: (800) 255-8341
FAX: (503) 287-2931
Contact: Mike Connley
DLR of *S, G, R4, other vehicles*
C-2

Portland
St. John's Truck & Equipment, Inc.
8435 N. Crawford
Portland, OR 97203
Tel: (503) 286-8336
Nation: (800) 222-8435
FAX: (503) 286-2941
MFR of *M*

Portland
Technology Development
3744 SE 99th Avenue
Portland, OR 97266
Tel: (503) 760-8144
FAX: (503) 760-1255
Contact: Bill Hannegan
MFR of *M*
C-2
D

Portland
US Vans
11564 SW Pacific Hwy.
Portland, OR 97223
Tel: (503) 245-4000
FAX: (503) 246-3825
Contact: David Wilson
R4

Portland
Western Wrecker Sales
12841 NE Whitaker Way
Portland, OR 97230
Tel: (503) 256-4200
FAX: (503) 256-4288
Contact: Carla Bryant
DLR of *W*

Prineville
Benare H. Workman & Sons, Incorporated
301030 Peters Road
Prineville, OR 97754
Tel: (503) 447-1297
Nation: (800) 422-4069
FAX: (503) 447-3222
MFR of *TB*
A-1

Redmond
Diamond B Trailer Works
7077 S. Hwy. 97
Redmond, OR 97756
Tel: (503) 923-7622
FAX: (503) 923-4119
Contact: Bob Earl
DLR of *T*

Roseburg
Bentley Welding
1510 SW Austin Road
Roseburg, OR 97470
Tel: (503) 679-7849
Contact: Wayne Bentley
MFR of *T*

Roseburg
Morgan Built, Inc.
1819 SW Austin Road
Roseburg, OR 97470
Tel: (503) 679-6999
FAX: (503) 679-3383
Contact: Dave Morgan
MFR of *T*
D

Roseburg
T & D Enterprises of Roseburg
959 Old Garden Valley
Roseburg, OR 97470
Tel: (503) 672-2819
Contact: Terry Lease
MFR of *T*

Salem
Earl Malm Trailer Sales
4130 Silverton Road, NE
Salem, OR 97305
Tel: (503) 581-2496
DLR of *T*

Salem
Northwest Mfg.
7905 State Street
Salem, OR 97301
Tel: (503) 362-5079
Contact: Ed Cox
REPAIR of *R1, R2*

Salem
Pioneer Machinery, Inc.
4355 Turner Road, SE
Salem, OR 97301
Tel: (503) 378-1756
Tel: (503) 585-9353
FAX: (503) 585-0908
Contact: Nick Nicholas
MFR of *CTB, TB*

Salem
Pummel Supply Co.
2365 Hoyt Street, SE
Salem, OR 97302
Tel: (503) 581-2437
MFR of *TB*

Salem
Wagers Trailer Sales
3282 Silverton Road, NE
Salem, OR 97303
Tel: (503) 585-7713
FAX: (503) 585-2564
DLR of *R1*

Salem
Warnock Enterprises
2317 38th Avenue, NW
Salem, OR 97304
Tel: (503) 585-4621
FAX: (503) 362-1521
R4

Sandy
Young Equipment
16765 SE 362nd Avenue
P.O. Box 1117
Sandy, OR 97055
Tel: (503) 668-4191
Nation: (800) 542-9255
FAX: (503) 668-3110
Contact: Gary Young
DLR of *S-2*
B-1, B-2, B-3, C-2:1
D ships a few.
(Units are shpped nationwide.)

Springfield
Baker Trailers, Inc.
1350 Clearwater Lane
Springfield, OR 97478
Tel: (503) 746-2241
Contact: Glenda Baker
MFR of *T*

Springfield
Collins Campers, Inc.
1635 N. 30th Street
Springfield, OR 97478
Tel: (503) 746-7212
FAX: (503) 746-5491
Contact: Vic Fitzpatrick
or Scott Keil
MFR of *R5*
C-2:1
D

Springfield
Excalibur, Incorporated
38751 Camp Creek Road
Springfield, OR 97478
Tel: (503) 747-5047
Contact: Clay Jack
MFR of *T*

Springfield
General Trailer
1420 South B Street
Springfield, OR 97477
Tel: (503) 746-8218
Tel: (503) 746-2506
Nation: (800) 624-4486
FAX: (503) 726-4707
Contact: Richard Pence
MFR of *S-2, T*

Springfield
Sturdy Built, Inc.
4396 Main Street
Springfield, OR 97478
Tel: (503) 747-1641
Contact: Mike Ward
MFR of *T*

Sutherlin
Warren Manufacturing
1630 W. Duke Road
Sutherlin, OR 97479
Tel: (503) 459-4263
Contact: Richard Warren
MFR of *T*

Sutherlin
Weebee & Associates
1774 W. Duke Road
Sutherlin, OR 97479
Tel: (503) 459-3519
MFR of *T*
C-2

Tigard
U. S. Vans
11564 SW Pacific Hwy.
Tigard, OR 97223
Tel: (503) 245-4000
FAX: (503) 246-3825
R4

Tualatin
Peerless Corporation
P.O. Box 447
Tualatin, OR 97062
Tel: (503) 639-6131
Nation: (800) 922-1338
Nation: (800) 331-3321
FAX: (503) 620-1187
Contact: Julie Birkey
MFR of *T*
B-2
D

Tualatin
Ryan Trailers
21175 SW 180th Street
Tualatin, OR 97062
Tel: (503) 692-3294
FAX: (503) 692-3294
Contact: Tim Farra
MFR of *ST: Passenger Vehicles*
B-2

Wilsonville
Z Products Autosport
30625 SW Boones Ferry Road
Wilsonville, OR 97070
Tel: (503) 246-4555
Nation: (800) 331-9027
Contact: Tim Knapp
R4
D

PENNSYLVANIA

Albion
Roger Bros. Corp.
100 Orchard Street
Albion, PA 16401
Tel: (814) 756-4121
Nation: (800) 441-9880
FAX: (814) 756-4830
Contact: Marilyn Madden
or Mark Kuly
MFR of *ST: Heavy Duty Lowbed*
D: Trailer Transit

Aliquippa
Vic's Van Daddy Shop
515 Green Garden Road
Aliquippa, PA 15001
Tel: (412) 495-3530
R4

Allentown
Allentown Brake & Wheel Service
5361 Oakview Drive
Allentown, PA 18104
Tel: (215) 395-0371
PA only: (800) 322-9584
NY, NJ, and DE only:
(800) 345-3031
FAX: (215) 395-7868
Contact: Bernard Bernan
MFR of *T*

Allentown
Mack Trucks, Inc.
(Executive Office: This is the World Headquarters)
2100 Mack Blvd.
Allentown, PA 18103
Tel: (215) 439-3011
FAX: (215) 439-3308
MFR of *TB*

Altoona
ABC Mack Sales, Inc.
2501 Beale Avenue
Altoona, PA 16601
Tel: (814) 943-8187
Nation: (800) 248-6225
FAX: (814) 946-1594
Contact: Bruce Brower
SALES of *Mack S-1*
C-1

Bala-Cynwyd
Rosen Cadillac
190 Presidential Blvd.
Bala-Cynwyd, PA 19004
Tel: (215) 667-7673
FAX: (215) 664-5529
Contact: Lisa Powers
DLR of *Limos*

Bensalem
Yard Truck Specialists/ Ottawa Trucks
1510 Ford Road
Bensalem, PA 19020
Tel: (215) 244-1773
Nation: (800) 445-1141
FAX: (215) 244-0317
Contact: Sue Anderson
DLR of *TB*

Berwick
Columbia Industries Inc.
9th & Oak Streets
P.O. Box 177
Berwick, PA 18603
Tel: (717) 759-1291
Contact: Bill Howek
MFR of *TB, U*
C-1

Bethel Park
Keystone Coach Works
4786 Liberty Road
Bethel Park, PA 15102
Tel: (412) 833-1900
FAX: (412) 833-1918
Contact: Dave Knaus
R4, H'cap Units

Bird in Hand
Andy's Body Shop
162 N. Rondks Road
P.O. Box 78
Bird in Hand, PA 17505
Tel: (717) 392-4238
Contact: David Andrews
R4

Blue Ball
M. H. Eby, Inc.
P.O. Box 127
Blue Ball, PA 17506
Tel: (717) 354-4971
Contact: Darryl Brensier
MFR of *T, TB*
D: Y-Tran

Blue Ball
Van House, The
1030 Main Street
Blue Ball, PA 17506
Tel: (717) 354-8140
Contact: Sherry Burkholder
R4

Blue Bell
Iveco Trucks of North America
4 Sentry Parkway
P.O. Box 1102
Blue Bell, PA 19422
Tel: (215) 825-3880
Nation: (800) 523-1156
FAX: (215) 874-8773
DLR of *TB, U*

Brooksville
Ti-Brook, Incorporated
Exit 14 of I-80
P.O. Box 300
Brooksville, PA 15825
Tel: (814) 849-2342
Nation: (800) 545-1549
PA only: (800) 545-1553
FAX: (814) 849-5063
Contact: Ralph Roudolph
MFR of *M, T*
C-2:2
D

Brownstown
Trans Equipment
Route 272
Brownstown, PA 17508
Tel: (717) 859-2095
MFR of *T*

Butler
Commonwealth Utility Equipment Company
129 Pillow Street
Butler, PA 16001
Tel: (412) 283-8400
Contact: Anthony Closkey
MFR of *TB, U*

Butler
Watt Camper
709 W. Old Route 422
Butler, PA 16001
Tel: (412) 287-5493
Contact: Francis Watt
MFR of *R5, R6*

Carlisle
Dawn Conversions, Inc.
1445 Holly Pike
Carlisle, PA 17013
Tel: (717) 243-5550
FAX: (717) 243-6542
Contact: Bruce Ruth
R4
C-1

Clarendon
Hoffman Coach Co.
US Route 6
P.O. Box 337
Clarendon, PA 15828
Tel: (814) 723-4550
Contact: Don Hoffman
MFR of *R1, R2*

Clearfield
Fullington GMC Sales
316 E. Cherry Street
Clearfield, PA 16830
Tel: (814) 765-2455
FAX: (814) 765-9572
Contact: Dick Fullington
DLR of *GMC Trucks*

Clifton Heights
Adaptive Driving Conversions, Inc.
319 E. Berkley Avenue
Clifton Heights, PA 19018
Tel: (215) 623-2080
FAX: (215) 284-4346
Contact: Michael Borkowski
H'cap R4, R4
C-1

Colmar
Advanced Tank Systems, Incorporated
301 Enterprises Lane
Colmar, PA 18915
Tel: (215) 822-1336
FAX: (215) 822-5591
Contact: Phil Raymond
MFR of *Liquid Handling Tank Trucks*

Conshohocken
Acroft Coachworks, Inc.
10 Oak Street
P.O. Box 674
Conshohocken, PA 19428
Tel: (215) 941-0303
Contact: John Fadel
DLR of *Limos*

Conshohocken
Alan Van Conversions
1516 Fayette Street
(At the rear, behind the movie store)
Conshohocken, PA 19428
Tel: (215) 828-2353
Contact: Randy Heines
R4

Conshohocken
Florig Equip. Co., Inc.
904 Ridge Pike
Conshohocken, PA 19428
Tel: (215) 825-0900
Nation: (800) 345-6171
FAX: (215) 825-0908
FAX: (215) 825-0909
Contact: Pat McFeeley or John Wood
MFR of *TB, T*

Delmont
Artman Parts & Equipment Company/ Mold Plastics, Inc.
350 Route 66, North
Delmont, PA 15626
Tel: (412) 468-4668
Tel: (412) 468-4242
FAX: (412) 468-4732
Contact: Jim Artman
MFR of *Sleeper Cabs, TB, U*
C-2
D

Denver
Gold Rush, Incorporated
430 S. Muddy Creek Rd.
Denver, PA 17517
Tel: (717) 336-4101
MFR of *T*

Denver
MGS, Incorporated
178 Muddy Creek Church Road
Denver, PA 17517
Tel: (717) 336-7528
Nation: (800) 952-4228
FAX: (717) 336-4071
Contact: Phil Hornberger or Katie Hershey
MFR of *UT, T, ST: Generator Trailers*
B-1:1, B-2: Several
D: Driveaway Company, and others

Denver
Sunline Coach Company
245 South Muddy Creek Road
Denver, PA 17517
Tel: (717) 336-2858
FAX: (717) 336-0527 (General Office)
FAX: (717) 336-4979 (Parts Department)
Contact: Herb Tester
MFR of *R5, R6*
B-1:3, working part-time
D: Quality Driveaway, Hoosier RV, and Rad Transport, all based in and near Elkhart, IN. (Most of those drivers live near the company.)

Dillsburg
Arndt Trailers, Inc.
1019 Pondtown Road
Dillsburg, PA 17019
Tel: (717) 432-5476
Contact: Kay Fetfro
MFR of *HT, UT*

Dillsburg
Shoop's Trailer, Inc.
715 Range End Road
Dillsburg, PA 17019
Tel: (717) 432-5212
MFR of *T*

Drums
Hildebrand Custom Truck Body
RR 2, Box 453
Drums, PA 18222
Tel: (717) 788-3405
FAX: (717) 788-3254
Contact: Lee Hildebrand
MFR of *TB, T*

Duncanville
Ansley & Lewis, Inc.
1280 Route 764
Duncanville, PA 16635
Tel: (814) 695-8336
PA & Area Code 301 of MD only: (800) 231-9817
FAX: (814) 695-9814
DLR of *R1, R5, R6*

Duncanville
Brumbaugh Truck Bodies
RD #5
P.O. Box 579
Duncanville, PA 16635
Tel: (814) 696-9552
Contact: Scott Emigh
MFR of *F*
D

Dunmore
Freuhauf Corporation
125 Monohan Avenue
Dunmore, PA 18512
Tel: (717) 344-1245
MFR of *T*

Ebensburg
Kasel Manufacturing Co.
722 Crescent Road
Ebensburg, PA 15931
Tel: (814) 472-9450
FAX: (814) 472-4117
Contact: George Lesak
MFR of *T*
D

Elizabeth
Laidlaw Transit, Inc.
1860 Scenery Drive
Elizabeth, PA 15037
Tel: (412) 384-3010
Contact: Gary Lee
MFR of *S*
C-1

- 268 -

Elizabethville
Swab Wagon Co., Inc.
One Chestnut Avenue
Elizabethville, PA 17023
Tel: (717) 362-8151
Contact: Tony Margerum
MFR of *TB, U*

Ephrata
Simon Ladder Towers, Incorporated
64 Cocalico Creek Road
Ephrata, PA 17522
Tel: (717) 859-1176
FAX: (717) 859-2774
Contact: Bill Martin
MFR of *F*
C-1

Erie
Erie Diesel & Truck Service, Incorporated
1504 W. 12th Street
Erie, PA 16501
Tel: (814) 454-7101
Contact: Gary Leslie
REPAIR of *TB, U*

Erie
Five Star International Trucks, Incorporated
6100 Wattsburg Road
Erie, PA 16509
Tel: (814) 825-6150
Nation: (800) 243-7241
FAX: (814) 825-8274
Contact: Peter Scheller
LEASING of *TB, U*

Erie
Garnon Truck Equipment, Incorporated
1617 Peninsula Drive
Erie, PA 16505
Tel: (814) 833-6000
FAX: (814) 833-6047
Contact: James H. Garnon
DISTRIBUTOR of
Morgan TB & XTB
C-2
D: Morgan Driveaway

Erie
Mack Truck Sales of Erie, Incorporated
960 W. 12th Street
Erie, PA 16501
Tel: (814) 454-2475
Contact: Peter Askey
DLR of *S-1*
C-1

Erie
Poplar White Truck, Inc.
436 W. 12th Street
Erie, PA 16501
Tel: (814) 454-1575
Nation: (800) 673-2475
FAX: (814) 456-2251
Contact: Robert Durst
DLR of *S-1*

Erie
Truck & Trailer Equipment, Inc.
1050 W. 12th Street
Erie, Pa 16501
Tel: (814) 452-3431
Contact: William Donor
DLR of *TB, U*

Exton
Wolfington Body Company, Incorporated
Route 100 & Penna. Tpk.
P.O. Box 218
Exton, PA 19341
Tel: (215) 458-8501
Nation: (800) 662-2435
FAX: (215) 458-0293
Contact: Jim Lewis
MFR of *U*
C-2

Fairless Hills
Strick Corporation
US Highway 1, Box 9
Fairless Hills, PA 19030
Tel: (215) 949-3600
FAX: (215) 949-4766
Contact: Frank Katz
MFR of *S-2*
C-2
D

Fleetwood
Imaginative Interiors
130 W. Main Street
Fleetwood, PA 19522
Tel: (215) 944-9795
Contact: John Luvensterger
MODIFIER of *R4*
C-1

Fredonia
J. C. Moore Industries
152 2nd Street
Fredonia, PA 16124
Tel: (412) 475-3185
FAX: (412) 475-2067
Contact: Gary A. Rhodes
DLR of *TB, U*
C-2
D

Freeport
Freeport Transport
1200 Butler Road
Freeport, PA 16229
Tel: (412) 295-2181
FAX: (412) 295-2710
Contact: Dawn Smetanick
MFR of *T*
C-1

Glen Rock
Mobility Independent Transportation
RR 2, Box 516
Glen Rock, PA 17327
Tel: (717) 233-6487
Tel: (717) 235-5899
Contact: Tim Hughes
H'cap R4

Greencastle
Danco Products
411 S. Cedar Lane
Greencastle, PA 17225
Tel: (717) 597-7185
Nation: (800) 453-2626
FAX: (717) 597-7106
Contact: Dan Reynolds
MFR of *TB*
C-2
D: Martin Freight

Greencastle
Fab Tech Industries, Inc.
80 Commerce Avenue
Greencastle, PA 17225
Tel: (717) 597-2310
FAX: (717) 597-5344
Contact: Dawn McClain
MFR of *TB*

Greencastle
Jerr-Dan Corporation
1080 Hykes Road
Greencastle, PA 17225
Tel: (717) 597-7111
Nation: (800) 926-9666
FAX: (717) 597-8509
Contact: Mike Miller
MFR of *U, Single-Car-Carrier TB, XTB*
C-2

Greensburg
Ranger Trailer Co., Inc.
215 N. Jefferson Avenue
Greensburg, PA 15601
Tel: (412) 837-2753
FAX: (412) 837-9310
Contact: Joseph Lonigro
MFR of *R1 Convs, R2, R3, H'cap R4, R5, CT, Mobile Photo Labs*
C-2:1

Greensburg
Universal Coach Co.
15 Rainbow Road
Greensburg, PA 15601
Tel: (412) 834-2391
Nation: (800) 242-1357
Contact: George Tarr
MFR of *Truck Cabs*
C-2

Harrisburg
Commonwealth International Trucks
1810 S. 19th Street
P.O. Box 1747
Harrisburg, PA 17105
Tel: (717) 986-1500
Contact: Harold Gooding
DLR of *S-1, Navistar Heavy Duty Trucks*

Harrisburg
Haveco
7408 Derry Street
Harrisburg, PA 17111
Tel: (717) 558-4301
FAX: (717) 231-6156
Contact: Greg Scizt
R4, H'cap R4

Harrisburg
Osterlund, Incorporated
711 Gibson Blvd.
Harrisburg, PA 17104
Tel: (717) 939-8795
FAX: (717) 564-1412
Contact: Jan Osterlund
MFR of *TB*
C-2
D

Hazelton
Craig Motors, Inc.
282 S. Church Street
Hazelton, PA 18201
Tel: (717) 454-8785
Nation: (800) 962-0808
FAX: (717) 454-2124
Contact: Charlie Desaulniers
DLR of *TB, U*
C-2

Hazelton
Montone Mfg. Co.
P.O. Box P
Hazelton, PA 18201
Tel: (717) 454-8742
Contact: Vincent Montone
MFR of *M, Dump T*

Hermitage
Century Wrecker Corp.
2755 Kirila Blvd.
Hermitage, PA 16148
Tel: (412) 981-3328
FAX: (412) 981-0277
Contact: Dan Sebasgian
MFR of *TB, W*

Hermitage
Schultz Truck Equipment
7006 E. State Street
Hermitage, PA 16148
Tel: (412) 342-2277
FAX: (412) 342-2610
Contact: Shirley Schultz
MFR of *TB, U*

Honey Brook
Schnure Mfg. Co., Inc.
RD #4, Supplee Road
Honey Brook, PA 19344
Tel: (215) 273-3352
MFR of *T*
B-2
D

Huntingdon Valley
M & M Custom Coach
1458 Country Line Road
Huntingdon Valley, PA 19006
Tel: (215) 355-7035
FAX: (215) 364-5479
Contact: Mary Vande
MFR of *R1*

Imperial
Imperial Truck Body & Equipment
934 Santiago Road
Imperial, PA 15126
Tel: (412) 771-8300
MFR of *TB*

Irwin
Cavalier Coach
11000 Route 30
Irwin, PA 15642
Tel: (412) 864-5700
Nation: (800) 345-VANS
FAX: (412) 864-7403
Contact: Bill Harrison
R4

Irwin
Serro Scotty RV
450 Arona Road
Irwin, PA 15642
Tel: (412) 863-3407
FAX: (412) 863-3880
Contact: Olga Reott
MFR of *R5, R6*
C-2:5

Jermyn
Grumman-Olson Mayfield
400 Penn Avenue
Jermyn, PA 18433
Tel: (717) 876-4560
MFR of *TB, U*

Jersey Shore
Hurlbutt Brothers Truck Body
Vilas Park
Jersey Shore, PA 17740
Tel: (717) 398-1113
DLR of *VTB, M*

Kingston
Wilkes Barre Mack Sales & Services
135 S. Wyoming Avenue
Kingston, PA 18704
Tel: (717) 288-9351
Nation: (800) 475-MACK
FAX: (717) 288-8944
Contact: Russell Springer
DLR of *S-1*

Kulpsville
Hessco Truck Body Corporation
Detweiler & Wambold Road
Kulpsville, PA 19443
Tel: (215) 256-4100
MFR of *TB*

Lancaster
Heil Company, The
P.O. Box 4807
Lancaster, PA 17604
Tel: (717) 397-7771
FAX: (717) 394-5908
Contact: Melissa Pepple
MFR of *Aluminum Tanker S-2*
D

Lancaster
Keystone Peterbilt, Inc.
1467 Manheim Pike
Lancaster, PA 17601
Tel: (717) 299-6630
DLR of *S-1*
C-2:6

Lancaster
Lancaster Truck Bodies
310 Richardson Drive
Lancaster, PA 17603
Tel: (717) 394-2647
Nation: (800) 732-0004
FAX: (717) 299-9540
DISTRIBUTOR of *TB*

Lebanon
Hewey Welding
RD #4, Box 2312
Lebanon, PA 17042
Tel: (717) 867-5222
Contact: Henry Wampler
MFR of *TB, U*

Lebanon
M. A. Brightbill Body Works, Incorporated
Route 422, East
Lebanon, PA 17042
Tel: (717) 272-7691
Nation: (800) 932-4625
Contact: Steve Shiner
DISTRIBUTOR of *TB, U*
C-1

Leeper
Pennstyle Campers, Inc.
Route 36
P.O. Box 155
Leeper, PA 16233
Tel: (814) 744-8537
Tel: (814) 744-8855
FAX: (814) 744-9450
Contact: Fred Oachs or Bill Wolter
MFR of *Cargo T, XT*
A-1, C-1

Leighton
Strick Corporation
RR 1
Leighton, PA 18235
Tel: (717) 386-5956
FAX: (717) 386-2816
Contact: Steve Nelson
MFR of *S-2, TB*
C-2
D

Leola
Glick's Trailer Shop
231 E. Main Street
Leola, PA 17540
Tel: (717) 656-9195
Contact: John Glick
MFR of *HT, LT*

Leola
Shasta Industries
40 Hess Road
Leola, PA 17540
Tel: (717) 656-2511
Nation: (800) 831-3123
PA Only: (800) SHASTA-1
DLR of *R1, R2, R3*
D: Horizon Transport, Wakarusa, IN (Toll-free numbers ring directly to Horizon.)

Leola
Skyline Corporation/ Nomad Travel Trailer
77 Horseshoe Road
Leola, PA 17540
Tel: (717) 656-2111
Nation: (800) 634-6366
FAX: (717) 656-3490
Contact: Jim Lovell or Paige Longnecker
MFR of *R1, R2, R3, R5, R6*
A-1
D

Linden
Willits Truck Body Shop
Pine Run Road
RD #1, Box 295
Linden, PA 17744
Tel: (717) 398-2878
FINAL ASSEMBLER of *TB*

Luzerne
Keller Wheelchair Lifts
197 Main Street
Luzerne, PA 18709
Tel: (717) 288-1004
FAX: (717) 288-8070
Contact: James Keller
H'cap R4, R4

Macungie
Mack Trucks, Assembly Division
7000 Alburtis Road
Macungie, PA 18062
Tel: (215) 439-3011
FAX: (215) 966-2051
Contact: Cindy Paulas
FINAL ASSEMBLER of *Mack Trucks*
D

Mammoth
Aliner/Alite
1 Main Street
P.O. Box 131
Mammoth, PA 15664
Tel: (412) 423-7440
FAX: (412) 423-8485
Contact: Mark Tait
MFR of *TC*
C-2:2
D: Morgan, Don Ray, Ideal Transport

Mann's Choice
Charles H. Burkett's Auto Rama
Route 96, RD #1
Mann's Choice, PA 15550
Tel: (814) 623-9696
MFR of *T*

Marion
Statler Body Works
5573 Main Street
Marion, PA 17235
Tel: (717) 375-2251
FAX: (717) 375-2252
Contact: Gary Winger
DLR of *TB, U*
C-2
D

McAdoo
Haulmark Industries, Incorporated
8 Kline Road
McAdoo, PA 18237
Tel: (717) 929-3761
FAX: (717) 929-2141
Contact: Jack Zimmerman **MFR** of *T*

Meadow Lands
Barr Cannon Body Company, Incorporated
2439 W. Pike Street
P.O. Box 546
Meadow Lands, PA 15347
Tel: (412) 745-6900
PA Only: (800) 438-2289
FAX: (412) 745-1853
Contact: Tim Cannon
MFR of *TB*
C-2

Mechanicsburg
New Harrisburg Truck Body Company
408 Sheeley Lane
Box 568
Mechanicsburg, PA 17055
Tel: (717) 766-7651
FAX: (717) 766-4289
Contact: Carol Forrest
MFR of *TB*

Mercer
Chevron, Incorporated
RD #7
Mercer, PA 16137
Tel: (412) 981-7500
FAX: (412) 981-4425
Contact: Linda Morlend or Ed Peters
MFR/DISTRIBUTOR of *W, Single-Car-Carrier TB*
D

Middleburg
Thor Industries
RD #3, Box 38
Middleburg, PA 17842
Tel: (717) 837-1663
Nation: (800) 548-7924
FAX: (717) 837-5274
Contact: Chris Rhodes
MFR of *R5, R6*
C-2:7

Mifflinburg
Remweld Trailers
RR 3
Mifflinburg, PA 17844
Tel: (717) 966-9188
Contact: Reuben Martin
MFR of *T*
B-2

Milroy
Hostetler Truck Bodies & Trailers
Route 322, Box 577
Milroy, PA 17063
Tel: (717) 667-3921
Nation: (800) 441-5161
FAX: (717) 667-3979
Contact: Fred Stock or Jim Knorr
MFR/DLR of *HT, TB*

Monaca
Roger's Kustom Shop
1500 Pennsyvania Avenue
Monaca, PA 15061
Tel: (412) 728-2299
R4
C-2

Monroeville
Cochran
4200 William Penn Hwy.
Monroeville, PA 15146
Tel: (412) 373-3333
Nation: (800) 860-3337
Contact: Betty Patski or Jim Bateman
DLR of *R4*
C-2

Montgomery
Grumman Long-Life Vehicles
Old Route 405
Road 1, Box 441
Montgomery, PA 17752
Tel: (717) 547-1681
FAX: (717) 547-6180
MFR of *Postal Trucks*
D

Montgomeryville
Quality Coach, Inc.
Stump Road & Commerce Drive
Montgomeryville, PA 18936
Tel: (215) 643-2211
FAX: (215) 362-1546
Contact: Marie Pierce
H'cap R4

Montoursville
Transport Designs, Inc.
240 Strieghbeigh Lane
Montoursville, PA 17754
Tel: (717) 368-1403
FAX: (717) 368-2398
Contact: Steve Mattey
MFR of *T*
D

Morgantown
McNeilus Truck & Manufacturing, Inc.
955 Hemlock Road
Morgantown, PA 19543
Tel: (610) 286-0400
MFR of *G, Mixer TB*

Morgantown
Morgan Corporation
1 Morgan Way
P.O. Box 588
Morgantown, PA 19543
Tel: (215) 286-5052
Nation: (800) 6-MORGAN
FAX: (215) 286-2220
FAX: (215) 286-2320
Contact: Dan Rupert
MFR of *TB*
C-2
D: Driveaway Company
NOTE: *"800" number reaches the closest plant to the caller. See also Morgan Corporation in Fontana, CA.*

Morgantown
Ronald M. Bressler
2563 Valley View Road
Morgantown, PA 19543
Tel: (215) 286-6013
R4, WConvs

Morrisville
Van & 4X4 Workshop
Bridge & Delmorr Ave.
Morrisville, PA 19067
Tel: (215) 295-5077
Contact: Mike Fletcher
R4
C-1

Myerstown
Kompact Kamp
RD #1
Hwy. 501, North
Myerstown, PA 17067
Tel: (717) 933-8070
Contact: Dennis Martin
MFR/DLR of *T, ST: Motorcycle T*
D

Nanticoke
Phoenix Mfg., Inc.
375 W. Union Street
Nanticoke, PA 18634
Tel.: (717) 735-1800
FINAL ASSEMBLER of *TB, U*

Nesquehoning
Kovatch Corporation
1 Industrial Complex
Nesquehoning, PA 18240
Tel: (717) 669-9461
Nation: (800) 235-3928
FAX: (717) 645-7007
Contact: Stan Ptaszkowski
MFR of *F*

New Castle
Cobra Mfg. Inc.
418 S. Cascade Street
New Castle, PA 16101
Tel: (412) 658-5681
Contact: Bob Pederson
MFR of *T*

New Castle
Galbreath Motor Co.
1807 Wilmington Road
New Castle, PA 16105
Tel: (412) 656-1075
Contact: Ed Galbreath
R4

New Castle
Starclass, Incorporated
3454 Elwood Road
New Castle, PA 16101
Tel: (412) 658-2865
Nation: (800) 422-2865
Contact: Raymond Moffett
MFR of *TB, U*

New Oxford
Wherley Trailer Mfg.
6480 York Road
New Oxford, PA 17350
Tel: (717) 624-2268
MFR of *T*

Norristown
Van Conversions, Inc.
925 S. Trooper Road
Norristown, PA 19403
Tel: (215) 666-9100
FAX: (215) 666-9102
Contact: Chip Pough or Jack Donovan
MFR of *R4*
NOTE: *Formerly in Valley Forge, PA*

Northumberland
Dorsey Trailers, Inc.
RD #1
Northumberland, PA 17857
Tel: (717) 275-5006
FAX: (717) 275-9529
Contact: Mike Gordy
MFR of *T, S-2*
D

Paxinos
Fleetwood Motor Homes of Pennsylvania
Route 487, RFD #1
P.O. Drawer 5
Paxinos, PA 17860
Tel: (717) 644-0817
Contact: Frank Nowicki
MFR of *R1, R2, R3*
D: Morgan Driveaway, Don Ray Driveaway

Philadelphia
Auto Truck & Trailer Body Company
820 N. 3rd Street
Philadelphia, PA 19123
Tel: (215) 592-9167
MFR of *TB*

Philadelphia
Carey International
6401 Passynuck Avenue
Philadelphia, PA 19153
Tel: (215) 492-8402
Nation: (800) 336-4646
RENTAL of *Limos*
C-2:12

Philadelphia
Memco Industries, Inc.
3050 North Hope Street
Philadelphia, PA 19433
Tel: (215) 423-7077
Contact: Susan Lies
MFR of *TB, U*
D

Philadelphia
S. J. Eskin, Incorporated
1408 N. 31st Street
Philadelphia, PA 19121
Tel: (215) 763-2000
FAX: (215) 763-2002
MFR of *TB, U*

Philadelphia
Van-Go, Incorporated
7990 Oxford Avenue
Philadelphia, PA 19111
Tel: (215) 722-4622
Nation: (800) 872-5371
FAX: (215) 722-4630
FINAL ASSEMBLER
of *T*

Pittsburgh
Access Services Unlimited, Incorporated
4801 Penn Avenue
Pittsburgh, PA 15224
Tel: (412) 363-2935
FAX: (412) 363-4318
Contact: Jere Walkow
R4, H'cap R4
C-2

Pittsburgh
Cornelius Arch Products, Incorporated
30 Pine Street
Pittsburgh, PA 15223
Tel: (412) 781-9003
Contact: Chuck Shelby
R4

Pittsburgh
Pittsburgh Elevator Co.
3862 East Street
Pittsburgh, PA 15214
Tel: (412) 321-6114
FAX: (412) 321-3997
R4

Pittsburgh
300 Vans, Incorporated
Camp Horne Road
Pittsburgh, PA 15202
Tel: (412) 761-9200
DLR of *R4*

Pittsfield
Ward's Custom Built Trailers
RD #2
Pittsfield, PA 16340
Tel: (814) 563-9217
FAX: (814) 563-9573
Contact: Jim Ward
MFR of *T*

Pottstown
Baker Equipment Engineering Company
3380 West Ridge Park
Pottstown, PA 19464
Tel: (215) 495-7091
FAX: (215) 495-7098
Contact: Tony Grasso
SERVICE CENTER
of *TB*
C-1

Pottstown
Phoenix Coach Works, Incorporated
39 Sheridan Lane
Pottstown, PA 19464
Tel: (215) 495-2266
Contact: Joe Kupski
MFR of *HT*

Pottstown
Pottstown Truck Sales, Incorporated
1402 W. High Street
Pottstown, PA 19464
Tel: (215) 323-8100
FAX: (215) 970-2275
Contact: Robert Slinn
DLR of *S-1, Heavy Duty Trucks*

Pottsville
Yaco Industries, Ltd.
1013 W. Market Street
Pottsville, PA 17901
Tel: (717) 622-2272
FAX: (717) 622-3292
Contact: Carol Lynch
MFR of *TB, U*
C-1

Prospect Park
Custom Auto World
1009 Lincoln Avenue
Prospect Park, PA 19076
Tel: (215) 461-7178
R4, 4-Wheel-Drive Convs

Reading
Viking Truck Sales, Inc.
1846 N. 5th Street
Reading, PA 19612
Tel: (215) 374-4914
Nation: (800) 438-4744
FAX: (215) 374-2493
Contact: Chuck Hirsch
DISTRIBUTOR of
TB, U

Revere
Cotner Trailer Mfg. Co.
Route 611, Box 237
Revere, PA 18953
Tel: (215) 847-2237
Contact: John Kazary
MFR of *HT*

Richfield
Gold Star Industries
RR 1, Box 538
Richfield, PA 17086
Tel: (717) 694-3171
Contact: Orville Brubaker
DISTRIBUTOR of *TC*

Saint Michael
Samco, Incorporated
Route 869
St. Michael, PA 15951
Tel: (814) 495-9632
FAX: (814) 495-4957
Contact: James Schrader
MFR of *TB*

Scottdale
Ken-Co Company, Inc.
RD #1, Box 826
Scottdale, PA 15683
Tel: (412) 887-7070
FAX: (412) 887-6727
Contact: Robert Kendi
MFR of *F*
C-1

Scranton
Simpson Motor Truck
319 Green Ridge Street
Scranton, PA 18509
Tel: (717) 342-0208
DLR of *Trucks*
C-2

Shickshinny
Scott Franklin's Custom Built Trailers
RR 1, Box 143-A
Shickshinny, PA 18655
Tel: (717) 256-7253
Contact: Scott Franklin
MFR of *T*

Shillington
Reading Body Works, Incorporated
Hancock Blvd. & Gerry Street, Box 650
Shillington, PA 19607-0650
Tel: (215) 775-3301
FAX: (215) 775-6513
Contact: Debbie Hartranft
MFR of *UTB*
C-2

Shoemakersville
Hill Manufacturing
869 Water Street
Shoemakersville, PA 19555
Tel: (215) 562-2207
FAX: (215) 562-2209
Contact: Bill Hill
MFR of *TB, U, T*

Skippeck
Heritage Coach Co.
4312 Skippeck Pike
Skippeck, PA 19474
Tel: (215) 584-8299
FAX: (215) 584-8313
Contact: Sue Langford
DLR of *H, Limos*

Somerset
Fleetwood Folding Trailers, Incorporated
RR 2
Somerset, PA 15501
Tel: (814) 445-9661
FAX: (814) 443-7340
Contact: Julie Cramer
DISTRIBUTOR of
Folding Campers, T
B-2

Somerset
J & J Truck Bodies
RD #2
Route 985, North
P.O. Box 735
Somerset, PA 15501
Tel: (814) 443-2671
Nation: (800) 777-2671
FAX: (814) 445-8475
Contact: Ann Swincinski
MFR of *TB*
C-2:7

Somerset
Somerset Welding & Steel, Incorporated
RD #2, Box 234-A
Somerset, PA 15501
Tel: (814) 443-2671
FAX: (814) 443-2621
Contact: Jerry Johnson
MFR of *TB, U*
C-2

State College
Vantasia Automotive
2231 E. College Avenue
State College, PA 16801
Tel: (814) 234-4506
FAX: (814) 238-8022
Contact: Bill Kalban
R4

Tamaqua
Tamaqua Truck & Trailer, Incorporated
RR 3, Box 12
Route 309
Tamaqua, PA 18252
Tel: (717) 386-5994
FAX: (717) 386-3162
Contact: Robin Wood
MFR of TB

Telford
Coach & Sail
158 Keystone Road
P.O. Box 232
Telford, PA 18969
Tel: (215) 453-8788
FAX: (215) 453-0605
Contact: Craig Bucce
or Marvin Neely
MFR of R4, TConvs, TC
REFURBISHER of R1, R2
C-2:2 (part-time)
D

Turtle Creek
Zoresco Equipment Co.
1241 Rodi Road
Turtle Creek, PA 15145
Tel: (412) 829-2120
FAX: (412) 829-7286
MFR of TB, U
C-2
D

Uniontown
Conaway Hearse & Limo Sales
305 Crossland Avenue
P.O. Box 1132
Uniontown, PA 15401
Tel: (412) 439-8800
FAX: (412) 439-6404
Contact: Barnetta Postories
DLR of H, Limos
C-2

Uniontown
Freuhauf Trailer Operations
60-D Lebanon Avenue
Uniontown, PA 15401
Tel: (412) 438-0565
FAX: (412) 439-5733
Contact: Cliff Burton
MFR of T
C-2
D

Warrington
Warrington Equipment Manufacturing Company
2051 Bunnell Road
Warrington, PA 18976
Tel: (215) 343-1714
FAX: (215) 343-2312
Contact: Don Mohr
MFR of TB, U-Haul T
D: U-Haul

Washington
Washington International Truck
1105 Fayette Street
Washington, PA 15301
Tel: (412) 222-8680
FAX: (412) 328-1970
Contact: Dave Blackburn
DLR of Trucks
C-2 (local)

Whitehall
Auto Truck Van & RV
Route 329
Whitehall, PA 18052
Tel: (215) 262-4941
Contact: Rich Malast
R4

Wilkes Barre
Voyton Brothers Truck Body Manufacturing
Parrish & High Streets
Wilkes Barre, PA 18702
Tel: (717) 822-6149
MFR of TB, U

Williamsport
Radiant Steel Products Company
205 Locust Street
Williamsport, PA 17701
Tel: (717) 322-7828
FAX: (717) 322-6838
Contact: Andrea Phillips
MFR of TB, U
D

Windber
Thiele Industries, Inc.
Route 56 at Spruce Street
P.O. Box 188
Windber, PA 15963
Tel: (814) 467-4504
FAX: (814) 467-4172
Contact: Sandy Conover
or Dave Romano
MFR of TB, U
C-2

York
York Mack, Incorporated
55 S. Fayette Street
York, PA 17404
Tel: (717) 792-2636
FAX: (717) 792-3543
Contact: Barry Trattner
DLR of TB, U, F
C-2
D

RHODE ISLAND

Johnston
Ocean State Custom Vans
391 George Waterman Road
Johnston, RI 02919
Tel: (401) 231-3211
R4

Johnston
Payette Truck Body Manufacturing Co.
65 Dyerville Avenue
Johnston, RI 02919
Tel: (401) 351-0711
MFR/FINAL ASSEMBLER of TB

Woonsocket
Beam Truck & Body, Incorporated
433 Cumberland Hill Rd.
Woonsocket, RI 02895
Tel: (401) 767-2639
FINAL ASSEMBLER of TB

Woonsocket
Janell Truck & Trailer Service, Incorporated
840 Cumberland Hill Rd.
Woonsocket, RI 02895
Tel: (401) 762-6363
Nation: (800) 556-3848
Nation: (800) 556-6492
FAX: (401) 766-6970
Contact: Glen Janell
MFR of TB
D: Driveaway Company

SOUTH CAROLINA

Barnwell
B & B Ford
1105 Dunbarton Blvd.
Barnwell, SC 29812
Tel: (803) 259-5524
Contact: Howard Bush
DLR of Trucks
C-1

Charleston
Herbert's Emergency Medical Service
2018 Herbert Street
Charleston, SC 29405
Tel: (803) 577-5655
FAX: (803) 577-8000
Contact: Bobby Herbert
H'cap R4

Columbia
Holiday Kamper & Boats
3630 Fernandina Road
Columbia, SC 29210
Tel: (803) 798-0450
Nation: (800) 848-3250
FAX: (803) 731-9791
Contact: Charlotte Hill
DLR of R1, R2
C-2

Columbia
Interstate Transportation Equipment
2511 Trotter Road
Columbia, SC 29209
Tel: (803) 776-5041
FAX: (803) 776-3527
Contact: Robert Coleman
MFR of TB, U
D

Columbia
Lee Transport Equipment, Incorporated
1300 Bluff Road
Columbia, SC 29201
Tel: (803) 799-7860
MFR of TB
C-1, C-2

Columbia
Trailmobile Trailers
324 Smith's Market Road
Columbia, SC 29212
Nation: (800) 743-4614
Contact: Richard Hawkins
MFR of T, S-2
(The 800 number is the Atlanta branch office.)

Dillon
Monitone Trailer Co.
P.O. Box 989
Dillon, SC 29536
Tel: (803) 774-3331
Contact: David Cunningham
MFR of T

Florence
American Luxury Coach
1714 S. Irby Street
Florence, SC 29505
Tel: (803) 665-2821
Contact: Theresa Jabelli
MFR of TB

Fort Mill
CSL Equipment Co.
300 Yorksouthern Drive
Fort Mill, SC 29715
Tel: (803) 548-4689
MFR of T

Greenville
Brannock's Custom Vans
46 Bell Road
Greenville, SC 29607
Tel: (803) 288-1387
Contact: Ralph Brannock
R4

Greenville
Christopher Truck Sales, Incorporated
1901 White Horse Road
Greenville, SC 29605
Tel: (803) 269-2131
FAX: (803) 295-2391
MFR of *TB*

Greenville/Easley
Keenan's World of Customizing/Kontinental Koaches
Route 8, Highway 153
Greenville/Easley, SC 29611
Tel: (803) 269-6470
FAX: (803) 269-4841
Contact: Jim Dendy
MFR of *R4*
A-1

Greenville
Long Trailer & Body Service
P.O. Box 5105
Greenville, SC 29606
Tel: (803) 277-7555
Contact: Joe Long
MFR of *T, TB*

Greenville
Quality Products
16 Santuck Street
Greenville, SC 29611
Tel: (803) 232-5549
Nation: (800) 477-5421
FAX: (803) 232-5007
Contact: Larry Robinette
MFR of *Tow Dollies*
C-2:3

John's Island
Action Vans
215 Main Road
John's Island, SC 29455
Tel: (803) 763-7681
FAX: (803) 763-8859
Contact: Patty Powell
R4

Leesville
King Manufacturing Co.
253 Ebenezer Road
Leesville, SC 29070
Tel: (803) 532-5733
Contact: C. B. King
MFR of *T*

Lexington
Swygert's Custom Van Shop
210 E. Main Street
Lexington, SC 29072
Tel: (803) 957-8805
Contact: Jerald Swygert
R4

Monetta
Monetta Farrier Specialities, Incorporated
RR 2, Box 403
Monetta, SC 29105
Tel: (803) 685-5101
Nation: (800) 654-5101
Contact: Sarah Schwartz
MFR of *TB*

Myrtle Beach
Grand Strand Trailers
430 Piedmont Avenue
Myrtle Beach, SC 29577
Tel: (803) 626-8202
MFR/DLR of *T*

Pamplico
Double A Body Builders
Highway 51, North
Pamplico, SC 29583
Tel: (803) 493-0065
Tel: (803) 493-5021
(Manufacturing Shop)
Contact: Ken Keenan
MFR of *R4*

Pamplico
Pamplico Truck & Body Works
912 N. Pamplico Hwy.
Pamplico, SC 29583
Tel: (803) 493-5950
REPAIR of *TB*

Piedmont
Travelier Truck & Van
I-85 at Highway 1153
P.O. Box 1130
Piedmont, SC 29673
Tel: (803) 269-4551
Tel: (803) 269-2716
Nation: (800) 682-2338
FAX: (803) 269-1686
Contact: Brady Freeman
R4, TConvs

Powdersville
Keenan's World of Customizing
Highway 153
Powdersville, SC 29611
Tel: (803) 269-6470
FAX: (803) 269-4841
Contact: Dennis Sledzianowski
MODIFIER of *R4*
A-1

Rock Hill
Interstate Vans
1020 Riverview Road
Rock Hill, SC 29732
Tel: (803) 324-8111
Contact: Bob Farn
R4, TConvs

Saint George
Carolina Coach Corp.
111 Metts Street
St. George, SC 29477
Tel: (803) 563-9654
MFR of *A, Mobile Units, Bloodmobiles*
C-2

Simpsonville
Vanco, Incorporated
Simpsonville, SC 29681
Tel: (803) 297-4544
R4

Spartanburg
Dixie Body and Truck Equipment
P.O. Box 945
Spartanburg, SC 29304
Tel: (803) 583-4655
Contact: Billy Beech
MFR of *TB*
C-1

Summerville
Baker Material Handling Corporation
2450 W. 5th North Street
Summerville, SC 29483
Tel: (803) 875-8000
Nation: (800) 627-1700
FAX: (803) 875-8329
Contact: Corey Lutinski
MFR of *Turret TB, Lift TB*
A-1

Sumter
Dixie Products, Inc.
1255 N. Lafayette Drive
Sumter, SC 29150
Tel: (803) 775-4391
Contact: Jan Dubose
MFR of *TB, U*

Winnsboro
Mack Trucks Assembly Division
US Route 231 &
SC Route 269
Winnsboro, SC 29180
Tel: (803) 635-7100
FAX: (803) 635-7229
Contact: Jill McIntosh
ASSEMBLER of
Mack S-1
D: Kenosha Transport

SOUTH DAKOTA

Armour
Mulder Fabrication Shop
P.O Box 491
Armour, SD 57313
Tel: (605) 724-2340
Contact: Ben Mulder
or Brian Mulder
MFR of *T*

Box Elder
Wykota Enterprises
Box Elder Road
P.O. Box 129
Box Elder, SD 57719
Tel: (605) 923-5831
Contact: Jack Chisolm
CONVERTER of *Trucks*

Brookings
Conveyance Vans, Inc.
2405 6th Street
Brookings, SD 57006
Tel: (605) 692-2236
R4, H'cap R4

Elk Point
Load King
Rose & Elm Streets
P.O. Box 427
Elk Point, SD 57025
Tel: (605) 356-3302
Nation: (800) 235-8210
FAX: (605) 356-3268
Contact: Brenda Schaffer
MFR of *S-2*
D

Faulkton
Classic Vans
P.O. Box 508
Faulkton, SD 57381
Tel: (605) 598-4437
R4

Flandreau
Dakota Coach
P.O. Box 308
Flandreau, SD 57028
Tel: (605) 997-2427
Nation: (800) 477-2939
FAX: (605) 997-2072
Contact: Richard Julson
or Michelle Jensen
CONVERTER of *U*
C-2:4-5

Huron
Huron Telelect, Inc.
601 Arizona Avenue, SW
Huron, SD 57350
Tel: (605) 352-0944
MFR of *TB*

Lake Preston
Joe Schnell
P.O. Box 37
Lake Preston, SD 57249
Tel: (605) 847-4448
SD only: (800) 540-5271
FAX: (605) 847-4449
Contact: Joe Schnell
MFR of *TB*

Letcher
Stunes' Welding
RR 1, Box 120
Letcher, SD 57359
Tel: (605) 996-8658
Contact: Ed Stunes
MFR of *TB*

Miller
Foreman Sales & Service
North Highway 14
Miller, SD 57362
Tel: (605) 853-2708
Nation: (800) 310-2708
FAX: (605) 853-3124
Contact: Doyle Foreman
DISTRIBUTOR of *U*

Mitchell
Dakota Mfg. Co., Inc.
1909 S. Rowley Street
Mitchell, SD 57301
Tel: (605) 996-5571
Nation: (800) 232-5682
FAX: (605) 996-5572
Contact: Lisa Munger
MFR of *T*
D

Mitchell
Trail King Industries, Incorporated
300 E. Norway
Mitchell, SD 57301
Tel: (605) 996-6482
Nation: (800) 843-3324
FAX: (605) 996-4727
Contact: Rick Sarris
MFR of *S-2*
D

Mitchell
Trail King Industries, Incorporated
22 S. Ohlman
Mitchell, SD 57301
Tel: (605) 996-3690
Nation: (800) 843-3324
FAX: (605) 996-4727
Contact: Rick Sarris
MFR of *S-2*
D

Rapid City
Backwoods Bungalow
RR 8, Box 740
Rapid City, SD 57702
Tel: (605) 348-9824
FAX: (605) 348-6224
Contact: Rena McKiernan
MFR of *TC*

Rapid City
Black Hawk Vans
3156 Haines Avenue
Rapid City, SD 57701
Tel: (605) 342--2104
Contact: Paul Bettmeng
R4

Rapid City
Midstate Camper Sales
5900 W. Highway 44
Rapid City, SD 57702
Tel: (605) 348-0623
Contact: Robert Truth, Jr.
DLR of *R1, R2*

Sioux Falls
Dakota Transportation Service, Incorporated
P.O. Box 1068
Sioux Falls, SD 57101
Tel: (605) 368-5306
FAX: (605) 368-2210
Contact: Arlene Meyer
MFR of *STB*

Sioux Falls
Jim Hawk Truck-Trailers, Incorporated
1401 E. Benson Road
Sioux Falls, SD 57104
Tel: (605) 338-6365
DLR of *S-2*

Sioux Falls
Marx Truck Trailers
2600 N. Westport
Sioux Falls, SD 57107
Tel: (605) 336-2371
DLR of *Cargo T, XT*

Sioux Falls
Northern Truck Equip.
P.O. Box 1104
Sioux Falls, SD 57101
Tel: (605) 543-5206
Contact: Liz Navratil
MFR of *TB*

Sioux Falls
R & R Conversions, Inc.
400 S. Marion Road
Sioux Falls, SD 57106
Tel: (605) 335-8646
FAX: (605) 334-3235
Contact: Roger Mofle
or Joel Niemeyer
R4

Sioux Falls
Schaap's Traveland, Inc.
3100 W. Russell
Sioux Falls, SD 57107
Tel: (605) 332-6241
DLR of *R1, R2*

Watertown
Duralite Corporation
South Highway 81
Watertown, SD 57201
Tel: (605) 886-5078
Nation: (800) 437-8931
Contact: Duane Althoff
MFR of *LT*

Watertown
Northern Truck Equip.
1414 5th Street, SE
Watertown, SD 57201
Tel: (605) 886-5816
FAX: (605) 886-5019
Contact: Tom Snyder
or Sandy Rosso
MFR of *TB*
C-1

Watertown
Simon Telelect
400 Oakwood Road
Watertown, SD 57201
Tel: (605) 882-4000
Contact: Terry Vanconent
MFR of *TB*

Webster
Harlow's School Bus Sales & Service
E. Highway 12
Webster, SD 57219
Tel: (605) 345-4023
Contact: Ron Black
DLR/REPAIR of *S*

Wessington
Vern's Mfg., Inc.
RR 2, Box 42
Wessington, SD 57381
Tel: (605) 458-2269
FAX: (605) 458-2269
Contact: Ray Crinefasser
MFR of *T*
B-1

Yankton
Hawkeye Manufacturing of South Dakota
P.O. Box 114
Yankton, SD 57078
Tel: (605) 665-8415
Contact: Steve Frick
MFR of *T*

Yankton
Road King, Incorporated
RR 2, Box 271-A
Yankton, SD 57078
Tel: (605) 665-5281
Contact: Terry Schramm
MFR of *T*
C-1

Yankton
Wilson Trailer Company
N. Highway 81, Box 795
Yankton, SD 57078
Tel: (605) 665-4441
DLR of *T*

TENNESSEE

Apison
Country Customs
11027 London Lane
Apison, TN 37302
Tel: (615) 236-4547
Contact: Danny Swafford
H'cap R4

Athens
Heil Company, The
P.O. Box 160
Athens, TN 37371-0160
Tel: (615) 745-5830
FAX: (615) 745-5863
Contact: Evelyn Moore
MFR of *S-2*
D

Bells
Evans Custom Trailers
RR 1
Bells, TN 38006
Tel: (901) 663-2466
Contact: Greg Evans
MFR of *T*

Bluff City
L & S Line Mfg. Co.
P.O. Box 640
Bluff City, TN 37618
Tel: (615) 538-4700
MFR of *T*
B-2

Chattanooga
Cherokee Utilities & Truck Equipment
522 W. 31st Street
Chattanooga, TN 37410
Tel: (615) 265-7189
Nation: (800) 365-7189
FAX: (615) 267-7280
Contact: Evetta Davis
FINAL ASSEMBLER
of *TB*

Chattanooga
Choo-Choo Customs, Incorporated
7801 Lee Highway
Chattanooga, TN 37421
Tel: (615) 899-5382
FAX: (615) 899-5611
Contact: Buck Karson
R4
C-2

Chattanooga
EMR Accessibility Lift Company
932 E. 11th Street
Chattanooga, TN 37403
Tel: (615) 267-5438
Contact: Buddy Hulgan
H'cap R4

Chattanooga
Heil Company, The
P.O. Box 8676
Chattanooga, TN 37414
Tel: (615) 899-9100
FAX: (615) 855-3478
Contact: Jane Chislom
MFR of *TB*
D
(This is the HQ.)

Chattanooga
River City Campers
3012 Rossville Blvd.
Chattanooga, TN 37407
Tel: (615) 622-4116
Contact: Mike Vaughn
MFR of *TC*

Chattanooga
Williamsburg Coach Company, Incorporated
4000 Hixson Pike
Chattanooga, TN 37415
Tel: (615) 870-5909
Contact: Gary Williams
R4

Clarksville
Clarksville RV Supercenter
550 Thun Road
Clarksville, TN 37040
Tel: (615) 889-9451
Tel: (615) 648-1800
DLR of R1, R2

Fayetteville
Patrick Trailer Sales
1924 Wilson Parkway
Fayetteville, TN 37334
Tel: (615) 433-4620
Contact: Charles Patrick
DLR of T

Fayetteville
T & W Machine
701 Lincoln Ave., South
Fayetteville, TN 37334
Tel: (615) 433-1577
Contact: Larry Stewart
MFR of TB

Franklin
J. D. Dunn Transportation/ Magnum Transportation
1228 Lakeview Drive
Franklin, SD 37064
Tel: (615) 790-8990
Region: (800) 641-0989
FAX: (615) 790-8989
Contact: Doug Dunn
or Randy Nemitz
DLR of U
C-2
NOTE: See Magnum Trans. in Charlotte, NC.

Gallatin
Wil Ro, Incorporated
1155 Highway 109, North
Gallatin, TN 37066
Tel: (615) 452-6119
Nation: (800) 879-1466
FAX: (615) 452-7078
Contact: Terry Whitaker
MFR of T

Germantown
Memphis Coach Co.
1870 Park Trail Drive
P.O. Box 38183
Germantown, TN 38138
Tel: (901) 853-4339
FAX: (901) 853-4350
Contact: Jim Bumpass
DLR of Limos
C-2

Grantwood
Klein Brothers Coach Company, Incorporated
310-B Wilson Pike Circle
Grantwood, TN 37027
Tel: (615) 661-9006
DLR/MFR of R1

Greeneville
Bluebird of Tennessee, Incorporated
1216 E. Church Street
Greeneville, TN 37743
Tel: (615) 638-4250
Nation: (800) 322-4024
Contact: Mike McCall
DISTRIBUTOR of S

Harriman
Woodsey Mfg. Co.
302 Sewamee Street
Harriman, TN 37748
Tel: (615) 882-7066
Contact: Henry Grigsby
MFR of Sportsman Camper T
D
(Open Tues.-Fri.)

Huntsville
Fruehauf Trailer Corp.
Highway 63
P.O. Box 200
Huntsville, TN 37756
Tel: (615) 663-3434
FAX: (615) 663-3438
MFR of M, Flatbed S-2
NOTE: This is one of 3 Fruehauf plant sites. See HQ listing in Detroit, MI.

Jackson
Custom Vans & 4 Wheel Drive Center
1082 US Hwy. 45 Bypass
Jackson, TN 38301
Tel: (901) 668-8084
Nation: (800) 467-8084
Contact: Ken Davis
R4

Johnson City
Crowder RV Center
4523 Bristol Highway
P.O. Box 3420
Johnson City, TN 37͞
Tel: (615) ͞
N͞
Not currently hiring.
͞͞30
Kim Pearman
DLR of R1, R2

Johnson City
Post & Company
1901 Southern Avenue
Johnson City, TN 37602
Tel: (615) 523-2101
FAX: (615) 523-5183
Contact: Carol Power
DLR of TB

Knoxville
Circle M Supreme Trailer Manufacturing
1810 Lovell Road
Knoxville, TN 37932
Tel: (615) 693-1783
MFR of T

Knoxville
Gregg Buddy Motor Homes
11730 Campbell Station
Knoxville, TN 37922
Tel: (615) 675-1986
DLR of R1, R2

Knoxville
O. G. Hughes & Sons, Incorporated
4816 Rutledge Pike
Knoxville, TN 37914
Tel: (615) 524-7525
Contact: George Taylor
MFR of Commercial R4
C-2:3

Knoxville
Phoenix Conversions
1401 N. Central Street
Knoxville, TN 37917
Tel: (615) 522-5400
FAX: (615) 525-5400
Contact: Scott Hayse
R4, H'cap R4
C-1

Knoxville
Post & Company
1901 Sutherland Avenue
Knoxville, TN 37921
Tel: (615) 523-2101
FINAL ASSEMBLER/
DLR of T, TB

Knoxville
RP Vans
4829 Newcom Avenue
Knoxville, TN 37919
Tel: (615) 524-7811
FAX: (615) 588-3416
Contact: Karen Burson
R4

Knoxville
Volunteer Bus Sales
P.O. Box 12220
Knoxville, TN 37912
Tel: (615) 524-3677
FAX: (615) 524-7980
Contact: Gene Emanual
DLR of U

Knoxville
World of Independence, Incorporated
6700 Asheville Highway
Knoxville, TN 37924
Tel: (615) 546-3477
FAX: (615) 546-1006
Contact: Terry Spear
R4, H'cap R4

LaFollette
Continental Factory Outlet
162 E. Central Avenue
LaFollette, TN 37766
Tel: (615) 562-0238
MFR/DLR of TC

Lake City
Trail Manor, Inc.
304 Church Street
P.O. Box 130
Lake City, TN 37769
Tel: (615) 426-7426
Contact: Keith Huesey
MFR of T

LaVergne
Allvan Corporation
5457 Murfreesboro Road
LaVergne, TN 37086
Tel: (615) 459-2511
Nation: (800) 899-9300
MFR of TB
C-2

Lebanon
Waco Truck Bodies, Incorporated
211 McCowan Drive
Lebanon, TN 37087
Tel: (615) 449-0960
MFR of TB

Madison
Medical Mobility, Inc.
903 Gallatin Road, South
Madison, TN 37115
Tel: (615) 865-8100
R4, H'cap R4

Madison
Peterbilt Motors, Inc.
P.O. Box 487
Madison, TN 37116-0487
Tel: (615) 865-8910
MFR of Trucks
C-2

Memphis
A Classic Limousine Service, Incorporated
7 S. McLain
Memphis, TN 38104
Tel: (901) 725-5466
Contact: Victoria Short
DLR of Limos

Memphis
Access Industries
2509 Summer Avenue
Memphis, TN 38112
Tel: (901) 323-5438
Nation: (800) 264-4304
FAX: (901) 323-5559
Contact: Theresa Walters
H'cap R4

Memphis
American Vans
7 McLean Blvd.
Memphis, TN 38104
Tel: (901) 725-9754
RENTAL of *Limos & Vans*

Memphis
Camper City
3492 Lamar
Memphis, TN 38118
Tel: (901) 795-9850
Contact: Robert Roop
DLR of *TC*

Memphis
Chuck Hutton Chevrolet-Geo
2471 Mount Moriah Road
Memphis, TN 38115
Tel: (901) 369-0666
FAX: (901) 365-9700
Contact: Harvey Rose
at (901) 369-0623
DLR of *R4*

Memphis
Great Dane Trailers, Inc.
1095 Harbor Avenue
Memphis, TN 38106
Tel: (901) 948-1611
FAX: (901) 946-6700
Contact: Jerry Driscol
MFR of *S-2*
D

Memphis
MCT Custom Truck Bodies, Incorporated
2900 Airways Blvd.
Memphis, TN 38132
Tel: (901) 332-2471
Contact: Rick Moore
MFR of *TB*
A-2, A-3 (Pulling low-boys)

Memphis
Mid-America International Trucks, Incorporated
1750 E. Brooks Road
Memphis, TN 38116
Tel: (901) 345-6275
FAX: (901) 396-3746
Contact: Dick Sweeby
DLR of *TB*

Memphis
Sully Corporation
792 S. Cooper
Memphis, TN 38104
Tel: (901) 726-9394
FAX: (901) 726-6708
Contact: Susanne Snyder
MFR of *Commercial R4*
C-2:4

Memphis
Tennessee Show Trucks
5438 Pleasant View Road
Memphis, TN 38134
Tel: (901) 386-5920
Contact: Ted Addison
R4

Memphis
Tri State Body Works
122 W. Carolina Avenue
Memphis, TN 38103
Tel: (901) 527-8774
Contact: George Katcter
MFR of *TB*

Memphis
Truck & Van Accessories
2811 Farrisview Blvd.
Memphis, TN 38118
Tel: (901) 360-8065
Nation: (800) 333-6511
FAX: (901) 795-6140
Contact: Sherry Bird
or Dale Ingram
R4, TConvs

Memphis
Vans to Go, Inc.
5472 Summer Avenue
Memphis, TN 38134
Tel: (901) 382-7676
RENTAL of *R4*

Milan
Darty Trailer Sales
359 Medina Highway
Milan, TN 38358
Tel: (901) 686-1458
Contact: J. R. Darty
DLR of *T*

Murfreesboro
Gem-Top East, Inc.
2204 NW Broad
Murfreesboro, TN 37130
Tel: (615) 890-0770
Nation: (800) 899-4368
FAX: (615) 895-3932
Contact: Bob Milsap
MFR of *TC*
C-2:4

Murfreesboro
Hank Williams Trailer Manufacturing
1762 Ghee Road
Murfreesboro, TN 37130
Tel: (615) 890-6143
MFR of *T*

Nashville
A & M Products
313 Alberta
Nashville, TN 37210
Tel: (615) 834-5154
H'cap R4

Nashville
Continental Conversions
2725 Nolensville Road
Nashville, TN 37211
Tel: (615) 244-3523
Contact: Ray Richardson
R4

Nashville
Custom Mobility, Inc.
2615 Lebanon Road, #B
Nashville, TN 37214
Tel: (615) 885-7592
FAX: (615) 885-7594
Contact: Peggy Williams
R4

Nashville
Fontaine Truck Equipment Company
508 Expressway Park Dr.
Nashville, TN 37210
Tel: (615) 244-9200
R4

Nashville
Homelift of Nashville, Incorporated
3901 Charlotte Avenue
Nashville, TN 37209
Tel: (615) 385-5438
Contact: Peppi Leland
H'cap R4

Nashville
Mighty Equipment Co.
491 Allied Drive
P.O. Box 110808
Nashville, TN 37211
Tel: (615) 834-2120
Nation: (800) 251-8177
FAX: (615) 331-7336
Contact: Shirley Younger
MFR of *Mixer TB*

Nashville
Neely Coble
319 Fessler's Lane
(I-40, E., Exit 212)
Nashville, TN 37210
Tel: (615) 244-8900
Nation: (800) 367-7712
FAX: (615) 726-2411
Contact: Dutch Bixler
DLR of *Trucks*
C-1

Nashville
Rogers Mfg. Co.
(MAIL: P.O. Box 100187
Nashville, TN 37224)
110 Transit Avenue
Nashville, TN 37210
Tel: (615) 244-9720
FAX: (615) 244-9719
Contact: Jimmy Jarrell
MFR of *M*
D

Nashville
Stringfellow, Inc.
2710 Locust Street
Nashville, TN 37207
Tel: (615) 226-4900
FAX: (615) 226-8685
Contact: John Retzz
MFR of *M*

New Market
Quality Built Trailers, Incorporated
1792 W. Hwy. 11, East
New Market, TN 37820
Tel: (615) 932-1936
Contact: Laura Jenkins
MFR of *HT*

New Tazewell
Homesteader, Inc.
1510 Cedar Lane
P.O. Box 900
New Tazewell, TN 37825
Tel: (615) 626-9040
FAX (615) 626-2739
Contact: Virgil Mayes
MFR of *R6*
B-2:2
D: Morgan Driveaway

Ooltewah
Miller Industries
8503 Hilltop Drive
P.O. Box 120
Ooltewah, TN 37363
Tel: (615) 238-4171
Nation: (800) 422-9730
FAX: (615) 238-5371
Contact: Stan Neeley
MFR of *W*
NOTE: Originally Century Wrecker Co., they have purchased "Challenger," "Holmes," "Champion," & "American Wheel-Lift," and moved them all to this site.
C-2

Pikesville
Flx Products Industries, Incorporated
RR 3, Box 520
Pikesville, TN 37367
Tel: (615) 447-2187
FAX: (615) 447-6502
Contact: Wayne Kohlmann
MFR of *TB*
C-2:5

Powell
Custom Medal Products
509 Bushy Valley West
Powell, TN 37849
Tel: (615) 938-4371
Contact: Colon Howell
MFR of *T*

Ridgetop
A & T Equip. Sales, Inc.
P.O. Box 499
Ridgetop, TN 37152
Tel: (615) 859-4336
FAX: (615) 859-0802
Contact: Jay Tate
DLR of *U*
D

Savannah
Savannah Machine Shop
1806 Pinhook Road
Savannah, TN 38372
Tel: (901) 925-5422
Contact: Jerry Halloway
MFR of *TB*

Soddy Daisy
Tennessee Trailers, Inc.
11297 Wall Street
Soddy Daisy, TN 37379
Tel: (615) 332-5353
Contact: Tom Burger
MFR of *T*
A-1

Sweetwater
Cherokee Mfg. Co.
Industrial Park Road
Sweetwater, TN 37874
Tel: (615) 337-6625
FAX: (615) 337-5730
Contact: Bob Leonard
MFR of *ST, HT*

Tullahoma
Lyn Mor, Incorporated
109 Montclair Street
Tullahoma, TN 37388
Tel: (615) 455-0009
DLR of *TC*

Union City
Terry Petty Chevrolet-Buick
524 E. Reelfoot Avenue
Union City, TN 38261
Tel: (901) 885-8150
FAX: (901) 885-7945
Contact: Terry Petty
DLR of *R4*

Walling
Rigsby Mfg. Co.
Route 1, Box 12
Walling, TN 38587
Tel: (615) 686-2125
Contact: Raymond Rigsby
MFR of *T*

TEXAS

Abilene
Corley-Wetsel Trucks, Incorporated
998 E. Highway 80
Abilene, TX 79601
Tel: (915) 677-8187
FAX: (915) 677-1261
Contact: Z. E. Corley
DLR of *Trucks*

Abilene
Kwik Kamp
5050 E. Highway 80
Abilene, TX 79601
Tel: (915) 673-KAMP
Nation: (800) 472-2901
FAX: (915) 673-5266
MFR of *T*

Abilene
Overland Tank & Trailer Manufacturing Company
4725 FM 18
P.O. Box 1640
Abilene, TX 79604
Tel: (915) 673-7132
MFR of *T*

Abilene
Western Trailer Equipment & Mfg.
1110 Highway 80, East
Abilene, TX 78601
Tel: (915) 673-8311
DLR of *T*

Alvarado
Travel Villa
Exit 27 of I-35, West
P.O. Box 412
Alvarado, TX 76009
Tel: (817) 477-2107
FAX: (817) 477-2242
Contact: Mark Sims
DLR of *R1, R2*

Amarillo
Action Control Systems
2420 Hobbs Road
Amarillo, TX 79109
Tel: (806) 352-0455
Contact: Ken Spencer
H'cap R4

Amarillo
Bowen Coach Company Mfg. & Distributing
1308 W. 6th Avenue
Amarillo, TX 79101
Tel: (806) 372-1206
Contact: E. D. Bowen
MFR of *TC*

Amarillo
Maverick Customs
3108 Amarillo Blvd.
Amarillo, TX 79106
Tel: (806) 381-7099
R4, TConvs

Amarillo
National Home Health Care
712 W. 7th Avenue
Amarillo, TX 79101
Tel: (806) 372-3215
H'cap R4
C-2

Anson
Wilson Trailer Mfg. Co.
2600 S. Commercial Ave.
Anson, TX 78501
Tel: (915) 823-2541
MFR of *T*

Arlington
American Shell Center, Incorporated
2006 E. Division Street
Arlington, TX 76011
Tel: (817) 261-1495
FAX: (817) 277-2518
Contact: Don Savage
DISTRIBUTOR of *TC*

Arlington
Cowboy Conversions, Incorporated
10001 N. Commercial
Arlington, TX 76017
Tel: (817) 472-9260
Tel: (817) 467-7845
FAX: (817) 468-3567
Contact: Melinda Ellison
R4
D: J & J, Packer

Arlington
DFW Camper Corral
808 E. Division Street
Arlington, TX 76011
Tel: (817) 460-8663
Contact: Kevin Moore
DLR of *TC*

Arlington
DFW Vans
3610 S. Cooper
Arlington, TX 76019
Tel: (817) 465-7810
Contact: Al Malconado
R4

Arlington
Executive Wheels
1901 Peyco Drive, South
Arlington, TX 76017
Tel: (817) 465-0678
R4, TConvs

Arlington
Galbreath, Incorporated
420 Dodson Lake Drive
Arlington, TX 76012
Tel: (817) 265-5125
Contact: Linda Eyster
MFR of *G*
C-2

Arlington
Interstate Trailers Inc.
1102 I-20, West
Arlington, TX 76017
Tel: (817) 465-5441
Nation: (800) 433-5384
FAX: (817) 438-8177
Contact: Mark Smith
or Troy Phelps
or Trish Flowers
MFR of *T*

Arlington
Johnson Aluminum Products, Incorporated
3305 W. Division Street
Arlington, TX 76012
Tel: (817) 461-7000
FAX: (817) 460-3450
Contact: Tom Johnson
MFR of *R1, R2*

Austin
Sportsmobile Texas, Inc.
9805 Gray Blvd.
Austin, TX 78758
Tel: (512) 835-4409
FAX: (512) 835-1293
Contact: John Kalbach
R4

Austin
Third Coast Vans & Acc.
1521 W. Anderson Lane
Austin, TX 78757
Tel: (512) 454-8597
Contact: Craig Oakes
R4, TConvs, Suburban Convs

Beaumont
American Recreational Vehicles, Incorporated
4848 W. Cardinal Drive
Beaumont, TX 77705
Tel: (409) 842-5060
DLR of *R1, R2*

Beaumont
Ayres Mfg., Inc.
1255 I-10, South
Beaumont, TX 77701
Tel: (409) 833-3381
Contact: Vaughn Ayers
MFR of *TC*

Beaumont
Modica Brothers Motorhomes
4450 College Street
(US Highway 90)
Beaumont, TX 77707
Tel: (409) 842-5546
FAX: (409) 842-1487
Contact: Tommie Modica
DLR of *HT*
D

Beaumont
*Tejas Manufacturing
& Supply, Incorporated*
5025 College Street
Beaumont, TX 77707
Tel: (409) 842-3377
FAX: (409) 842-1635
Contact: Greg Anderson
DLR of *TC*

Beaumont
Wheeler Truck Body
500 S. 4th Street
Beaumont, TX 77701
Tel: (409) 832-8407
FAX: (409) 832-8406
Contact: Corky Wheeler
MFR of *TB*

Belton
Sunbelt RV Center, Inc.
I-35, South
Belton, TX 76513
Tel: (817) 939-1792
Contact: Al Otmer
DLR of *R1, R2*

Brenham
Fantasia Coaches
1607 Loop 577
Brenham, TX 77833
Tel: (409) 830-1477
FAX: (409) 830-7199
Contact: Jim Swingholm
CONVERTER of *Busses
into RVs*
C-1

Brownsville
Eagle Bus Mfg.
2045 Les Mauldin Blvd.
Brownsville, TX 78521
Tel: (210) 541-3111
Nation: (800) 531-4536
FAX: (210) 541-9661
Contact: Victor Resenders
MFR of *U*
C-1

Brownsville
Vanego Convs., Inc.
4614 N. Expressway
Brownsville, TX 78521
Tel: (210) 350-5445
Contact: Fabian Chavez
R4

Brownwood
*Imco Manufacturing-
Engineering, Inc.*
Milan Drive/Camp Bowie
P.O. Box 748
Brownwood, TX
76804-1748
Tel: (915) 643-1141
FAX: (915) 646-6160
Contact: James Isom
MFR of *T*
B-2:1

Bryan
*Global Tank & Trailer
Manufacturing, Inc.*
Highway 21, West
Bryan, TX 77801
Tel: (409) 775-0087
DLR of *T*

Bryan
Gooseneck Trailers
(MAIL: Box 832
Bryan, TX 77803)
4400 Highway 21, East
Bryan, TX 77806
Tel: (409) 778-0034
Nation: (800) 648-8900
FAX: (409) 778-0615
Contact: Milton Dockery
MFR of *GT, HT, LT, UT*
B-2

Buda
Wiley Trailers
200 Hy Road
Buda, TX 78610
Tel: (512) 295-7391
Contact: Don Wiley
MFR of *T*

Burleson
LCS Conversions
12 Eldorado Drive
Burleson, TX 76028
Tel: (817) 295-7676
Contact: Larry Sailors
R4
C-1

Carrolton
*Ballistic Transport
Security Systems*
1833 N. I-35
Carrolton, TX 75006
Tel: (214) 242-7027
FAX: (214) 243-5699
Contact: Billy Brown
MFR of *Armored Cars*
D: Rodeway

Cedar Hill
Cruise America
480 Highway 67
Cedar Hill, TX
75106-1720
Tel: (214) 526-1224
Nation: (800) 225-1755
DLR/RENTAL of *R1, R2*
(For more data, see the
HQ listing, Mesa, AZ.)

Cleburne
Supreme Corporation
500 West Commerce
Cleburne, TX 76031
Tel: (817) 641-6282
Nation: (800) 950-2230
Contact: David Banton
MFR of *TB*
C-2:5

Clifton
Davis Truck Equipment
P.O. Box 33
Clifton, TX 76634
Tel: (817) 675-8377
FAX: (817) 675-6628
Contact: Danny NcNeil
MFR of *TB*
C-1:3

Conroe
*Odom Trailer
Manufacturing Co., Inc.*
213 Porter Road
Conroe, TX 77301
Tel: (409) 539-3324
FAX: (409) 539-1992
MFR of *T*

Corpus Christi
CC Motor Homes
1314 S.P.I.D.
Corpus Christi, TX 78416
Tel: (512) 854-5383
FAX: (512) 851-9578
Contact: Ron Carothers
DLR of *R1, R2*
C-2

Crockett
Travel Quest
Loop 304, South
Crockett, TX 75835
Tel: (409) 544-2175
Contact: Marilyn Raines
R4, Suburban Convs

Dallas
*Bond Equipment
Company, Incorporated*
2946 Irving Blvd.
Dallas, TX 75247
Tel: (214) 637-0760
Contact: Gary Bond
DLR of *TB*

Dallas
*Fontaine Truck
Equipment Company*
3030 Irving Blvd.
Dallas, TX 75247
Tel: (214) 631-8810
FAX: (214) 631-0110
Contact: Mike Stanley
FINAL ASSEMBLER
of *TB*

Dallas
*Lasseter Bus
Company, Incorporated*
4455 Alpha Road
Dallas, TX 75244
Tel: (214) 991-9822
DLR of *S*

Dallas
*Southwest Metrotrans/
Southwest Professional*
3910 E. Overton Road
P.O. Box 8775
Dallas, TX 75216
Tel: (214) 371-7715
Tel: (214) 371-3474
FAX: (214) 371-3597
Contact: Connie Tipps
or Bill Meyers
DLR of *U, H, Limos*

Decatur
Trucks-N-Stuff
RR 5
Decatur, TX 76234
Tel: (817) 627-5854
Contact: Danny Lagunas
TConvs, Suburban Convs

Denton
Peterbilt Motors Co.
3200 Airport Road
Denton, TX 76207
Tel: (817) 566-7100
Contact: Ed Moser
MFR of *Trucks*

Duncanville
Pro Van Company
743 N. Merrill Avenue
Duncanville, TX 75137
Tel: (214) 298-8876
Contact: Neil Hieb
R4

Duncanville
U. S. Coachworks
802 Mercury
Duncanville, TX 75037
Tel: (214) 709-8656
FAX: (214) 709-4133
Contact: Steve Ashcraft
MFR of *Bloodmobiles,
Medical-mobiles*

Eagle Lake
Trailer Enterprises Inc.
500 Glen Flora Road
Eagle Lake, TX 77434
Tel: (409) 234-3533
Contact: Greg Slair
MFR of *T*

El Paso
AM Medical
2101 Montana Avenue
El Paso, TX 79903
Tel: (915) 532-3145
H'cap R4

El Paso
Asmar Truck Equipment
7713 Alameda Avenue
El Paso, TX 79915
Tel: (915) 778-9548
Contact: Kwan Sandobal
DLR of *TB*

El Paso
Bill's Campers
7429 Alameda Avenue
El Paso, TX 79915
Tel: (915) 778-4808
MFR of *TC*

El Paso
Border International Truck, Incorporated
1213 N. Zaragosa Road
El Paso, TX 79907
Tel: (915) 858-4644
Nation: (800) 678-7007
FAX: (915) 858-2477
Contact: Ed Dyers
DLR of *Trucks*

El Paso
El Paso Armor
6100 Fiesta Drive
El Paso, TX 79912
Tel: (915) 585-0001
FAX: (915) 833-2194
Contact: Lynn Robinson
MFR of *Armored Cars*

El Paso
Mobility Products/ Street Toys
8409 Lockheed Drive
Suite 19
El Paso, TX 79925
Tel: (915) 779-2200
Contact: Eric Green
or Tom Carter
MFR of *R4, H'cap R4*

El Paso
Truck Cab, Inc.
13675 Gateway Blvd., W.
El Paso, TX 79927
Tel: (915) 858-4000
FAX: (915) 858-0323
DLR of *TC*

Ferris
D & H Bus Repair
P.O. Box 275
Ferris, TX 75125
Tel: (214) 255-4494
Contact: Gerald Taylor
or Mike Kipp
MFR of *U*

Fort Worth
AA Truck Sleeper, Inc.
2517 Minnis Drive
Ft. Worth, TX 76117
Tel: (817) 284-1689
Nation:
(800) AASLEEPER
FAX: (817) 834-4784
Contact: Larry Miller
MFR of *Truck Sleepers*

Fort Worth
Auto Truck and Van Center
1516 Hemphill Street
Ft. Worth 76104
Tel: (817) 924-1704
R4, T Convs

Fort Worth
Clifton Metal Products
2001 E. Loop 820, South
Ft. Worth, TX 76112
Tel: (817) 451-5228
FAX: (817) 451-5211
Contact: H. J. Clifton, Jr.
MFR of *TB, T*
A-1

Fort Worth
Cowtown Fiberglass & Topper Manufacturing
6200 S. Freeway
Ft. Worth, TX 76134
Tel: (817) 293-9100
Contact: Jerry Smith
MFR of *TC, Van Tops*

Fort Worth
Fort Worth Fabrication, Incorporated
5316 Blue Mound Road
Ft. Worth, TX 76106
Tel: (817) 625-2321
Nation: (800) 944-8265
FAX: (817) 625-2322
Contact: Robert Montgomery
MFR of *T*

Fort Worth
Fort Worth Truck Supply
411 Grand Avenue
Ft. Worth, TX 76106
Tel: (817) 625-1117
FAX: (817) 429-8209
Contact: Betty Ford
MFR of *CTB*

Fort Worth
Lift Aids, Incorporated
2381 Pecan Court
Ft. Worth, TX 76117
Tel: (817) 834-3881
Contact: Connie Stauffer
H'cap R4

Fort Worth
Regency Conversions
2800 Golden Triangle Blvd.
Ft. Worth, TX 76131
Tel: (817) 847-7171
FAX: (817) 827-1738
Contact: Sherry Brown
MFR of *R4*
C-2:3
D: Morgan Driveaway

Fort Worth
RV World
5213 Airport Freeway
Ft. Worth, TX 76117
Tel: (817) 831-2526
DLR of *R1, R2*

Fort Worth
Tra-Tech Conversions
(MAIL: P.O. Box 161489
Ft. Worth, TX 76161)
2724 Bryan Avenue
Ft. Worth, TX 76104
Tel: (817) 232-4900
FAX: (817) 927-8748
Contact: Greg Carmen
R4
C-2
D: J & J Transport

Fort Worth
Trailmaster Tanks, Inc.
1121 Cantrell Sansom Rd.
Ft. Worth, TX 76131
Tel: (817) 232-0900
Nation: (800) 621-2563
FAX: (817) 232-8954
MFR of *T*

Fort Worth
U-Haul/ FW Mfg. Co., Inc.
5335 Wichita Street
Ft. Worth, TX 76119
Tel: (817) 534-6704
FAX: (817) 531-1685
Contact: Debbie Heels
MFR of *U-Haul Trucks & Trailers*
C-2 take them to the rental sites.

Fort Worth
Western Hauler
2420 White Settlement Road
Ft. Worth, TX 76107
Tel: (817) 332-1121
Contact: Wayne Bell
DLR of *HT, LT*
B-2

Garland
Accent Vehicles, Inc.
175 E. I-30, #I
Garland, TX 75043
Tel: (214) 240-9056
Nation: (800) 241-8839
Contact: Thomas Wright
H'cap R4
A-1, C-2:1

Garland
Marmon Motor Company
102 N. Shiloh Road
Garland, TX 75042
Tel: (214) 276-5121
FAX: (214) 272-1240
Contact: John Scolastico
MFR of *Trucks*
C-2

Garland
Merry Miler, Inc.
35337 National Circle
Garland, TX 75041
Tel: (214) 287-5000
MFR of *R4*

Gatesville
Kalyn, Incorporated
US Highway 84
Box 487
Gatesville, TX 76528
Tel: (817) 865-7235
Nation: (800) 525-9689
FAX: (817) 865-7234
Contact: Stephanie Cooper
MFR of *CT*
D

Grandview
Luxury Conversions, Inc.
P.O. Drawer 464
Grandview, TX 76050
Tel: (817) 866-2901
FAX: (817) 866-2644
Contact: Dorthy Wilcox
MFR of *R4*
C-2:3

Henderson
Competition Trailers, Incorporated
P.O. Box 698
Henderson, TX 75652
Tel: (903) 657-1096
FAX: (903) 657-0223
Contact: Sam Harris
MFR of *T*

Henderson
Galyean Equipment Company, Incorporated
1225 Industrial Drive
Henderson, TX 75652
Tel: (903) 657-7561
FAX: (903) 657-1412
Contact: Alan Galyean
MFR of *T*

Hewitt
Trans-Con Van Conversions
9000 Van American Dr.
Hewitt, TX 76643
Tel: (817) 666-7781
Contact: Walt Jones
MFR of *R4*
D: Morgan Driveaway

Houston
Al Tucker Trailers
7401 North Loop, East
Houston, TX 77028
Tel: (713) 672-7578
FAX: (713) 676-2414
Contact: Tom Tucker
MFR of *T*
A-1

Houston
American Gear &
Supply Company, Inc.
5400 Cedar Crest
Houston, TX 77087
Tel: (713) 643-4321
FAX: (713) 643-8912
Contact: Phil Hampton
MFR of *CTB*

Houston
Anaheim Industries
2305 Bennington
Houston, TX 77093
Tel: (713) 697-3160
Tel: (713) 697-6212
FAX: (713) 697-4675
Contact: Linda Wilson
MFR of *R4*
C-2:5

Houston
Best Trailers
4506 Lauder Road
Houston, TX 77039
Tel: (713) 442-4770
Contact: Mark Taylor
DLR of *T*

Houston
Cruise America
11380 Eastex Freeway
Houston, TX 77093
Tel: (713) 931-3564
DLR/RENTAL of *R1, R2*
(For more data, see the
HQ listing, Mesa, AZ.)

Houston
Custom Vans of Houston
50 W. Canino Road
Houston, TX 77037
Tel: (713) 448-8183
FAX: (713) 448-0950
Contact: Les Muguerda
R4
C-1

Houston
Frazer, Incorporated
7219 Rampart Street
Houston, TX 77081
Tel: (713) 772-5511
Contact: John Griffin
MFR of *A*

Houston
Freedom Wheels
580 T.C. Jesture
(Off I-10)
Houston, TX 77007
Tel: (713) 864-1460
FAX: (713) 464-1480
Contact: Randy Randall
H'cap Convs
D

Houston
G. T. Johnson Sales
& Service
11414 Gulf Freeway
Houston, TX 77034
Tel: (713) 943-9272
Contact: Ricky Box
DLR of *TC*

Houston
General Body Mfg.
Company of Texas
7110 Jensen Drive
P.O. Box 16278
Houston, TX 77093
Tel: (713) 692-5177
FAX: (713) 692-0700
Contact: Carl Sleeper
MFR of *TB*
C-2:3

Houston
Holiday World, Inc.
8224 North Freeway
(I-45, North)
Houston, TX 77037
Tel: (713) 448-0035
Contact: Michael Peay
DLR of *R1, R2*

Houston
Holiday World, Inc.
11400 Gulf Freeway
(I-45, South)
Houston, TX 77034
Tel: (713) 943-1331
FAX: (713) 943-8925
Contact: Michael Peay
DLR of *R1, R2*

Houston
Imperial Van & Acc.
6726 Loma Vista Street
Houston, TX 77085
Tel: (713) 721-9677
Contact: Bonni Iledan
R4

Houston
Independence Vans
of Texas
1789 Upland Drive
Houston, TX 77043
Tel: (713) 468-4683
R4

Houston
Koenig, Incorporated
2301 Central Parkway
Houston, TX 77092
Tel: (713) 688-4414
Nation: (800) 346-8988
FAX: (713) 688-0275
Contact: Roger Clemmett
MFR of *CTB*

Houston
Lifts Aids of Houston,
Incorporated
6270 Brookhill
Houston, TX 77087
Tel: (713) 645-2714
FAX: (713) 645-1461
Contact: Jim Hickok
H'cap R4

Houston
McClain Trailer Mfg. Co
7202 Cowart Street
Houston, TX 77020
Tel: (713) 575-2761
FAX: (713) 921-4543
MFR of *T*

Houston
New World Van
Accessories and
Conversions
6025 Bissonnet
Houston, TX 77081
Tel : (713) 661-3731
FAX: (713) 661-4852
Contact: Chris Leverier
R4

Houston
Republic Trailer & Mfg.
8516 Hempstead Road
Houston, TX 77008
Tel: (713) 869-9201
MFR of *T*

Houston
Sam & Sons Truck
Equipment
8902 East Hardy Road
Houston, TX 77093
Tel: (713) 694-3077
Contact: William Brown
MFR of *TB*

Houston
Strong Mixers, Inc.
13515 Ann Louise
Houston, TX 77086
Tel: (713) 847-0111
Nation: (800) 822-0004
FAX: (713) 820-5569
Contact: Jane Shriver
MFR of *Concrete Mixer*
TB

Houston
Texas Stagecoach
5136 Highway 6, North
Houston, TX 77084
Tel: (713) 855-7777
FAX: (713) 855-7077
Contact: Grant Gilchrist
MFR of *R4*
C-2:3

Houston
Trailer Wheel & Frame
Company
6839 S. Loop, East
Houston, TX 77087
Tel: (713) 649-2424
Tel: (713) 931-2910
Contact: Ron Wickes
MFR of *W*

Hutchins
McNeilus Truck &
Manufacturing, Inc.
1101 S. I. H. 45
Hutchins, TX 75141
Tel: (214) 225-2313
Contact: Wes Austin
MFR of *Cement Mixer*
TB

Irving
GMC Truck Division,
Houston Marketing
130 E. Carpenter Fwy.
Suite 300
Irving, TX 75062
Tel: (214) 541-5150
Nation: (800) 462-8782
MFR of *TB*
D: Cooper Transport

Irving
LES Distributors, Inc.
6025 Commerce Drive
Suite 545
Irving, TX 75062
Tel: (214) 751-0488
Nation: (800) 527-2939
FAX: (214) 550-8720
Contact: Lynn Hicks
DISTRIBUTOR of *R4*

Kilgore
Herrin Welding Service,
Incorporated
RR 4, Box 250
Kilgore, TX 75662
Tel: (903) 984-7139
Contact: Bill Herrin
MFR of *TB*

Laredo
Laredo Coachworks
403 Maher Avenue
Laredo, TX 87041
Tel: (210) 724-5021
FAX: (210) 727-4924
Contact: John Adams
MFR of *Limos*
C-1

Lewisville
Champion Trailer
Manufacturing, Inc.
1620 E. Highway 121
Lewisville, TX 75056
Tel: (214) 221-4422
FAX: (217) 394-5680
Contact: Bee Peck
MFR of *T*

Longview
Country Conversions
515 W. Marshall Avenue
Longview, TX 75601
Tel: (903) 758-3632
R4

Longview
Dealers' Truck Equip.
P.O. Box 631
Longview, TX 75606
Tel: (903) 758-4451
FAX: (903) 758-4483
Contact: Larry Painter
MFR of TB
C-2
D: Gibson Transport

Longview
Fleetwood Travel Trailers of Texas, Inc.
810 Prowler Drive
P.O. Box 7909
Longview, TX 75607
Tel: (903) 759-9451
Contact: Roger Pugh
MFR of R5, R6
D: Selman Trucking, Barrett

Longview
Hayes Trailer Sales
5009 Judson Road
Longview, TX 75605
Tel: (903) 663-3488
FAX: (903) 663-3406
Contact: Becky Eason or David Hayes
DLR of R1, R2

Longview
Just Cruisin'
1204 W. Marshall Ave.
Longview, TX 75604
Tel: (903) 753-1888
FAX: (903) 757-6974
Contact: Jim Wortham
R4

Lott
P & S Camper Mfg., Inc.
Hwy. 320 at Hwy. 77
P.O. Box 209
Lott, TX 76656
Tel: (817) 584-2771
FAX: (817) 584-2834
Contact: David Pomycal
MFR of TC
A-1, C-2:1

Lubbock
American Kar 'N Van
111 Slaton Road
Lubbock, TX 79404
Tel: (806) 745-5556
R4

Lubbock
Pharr RV, Incorporated
320 N. Loop 289
Lubbock, TX 79403
Tel: (806) 765-6088
Nation: (800) 952-2389
Contact: Harold Pharr
DLR of R1, R2

Lubbock
Premium Pick-up
1701 Broadway Street
Lubbock, TX 79401
Tel: (806) 747-2453
FAX: (806) 747-7207
Contact: Cody Bowman
TConvs

Lufkin
Lufkin Industries (Trailer Division)
Highway 69, South
P.O. Box 849
Lufkin, TX 75901
Tel: (409) 634-2211
FAX: (409) 637-5244
MFR of T
B-2

Malakoff
Malakoff Truck and Body Works
Highway 31 West
Box 205
Malakoff, TX 75148
Tel: (903) 489-1418
MFR of TB

Mansfield
Nu Van Technology, Inc.
2155 FM 1187
Mansfield, TX 76063
Tel: (817) 477-1734
FAX: (817) 473-3942
Contact: Gary Ashford
MFR of T
D

Mansfield
Road Star Vehicles
2850 N. Main Street
Mansfield, TX 76063
Tel: (817) 561-1899
Contact: Scott Ryder
R4
C-1

Mansfield
Skyline RV
606 S. 2nd Avenue
Mansfield, TX 76063
Tel: (817) 477-3161
Nation: (800) 962-7773
FAX: (817) 477-4315
Contact: Charles Jordan
MFR of R5, R6
D

Mansfield
Traveltime Vans
300 S. Westyria
Mansfield, TX 76063
Tel: (817) 473-8415
DLR of R4

Mansfield
Tiara Motorcoach of Texas
108 Sentry Drive
Mansfield, TX 76063
Tel: (817) 473-7353
FAX: (817) 473-7935
CONVERTER of U, Trucks, and Suburbans

Mansfield
Unique Conversions, Inc.
P.O. Box 672
Mansfield, TX 76063
Tel: (817) 477-5251
FAX: (817) 477-1537
Contact: Rita Marshall
MFR of R4
C-2:6

McGregor
Companion Van Company, Incorporated
Blue Bonnet Industrial Pk
McGregor, TX 76657
Tel: (817) 840-3271
Nation: (800) 227-5733
FAX: (817) 840-2465
MFR of R4
(This location is HQ.)

McGregor
Duster Campers
103 N. Garfield Street
McGregor, TX 76657
Tel: (817) 840-3770
FAX: (817) 840-4313
Contact: Richard Eberspacher
REFURBISHER of R1, R3
MODIFIER/CUSTOMIZER of HT, LT, Race Car T, Medical T, Haz-Mat T, Command Post T, R5, R6
A-1

McKinney
Fero Trailer Mfg.
1455 E. Highway 380
McKinney, TX 75069
Tel: (214) 542-8185
MFR of T

Mesquite
Holiday World, Inc.
4630 Highway 67
Mesquite, TX 75150
Tel: (214) 328-4151
TX Only: (800) 225-1434
Contact: Jim Anderson
DLR of R1, R2

Mesquite
Show Trucks USA, Inc.
411 Lawson Road
Mesquite, TX 75181
Tel: (214) 557-1900
Nation: (800) 456-9395
MFR of R4, TConvs
C-2:3

Midland
Brenderup Horse Trailers
2801 Rankin Highway
Midland, TX 79702
Tel: (915) 684-8372
MFR of HT

Mineola
Hackco Van Conversions
403-1/2 W. Broad St., #A
Mineola, TX 75773
Tel: (903) 569-9712
Contact: David Hackler
R4

Mount Pleasant
Diamond C Trailer Mfg.
Route 9, Box 577
Mt. Pleasant, TX 75455
Tel: (903) 572-2834
MFR of T

Mount Pleasant
Ehrlish Trailer Mfg.
Route 1, Box 340
Mt. Pleasant, TX 75455
Tel: (903) 572-4483
MFR of T

Nacogdoches
Foretravel, Incorporated
929 W. Stallings Drive
Nacogdoches, TX 75961
Tel: (409) 634-2211
FAX: (409) 564-0391
Contact: Tip Harris
MFR of R1, R2
C-2

Odessa
Big Tex Trailer Manufacturing, Inc.
12400 I-20, East
Odessa, TX 79765
Tel: (915) 563-0300
FAX: (915) 563-0739
MFR of T

Odessa
Watco Truck Rigging, Incorporated
1550 Laredo
Odessa, TX 79761
Tel: (915) 333-1629
FAX: (915) 333-3707
Contact: Johnny Watkins
MFR of TB

Ore City
Blacksmith Trailers
Box 549
Ore City, TX 75683
Tel: (903) 968-3137
Contact: Dave Storts
MFR of *T*

Pharr
RV Greenway Center
1315 W. US Highway 83
Pharr, TX 78577
Tel: (210) 783-1699
Contact: Carrie Marks
REPAIR of *T, R1, R2*

Pipe Creek
Texas Custom Coach
HCR 2, Box 6611
Pipe Creek, TX 78063
Tel: (210) 510-4224
Contact: Jack Brannan
MFR of *R1, R2*

Plainview
Bothwell Enterprises
I-27 South, Route 1
Plainview, TX 79072
Tel: (806) 293-2961
FAX: (806) 293-7011
Contact: R.T. Bothwell
DLR of *U*

Plano
Ozanne Limousine Sales
2504 Kelsey Drive
Plano, TX 75075
Tel: (214) 424-0577
FAX: (214) 423-1806
Contact: John Ozanne, Sr.
or John Ozanne, Jr.
DLR of *Limos*

Porter
Pegasus Autohaus
1805 FM 1314
Porter, TX 77365
Tel: (713) 354-3288
FAX: (713) 354-3290
Contact: John Bullock
MFR of *R1, R2*

Richardson
Roadrunner Vans, Inc.
805 S. Sherman Street
Richardson, TX 75081
Tel: (214) 783-8155
FAX: (214) 783-7382
Contact: Hank Sokol
MFR of *R4*
C-1

Round Rock
Royal Vans of Texas
204 Texas Avenue
Round Rock, TX 78664
Tel: (512) 244-1616
FAX: (512) 244-2553
MFR of *R4*
A-1

San Antonio
*Alamo Trailer &
Truck Repair*
4100 Factory Hill Street
San Antonio, TX 78219
Tel: (210) 337-7900
MFR of *T*

San Antonio
AMA Enterprises, Inc.
3813 Pleasanton Road
San Antonio, TX 78221
Tel: (210) 924-6482
FAX: (210) 927-4448
Contact: Henry Acuna
MFR of *TB*
C-1

San Antonio
Commercial Body Corp.
142 Gimbler
P.O. Box 1119
San Antonio, TX 78219
Tel: (210) 224-1931
Nation: (800) 292-1931
FAX: (210) 224-6885
Contact: Steve Masterson
MFR of *CTB*
C-2:5 part-timers
D: Northwest, Central

San Antonio
EMS Enterprises
17585 W. Blanco Road,
#145
San Antonio, TX 78212
Tel: (210) 492-9775
Contact: Steve Fitmer
R4

San Antonio
*Executive Armoring
Corporation*
4836 Whirlwind
San Antonio, TX 78217
Tel: (210) 654-3905
Contact: Lauren Bryner
ARMORING of *Vehicles*
C-1

San Antonio
Home Elevator of Texas
4335 Vance Jackson Road
San Antonio, TX 78230
Tel: (210) 340-5702
Contact: Don Zimmerman
R4

San Antonio
Pak-Mor Mfg. Co.
P.O. Box 14147
San Antonio, TX 14147
Tel: (210) 923-4317
MFR of *TB*

San Antonio
Para-Driving Aids
4714 Broom Street
San Antonio, TX 78217
Tel: (210) 655-5438
FAX: (210) 655-5573
Contact: Dan Hansen
H'cap R4

San Antonio
*Royal Coach Van
Conversions*
1420 Roosevelt Avenue
San Antonio, TX 78210
Tel: (210) 532-8874
Contact: Ceasar
Villagonez
R4

Sanger
Perrico Trailer & Mfg.
905 E. Chapman Drive
P. O. Box 738
Sanger, TX 76266
Tel: (817) 458-3929
MFR of *T*

Seagoville
Custom Seats of Texas
1702 N. Highway 175
Seagoville, TX 75159
Tel: (214) 287-7328
Nation: (800) 742-9226
Contact: Jason Burks
MODIFIER of *R4*

Sherman
Custom Bodies, Inc.
1701 Texoma Drive
Sherman, TX 75090
Tel: (903) 892-0561
FAX: (903) 892-0562
Contact: Jim Lewis, Sr.
MFR of *TB, U*

Sherman
Du Tec
RR 1
Sherman, TX 75090
Tel: (903) 868-1917
MFR of *TB*

Sherman
*Sloan Kwik Load
Trailer Manufacturing*
Route 2, Box 100
Sherman, TX 75090
Tel: (903) 893-7133
MFR of *Load T*

Silver Springs
*Custom Welding &
Trailer Manufacturing*
Route 2, Box 239
Silver Springs, TX 75482
Tel: (903) 488-3718
MFR of *T*

Sinton
*Ross Stanford's Trailer
Manufacturing*
(MAIL: P.O. Box 10001
Corpus Christi, TX
78410)
S Highway 77
Sinton, TX 78387
Tel : (512) 364-5090
MFR of *T*

Springtown
Deerskin Mfg. Co.
P.O. Box 127
Springtown, TX 76082
Tel: (817) 523-5535
FAX: (817) 523-6685
Contact: Andy Deerskin
MFR of *TB*

Stafford
Rolligon Corporation
10635 Brighton Lane
Stafford, TX 77477
Tel: (713) 495-1140
FAX: (713) 495-1145
Contact: Derrick Deedon
MFR of *TB*

Sulphur Springs
Cromer Custom Vans
1020 Main Street
Sulphur Springs, TX
75482
Tel: (903) 885-3262
R4

Sumner
PJ Trailer Service
Farm Road 2352
Sumner, TX 75486
Tel: (903) 785-6879
MFR of *T*

Teague
Bossier Chrysler-Dodge
Highway 84
Teague, TX 75860
Tel: (817) 739-2521
Nation: (800) 284-0360
FAX: (817) 739-5148
Contact: Randy Pretzer
DLR of *Trucks*

Temple
Steelworld of Texas
3321 Parkway Drive
Temple, TX 76503
Tel: (817) 773-1585
Contact: Don Kessler
MFR of *TB*
D

Tyler
*Nick's Trailer
Hitch Shop*
5592 FM 14
Tyler, TX 75706
Tel: (903) 593-1808
Contact: Susan Nicks
MFR of *T*

Tyler
Smith Tank & Equip. Co.
P.O. Box 2014
Tyler, TX 75710
Tel: (903) 597-5541
Contact: Greg Bohnam
MFR of *TB*

Tyler
Tyler RV Center
935 NE Loop 323
Tyler, TX 75708
Tel: (903) 597-1471
Contact: Brad Shaw
DLR of *R1, R2*

Victoria
Clegg Industries
700 Bobwhite
Victoria, TX 77901
Tel: (512) 578-0291
Nation: (800) 576-9811
FAX: (512) 576-9811
Contact: John Clegg
MFR of *T*
NOTE: *Formerly Weathermaster Mfg. Co.*

Victoria
Vans of Victoria
3207 Houston Highway
Victoria, TX 77901
Tel: (512) 798-7207
Contact: William A. Krause
R4

Waco
Hafford Equipment
3325 S. I-35
Waco, TX 76706
Tel: (817) 752-4397
Nation: (800) 792-3027
FAX: (817) 756-1997
Contact: Pete Rebando
MFR of *TB*

Waco
Leggott Trailers
3015 S. I-35
Waco, TX 76706
Tel: (817) 754-5512
Nation: (800) 525-WACO
FAX: (817) 754-4452
Contact: Tom Legott
DLR of *HT*

Waco
Transportation Concepts
(MAIL: P.O. Box 20127
Waco, TX 76062-0127)
9000 Van American Dr.
Waco, TX 76710
Tel: (817) 666-7781
Tel: (817) 666-7784
Contact: Sharon Nichols
R4
D

Waco
*Wells Cargo, Inc.,
Texas Division*
P.O. Box 7128
Waco, TX 76714
Tel: (817) 772-1740
Nation: (800) 348-7553
FAX: (817) 772-7673
Contact: Tina La Piere
at (219) 264-9661
MFR of *ST*
B-1

Webster
Cadillac Custom Vans
12430 Galveston Road
Webster, TX 77598
Tel: (713) 486-9739
R4

Wichita Falls
*Longhorn Trailer &
Body Company*
1141 Sheppard Access Rd
Wichita Falls, TX 76304
Tel: (817) 322-5259
TX Only: (800) 772-0855
DLR of *TB, T*

Wichita Falls
Otis Thomas Sales
2606 Jacksboro Highway
Wichita Falls, TX 76302
Tel: (817) 767-1234
DLR of *R1, R6*

Woodson
Jones Trailer Co., Inc.
300 Jom Street
Woodson, TX 76491
Tel: (817) 345-6759
Nation: (800) 336-0360
Contact: Danny Jones
MFR of *T*

UTAH

Clearfield
Utility Trailer Mfg.
Freeport Center, Bldg. 14
Clearfield, UT 84015
Tel: (801) 328-2382
FAX: (801) 773-9051
Contact: Steve Smith
MFR of *T*

Kaysville
*Blaine Jensen & Sons
RV Center*
220 N. 550 W.
(Exit 331 of I-15)
Kaysville, UT 84037
Tel: (801) 261-0481
Nation: (800) 424-8844
FAX: (801) 269-0987
Contact: Dick Jones
DLR of *R1, R2*

Kearns
Tuff Trailer Mfg.
4800 S. 5200 W.
Kearns, UT 84118
Tel: (801) 965-8833
MFR of *T*

Logan
Logan Coach
290 S. 400 W
Logan, UT 84321
Tel: (801) 752-3737
Contact: Jason Smart
MFR of *T*
B-2
D

Logan
Walton Products
150 W. & 2450 N.
Logan, UT 84321
Tel: (801) 753-2022
Nation: (800) 321-8818
MFR of *T*

Midvale
Jordan Camper
7000 State Street
Midvale, UT 84047
Tel: (801) 255-1512
Contact: Paul Glover
DLR of *TC*

Murray
Joseph Clair Clayton
5850 S. 300 W.
Murray, UT 84107
Tel: (801) 263-8953
Contact: Joseph Clayton
MFR of *T*

Oakley
*5 Bar Dash Custom
Trailers Mfg., Inc.*
North Beanh Road
Oakley, UT 84055
Tel: (801) 783-5575
MFR of *HT*

Ogden
Custom Welding
1182 W. & 3050 S.
Ogden, UT 84401
Tel: (801) 621-5432
Contact: Craig Smith
MFR of *T*

Ogden
Interwest Medical
4031 Riverdale Road
Ogden, UT 84405
Tel: (801) 394-4000
Nation: (800) 947-9797
FAX: (801) 394-6853
H'cap R4
C-1

Ogden
*T-J Horse Trailer &
Repair*
2914 Pennsylvania Ave.
Ogden, UT 84401
Tel: (801) 627-0885
FAX: (801) 627-0884
Contact: Larry Ropelato
MFR of *HT*

Ogden
Vogt Manufacturing
1441 W. 2550 S.
Ogden, UT 84401
Tel: (801) 627-1017
Tel: (801) 392-1759
MFR of *HT*

Ogden
Wells Cargo Trailer Mfg.
1741 W. 2550 S.
Ogden, UT 84401
Tel: (801) 266-1552
Tel: (801) 621-3637
Nation: (800) 348-7553
FAX: (801) 392-5443
Contact: Jack Klepinger
MFR of *Cargo T, ST*
B-2

Ogden
Wells Western Trailer
808 N. Highway 91
Ogden, UT 84404
Tel: (801) 782-7389
Contact: Jason Wells
MFR of *T*

Pleasant Grove
Interwest Medical
60 E. State Road
Pleasant Grove, UT 84062
Tel: (801) 785-1000
H'cap R4

Providence
Pickett Welding Co.
281 E. 200 N.
Providence, UT 84332
Tel: (801) 752-7083
Contact: Farrell Pickett
MFR of *T*

Provo
*Arko Upholstery
Unlimited*
1460 N. State Street
Provo, UT 84604
Tel: (801) 375-5522
MODIFIER of *R4*

Salt Lake City
Custom Van of Utah
3665 S. 300 W.
Salt Lake City, UT 84115
Tel: (801) 266-1552
Nation: (800) 688-6402
FAX: (801) 268-3011
Contact: Sandy May
MFR of *R4*
D: Ryder Transport

Salt Lake City
H & K Truck Equipment
751 W. 300 S.
Salt Lake City, UT 84104
Tel: (801) 355-0531
UT Only: (800) 662-8962
FAX: (801) 355-9242
Contact: Al Lopez
DLR of *TB*
C-2:2
D

Salt Lake City
Intermountain Peterbilt, Incorporated
2858 S. 300 W.
Salt Lake City, UT 84115
Tel: (801) 486-2391
Tel: (801) 486-8781
MFR of *Trucks*
C-1, C-2

Salt Lake City
Intermountain Sports
4225 S. 500 W.
Salt Lake City, UT 84123
Tel: (801) 266-4449
FAX: (801) 265-0461
Contact: Bill McGrew
DLR of *R1, R2*
C-2

Salt Lake City
Interwest Medical
235 E. 6100 S.
Salt Lake City, UT 84107
Tel: (801) 262-5661
Contact: Val Christensen
R4, H'cap R4

Salt Lake City
New Image Vans
1425 S. 300 W.
Salt Lake City, UT 84115
Tel: (801) 487-8919
Contact: Tuong Dang
R4

Salt Lake City
Para Quad Marketing, Incorporated
2572 SW Temple
Salt Lake City, UT 84115
Tel: (801) 487-0111
Contact: Tom Flandro
R4, H'cap R4

Salt Lake City
Salt Lake City Mack Sales & Service
2795 S. 300 W.
Salt Lake City, UT 84115
Tel: (801) 486-4111
Contact: Steve Sturdevant or Vic Adams
DLR of *Mack Trucks*

Salt Lake City
Salt Lake Valley Custom Vans & GMC
725 W. 3300 S.
Salt Lake City, UT 84119
Tel: (801) 265-1511
FAX: (801) 265-1660
Contact: Debbie Nielsen
R4

Salt Lake City
Top-It of Salt Lake
5567 S. 320 W.
Salt Lake City, UT 84107
Tel: (801) 262-5904
FAX: (801) 262-5964
Contact: Keith Bererton
DLR of *TC*

Salt Lake City
Twamco Trailer Manufacturing Co., Inc.
1920 W. 3500 S.
Salt Lake City, UT 84119
Tel: (801) 972-8325
FAX: (801) 973-0224
Contact: Chuck Charlestodd
MFR of *T*
B-2

Salt Lake City
Vacation Village
4231 S. State Street
Salt Lake City, UT 84107
Tel: (801) 262-7666
FAX: (801) 266-9072
Contact: Mark Riley
DLR of *Campers*

Salt Lake City
Williamsen Mfg., Inc.
P.O. Box 26864
Salt Lake City, UT 84101
Tel: (801) 975-0800
Tel: (801) 793-9400
FAX: (801) 973-2838
Contact: Bruce Joehansen
DLR of *TB*
C-2:2
D

Sandy
Ardell Brown RVs
9200 S. State
Sandy, UT 84070
Tel: (801) 255-9200
FAX: (801) 255-4670
Contact: Angela Christensen
DLR of *R1, R2*

Tremonton
Trump Wheatley
659 W. Main Street
Tremonton, UT 84337
Tel: (801) 257-3328
Contact: Glen Trump
DLR of *TC*
D

Vernal
B & D RV Center
1570 W. Highway 40
Vernal, UT 84008
Tel: (801) 789-1970
DLR of *TC*

VERMONT

Hinesburg
Iroquois Mfg. Co., Inc.
RD #2, Box 550
Hinesburg, VT 05461
Tel: (802) 482-2155
FAX: (802) 482-2962
Contact: Ryan Lyman
MFR of *TB*

VIRGINIA

Ashland
Dixie Trailer, Inc.
P.O. Box 169
Ashland, VA 23005
Tel: (804) 798-6006
FAX: (804) 798-6008
Contact: Jimmy Face
MFR of *TB, T*
C-2:3

Atkins
Utility Trailer Mfg.
State Highway 788
P.O. Box 230
Atkins, VA 24311
Tel: (703) 783-8800
MFR of *T, S-2*

Berryville
Batterson Trailer Sales
RR 3, Box 6220
Berryville, VA 22611
Tel: (703) 955-3328
FAX: (703) 955-4035
Contact: Roy Batterton
DLR of *HT*

Bluefield
American La France
600 Mountain Lane
Bluefield, VA 24605
Tel: (703) 326-1121
Nation: (800) 932-3523
FAX: (703) 322-3666
Contact: Maggy Asbury
SERVICE CENTER of *F*
C-2

Bristol
Branson Body Works, Incorporated
225 Stagecoach Road
Bristol, VA 24201
Tel: (703) 669-4311
FAX: (703) 669-8633
Contact: Ralph Branson
MFR of *T*

Bristol
Bristol Horse Vans
225 Stagecoach Road
Bristol, VA 24201
Tel: (703) 669-8633
MFR of *HT*

Chantilly
Van Stand, The
4270 Henninger Ct., #K
Chantilly, VA 22021
Tel: (703) 631-8338
Contact: Gary White
R4

Chesapeake
RSO, Ltd.
3737 Holland Blvd.
Suite A
Chesapeake, VA 23323
Tel: (804) 485-3619
FAX: (804) 485-2825
Contact: Richard Ott
R4, H'cap R4
D

Chilhowie
Special Interest Automobile Trailers
Exit 35 of I-81
Chilhowie, VA 24319
Tel: (703) 646-8416
Contact: Tim Tool
DLR of *T*
B-2:3

Cloverdale
Cavalier Equipment Corporation
2974 Lee Highway, South
Cloverdale, VA 24077
Tel: (703) 992-3355
FAX: (703) 992-2150
Contact: Mark Powell
MFR of *G*
C-2 (Local)
D

Dublin
Volvo GM Heavy Truck Corporation
Route 643
P.O. Box 1126
Dublin, VA 24084
Tel: (703) 674-4181
FAX: (703) 674-0391
Contact: Steve Plastek
FINAL ASSEMBLER of *TB*
D: Kuehl

Duffield
Pak-Mor Mfg. Co.
P.O. Box 326
Duffield, VA 24244
Tel: (703) 431-2601
FAX: (703) 431-4296
Contact: Wayne Bishop or Charles McDonald
MFR of *TB*
D

Emporia
Old Dominion Motor Coach Corporation
1201 Wiggins Road
Emporia, VA 23847
Tel: (804) 634-4812
Contact: Mark Yehets
R4

Evington
Sonny Merryman, Inc.
(MAIL: P.O. Box 495, Rustberg, VA 24588)
Route 1, Box 489
Route 29, South
Evington, VA 24450
Tel: (804) 821-1000
FAX: (804) 821-8203
Contact: Vicki Overstreet
MFR of *U*
C-2:8

Fredericksburg
Probilt Fabricators, Inc.
207 Willow Street
Fredericksburg, VA 22405
Tel: (703) 373-2358
FAX: (703) 899-0513
Contact: Charles Stern
MFR of *TB*

Hampton
Van House, The
2002 E. Pembroke Ave.
Hampton, VA 23664
Tel: (804) 851-8000
FAX: (804) 850-3653
Contact: Doug Wornom
R4
C-2

Leesburg
Mini Manor Industries
346 C. E. Market Street
Leesburg, VA 22075
Tel: (703) 777-1557
Contact: Dan Cox
REPAIR of *R1, HT*

Lynchburg
Truck Body Corporation
4401 Richmond Highway
P.O. Box 10906
Lynchburg, VA 24506
Tel: (804) 847-7787
Nation: (800) 828-6492
FAX: (804) 847-7792
MFR of *TB*

Petersburg
Wooden Leg Van Shop
214 Grove Avenue, #A
Petersburg, VA 23803
Tel: (804) 861-5255
Contact: Jim Warehime
R4

Portsmouth
Gosport Automotive Center
2100 Portsmouth Blvd.
Portsmouth, VA 23704
Tel: (804) 393-4021
Contact: Frankie Eats, Jr.
R4

Portsmouth
Lifestyle Vans
4212 Portsmouth Blvd.
Portsmouth, VA 23701
Tel: (804) 465-2857
Contact: Sonya Medlin
R4
D: Low-Boy Carrier (Conversion vans are transported on trailers.)

Portsmouth
Wilbar Truck Equip, Inc.
2808 Frederick Blvd.
Portsmouth, VA 23707
Tel: (804) 397-3200
FAX: (804) 393-0981
Contact: Keith Chirorz
FINAL ASSEMBLER of *TB*

Richlands
Burks' Truck Body, Inc.
2950 S. Front Street
Richlands, VA 24641
Tel: (703) 964-5866
FAX: (703) 963-3035
Contact: Alan Rife
MFR of *TB*

Richlands
Virginia Metal Products Company
2706 Clinch Street
Richlands, VA 24641
Tel: (703) 963-1061
Contact: Homer Nelson
MFR of *T*

Richmond
Arrow Auto Interiors & Paradapt Service
232 E. Belt Blvd.
Richmond, VA 23224
Tel: (804) 233-8267
FAX: (804) 233-8284
Contact: Kay Potter
R4, H'cap R4

Richmond
Baker Equuipment Engineering Company
(MAIL: P.O. Box 25609 Richmond, VA 23260)
1700 Summit Avenue
Richmond, VA 23230
Tel: (804) 358-0481
FAX: (804) 342-6888
Contact: Reid Snider
MFR of *Man-Lift Trucks, TB*
D

Richmond
Crenshaw Corporation
1700 Commerce Road
Richmond, VA 23224
Tel: (804) 231-6241
MFR of *TB*

Richmond
Cushing Manufacturing & Equipment Company
2901 Commerce Road
Richmond, VA 23234
Tel: (804) 231-1161
Nation: (800) 252-1161
FAX: (804) 230-4045
Contact: Ross Jennings
REPAIR of *CT*

Richmond
Eubanks Trucks
3800 N. Hopkins Street
Richmond, VA 23224
Tel: (804) 232-6716
VA only: (800) 446-5010
FAX: (800) 552-4010
DLR of *Used VTB*
C-1

Richmond
McGeorge RV & Marine Center
6200 W. Broad Street
Richmond, VA 23230
Tel: (804) 285-9071
FAX: (804) 285-2253
Contact: Bob Melson
DLR of *R1, R2*

Richmond
Overland Bus Sales
6020 Midlothian Turnpike
Richmond, VA 23225
Tel: (804) 233-1164
Nation: (800) 877-1699
FAX: (804) 233-1169
Contact: John Davis
DLR of *U*

Richmond
Van Conversions
5255 Hull Street Road.
Suite L
Richmond, VA 23224
Tel: (804) 233-5658
FAX: (804) 231-4698
Contact: Edna Hudges
R4

Roanoke
General Truck Body Co.
1919 10th Street, NW
Roanoke, VA 24012
Tel: (703) 362-1861
R4

Roanoke
Roanoke Seat Cover Shop
2901 Williamson Rd, NW
Roanoke, VA 24012
Tel: (703) 563-4919
Contact: Virginia King
R4

Salem
Salem Quality Equipment, Incorporated
501 8th Street
Salem, VA 24153
Tel: (703) 389-6000
Contact: Kim Gillispie
MFR of *U, VBT*
C-2:5

South Boston
Jack Slagle
Highway 58, East
Box 15
South Boston, VA 24592
Tel: (804) 575-7905
Nation: (800) 446-8896
FAX: (804) 572-3373
Contact: Jack Slagal
MFR of *F*
C-2
D

South Hill
Hazelwood Trailer Manufacturing Co.
201 Maple Lane
South Hill, VA 23970
Tel: (804) 447-7365
MFR of *CT*

Springfield
Lee's Custom Trim
7516 Fullerton Road
Springfield, VA 22153
Tel: (703) 569-1788
FAX: (703) 569-7156
Contact: Roy Lee
R4, TConvs

Vienna
Melody Coach Industries, Incorporated
2830 Gallows Road
Vienna, VA 22180
Tel: (703) 560-6424
FAX: (703) 207-9872
Contact: James Clark
R4

Winchester
Fleetwood Travel Trailers of Virginia
380 Battaile Drive
P.O. Box 2370
Winchester, VA 22601
Tel: (703) 662-3436
FAX: (703) 662-1566
MFR of *R5, R6*
D

Woods Cross Roads
Henry's Step Vans
Route 16 & Route 17
P.O. Box 30
Woods Cross Roads, VA 23190
Tel: (804) 693-7514
MFR of *T, TB*

WASHINGTON

Auburn
Auburn RV
2536 Auburn Way, North
Auburn, WA 98002
Tel: (206) 833-3368
Nation: (800) 822-8422
FAX: (206) 939-4029
Contact: Donna Parker
DLR of *R1, R2*

Auburn
Bothell Brothers Chevrolet, Incorporated
1600 Auburn Way, North
Auburn, WA 98002
Tel: (206) 833-2000
FAX: (206) 939-7794
Contact: Dick Matson
R4
C-2

Auburn
Fry's Welding, Inc.
3240 B Street, NW
Auburn, WA 98001
Tel: (206) 939-1258
FAX: (206) 939-4028
Contact: Dave Fry
MFR of *T*
B-1

Bellevue
Superior Auto Trim
12766 Bellevue Redmond Road
Bellevue, WA 98005
Tel: (206) 454-5860
FAX: (206) 462-0907
Contact: Maurice Pilgrim or Phil Falcone
R4

Bellingham
Quality Big Boat Custom Trailer Manufacturing
415 Fieldston Road
Bellingham, WA 98225
Tel: (206) 671-5068
Contact: George Manchester
MFR of *T*

Bremerton
Soundline Trailers & Manufacturing
233 Bruin Avenue
Bremerton, WA 98312
Tel: (206) 373-9421
Contact: Brian Hofer
MFR of *T*

Chehalis
Alaskan Campers, Inc.
280 NW Chehalis Avenue
Chehalis, WA 98532
Tel: (206) 748-6494
Contact: Judy Wheat
MFR of *TC*

Chehalis
Wilson's Trailers
153 La Brea Road
Chehalis, WA 98532
Tel: (206) 748-0959
Contact: Trev Wilson
MFR of *T*

Clarkston
Heliarc Boat
3010 Riverside Drive
Clarkston, WA 99403
Tel: (509) 758-1257
DLR of *BT*

Clarkston
On Spec Trailer
3022 Riverside Drive
Clarkston, WA 99403
Tel: (509) 243-4878
MFR of *T*

Clarkston
Simmons' Trailer Systems
102 14th Street
Clarkston, WA 99403
Tel: (509) 758-1112
FAX: (509) 758-1116
Contact: Ron Simmons
MFR of *S-2*

Des Moines
Sunrise Automobile
22727 Marine View Drive
Des Moines, WA 98198
Tel: (206) 824-2200
Contact: Ross Dick
MFR of *Limos*
D

Ellensburg
Centerline Fabricators, Incorporated
1442 Cascade Way
Ellensburg, WA 98926
Tel: (509) 925-2847
FAX: (509) 925-2934
Contact: Clete Samuelson
MFR of *T*

Everett
Aalbu Brothers
2927 Grand Avenue
Everett, WA 98201
Tel: (206) 252-9751
FAX: (206) 252-1050
Contact: Cal Fergason
MFR of *CTB*

Garfield
Ed-Ka Mfg., Inc.
213 E. Main
Garfield, WA 99130
Tel: (509) 635-1521
Contact: Darryl Dutkey
MFR of *T*

Kelso
Action Welding
1814 Baker Way
Kelso, WA 98626
Tel: (206) 425-5250
Contact: Dave Williams
MFR of *T*

Kent
Bert Well Industries, Inc.
7848 S. 202nd Street
Kent, WA 98032
Tel: (206) 872-3430
Contact: Ralph Stewart
MFR of *TB*
C-2:4

Kent
Flxible Corporation
19130 84th Ave., South
Kent, WA 98032
Tel: (206) 872-7123
Nation: (800) 426-9350
FAX: (206) 395-3437
Contact: Rick Glastin
MFR of *U Acc.*
A-1
NOTE: *See also Flxible in Delaware, OH and Loudonville, OH.*

Kent
Tork Lift Control/ Weld Kent, Inc.
315 Central Ave., North
Kent, WA 98032
Tel: (206) 854-1832
FAX: (206) 854-8003
Contact: Jahn Kay
MFR of *T*

Kent
Valley I-5 RV
23051 Military Road, S.
Kent, WA 98032
Tel: (206) 824-7170
WA, AK: (800) 562-2323
FAX: (206) 878-7050
Contact: Jan Parsons
DLR of *R1, R2*

Kent
Van Master Conversions
1513-A S. Central Ave.
Kent, WA 98032
Tel: (206) 854-2100
FAX: (206) 854-1350
Contact: Larry Jacobs
R4

Lynden
Crabtree RV Rental
8205 Berethusen Road
Lynden, WA 98264
Tel: (206) 354-3058
Contact: Brent Crabtree
RENTAL of *RVs*

Lynnwood
Sturdy Weld
15405 Highway 99
Lynnwood, WA 98037
Tel: (206) 743-9772
Contact: Shirley Jelloson
MFR of *T*

Lynnwood
Van Warehouse, The
4918 184th Place, SW
Lynnwood, WA 98037
Tel: (206) 672-8267
Contact: Dwayne Yearno or Matt Yearno
R4, TConvs
A-1

Monroe
Charmac of Washington
17461 147th Street, NE
Space # 19 & 21
Monroe, WA 98272
Tel: (206) 794-9224
DLR of *HT, LT, CT*

Mount Vernon
John's Auto Toggery
1220 S. 2nd Street
Mt. Vernon, WA 98273
Tel: (206) 336-2744
Contact: Jake Pederson or Kitty Pederson
R4

Mount Vernon
Quality RV & Horse Trailer
901 W. Division Street
Mt. Vernon, WA 98273
Tel: (206) 428-6633
DLR of *HT*

Mount Vernon
Smiley's, Incorporated
1600 Memorial Highway
P.O. Box 737
Mt. Vernon, WA 98273
Tel: (206) 424-7338
FAX: (206) 424-5014
Contact: Dale Smiley
MFR of *CTB*

Olympia
Baydo's Trailer Sales
2411 E. 4th
Olympia, WA 98506
Tel: (206) 357-3811
FAX: (206) 357-3826
Contact: Diane Baydo
DLR of *R1, R2*

Pasco
Gibb's Trailer Mfg. & Repair
320 S. Main
Pasco, WA 99301
Tel: (509) 547-8241
MFR of *T*

Pasco
Smith Truck & Tractor, Incorporated
216 S. 6th Avenue
Pasco, WA 99301
Tel: (509) 547-8835
Contact: Ralph Smith
MFR of *TB*

Port Angeles
Lincoln Industrial Corp./ Lincoln Welding
4130 Tumwater Truck
Port Angeles, WA 98362
Tel: (206) 457-6122
FAX: (206) 452-4773
Contact: Barb Iring
MFR of *T*
B-2:2
D

Port Townsend
Mobile Logic, Inc.
9495 SR 20
Port Townsend, WA 98368
Tel: (206) 385-3509
Contact: Steve Taylor
MFR of *T*

Puyallup
Goldwing, Incorporated
5101 Pioneer Way, East
Puyallup, WA 98371
Tel: (206) 845-7523
MFR of *T*
B-1 (Local)

Puyallup
Van Factory, Inc., The
14009 Canyon Road, East
Puyallup, WA 98373
Tel: (206) 866-8362
FAX: (206) 535-1692
Contact: Dan Beaulaureier *R4*

Rainier
Horse Trailers Only
301 Binghampton St., W.
Rainier, WA 98576
Tel: (206) 446-7266
MFR of *Custom HT*

Redmond
A Mobility Independence Center
7500 159th Place, NE
Redmond, WA 98052
Tel: (206) 883-9718
Nation: (800) 735-7236
FAX: (206) 861-4292
Contact: Barry Pearle
R4, H'cap R4

Redmond
Evergreen Mobile Co.
P.O. Box 687
Redmond, WA 98073-0687
Tel: (206) 383-4172
WA only: (800) 488-0441
FAX: (206) 881-6814
Contact: Dale Goebel
MFR of *T*
B-2

Richland
B & B Enterprises
86 Wellsian Way
Richland, WA 99352
Tel: (509) 943-5884
Contact: Brian Brittian
MFR of *T*

Seattle
Allied Body Works, Inc.
625 S. 96th Street
Seattle, WA 98108
Tel: (206) 763-7811
FAX: (206) 763-8836
Contact: Rich Minice
MFR of *T*
B-2
D

Seattle
Chef's Mobility Conversions, Inc.
1425 NW Ballard Way
Seattle, WA 98107
Tel: (206) 783-2700
Contact: Bob Poeppel
R4, H'cap R4

Seattle
FruehaufTrailers
9426 8th Avenue, South
Seattle, WA 98108
Tel: (206) 762-5800
FAX: (206) 763-4792
MFR of *T*
C-2
D

Seattle
George Heiser Body Company, Incorporated
725 S. Hanford Street
Seattle, WA 98134
Tel: (206) 622-7985
Contact: John Ochs
MFR of *TB*
C-2

Selah
Comet Trailer Corp.
501 S. First Street
P.O. Box 460
Selah, WA 98942
Tel: (509) 697-4800
FAX: (509) 697-8126
Contact: Steve Owens
MFR of *FTB, VTB, S-2*

Snohomish
Rich's Northwest Mobility
7821 Maltby Road
Snohomish, WA 98290
Tel: (206) 481-6546
FAX: (206) 487-8976
R4

Spokane
Alloy Trailers, Inc.
(MAIL: P.O. Box 19208
Spokane, WA 99219)
S. 3025 Geiger Blvd.
Spokane, WA 99204
Tel: (509) 455-8650
FAX: (509) 747-4811
Contact: Bob Urban
MFR of *TB, T*
C-2:3
D

Spokane
Amwest Manufacturing
E. 5805 Sharp Ave., #D-4
Spokane, WA 99212
Tel: (509) 535-0625
Contact: Bruce Jones
MFR of *R1, TC*

Spokane
E-Z Loader Boat Trailers
717 N. Hamilton Street
Spokane, WA 99220
Tel: (509) 489-0181
Contact: Cassandra Willard
MFR of *T*
A-1, B-2

Spokane
Fabrication & Truck Equipment
P.O. Box 11435
Spokane, WA 99211
Tel: (509) 535-0363
Nation: (800) 456-0363
FAX: (509) 534-1623
Contact: Mel Mackey
MFR of *TB*
C-2

Spokane
Goldenwest Mfg., Inc.
E. 1414 Holyoke Avenue
Spokane, WA 99207
Tel: (509) 484-3842
WA only: (800) 743-3842
FAX: (509) 484-3858
MFR of *R4*

Spokane
Meili Manufacturing
N. 3511 Market Street
Spokane, WA 99207
Tel: (509) 489-9180
FAX: (509) 482-7609
Contact: Tim Clinton
MFR of *Truck Canopies*
A-1 (Local)

Spokane
Roamin' Chariot Industries
E. 3342 Trent Avenue
Spokane, WA 99202
Tel: (509) 535-9634
Contact: Neil Christen
MFR of *TC*

Sumner
Royal Aire Vans, Inc.
P.O. Box 1462
Sumner, WA 98390
Tel: (206) 863-6191
Contact: Scott Christian
MFR of *R1*

Sunnyside
Star Transport Trailers, Incorporated
P.O. Box 403
Sunnyside, WA 98944
Tel: (509) 837-3136
Contact: Gene Waller
MFR of *T*

Tacoma
Atwood Trailers
9804 Sales Road, South
Tacoma, WA 98444
Tel: (206) 582-0502
Contact: Dale Atwood
or Beverly Atwood
MFR of *T*

Tacoma
Baydo & Sons RV
10130 S. Tacoma Way
Tacoma, WA 98499
Tel: (206) 582-4176
Nation: (800) 742-6554
FAX: (206) 582-4119
Contact: Jeff Cridlebaugh
DLR of *R5, R6*

Tacoma
Baydo's Trailer Sales
74th S. Tacoma Way
Tacoma, WA 98409
Tel: (206) 475-1411
Nation: (800) 422-9367
FAX: (206) 472-1702
Contact: Tim Baydo
DLR of *R1, R2*

Tacoma
Budget Truck & Van Accessories
10007 Lakeview Ave, SW
Tacoma, WA 98499
Tel: (206) 588-9053
Contact: David Buck
R4
A-1

Tacoma
Cruise America
7833 S. Tacoma Way
Tacoma, WA 98409
Tel: (206) 474-9511
DLR/RENTAL of *R1, R2*
(For more data, see the HQ listing, Mesa, AZ.)

Tacoma
Guenther Fabrication
406 112th Street, East
Tacoma, WA 98445
Tel: (206) 536-1066
Contact: Brock Guenther
MFR of *T*

Tacoma
Holte Truck Equipment
2545 Jefferson Avenue
Tacoma, WA 98402
Tel: (206) 272-6414
FAX: (206) 272-0570
Contact: Mickey Staylen
FINAL ASSEMBLER of *TB*

Tacoma
Northwest Conversions, Incorporated
4732 S. Washington St.
Tacoma, WA 98409
Tel: (206) 475-9060
Contact: Ron Pelland
R4

Tacoma
Spirit Trailer Mfg.
10013 Lakeview Ave, SW
Tacoma, WA 98499
Tel: (206) 581-3818
MFR of *T*

Tacoma
Tveten Motor Company
5610 116th Street, SW
Tacoma, WA 98424
Tel: (206) 922-7770
Contact: Wanda Lang
DLR of *R1, R2*

Toledo
Better Weigh Mfg.
Exit 57 & I-5
Toledo, WA 98591
Tel: (206) 864-6800
Contact: Sam Tomes
MFR of *T*

Touchet
Rea Trailers Inc.
Route 1, Box 174
Touchet, WA 99360
Tel: (509) 394-2305
MFR of *T*

Tukwila
Kenworth Truck Co.
Seattle Mfg. Factory
8801 E. Marginal Way, South
Tukwila, WA 98108
Tel: (206) 764-5400
Tel: (206) 764-5500
MFR of *S-1*

Vancouver
Attbar, Incorporated
6205 NE 63rd Street
Vancouver, WA 98661
Tel: (206) 694-5662
FAX: (206) 694-3043
MFR of *TB*
D

Vancouver
Buz's Equipment Trailers
5815 NE 78th Street
Vancouver, WA 98665
Tel: (206) 694-9116
MFR of *T*

Vancouver
Pac 'Orse Systems
606 NW 94th Street
Vancouver, WA 98665
Tel: (206) 574-1999
Nation: (800) 722-6773
Contact: Freeman Cochren
MFR of *ST: Cart for Hunters*

Vancouver
Pro-Tech Industries, Inc.
NE 3rd Court
Vancouver, WA 98666
Tel: (206) 573-6641
FAX: (206) 573-6687
Contact: Dave Wager
MFR of *Aluminum TB*
C-2
D

Vancouver
Van Mart
7500 B NE 16th Avenue
Vancouver, WA 98665
Tel: (206) 695-6499
Contact: Al Lasko
R4, TConvs

Veradale
Macklin Welding
15722 E. Sprague Avenue
Veradale, WA 99037
Tel: (509) 926-3597
Contact: Bill Macklin
MFR of *T*

Wenatchee
Frank Parker Mfg. Co.
2127 Duncan Drive, N.
Wenatchee, WA 98801
Tel: (509) 663-5923
Contact: Doug Parker
MFR of *T*

Woodinville
Garland Custom Trailers Corporation
23205 Woodinville Hwy.
Woodinville, WA 98072
Tel: (206) 483-5626
Contact: Jim Garland
MFR of *T*
B-2:4

Yakima
Carrier Transports Inc.
1008 N. 1st Street
Yakima, WA 98901
Tel: (509) 248-9800
Contact: Jim Kunz
MFR of *T*
B-2:4

Yakima
Direct Connection
1802 W. Nob Hill Blvd.
Yakima, WA 98902
Tel: (509) 248-9626
Contact: Dane Lukehart
MFR of *R1, R4, TConvs*
C-1

Yakima
Trail Wagons/Chinook
1100 E. Lincoln Avenue
P.O. Box 2589
Yakima, WA 98901
Tel: (509) 248-9026
Nation: (800) 592-8886
FAX: (509) 248-9054
Contact: Sam Alzerez
MFR of *R4, TConvs*
D: Better-All Transport

Yakima
Western Recreational Vehicles, Incorporated
3401 W. Washington Ave
P.O. Box 9547
Yakima, WA 98909
Tel: (509) 457-4133
FAX: (509) 457-8184
Contact: Robert Hillis
MFR of *R5, R6, TC*

WEST VIRGINIA

Alderson
Double M Livestock Trailers
401 Riverview Drive
Alderson, WV 24910
Tel: (304) 445-7991
DLR of *LT*

Belle
Lockwood Van Corp.
2302 E. DuPont Avenue
Belle, WV 25015
Tel: (304) 949-2400
Nation: (800) 998-7762
FAX: (304) 949-1890
Contact: Chuck Moore
MFR of *R4, H'cap R4*
C-2:1-2

Clarksburg
Harry Green Chevy-Geo-Jeep-Eagle
Route 50, East
Clarksburg, WV 26301
Tel: (304) 624-6304
WV only: (800) 352-4389
FAX: (304) 624-2000
Contact: Sharon Shippley
DLR of *R4*

Mineral Wells
Benson Truck Bodies
I-77 & Route 14, South
Mineral Wells, WV 26150
Tel: (304) 489-9020
FAX: (304) 489-2828
MFR/DLR of *TB*

Nitro/Charleston
West Virginia Truck & Trailer Company
Property Road
P.O. Box 598
Nitro, WV 25143
Tel: (304) 755-0113
FAX: (304) 755-1163
REPAIR of *Trucks, T*

Parkersburg
Ravens Metal Products, Incorporated
Route 95 & Rayon Drive
Parkersburg, WV 26102
Tel: (304) 275-4247
Nation: (800) 860-6201
FAX: (304) 424-6213
Contact: Robert Kohner
DLR of *T*

Petersburg
Iman Truck Body Shop
15 Creek Street
Petersburg, WV 26847
Tel: (304) 257-1028
Contact: Curtis Iman
MFR of *TB*

St. Albans
Unit Rig & Equip. Co.
104 Smiley Road
St. Albans, WV 25177
Tel: (304) 755-0711
FAX: (304) 775-0714
Contact: John Willard
MFR of *Off-Highway Mining Trucks*
D

Vienna
Custom Vans of Vienna
3101 Grand Central Ave.
Vienna, WV 26105
Tel: (304) 295-8414
FAX: (304) 295-4065
Contact: Mark Srogi
R4

Wheeling
Specialty Auto Center
2154 Main Street
Wheeling, WV 26003
Tel: (304) 232-0369
WV only: (800) 285-0369
FAX: (304) 232-8381
Contact: Lenny Schwartz
R4

WISCONSIN

Antigo
Marckx Handi-Vans
1122 S. Dorr Street
Antigo, WI 54409
Tel: (715) 623-4026
H'cap R4

Appleton
Jeff's Auto Body & Custom Specialty
1134 W. Wisconsin Ave.
Appleton, WI 54914
Tel: (414) 734-2440
Contact: Jeff Kamts
R4

Appleton
Pierce Mfg., Inc.
P.O. Box 2017
Appleton, WI 54911
Tel: (414) 832-3000
FAX: (414) 832-3084
Contact: Rue Westinberger
MFR of *F*

Bangor
Wehr's Chevrolet
I-90 & Highway 162
Bangor, WI 54614
Tel: (608) 486-2321
Nation: (800) 562-0907
FAX: (608) 486-4407
Contact: Dick Marking
DLR of *HT*
B-1

Big Bend
Refuse Equipment/ Huge Haul, Incorporated
S. 88 W. 23105 Wynn Dr.
P.O. Box 79
Big Bend, WI 53103
Tel: (414) 662-5500
Contact: Don Wene
FINAL ASSEMBLER of *G, XTB*

Brookfield
Select Vehicle Distributing
(MAIL: P.O. Box 347
Brookfield, WI 53008)
21000 W. Capitol Drive
Brookfield, WI 53005
Tel: (414) 781-7711
DISTRIBUTOR of *R4*

Burlington
LDZ/Lynch Display Vans
180 Industrial Drive
Burlington, WI 53105
Tel: (414) 763-0147
Nation: (800) 558-5986
FAX: (414) 763-0156
Contact: Larry LaGuardia
MFR of *R4*
C-2:6-8

Butler
DMC Vans/ DM Conversions, Ltd.
12651 W. Silver Spring Drive
Butler, WI 53007
Tel: (414) 781-1170
FAX: (414) 783-2289
Contact: Pat Campbell
R4
C-2:10

Clintonville
Seagrave Fire Apparatus, Incorporated
105 E. 12th Street
Clintonville, WI 54929
Tel: (715) 823-3194
Tel: (715) 823-2304
FAX: (715) 823-5768
Contact: Bob Hoffman or Jim Engleson
MFR of *F*
C-2:3

Clintonville
Utility Tool & Body Company, Incorporated
151 E. 16th Street
P.O. Box 360
Clintonville, WI 54929
Tel: (715) 823-3167
FAX: (715) 823-5274
Contact: Tom Kenfield
MFR of *TB*
C-2:4

Coloma
RNCO Body Company
Highway CH
P.O. Box 9
Coloma, WI 54930
Tel: (715) 228-2972
Contact: James Rox
MFR of *TB*
A-1

Cottage Grove
Stainless Tank & Equipment, Incorporated
4776 Highway TT
Cottage Grove, WI 53527
Tel: (608) 837-5121
FAX: (608) 837-5126
Contact: Paul Kruger
MFR of *Stainless Steel Tanker TB*

Crandon
Rosa Trailer Mfg.
RR 2, Box 657
Crandon, WI 54520
Tel: (715) 478-3435
Contact: Dennis Rosa
MFR of *T*

De Pere
Dorsch Ford
715 N. 8 De Pere
De Pere, WI 54115
Tel: (414) 336-5701
FAX: (414) 337-4293
Contact: Kathy Rost
DLR of *R4*

Eau Claire
Northwest Enterprises, Incorporated
5100 State Road 93, S.
Eau Claire, WI 54701
Tel: (715) 834-8426
Nation: (800) 462-9641
FAX: (715) 834-4507
Contact: Orville Anderson or Shirley Anderson
DLR of *TB*

Elk Mound
Gullickson Trailer Sales & Service, Incorporated
RR 2, Box 2454
Elk Mound, WI 54739
Tel: (715) 874-6552
Contact: Malcom Gullickson
MFR of *T*
B-2

Fond Du Lac
Emerich Mfg. Co.
N. 8427 Lakeview Road
Fond Du Lac, WI 54935
Tel: (414) 921-9630
Contact: Pat Emerich
MFR of *T*

Fond Du Lac
S. J. Krueger Enterprises
333 Fond Du Lac Avenue
Fond Du Lac, WI 54935
Tel: (414) 921-0323
Contact: Steve Krueger
R4

Grantsburg
North Country Metals
213 N. Pine Street
Grantsburg, WI 54840
Tel: (715) 463-5334
Contact: Ann Anmundson
MFR of *T*

Green Bay
Bach Mobilities, Inc.
1000 Centennial Street
Green Bay, WI 54304
Tel: (414) 432-7575
Nation: (800) 828-2224
Contact: Don Ferenbach or Dee Benson
H'cap R4

Green Bay
NEW Vans & Custom
1800 Velp Avenue
Green Bay, WI 54303
Tel: (414) 499-3991
FAX: (608) 499-8531
Contact: Scott Wesa
TConvs

Green Bay
Olson Trailer & Body Builder Company
2740 S. Ashland Avenue
Green Bay, WI 54304
Tel: (414) 499-0881
Contact: Roger Yakel
MFR of *T*

Green Bay
Witt Intensive Care
3201 Market Street
Green Bay, WI 54304
Tel: (414) 336-9488
Contact: Graig Zachman
R4, H'cap R4

Jackson
Jackson Body Co., Inc.
N. 168 W. 20640 Main St
Jackson, WI 53037
Tel: (414) 677-3133
WI only: (800) 491-4133
FAX: (414) 677-4675
Contact: William Tilbert
MFR of *T, TB*

Janesville
Auto Magic
265 S. River Street
Janesville, WI 53545
Tel: (608) 756-2886
Contact: Mike Olver
R4

Janesville
Featherlite Trailers Division - Fagan
3601 E. Milwaukee
Janesville, WI 53546
Tel: (608) 752-1331
Contact: Pat Fagan
DLR of *T*
B-2:12

Janesville
GM Corp. Truck & Bus
1000 Industrial Avenue
Janesville, WI 53546
Tel: (608) 756-7791
Contact: Nick Matich
MFR of *TB*
D: Jadco

Janesville
Morgan Corporation
2 Morgan Way
Janesville, WI 53545
Tel: (608) 756-4577
Contact: Roger Cardoni
MFR of *TB*

Kenosha
State Line Caps & Custom Truck Center
12700 Green Bay Road
Kenosha, WI 53142
Tel: (414) 694-1818
Contact: Mike Jensen
R4

La Crosse
Bruin Enterprises
1708 Barnabee Road
La Crosse, WI 54601
Tel: (608) 788-6957
Contact: Mike Jerraue
R4

La Crosse
Midwest Off-Road Center, Incorporated
20 Copeland Avenue
La Crosse, WI 54603
Tel: (608) 784-9980
Nation: (800) 626-1001
FAX: (608) 784-1330
Contact: Greg Gerlack
R4

Lake Geneva
Geneva Fontana Specialty Vehicles
1070 Carey Street
P.O. Box 879
Lake Geneva, WI 53147
Tel: (414) 248-0244
Nation: (800) 248-0244
FAX: (414) 248-5628
Contact: Dave Jones
MFR of *R4, H'cap R4, Blazer Convs, Suburban Convs, TConvs*
NOTE: *Formerly CTI. Several plants are located on Carey Street; all are reached via the above phone numbers.*

Lake Geneva
Leathercraft of Wisconsin
1065 Carey Street, #B
Lake Geneva, WI 53147
Tel: (414) 248-5630
Contact: Marge Woodley
R4

Madison
Custom RV Services, Inc.
4107 Hansen Road
Madison, WI 53704
Tel: (608) 241-1412
Contact: Scott Skalitzky
R4

Madison
Fedele Auto Expo
2205 Rimrock Road
Madison, WI 53713
Tel: (608) 255-7110
FAX: (608) 255-5452
Contact: Denny Fedele
DLR of *R4, Trucks*

Madison
Madison Auto & Van Conversion
3802 Packers Avenue
Madison, WI 53704
Tel: (608) 242-4122
R4

Madison
Transit Auto Body, Inc.
4601 Pflaum Road
Madison, WI 53704
Tel: (608) 249-8030
Contact: Larry Johnson or Chip Wimmler
R4
C-2

Madison
Unique Vehicles
6140 Cottonwood Drive
Madison, WI 37019
Tel: (608) 277-0644
WI only: (800) 648-1346
Contact: Stephanie Shaw
R4

Madison
Wisconsin Bus Sales & Service
4212 Robertson Road
Madison, WI 53714
Tel: (608) 249-6460
WI only: (800) 346-6460
FAX: (608) 249-6454
Contact: Amy Kiefer or Tim Kiefer
DLR of *S*
C-2

Marion
Marion Body Works, Inc.
211 W. Ramsdell Street
P.O. Box 500
Marion, WI 54950
Tel: (715) 754-5261
FAX: (715) 754-2776
Contact: Curt Kjendelen or Dorothy Egdorf
MFR of *TB*
C-2

Marion
Welch Fire Equipment Corporation
930 E. Prospect Avenue
Marion, WI 54950
Tel: (715) 754-5225
MFR of *F*

Mauston
Bar-Bel Fabricating Company, Incorporated
N. 3760 Hwys. 12 & 16
Mauston, WI 53948
Tel: (608) 847-4131
Nation: (800) 468-0345
FAX: (608) 847-6911
Contact: Janelle Fleggy
MFR of *Tanker T*

Menasha
Toys for Trucks
W. 7158 US Highway 10 #114
Menasha, WI 54952
Tel: (414) 734-4272
Contact: Mike Larson
TConvs

Menomonee Falls
Beta Mfg. Co., Inc.
W. 161 N. 9116
Menomonee Falls, WI 53051
Tel: (414) 251-2677
FAX: (414) 251-5832
Contact: Stan Waller
MFR of *T*

Merrill
Geri-Vans
W. 4599 Pope Road
Merrill, WI 54452
Tel: (715) 536-7900
H'cap R4

Milwaukee
Business Vans, Inc.
6944 N. Teutonia Avenue
Milwaukee, WI 53209
Tel: (414) 351-5611
Contact: Ed Hdorosky
R4

Milwaukee
Caravans, Incorporated
424 W. Cherry Street
Milwaukee, WI 53212
Tel: (414) 264-2000
FAX: (414) 264-7460
Contact: John Doherty
R4
C-2

Milwaukee
Custom Craft Vehicles
960 W. Armour Avenue
Milwaukee, WI 53221
Tel: (414) 744-8118
FAX: (414) 744-8123
Contact: Andy Varbeski
MFR of *R4*

Milwaukee
F. Barkow, Incorporated
2830 N. Fratney Street
Milwaukee, WI 53212
Tel: (414) 332-7311
Nation: (800) 558-5580
FAX: (414) 332-8217
MFR of *Glass-Rack TB*

Milwaukee
Meda-Care Vans, Inc.
424 W. Cherry Street
Milwaukee, WI 53212
Tel: (414) 264-7433
H'cap R4

Milwaukee
Mobility Unlimited, Inc.
7030 W. National Avenue
Milwaukee, WI 53214
Tel: (414) 774-3085
FAX: (414) 774-8510
R4, H'cap R4

Milwaukee
Monroe Truck Equip.
11811 W. Silver Spring Drive
Milwaukee, WI 53225
Tel: (414) 462-7650
Nation: (800) 874-6900
Contact: Erica Schwoegler
DLR of *TB*

Milwaukee
Schesinger Chevy & Geo, Incorporated
8711 W. Brown Deer Rd.
Milwaukee, WI 53224
Tel: (414) 355-2500
Contact: Jim Johnson
R4

Monroe
Monroe Truck Equipment, Inc.
1051 W. 7th Street
Monroe, WI 53566
Tel: (608) 328-8127
Nation: (800) 356-8134
FAX: (608) 328-4278
Contact: Walt Althas
MFR of *F*
C-2:20

Neenah
Witt Intensive Care
2380 Holly Road
Neenah, WI 54956
Tel: (414) 734-9488
Nation: (800) 722-9488
Contact: Rick Monday
R4, H'cap R4
C-1 to Green Bay
(This is Corporate Headquarters.)

Neillsville
Abby-Vans
W 5821 Todd Road
Neillsville, WI 54456
Tel: (715) 743-3344
R4

Oshkosh
Leach Company
2737 Harrison Street
Oshkosh, WI 54901
Tel: (414) 231-2770
Contact: Erica Schmidt
DLR of *TB*
D

Oshkosh
Oshkosh Truck Corp.
P.O Box 2566
Oshkosh, WI 54903
Tel: (414) 235-9150
FAX: (414) 233-9624
Contact: Peter Losling
MFR of *F*

Pewukee/Waukesha
Peterbilt
(MAIL: P.O. Box 49
Waukesha, WI 53187)
N. 11 W. 24500 Hwy. TJ
Pewaukee, WI 53072
Tel: (414) 547-0001
Nation: (800) 558-0524
WI only: (800) 242-2033
MFR of *S-1*
C-2:20

Phelps
Wisconsin Trailer Co.
2527 SR 17
Phelps, WI 54554
Tel: (715) 545-2000
FAX: (715) 545-2693
Contact: Bev Mueller
MFR of *T*
B-2:2

Rice Lake
Johnson Truck Bodies Division
215 E. Allen Street
P.O. Box 480
Rice Lake, WI 54868
Tel: (715) 234-7071
Nation: (800) 922-8360
FAX: (715) 234-4628
Contact: Ron Ricci
MFR of *TB*
C-2
D: Auto Driveaway

Rhinelander
Lincoln Conversion
1478 Chippewa Drive
P.O. Box 1418
Rhinelander, WI 54501
Tel: (715) 369-5000
Contact: Pete Kowapash
CONVERTER of *Limos*

Schofield
Campmobile Vans
5403 Normandy Street
Schofield, WI 54476
Tel: (715) 359-4709
Contact: Marco Meade
R4

Schofield
Sport Cam Industries
9306 Weston Avenue
Schofield, WI 54476
Tel: (715) 355-1257
FAX: (715) 359-5672
Contact: Rob Zoromski
MFR of *R1*
C-2:1

Shell Lake
West Side Livestock Trailer
S. Semm Street
Shell Lake, WI 54871
Tel: (715) 468-7714
DLR of *LT*

Stevens Point
Advantage Vans
2523 Post Road
Stevens Point, WI 54481
Tel: (715) 341-2712
FAX: (715) 341-2736
Contact: Buryl Thompson
R4

Stoughton
Stoughton Trailers, Inc.
416 S. Academy
Stoughton, WI 53589
Tel: (608) 673-2500
Nation: (800) 227-5391
MFR of *S-2*

Valdera
A & J Vans, Inc.
333 Washington Street
Valdera, WI 45245
Tel: (414) 775-9333
FAX: (414) 775-4104
Contact: John Kuphs
R4
C-2:15-20

Waukesha
Jack Griffin Ford, Inc.
1940 E. Main Street
Waukesha, WI 53186
Tel: (414) 542-5781
Contact: Jim Griffin
DLR of *R4*

Waukesha
Joe Carini Lincoln-Mercury
1583 E. Moreland Blvd.
Waukesha, WI 53186
Tel: (414) 547-0031
FAX: (414) 547-6692
Contact: Dave Heidel
DLR of *Limos, F*

Waupaca
Traile-et
107 Tower Road
P.O. Box 499
Waupaca, WI 54981
Tel: (715) 258-8565
FAX: (715) 258-8593
Contact: Debra Braatz
MFR of *T*
B-2:4

West Allis
Excalibur Automobile Corporation
1735 S. 106th Street
West Allis, WI 53214
Tel: (414) 771-7171
FAX: (414) 771-8941
Contact: Dean LePoidevin
MFR of *Limos*
D

West Bend
Damon Corporation
805 Mulberry Drive
West Bend, WI 53095
Tel: (414) 338-9444
MFR of *R1, R2, R5, R6 and Mini Homes*
(This is only a Sales Office.)

West Bend
Unique Productions
1002 Decorah Road
West Bend, WI 53095
Tel: (414) 675-2748
R4

WYOMING

Buffalo
Bolinger Welding
141 Highway 16, East
Buffalo, WY 82834
Tel: (307) 684-5515
Contact: Kim Bolinger
MFR of *T*
C-1

Casper
Blair's Custom Trailers
5107 Abbott
Casper, WY 82604
Tel: (307) 235-3975
Contact: Wayne Blair
MFR of *Flatbed T, CT*

Casper
Cole Custom Coach
350 N. Beech Street
Casper, WY 82601
Tel: (307) 237-7512
Contact: Bill Cole
or Linda Cole
MFR of *R1*

Casper
RV Smith Sales & Service
3500 E. Yellowstone
Casper, WY 82604
Tel: (307) 234-5617
DLR of *R1, R2*

Casper/Mills
Teton Homes
(MAIL: P.O. Box 2349
Mills, WY 82644)
3283 North 9-Mile Road
Casper/Mills, WY 82604
Tel: (307) 235-1525
FAX: (307) 577-6027
Contact: Torry Ingrams
MFR of *R5, R6*
B-2

Cheyenne
Jolley Rogers RV & Truck
6102 E. Hwy. 30
Cheyenne, WY 82001
Tel: (307) 634-8457
Contact: Patty Jones
DLR of *R1, R2*

Cheyenne
Wyoming Steel Products
212 N. Avenue D
Cheyenne, WY 82007
Tel: (307) 634-8621
FAX: (307) 778-3091
MFR of *CT*

Dubois
Wind River Livestock & Trailer
4 Absroka Court
Dubois, WY 82513
Tel: (307) 455-3525
DLR of *LT*

Evansville
Ameri-Tech Equip. Co.
970 Oildale
Evansville, WY 82636
Tel: (307) 234-9921
FAX: (307) 234-3432
MFR of *UB*

Greybull
Stockwell Mfg. Co.
125 S. 6th Street
Greybull, WY 82426
Tel: (307) 756-4711
MFR of *TB, HT, LT, CT, XT, S-2*

CANADA

Manufacturers, Modifiers, Final Assemblers, and Selected Dealers of Recreational and Specialty Vehicles

ALBERTA

Bowden
White Line Mfg. & Distribution Co., Ltd.
Box 190
Bowden, AB T0M 0K0
Tel: (403) 224-3321
Contact: Elwood Fyten
MFR of *HT, GT, LT*
B-1

Calgary
Cascade Vans & Interiors
3831 12th Street, NE
Calgary, AB T2E 6M5
Tel: (403) 250-3861
R4

Calgary
Dwornik Welding, Ltd.
4226-C Ogden Road, SE
Calgary, AB T2G 4V3
Tel: (403) 262-9944
Contact: Mike Dwornik
REPAIR of *VTB, XTB*

Calgary
Intercontinental Truck Body
2915 21st Street, NE
Suite 109
Calgary, AB T2E 7T1
Tel: (403) 291-0524
DLR of *TB*
(This location is just a Sales office. See also Coaldale, AB.)

Calgary
Matt's Mfg., Ltd.
8512 44th Street, SE
Box 18, Site 4, RR 5
Calgary, AB T2P 2G6
Tel: (403) 279-9353
Contact: Steve Plesa
MFR of *T, UT, ST*

Calgary
Vantech Van Conversions, Ltd.
1420 40th Avenue, NE
Bay #2
Calgary, AB T2E 6L1
Tel: (403) 250-1159
R4

Coaldale
Intercontinental Truck Body, Ltd.
1806 11th Street
Box 1300
Coaldale, AB T0K 0L0
Tel: (403) 245-4427
Tel: (403) 345-6078
Nation: (800) 661-1030
Contact: Jake Van Seters
MFR of *Aluminum TB*
(See also Calgary, AB.)

Edmonton
Advanced Engineering Products
10498 17th Street
Edmonton, AB T6P 1V8
Tel: (403) 467-8891
FAX: (403) 467-0950
Contact: Don Campbell
MFR of *Specialty Tankers*
D: Tri-Line Expressways

Edmonton
Armand Truck Body & Body Works, Ltd.
6730 Yellowhead Trail
Edmonton, AB T5B 4J7
Tel: (403) 471-2258
MFR of *STB*

Edmonton
Custom Hoist & Truck Body, Ltd.
11233 67th Street, NW
Edmonton, AB T5B 1M8
Tel: (403) 471-5487
MFR of *TB*

Edmonton
Deluxe Van & Body, Ltd.
8825 126th Avenue
Edmonton, AB T5B 1G8
Tel: (403) 474-6411
FAX: (403) 474-5628
MFR of *T, VTB*

Edmonton
Edmonton Auto Spring Works, Ltd.
9502 102nd Avenue
Edmonton, AB T5H 0E3
Tel: (403) 422-6892
MFR of *UT*

Edmonton
General Body & Equipment, Ltd.
8124 Davis Road
Edmonton, AB T6E 4H2
Tel: (403) 468-5331
FAX: (403) 465-5301
MFR of *TB*
C-2 (AB only)

Edmonton
Roadway Trailers, Ltd.
6925 103rd Street
Edmonton, AB T6H 2J1
Tel: (403) 434-7576
Contact: Amol Shapka
MFR of *Industrial T*

Edmonton
Vantage Vans, Inc.
5705 99th Street, NW
Edmonton, AB T6E 3N8
Tel: (403) 438-1444
R4

Edmonton
Western Truck Equipment, Ltd.
4308 74th Avenue
Edmonton, AB T6B 2K3
Tel: (403) 466-8063
FAX: (403) 468-1577
Contact: Rob Pondgrass
MFR of *UTB, TB*
A-1

Lethbridge
Royal Trailer Company, Ltd.
226 36th Street, North
Lethbridge, AB T1H 3Z7
Tel: (403) 328-5835
FAX: (403) 328-0772
Contact: Dave Dubin
MFR of *CT*
B-2
D

Lloydminster
First Truck Centre, Inc.
5105 63rd Street
Lloydminster, AB
T9V 2E7
Tel: (403) 875-6211
DLR of *Trucks*
DPU drivers are used.

Medicine Hat
Wittke Waste Product
1496 Brier Park Crecent, NW, Box 1180
Medicine Hat, AB
T1A 7H3
Tel: (403) 527-8806
CANADA only:
(800) 387-8193
FAX: (403) 529-1821
FINAL ASSEMBLER of *G*

Red Deer
Superior Emergency Equipment, Ltd.
6430 Golden West Ave.
Red Deer, AB T4P 1A6
Tel: (403) 346-8884
MFR of *F*
C-2

Red Deer
Travelaire Trailer Canada, Ltd.
6702 Golden West Ave.
Red Deer, AB T4P 1A8
Tel: (403) 347-6641
FAX: (403) 346-6080
Contact: Bob McDonald
MFR of *R6*
B-2 (Canadians only)

Saint Albert
Pacemaker Vans, Ltd.
Rayborn Estates
St. Albert, AB T8N 5C5
Tel: (403) 459-0066
R4

Strome
Quicksilver Mfg., Ltd.
Box 160
Strome, AB T0B 4H0
Tel: (403) 376-3502
Contact: Jim Rasmussen
MFR of *Truck Tanks*
A-1

BRITISH COLUMBIA

Abbottsford
Hub Fire Engines & Equipment, Ltd.
3175 McCallum Road
P.O. Box 10
Abbottsford, BC
V2S 4N7
Tel: (604) 859-3214
FAX: (604) 859-5821
Contact: Mike Green
MFR of *E, F*
C-1

Abbottsford
L & H Leisure Vehicles, Ltd.
33177 S. Fraser Way
Abbottsford, BC
V2S 2B1
Tel: (604) 853-0381
Tel: (604) 853-ABBY
MFR/DLR of *"Abby Motor Coach" (R4, R4-B)*
NOTE: *Because no other dealers sell these, driving opportunity is very limited.*

Abbottsford
Western Canadian Recreational Vehicles, Ltd.
33541 MacLure Road
Abbottsford, BC
V2S 4N3
Tel: (604) 852-5731
FAX: (604) 852-6721
Contact: Don Kyle
MFR of *R1, R2, R3, R5, R6*

Aldergrove
Norco Trailer Mfg., Ltd.
3181 260-B Street
Aldergrove, BC
V4W 2Z6
Tel: (604) 856-3124
MFR of *T*

Burnaby
Howard Distributors
4550 Longheed Highway
Burnaby, BC V5C 2Z5
Tel: (604) 291-6474
FAX: (604) 291-0652
FAX: (604) 291-0796
Contact: Mike Meyer
MAJOR DLR of *Limos, H*
NOTE: *2nd FAX reaches Mr. Meyer directly.*
NOTE: *This dealer obtains all his units via DPU drivers that he sends to Ohio, from here. Drivers are insured by, and paid by, this dealer. Units are picked up from Superior Coaches, Lima, OH & Eureka Coach, Norwalk, OH.*

Burnaby
Pacific Coast Van & RV, Ltd.
7454 6th Street
Burnaby, BC V3N 4P9
Tel: (604) 525-6332
FAX: (604) 525-5663
MFR of *R4*
NOTE: *Driving opportunities extremely limited.*

Coquitlam
Quality Truck Bodies, Ltd.
#2 228 Cayer Street
Coquitlam, BC V3K 5B1
Tel: (604) 520-3220
FAX: (604) 464-1212
MFR of *TB*

Cranbrook
Freightliner of Cranbrook, Ltd.
301 Slater Road
Cranbrook, BC V1C 4Y5
Tel: (604) 489-4741
FAX: (604) 489-3153
Contact: Jack Chisholm
MFR of *Slide Kits for TB C-2*

Duncan
Promac Industries, Inc.
2940 Jacob Road
Duncan, BC V9L 3X9
Tel: (604) 746-5181
FAX: (604) 746-4799
Contact: Phil Humber
MFR of *T*

Fort Langley
Truck Specialists
#5 19695 96th Avenue
Ft. Langley, BC V0X 1J0
Tel: (604) 888-4606
REPAIR of *Heavy Duty Trucks*

Fort Saint John
Peace Country Freightliner/ Mercedes-Benz
11824 Alaska Highway
Ft. St. John, BC V1J 4H9
Tel: (604) 785-5655
FAX: (604) 785-0084
Contact: Joe Jackson
MFR of *S-1*

Kamloops
Freightliner/ Mercedes-Benz Truck Center
1867 Versatile Drive
Kamloops, BC V1S 1C5
Tel: (604) 374-6688
FAX: (604) 372-0883
Contact: Mike McPhee
MFR of *S-1*

Kamloops
Kamloops Mack Trucks, Incorporated
2065 W. Trans-Canada Highway
Kamloops, BC V1S 1A7
Tel: (604) 374-3883
DLR of *S-1*

Kelowna
Kelowna Freightliner Truck Sales
#103 2485 Ross Road
Kelowna, BC V1Z 1M2
Tel: (604) 769-7255
FAX: (604) 769-3032
Contact: Bob Boose
MFR of *S-1 D*

Kelowna
Reidco Metal Industries, Incorporated
4290 Highway 97, North
Kelowna, BC V1V 1M4
Tel: (604) 765-2941
FAX: (604) 765-2950
Contact: Rene Elyzen
MFR of *TB A-1 D*

Kelowna
Security RV Mfg., Ltd.
1345 Industrial Road
Kelowna, BC V1Z 1G4
Tel: (604) 769-2007
FAX: (604) 769-3544
MFR of *R5*

Langley
B & H Equipment, Ltd.
200 20628 Mufford Crescent
Langley, BC V3A 4P7
Tel: (604) 530-9764
MFR of *FTB, UTB*

Langley
Collins Manufacturing Company, Ltd.
9835 199-A Street
RR 5
Langley, BC V3A 4P8
Tel: (604) 888-2812
FAX: (604) 888-7689
Contact: Mike Sondergaard
MFR of *TB*

Langley
Dynamic Specialty Vehicles
201 19670 Landmark Way
Langley, BC V3A 7Z5
Tel: (604) 534-3500
FAX: (604) 534-6600
Contact: Bill Jones
MFR/DLR of *A, Paratransit Vehicles*
DLR of *Minibusses*
NOTE: *They obtain their Minibusses from Goshen Coach, Elkhart, IN, USA. Most are delivered by drivers originating at the plant. A few are picked up by regular workers for THIS company as C-1 drivers doing DPUs.*

Langley
Truck West, Ltd.
9737 197-B Street
RR 5
Langley, BC V3A 4P8
Tel: (604) 888-8788
REPAIR of *Heavy Duty Trucks*

Lumby
Timer Truck
Highway 6, Box 670
Lumby, BC V0E 2G0
Tel: (604) 547-2200
REPAIR of *Heavy Duty Trucks*

Maple Ridge
XTC Industries, Ltd.
23332 River Road
Maple Ridge, BC
V2X 7G1
Tel: (604) 467-1508
MFR of *R4*

Nanaimo
De Iago Trailer Manufacturing, Ltd.
4446 Wellington Road
Nanaimo, BC V9T 2H3
Tel: (604) 758-6658
MFR of *T*

New Westminster
Canadian Aerial
866 Derwent Way
New Westminster, BC
V3M 5R1
Tel: (604) 525-1074
FAX: (604) 524-0671
Contact: Hugh Spencer
MFR of *Cube VTB C-2 (deliver to USA only.)*

New Westminster
Commercial Body Builders, Ltd.
591 Chester Road
New Westminster, BC
V3M 6G7
Tel: (604) 526-6126
Contact: John Barker
MFR of *UTB*

Oliver
General Coach
9316 348th Avenue
P.O. Box 700
Oliver, BC V0H 1T0
Tel: (604) 498-3471
FAX: (604) 498-3240
MFR of *R1, R2, R5 DPU*

- 294 -

Penticton
Okanagan Mfrs., Ltd.
316 Dawson
Penticton, BC V2A 3N6
Tel: (604) 493-1535
FAX: (604) 492-6110
Contact: Pat Turner
MFR of *R4*

Prince George
Arctic Mfg., Ltd.
3323 Hart Highway
Prince George, BC
V2K 1M8
Tel: (604) 962-9631
FAX: (604) 962-7500
Contact: Blair Stender
MFR of *Logging T*

Prince George
Prince George Truck & Equipment
8982 Sintich Road
RR 8
Prince George, BC
V2N 4M6
Tel: (604) 561-1234
REPAIR of *Logging Trucks*
DLR of *Volvo and GM Trucks*

Quesnel
Campmaster Trailer Manufacturers
1216 Highway 97, North
Quesnel, BC V2J 4E1
Tel: (604) 747-1097
MFR of *T*

Richmond
Able Trailer Mfg., Ltd.
8900 River Road
Richmond, BC V6X 1Y7
Tel: (604) 278-0321
MFR of *T*

Richmond
Get-Away International Manufacturing, Inc.
9400 River Road
Richmond, BC V6X 1Y9
Tel: (604) 270-1152
FAX: (604) 273-0546
Contact: Paul Bergin
R4

Richmond
Minoru Truck Bodies
11860 Machrina Way
Richmond, BC V7A 4V1
MFR of *TB*

Richmond
Road Runner Trailer Manufacturing
7280 River Road
Richmond, BC V6X 1X5
Tel: (604) 278-3484
FAX: (604) 276-1494
MFR of *BT, CT*

Sidney
Professional Components, Ltd.
2974 Henry Avenue
Box 2175
Sidney, BC V8L 3S6
Tel: (604) 656-6165
FAX: (604) 655-4334
Contact: Dave Smith
MFR of *A*
C-2

Smithers
RSP Energy, Ltd.
2965 Tatlow Road
P.O. Box 3637
Smithers, BC V0J 2N0
Tel: (604) 847-4301
FAX: (604) 847-4432
MFR of *TB*
C-1

Surrey
Brentwood Trailer Manufacturing Company, Ltd.
7800 Anvil Way
Surrey, BC V3W 4H7
Tel: (604) 590-8108
MFR of *M, Construction M, Logging S-2, other S-2*

Surrey
Columbia Remtek, Inc.
19325-B 96th Avenue
Surrey, BC V4N 4C4
Tel: (604) 888-9211
FAX: (604) 888-9011
MFR of *T*
B-1

Surrey
Intercontinental Truck Body
5285 192nd Street
Surrey, BC V3S 4N9
Tel: (604) 576-2971
Tel: (604) 649-3479
FAX: (604) 576-1304
MFR of *FTB, Cargo TB, GT, XTB, S-2*
C-1 (deliver within BC only.)
D: Their plant in Alberta ships to other locations.
NOTE: *Also mfr. a very unique R1 which has a built-in garage under the master bedroom!*

Surrey
Nahanni Industries, Ltd.
19500-C 56th Avenue
Surrey, BC V3S 6K4
Tel: (604) 533-4841
FAX: (604) 533-8400
Contact: Rich Vaughn-Smith
MFR of *Dump T*
A-1
D

Surrey
Peterbilt Truck Pacific, Incorporated
19470 96th Avenue
Surrey, BC V4N 4C2
Tel: (604) 888-1411
Nation: (800) 663-4693
FAX: (604) 888-0577
DLR of *S-1*

Terrace
Bytown Freightliner/ Mercedes-Benz Trucks
5408 Highway 16, West
Terrace, BC V8G 4V1
Tel: (604) 635-4938
FAX: (604) 635-9535
DLR of *Trucks*

Vancouver
ABC Dump Truck & Dispatch
3767 Penticon Street
Vancouver, BC
V5M 4H2
Tel: (604) 434-8811
RENTAL of *M*

Vernon
Anser Industries, Inc./ Anser Manufacturing
RR 5, Site 16, Comp. 21
Vernon, BC V1T 6L8
Tel: (604) 545-7070
FAX: (604) 542-0720
Contact: Randy Shultz
MFR of *Logging T*

Winfield
AGM Steel Industries
P.O. Box 100
Winfield, BC V0H 2C0
Tel: (604) 766-2424
FAX: (604) 766-2255
Contact: Dwayne Armeneau
MFR of *U Bodies*
D

MANITOBA

Brandon
Picadilly Trailer Sales, Ltd.
320 Highland Avenue
Box 355
Brandon, MB R7C 1A9
Tel: (204) 728-8570
FAX: (204) 725-3312
Contact: Darcy Snyder
DLR of *R1, R2, R5, R6, TC*
DPU drivers are used.

Rosemont
Midland Mfg., Ltd.
P.O. Box 249
Rosemont, MB
R0G 1W0
Tel: (204) 746-2348
FAX: (204) 746-2286
Contact: Jack Fleming
MFR of *T, CT*

Winkler
Load Line Mfg., Inc.
Box 2319
Winkler, MB R0G 2X0
Tel: (204) 325-4789
Tel: (204) 325-4378
FAX: (204) 325-4055
MFR of *Dump T*

Winkler
Triple E Canada, Ltd., RV Division
301 Robin Boulevard
P.O. Box 1230
Winkler, MB R0G 2X0
Tel: (204) 325-4361
Contact: Howard Ginter
MFR of *R1, R2*
C-2

Winnipeg
Arne's Welding
835 Mission Street
Winnipeg, MB R2J 0A4
Tel: (204) 233-7111
FAX: (204) 231-1252
Contact: Alex Maciejkow
MFR of *Dump T*

Winnipeg
Canadian Anglo Machine & Iron Works, Incorporated
2475 Day Street
Winnipeg, MB
R2C 2X5
Tel: (204) 222-2788
FAX: (204) 224-2502
Contact: John Prohaska
MFR of *CTB*
D: Tri-Line Expressways, Big Freight Transport, Rymer Transportation

Winnipeg
Chuck's Van Conversions
601 Washington Avenue
Winnipeg, MB
R2K 1M4
Tel: (204) 668-5011
R4

Winnipeg
Fort Garry Industries, Ltd.
460 McPhillips Street
Winnipeg, MB R2X 2G8
Tel: (204) 586-8261
FAX: (204) 956-1786
Contact: Rick Shshe
MFR of *F*
C-1

Winnipeg
Grainmaster Mfg., Ltd.
Lot 18, Springfield Road
Box 9, Station F
Winnipeg, MB R2L 2A5
Tel: (204) 224-1697
MFR of *Grain TB*

Winnipeg
Great West Van Conversions, Inc.
Box 33, Group A
RR 1-B
Winnipeg, MB R3C 4A3
Tel: (204) 338-9303
R4

Winnipeg
Motor Coach Industries
1149 St. Matthews Ave.
Winnipeg, MB R3J 0J8
Tel: (204) 786-3301
DLR of Tour *U*
D

Winnipeg
Van Craft
Box 11, Group 6-A
RR 1-B
Winnipeg, MB R3C 4A3
Tel: (204) 338-9305
FAX: (204) 339-1245
Contact: Richard Willard or Carl King
R4

NEW BRUNSWICK

Cap-Pele
Laundry Truck Body Manufacturing
RR 2, Box 8, Site 24
Cap-Pele, NB E0A 1J0
Tel: (506) 577-2878
MFR of *Laundry TB*

Centreville
BWS Mfg., Ltd.
P.O. Box 420
Centreville, NB E0S 1H0
Tel: (506) 276-4569
FAX: (506) 276-4380
Contact: Paul Eggart
MFR of *ST*

Centreville
Metalfab, Ltd.
P.O. Box 8
Centreville, NB E0J 1H0
Tel: (506) 276-4551
FAX: (506) 276-3648
Contact: Alan Green
MFR of *F*
C-1, C-2

Hartland
Craig's Machine Shop, Ltd.
P.O. Box 328
Hartland, NB E0J 1N0
Tel: (506) 375-4493
FAX: (506) 375-4848
MFR of *T*

Moncton
Alniver
925 Champlain Street
Moncton, NB E1C 8R9
Tel: (506) 857-2222
Tel: (506) 634-2336
FAX: (506) 858-0265
Contact: Alfred Thebau
MFR of *T*

Saint Jacques
Dynamic Fiber, Ltd.
32 Rue Industriel
St. Jacques, NB E0L 1K0
Tel: (506) 739-6666
FAX: (506) 735-7444
Contact: Bob Cyr
MFR of *Fiberglass TB*

Saint John
G. R. Patstone, Ltd.
P.O. Box 1081
St. John, NB E2L 4E9
Tel: (506) 633-7602
FAX: (506) 634-1445
Contact: Al Thompson
MFR/INSTALLER of *TB*

Saint John
Universal Sales, Ltd.
1150 Fairville Boulevard
St. John, NB E2M 3W2
Tel: (506) 634-2300
FAX: (506) 634-2324
Contact: Dom Leger
REPAIR of *Trucks*
(This is the TB Division)

NEWFOUNDLAND & LABRADOR

Saint Johns
Royal Freightliner/ Division of Royal Garage
P.O. Box 1210
St. Johns, NF A1C 5N2
Tel: (709) 745-3406
FAX: (709) 745-6309
Contact: Eric Arsenault
DLR of *Freightliner Trucks*
C-2

NOVA SCOTIA

Amherst
General Eastern Homes, Ltd.
283 Church Street
Amherst, NS B4H 3E2
Tel: (902) 667-1600
FAX: (902) 667-0212
MFR of *R2*

Dartmouth
CTS Container & Trailer Services, Ltd.
120 Joseph Zatzman Dr.
Dartmouth, NS B3B 1M4
Tel: (902) 468-1960
FAX: (902) 468-2072
Contact: Andrew Allardice
MFR of *T, ST, TB*
C-1 (Local)

Truro
Nova Enterprises, Ltd.
Exit 13, Highway 102
Box 1229
Truro, NS B2N 5N2
Tel: (902) 895-6381
FAX: (902) 893-7603
Contact: Bruce Morrison
MFR of *S-1*
C-1

Truro
Wilson's Truck Bodies
Box 808, Meadow Drive
Truro, NS B2N 5E8
Tel: (902) 895-2848
FAX: (902) 893-3523
Contact: Harold Goswell
MFR of *TB*
D: FOB Truro

Wolfville
Lantz Truck Body, Ltd.
Belcher Street
Wolfville, NS B0P 1X0
Tel: (902) 542-9797
MFR of *TB*

Yarmouth
Tri-Star Industries, Ltd.
88 Forest Street
Yarmouth, NS B5A 4B4
Tel: (902) 742-9254
Contact: Keith Condon
CONVERTER of *Vehicles*

ONTARIO

Aurora
Riexinger Tankers
16 Fortecon Drive
Aurora, ON L0H 1G0
Tel: (905) 727-0670
FAX (905) 727-6139
Contact: Roy Riexinger
MFR of *Stainless Steel Milk Tankers*

Aylmer
Wiltsie Truck Bodies, Ltd.
686 Talbot, West
Box 216
Aylmer, ON N5H 2R9
Tel: (519) 773-2066
FAX: (519) 765-1432
MFR of *TB*
C-1

Azilda
Sudbury Custom Vans, Ltd.
200 Notre Dame, West
Azilda, ON P0M 1B0
Tel: (705) 983-2442
R4

Barrie
Canadian Crane & Hoist Manufacturing, Ltd.
75 Welham Road
RR 8
Barrie, ON L4M 6E7
Tel: (705) 726-5951
MFR of *Cranes*

Bolton
Multi-Van, Incorporated
375 Wilton Drive
Bolton, ON L7E 5T2
Tel: (905) 857-3171
FAX: (905) 857-0127
Contact: Diane Patterson
MFR of *TB*

Bond Head
Durabody & Trailers, Ltd
P.O. Box 12
Bond Head, ON
L0G 1B0
Tel: (905) 775-5338
FAX: (905) 775-8748
Contact: Lowell Tipping
MFR of *T*
D

Bothwell
Comptank Corporation
RR 2
Bothwell, ON N0P 1C0
Tel: (905) 695-2915
FAX: (905) 695-2114
MFR of *Tanker T & TB*
D: Trailer Transit

Brampton
Babcock Motor Bodies/ Commercial Vans, Inc.
12 Chelsea Lane
Brampton, ON L6T 3Y4
Tel: (905) 791-8100
FAX: (905) 791-8057
Contact: Mike Davis
MFR of *FTB, STB*
C-1

Brampton
Trailcraft Mfg., Ltd.
8 Tillbury Court
Brampton, ON L6T 3T4
Tel: (905) 450-1144
FAX: (905) 450-6327
Contact: Jim Selva
MFR of *BT*
C-1

Brantford
Canadian Blue Bird Sales Company
P.O. Box 880
Brantford, ON N3T 5R7
Tel: (519) 752-9700
FAX: (519) 752-9893
MFR of *S, U*

Brantford
Go Vacations Industries, Incorporated
66 Mohawk Street, Unit 7
Brantford, ON N3S 2W3
Tel: (519) 751-0033
FAX: (519) 759-5652
MFR of *R2, R4*
DLR of *TC*

Cambridge
Dynasty Vans, Inc.
190 Turnbull Court
Cambridge, ON N1T 1J1
Tel: (519) 622-3130
R4

Cambridge
Frink Canada
777 Laurel Street
P.O. Box 3040
Cambridge, ON
N3H 4S3
Tel: (519) 653-6234
FAX: (519) 653-2527
MFR of *TB*

Cambridge
MacDonald Steel, Ltd.
1556-C Industrial Road
Cambridge, ON
N3H 4S6
Tel: (519) 653-5795
FAX: (519) 650-0343
MFR of *Truck Cabs*
D

Cobourg
Larry's Custom Trailer Manufacturing, Inc.
Industrial Park Road
Cobourg, ON K9A 4K1
Tel: (905) 355-5154
MFR of *Dump T*

Concord
Breda Machinery, Ltd.
131 Staffern Drive
Concord, ON L4K 2R2
Tel: (905) 738-0456
FAX: (905) 738-7843
Contact: Tony Breda
MFR of *Low-bed T*

Concord
Westdale Enterprises, Incorporated
15 Connie Crescent, #29
Concord, ON L4K 1L3
Tel: (905) 738-0778
MFR of *Custom R1*
C-2:4

Cornwall
Gravely Trailer Sales
2215 Vincent Massery Dr.
Cornwall, ON L4K 2R2
Tel: (613) 933-3200
DLR of *R5*
DPU drivers are used.

Cornwall
Travelite Trailers, Inc.
P.O. Box 134
Cornwall, ON K6H 5S7
Tel: (613) 931-1006
FAX: (613) 931-1464
RENTAL of *S-2*

Dundalk
Alumi-Bunk Corporation
P.O. Box 130
Dundalk, ON N0C 1B0
Tel: (519) 923-2016
FAX: (519) 923-2672
Contact: Eric Jain
MFR of *Sleeper Bunks, Dump T*
C-1

Elmira
Explorer Fabricating, Incorporated
53 Arthur Street, North
Elmira, ON N3B 2Z7
Tel: (519) 669-5720
FAX: (519) 669-8331
MFR of *LT*

Enterprise
Doyle's RV & Custom Vans
Main Street
Enterprise, ON K0K 1Z0
Tel: (613) 358-2241
R4

Grimsby
ABI Leisure
726 Broad Street, East
Grimsby, ON N1A 2X2
Tel: (905) 774-8891
FAX: (905) 774-7153
Contact: Dan Naylor
MFR of *R6*
D: RV Driveaway

Guelph
Walinga, Incorporated
RR 5
Guelph, ON N1H 6J2
Tel: (519) 824-8520
FAX: (519) 824-5651
Contact: Terry Medemblik
MFR of *T*

Hamilton
Cascade Truck Bodies
95 Cascade Street
Hamilton, ON L8E 3S7
Tel: (416) 573-8100
MFR of *TB*

Hamilton
Excel Fiberglass
36 Morley Street
Hamilton, ON L8H 3R7
Tel: (905) 561-8112
MFR of *Fiberglass TB*

Hanover
Hanover Truck Bodies, Ltd.
631 13th Avenue
Hanover, ON N4N 3O3
Tel: (519) 364-2070
MFR of *TB*

Havelock
Marten Mfg., Ltd.
Concession Street, North
P.O. Box 134
Havelock, ON K0L 1Z0
Tel: (705) 778-3371
Contact: Jeff Taylor
MFR of *T*

Hearst
Maurice Welding Shop, Incorporated
Highway 11, East
P.O. Box 538
Hearst, ON P0L 1N0
Tel: (705) 372-1331
FAX: (705) 362-7024
Contact: Marcel Boissonneault
MFR of *T*

Hensall
General Coach
73 Mill Street
P.O. Box 10
Hensall, ON N0M 1X0
Tel: (519) 262-2600
FAX: (519) 262-2340
MFR of *R1, R2, R5*

Keswick
JC Trailers & Equipment, Ltd.
25975 Woodbine
Keswick, ON L4P 3E9
Tel: (905) 889-0280
FAX: (905) 476-6751
Contact: John Csiki
MFR of *Industrial T*

Kitchener
Home Park & Motorhomes
100 Shirley Avenue
Kitchener, ON N2B 2E1
Tel: (519) 745-1169
FAX: (519) 745-1160
Contact: Ray Wickham
MFR of *R4*

Kitchener
Sturdy Truck Body, Ltd.
196 River Bend Drive
Kitchener, ON N2B 2G8
Tel: (619) 743-0224
MFR of *TB*

Lindsay
Clarke Trailers
RR 2
Lindsay, ON K9V 4R2
Tel: (705) 324-2700
MFR of *HT, LT*

Lindsay
Fleetwood Canada, Ltd./Industries of Ontario, Ltd.
70 Mt. Hope Street
P.O. Box 485
Lindsay, ON K9V 4R5
Tel: (705) 324-0095
FAX: (705) 324-8370
MFR of *R1, R5, R6*

Listowel
Starcraft Recreational Products, Ltd.
801 Tremaine Ave., South
RR 4
Listowel, ON N4W 3G9
Tel: (519) 291-1391
MFR of *R4*
NOTE: *Driver opportunity for students! "Sometimes it's hard to find a student to drive."*

London
Contran Mfg., Ltd.
529 Phillips Street
London, ON N6B 1A1
Tel: (519) 433-6147
FAX: (519) 433-6149
Contact: Jim Balch
MFR of *TB*
D

London
General Motors of Canada, Ltd.
P.O. Box 5160
London, ON N6A 4N5
Tel: (519) 452-5000
Contact: Patricia Giniac
MFR of *Armored Cars*
C-2

Markham
Marine Cradle Shop
66 Bullock Drive, Unit 4
Markham, ON L3P 3P2
Tel: (905) 294-3507
MFR of *BT*

Millgrove
Taylor's Travel Center
915 Highway 6
Millgrove, ON L0R 1V0
Tel: (905) 689-8609
FAX: (905) 689-6167
Contact: Brad Taylor
CUSTOMIZER of *R5*

Mississauga
Alcan Truck Bodies
6450 Viscount Road
Mississauga, ON
L4V 1H3
Tel: (905) 672-2460
MFR of *TB*

Mississauga
Canadian Kenworth Company
6711 Mississauga
Mississauga, ON
L5N 4J8
Tel: (905) 858-7000
FAX: (905) 858-2971
MFR of *Trucks*

Mississauga
Dominion Truck Bodies, Ltd.
1375 Britannia Road, East
Mississauga, ON
L4W 1C7
Tel: (905) 670-7470
MFR of *TB*

Mississauga
Freightliner of Canada, Ltd.
3880 Nashua Drive
Mississauga, ON
L4H 1M5
Tel: (905) 677-4961
Corporate HQ

Mississauga
Ontario Bus Industries, Incorporated
5395 Maingate Drive
Mississauga, ON
L4W 1G6
Tel: (905) 625-9510
FAX: (905) 625-5218
Contact: Patrick Scully
MFR of *Transit U*
C-2

Mississauga
Superior Custom Vans
9412 Haines Road
Units 1, 2, 3, & 4
Mississauga, ON
L4Y 1Y6
Tel: (905) 273-7956
R4

Mississauga
Thru-Way Trailer
3611 Erindale Station Rd.
Mississauga, ON
L5C 2S9
Tel: (905) 270-4611
FAX: (905) 270-9848
Contact: Jerry Collis
MFR of *S-2*

Mississauga
Wilcox Bodies, Ltd.
6215 Mississauga Rd., N.
Mississauga, ON
L5N 1A4
Tel: (905) 826-3722
FAX: (905) 826-4585
Contact: Doug Jane
MFR of *TB*
C-2

Mount Albert
TJ Welding, Ltd.
Highway 48
P.O. Box 98
Mount Albert, ON
L0G 1M0
Tel: (905) 473-2504
FAX: (905) 473-6886
Contact: Frank Goneau
MFR/REPAIR of *T*

New Liskeard
Mik Mak Fabrication, Ltd.
RR 1
New Liskeard, ON
P0J 1P0
Tel: (705) 647-4667
FAX: (705) 647-8222
MFR of *Sleeper Cabs for S-1*
C-1

North York
Yamaha Motor Canada, Ltd.
480 Gordon Baker Road
North York, ON
M2H 3B4
Tel: (416) 498-1911
Corporate HQ for Canada

Norwich
Holland Equipment, Ltd.
20 Phoebe Street
P.O. Box 339
Norwich, ON N0J 1P0
Tel: (519) 863-3414
FAX: (519) 863-2398
Contact: Dan Hunski
MFR of *T*
C-2

Oakville
Firan Corporation
353 Iroquois Shore Road
Oakville, ON L6H 1M3
Tel: (905) 844-2870
FAX: (905) 844-2907
Corporate HQ

Oakville
Ford Motor Company of Canada, Ltd.
Canadian Road
Box 2000
Oakville, ON L6J 5E4
Tel: (905) 845-2511
ASSEMBLER of *Trucks*

Orillia
IMT Cranes Canada, Ltd.
385 West Street, South
Orillia, ON L3V 6K8
Tel: (705) 325-7458
FAX: (905) 325-7624
MFR of *Crane Trucks*

Oshawa
General Motors of Canada
1908 Colonel Sam Drive
Oshawa, ON L1H 8P7
Tel: (905) 644-5000
MFR of *Trucks, Cars*

Oshawa
Motor City Trailer Manufacturing, Ltd.
555 Hastings Avenue
Oshawa, ON L1H 7R5
Tel: (416) 723-3457
MFR of *T*

Oshawa
PK Welding & Fabrication, Ltd.
747 Bloor Street, West
Oshawa, ON L1J 5Y6
Tel: (905) 571-1701
FAX: (905) 571-3483
MFR of *E, R, T*

Ottawa
Capitol Truck Bodies
1461 Star Top Road
Ottawa, ON K1G 3W5
Tel: (613) 745-6327
MFR of *TB*

Ottawa
Luxury Motor Homes
Highway 17 & 155, South
RR 2, Carlton Place
Ottawa, ON K2C 3V3
Tel: (613) 257-1299
FAX: (613) 257-4586
DLR of *R1, R2, R5, R6*
C-1 (Canada only)

Ottawa
Malmberg Truck Trailer Equipment, Incorporated
1621 Michael Street
Ottawa, ON K1B 3T6
Tel: (613) 741-3360
MFR of *UTB*

Ottawa
Vans Plus, Ltd.
888 Boyd Avenue
Ottawa, ON K2A 2E3
Tel: (613) 728-8530
FAX: (613) 728-5895
R4

Peterborough
Bruce Custom Fabricating
RR 1
Chemong Road
Peterborough, ON
K9J 6X2
Tel: (705) 743-0414
FAX: (705) 743-0434
MFR of *Bunk T for Boats*
B-1

Petrolia
Jay-B Van Conversions
4525 Petrolia
Petrolia, ON N0N 1R0
Tel: (619) 882-3410
R4

Renfrew
Renfrew RV
620 Stewart Street
Renfrew, ON K7V 4A6
Tel: (613) 432-9051
FAX: (613) 432-7816
Contact: Doug Kinnear
DLR of *R1, R2, R5, R6*

Ridgetown
Waltron
55 Marsh Street
P.O. Box 99
Ridgetown, ON N0P 2C0
Tel: (519) 674-5488
FAX: (519) 674-5480
Contact: Ron McLain
MFR of *BT*
B-2
D

Scarborough
Fiba Canning, Inc.
2651 Markham Road
Scarborough, ON
M1X 1X4
Tel: (416) 299-1142
FAX (416) 299-0349
Contact: Jerry Marsiske
MFR of *T*

Scarborough
General Motors of Canada, Ltd.
1901 Eglinton Ave., East
Scarborough, ON
M1L 2L8
Tel: (416) 750-2500
Corporate HQ for GM Union Personnel

Scarborough
Scarborough Metal
285 Raleigh Avenue
Scarborough, ON
M1K 1A5
Tel: (416) 266-7132
FAX: (416) 266-0197
Contact: Andy Lange
MFR of *TB*

Scarborough
Truck Equipment & Service Company, Ltd.
2215 Midland Avenue
Scarborough, ON
M1S 3A7
Tel: (416) 291-6265
FAX: (416) 291-0604
MFR of *TB*

Stouffville
Earl Hoover's Machine & Welding, Ltd.
5892 Main Street
Stouffville, ON L0H 1L0
Tel: (905) 640-2712
FAX: (905) 640-2718
Contact: David Hoover
MFR of *TB*

Stratford
National Engineering & Science Accessories, Inc.
367 Water Street
P.O. Box 22001
Stratford, ON N5A 6S8
Tel: (519) 271-6710
FAX: (519) 271-6454
Contact: Sandon Cox
MFR of *TB*
D

Strathroy
Glendale RV
145 Queen Street
Strathroy, ON N7G 3J6
Tel: (519) 245-4540
Tel: (519) 245-1600
FAX: (519) 245-5149
Contact: Len McDougall
MFR of *R6*

Strathroy
Pollock Truck Rentals
#30 Highway 81, North
Strathroy, ON
N7G 3J6
Tel: (519) 245-3000
MFR of *TB*
RENTAL of *Trucks*
(This is the Corporate HQ.)

Sudbury
Northland Truck Sales, Ltd.
2050 Regent St., South
Sudbury, ON P3E 3T9
Tel: (705) 522-3630
DLR of *Trucks*

Sutton West
Vancraft Van Conversions
Highway 48, South
Sutton West, ON
L0E 1R0
Tel: (905) 722-6531
R4

Thunder Bay
Superior Custom Trailers, Ltd.
1185 Roland Street
Thunder Bay, ON
P7B 5M5
Tel: (807) 623-5107
FAX: (807) 623-9062
Contact: Henry Poirier
MFR of *Logging T*

Timmins
Porcupine Trailers, Ltd.
2010 Riverside Drive
Timmins, ON P4N 7W7
Tel: (705) 267-7195
FAX: (705) 268-9731
Contact: Mr. Jackie Larochelle
MFR of *Logging T*

Toronto
Advanced Vans, Ltd.
1872 Kipling Avenue
Toronto, ON M9W 4J1
Tel: (416) 241-9411
R4

Toronto
*Algood's Truck Bodies
(Div. of Alcan Corp.)*
6450 Viscount
Toronto, ON L4V 1K8
Tel: (905) 672-2460
FAX: (905) 672-3963
MFR of *TB Kits*
*D: K-Tryel,
Rymer Transport,
X-Press Transportation*

Toronto
Back Motor Bodies
391 Alliance Avenue
Toronto, ON M6N 2J1
Tel: (416) 763-5255
FAX: (416) 763-0293
Contact: Gabriel Falcone
MFR of *TB*
C-2
D

Toronto
Central Truck Body Company, Ltd.
820 Garyray Drive
Toronto, ON M8L 1X1
Tel: (416) 749-2447
MFR of *TB*

Toronto
Diesel Equipment, Ltd.
139 Laird Drive
Toronto, ON M4G 3V5
Tel: (416) 421-5851
FAX: (416) 421-7663
Contact: Sales Dept.
MFR of *TB*

Toronto
Lil' Al's Custom Vans, Ltd.
1194 Weston Road
Toronto, ON M6M 4P4
Tel: (416) 244-1665
R4

Toronto
Mack Canada, Inc.
1350 Queensway
Toronto, ON M8Z 1S5
Tel: (416) 255-1311
DLR/SERVICE of *Mack Trucks*

Toronto
Mond Industries
225 Evans Avenue
Toronto, ON M8Z 1S5
Tel: (416) 259-8405
FAX: (416) 251-1839
Contact: Pat Dilillo
MFR of *T*

Toronto
Toronto Vans, Ltd.
1498 Midland Avenue
Toronto, ON M1P 3B9
Tel: (416) 755-5500
R4

Toronto
Unicell, Ltd.
50 Industrial Street
Toronto, ON M4G 1Y9
Tel: (416) 421-6845
FAX: (416) 421-5182
Contact: Russ Hollingshead
MFR of *TB*

Uxbridge
L. B. Moore Company, Ltd.
RR 1
Uxbridge, ON L0C 1K0
Tel: (905) 852-9711
FAX: (905) 852-4897
MFR of *T*

Weston
Central Truck Body Company, Ltd.
820 Garyray Drive
Weston, ON M9L 1X1
Tel: (416) 749-2447
FAX: (416) 749-7495
Contact: Tom Varga
MFR of *Aluminum TB*

Windsor
Chrysler Canada, Ltd.
2450 Chrysler Center
P.O. Box 1621
Windsor, ON N9A 4H6
Tel: (519) 973-2000
FAX: (519) 973-2799
Contact: Sales Dept.
(FAX number reaches Sales Department.)
MFR of *Vans*
(All units are picked up by CPU drivers.)

Woodstock
Teledyne Canada Metal Products
460 Industrial Avenue
P.O. Box 366
Woodstock, ON
N4S 7X6
Tel: (519) 537-2355
FAX: (519) 537-8613
Contact: Bert Clay
MFR of *TB*

PRINCE EDWARD ISLAND

Vernon Bridge
Drake Truck Bodies
Vernon RR 1
Vernon Bridge, PEI
C0A 2E0
Tel: (902) 651-2782
FAX: (902) 651-2786
Contact: Mr. Allison Drake
MFR of *TB (All types)*
C-1

QUEBEC

Ayer's Cliff
Everest Equipment
1077 Westmount Street
P.O. Box 390
Ayer's Cliff, PQ
J0B 1C0
Tel: (819) 838-4257
FAX: (819) 838-5653
Contact: Ron Stewart
MFR of *M*
D: DeKato Brothers

Beauce
Manac, Incorporated
2275, 107e Rue C.P. 490
Saint George, East
Beauce, PQ G5Y 5C9
Tel: (418) 228-2018
FAX: (418) 227-3344
Contact: Dennis LaRochelle
MFR of *T*
C-1

Beloeil
Demers, Paul & Fils, Incorporated
28 Richelieu
Beloeil, PQ J3G 4N5
Tel: (514) 467-4683
FAX: (514) 467-6526
Contact: Yves Martin
MFR of *A, H, Limos*
C-2 (Canadians Only)

Chambly
Remtec, Incorporated
933 Simard
Chambly, PQ J3L 4B7
Tel: (514) 658-6671
FAX: (514) 658-9629
MFR of *T*
C-2
D

Granby
Parco-Hesse Corp., Inc.
1060, Rue Andre Line
Granby, PQ J2J 1J9
Tel: (514) 378-4696
FAX: (514) 378-3614
Contact: John Hannon
MFR of *Beverage T*
D

Laval
Fourgons Transit, Inc.
3600 Boul. Industriel
Laval, PQ H7L 4R9
Tel: (514) 382-0104
FAX: (514) 383-5636
Contact: Louie LeClair
MFR of *TB (All types)*

Montreal
Bedard Tanker
5785 Place Turcot
Montreal, PQ H4C 1V9
Tel: (514) 937-1670
FAX: (514) 937-2190
Contact: Nabil Attirgi
MFR of *Tanker S-2*

Notre-Dame-De-Pierreville
Caminos Pierre Thibault, Incorporated
297 Chenal Tardif
Notre-Dame-De-Pierreville, PQ
J0G 1G0
Tel: (514) 568-7020
FAX: (514) 568-3049
Contact: Carl Thibault
MFR of *E, F*
C-1

Quebec
Ideal Body, Incorporated
225 St. Sacrament Ave.
Quebec, PQ G1N 3X8
Tel: (418) 687-4040
FAX: (418) 587-1111
Contact: Bob LaRochelle
MFR of *TB (All types)*

Quebec
Phil La Rochelle Equipment, Inc.
250 2nd Avenue
Quebec, PQ G1L 3A7
Tel: (418) 522-8222
FAX: (418) 522-3115
Contact: Sylvie Verrolault
MFR of *T*
C-2 (Deliver within Canada only; all units going to the USA are picked up by CPU drivers.)

Riviere-du-Loup
Camions Freightliner Riviere-du-Loup
108 Rue Fraser
Riviere-du-Loup, PQ
G5R 1C8
Tel: (418) 862-3192
DLR of *Freightliner Trucks*

St.-Alexandre-D'Iberville
Jean-March Vigeant, Incorporated
497 Saint-Denis
St.-Alexandre-D'Iberville, PQ J0J 1S0
Tel: (514) 346-4089
FAX: (514) 346-6837
Contact: Jean-Marc
MFR/INSTALLER of *Sleeper Cabs for S-1*

St.-Evariste-de-Forsyth
Deloupe Trailers & Floats, Incorporated
120 Rue de Parc Industriel
St.-Evariste-de-Forsyth, PQ G0M 1S0
Tel: (418) 459-6443
FAX: (418) 459-6571
Contact: Eve Yves
MFR of *T*
C-2

St.-Felix-de-Valois
Bibeau Freres, Inc.
4611 Castel-d'Autrey
St.-Felix-de-Valois, PQ
J0K 2M0
Tel: (514) 889-5505
FAX: (514) 889-8166
Contact: Mr. Danielle Bibeau
MFR of *M*
D

St.-Gabriel-de-Brandon
Les Ateliers Beau-Roc, Incorporated
1750 Route 348 Ouest
Saint-Gabriel-de-Brandon, PQ J0K 2N0
Tel: (514) 835-3404
FAX: (514) 835-1033
Contact: Andre Rocheau
MFR of *M*
C-2
D: Je Boushad

St.-Pascal-de-Kamouraska
La Compagnie Normand, Ltee.
C.P. 608, 340 Dieme Rue
St.-Pascal-de-Kamouraska, PQ
G0L 3Y0
Tel: (418) 492-2712
MFR of *T (All types)*

St.-Philippe-de-Laprairie
Van Conversions
15 Edward VII
St.-Philippe-de-Laprairie, PQ J0L 2K0
Tel: (514) 659-1449
R4

Ste. Clair
Prevost Car, Inc.
35 Boul. Gagnon
Ste. Clair, PQ G0R 2V0
Tel: (418) 883-3391
FAX: (418) 883-4157
Contact: Michael Rochette
MFR of *Luxury U, Tour Busses, Luxury R1*
C-2

Sherbrooke
Diesel, Incorporated
(Div. of Kenworth Corp.)
1175 Galt, East
Sherbrooke, PQ G1J 1Y7
Tel: (819) 569-2575
FAX: (819) 569-2577
Contact: Gerard Laemilan
MFR of *S-1*

Terrebonne
Tibotrac, Incorporated
2900 Cote Terrebonne
Terrebonne, PQ J6W 5E1
Tel: (514) 471-7250
FAX: (514) 471-9411
Contact: Robin Tibault
MFR of *F*
C-2

Thetford Mines
Bonaire Leisure Industries, Incorporated
2885 Smith Boulevard
Thetford Mines, PQ
G6G 6P6
Tel: (418) 335-5259
FAX: (418) 338-9304
Contact: Serge Langlois
MFR of *R6, Folding R6*

Victoriaville
Poudrier Freres, Ltee.
C.P. 56, 430 Reu Cantin
Victoriaville, PQ
G6P 7E6
Tel: (819) 758-6223
FAX: (819) 758-6745
Contact: Marc-Aurele Cliche
MFR of *M*
C-1

SASKATCHEWAN

Battleford
Double D Truck & Body
122 Industrial Drive
Battleford, SK S0M 0E0
Tel: (306) 937-2255
DLR/REPAIR of *Trucks*

Drinkwater
Brown Industries, Ltd.
P.O. Box 63
Drinkwater, SK S0H 1G0
Tel: (306) 693-4992
FAX: (306) 694-5633
MFR of *Low-bed Canopies*

Estevan
Shelter Industries, Ltd.
200 Highway 18, West
P.O. Box 845
Estevan, SK S4A 2A7
Tel: (306) 634-7255
FAX: (306) 634-7597
MFR of *R6*

Humboldt
Commercial Industrial Mfg., Ltd. (CIM)
Highway 5, East
Humboldt, SK S0K 2A0
Tel: (306) 682-2505
FAX: (306) 682-4516
MFR of *TB (All Types)*

Kindersley
Boychuk Industries, Ltd.
1015 9th Avenue, West
P.O. Box 2110
Kindersley, SK S0L 1S0
Tel: (306) 463-6511
FAX: (306) 463-3511
DLR of *T, R1*

LaFleche
De Cap Trailer Manufacturing, Ltd.
Box 535
LaFleche, SK S0H 2K0
Tel: (306) 472-5506
MFR of *Belly-dump gobble T*

Pilot Butte
Lift-Off Stock Trailer Manufacturing
Box 539
Pilot Butte, SK S0G 3Z0
MFR of *LT*

Regina
Custom Creations, Ltd.
230 Hodsman Road
Regina, SK S4N 5X4
Tel: (306) 721-3333
FAX: (306) 721-1333
R4
C-1

Regina
Fort Garry Industries, Ltd.
1572 Elliott Street
P.O. Box 904
Regina, SK S4P 3B1
Tel: (306) 757-5606
FAX: (306) 781-7926
REPAIR of *TB*

Regina
Van-Decor Enterprises, Ltd.
RR 2
(6 miles W. on Dudney Avenue)
Regina, SK S4P 2Z2
Tel: (306) 525-5122
MFR of *R4*

Saskatoon
Crestline Coach, Ltd.
802 57th Street, East
Saskatoon, SK S7K 5Z1
Tel: (306) 934-8844
FAX: (306) 242-5838
Contact: Sales Dept.
MFR of *A*
C-2
D

Saskatoon
WRT Equipment
818 43rd Street, East
Saskatoon, SK S7K 3V1
Tel: (306) 244-0423
FAX: (306) 653-1292
Contact: Order Desk
MFR of *T*

EUROPE

SPECIAL NOTE: It may or may not be possible to pursue this lifestyle regularly in Europe. It is recommended that, should you go there, you contact. companies from this listing with the idea of taking a single run, and see what develops from there. Unlike the other continents, only a fraction of Europe's companies are presented in this book.

AUSTRIA

Salzburg
Ford Motor Company (Austria) KG
Fuerbergstr. 51
Salzburg 5020

Vienna
Oesterreichische Automobilfabrik Deaf Graef & Stift AG
Bruennerstr. 72
Vienna 1210

Vienna
Wolfgang Denzel Kraftfahrzengeaktiengsellschaft
Parkring 12
Vienna 1010

Vienna
F.M. Tarbuk & Co.
Davidgasse 90
Vienna 1100

BELGIUM

Antwerp
BMW Belgium N.V.
Pierstraat 229
Antwerp 2550

Brussels
Alfa Romeo Benelux S.A.
Ch. De Zellik 65
Brussels, Brabant 1080

Brussels
S.B.A. Citroen S.A.
Place De Liyser 7
Brussels, Brabant 1040

DENMARK

Copenhagen
Petersen Automobiler A/S Svend
Jagtvej 155
Kobenhavn, Copenhagen
DK-2200

Copenhagen
Skandinavisk Motor Co. A/S
Park Allee 355
Glostrup, Copenhagen
DK-2600

Haderslev
Diesel-Garden Haderslev A/S
Sverigesvej 4-6
Haderslev, Sjylland
DK-6100

Soeborg
General Motors Danmark
Tobaksvejen 22
Soeborg, Vsjaelland
DK-2860

FINLAND

Helsinki
Autonovo OY
Abraham Wetterintie 4
Helsinki, Uusimaa 00811

Helsinki
Suomen General Motors OY
Kutojatie 8
Helsinki, Uusimaa 00101

Jyvaskyla
Are Vhtymae
Aren Aukio
Jyvaskyla, Kesk-Suomi
40101

Vantaa
Korpivaara OY
Korpikontiontie 2
Vantaa 45
Vantaa, Uusimaa 00810

FRANCE

Anneyron
Lafuma SA
Route de St. Rambert
D'Albon
Anneyron, Drome 26140

Cohors
Quercymetal
Zone Industrielle
D'Eglandieres
Cohors, Lot 46001

Dreux
Veleclair
16 Rue de Moronval
Dreux, Eure-Loire 28100

Jarny
LeClerc SA
58 Av. de La Republigne
Jarny, Meur-Mos 54800

Paris
Chardonnet (STE)
48 Av. Kleber
Paris 75016

Saint-Nazaire
Ateliers de Constructions Mecaniques de L'Atlantigue
Le Point Du Jour
Saint-Nazaire, Lor-Atlan
44600

Seclin
Sterckeman (Caravanes)
211 Rue M. Bouchery
Seclin, Nord 59113

GREECE

Thessalonika
Katsaros Ippokratis & Sons S.A.
6 Aghion panton St.
Thessalonika, Mecedonia

ICELAND

Reykjavik
Hexla HF
Laugaegur 170-172
Reykjavik 105

REPIBLIC of IRELAND

Dublin
Austin Rover Ireland, Ltd.
Ballymount Cross
Ballymount Rd.
Walkinstown
Dublin 12

ITALY

Verona
Autogerma SPA
Via Germania 33
Verona, VR 37100

NETHERLANDS

Amsterdam
Leonard Lang BV
Daniel Goedkoopstraat 9
Amsterdam, NL 1009 DB

NORWAY

Kolbotn
Ford Motor Norge A/S
Kongeveien 47
Kolbotn, Akershus
N-1410

Kolbotn
Volvo Norge A/S
Mastemyr
Industriomraade
Kolbotn, Akershus
N-1410

Oslo
Motordrift A/S
Brynsengvelan 1
Oslo, Akershus N-1324

AUSTRALIA

Manufacturers, Modifiers, Final Assemblers, Selected Dealers, and Transporters of Recreational and Specialty Vehicles

NEW SOUTH WALES

Albury
Inter-Trucks Pty., Ltd.
330 Kiewa Street
Box 65
Albury, NSW 2640
Tel: (060) 21-1077
FAX: (060) 21-7477
Contact: B. Hully, SM
DLR of R4, Comm'l Vans, TConvs, M XTB, S-2
Hours: Mon.-Sat., 8-5:30

Albury
J.D. Phillips Pty., Ltd.
Corner of Young & Smollett Streets
Box 334
Albury, NSW 2640
Tel: (060) 21-2911
FAX: (060) 21-6617
Contact: W.M. Reid, Mgr.
DLR of BT

Alexander
Eimco Australia
65-A Ashmore Street
Box 131
Alexander, NSW 2015
Tel: (02) 517-1855
FAX: (02) 517-1566
Telex: 20027
Contact: G. Marsden
MFR of Mini-busses

Bankstown
Traction Controls Pty., Ltd.
47 Birch Street
Bankstown, NSW 2200
Tel: (02) 709-4144
Telex: 73316
Contact: D.A. Johnson
MFR of Electric Road Vehicles

Botany
Botany Cranes & Forklift Services Pty., Ltd.
1681 Botany Road
Box 181
Botany, NSW 2019
Tel: (02) 666-6366
A-H: (02) 669-1104
FAX: (02) 666-3601
Contact: C.O. Bourke
MFR of S-2

Broadmeadow
Kelrit Pty., Ltd.
Unit 12/50, Clyde Street
Box 81
Broadmeadow, NSW 2292
Tel: (049) 69-5277
A-H: (049) 32-6186
FAX: (049) 62-2370
Contact: K.D. Wethered
MFR of STB
Hours: Mon.-Fri., 7:30-4

Brookvale
Tracer Trailers Pty., Ltd.
28 Orchard Road
Brookvale, NSW 2100
Tel: (02) 938-1263
Tel: (02) 938-2614
Contact: R.J. Kemp
MFR of BT

Caringbah
LNC Industries Pty., Ltd.
86-90 Woodfield Blvd.
Caringbah, NSW 2229
Tel: (02) 525-8544
Tel: (02) 525-8332
FAX: (02) 525-7601
Telex: 20149 LSK
Contact: D. Fletcher
DLR of R4, Comm'l Vans, TConvs, M, TB & U Chassis

Carrington
Marlin Truck Bodies Pty., Ltd.
Young Street
Box 29
Carrington, NSW 2294
Tel: (049) 69-2006
Tel: (049) 69-6369
Contact: M. McNally
MFR of M, HTB, LTB, Oilfield TB, Refig. & Insul. TB, Tanker TB, STB, S-1
Hours: Mon.-Fri., 7:30-4

Chatswood
Boeing Sales Pty., Ltd.
20 Smith Street
Chatswood, NSW 2067
Tel: (02) 406-4404
Tel: (02) 406-5057
FAX: (02) 417-7185
Contact: G.W. Bruckner or U.K. Bruckner
DLR of BT

Chatswood
Volvo Australia Pty., Ltd.
350 Eastern Valley Way
Box 1033
Chatswood, NSW 2067
Tel: (02) 406-0011
FAX: (02) 406-4071
Telex: 26595
Contact: J. Walldorf
MFR of U, STB

Chester Hill
RFW Truck Mfg. Co.
(Div. of Permatrak Pty., Ltd-NSW)
56 Boundary Rd.
Box 76
Chester Hill, NSW 2162
Tel: (02) 644-1304
Tel: (02) 644-6708
FAX: (02) 644-8108
Telex: 73224
Contact: R.F. Whitehead
MFR of M, XTB

Darling Harbour
S & M Contract Furniture Pty., Ltd.
(MAIL: Box 3311 Sydney, NSW 2001)
Unit 6, Corner of Pyrmont Bridge Road & Union St.
Darling Harbour, NSW 2007
Tel: (02) 692-0000
Contact: R. Knapp
MFR of Light-duty UTB

Dubbo
Airlink Pty., Ltd.
Hangar 1, Dubbo Airport
Dubbo, NSW 2830
Tel: (068) 82-4435
Contact: A.Wayland or D. Miller
MFR of Aircraft Refuelling Vehicles

Homebush
Pathfinder Boatland Pty., Ltd.
31 Parramatta Road
Homebush, NSW 2140
Tel: (02) 764-2500
Tel: (02) 764-2947
Contact: R. Pym, GM
DLR of BT
Hours: 7 Days/wk., 9-5

Leichhardt
Ajax Sheet Metal Pty., Ltd
68 Jarrett Street
Leichhardt, NSW 2040
Tel: (02) 569-8026
Contact: G. Birchell
MFR of HT, HTB
Hours: M-Thur., 7:30-4
Fri., 7:30-1

Lidcombe
Commercial Welding Pty., Ltd.
8-10 Nicholas Street
Lidcombe, NSW
Tel: (02) 649-7759
Tel: (02) 649-5569
Contact: R.P. Beaver
MFR of *Tanker TB*

Lidcombe
Lansing Australia Pty., Ltd.
12 Carter Street
Box 161
Lidcombe, NSW 2141
Tel: (02) 648-0211
FAX: (02) 647-1287
Telex:121521 Lans
Contact: D. McEvoy, GM
MFR of *Industrial Vehs.*

Lismore
Lismore Machinery Co. Pty., Ltd.
59 Conway Street
Box 496
Lismore, NSW 2840
Tel: (066) 21-2591
Contact: B. Winterbon
DLR of *R4, Comm'l Vans, TConvs, Oilfield TB, 4WD Vehs., UTB, XTB, Mini-busses, S-1*

Liverpool
Viscount Caravans Pty., Ltd.
2-20 Orange Grove Rd.
Box 187
Liverpool, NSW 2170
Tel: (02) 602-1144
FAX: (02) 601-7348
Telex: 22776
Contact: P.H. Dykes
MFR of *R5, R6*

Milperra
Mercedes-Benz (NSW) Pty., Ltd.
75-89 Ashford Avenue
Box 52
Milperra, NSW 2214
Tel: (02) 771-1500
Contact: A.R. Dessaix
DLR of *M, LTB, Grain TB, Tanker TB, STB, XTB, S-1, Specialized Mobile Offices & Display Vehicles*

Miranda
U.D. Australia Pty. Ltd.
1 Kumulla Road
Box 453
Miranda, NSW 2228
Tel: (02) 525-0288
FAX: (02) 524-8981
Contact: R.A. O'Hara
DLR of *U, STB, Truck Chassis*

Moorebank
Fodens (Distributors) Pty., Ltd.
353 Newbridge Road
Moorebank, NSW 2170
Tel: (02) 602-9211
Telex: 23071
Contact: R.J. Ireland
MFR of *M, Tanker TB, Liquid Oxygen TB, STB, XTB, S-1, S-2*
Hours: Mon.-Fri., 8:30-5
Sat., 8:30-Noon

Moorebank
JRA, Ltd.
(MAIL: Box 59
Liverpool, NSW 2170)
Corner of Church &
Heathcote Roads
Moorebank, NSW 2170
Tel: (02) 600-0022
FAX: (02) 602-1759
Telex: 25375
Contact: A. Rae
MFR of *R4, Armored Cars, many types of U, Tanker TB, XTB, Medical Vans, Bookmobiles, HT*
Hours: Mon.-Fri., 8:30-5

Mortdale
Gritter Instruments Mfg. Co. Pty., Ltd.
61 Boundary Road
Box 30
Mortdale, NSW 2223
Tel: (02) 570-1477
FAX: (02) 570-1246
Contact: F. Gritter
DLR of *Mobile Dental Vans*
Hours: Mon.-Fri., 8-4:30

Murwillumbah
Ebbott & Fenner Pty., Ltd.
Prospero Street
Box 815
Murwillumbah, NSW 2484
Tel: (066) 72-2555
Contact: Mrs. V.E.K. Ebbott
DLR of *R4, M, VTB, U, S-2*

Murwillumbah
Partridge & Walker Pty., Ltd.
1 Brisbane Street
Box 107
Murwillumbah, NSW 2484
Tel: (066) 72-2788
Contact: D.R. Stainley
DLR of *R4, TConvs, Light-duty TB, Heavy-duty TB, S-1, M, U, Mini-busses*

North Ryde
Gilbarco Australia, Ltd.-NSW
Branch 12 Talavera Road
Box 63
North Ryde, NSW 2113
Tel: (02) 888-4888
Telex: 20832
Contact: P.M. Beverley
MFR of *Aircraft Refuelling Trucks*

Peakhurst
Scott's Refrigerated Freightways Pty., Ltd.
5 Lorraine Street
Peakhurst, NSW 2210
Tel: (02) 53-8123
Tel: (02) 534-4797
FAX: (02) 534-6438
Contact: D.J. Scott
MFR of *Refrig. TB*

Port Kembla
Garnock Engineering Co. Pty., Inc.
(Primbee Division)
Five Islands Road
Box 199
Port Kembla, NSW 2505
Tel: (042) 74-0388
Tel: (042) 74-0274
FAX: (042) 76-1313
Contact: N. Shearman
MFR of *Cement TB, Grain TB, Special-purpose Tanker TB*

Port Kembla
M & S Kembla Truck Bodies Pty., Ltd.
Lot B, Shellharbour Rd.
Port Kembla, NSW 2505
Tel: (042) 74-3003
Contact: A. Mori
MFR of *Low-boy T*
Hours: Mon.-Fri., 9-4

Pymble
Rheem Australia, Ltd.
(Container Products Div.)
9-11 Bridge Street
Box 520
Pymble, NSW 2073
Tel: (02) 488-9400
FAX: (02) 488-9455
Telex: 71431
Contact: B.A. Cridland
MFR of *Cement-carrying Vehicles*

Queanbeyan
Durelink Pty., Ltd.
10 Endurance Avenue
Box 487
Queanbeyan, NSW 2620
Tel: (062) 97-3177
Tel: (062) 97-6266
Contact: C.A. Besselink
MFR of *HT, XT*

Regents Park
Wreckair Pty., Ltd.
(MAIL: Box 184
Chester Hill, NSW 2162)
2 Chisholm Road
Regents Park, NSW 2143
Tel: (02) 645-4000
FAX: (02) 645-1506
Telex: 25285
MFR of *R1, R2, Light-duty UTB, Heavy-duty UTB, M*

Smithfield
Cryofab Industries, Ltd.
45 Sammut Street
Box 48
Smithfield, NSW 2164
Tel: (02) 609-1438
Telex: 72689
Contact: R. Beckhaus
MFR of *most types of Tanker TB, STB*

Smithfield
Hockney Alcan Pty., Ltd.
2-4 Dupas Street
Box 487
Smithfield, NSW 2164
Tel: (02) 609-4428
Telex: 23378
Contact: P.K. Hockney
MFR of *Cement TB, Grain TB, Insul. & Refrig. TB, Tanker TB, STB*
Hours: Mon.-Fri., 8-4:30

Smithfield
Panther Engineering Pty., Ltd.
193-197 Warren Road
Smithfield, NSW 2164
Tel: (02) 604-6300
Contact: J.E. Faulder
MFR of *S-2*
Hours: M-F, 8:30-4:30

Sydney
Daewoo Corporation
(Liason Office)
(MAIL: Box H157
Sydney, NSW 2001)
Suite 2120, Australia Sq.
Sydney, NSW 2000
Tel: (02) 27-8846
Tel: (02) 232-3701
FAX: (02) 233-5616
Telex: 24890
Contact: Tae-Hee Lee
MFR of *TB Chassis*

Sydney
Hastings Deering Corp., Ltd.
44 Market St., 19th Floor
Sydney, NSW 2000
Tel: (02) 290-1922
FAX: (02) 290-3992
Telex: 70390
Contact: C.W. Horsely
DLR of *R4, TB, S-1*

Sydney
Nichimen Company (Australia) Pty., Ltd.
9th Floor, Gulf House
55 Young Street
Box H90, Australia Sq.
Sydney, NSW 2000
Tel: (02) 251-1033
FAX: (02) 233-6040
Telex: 122093
Telex: 120295
Contact: H. Ebihara
DLR of *R4, Comm'l Vans, TConvs, Medium-duty TB*

Sydney
Nissan Motor Company (Australia) Pty., Ltd.
5th Floor, 66 Barry St., N.
Sydney, NSW 2060
Tel: (02) 925-0122
FAX: (02) 967-6818
Telex: 71519
Contact: P. McInerney or D. Levy
MFR of *Light-duty TB, Medium-duty TB, 4WD Vehicles*

Sydney
Peko-Wallsend Group, Ltd.
10 Loftus Street
Box R-211, Royal Exch.
Sydney, NSW 2000
Tel: (02) 250-1100
FAX: (02) 251-1558
Telex: 121107 Pkosyd
Contact: K.W. Halkerston
TRANSPORTER CO.

Sydney
Unicoopjapan (Australia) Pty., Ltd.
6th Floor, Barclays House
25 Bligh Street
Sydney, NSW 2000
Tel: (02) 232-5322
FAX: (02) 233-1135
Telex: 24522
Contact: M. Ozawa
DLR of *Coach Chassis*

Sydney
Vanreid Industries Pty., Ltd.
189 Elizabeth Street
Box E-18
Sydney, NSW 2000
Tel: (02) 264-6431
Contact: P.M. Reid
MFR of *STB*

Tamworth
Tamworth Hydraulics
(MAIL: Box W116 West Tamworth)
Corner of Barnes & Denison Streets
Tamworth, NSW 2340
Tel: (067) 65-7966
FAX: (067) 65-7327
Contact: D. Rowland
MFR of *STB*
Hours: Mon.-Fri., 8-4:30

Taren Point
Classic Trailers Mfg. Pty., Ltd.
126 Taren Point Road
Taren Point, NSW 2229
Tel: (02) 525-7599
FAX: (02) 525-9228
Contact: J. Besnard
MFR of *Low-boy T*
Hours: M-F, 8:30-4:30
Sat., 9-3

Taren Point
Theiss Toyota, Pty., Ltd.
(MAIL: Box 187 Caringbah, NSW 2229)
2-28 Alexander Avenue
Taren Point, NSW 2229
Tel: (02) 526-3333
FAX: (02) 525-9852
Telex: 21285
Contact: J.H. Conomos
MFR of *R4, Pickup Trucks, Light-duty TB, Medium-duty TB, 4WD Vehicles, M, U, Mini-busses, STB*

Unanderra
Brentwood Engineering Pty., Ltd.
Berkeley Road
Box 200
Unanderra, NSW 2528
Tel: (042) 71-7511
FAX: (042) 71-6845
Telex: 29230
Contact: J. Badman
MFR of *Fire-fighting T, Dump T, Lowboy T, HT, LT*

Vineyard
H.M. Kuipers & Sons Pty., Ltd.
31 Boundary Road
Vineyard, NSW 2765
Tel: (02) 627-1703
Contact: G. Kuipers
MFR of *STB*
Hours: Mon.-Fri., 7-4

Wallsend
Arthur Priestly Pty., Ltd.
John Street
Box 55
Wallsend, NSW 2287
Tel: (049) 51-1700
Contact: A. Priestly
MFR of *M, STB, XTB*
Hours: Mon.-Fri., 7-3:30

Wetherill Park
LNC Distribution Pty., Ltd.
(MAIL: Box 127 North Ryde, NSW 2113)
250 Victoria Street
Wetherill Park, NSW 2164
Tel: (02) 725-9111
FAX: (02) 725-2240
Telex: 20192
Contact: J. Richardson
DLR of *R4, Comm'l Vans, Pickup Trucks, UTB, S-2*

QUEENSLAND

Acacia Ridge
Denning
(Div. of JRA, Ltd.)
Landseer Street
Box 26
Acacia Ridge, Qld 4110
Tel: (07) 343-1151
Telex: 43022
Contact: W.E. Rolls
MFR of *U*

Acacia Ridge
Luya Julius
66 McCotter Street
Box 359
Acacia Ridge, Qld 4110
Tel: (07) 237-2000
Telex: 43415
Contact: K.D. Noyes
TRANSPORTER CO.
Hours: Mon.-Fri., 8-5

Archerfield
G.B.W. Operations
170 Beatty Road
Box 371
Archerfield, Qld 4108
Tel: (07) 277-7260
MFR of *U*

Archerfield
John Shephard Trailers Pty., Ltd.
999 Beandesert Road
Box 205
Archerfield, Qld 4108
Tel: (07) 277-6888
FAX: (07) 277-6218
Contact: D. Bryant
MFR of *M, TB Chassis*
Hours: Mon.-Fri., 7-5

Bulimba
Annand & Thompson Holding Pty., Ltd.
(Subsid. of LNC Ind. Pty., Ltd.)
30 Johnston Street
Box 146
Bulimba, Qld 4171
Tel: (07) 399-0999
FAX: (07) 395-7783
Telex: 41174
Cotnact: W.J. Thompson
DLR of *R4, Taxis, 4WD Vehicles, X-Country Vehicles*

Bulimba
Rheem Australia, Ltd.
55 Oxford Street
Box 7
Bulimba, Qld 4171
Tel: (07) 399-2122
FAX: (07) 395-7222
Telex: 40294
Contact: J.E. Bamford
MFR of *Cement-carrying Vehicles*

Bundaberg
Nev Loxton, Pty., Ltd.
4 Takalvan Street
Box 710
Bundaberg, Qld 4670
Tel: (071) 72-9911
Telex: 49605
MFR of *M, Medium-duty TB, Heavy-duty TB, 4WD Vehicles, S-2*

Carole Park
Fibre Glass Industries
28 Antimony Street
Carole Park, Qld 4300
Tel. (07) 271-1200
Contact: E.C. Stacy
MFR of *Insulated TB*

Chermside
Byrne Ford Pty., Ltd.
Cor. Hamilton Road & Charlotte Street
Box 63
Chermside, Qld 4032
Tel: (07) 359-8122
FAX: (07) 530-2513
Telex: 42202 BYRNFO
Contact: E.A. Byrne, GM
DLR of *R4, Oilfield TB, XTB, Bus Chassis*
Hours: Mon.-Fri., 8-5
Sat., 8-12

Coopers Plains
Bunnco Stock Crates Pty., Ltd.
(MAIL: Box 234,
Archerfield, Qld 4108)
112 Boniface Street
Coopers Plains Qld 4108
Tel: (07) 277-5132
Contact: B.S. Bunn
MFR of *LT, & S-2: LT*
Hours: 7:30-4

Darra
Brown & Hurley Used Trucks Pty., Ltd.
(MAIL: Box 107,
Brisbane Mkt., Qld 4106)
2632 Ipswich Road
Darra, Qld 4076
Tel: (07) 375-4021
FAX: (07) 375-3449
Telex: 40465
Contact: D. Muir
REFURBISHER of *TB*
Hours: Mon.-Fri., 8-4:30

Eagle Farm
Blackwood Hodge (Australia) Pty., Ltd.
(MAIL: Box 171,
Hamilton Central, Qld 4007)
Links Avenue
Eagle Farm, Qld 4007
Tel: (07) 268-2146
FAX: (07) 868-1220
Telex: 40225
MFR of *S-1*

Eagle Farm
Burnco
(MAIL: Box 85
Hamilton Central
Qld 4007)
981 Kingsford Smith Dr.
Eagle Farm, Qld 4007
Tel: (07) 268-5144
FAX: (07) 868-1070
Telex: 43656
Contact: R.W. Bruns, GM
MFR of *Tanker TB: Petroleum, Bulk Liquids, LP Gas, Acft. Refuelling*
Hours: M-F, 8:30-4:30

Eagle Farm
Embeess Pty., Ltd.
(Sub. of F. Rogers & Sons Pty., Ltd.)
(MAIL: Bx 145, Hamilton Central, Qld 4007)
39 Harvey Street
Eagle Farm, Qld 4007
Tel: (07) 268-4522
FAX: (07) 271-156
Telex: 43094
Contact: M.M. Rogers
MFR of *U, TB*
NOTE: *FAX & Telex both reach F. Rogers & Sons.*

East Acacia Ridge
Volgren Industries Coaches Pty., Ltd.
(MAIL: Box 169
Archerfield, Qld 4108)
11 Colebard Street
East Acacia Ridge, Qld 4110
Tel: (07) 277-8477
FAX: (07) 875-1064
Telex: 144788
MFR of *U*

Geebung
Austral Group-Mfg.
(MAIL: Box 170
Nundah, Qld 4012)
356 Bilsen Road
Geebung, Qld 4034
Tel: (07) 265-0555
FAX: (07) 265-6399
Telex: 42256 Auspec
Contact: D. Reeves, GM
MFR of U
DLR of *Double-deck U*
Hours: Mon.-Fri., 8-4:30

Maryborough
Tarrant's Pty., Ltd.
267 Adelaide Street
Box 132
Maryborough, Qld 4650
Tel: (07) 22-2999
Contact: A.H. Frank, GM
DLR *of R4, Pickup Trucks, Light-duty TB, Medium-duty TB, M, Bus Chassis*

Moorooka
Pinnacle Engineering Pty., Ltd.
Unwin Street
Box 46
Moorooka, Qld 4105
Tel: (07) 845-9055
FAX: (07) 892-4215
Telex: 40472 BR296
Contact: D. Hoggan or R.K. Pinna
MFR of *Stainless Steel Tanker TB*

Mount Isa
Bell & Moir Corp., Pty., Ltd.
81 Marian Street
Box 108
Mount Isa, Qld 4825
Tel: (07) 43-3066
Telex: 79945
Contact: J.B. Singh, Mgr.
DLR of *R4, M, 4WD Vehicles, XTB*
*Hours: Mon.-Fri., 8-5:30
Sat., 8-12:30*

Newstead
Cromack & Tranter Road Transport
75 Newstead Terrace
Newstead, Qld 4006
Tel: (07) 52-2193
Contact: F. Cromack
TRANSPORTER CO.

Newstead
Eagers Holdings/Retail Pty., Ltd.
95 Breakfast Creek Road
Box 41
Newstead, Qld 4006
Tel: (07) 253-9209 (Corp.)
Tel/FAX: (07) 252-3607 (Sales)
Telex: 40102
Contact: N.J. Heywood
DLR *of A, R4, M, UTB, XTB, S-2*

Newstead
Gilbarco Australia, Ltd.
(MAIL: Box 698,
Fortitude Valley, Qld 4006)
35-47 Longland Street
Newstead, Qld 4006
Tel: (07) 252-3121
FAX: (07) 252-2717
Telex: 41490
Contact: J.R. Ridley, Mgr.
MFR of *Aircraft Refuelling Trucks*

North Rockhampton
Chippindale Motor Co. Pty., Ltd.
Corner of Bruce Hwy. & Alexander Street
Box 5215
North Rockhampton, Qld 4701
Telex: 49007
Contact: R.W. Chippindale
DLR *of R4, M, LTB, U, Refrig. & Insul. TB, XTB*
Hours: 8:30-5:30

Nudgee
Forbes Engineering Holding Pty., Ltd.
14 Hurricane Street
Nudgee, Qld 4014
Tel: (07) 267-7400
FAX: (07) 267-7823
Contact: M. Forbes, Mgr.
MFR of *Special-purpose Tanker TB*

Nudgee
Hydraulics & Fabrication Pty., Ltd.
43 Raubers Road
Nudgee, Qld 4014
Tel: (07) 267-6511
FAX: (07) 267-8252
Telex: 40472 BR1156
Contact: D.D. Hunter
MFR of *S-2*

Nundah
Nundah Motors Pty. Ltd.
(Sub. of Eagers Holdings, Ltd. - Qld.)
Corner of Sandgate Road & Wood Street
Box 18
Nundah, Qld 4012
Tel: (07) 266-1333
FAX: (07) 252-3607
Telex: 40102
Contact: J.R. Menzies,
DLR *of R4, Pickup Trucks, Light-duty UTB, Heavy-duty UTB, A, LP-Gas TB*
*Hours: Mon.-Fri., 8:30-5
Sat., 8:30-1*

Richlands
Mack Trucks Australia Pty., Ltd.
(MAIL: Box 364
Darra, Qld 4076)
616 Boundary Road
Richlands, Qld 4077
Tel: (07) 375-3333
FAX: (07) 375-3469
Telex: 42306
Contact: N.C. Hewton
MFR of *M, Grain TB, LTB, UTB, Tanker TB, XTB, S-1, S-2*

Rocklea
Abaleton Pty., Ltd.
(MAIL: Box 389
Archerfield, Qld 4108)
24 Reginald Street
Rocklea, Qld 4106
Tel: (07) 277-7693
A-H: (07) 288-3346
Contact: J. Tanbe
MFR of *U, TB*
Hours: Mon.-Fri., 7-5

Rocklea
Drake Trailers
Andrew Street
Rocklea, Qld 4106
Tel: (07) 277-2448
Tel: (07) 277-5888
FAX: (07) 277-1248
Contact: J. McKay, Mgr.
MFR of *TB, Low-boy T*
Hours Mon.-Fri., 8-4:30

Rocklea
Duce Commercial Motors
(MAIL: Box 85
Archerfield, Qld 4108)
Ipswich Road
Rocklea, Qld 4106
Tel: (07) 277-5144
FAX: (07) 277-8802
Telex: 41446
Contact: D. Clamp
DLR of R4, M, LTB,
Grain TB, Insul. & Refrig.
TB, Tanker TB, STB,
XTB, S-2
Hours: Mon.-Fri., 8-5
Sat., 8-11

Rocklea
Haulmark Mfg. Co. Pty., Ltd./ Haulmark Trailers
(MAIL: Box 107
Archerfield, Qld. 4108)
1848 Ipswich Road
Rocklea, Qld 4106
Tel: (07) 277-3666
FAX: (07) 277-0296
Telex: 41695
Contact: B. Quinn
MFR of S-2

Rocklea
Hockney Alcan
(Div. of Hockney Pty., Ltd.)
(MAIL: Box 182
Moorooka, Qld 4105)
45 Suscatand Street
Rocklea, Qld 4106
Tel: (07) 277-2966
FAX: (07) 277-5471
Contact: L. Singleton
MFR of Tanker TB

Rocklea
Lusty Engineering Pty., Ltd.
100 Grindle Road
Rocklea, Qld 4106
Tel: (07) 277-7477
FAX: (07) 875-1296
Telex: 43408
Contact: G.R. Lusty
MFR of LT, Low-boy T

Rocklea
Wreckair Pty., Ltd.
Corner of Boundary Road
& Ipswich Road
Rocklea, Qld 4106
Tel: (07) 848-0325
Telex: 41827
Contact: C. Holmes
MFR of R1, R2, M,
Light-duty UTB,
Heavy-duty UTB
Hours: Mon.-Fri., 7-5

Scarborough
Jonkers Enterprises Pty. Ltd.
660 Oxley Avenue
Scarborough, Qld 4020
Tel: (07) 203-6611
A-H: (07) 285-1068
Contact: R. Jonkers
MFR of UTB

Southport
Lockhart Motors
70 Nerang Street
Box 381
Southport, Qld 4215
Tel: (075) 32-2622
Contact: D.S. Lockhart
DLR of Commercial
Vans, Pickup Trucks, TB
Hours: Mon.-Fri., 8-5:30
Sat., 8-12

Springwood
Springdale Caravan Mart Pty., Ltd.
3362 Pacific Highway
Box 129
Springwood, Qld 4127
Tel: (07) 208-2098
DLR of R6, UT
Hours: Mon.-Fri., 8-6
Sat., 8:30-5:30

Tenerife
Mayfairs Wholesale Pty., Ltd.
(MAIL: Box 75
Lutwyche, Qld 4030)
8 Skyring Terrace
Tenerife, Qld 4005
Tel: (07) 252-8016
FAX: (07) 252-4610
Telex: 41913
DLR of BT

Toowoomba
Allan Flohr Ford
Corner of Anzac Avenue
& James Street
Box 6247
Toowoomba, Qld 4350
Tel: (076) 34-3233
FAX: (076) 33-1785
Telex: 40030
MFR of Agricultural
Vehicles

Toowoomba
Rex Burrell Group
211 Anzac Avenue
Toowoomba, Qld 4350
Tel: (076) 34-2087
FAX: (076) 39-2087
MFR of R5, R6

Townsville
Mike Carney Toyota
Corner of Duckworth St.
& Dalrymple Road
Box 5088-MC
Townsville, Qld 4810
Tel: (077) 79-6799
FAX: (077) 79-6150
Telex: 47261
MFR of UTB

Townsville
Townsville Transport & Services Pty., Ltd.
122 Walker Street
Box TMC 5422
Mt. Isa House
Townsville, Qld 4810
Tel: (077) 72-1211
Telex: 47012
Contact: J.R. Casas, GM
TRANSPORTER CO.
Hours: M-F, 7:30-4:45

Virginia
Palm Machinery
1880 Sandgate Road
Virginia, Qld 4014
Tel: (07) 265-1799
Contact: G. Palm, GM
MFR of 4WD Vehs., M

Wacol
F. Rogers & Sons Pty., Ltd
(MAIL: Box 114
Darra, Qld 4076)
95 Industrial Avenue
Wacol, Qld 4076
Tel: (07) 271-1744
FAX: (07) 271-1156
Telex: 43094
Contact: M.M. Rogers
MFR of M, U

Wacol
Progress Mfg. Co. Pty., Ltd.
(MAIL: Box 75
Lutwyche, Qld 4030)
Viking Drive
Wacol, Qld 4076
Tel: (07) 271-1122
FAX: (07) 252-4610
Telex: 41913
MFR of BT

Wacol
Rosenthal Enterprises Pty., Ltd.
8 Priority Street
Wacol, Qld 4076
Tel: (07) 271-1477
Telex: 40472
Contact: G. Rosenthal
MFR of Fiberglass TB

Wacol
Western Star Trucks (Australasia) Pty., Ltd.
(MAIL: Box 415
Darra, Qld 4076)
72 Formation Street
Wacol, Qld 4076
Tel: (07) 271-1788
FAX: (07) 271-2047
Telex: 140989
Contact: R.M. Shand, GM
MFR of STB
Hours: Mon.-Fri., 7-5

Zillmere
Hagglunds Denison Pty., Ltd.
509 Zillmere Road
Box 62
Zillmere, Qld 4034
Tel: (07) 263-3133
FAX: (07) 263-3835
Telex: 40424
Contact: J. Rooney
MFR of Military
Personnel Carriers, STB

SOUTH AUSTRALIA

Adelaide
Commercial Motor Vehicles, Ltd.
(MAIL: Box 2238
Adelaide, SA 5001)
241 Flinders Street
Adelaide, SA 5000
Tel: (08) 244-1400
Telex: 82578
Contact: J.A. Crawford
MFR of STB

Adelaide
Yorke Motors Group of Companies
(MAIL: Box 1406
Adelaide, SA 5001)
271 Pulteney Street
Adelaide, SA 5000
Tel: (08) 223-4000
Telex: 89858
Contact: R.N. Sprod
DLR of R4, Pickup
Trucks, Medium-duty
Trucks, U, S-2

Blair Athol
Wreckair Pty., Ltd.
152 Grand Junction Road
Box 106
Blair Athol, SA 5084
Tel: (08) 349-4922
FAX: (08) 349-4948
Telex: 88124
Contact: M. Rich
MFR of R1, R2, M,
Light-duty UTB,
Medium-duty UTB,
Heavy-duty UTB

Cavan
Sheppard United Tankers Pty., Ltd.
(MAIL: Box 263
Blair Athol, SA 5084)
1184 Churchill Road
Cavan, SA 5094
Tel: (08) 262-2010
Contact: E.W. Butcher
MFR of *Stainless Steel Tanker TB*

Cheltenham
Maughan Thiem Motor Co. Pty., Ltd.
(MAIL: Box 108
Alberton, SA 5014)
1013 Port Road
Cheltenham, SA 5014
Tel: (08) 47-5588
Telex: 88162 Contact: A.B. Chambers
DLR *of R4, Commercial Vans, Pickup Trucks, TB Chassis*
Hours: M-F, 8:30-5:30
Sat., 8:30-11:30 a.m.

Clovelly Park
Mitsubishi Motors Australia, Ltd.
(MAIL: Box 1851
Adelaide, SA 5001)
1284 South Road
Clovelly Park, SA 5042
Tel: (08) 275-7111
FAX: (08) 275-6841
Telex: 82204
Contact: M.T. Quinn
MFR of *Light-, Med.-, & Heavy-duty Trucks, S-1, Truck Chassis*

Edwardstown
Adelaide Outboard Service Pty., Ltd.
108 Daws Road
Edwardstown, SA 5039
Tel: (08) 276-5622
A-H: (08) 381-6146
Contact: D. Fitch
DLR *of BT*
Hours: Mon.-Fri., 8-5:15
Sat., 8:30-Noon

Elizabeth
Static Engineering Pty., Ltd.
6 Oldham Road
Box 95
Elizabeth, SA 5112
Tel: (08) 255-2355
FAX: (08) 255-4404
Telex: 88906
Contact: Dr. W. Verschoor
MFR of *Lift TB for Aircraft Loading*

Findon
Gilberco Australia, Ltd.
(MAIL: Box 21
Seaton, SA 5023)
46 Crittendon Road
Findon, SA 5023
Tel: (08) 45-1788
FAX: (08) 45-3139
Contact: D.W. Jones
MFR of *Aircraft Refuelling Trucks*

Fullarton
Diesel Motors Pty., Ltd.
(MAIL: Box 115
Glen Osmond, SA 5064)
288 Glen Osmond Road
Fullarton, SA 5063
Tel: (08) 79-1678
Telex: 88145
Contact: J. Scott, GM
DLR *of TB, S-2*

Gillman
Mayne Nickless Transport Management
(MAIL: Box 83
Rosewater East, SA 5013)
Bedford Street
Gillman, SA 5013
Tel: (08) 47-5288
FAX: (08) 47-3942
Telex: 88902
MFR of *Vehicle-transport TB, S-2*

Hampstead Gardens
Kessner Trailers
95 Mullers Road
Hampstead Gardens, SA 5086
Tel: (08) 261-2495
Contact: D.J. Kessner
MFR of *R5, R6, Mobile Offices & Display Units*

Malvern
Fairway Ford Pty., Ltd.
(MAIL: Box 196
Unley, SA 5061)
321 Unley Road
Malvern, SA 5061
Tel: (08) 272-3000
FAX (08) 272-3909
Contact: G. Hannaford
MFR of *R4, TB*

Mile End
J.H. Southcott Industries Pty., Ltd.
3 Rosalyn Street
Mile End, SA 5031
Tel: (08) 352-8522
MFR of *Specialty Vehicles*

Mile End
United Motors Retail, Ltd.
(MAIL: Box 443
Adelaide, SA 5001)
71 Richmond Road
Mile End, SA 5031
Tel: (08) 297-9666
Telex: 82230
Contact: V.P. Kean
DLR of *R4, Pickup Trucks, Light-, Medium-, & Heavy-duty Trucks, M, UTB, A, S-1, S-2, U, Mini-busses*

Mile End South
Coldstream Pty., Ltd.
(MAIL: Box 43 (C/-)
Unley, SA 5061)
309 South Road
Mile End South, SA 5031
Tel: (08) 352-5199
Tel: (008) 271-0314
MFR of *Refrig. TB*

Mt. Gambier
Scotts Transport Industries Pty., Ltd.
Millicent Road
Box 504
Mt. Gambier, SA 5290
Tel: (087) 25-5222
FAX: (087) 25-7578
Telex: 80020
Contact: L.A. Byrne, GM
TRANSPORTER CO.
Hours: Mon.-Fri., 8:30-5
Sat., 8-12

Oaklands Park
Marion Toyota
310 Diagonal Road
Box 41
Oaklands Park, SA 5046
Tel: (08) 296-4311
FAX: (08) 296-2655
Contact: I. Sowton
DLR of *R4, Pickup Trucks, 4WD Vehicles*

Plympton
Lansing Australia Pty., Ltd.
20 Starr Avenue
Plympton, SA 5037
Tel: (08) 376-0344
FAX: (08) 294-4805
Contact: R. Polley
MFR of *Industrial Vehs.*

Port Adelaide
Danzas Wills Int'l.
17-21 Divett Street
Box 111
Port Adelaide, SA 5015
Tel: (08) 240-0715
Telex: 88134
Contact: P.A. Cullen
TRANSPORTER CO.

Regency Park
Mazda (SA)
(MAIL: Box 163
Welland, SA 5007)
589 South Road
Regency Park, SA 5010
Tel: (08) 286-3999
FAX: (08) 45-4325
Contact: I. Digby
DLR of *R4, Pickup Trucks, Commercial Vans*

Royal Park
Industrial Corp. Ltd.
11-15 Frederick Road
Royal Park, SA 5014
Tel: (08) 341-1377
FAX: (08) 341-1677
Contact: E.D. Hancock
MFR of *Agricultural Vehicles*

Somerton Park
John H. Ellers Pty., Ltd.
(MAIL: Box 68
Glenely, SA 5045)
278-288 Brighton Road
Somerton Park, SA 5044
Tel: (08) 296-4866
FAX: (08) 296-7112
Contact: G.D. Ellers
DLR of *R4*
Hours: M-F, 8:30-5:30
Sat., 8-12

Wingfield
L.M. Transport Equipment
40 Cormack Road
Wingfield, SA 5013
Tel: (08) 45-6443
Tel: (08) 45-8793
Telex: 89085
Contact: B. Lucas
MFR of *GTB, LTB, STB, Vehicle-transport Vehicles, S-2*

Wingfield
Rheem Australia, Ltd.
(Container Products Div.)
553 Grand Junction Road
Wingfield, SA 5013
Tel: (08) 45-7633
FAX: (08) 347-0588
Telex: 82348
Contact: P. Roberts, S.M.
MFR of *Cement-carrying Vehicles*

TASMANIA

Hobart
Co-Operative Motors, Ltd.
(MAIL: Box 86-A
Hobart, Tas 7001)
199 Collins Street
Hobart, Tas 7000
Tel: (002) 30-1901
FAX: (002) 34-4497
Contact: W.J. Carrick,
DLR of TB

Lindisfarne
Wreckair Pty., Ltd.
308 East Derwent Hwy.
Lindisfarne, Tas 7015
Tel: (002) 43-8766
FAX: (002) 43-5282
Telex: 58158
Contact: N. Lovell
MFR of R1, R2, Light- to Heavy-duty UTB

Moonah
Bender's Truck Sales Pty., Ltd.
123 Albert Road
Box 259
Moonah, Tas 7009
Tel: (002) 28-0041
FAX: (002) 28-2073,
Attn: Judy
Contact: R.T. Bender
MFR of STB

Moonah
King Trailer Industries Pty., Ltd.
5-9 Florence Street
Moonah, Tas 7009
Tel: (002) 28-4158
Contact: R. King
MFR of R5, R6
Hours: Mon.-Fri., 9-5

Mornington
Gilbarco Australia, Ltd.
110 Mornington Road
Mornington, Tas 7018
Tel: (002) 44-3644
Contact: G. Hall
MFR of Aircraft Refuelling Trucks

Rocherlea Launceston
Rheem Australia, Ltd.
(Container Products Div.)
East Tamar Highway
Rocherlea Launcestoon, Tas 7250
Tel: (003) 26-3477
Telex: 58850
Contact: L.J. Knowles
MFR of Cement-carrying Vehicles

VICTORIA

Airport West
Gilbarco Australia, Ltd.
(MAIL: Box 262
Neddrie, Vic 3042)
42 Moore Road
Airport West, Vic 3042
Tel: (03) 338-1011
FAX: (03) 338-3702
Contact: K. Burt
MFR of Aircraft Refuelling Trucks

Ballarat
MBI Engineering Services
902 LaTrobe Street
Ballarat, Vic 3350
Tel: (053) 35-8450
FAX: (053) 36-1269
Contact: J.E. Miller, GM
MFR of Specialty Vehicles
Hours: M-F, 8-12 & 1-5

Bayswater
Hagglunds Denison Pty., Ltd.
(MAIL: Box 46
Mt. Waverley, Vic 3149)
12/42 Stud Road
Bayswater, Vic 3153
Tel: (03) 720-5055
FAX: (03) 720-5056
Telex: 35359
Contact: J. Binks
MFR of Military Personnel Carriers, STB

Brooklea
Rheem Australia, Ltd.- Container Products Div.
(MAIL: Box 221
W. Footscray, Vic 3012)
521 Geelong Road
Brooklea, Vic 3012
Tel: (03) 314-0777
FAX: (03) 314-4842
Telex: 30804
Contact: K.W. Hartley
MFR of Cement-carrying Vehicles

Brunswick
Cameron & Jason Pty., Ltd.
44 Phoenix Street
Brunswick, Vic 3056
Tel: (03) 387-1633
Tel: (03) 387-2055
Tel: (03) 387-1077
FAX: (03) 388-1161
Contact: H. Jason
MFR of Water Tanker TB
Hours: M-F, 7:45-4:15
Sat., 7-11 a.m.

Brunswick
J.J. McGrath (Australia) Ply., Ltd.
225 Brunswick Road
Box 75
Brunswick, Vic 3056
Tel: (03) 380-4134
Contact: V. McGrath
MFR of Aircraft Refuelling Trucks, XTB

Campbellfield
Ford Motor Company of Australia, Ltd.
1735 Sydney Road
Box PMB 6
Campbellfield, Vic 3061
Tel: (03) 359-8211
FAX: (03) 357-1824
Telex: 30624
Contact: W.L. Dix
MFR of R4, TB

Clayton
The Nissan Motor Mfg. Co. (Australia), Ltd.
1508-1550 Centre Road
Box 22
Clayton, Vic 3168
Tel: (03) 542-6666
FAX: (03) 543-4629
Telex: 30502
Contact: L. Daphne
MFR of Light-to-Medium Duty Vans & Trucks, 4WD Vehicles

Clayton
Transfield Pty., Ltd.
(RP/C Div., Victoria)
84 Fairbank Road
Box 181
Clayton, Vic 3168
Tel: (03) 546-0011
Contact: K. O'Brien, GM
MFR of R4, Pickup Trucks, Light-, Med.-, & Heavy-duty Trucks, S-1, S-2, Tanker Vehicles, Limos, STB, Refrig. & Insulated TB

Clayton South
Austral Insulation Pty., Ltd.
(MAIL: Box 188
Clayton, Vic 3168)
13-19 Eileen Road
Clayton South, Vic 3169
Tel: (03) 548-3233
FAX: (03) 548-1057
Telex: 134942
Contact: N. Scott, GM
MFR of Insulated TB

Coburg
Wreckair Pty., Ltd.
240 Sydney Road
Coburg, Vic 3058
Tel: (03) 383-2111
Tel: (03) 353-4411
FAX: (03) 386-7667
Telex: 33679
Contact: M. Conruy
MFR of R1, R2, M, Light-to Heavy-duty UTB
Hours: Mon.-Fri., 7-5

Fitzroy
Hermes Overseas Baggage Agency
72 Johnston Street
Fitzroy, Vic 3065
Tel: (03) 417-5537
Contact: H. Thodis, GM
MFR of Commercial Vans, Pickup Trucks
Hours: Mon.-Sat., 8-6

Geelong
J.C. Brown Mfg. Pty., Ltd.
7 Barwon Terrace, S.
Box 9
Geelong, Vic 3220
Tel: (052) 21-3177
FAX: (052) 21-8442
Telex: 37613
Contact: R.K. Griffiths
MFR of Stainless Steel Tank TB
Hours: M-F, 7:30-5:30

Keon Park
Tieman Industries Pty., Ltd.
(MAIL: Box 68
Reservoir, Vic 3073)
4 Keon Pde.
Keon Park, Vic 3073
Tel: (03) 460-5111
Telex: 32213
Contact: A. Turner
MFR of Tanker Vehicles
DISTRIBUTOR for Blue Giant Equipment of Canada (Canada) & Maxon Industries, Inc. (USA)

Melbourne
Amalgamated Marine Engineers Pty., Ltd.
(MAIL: Box 4091
Melbourne, Vic 3001)
88-102 Normandy Rd., S. Melbourne, Vic 3205
Tel: (03) 699-7277
FAX: (03) 699-3425
Telex: 139670
Contact: K.F. Saville
MFR of TB: Petroleum, Bulk Liquids, Liquid Oxygen

Melbourne
International Harvester Australia, Ltd.
(MAIL: Box 4305
Melbourne, Vic 3001)
211 Sturt Street, S.
Melbourne, Vic 3205
Tel: (03) 697-7209
FAX: (03) 697-7205
Telex: 30534
Contact: D.A. Eagle
MFR of *M, STB, S-2, U, Military Personnel Vehicles, Medical Units, Bookmobiles, XTB*
Hours: Mon.-Fri., 8-4:30

Melbourne
V Line
State Transport Authority
589 Collins Street
Melbourne, Vic 3000
Tel: (03) 619-1111
FAX: (03) 619-4143
Telex: 33801
TRANSPORTER CO.
Hours: M-F, 8:30-4:45

Moorabbin
Heuch Refrigeration Pty., Ltd.
Corner of Simpson Street & Powlett Street
Moorabbin, Vic 3189
Tel: (03) 555-7755
FAX: (03) 555-5451
Telex: 39459
Contact: J.C. Heuch
MFR of *Refrig. TB*

Moorabbin
Vicoach Industries Pty., Ltd.
(MAIL: Box 112
Cheltenham, Vic 3192)
8 Simpson Street
Moorabbin, Vic 3189
Tel: (03) 553-1255
FAX: (03) 555-7951
Telex: 37706
Contact: W. Fairweather
DLR *of U*

Mordialloc
Bullet Resistant Equipment Co. Pty., Ltd.
(Div. of Kenbrock Group)
7 Hinkler Road
Mordialloc, Vic 3195
Tel: (03) 587-2311
FAX: (03) 580-6572
Telex: 135049
Contact: J. Schmid, GM
MFR of *Armored Cars, Security Vehicles*

Mount Waverley
Furnace Engineering Pty., Ltd.
(MAIL: Private Bay 11)
11 Gilby Road
Mt. Waverley, Vic 3149
Tel: (03) 544-2922
FAX: (03) 544-2723
Telex: 33539
Contact: R.G. Simpson
MFR of *Vehicle-transport TB, STB, S-2*

Mount Waverley
Lansing Australia Pty., Ltd.
6 Expo Court
Box 324
Mt. Waverley, Vic 3149
Tel: (03) 543-4455
FAX: (03) 543-5175
Contact: L.J. Allen
MFR of *Industrial Vehs.*

Northcote
Emco Wheaton Australia Pty., Ltd.
(MAIL: Box 203
Fairfield, Vic 3078)
145 Heidelburg Road
Northcote, Vic 3070
Tel: (03) 486-2333
FAX: (03) 486-2370
Telex: 34044
Contact: G. Smith
MFR of *Tanker TB: Aircraft Refuelling Trucks*
Hours: Mon.-Fri., 8:15-5

Oakleigh
Edgerows Pty., Ltd./ Brents Motors
Corner of Dandenong Rd. & Warrigal Rd.
Oakleigh, Vic 3166
Tel: (03) 568-0888
Telex: 34296
Contact: B. Forshaw
MFR of *S-2*
Hours: Mon.-Sat., 8:30-6

Oakleigh
Merlin Fiberglass Pty., Ltd.
28-34 Westminster Street
Oakleigh, Vic 3166
Tel: (03) 568-1026
FAX: (03) 563-1501
Contact: I.T. Hollinrake
MFR of *Fiberglass TB*

Port Melbourne
AMI Toyota, Ltd.
(MAIL: Box 2006-S
Melbourne, Vic 3001)
155 Bertie Street
Port Melbourne, Vic 3207
Tel: (03) 647-4444
Contact: D.L. Wallin
MFR of *Vans*

Port Melbourne
Fleetxpress Pty., Ltd.
61 Bertie Street
Box 73
Port Melbourne, Vic 3207
Tel: (03) 645-1155
Telex: 30072
Contact: J.F. Hogan
TRANSPORTER CO.

Port Melbourne
Holden's Motor Co.
(MAIL: Box 1714,
Melbourne, Vic 3001)
241 Salmon Street
Port Melbourne, Vic 3207
Tel: (03) 647-1111
FAX: Rapifax (03) 647-1111
Telex: 30168
Contact: C.S. Chapman
MFR of *Vans* (Parent Co.: General Motors Corp., USA)

Shepparton
Goulburn Valley Engineering Works
53 Archer Street
Box 866
Shepparton, Vic 3630
Tel: (058) 21-2266
Contact: D.H. Kerambrun
MFR of *TB*

Spotswood
Hockney Alcan
(MAIL: Box 133
Newport, Vic 3015)
Sutton Street
Spotswood, Vic 3015
Tel: (03) 391-6211
FAX: (03) 391-7243
MFR of *Stainless Steel Tanker TB*

Springvale
Emptor Pty., Ltd.
212 Springvale Road
Box 114
Springvale, Vic 3171
Tel: (03) 546-4100
FAX: (03) 546-0119
Contact: F.J. Donovan
DLR *of R4, TB*
Hours: Mon.-Fri., 7-6
Sat., 8:30-6

Thomastown
L.R. Alderson
196 Settlement Road
Thomastown, Vic 3074
Tel: (03) 465-4033
Telex: 33511
Contact: R.T. Cahill, GM
MFR of *LP-Gas Vehicles*

Thornburg
Lucar (Victoria) Pty., Ltd.
11 Anderson Road
Thornburg, Vic 3071
Tel: (03) 480-4311
Telex: 33409
Contact: A. McCristal
MFR of *R4, Pickup Trucks, U, Dental Vans, Bookmobiles, X-Ray & Medical Units*

Thornbury
S.J. Brown Pty., Ltd.
286 Darebin Road
Thornbury, Vic 3071
Tel: (03) 489-0212
MFR of *BT*

Tullamarine
Ansair
Garden Drive
Box 63
Tullamarine, Vic 3043
Tel: (03) 339-6717
Contact: A.D. Callanay
MFR of *U, UTB*
Hours: M-F, 8:30-4:15

Wangaratta
West City Autos Pty., Ltd.
52-60 Parfitt Road
Box 406
Wangaratta, Vic 3677
Tel: (057) 21-4461
Tel: (057) 21-4462
Telex: 56141
Contact: G.W. Price
MFR of *R4, Pickup Trucks, Lt.- & Med.-duty Trucks, M, U*
Hours: M-F, 8:30-5:30
Sat., 9-12

WESTERN AUSTRALIA

Bayswater
Commercial Body Builders Pty., Ltd.
30 Jackson Street
Bayswater, W.A. 6053
Tel: (09) 279-2019
Contact: G. Taylor
MFR of *U, Truck Chassis*

Bayswater
Master Engineering
120 Beechboro Road
Bayswater, W.A. 6053
Tel: (09) 271-2229
Contact: P. Long
MFR of *BT*
Hours: Mon.-Fri., 8-5
Sat., 8:30-12

Belmont
Boomerang Engineering Pty., Ltd.
14-16 Wheeler Street
Belmont, W.A. 6104
Tel: (09) 277-2522
A-H: (09) 446-3396
A-H: (09) 271-9854
FAX: (09) 479-1270
Telex: 93957
Contact: P. Travaglini
MFR of *Lowboy T, S-2*

Belmont
Gilbarco Australia, Ltd.
Cleaver Terrace
Box 135
Belmont, W.A. 6104
Tel: (09) 277-1211
Telex: 93085
Contact: K.G. White
MFR of *Aircraft Refuelling Trucks*

East Victoria Park
Polmac Trailers
29 Welshpool Road
East Victoria Park,
W.A. 6101
Tel: (09) 361-8388
A-H: (09) 451-2693
Contact: E. Pollard, Mgr.
MFR of *BT*
Hours: M-F, 7:45-5:30

Freemantle
Gardner Brothers & Perrott (WA) Pty. Ltd.
20 Stack Street
Box 654
Freemantle, W.A. 6160
Tel: (09) 335-9000
FAX: (09) 430-4659
Contact: M.D. Perrott
MFR of *Water Tanker TB*

Freemantle
Rheem Australia, Ltd.
144 Carrington Street
Freemantle, W.A. 6160
Tel: (09) 337-3411
FAX: (09) 331-1379
Telex: 92246
Contact: J. Havercroft
MFR of *Cement-carrying Vehicles*

Jandakot
Bevron Fibreglass Pty., Ltd.
(MAIL: Box 72
Hamilton Hill, WA 6163)
21 Spencer Street
Jandakot, W.A. 6164
Tel: (09) 417-9533
Contact: R.T. Cary, Mgr.
MFR of *Fiberglass TB, Refrig. & Insulated TB*

Kewdale
J.W. Bolton Pty., Ltd.
(MAIL: Box 111
Cloverdale, WA 6105)
9 Bradford Street
Kewdale, W.A. 6105
Tel: (09) 350-6966
Telex: 96871
Contact: J.W. Bolton
MFR of *TB*

Maddington
Fleetwood Corp. Ltd.
(MAIL: Box 145
Gosnells, WA 6110)
1964 Albany Highway
Maddington, W.A. 6109
Tel: (09) 459-2511
FAX: (09) 459-0424
Contact: J. Wood
MFR of *R5, R6*

Malaga
Begley Engineering Services
(MAIL: Box 264
Mirrabooka, WA 6061)
Lot 19, Camboon Road
Malaga, W.A. 6062
Tel: (09) 275-7327
Telex: 95316
Contact: M.G. Begley
MFR of *Aircraft Refuelling Vehicles*

Melville
Laurie Chivers & Co.
(MAIL: Box 146
Applecross, WA 6153)
104 Rome Road
Melville, W.A. 6156
Tel: (09) 330-4208
Contact: L. Chivers, Mgr.
MFR of *BT*
Hours: Mon.-Fri., 8-5
Sat., 8-12:30

O'Connor
Howard Porter Pty., Ltd.
(MAIL: Box 76
Hamilton Hill, WA 6163)
Corner of Jones Street & Murphy Street
O'Connor, W.A. 6163
Tel: (09) 337-3533
A-H: (09) 384-1527
FAX: (09) 331-2931
Telex: 92086
Contact: C.R. Stewart
MFR of *A, R4, M, GTB, LTB, Tanker TB, STB, XTB, Busses, Mini-busses, Bookmobiles, HT*

O'Connor
Windrush Yachts
1 Rawlinson Street
O'Connor, W.A. 6163
Tel: (09) 337-4323
Contact: J. McFarlane
MFR of *BT*

Osborne Park
George Moss, Ltd.
(MAIL: Box 136
Mt. Hawthorne, WA 6016)
461 Scarborough Beach Road
Osborne Park, W.A. 6017
Tel: (09) 446-8844
FAX: (09) 446-3404
Telex: 92645
Contact: F.A. Quilty
MFR of *STB*

Osborne Park
Northwest Engineering Pty., Ltd.
52 King Edward Road
Osborne Park, W.A. 6017
Tel: (09) 446-8687
Contact: J. Travaglini
MFR of *M*
Hours: M-F, 7:30-5:30

Perth
Automotive Holdings, Ltd.
284 Aberdeen Street
Perth, W.A. 6000
Tel: (09) 328-5644
FAX: (09) 328-4347
Telex: 92439
Contact: V.C. Wheatley
MFR of *R4, Pickups*

South Guildford
Wigmore's Tractors Pty., Ltd.
(MAIL: Box B-83
Perth, WA 6001)
128 Great Eastern Hwy.,
South
Guildford, W.A. 6055
Tel: (09) 378-1000
FAX: (09) 279-9159
Telex: 92012
Contact: F. Johnson, CEO
DLR of *M*

Welshpool
Alma Engineering Pty., Ltd.
(MAIL: Box 1
Cloverdale, WA 6105)
73 Division Street
Welshpool, W.A. 6106
Tel: (09) 350-5977
Contact: R.C. Walliss
MFR of *Dump T*

Welshpool
Wreckair Pty., Ltd.
140 Welshpool Road
Welshpool, W.A. 6106
Tel: (09) 451-9555
FAX: (09) 458-9092
Telex: 94649
Contact: D. Loxton, Mgr.
MFR of *R1, R2, M, Light- to Heavy-duty UTB*
Hours: Mon.-Fri., 7:30-5

Wembley
Bosich Holdings Pty., Ltd.
20 Roydhouse Street
Wembley, W.A. 6014
Tel: (09) 381-4655
Telex: 93609
Contact: M. Bosich
MFR of *STB*

Willetton
Hagglunds Denison Pty., Ltd.
5 Whyalla Street
Box 213
Willetton, W.A. 6155
Tel: (09) 457-5582
Telex: 93219
Contact: J. Horton, SM
MFR of *Military Personnel Carriers, STB*

SECTION 4

Transporter Companies of the USA and Canada

The listings in this section begin with Auto Driveaway. That's because this transporter is so readily available to drivers in most of America, and in much of Canada, and the information presented is so detailed. The other major transporters follow, mostly alphabetically. When you write, all Auto Driveaway addresses should start with the agent's name, then: Auto Driveaway Company... unless otherwise noted. States are alphabetical in this list by their *full spellings* -- **not** by their two-letter postal abbreviations.

TIP: **Please be aware that new transporter company offices and agencies open with frequency. For example, as you read these words, there may well be an *Auto Driveaway* office in your own city that is *not* listed below because it opened after our research was completed. Therefore, you should always check your telephone directory for *each* of the transporters in this section if you find that your city is not included. That situation may have changed.**

Auto Driveaway -- USA

KEY

ADC	--	Auto Driveaway Co.
D/S	--	Driveaway Service
RVT	--	RV Transport Office
PDD	--	Pro Driver Division

NATIONAL HEADQUARTERS

310 S. Michigan Ave.   Tel.: (312) 341-1900
Chicago, IL 60604   Nation: (800) 346-CARS

State	City	Agent's Name(s)	Address	Type	Telephone
AZ	Phoenix	Barbara Jones Frank Jones	3920 E. Indian Sch'l. Rd. Suites 14 & 15 Phoenix, AZ 85018	ADC	(602) 952-0339
AZ	Tucson	Ken Zettel Helen Zettel	4420 E. Speedway, #201 Tucson, AZ 85712	ADC	(520) 323-7659
CA	Chico	Ron Speed	RV Transport Office 1020 Marauder Avenue Chico, CA 95926	RVT	(916) 893-0527
CA	Long Beach	Robert Daley	2735 E. Carson St. Lakewood, CA 90712	ADC	(310)421-0313
CA	Los Angeles	Bob Aschenbrenner	3407 W. 6th St. Suite 525 Los Angeles, CA 90020	ADC	(213) 666-6100
CA	Riverside	Rick Atencio	RV Transport Office 2501 Rubidoux Blvd. Suite A Riverside, CA 92509	RVT	(909) 788-0500

State	City	Contact	Address	Type	Phone
CA	San Diego	Arlette Stein Veronique Stein	4645 Park Blvd. San Diego, CA 92116	ADC	(619) 295-8006 (619) 295-8060
CA	San Francisco	Michael Smith	350 Townsend St. Suite 208 San Francisco, CA 94107	ADC	(415) 777-3740
CA	San Jose	John Ortiz	3275 Stevens Creek Blvd. Suite 204 San Jose, CA 95117	ADC	(408) 984-4999
CO	Denver	Ted Joens	5777 E. Evans Avenue Suite 109 Denver, CO 80222	ADC	(303) 757-1211
DC	Dist. of Columbia	------	See Arlington, VA. That office serves Washington, D.C.		
FL	Fort Lauderdale	John Muller	4971 N.E. 9th Avenue Fort Lauderdale, FL 33334	ADC	(954) 771-4059
FL	Fort Myers	Peter Lyon Diane Lyon	10550 Daniels Parkway Fort Myers, FL 33913	ADC	(941) 768-2345
FL	Jacksonville	Manager	5991 Chester Avenue Suite 108 Jacksonville, FL 32217	ADC	(904) 737-9500
FL	Miami Beach	Barry Halpern Carol Halpern	2500 E. Hallandale Beach Blvd., Suite A Hallandale, FL 33009	ADC	(954) 456-2277 (954) 456-2285
FL	Orlando	Wendy Geller Alan Kornman	1 Purlieu Pl. (Driggs Dr.) Suite 131 Winter Park, FL 33792	ADC	(407) 678-7000
FL	Tampa	Don Harries	2401 W. Kennedy Blvd. Suite A Tampa, FL 33609	ADC	(813) 254-8411
GA	Atlanta	Dick Dennis	3312 Piedmont Road Suite 422 Atlanta, GA 30305	ADC	(404) 364-0464
GA	Atlanta	Mike Brown	3455 N. Desert Drive Suite 108 East Point, GA 30344	D/S	(404) 305-8000
IL	Chicago	Mike Van Der Haegen	310 S. Michigan Avenue Suite 1401 Chicago, IL 60604	ADC	(312) 939-3600
IN	Elkhart	Dick Miller	Pro Driver Division 1550 W. Lusher Avenue Elkhart, IN 46517	PDD	(219) 522-3000

State	City	Contact	Address	Type	Phone
IN	Howe	Dennis Skoczylas	Pro Driver Division 5580 N. State Road 9 Howe, IN 46746	PDD	(219) 562-2500
IN	Indianapolis	Wayne Moss	2559 E. 55th Place Indianapolis, IN 46220	ADC	(317) 259-7060
KS	Kansas City	Sharie Bell	7930 State Line Road Suite 203 Prairie Village, KS 66208	ADC	(913) 381-2125
KS	Wichita	Carl Nelson	3340 W. Douglas Suite 1 Wichita, KS 67203	ADC	(316) 945-2882
KY	Louisville	Debra Young	2210 Goldsmith Lane Suite 214 Louisville, KY 40218	ADC	(502) 456-4990
LA	New Orleans	Don Vickrey Joanne Vickrey	7809 Airline Highway Suite 207-B Metairie, LA 70003	ADC	(504) 737-0266
MA	Boston	Larry Sprince	1170 Commonwealth Av. Boston, MA 02134	ADC	(617) 731-1261
MI	Detroit	Harold Long Sue Olson	28605 Grand River Ave. Detroit, MI 48336	ADC	(810) 442-2335
MI	Grand Rapids	Paul Schultz	5600 S. Division, SE Kentwood, MI 49548	ADC	(616) 530-0187
MN	Minneapolis	Barry Wilmert	6950 France Avenue, S. Galleria Offices, #109 Edina, MN 55435	ADC	(612) 926-0262 (612) 926-3150
MN	St. Paul	Dick Asmussen	1133 Rankin, Suite 328-A St. Paul, MN 55116	D/S	(612) 698-6929
MO	St. Louis	Barbara Lynch	1155 Francis Place St. Louis, MO 63117	ADC	(314) 726-2886
NE	Omaha	Steve Westerfield	3506 Keystone Drive Omaha, NE 68134	ADC	(402) 571-5010
NJ	Hackensack	Mike Rossi	520 S. River St., Suite 101 Hackensack, NJ 07601	ADC	(201) 440-0707
NM	Albuquerque	Manager	(Office was changing location as this printing was researched in Dec., 1996.)	ADC	(505) 345-4317

NY	Buffalo	Manager	(Office was changing Location as this printing was Researched in Dec., 1996.)	ADC	(716) 743-1491
NY	New York City	Don Clarkin	264 W. 35th St. Suite 500 New York City, NY 10001	ADC	(212) 967-2344 (212) 967-2345 (212) 967-2346
NY	Syracuse	Bob Waters Maureen De Santis	116 Maple Drive P.O. Box 247 Fayetteville, NY 13066	ADC	(315) 445-0809
NC	Charlotte	Steve Horn	1222 W. Craighead Road Charlotte, NC 28256	ADC	(704) 921-0007
NC	Charlotte	David Norton	Pro Driver Division 1222 W. Craighead Road Charlotte, NC 28256	PDD	(704) 597-5766
NC	Greensboro	Joan Schneiderman Ken Schneiderman	501 W. Lee St. Greensboro, NC 27406	ADC	(910) 272-2153
OH	Cincinnati	Mary Hinkle	5721 Cheviot Road Room 5 Cincinnati, OH 45247	ADC	(513) 385-6654
OH	Cleveland	Frank Kodman Erna Kodman	20575 Center Ridge Road Cleveland, OH 44116	ADC	(216) 331-1495
OH	Columbus	Bill Huber	4540 Indianola Avenue Columbus, OH 43214	ADC	(614) 261-8170
OK	Oklahoma City	Greg Ruch Joyce Ruch	2508 N.W. 39th St. Oklahoma City, OK 73112	ADC	(405) 943-8443
OR	Portland	John Case	434 N.W. Hoyt St. Portland, OR 97209	ADC	(503) 294-2955
PA	Philadelphia	Russ Schilling	Mount Carmel & Roberts Avenues Glenside, PA 19038	ADC	(215) 884-6662
PA	Pittsburgh	Don Addlespurger	1100 Washington Ave. Suite 106 Carnegie, PA 15106	ADC	(412) 276-6922 (412)276-6923
PA	Reading	Mary Rose	Pro Driver Division 3907 Pottsville Pike (Front) Reading, PA 19605 *Mailing Address:* P.O. Box 15063 Reading, PA 19612-5063	PDD	(610) 929-1800

TN	Memphis	Bailey Barry David Matthews	6401 Poplar Avenue Suite 557 Memphis, TN 38119	ADC	(901) 685-3360
TN	Nashville	Al Morris	333 S. Gallatin Road Suite 12 Madison, TN 37115	ADC	(615) 244-8000
TX	Dallas	Ed Wood	13610 Midway Road Suite 232 Dallas, TX 75244	ADC	(972) 233-5533 (972) 233-5534
TX	San Antonio	Tom Williams Mary Jane Williams	105 N. Alamo Room 501 San Antonio, TX 78205	ADC	(210) 226-1676 (210) 226-1719
UT	Salt Lake City	Todd Abelhaucen	6000 S. 300 W., Bldg. B Salt Lake City, UT 84107	ADC	(801) 262-3662
VA	Arlington	Bernie Wright	1022 N. Fillmore Arlington, VA 22201	ADC	(703) 524-7300 (703) 524-7301
VA	Richmond	Mac Perkinson	4905 Radford Avenue Room 105 Richmond, VA 23230	ADC	(804) 353-9390
WA	Seattle	Rich Mather	13470 M.L. King Way, S. (*Formerly* Empire Way) Seattle, WA 98178	ADC	(206) 235-0880
WI	Janesville	Phil Owens Ray Norton	1611 Randolph Road Janesville, WI 53545	ADC	(608) 755-1711
WI	Milwaukee	Roy Lamberty	9039-A W. National Ave. Suite 3 Milwaukee, WI 53227	ADC	(414) 327-5252 (414) 327-6778 (414) 327-6779 (414) 327-3269 (414) 962-0008

Auto Driveaway -- CANADA

AB	Calgary	Bridget Palmer Barry Palmer	Brentwood Village Mall 232-G 3630 Brentwood Rd., NW Calgary, AB T2L 1K8	ADC	(403) 289-7854
BC	Vancouver	Leslie Ann Coyle	1080-A Marine Drive North Vancouver, BC V7P 1S5	ADC	(604) 985-0936
MB	Winnipeg	Gordon Reimer Arnold Reimer	1579 Dugald Road Winnipeg, MB R2J 0H3	ADC	(204) 663-2966

Auto Driveaway -- CANADA
(Continued)

NS	Halifax	Gerry Giovannetti	1550 Bedford Highway Suite 600, Sun Tower Bedford, NS B4A 1E6	ADC	(902) 832-1240
ON	Toronto	Joseph Aprile	6120-A Yonge Street Suite 2 North York, ON M2M 3W7	ADC	(416) 222-4700
PQ	Montreal	Albert Paquette	2421 Guenette Ville St. Laurent Montreal, PQ H4R 2E9	ADC	(514) 956-1046

= = = END OF THE AUTO DRIVEAWAY LISTINGS = = =

Arkansas Delivery Service
Highway 365, S.
P.O. Box 1677
Conway, AR 72032
Tel. (501) 329-6634
Contact: Bill Hobbs
C-2:35

Automotive Services, Inc.
2001 W. Fourth Plain Blvd.
Vancouver, WA 98660
Tel. (206) 693-5835
Portland, OR Line: (503) 283-2273
Nation, Except WA: (800) 843-4564
WA Only: (800) 843-4564
C-1:24, C-2:1

=== REMINDER ===

There are many specific things to keep in mind when you consider applying for a Road Rat position with transporter companies. Transporter companies are excellent places for which to work, as long as you know the secrets for being successful when doing so. This is a very detailed and comprehensive book, so this reminder is placed here to point you, once again, in the direction of the portions of the text that provide you with the knowledge you need, regarding transporters. If you skimmed too quickly over any of these, or if you skipped any altogether, then I strongly urge you to return to those sections. Read them carefully and thoroughly **BEFORE** you apply to transporter companies. This will enable you to present yourself as a very *well-informed* applicant. *And* it will tell you exactly how to begin working for a *comfortable* living wage. Here are the places that give you specific details about working for transporters:

Pages ix - xii, 161-166, & 170 -- Information you **NEED** to know before working for **ANY** company.
Pages 3-7 -- Valuable background data pertaining to the availability of work.
Pages 10-14 -- Distinguishing between the types of work, and the types of companies.
Pages 19-23 -- Presenting yourself as an applicant to any company, *including* the transporters.
Pages 111-119 -- *Interlock*. And Pages 135-149 -- The **Ameripass**. To be *successful* as a Road Rat working for a transporter company, you **MUST** employ *one or the other* of these methods!
Pages 156-159 -- Answers to some of the most important questions. Please review these.

A. Anthony Driveaway/Truckaway

NATIONAL HEADQUARTERS

300-2 Route 17, South
Lodi, NJ 07644
Tel.: (201) 777-8100
Nation: (800) 659-9903

State	City	Address	Telephone(s)
CA	Los Angeles	429 N. Anaheim Blvd. Orange, CA 92668	(714) 634-8848 (800) 336-1777
GA	Marietta	2010-B Airport Indus. Dr. Marietta, GA 30062	(404) 951-8013 (800) 526-1778
IL	Chicago	1020 W. Van Buren Chicago, IL 60607	(312) 226-6616 (800) 348-8049
TX	Dallas	5307 E. Mockingbird Lane Suite 214 Dallas, TX 75206	(214) 823-2820 (800) 229-8270
TX	San Antonio	28155 Boerne Stage One Boerne, TX 78006	(210) 981-2395 (800) 451-9495
VA	Warrenton	5860 Ridgecrest Ave Warrenton, VA 22186	(703) 349-8471 (800) 728-2211

* *

SPECIAL NOTE

While some of the transporters listed in this section are relatively small, most of what you see here are the larger ones. That is because there are perhaps 100 or more across the continent which normally serve only a few factories. Three or less is typical, and many serve only one. Wherever possible, such small transporters have been indicated by name in the Manufacturers' section, as part of the individual manufacturer's data. When you see a transporter that is listed there, but not here, then you should contact the manufacturer directly, to obtain more information about the transporter that serves him. Also... large-font headings in this section should not be construed as a measure of a company's importance. A larger heading simply indicates that *several sites are listed* below it.

* *

Barrett Mobile Home Transport

NATIONAL HEADQUARTERS

2910 University Drive, S.
Box 9679
Tel.: (701) 237-5352
Nation: (800) 535-2848

MAJOR BRANCH OFFICE

56960 Elk Park Drive
Elkhart, IN 46516
Tel.: (219) 522-7551
Nation: (800) 433-5690

DISPATCH OFFICES THROUGHOUT THE USA
(Alphabetized by the way the states' complete names are spelled.)

State	City	Telephone	State	City	Telephone
AL	Gardendale	(205) 631-6224	OR	Forest Grove	(503) 359-4294
AL	Irvington	(205) 957-3025	OR	McMinnville	(503) 472-0975
AZ	Tucson	(602) 883-1798	OR	Molalla	(503) 829-6938
CO	Salida	(719) 539-6015	OR	Springfield	(503) 747-1837
GA	Ocilla	(912) 468-5814	PA	Clarion	(814) 764-3364
ID	Boise	(208) 342-6806	PA	Leola (#1)	(717) 656-3020
ID	New Plymouth	(208) 278-3042	PA	Leola (#2)	(717) 656-2442
ID	Twin Falls	(208) 733-2192	SD	Aberdeen	(605) 225-8975
IN	Middlebury	(219) 825-5891	SD	Harrisburg	(605) 743-5994
KS	Chanute	(316) 431-1839	TN	Memphis	(901) 725-9725
KS	Shawnee	(913) 268-4488	TX	Corpus Christi	(512) 882-9941
MI	Sault Ste. Marie	(906) 635-0450	TX	Longview (#1)	(214) 759-5476
MN	Mankato	(507) 625-1461	TX	Longview (#2)	(214) 643-9951
MN	Montevideo	(612) 269-8113	TX	Splendora	(713) 689-3774
MS	Pearl	(601) 932-2709	TX	Springtown	(817) 677-5422
MO	Springfield	(417) 831-6822	UT	Bountiful	(801) 298-5827
MT	Stevensville	(406) 728-9585	WA	Bremerton	(206) 479-8312
NE	Gering	(308) 436-3856	WA	Chehallis	(206) 748-1472
NV	Carson City	(702) 882-1811	WA	Deer Park	(509) 276-8133
NV	Tonopah	(702) 482-5924	WA	Moses Lake	(509) 766-1242
NV	Winnemucca	(702) 623-5449	WA	Puyallup	(206) 845-3912
NM	Aztec	(505) 334-3667	WA	Sedro Wooly	(206) 724-5001
NM	Las Vegas	(505) 526-6457	WA	Spokane	(509) 487-8198
ND	Bismarck	(701) 255-0808	WA	Startup	(206) 793-0711
ND	Devil's Lake	(701) 662-3073	WA	Woodland	(206) 225-7396
ND	Fargo	(701) 293-0571	WI	Fremont	(414) 667-4309
OH	Hillsboro	(513) 393-5084	WI	Marshfield	(715) 389-2089
OH	Holmesville	(216) 674-9336	WI	Mount Hope	(608) 988-4561
OK	Norman	(405) 360-3364	WI	Spring Valley	(715) 778-4468
OR	Bend	(503) 382-2323			

Bennett's Motor Express

28826 U.S. Hwy. 20, W.
P.O. Box 4575
Elkhart, IN 46514
Tel.: (219) 293-2537
250 Drivers
(35 of these drive R4)

P.O. Box 569
McDonough, GA 30253
Tel.: (404) 957-1866
Nation: (800) 866-5500
Contact: Marcia Garrison-Taylor

Brock's Mobile Home Transport

5421 Eastside Road
Redding, CA 96001
Tel.: (916) 246-9443
Contact: Jim Brock
A-1, B-2, B-3, C-2
(Total of 15 drivers)

* *

Don Ray Driveaway
(5 Locations)

Decatur, Indiana
(Headquarters)

1400 S. 13th Street
Decatur, IN 46733
Tel.: (219) 724-4644
Nation: (800) 336-6729
Contact: Don Ray, President

Bristol, Indiana

506 Vistula Street
Bristol, IN 46507
Tel.: (219) 848-7619
Nation: (800) 848-7619

Paxinos, Pennsylvania

P.O. Box 153
Paxinos, PA 17860
Tel.: (717) 648-4211

Chico, California

4950 Cohasset Road, #9
Chico, CA 95927
Tel.: (916) 893-2377

Riverside, California

2431 Rubideaux, Bldg. #11
Riverside, CA 92509
Tel.: (909) 686-4369

* *

Horizon Transport

407 E. Wabash Avenue
Wakarusa, IN 46573
Tel.: (219) 862-2161
Nation: (800) 320-4055
FAX: (219) 862-4860
Contact: Marion Schrock
　　　　 or Jim Miller
All drivers are C-1.

Knudsen Enterprises

(MAIL: P.O. Box 7161
McLean, VA 22106)
7115 Leesburg Pike
Falls Church, VA 22043
Tel.: (703) 241-0920
FAX: (703) 241-0921
Contact: John Knudsen

Ladd Transit Service

1050 N.W. "T"
Richmond, IN 47374
Tel.: (317) 966-0815
Drivers: 50 during summer
　　　　 20 rest of year

Lundin's Driveback, Ltd.

R.R. #1
Trenton, ON K8V 5P4
Canada
Tel.: (613) 394-3313
FAX: (613) 394-5994
Dispatcher: Dave Pyatt

Drivers work out of
Woodstock and Trenton.
ALL trips are assigned by Dave,
from Trenton.
Number of Drivers: In Trenton: Around 50
　　　　　　　　　　 In Woodstock: 5 to 10

Morgan Driveaway

(NOTE: All "800" numbers listed below ring into the Headquarters.)

Headquarters

P.O. Box 1168 *[ZIP 46515]*
28651 U.S. Route 20, W.
Elkhart, IN 46514
Nation: (800) 289-7565
Nation: (800) 289-5623

Regional Office

8-C Craftman Court
Greer, SC 29650
Tel.: (803) 879-4865
WATS: (800) 456-6115
WATS: (800) 879-4865
FAX: (803) 879-7664

Regional Office

2400 Progress Way
Woodburn, OR 97071
Tel.: (503) 981-3450
WATS: (800) 950-0117
FAX: (503) 981-7949
(Inquire FIRST with HQ.)

Morgan has many more terminals, coast-to-coast. Inquire with HQ.

* *

Here's one specifically for Truckers who want to be Road Rats... but still drive large trucks...

Pride Truck Delivery, Ltd.

(MAIL: P.O. Box 130
Fort Langley, BC V1M 2R5
Canada)

21956 88th Avenue
Langley, BC V3A 6X5
Canada

Contact: Peg Macmillan
C-2:4   Full-time
C-2:4-5 Part-time & on-call

NOTE: Driver applicant must send resume and driver abstract (driving record) *to Peg* at the *mailing* address. These are kept on file for as long as necessary; they're not discarded after a short time, as happens in many places. Drivers must have a Class "1" CDL (that's the Canadian equivalant of a USA Class "A" CDL) with Dangerous Goods and Air endorsements. All vehicles are tractor-trailers, and many of these are aircraft refuellers. Full-time drivers work locally. On-call drivers deliver throughout British Columbia and on rare occasions into Alberta. Never farther east, and only rarely into the USA.

Selman Trucking

4759 S. 132nd Street
Omaha, NE 68137
Tel.: (402) 895-8138
Nation: (800) 228-0879
*Serves **all** of Fleetwood's R5 & R6 plants.*
B-3 drivers dispatched from all sites.

Southern Transfer Services

2913 McCoy Road
Orlando, FL 32812
Tel.: (407) 859-1942
FL Only: (800) 553-4737
FAX: (407) 859-5678
Contact: Kit Kirk.
C-2:30. Living nearby helps!

Transfer Drivers, Inc.

10920 E. McKinley Highway
Osceola, IN 46561
Tel.: (219) 674-6985
Nation: (800) 678-7013
30 USA Terminals; Agents in every state. Ask HQ for the location of the nearest one.

Transit Homes of America

HEADQUARTERS

530 S. Diamond St.
P.O. Box 5155
Boise, ID 83705
Tel.: (208) 362-8640
Nation: (800) 345-0323

MAJOR TERMINAL

1607 Industrial Road
Nampa, ID 83687
Tel.: (208) 467-5766
Tel.: (208) 888-3944
Nation: (800) 433-5007

78 Terminals in the USA

APPENDIX 2
THE TECHNICAL STUFF

This supplemental information may or may not be useful to you, so that's why I've put it at the very end of the book. Thus, it won't be getting in your way as you flip back and forth through the more important material. Many readers will want to know more of the specific details about some of the topics in this book, however, and those are provided here.

1. More Information on BUS Travel
Primary Details: Part III, Chapter 4

By far, the very least-expensive bus travel is via *Greyhound's Ameripass*. That's the good news. The bad news is that in July, 1994 Greyhound again increased the price of these versatile tickets! Just to give you an idea how much things have changed since I first started, the *Ameripass* then could be purchased in a *60-day* version for only $250.00 Today, the price of the longest-duration pass (30-day) is more than *quadruple* that rate per day, far exceeding the inflation rate over that time frame. Agents with whom I've discussed this were quite surprised that it rose so drastically! Despite all this, the *Ameripass* remains the least expensive way to make return trips *except* via Interlock, or when special air fares are *consistently* available. But that's only true if you buy the 30-day version, which costs $550.00. That translates to **a daily cost of $18.33.**

By comparison, the ticket would have cost you **only $4.17/day in 1977.** Just so you can see how out-of-line with inflation rates that truly is, the price of *gasoline* between 1977 and 1994 only *doubled.*

The scenarios provided in the chapter dealt only with real-world situations, for the purpose of providing you with a *realistic* picture of the earnings that could be attained when working for a *typical* transporter company. However, you might find it interesting to see what would be possible if you could find a transporter company that was situated in a major hub city for airlines, on one coast, which would send you *only* to dealerships located in *another* major hub city, on the opposite coast. That way, *all* your runs would be *transcontinental.*

The list on the next page will provide all the variables upon which *these* calculations are based. For the sake of keeping these figures meaningful when you compare them to the real-world situations provided in the chapter, I've kept ALL the variables *identical* in terms of the gasoline mileage of the RVs driven, the price of gas per gallon, and the amount per mile that the company pays you. And, as before, we use the widely-used payment method in which all the funds for trip expenses *and* the driver's pay are *combined.* Thus, in these scenarios, as with the case of the ones in the chapter, the driver gets to keep whatever money is left over at the end of the trip, as his or her pay. These scenarios, then, represent the very MOST that transporter-company Road Rats could expect to earn, under the most IDEAL *conditions,* if they choose *not* to use Interlock.

The *IDEAL* Transporter Company Situation

1. Your hypothetical transporter company is based in Washington, D.C.
2. You are paid 41 cents per mile. You take everything out of that, and then get to keep whatever remains at the end of the trip as your profit.
3. The units you drive average 8 miles per gallon.
4. Your company sends you *only* to Los Angeles. The run is 2,754 miles long. And *they keep you as busy as you want to be.* **Total Funding: $1,129.14** per trip.
5. At your chosen pace, each trip takes 4 days to drive. That's a pretty average pace.
6. Return *bus* trips from L.A. to Washington, D.C each take 3 days and 3 nights.
7. Overall average gasoline cost is $1.17^9 per gallon.
8. Based on items 3 and 4, your fuel will require 14.7 cents per mile of your pay, and leave you with 28.3 cents per mile from which you will buy your meals, return transportation, and take your profit. **Total Fuel Cost: $404.83** per trip.
9. Your meals average $12.00 per day, for the number of days that elapse from the time you start your run until you get back to the company.
10. After subtracting the fuel cost (but not meals eaten en route), you have $724.31 remaining after each run, from which to pay for return transportation, all meals, and from which to take your profit.

Here are the RESULTS of the three scenarios, based on the facts just presented...

Scenario #1
All Returns by *Greyhound Ameripass*

In a 35-day period (4 days for the first drive out, plus the 31 days your *Ameripass* was valid), you had no delays, and were able to accomplish 5 round trips. After deducting fuel, bus ticket, and meals, you earned:

$2,651.55 Total Profit, @ $75.76/day

For a 345-day work year, that equals **$26,136.70**
For a 50-week work year, that equals **$26,515.50**

* *

Scenario #2
All Returns on a Discount Airline

This time, you *didn't* use an *Ameripass*. Instead, you returned via *Mark Air* at $149.00 per trip (which is what they were charging at the time this was researched, in 1994). The returns now took one day instead of three, so you were able to drive to L.A. 7 times in 35 days. You encountered no delays, and over the 35 day-day period, you earned:

$3607.17 Total Profit, @ $103.06/day

For a 345-day work year, that equals **$35,556.39**
For a 50-week work year, that equals **$36,071.70**

* *

Scenario #3
All Returns on a Major Airline, at Best Discount Available

Wonderfully-discounted airfares aren't always available. So this scenario is identical to the last one, except that *Delta* or *Continental* are used. When this was researched, they were charging $299 for the same route, one-way. Everything else is the same. For 7 trips to L.A. in 35 days, you earned:

$2,557.17 Total Profit, @ $73.06/day

For a 345-day work year, that equals **$25,206.39**
For a 50-week work year, that equals **$25,571.70**

What a surprise! THAT'S *almost identical* to the money you'd make by riding the *bus,* using a *Greyhound Ameripass!* The only trouble is, you had to *work* almost *30% harder* to *obtain* it! You drove *an extra 5,508 miles* during the 35-day period for slightly *less* money!

* *

So... great! All those earnings figures come in at over $25,000 per year, even when allowing three weeks for vacation. Does this mean that a driver working solely for one transporter company can make decent money even if he *doesn't* employ the techniques of Interlock and/or Maximization?

Even though all of these scenarios showed potential annual earnings close to the national average (in the mid-1990s) for individual income, we must remember that this was an IDEAL situation, not a real-world one, and was used for the sole purpose of showing you the MOST money you *ever* could possibly expect to earn, when working solely for *ONE transporter company,* using *NO Interlock.* In the real world, you are never *likely* to be able to find a transporter in a hub city that will feed you a constant diet of runs across the continent to another airline hub, although it is a remote possibility. (If you are lucky enough to get into such a situation, compare your *own* results to the scenarios above!)

Also, you have to keep a couple of other things in mind. Ask yourself how long you could make *transcontinental trips between the same two cities* without becoming *bored stiff!?* One of the nicest things about being a Road Rat is the tremendous *variety* the job provides in your life. I can't imagine a Road Rat being able to stand this sort of "ideal" routine for more than a few months, tops. It reminds me of the man in an old *"Twilight Zone"* episode who died and found that everything he ever wanted was being handed to him on a silver platter. After awhile, he got completely bored with it all, and said to his servant, "If this is what heaven is like, I think I'd be happier if you sent me down to the other place." Whereupon the servant (played by Burl Ives, if I recall correctly), with an evil, devilish grin replied with something close to, "Heaven? Whoever said you were *there?* This *IS* the 'other place.'"

Secondly, in Scenarios #2 and 3, unlike the long bus rides, returning by *air* afforded you *no time at all to unwind and relax.* Even those harried and hassled folks who have 9-to-5 jobs and commute to work usually at least have their *weekends!* So this aspect is far from "ideal," too! Such a Road Rat probably would be a burnout case in less than two months.

Things are not always as "ideal" as they might at first appear. Maybe you wouldn't be so "lucky" after all, if you happened to find a situation like *this* one, in which to work. Money isn't everything, remember. The *happiest* Road Rats usually are ones who have a *comfortable* income, enjoy the *freedom* that this lifestyle affords, like *variety,* and love to *travel.* Working for the *average* transporter company, a driver can *achieve* these objectives simply by using Interlock or *Ameripasses.*

Working Steadily for an "Ideal" Transporter Company

CONCLUSIONS

1 -- In a *perfect* scenario, if you take reasonable periods of time off, you could earn over **$25,000 a year**, working *solely* for a transporter, just by *riding the bus* home, using an *Ameripass*.

2 -- In a *perfect* scenario, if you took reasonable periods of time off, you could earn over **$35,000 a year**, working *solely* for a transporter, *IF* you could *almost always* obtain *deeply-discounted* air fares. BUT, you would have to actually **drive 30% more of the time** than you would if returning by bus, in order to achieve this!

3 -- In a *perfect* scenario, if you took reasonable periods of time off, you could earn **$25,000 a year**, working *solely* for a transporter company, by obtaining *normally*-available discount air fares. BUT again, you would have to **drive 30% more miles** than you would if returning by bus, in order to achieve this!

Okay. Before leaving the bus behind, let's put this all together in *one* table, so that you can directly compare the "typical" outcomes in *Part III, Chapter 4* with the "ideal" ones in this *Appendix*.

Comparison Table

Anticipated Earnings *Without* Using Interlock, When Working for One Transporter Company:

"TYPICAL" Situation *vs.* "IDEAL" Situation

Earnings for a 345-day Work Year

	"Typical" Co.	"Ideal" Co.
Scenario #1 (pp. 137 & 322) -- *Ameripass* ONLY --	$19,659.58	$26,136.70
Scenario #2 (p. 138) -- *Ameripass* Returns Combined with 2 cut-rate Air Returns --	$17,919.79	- - - - -
Scenario #3 (p. 139) -- No *Ameripass*. Single Tickets Purchased, as Appropriate --	*- $11,005.50*	- - - - -
Scenario #2 (p. 322) -- No *Ameripass*. All Returns on Discounted plane tickets --	- - - - -	$35,556.39
Scenario #3 (p. 323) -- No *Ameripass*. All Returns via Coach Airplane Tickets --	- - - - -	$25,206.39

BOTTOM LINE: When working for a transporter company, *ALWAYS* make your returns via *either* Interlock, or by using *Greyhound Ameripasses*.

2. More Information on TRAIN Travel
Primary Details: Part III, Chapter 5

A discussion of rail fares can be just as complicated as one of air fares, even though we're talking about just one carrier! For that reason, we'll take it step-by-step, starting with *Amtrak's* primary *round-trip* ticket, "All Aboard, America!" That's the closest to the "USA Railpass" that *North Americans* can come. This will be followed with a few more words on using *sleeping* accommodations on *Amtrak*. That's information that everyone who likes to ride trains can use, no matter where they happen to live. And finally, we'll provide a good overview of the "USA Railpass," which is America's closest equivalent to the "Eurailpass"... information that can be helpful to all Handbook owners living *outside* of North America. All set? Okay! Here comes the *"Twentieth Century Limited"*... er... the *"Pacemaker!"* Oops. Wrong *year* again!! Would you believe *"The Coast Starlight?"* Or, *"The Desert Wind?"* Right. *Those* names work, in the 1990s!

"All Aboard, America!"

These fares do *not* apply to travel in Canada on *Via*, nor do they apply to *Amtrak's Auto-Train*, nor to the *Metroliners* which ply the Northeast Corridor. They *do* apply to all **other** *Amtrak* system trains.

"All Aboard, America" is a ticket of *limited flexibility* that almost always is purchased for *round-trip* purposes. You are permitted **up to 3 stopovers** and may take **up to 45 days** to complete your journey. Since Road Rats normally don't use round-trip tickets in the line of duty, I decided to confine discussion of this particular *Amtrak* ticket to this Appendix. You normally will find it difficult to schedule return runs using this type of ticket because restrictions apply that usually are inconsistent with being able to schedule *one-way* return trips. But just in case you can make it work somehow, or wish to take a vacation this way, these are the basic facts.

Amtrak's America is divided into three zones, and these figure importantly in the fares you pay using "All Aboard, America!" The western and central zones meet at Wolf Point (MT), Cheyenne, Denver, Albuquerque, and El Paso. The central and eastern zones have Chicago, St. Louis, Memphis, and New Orleans in common. These should not be confused with *time* zones, because the western/central *Amtrak* division line is entirely *within* the Mountain Time Zone, and the other one is entirely *within* the Central Time Zone. Cities *on* these dividing lines are common to *both* of the zones they occupy. For example, travel within the region between Chicago and New York would be entirely within one zone... and so would be travel within the area between Chicago to Omaha. However, travel involving New York and Omaha as the extremes would involve *two* zones. Finally, you *may* choose to "zig-zag" a *lot* within your zones(s) -- using diverse routes -- when paying these "Zone" fares. (It would be similar to using an *Ameripass* to roam the country on *Greyhound*, **but** with *major* restrictions on changes and stopovers, and advanced booking on *specific* trains being absolutely required. *Also* unlike the bus pass, it is **not** permissible to *backtrack* over the same routes, while you travel.) Or you may pay a "Point-to-Point" fare, and sacrifice that flexibility, for somewhat less money.

If you kept all of *that* straight, you're home free. The *rest* of this is much *easier* to understand!

Up to three stopovers are permitted (at no extra charge) when using an "All Aboard America" ticket, and the routes and dates must be reserved before ticketing, or at the time of purchasing the ticket. In the table at the top of the next page, fares are shown **regular fare first,** and then the **"Senior Fare," for those 62 and over, after the slash.** In 1994, the Peak season was June 17-August 21, and Dec. 16-Jan 4, 1995. All other dates are Off-Peak. According to *Amtrak,* these are close approximations to the dates of their seasons from one year to the next, with variations of only a few days.

"All Aboard, America" ZONE Fares in Effect in Mid-1994

Zones Crossed:	Within 1 Zone	Within 2 Zones	All 3 Zones
Peak	-- $198/169	$278/237	$338/288
Off-Peak	-- $178/152	$238/203	$278/237

Maximum round-trip fares on *Amtrak* over the longest distances vary between $254 and $494.

That's right. An off-peak New York-to-Los Angeles *round trip* might cost you as little as $254/216, or as much as *nearly $500* (or exactly $420, senior fare) depending on the *degree to which the train is already booked* at the time you make your reservation! Fares increase as the seats are sold. Remember, though, **it's the round-trip fares that vary.** (*Compare:* If you purchase an off-peak **Point-to-Point** *one-way* ticket *before* the train is too fully booked, it'll probably cost you the Excursion Fare of $247. Or $210 if you're a senior.)

Sleeping on *Amtrak* When Cost is *Not* a Limiting Factor

The *details* on sleeping accomodations are presented in Part III, Chapter 5, but at the risk of being a bit redundant with some of the material presented earlier, let's think on this particular **type** of travel expense just a bit further.

If you are a retiree who already *has* a good, comfortable income from pension(s), social security, investments, or a combination of these, then you might have decided to become a Road Rat **not** for the income, but instead for the **sheer adventure of experiencing paid travel.** You might even be delighted to do this without earning *anything!* And in that event, being able to ride trains and planes in style, without having to touch your retirement funds, just might be the best of all possible worlds! Then, by all means, *go for it!!*

Even though this Handbook is designed primarily to help people to get into the Road Rat lifestyle and make a comfortable living, it *also* is for anyone who just wants to get out there and have a wonderful time, *without* being particularly concerned about earnings levels, if they so desire. So if you're in *that* very comfortable position, then simply study this book to learn all the techniques that keep this job hassle-free and stress-free. And then if you wish to spend *extra* money on hotels, accomodations... *and sleeping rooms on trains...* then do it *all,* in the style in which you can *afford* to be accustomed! And have a great time!!

"USA Railpass"

It used to be possible for Americans (including Canadians) to purchase a "USA Railpass" and just ride on *Amtrak* to their heart's content in much the same way that people can ride on *Greyhound* today, using an *Ameripass.* Not anymore. *Amtrak* tells me that's because its trains are too fully booked, so seats for walk-on passengers are unavailable.

(This made me wonder how the foreign tourists holding "USA Railpasses" can get on them, but perhaps that results in several passengers spending much of the trip in the lounge car, or standing. I've noticed that the European trains are pretty crowded during the summertime. But using a "Eurailpass" in the *wintertime, late spring, or early- to mid-autumn* is a great experience!

Having clear memories of the fabulous passenger rail service of the '50s and '60s, I just had to ask! If rail travel enjoys *that* degree of popularity in America, then why not add *more trains,* and *expand* the *Amtrak* routes? The answer was puzzling. Too *expensive,* they said.

Now, when one is in the business of transporting passengers, and the fares frequently are as high or higher than those charged for air travel, why wouldn't this *pay* for more rolling stock, and more track? After all, the airlines manage to keep buying planes that cost tens of millions of dollars, and that's how *they* make *their* money...?

If you have some time, perhaps it wouldn't hurt to pose that question to *Amtrak.* (Doing that *in writing* works best.) If *enough* of us ask, maybe it'll provide some incentive for them to act.

For those who happen to be reading this who *live outside of North America,* you can purchase the "USA Railpass" from your travel agent, and the fares that existed in mid-1994, when this was researched, are as follows, expressed in *U.S. dollars:*

"USA Railpass"

Off-Peak Season (Jan. 1-May 29 & Aug. 29-Dec. 31, inclusive)

Adults (age 16 & over)	-- $218.00 --	15-Day Pass
Children (age 2 - 15)	-- $109.00 --	15-Day Pass
Adults (age 16 & over)	-- $319.00 --	30-Day Pass
Children (age 2 - 15)	-- $160.00 --	30-Day Pass

Peak Season (May 31-Aug. 28, inclusive)

Adults (age 16 & over)	-- $318.00 --	15-Day Pass
Children (age 2 - 15)	-- $159.00 --	15-Day Pass
Adults (age 16 & over)	-- $399.00 --	30-Day Pass
Children (age 2 - 15)	-- $200.00 --	30-Day Pass

If for any reason you can't obtain all the information that you need on *Amtrak* from your travel agent, or if you wish to obtain the *latest* information, you should write to the following address:

Amtrak International Sales
60 Massachusetts Avenue, N.E.
Washington, DC 20002, USA

While it's unfortunate that those living in North America cannot use the "USA Railpass," *Amtrak* does run *specials* with frequency, and basic fares fluctuate. Interestingly, even though the peak and off-peak periods are pretty stable when the "big picture" is observed, they can vary wildly within *Amtrak* when *individual* aspects are involved. For example, the peak fare period for the "All Aboard America" fare is *different* from that of the "USA Railpass," and both of those are quite different from the peak fare periods that apply to *accomodations* on board! In fact, it is possible to find that peak fare periods even vary from one *train* to another! That's why it is very important to use the figures and dates on these pages *for guidance only.* All of the peak- and off-peak-period dates and fares were accurate as of August 20, 1994. And as we've said before, if the economic balloon doesn't go up worldwide over the next few years, these will probably be good ballpark figures to use in your preliminary planning for as long as this book is current (through 1998).

BEWARE of Card-Devouring ATMs!!

This advice rightfully belongs in either Chapter 7 or 8 of Part II, but was added too late for inclusion there. This is **critically-important** advice!! Read it carefully and please heed it well!

Most automatic teller machines (ATMs) require that you *INSERT* your ATM or credit card before it will function. **STAY AWAY FROM THOSE!!!** Once one of those has engulfed your card, you are *completely* at that machine's mercy! And such ATMs can be anything *BUT* "user-friendly!"

In early 1994, I attempted to use my card at an ATM in northern Delaware, and was unaware that my account balance was lower than the amount of withdrawal I requested. It returned my card with a slip that informed me of this. I reinserted the card and asked for a readout of my current balance. Then I phoned my office and simply had a staff member make a deposit to cover the amount I needed.

At 8 p.m., I stopped at an ATM located behind a bank in downtown Liberty, NY, and attempted again to make the withdrawal. Instead of giving me the money, it *KEPT* the card and on the screen appeared a message, "Card is being retained for the protection of the customer." *Some* "protection!" I was on my way to *Syracuse*, over 100 miles away! *Without* my card!

The next morning I called the bank in Liberty to tell them I was about to drive down there to retrieve my card. They told me not to bother -- they'd already **destroyed** it!! To add insult to injury, they told me that this procedure was in compliance with a directive from my *own* bank, in Waterloo, Iowa. Seconds later, I had *them* on the line and I don't mind telling you that I was breathing *fire* at *that* point!

They told me that the card had been "captured" by the machine because I'd attempted to make a *second* withdrawal in the *same day* while funds were not available. (The deposit had been credited to my account just minutes *after* my card had been scarfed up in Liberty.) And because the card was captured out-of-state, the bank in Liberty had been electronically directed by my home bank to *destroy* it!

SOLUTION: **DON'T LET THIS HAPPEN TO *YOU*!! Find ATMs along routes you use, which do *NOT* require card insertion, but instead allow you to SWIPE card through a *scanner*. SUCH AN ATM IS *ABSOLUTELY INCAPABLE* OF CAPTURING YOUR CARD!! Use *ONLY* ATMs that are of *that* type, and allow yourself to make *NO EXCEPTIONS* to that rule! Make a *list* of all such ATMs that you find, and *keep it with you on all your trips.***

I've discovered that MOST truck stops have *GOOD* ATMs! The same is true of MANY mini-mart/gas station combinations. Try those locations *first*. Banks seem to be the biggest offenders in this regard; very FEW of those have good ATMs. **TIP:** As you travel, develop a *list* of all those that can be *useful* to you. **It is in your best interests to *avoid* all ATMs capable of capturing your card!**

Public service: You may FREELY copy *this page* and distribute it to *ANYONE!*   --XANADU Ent., Evansdale, IA 50707-0147.

You are Invited to Join Me on this Wondrous Cruise!

If you are reading these words, **you are entitled to a discount of $200 per person --** *whether or not you happen to own this book.* An entire chapter describes this adventure, starting on Page 104.

You may choose *any* cruise, *whether or not* I happen to be on it, and *still* receive this special discount. If you *can* join me, though, I'd love to have the chance to meet you. In 1997, I will be on the September 16 - Oct. 1 Volga cruise from Moscow, to Makareyev Monastery, and back to Moscow, followed by the included motor coach tour to St. Petersburg. Three days will be spent seeing the wonders of St. Petersburg, upon arrival there.

This special offer is available until at least Dec. 31, 1998. So if you can't go in 1997, you still may obtain the discount in 1998, and possibly beyond. (And I'm hoping to take one of these cruises annually, so if you'd like to join me, simply ask the folks at International Cruises & Tours which one I'm scheduled on, for each year after 1997. They should have that information available for you by the fall of each previous year.)

The Most Unique Tours of the World

- Educational • Only Meet-the-People Program • Personal Escorts • Professional Guides

You are invited by Elizabeth and Mark to be Craig Chilton's Special Guest as he returns again to Russia!

Notes from Elizabeth and Mark:

Dear Friend,

Mark and I have organized and escorted more than 70 trips to Russia since 1990. We used to book thousands, but that no longer works in Russia - you miss out on meeting the great people. So we invite you to join Craig on one of our unparalled adventures.

You'll sail from Moscow to Nizhni Novgorod and see sights other tour passengers never see, all from the comfort of our deluxe boat. You'll love our unique meet-the-people program.

To help you get to know the people of Russia, we have a 12-1 translator ratio.

Craig leaves the U.S. September 16. The temperature will be wonderful. Sites stunning. The memories forever.

Liz Stoddard

International Cruises & Tours
• 2476 N. University Pkwy B-1 • Provo, UT 84604 •
(Toll Free) 1-888-827-8357 or 1-801-344-8747

After you've experienced the warmth, hospitality, and friendliness of the Russian people, who at long last live in a free land, you'll never see the world in quite the same way again. It's the ultimate adventure in learning, and making new friends.

Here are a few comments by earlier Volga River cruise participants...

"You have some of the finest musicians in the world aboard your ship."

"We were most impressed with the young interpreters -- patient, intelligent, very frank and open. A credit to Russia. A great experience."

"The price is a best buy. The music was an unexpected delight. We'd do it again in a minute."

The complete details of how to obtain a *free* color brochure at *no obligation,* **and** how to obtain the special discount, are provided on Page 108. The phone numbers are in the insert, above. Don't "miss the boat" by waiting too long, though. The best staterooms tend to be booked early. Welcome aboard!

SPREAD THE OPPORTUNITY!

If you love the Road Rat lifestyle, and are being helped by this book, it was because *someone* cared enough to make it available to you. That might have been the author, via a talk show or TV appearance. Or you might have obtained it in a bookstore, because the store thought it worthy to carry. Or you may have been given an order blank, like those below, by a friend or loved one. Or -- perhaps your friend used one of those to order the book, and then provided it to you as a gift. But somebody wanted, at least a little bit, to give you this opportunity to enjoy life more than ever.

So here's *your* chance to help others. (And if these aren't enough, *copies* of them *are* fine.)

ORDER FORM

Please send ____ copy(ies) of the *1995-97 Edition* of **How to Get Paid $30,000 a Year to Travel (Without Selling Anything).** (*Mail to:* TRAVEL, P.O. Box 3147, Dept BK, Waterloo, IA 50707-0147 USA)

Name:_____

MAILING Address:_____

City:_____ State/Province:_____ Code:_____

Enclosed is **$28.95 (US funds) per book, which includes the shipping.** Check or money order.
Iowa residents only: Please add $1.16 per book sales tax. Canadians: No additional charges.
For **Air Mail** shipment to *overseas* points, please add $10.00 postage, per book.

ORDER FORM

Please send ____ copy(ies) of the *1995-97 Edition* of **How to Get Paid $30,000 a Year to Travel (Without Selling Anything).** (*Mail to:* TRAVEL, P.O. Box 3147, Dept BK, Waterloo, IA 50707-0147 USA)

Name:_____

MAILING Address:_____

City:_____ State/Province:_____ Code:_____

Enclosed is **$28.95 (US funds) per book, which includes the shipping.** Check or money order.
Iowa residents only: Please add $1.16 per book sales tax. Canadians: No additional charges.
For **Air Mail** shipment to *overseas* points, please add $10.00 postage, per book.

ORDER FORM

Please send ____ copy(ies) of the *1995-97 Edition* of **How to Get Paid $30,000 a Year to Travel (Without Selling Anything).** (*Mail to:* TRAVEL, P.O. Box 3147, Dept BK, Waterloo, IA 50707-0147 USA)

Name:_____

MAILING Address:_____

City:_____ State/Province:_____ Code:_____

Enclosed is **$28.95 (US funds) per book, which includes the shipping.** Check or money order.
Iowa residents only: Please add $1.16 per book sales tax. Canadians: No additional charges.
For **Air Mail** shipment to *overseas* points, please add $10.00 postage, per book.

ORDER FORM

Please send ____ copy(ies) of the *1995-97 Edition* of **How to Get Paid $30,000 a Year to Travel (Without Selling Anything).** (*Mail to:* **TRAVEL, P.O. Box 3147, Dept BK, Waterloo, IA 50707-0147 USA**)

Name:_____

MAILING Address:_____

City:_____ State/Province:_____ Code:_____

Enclosed is **$28.95 (US funds) per book, which includes the shipping.** Check or money order.
Iowa residents only: Please add $1.16 per book sales tax. Canadians: No additional charges.
For **Air Mail** shipment to *overseas* points, please add $10.00 postage, per book.

- -

ORDER FORM

Please send ____ copy(ies) of the *1995-97 Edition* of **How to Get Paid $30,000 a Year to Travel (Without Selling Anything).** (*Mail to:* **TRAVEL, P.O. Box 3147, Dept BK, Waterloo, IA 50707-0147 USA**)

Name:_____

MAILING Address:_____

City:_____ State/Province:_____ Code:_____

Enclosed is **$28.95 (US funds) per book, which includes the shipping.** Check or money order.
Iowa residents only: Please add $1.16 per book sales tax. Canadians: No additional charges.
For **Air Mail** shipment to *overseas* points, please add $10.00 postage, per book.

- -

ORDER FORM

Please send ____ copy(ies) of the *1995-97 Edition* of **How to Get Paid $30,000 a Year to Travel (Without Selling Anything).** (*Mail to:* **TRAVEL, P.O. Box 3147, Dept BK, Waterloo, IA 50707-0147 USA**)

Name:_____

MAILING Address:_____

City:_____ State/Province:_____ Code:_____

Enclosed is **$28.95 (US funds) per book, which includes the shipping.** Check or money order.
Iowa residents only: Please add $1.16 per book sales tax. Canadians: No additional charges.
For **Air Mail** shipment to *overseas* points, please add $10.00 postage, per book.

- -

ORDER FORM

Please send ____ copy(ies) of the *1995-97 Edition* of **How to Get Paid $30,000 a Year to Travel (Without Selling Anything).** (*Mail to:* **TRAVEL, P.O. Box 3147, Dept BK, Waterloo, IA 50707-0147 USA**)

Name:_____

MAILING Address:_____

City:_____ State/Province:_____ Code:_____

Enclosed is **$28.95 (US funds) per book, which includes the shipping.** Check or money order.
Iowa residents only: Please add $1.16 per book sales tax. Canadians: No additional charges.
For **Air Mail** shipment to *overseas* points, please add $10.00 postage, per book.

- -

Did You Get Your Inserts?

This Handbook always contains special insertions when it is shipped, which provide *additional* useful materials and information to its travel-oriented purchasers.

Occasionally, these are no longer in the book when it is received. This is most likely to occur when the Handbook is purchased in a bookstore, because they can get lost on the way to the shelf, or browsers can accidentally drop them. Not as often, they are accidentally omitted.

If you found *no* inserts in this Handbook, we will be glad to replace them for you, *free of charge.*

Just drop us a note, or call us, and we'll get another set right in the mail to you! Here's where we can be reached:

**XANADU Enterprises
P.O. Box 3147
Waterloo, Iowa 50707-0147**

Tel.: (319) 234-0676

(The address shown above is identical to the one on the back of this book's title page. This note is being added to save you confusion on that. "Waterloo," and "Evansdale" are *interchangeable.* We wanted you to be aware of this because Directory Assistance operators outside of Iowa frequently don't have Evansdale in their database. But they can *always* access its larger counterpart, Waterloo.)

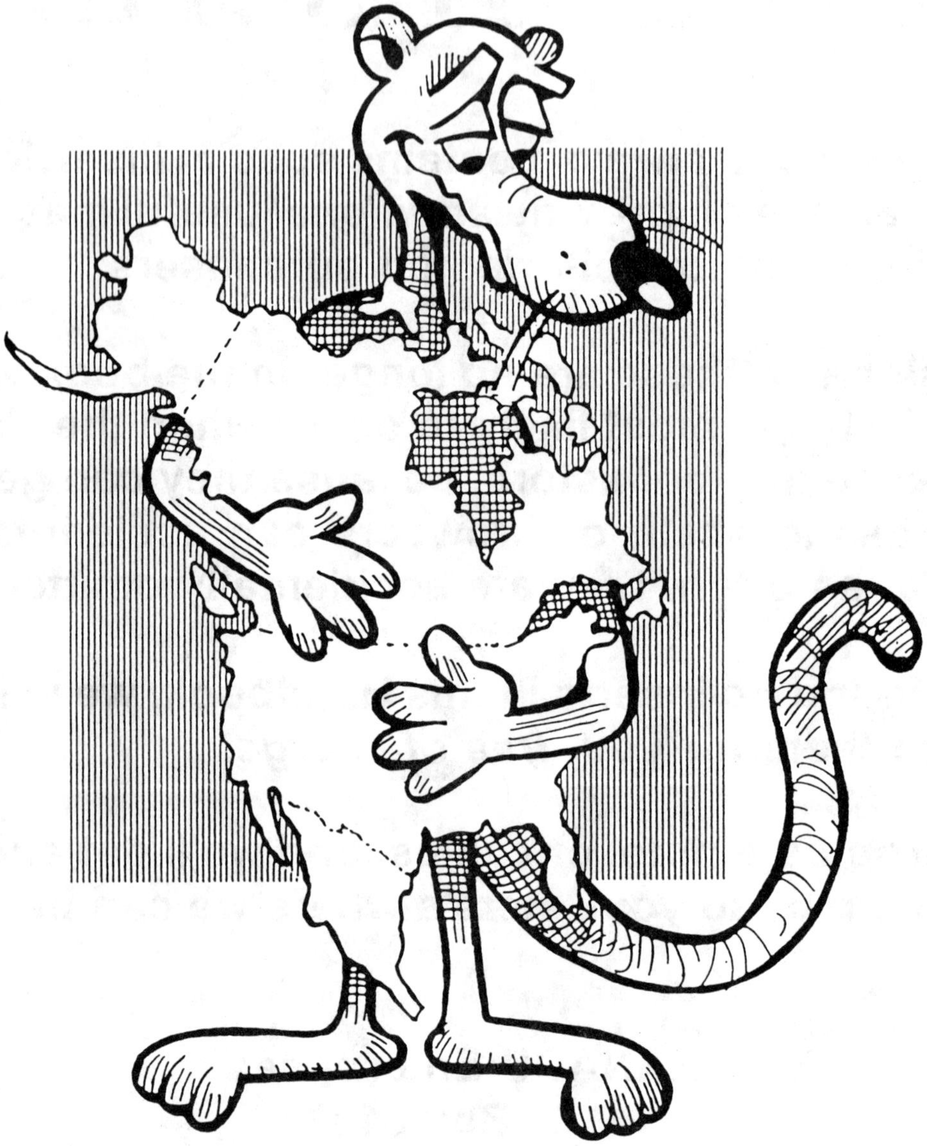

The Latest Information!

BRAND-NEW INFORMATION!!

* *

U.S. SOCIAL SECURITY GUIDE

These are the established thresholds for earnings that may be attained before reductions start to apply with respect to Social Security benefits to retirees in the USA. As earnings increase beyond these limits in the given calendar year, benefit payments are proportionately reduced. A person falling within these age ranges should refer to pages 120 and 121 for suggestions on how to proceed in light of this information.

This printing provides the figures that applied in 1996, and the *projected* figures for 1997-2002, for those in the age group 65-69. (As you can see, this situation soon will improve dramatically! *Especially* when the Twenty-First Century *officially* begins, on Jan. 1, *2001*.) To *obtain* figures for the age group 62 thru 64 after 1996, and to *verify* the projected figures for age group 65 thru 69 for those years, simply phone your nearby Social Security office every year. Then you may print those figures in the spaces provided.

Age Range	1996	1997	1998	1999	2000	2001	2002
62 through 64	$8,280	8,640	_____	_____	_____	_____	_____
65 through 69	$12,500	13,500	14,500	15,500	17,000	25,000	30,000
70 and Over	--	Earn as much as you'd like and still get *full* benefits. No limit!					

* *

3rd Printing Update

Each time a given edition of a book is reprinted, there's a golden window of opportunity to correct previous errors, and to update its information. Even though only 2 years have passed since the first printing of this edition, many changes have been implemented, affecting no less than 100 pages of this book, including full updating of more than 500 company listings. In addition, we put three "Notes" pages in the back, in the First Printing, to allow us to insert new information in successive printings. As the "Notes" space *decreases*, the book's information *increases*, and your Handbook becomes even more useful to you!

TELEPHONES
(Please refer back to Pages 74-75 and 86-89 for background data.)

There is a fabulous *exception* to the information provided regarding small, "rinky-dink" long distance carriers that overcharge. You can save a great deal of money through the PROPER use of pre-paid phone cards, which commonly are sold in vending machines that are easy to find these days in truck stops, airports, convenience stores, and now even from the *U.S. Postal Service*. AND, in late 1995, a *new,* and very special card, available **ONLY** to Road Rats and their family members and friends, became available directly from *us*, here at XANADU Enterprises! It's called the **"Road Rat Pre-Paid Phone Card."**

Enclosed within this book, you should find a packet of inserts. Or it may be mounted inside the back cover of the book. One of the inserts is a color flyer that illustrates the *standard* Road Rat Card, and provides ordering information. (*Please note:* If that packet of inserts did *not* come with your book, please notify us, and we will provide you with a replacement packet at no charge. **See page 335**.)

What *IS* a Pre-Paid Phone Card?

All pre-paid phone cards are *debit* cards, and they all work basically the same way. To make a long-distance call, you simply dial a toll-free number (which, as of 1996, can be either a "1-800" number or a "1-888" number), and then the PIN number that is unique to the card... and then the number you are calling. The cost of your call will automatically be deducted from the value of your card, each time.

Every time you make a call, you will get a message -- either after you dial the PIN number, or after you've dialed the number you're calling -- which will tell you the amount of time remaining on your card. This is especially helpful if your card is running low, so that you can plan accordingly.

From that point on, your call proceeds normally, just as though you were using a telephone credit card. Should the card's balance become low, you will get a one-minute warning before it expires, so that you can disconnect gracefully from your conversation.

Pre-paid phone cards got their start in Europe during the 1980s, and are immensely popular and commonly-used there. They reached the USA around 1990, and only by the mid-'90s were they coming into use in Canada. When in British Columbia in April, 1996, I found a vending machine for the cards on board the Tsawwassen Ferry, which connects hourly across the Georgia Strait from Vancouver to Vancouver Island, near Victoria. Unfortunately, there were three major drawbacks: (1) *Nowhere* on the machine was there any information to tell the prospective customer the **RATE** at which the card would be consumed... and (2) that rate turned out to be **a whopping 60 cents per minute!** (3) The card was *not* renewable. That means that if a person chose to use such cards to make their long-distance calls, they would just about have to carry along *two* of them, most of the time, so they'd have one to use after the first one expired.

So -- You should always be sure of these three things before you buy a pre-paid phone card: Be sure you KNOW the **rate** at which you will be charged for your calls, and be sure that the rate is **FAIR**. (These days, 25 cents per minute is a good rate, and more is too high.) And always have a card that can be **easily renewed**. That way, you can actively continue using the SAME card for years, if you so desire.

WHY Use a *Pre-Paid* Phone Card?

A pre-paid phone card is one of the most valuable and economical tools that the Road Rat can have. As we already have discussed, you'll be using the phone a lot while you're out on the road, and that means paying for your calls in any of *four* ways. You can put the coins into a pay phone... and you already know how *that* can rip you off! Or secondly, you can use a telephone credit card and use the *pay phone's* own carrier to route your call. That can be *worse!* Third, you can use a major carrier's credit card such that you access ONLY the *card's* carrier for your call. (That's usually second-best.) And finally, you can choose to use a renewable, low-cost pre-paid (debit) phone card. And *that* method is by *FAR* the *least* expensive!

Don't be fooled by the new breed of pay phones that are cropping up which allow you to call anywhere in the lower 48 states for only 25 cents per minute. That *sounds* just as good as a 25-cent-per-minute pre-paid phone card at first, but there are two major shortcomings that can cost you, inconvenience you, or both. It'll *usually* cost you, because there's normally a 4-minute minimum required for such calls, and that means the call will cost you a dollar, even if you only talk for a minute or two. And it'll inconvenience you, unless you're wildly enthusiastic about carrying around a pocketful of quarters. (Not to mention the hassle of having your call interrupted over and over with requests for additional coins!)

If you have an economical pre-paid phone card, you know that you will ALWAYS save substantially on your long-distance calls while on the road, and you'll never have to worry about those calls showing up on a bill -- because you've *already paid* for them!

Be aware, too, that if you choose to use a carrier's *credit* card instead, then besides having to face a phone bill each month, there's some *extra* expense involved ... even if the carrier is one of the "Big Three." For example, *AT&T* will clobber you with an **80-CENT surcharge** for the first minute when you use their credit card! But when you use a pre-paid phone card, there is *NO* surcharge. You pay a flat rate per minute, and if that rate is 25 cents, and you make a call that is only one minute long, then 25 cents is ALL you pay for your call. Think about that. MANY of the calls you'll be making will be simple and brief check-in calls, which will only take a minute or less. All such calls will cost you just 25 cents each, night or day, 7 days a week (if you use the Road Rat Card), and the savings are tremendous.

Oh -- almost forgot! Phone cards have quickly become a great collector's item, worldwide. And the Road Rat card already is in demand from that standpoint, because **ONLY** Road Rats and their friends can obtain them! So it may even gain value for you, while you use it. And every Christmas, we issue a special, commemorative card. So that it can be a collectable, we make it available without quantity restriction until March first of the next year, unless fewer than 500 of that card were sold by that time. In that event, after March 1st, the card for the previous Christmas continues to be available until 500 have been sold, and that ends its run. A few of the **first** issue ("Christmas '95") are still available, as of January, 1997. If you'd like one or more, please inquire. (Those who order, but don't request a special card, will receive the standard card shown on the color brochure.) *Both* Road Rat Cards are 25 cents per minute, and are renewable.

REASONABLY-PRICED GASOLINE IN GEORGIA *SURVIVES!*

It's all good news in Georgia! On Feb. 24, 1995, the Georgia Legislature *abandoned* an effort to raise gasoline taxes by 5 cents per gallon! Georgia currently has the nation's *best* gasoline prices, and now *will continue* in that category. (In December, 1995, I purchased regular unleaded there for 0.79^9/gallon, and as recently as mid-1994, it was as low as 0.74^9!). Kudos to Georgia residents who *resisted* the increase! But don't let your guard down. Remember that *Congress* passes unpopular things like congressional pay raises at midnight when no one's looking! So keep the pressure on; keep up the good work!!

TRANSPORTER COMPANIES GAIN SLIGHTLY SINCE 1995

Our research has revealed a gradual trend toward an increase in the number of Road Rats who work for transporters compared to those working directly for manufacturers. It's too early to know whether or not the trend will continue, or even whether it will be long-term, but for driver candidates seeking to work directly for a manufacturer, best advice for now is to start out with a transporter if work for a manufacturer or for a dealer isn't immediately available. Remember, a Semi-Permanent Interlock **(see p. 115)** involving two transporters that are 500 miles or more apart can provide a nice income. Meanwhile, up to 30% of maufacturers, and a similar percentage of dealers, continue to employ drivers, and the majority of such drivers continue to be independent contractors.

CONSIDER THE "CLASS B" CDL

On **page 133**, we looked at the advantages of having Class A CDL, but even if you choose not to acquire one of those, the easier-to-obtain Class B one might be well worth your consideration. That one allows you to drive a very wide range of vehicles and has the advantage of opening the door for you of the many companies out there that want their drivers to have *some* level of CDL. Even when a company doesn't require its drivers to hold CDLs, *having* one can give you a very nice edge, when making applications over those who don't. And if a company has a wide range of vehicle sizes, that will give you the capability to drive them *all,* and therefore never miss out on a nice run.

USEFUL NOTES

Just as I wrote this book, and the ones before it, by taking note of special circumstances and opportunities along the road, you now can ADD to your knowledge, by putting **YOUR OWN** special observations on this page!